Springer Proceedings in Business and Economics

Springer Proceedings in Business and Economics brings the most current research presented at conferences and workshops to a global readership. The series features volumes (in electronic and print formats) of selected contributions from conferences in all areas of economics, business, management, and finance. In addition to an overall evaluation by the publisher of the topical interest, scientific quality, and timeliness of each volume, each contribution is refereed to standards comparable to those of leading journals, resulting in authoritative contributions to the respective fields. Springer's production and distribution infrastructure ensures rapid publication and wide circulation of the latest developments in the most compelling and promising areas of research today.

The editorial development of volumes may be managed using Springer Nature's innovative EquinOCS, a proven online conference proceedings submission, management and review system. This system is designed to ensure an efficient timeline for your publication, making Springer Proceedings in Business and Economics the premier series to publish your workshop or conference volume.

This book series is indexed in SCOPUS.

Katerina Berezina · Lyndon Nixon · Aarni Tuomi

Editors

Information and Communication Technologies in Tourism 2024

ENTER 2024 International eTourism Conference, Izmir, Türkiye, January 17–19

 Springer

Editors
Katerina Berezina
Department of Nutrition and Hospitality
Management
University of Mississippi
University, MS, USA

Lyndon Nixon
School of Applied Data Science
MODUL University Vienna
Vienna, Austria

Aarni Tuomi
Haaga-Helia University of Applied Sciences
Helsinki, Finland

ISSN 2198-7246   ISSN 2198-7254 (electronic)
Springer Proceedings in Business and Economics
ISBN 978-3-031-58838-9   ISBN 978-3-031-58839-6 (eBook)
https://doi.org/10.1007/978-3-031-58839-6

This Springer imprint is published by the registered company Springer Nature Switzerland AG
The registered company address is: Gewerbestrasse 11, 6330 Cham, Switzerland

Paper in this product is recyclable.

Foreword

As we come together for the ENTER24 conference organized by IFITT and IFITT Türkiye, we find ourselves in the heart of beautiful İzmir, the pearl of the Aegean, with its 8,500 years of history and unique geography. We are at the intersection of innovation and tradition, exploring the dynamic interaction of information and communication technologies (ICTs) within the travel and tourism sector.

For over 30 years, the ENTER conference has been a pioneer in advancing the development of the impacts of ICT usage in the industry, leading the way in knowledge sharing, exchange, and facilitation. The theme of this year, "Challenging the Next 30 Years of Tourism," guides us into a realm of exploration and anticipation.

While focusing on the transformation brought about by the World Wide Web just three decades ago, we now stand on the threshold of a similar transformative disruption triggered by technologies such as augmented realities, productive artificial intelligence, and the Internet of Things. IFITT, in collaboration with IFITT Türkiye Chapter, warmly invites the global e-tourism community, academics, technology and travel businesses, destinations, and non-governmental organizations to contribute to this significant discourse.

The ENTER24 conference serves as a platform to shape the future of the tourism industry, functioning as a nexus for collaboration, innovation, and learning. The questions posed this year delve into how technology will shape marketing, business growth, and development; the role of digital-focused workplaces in the future of tourism; and how technology can contribute to sustainability, new professions, global and local development, cultural heritage, entrepreneurship, digitalization, climate change, mobility, energy, health, and well-being. These questions, among others, guide us as we navigate the uncharted waters of the next 30 years.

While the ENTER24 conference encourages participants to engage in interactive and inspiring discussions, this event will bring together academia, students, professionals, the business world, public institutions, and organizations. We will share the latest research and case studies on emerging and innovative ICT concepts, applications, and business models.

As we embark on this intellectual journey, this carefully prepared publication by those who contribute to the collective wisdom shaping the future of e-tourism will not only be a valuable resource but will also pave the way for the creation of many new business models in the tourism perspective of the next 30 years.

I express my sincere gratitude to the invaluable academic community, colleagues, the business world, public institutions, and students who have contributed to this remarkable publication. May our time together at ENTER24 be filled with lively discussions, shared insights, and a collective commitment to advancing the science and practice of tourism.

Wishing you an excellent experience and a unique journey on this exciting adventure!

Mine Gunes Kaya
President of IFITT Türkiye/
IFITT International Board Member/
ENTER24 Local Chair

Preface 2024

The 31st Annual International eTourism Conference ENTER24@Izmir is a premier global forum for researchers, practitioners, and policymakers to exchange ideas and explore new frontiers in the field of technology in tourism and hospitality. The conference takes place in person from January 17–19, 2024, in Izmir, Turkey. ENTER24 is organized by the IFITT Türkiye Chapter, which is among the largest and most active IFITT communities.

The theme of the conference is "Challenging the Next 30 Years of Tourism." For more than 30 years, information and communication technologies (ICTs) have been revolutionizing travel, tourism, and hospitality. Over all these years, the ENTER conference has been at the forefront of facilitating the discussion, exchange, and development of knowledge about the use and impact of new ICTs in the travel, tourism, and hospitality industry. While we have learned a lot in this journey, ICTs continue to evolve and reshape the businesses and societies.

Thirty years ago, at the dawn of the World Wide Web, we could have never imagined everything that has happened since. Now, we are likely to be on the cusp of a similar, transformational disruption through technology, as extended realities, generative artificial intelligence, and the Internet of Things bring new disruptions. At this milestone, ENTER24 shares the works of the academic and professional research community to challenge the next 30 years of tourism and hospitality and prepare both tourists and tourism stakeholders for what the future will bring.

The research track of ENTER24@Izmir received a total of 75 full and short paper submissions. Each paper was reviewed by a panel of experts using a double-blind review process. As a result, 25 full papers and 21 short papers were accepted for publication in the conference proceedings. The papers in this volume advance the current knowledge base of ICT and tourism and hospitality in a variety of areas including:

- Digital immersive technologies (e.g., virtual reality and metaverse),
- Social media and user-generated content,
- Recommender systems and travel planning,
- Workplace transformation and digital nomadism.

In addition to the regular research track, ENTER24@Izmir will also feature two special research sessions on:

- Artificial General Intelligence (AGI) in Tourism and Hospitality, and
- The Use of Emerging Technologies in Tourism Education.

The research track of ENTER24 also includes for the first time a Posters & Demos session. The posters and demos category is intended for various types of research, teaching, and practice outputs that are of interest to the ENTER community and align with the conference theme. This category includes but is not limited to industry cases, teaching cases, early research, research methods demonstrations, and technology/software/app/code demonstrations, facilitating the sharing of innovative research and tourism technology practices. Accepted posters and demos are available to all IFITT members in the membership area on the IFITT website. We hope that this new presentation format will be embraced by the IFITT community and will become a tradition for future ENTER conferences.

We envision that this proceedings will serve as a valuable source of information on the state of the art in ICT in tourism and hospitality research. We would like to thank all authors who chose ENTER24 and this proceedings as a publication vehicle for their research. Also, we share sincere gratitude to all members of the ENTER24@Izmir Scientific Committee who ensured the rigorous review process of the works selected for this conference. We appreciate the work of ENTER24 conference chair Dr. Jelena Dorčić for bringing all the pieces together to make a successful ENTER24 conference. Finally, we would like to thank the IFITT President Dr. Juho Pesonen and the entire IFITT Board for their vision and support of the ENTER24 research track, as well as the IFITT Türkiye Chapter and the professional conference organizer Red & More for unique Turkish hospitality and coordination at the conference destination.

Katerina Berezina
Lyndon Nixon
Aarni Tuomi
ENTER24 Research Track Co-chairs

Organization

ENTER24 Scientific Committee

Marina Abad	University of Deusto
Aurkene Alzua-Sorzabal	Deusto University
Mark Ashton	University of Surrey
Rodolfo Baggio	Bocconi University
Matthias Braunhofer	Microsoft
Claudia Brözel	University of Applied Science for Sustainable Development
Dimitrios Buhalis	Bournemouth University
Jacques Bulchand-Gidumal	University of Las Palmas de Gran Canaria
Lorenzo Cantoni	USI - Università della Svizzera italiana
Ekaterina Chevtaeva	Zayed University
Yeongbae Choe	Gachon University
Namho Chung	Kyung Hee University
Cynthia Corrêa	University of São Paulo
Giacomo Del Chiappa	University of Sassari
Amra Delić	University of Sarajevo
Roman Egger	Salzburg University of Applied Sciences
Berta Ferrer-Rosell	University of Lleida
Matthias Fuchs	Mid Sweden University
Damianos Gavalas	University of the Aegean
Robert Goecke	Munich University of Applied Sciences
Maria Rosario González	University of Seville
Ulrike Gretzel	University of Southern California
Vincent Grèzes	University of Applied Sciences Western Switzerland
Noor Hazarina Hashim	Universiti Teknologi Malaysia
Jesus Herrero	Tecnalia
Wolfram Höpken	Ravensburg-Weingarten University of Applied Sciences
Sergio Ibano Sanchez	University of Zaragoza
Dietmar Jannach	University of Klagenfurt
Jin Young Kim	Kyung Hee University
Yoo Ri Kim	University of Central Florida
Stefan Klein	University of Münster
Chulmo Koo	Kyung Hee University
Jan Krasnodebski	Expedia
Rob Law	The Hong Kong Polytechnic University

Seul Ki Lee	Sejong University
Rosanna Leung	National Kaohsiung University of Hospitality and Tourism
Daniel Leung	The Hong Kong Polytechnic University
Gang Li	Deakin University
Andreas Liebrich	Hochschule Luzern - Wirtschaft
Anyu Liu	University of Surrey
Bernd Ludwig	University Regensburg
Estela Marine-Roig	University of Lleida
Eva Martin-Fuentes	University of Lleida
David Massimo	Free University of Bozen-Bolzano
Christian Maurer	IMC University of Applied Sciences Krems
Luiz Mendes-Filho	Federal University of Rio Grande do Norte
Elina Michopoulou	University of Derby
Valeria Minghetti	CISET – Ca' Foscari University
Kasha Minor	Cardiff Metropolitan University
Jean-Claude Morand	CYBERSTRAT
Antonio Moreno	URV
Jamie Murphy	University of Eastern Finland
Stefan Neubig	Outdooractive
Barbara Neuhofer	Salzburg University of Applied Sciences
Elena Not	Fondazione Bruno Kessler
Peter O'Connor	ESSEC
Juho Pesonen	University of Eastern Finland
Ilona Pezenka	FHWien der WKW University of Applied Sciences for Management & Communication
Mattia Rainoldi	IMC Krems University of Applied Sciences
Francesco Ricci	Free University of Bozen-Bolzano
Jia Rong	Victoria University
Laurens Rook	Delft University of Technology
Roland Schegg	HES-SO Valais
Marianna Sigala	Sheffield Hallam University
Brigitte Stangl	University of Surrey
Jason Stienmetz	MODUL University
Dandison Ukpabi	University of Jyväskylä
Vania Vigolo	University of Verona
Katerina Volchek	Deggendorf Institute of Technology
Bruce Wan	Hong Kong Metropolitan University
Christian Weismayer	MODUL University
Wolfgang Wörndl	Technical University of Munich
Yerin Yhee	Kyung Hee University
Kyung-Hyan Yoo	William Paterson University

ENTER24 Acknowledgements

We would like to thank the Izmir Development Agency for its contribution to the publication of the conference proceedings in open access format that makes ENTER24 research available to the global community.

Contents

Immersive Technologies in Tourism

Technology for Enhanced Experiences

Technology for Marketing, Business Growth, and Development

Technology for Smartness and Disruption

Technology for Sustainability, Health, and Well-being

Reimagining Travel Planning

UGC and Social Media

Editors' Bios

Dr. Katerina Berezina is an Associate Professor and a Hospitality Management Program Director in the Department of Nutrition and Hospitality Management at the University of Mississippi, USA. Her research interests are in the areas of information technology in hospitality and tourism, electronic distribution, and revenue management. Her recent works explored the use of service robots and virtual reality in hospitality and tourism. She serves as the Managing Editor of the Journal of Hospitality and Tourism Technology.

Dr. Lyndon Nixon is an Assistant Professor in the School of Applied Data Science at MODUL University Vienna. His research interests cover the visual classification of photography to automatically extract the touristic destination image from social networks such as Instagram; the use of deep learning for predictive analytics in open domains such as predicting the next trending topic in online channels; the extraction and modeling of knowledge, e.g., about events, in graph structures, and their combination with neural networks to improve computational understanding of the world.

Dr. Aarni Tuomi is Senior Lecturer at Haaga-Helia University of Applied Sciences, Finland. His research, teaching, and consultancy projects explore the intersection of emerging technologies and service business. His research has explored, e.g., service robotics, artificial intelligence, digital platforms, and food technology, as well as experience design and innovation. His work is regularly featured in industry trade magazines and his research has been published in top academic journals, e.g., Annals of Tourism Research and Psychology & Marketing.

AI for Future Tourism and Hospitality

Preference Management in a Single User Group Recommender System

Hanif Emamgholizadeh[1]([✉]), Amra Delić[2], and Francesco Ricci[1]

[1] Free University of Bozen-Bolzano, Bolzano, Italy
`hemamgholizadeh@unibz.it`
[2] University of Sarajevo, Sarajevo, Bosnia and Herzegovina
`adelic@etf.unsa.ba`

Abstract. Group recommender systems (GRSs) support groups of users to find items, e.g., restaurants, that suit, as much as possible, all the group members' preferences. We consider a GRS scenario where a single member of the group, the organizer, uses the system to find and choose a suitable restaurant for the entire group. We present a novel GRS that helps the organizer to: enter the preferences of all the group members, recall them, and manage incompatible preferences. In the system's experimental evaluation, we have found that the designed functionality for recalling group members' preferences and managing incompatible preferences improve the quality of the organizer's choice.

Keywords: Group Decision-Making · Group Recommender System · Recommender Systems

1 Introduction

Groups often need to identify a product or service to consume together. For instance, when a group of friends is planning a vacation, they may look for an itinerary that satisfies all their wishes and wants. Group Recommender Systems (GRSs) employ special recommendation techniques designed to aid groups in their decision-making process. They can acquire the group members' preferences and suggest items that satisfy them as much as possible [1].

In some decision-making scenarios, group members actively participate in the process, by expressing their preferences and discussing alternative options. However, sometimes just a single group member, here called the organizer, may be involved in evaluating options and making a choice, by considering all the group members' preferences, according to his/her knowledge of them. This is a challenging application scenario for GRSs that, despite the absence of the group members' active participation to the preference elicitation, and options discussion phases, is not necessarily simpler to address.

When an organizer searches for a convenient restaurant for his/her group, the following tasks should be supported: (i) *recalling or anticipating group members' preferences, depending on the available knowledge of them*; (ii) *reconciling*

K. Berezina et al. (Eds.): ENTER 2024, SPBE, pp. 3–15, 2024.
https://doi.org/10.1007/978-3-031-58839-6_1

possibly incompatible preferences of the group members; and (iii) *identifying a restaurant that offers at least one dish suited for each group member's preferences*.

To support these tasks we have designed a novel version of MyFoodGRS[1] [2,3], a GRS that enables an organizer to set a group, enter and revise the group members' preferences, evaluate restaurants' qualities, and make an informed choice for his/her group. The food preferences of a group member are specified by the organizer as a set of preferred food categories, and each dish, i.e., a meal included in the menu of a restaurant, belongs to one category. We consider ten food categories: *Pasta, Red Meat, Fish, Rice, Burger, Pizza, Salad, Soup, White Meat, Chinese Noodle*.

MyFoodGRS also helps the organizer to recall or anticipate a group member's preferences (i.e., make reasonable guesses), if she/he does not have this knowledge, by using demographic and preferred cuisines information that may be more easily available [4]. MyFoodGRS uses this information in a machine learning model as predictive features of the group member's food preferences. Moreover, group members' preferences may be incompatible: for instance, it could be hard to find a place that serves Pizza (preference of a member) and also Fish (preference of another member). Hence, by utilizing an association rules component, MyFoodGRS assists the organizer in expanding the already entered food preferences of the group members and discovering new alternative preferences of the group members. In summary, we make the following contributions:

- We present a novel version of MyFoodGRS that supports a single group member (organizer) in entering/revising group members' preferences and making a decision, i.e., selecting a restaurant, on behalf of the group.
- We introduce machine learning solutions that aid the organizer to recall and anticipate group members' preferences and resolve issues related to incompatible preferences that hinder the possibility to find an appropriate restaurant for the group.
- We report the results of an ablation study, aimed at evaluating the supporting functionalities (i.e., recalling and anticipating group members' preferences, and resolving incompatible preferences). The main result indicates that the designed functionalities help the organizer to make better choices, decreasing the discrepancy between individuals' preferences and actual group choice, and increasing the group members' evaluation (rating) of the organizer's choice.

In the rest of the paper, a brief overview of the GRSs state-of-the-art is provided in Sect. 2, in Sect. 3 we describe the usage of MyFoodGRS in the target application scenario. Then, Sect. 4 describes the implementation of the preference management and recommendation functions. The designed user study and its results are described in Sects. 5 and 6. We conclude the paper by discussing its limitations and future works in Sect. 7.

---

[1] myfoodgrs.inf.unibz.it:8080.

2   Related Work and Research Gaps

Recommender Systems (RSs) help their users to find content that meets their preferences and needs [5]. Group Recommender Systems (GRSs) are RSs that provide personalized content to a group of people; their main challenge is to properly aggregate the preferences of the group members, such that the recommendations satisfy everybody in the group [1].

A variety of GRSs have been proposed to address the specific requirements of the group recommendation task [1,6]. However, we have found that only two, namely, Intrigue [7] and Rempad [8], are addressing an application scenario similar to that of MyFoodGRS, as they both support an organizer to make a decision on behalf of an entire group. Intrigue enables a tour leader to insert group members' information and generate recommendations to satisfy different subgroups. Rempad supports organizers in selecting multimedia content for reminiscence therapy sessions. In comparison to Intrigue, which is suggesting a set of points of interest (POIs), recommending a single restaurant satisfying a wide spectrum of food preferences is harder, as more constraints must be satisfied. Moreover, differently from Rempad, in our scenario the organizer has a more limited knowledge of the individual group members' preferences, hence requires some system support.

From another point of view, commercial restaurant finders, such as TripAdvisor, are designed for individuals seeking restaurants for their group, but they do not explicitly provide support functionalities such that the selected item actually fits all the group members' needs and wants. In fact, none of them support the organizer in facing the two key tasks mentioned in the Introduction, namely, recalling and anticipating other group members' preferences and helping the organizer in dealing with incompatible preferences.

Our approach is motivated by Logue and Smith [4], who introduce age, thinness, sensation seeking, and ethnic background (i.e., the main cuisine of the users on which they were raised) as predictors of food preferences for adult humans. They show that by using these features one can predict food preferences of individuals. They also model patterns of food preferences by establishing relations between them. For instance, they have found that the tendency to prefer junk dishes is correlated with a tendency to prefer meat and potatoes, and breakfast dishes. We have implemented these ideas in machine learning models to support the organizer to expand the initially entered group members' preferences.

3   MyFoodGRS Interaction Design

Let's assume that Jack is arranging a dinner for a group including also Jim and Frank. The interaction with MyFoodGRS starts in the GROUP tab, where Jack can customize the system behavior and set up the group (Fig. 1a). Then, he can enter his and the other group members' (known) food preferences, i.e., favorite food categories (Fig. 1b). The preferences of a group member are considered to be "alternative" ones, i.e., they are expressing OR conditions. The system assigns a

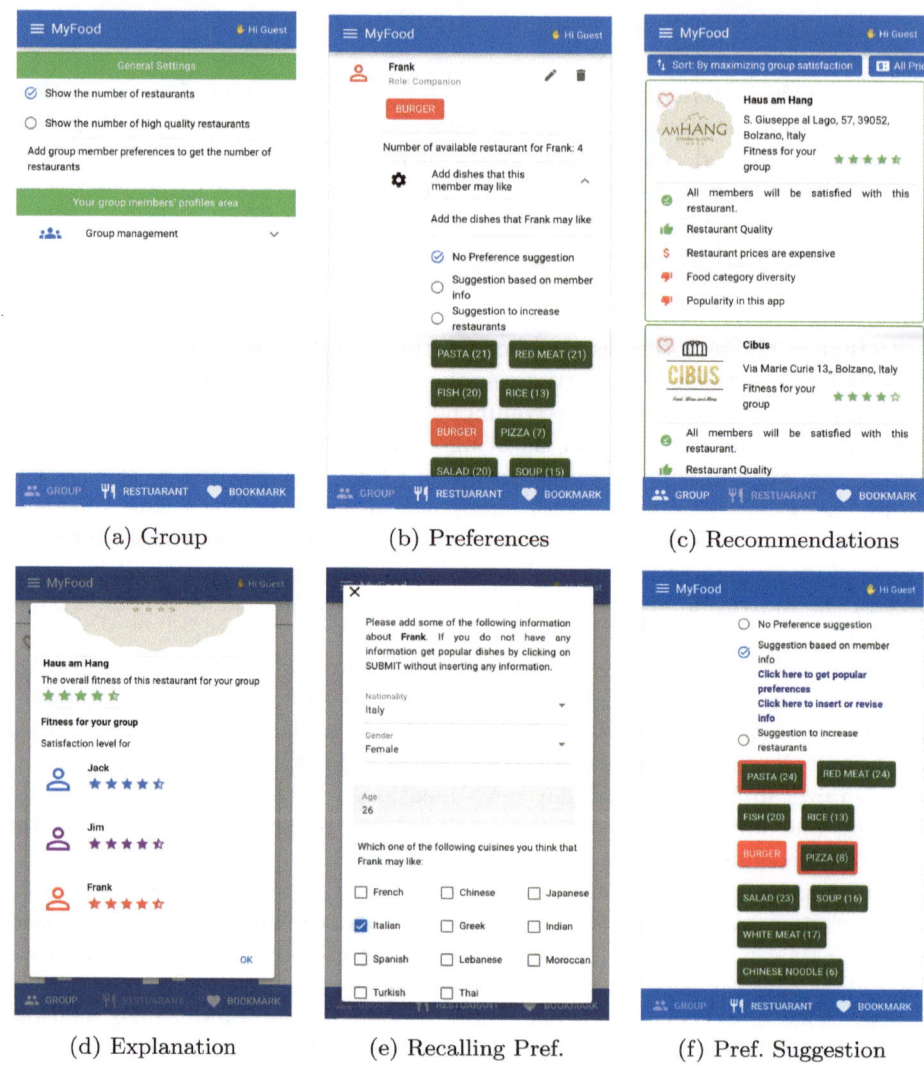

Fig. 1. Application screenshots

color to each group member (e.g., red to Frank), that always indicates the group member and his/her preferences in the various system screens.

Jack, the organizer, can also access two preference management functionalities: one helps Jack to recall Jim or Frank's preferences and another helps him to overcome the difficulty of finding a suitable restaurant in case of incompatible preferences. Recalling preferences highlights possible preferences of a group member as soon as he/she is introduced in the system by the organizer, whereas the incompatible preference suggestion support requires that an initial set of group members' preferences have been entered by the organizer. To recall a group member's preferences, Jack can click on "Suggestion based on member's info" and input member information: nationality, gender, age, or preferred cuisines (Fig. 1e). Suggested preferences for a group member are indicated by adding a border, of the member's distinguishing color, around preferences not yet attributed (hence in green) to the group member (Fig. 1f). Suggestions for overcoming incompatible preferences are also indicated in a visually similar way.

The organizer (Jack), after having entered some group members' preferences, can access the system's recommendations in the RESTAURANT tab (Fig. 1c), where restaurants are ranked based on their "Fitness to the group" (see Sect. 4 for the technical details). For a better assessment of the restaurant's suitability for the group, clicking on its card (Fig. 1c) displays restaurant details: (a) popularity of the restaurant in the system; (b) fitness for the group, showing the predicted group score of the restaurant (see Sect. 4) and detailed information about the suitability of the restaurant for each group member; (c) similarity to the groups who bookmarked this restaurant in the past, that is, showing to what extent other groups who bookmarked this restaurant are similar to the organizer's group; (d) TripAdvisor score of the restaurant; and (e) food categories and dishes diversity on the restaurant menu.

When the organizer reaches the last recommendation in the list that satisfies all the group members, if he is not satisfied with any of the recommended restaurants, is invited to use the two preference management supporting functionalities we mentioned above. Hence, by clicking on the REVISE button, the organizer is redirected to the GROUP tab, where the two preference management functionalities are available.

Finally, the organizer can bookmark some restaurants and access them by using the Bookmark tab. Bookmarked restaurants can be compared side-by-side and one of them can be finally chosen for the group.

4   Recommendation and Interaction Management

To sort the recommendations, the organizer can select one of the three available ranking algorithms, while two machine learning models are supporting the organizer in, recalling and anticipating the other members' preferences, and dealing with incompatible preferences.

4.1   Recommendations Ranking

Popularity. The first ranking algorithm is not adapted to the group preferences and it is based only on the restaurants' popularity score: how frequently a restaurant was bookmarked in MyFoodGRS by other groups. Popularity ranking is used by default when no users' preferences are entered.

Fitness for the Group. Let q_r be the quality score of the restaurant r, which is the TripAdvisor five star rating, and $\boldsymbol{p_r} = (r_1, r_2, \ldots, r_c)$ the profile of the restaurant r: c is the number of food categories and $r_j = 1$ if at least one dish in the restaurant menu is in category j ($r_j = 0$ otherwise). Furthermore, let $u \in G$ be a member of the group G, and $\boldsymbol{p_u} = (u_1, u_2, \ldots, u_c)$ the profile of u: $u_j = 1$ if category j is preferred by u ($u_j = 0$ otherwise). The predicted satisfaction score $s_{r,u}$ of restaurant r for u is calculated as follows:

$$s_{r,u} = \max(\boldsymbol{p_r} \odot \boldsymbol{p_u} \cdot q_r) \tag{1}$$

where $\odot$ is the element-wise multiplication of the vectors $\boldsymbol{p_u}$ and $\boldsymbol{p_r}$, and $\max(\cdot)$ is the maximum value of the elements in the vector. Hence, u has a non-null satisfaction when there is at least one dish in the restaurant's menu that fits u preferences, and the satisfaction level is equal to the TripAdvisor rating of the restaurant. Finally, by using the *Average Aggregation Strategy* [1], the satisfaction score of the group G for the restaurant r is defined as the average of the $s_{r,u}$ scores of all the users $u \in G$. This average score is then used to rank restaurants according to their fitness for the group.

Collaborative Based Ranking. In the third ranking algorithm, restaurants are sorted by a collaborative filtering approach: the score of a restaurant is proportional to the number of similar groups who bookmarked it. The similarity of the two groups is estimated by considering the group members' preferences. In particular, the similarity between the organizer's group and a group who bookmarked the target restaurant is calculated as the Jaccard similarity of the two groups, where a group is represented by the "OR" of its group members' profiles $\boldsymbol{p_u}$. Then, the score of the restaurant is calculated as the ratio of (i) the number of groups who bookmarked the restaurant and have Jaccard similarity with the organizer's group greater than a threshold (0.6 in our case), to (ii) the number of all groups who bookmarked the restaurant.

4.2   Reconstructing Group Members Preferences

For supporting the organizer in recalling or anticipating the other group members' preferences we have implemented a model that, taking into account a group member's nationality, gender, age, and preferred cuisines, predicts the member's preferred food categories. A cuisine is often linked to a particular culture or provenance area, and by knowing that a user likes a cuisine, e.g., Italian, one can predict user's preferred food categories, e.g., Pasta.

There are two situations in which the organizer may need support to recall or anticipate group members' preferences. First, when the organizer does not know the group member. In this case, the system could only make a generic suggestion, i.e., that the group member may like the most popular food categories. Conversely, when the organizer has some information about a group member, such as demographic data or preferred cuisines, then the system can use of a predictive model.

We have therefore trained a Support Vector Machine (SVM) model which takes as input nationality, age, gender, and/or preferred cuisines (depending on the available information), and predicts the top two preferred food categories. We employed Scikit-learn's SVM for training. We have optimized the regularization term and the kernel with Grid search. The training data is the collection of users' profiles entered by the subjects that participated in the experimental evaluation.

4.3   Dealing with Incompatible Preferences

When the group members have incompatible preferences, i.e., there is no restaurant that offers at least one dish in one of the preferred food categories of each group member, MyFoodGRS suggests alternative preferences for the group members. It is implemented by taking into consideration food preference patterns. For instance, users who like Pasta often also like Pizza. To this end, we have used fpgrowth[2] [9]. This algorithm extracts the most frequent patterns of food category preferences, and then, based on the declared user's preferences, predicts other possible preferences of the group member.

5   Methodology

We now focus on the evaluation of the usefulness of the two proposed supporting functionalities: helping the organizer to (i) recall and anticipate the preferences of the group members, and (ii) deal with incompatible preferences. To this end, we have conducted a user study, which will be now described, providing details on the design, i.e., independent and dependent variables, data collection procedure, and resulting measures. At the end, we will elaborate on the conducted analyses.

The **user study** was designed to assess whether the two proposed supporting functionalities enhance the organizers' ability to make better decisions. The "goodness" of a decision is quantified with two constructs, (a) the individual loss, i.e., how well the group choice aligns with the group members' individual preferences [10], and (b) the group score, i.e., how highly the group members rate the selected option as appropriate for the group. The operationalization of these constructs will be in detail described below. These constructs are the dependent variables of our analysis - we measure how good the choice of the organizer is, depending on the supporting functionalities in the system.

The realization of the independent variables is done with four variants of the system. Namely, V_N does not offer any of the two supporting functionalities. V_R provides support for *Recalling* preferences, V_I provides support for *Overcoming Incompatible* preferences, and finally, the variant V_{RI} provides both supporting functionalities. As an extraneous condition, that can affect the quality of the organizer's choice, we have considered the level of information about the group members available to the organizer. To this end, we have defined three types of groups: (i) G_N - *Groups with no information*, i.e., only group members' demographic information (age, gender, and nationality) is available, (ii) G_P - *Groups with partial information*, i.e., demographic information and preferred cuisines of the group members are available, and (iii) G_F - *Groups with full information*,

---

[2] https://rasbt.github.io/mlxtend/user_guide/frequent_patterns/fpgrowth/.

i.e., demographic information, preferred cuisines, and preferred food categories are revealed to the organizer. During the experiment stage, we followed the A/B testing experimental design [11]. We note that for each group, all the group members played the role of "organizer", they were provided with one of the introduced system variants, and they were shown different levels of information about their fellow group members.

Data Collection Procedure was organized in three stages, *Before Decision-Making, Decision-Making,* and *After Decision-Making.* In the *Before Decision-Making* stage, each participant was introduced to the overall procedure with an explanatory movie, and entered personal demographic information (age, gender, and nationality), preferred food categories, and preferred cuisines. The system also randomly selected for each user 10 restaurants such that each restaurant had at least one of the user's food preferences in their menu, and asked the users to rate them based on their preferences.

After all the involved users had performed the Before Decision-Making stage, the system automatically constructed groups of different sizes (containing from 2 to 5 members). Then, started the Decision-Making stage where each group member was asked to independently interact with a variant of the system and to play the role of the organizer of the group. Note that a user was often assigned to more than one group. In this stage, the system also showed different levels of information about other group members to the organizer, depending on the *group type* to which a particular user was assigned. The task for the organizer was: *Imagine that you are responsible for finding a proper restaurant for a group of people. This is a group of people that you might or might not know. Based on the information about the group members provided in the system, and with the help of the system's functionalities, your task is to select one restaurant that you believe will make the group (all group members) happy.* In parallel, all the other group members performed the same procedure. This stage was completed when all the organizers selected a restaurant for their group.

In the *After Decision-Making* stage, the restaurants selected by the organizers were evaluated and rated by their fellow group members. Firstly, they rated each restaurant selected by an organiser of their group, if that was not already rated in the first stage (where they already provided their individual ratings for 10 restaurants). Then, they provided a different type of rating to these restaurants, which is called group score: considering how appropriate the restaurants were for the entire group, i.e., by taking into consideration the preferences of all the group members.

The participants were faculty members of the Free University of Bozen-Bolzano and bachelor students at the University of Sarajevo. Altogether, 95 participants were involved, and 60 groups were generated: each user participated in two groups and very few in three groups. However, not all the participants completed all the initiated evaluation sessions (195) in their groups, and we obtained 153 evaluations (26 users completed one evaluation, 53 two evaluations, and 7 three evaluations). In each evaluation, a user rated the choices made by the other group members when they acted as organizers, and overall we collected

492 ratings and group scores for restaurants chosen by group members acting as organizers. Participants were from 11 countries, mainly Bosnia, Italy, and Iran. 54% are males and 46% females, with an average age of 21. The minimum number of organizer's choice ratings/group-scores that the combination, i.e., the variant of the system and group type (altogether 12 combinations), received was 25, the maximum was 56, with the mean of 41.

Measures represent the concepts over which we hypothesize to see the effects of the previously defined independent variables. More precisely, we are interested in how the two proposed supporting functionalities influence the "goodness" of the organizer's choice, given the different levels of information availability. The two concepts that measure the "goodness" of the organizer's choice are individual loss and group score. Individual loss quantifies the difference between the maximum rating an individual would give to the best restaurant that he/she would have selected for themselves and the rating that the user gave to a restaurant that the organizer in his/her group selected. Secondly, we consider the already defined group score: the group member's rating for an organizer's choice, considering the preferences of the other group members.

Analyses. In order to evaluate the effectiveness of the two proposed supporting functionalities in terms of the organizer's choice quality, the *Cumulative Link Model* (CLM) [12] (also known as two-way ordinal regression, or proportional odds model [13]) with the help of R package **ordinal** [14,15] was used. This analysis is the most similar to the factorial (two-way) ANOVA [16,17], which is suitable when there is more than one independent, categorical variable, and the goal is to measure the effect of each variable as well as their interaction on a continuous dependent variable. However, in our case, the dependent variables are ordinal (not continuous), i.e., individual loss takes integer values from 0 to 4 (lower is better), and group score takes also integer values from 1 to 5 (higher is better), and for both, order of values is relevant. To this end, factorial ANOVA was not a suitable choice, and the CLM was instead utilized. The significant results are interpreted as "there is a significant effect of the independent variable on the dependent variable". The assumption that CLM needs to meet in order to be applicable for the data is the *proportional odds assumption* [18], which in our case was not violated.

6   Results

The output of the CLM is shown in Table 1, and indicates that the system variant has a significant effect on individual loss as well as on group score: there are differences in the quality of the organizer's choice with respect to different variants of the system. Conversely, no significant effects were found for the group type (i.e., the level of information about the group members that was provided to the organizer), nor the interaction effect of the two independent variables. Therefore, we hypothesize that depending on the group type, different system variants provided different levels of support, however leading to the same quality levels of the organiser's choice. Nevertheless, both models are significant, indicating that their predictive power is significantly better than that of models using only intercept values.

Table 1. Cumulative link model output

	Df	Individual Loss χ^2	p-value	Group Score χ^2	p-value
system variant	2	17.579	**0.000**	9.673	**0.021**
group type	3	0.376	0.828	1.673	0.433
interaction effect	6	4.205	0.648	10.020	0.123
Model		22.41	**0.021**	21.583	**0.027**

Next, since we have four variants of the system, we were interested in which variants actually excel in terms of the two dependent variables. Since the level of available information did not play a role in the quality of the organizer's choice, we proceeded with a simpler analysis of variance for an ordinal (rank) variable, i.e., the Kruskal-Wallis test and the post-hoc Dunn test.

Kruskal-Wallis test indicates significant differences between the four system variants, for individual loss with p-value of 0.000, as well as for the group score variable with p-value of 0.019 (which was expected given the previously presented results). The results of the Dunn test are provided in Table 2 (the reported p-values are adjusted for multiple comparisons using the Bonferoni correction [19]. The table only shows significant differences due to the page limit. It is found that individual loss is lower and group score is higher when the organizer's choice was made within the variant that provides support for both recalling/anticipating and dealing with incompatible preferences, in comparison to the organizer's choices made within the variant with no supporting functionalities, and the variant which only provided support for recalling group members' preferences. Furthermore, the individual loss was significantly lower for the organizer's choice when the support for incompatible preferences was provided in comparison to when support for recalling preferences was given. Here, no significant differences were observed for the group score. These differences are also visualized in Fig. 2.

Table 2. Dunn test results

Comparison	Individual Loss Z-value	p-value	Group Score Z-value	p-value
V_I to V_R	**−3.077**	**0.006**	0.925	0.532
V_N to V_{RI}	**2.590**	**0.0191**	−2.481	**0.039**
V_R to V_{RI}	**3.517**	**0.002**	−3.029	**0.014**

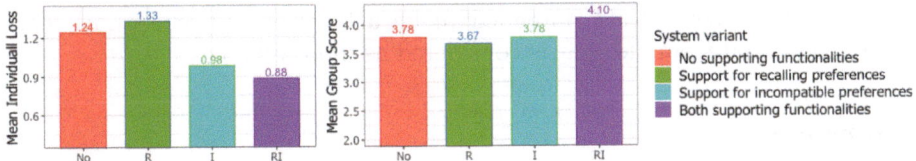

Fig. 2. Differences in mean values of individual loss and group score over system variants (for individual loss, lower is better, and for group score, higher is better)

7   Conclusion and Future Work

We have here presented MyFoodGRS; it assists a group member (organizer) to choose a restaurant on behalf of the entire group. We have evaluated two supporting functionalities: recalling and anticipating group members' preferences, and dealing with possibly incompatible preferences within the group. The first one utilizes a machine learning model that predicts the most probable member's individual preferences based on available demographics or preferred cuisine data. The second one makes use of association rule mining to extend the preferences of a group member entered by the organizer. In our ablation analysis, we found that the variant offering both supporting functionalities resulted in significantly better choices, i.e., choices for which individual loss of group members is significantly lower, and their rating for the choice is significantly higher, in comparison to choices made with variants of the system that do not provide these functionalities. Moreover, the variant that only provides support for recalling and anticipating group members' preferences did not result in significantly better choices.

We would like to highlight some of the limitations of this study. First of all, we acknowledge that the number of food categories that we used (only 10) is a limiting factor in fully expressing food related preferences. Additionally, our participants were mostly bachelor students and may not be representative of real-world users. Furthermore, we expected to observe certain differences in the usefulness of the proposed supporting functionalities in relation to the level of available information about the group members, but this was not the case, and in order to better understand this, additional analysis, with an extended data sample is necessary. We speculate, that the recalling functionality may have not been effective for at least three reasons. First, because of a sub-optimal machine learning model that we have used and the limited training data. Secondly, because of the low variability of the users' demographics in our data sample, as most of the participants are from Bosnia and of similar age. Third, the usefulness of the proposed functionality may have been reduced by the small number of food categories.

We acknowledge as well that randomly formed groups do not represent typical groups, which tend to be composed by more similar individuals. As part of our future work, we aim to conduct a larger experiment with established groups.

This new experiment is also intended to be a between-subjects study, which requires more data samples but is considered as more reliable.

References

1. Masthoff, J., Delić, A.: Group recommender systems: beyond preference aggregation. In Ricci, F., Rokach, L., Shapira, B. (eds.) Recommender Systems Handbook, pp. 381–420. Springer, New York (2022)
2. Emamgholizadeh, H., Delic, A., Ricci, F.: Supporting a group member to make a group choice. In: Adjunct Proceedings of the 31st ACM Conference on User Modeling, Adaptation and Personalization, pp. 96–99 (2023)
3. Emamgholizadeh, H., Bazzanella, B., Molinari, A., Ricci, F.: Single user group recommendations. In: Adjunct Proceedings of the 30th ACM Conference on User Modeling, Adaptation and Personalization, pp. 308–313 (2022)
4. Logue, A.W., Smith, M.E.: Predictors of food preferences in adult humans. Appetite **7**(2), 109–125 (1986)
5. Ricci, F., Rokach, L., Shapira, B.: Recommender systems: techniques, applications, and challenges. In: Ricci, F., Rokach, L., Shapira, B. (eds.) Recommender Systems Handbook, pp. 1–45. Springer, New York (2022). https://doi.org/10.1007/978-1-0716-2197-4_1
6. Felfernig, A., Boratto, L., Stettinger, M., Tkalčič, M.: Group Recommender Systems. SECE, Springer, Cham (2018). https://doi.org/10.1007/978-3-319-75067-5
7. Ardissono, L., Goy, A., Petrone, G., Segnan, M., Torasso, P.: Intrigue: personalized recommendation of tourist attractions for desktop and hand held devices. Appl. Artif. Intell. **17**(8–9), 687–714 (2003)
8. Bermingham, A., O'Rourke, J., Gurrin, C., Collins, R., Irving, K., Smeaton, A.F.: Automatically recommending multimedia content for use in group reminiscence therap. In: Proceedings of the 1st ACM International Workshop on Multimedia Indexing and Information Retrieval for Healthcare, pp. 49–58 (2013)
9. Han, J., Pei, J., Yin, Y.: Mining frequent patterns without candidate generation. ACM SIGMOD Rec. **29**(2), 1–12 (2000)
10. Baltrunas, L., Makcinskas, T., Ricci, F.: Group recommendations with rank aggregation and collaborative filtering. In: Proceedings of the Fourth ACM Conference on Recommender Systems, pp. 119–126. ACM (2010)
11. Kohavi, R., Longbotham, R.: Online controlled experiments and A/B tests. In: Sammut, C., Webb, G.I. (eds.) Encyclopedia of Machine Learning and Data Mining, pp. 1–11. Springer, Boston, MA (2015). https://doi.org/10.1007/978-1-4899-7687-1_891
12. Agresti, A.: Categorical Data Analysis, vol. 792. Wiley (2012)
13. McCullagh, P.: Regression models for ordinal data. J. Roy. Stat. Soc.: Ser. B (Methodol.) **42**(2), 109–127 (1980)
14. Haubo, R., Christensen, B.: Cumulative link models for ordinal regression with the R package ordinal 2018 (2018)
15. Mangiafico, S.S.: Summary and analysis of extension. Program Eval. R Version 1(1) (2016)
16. Yates, F.: The analysis of multiple classifications with unequal numbers in the different classes. J. Am. Stat. Assoc. **29**(185), 51–66 (1934)
17. Fujikoshi, Y.: Two-way ANOVA models with unbalanced data. Discret. Math. **116**(1–3), 315–334 (1993)

18. Strand, S., Cadwallader, C., Firth, D.: Using Statistical Regression Methods in Education Research. University of Southampton, ESRC National Centre for Research Methods (2011)
19. Benjamini, Y., Hochberg, Y.: Controlling the false discovery rate: a practical and powerful approach to multiple testing. J. Roy. Stat. Soc.: Ser. B (Methodol.) **57**(1), 289–300 (1995)

How Distinct and Aligned with UGC is European Capitals' DMO Branding on Instagram?

Lyndon J. B. Nixon[(⊠)]

Modul University Vienna, Am Kahlenberg 1, 1190 Vienna, Austria
lyndon.nixon@modul.ac.at

Abstract. Destination positioning refers to destinations identifying their most distinct attributes and focusing on these in their marketing activities in order to distinguish themselves from competitors, develop a brand identity and highlight uniqueness. In this paper, we consider 9 European capitals and analyse their visual marketing on Instagram to identify how truly distinct their destinations are being presented online. By comparing between them as well as comparing to the perceived destination image measured from visitor photos on the same platform, we present a methodology for identifying each destinations distinct attributes and measuring how well DMOs are positioning themselves with respect to competing destinations, with recommendations for improving their positioning.

Keywords: Destination Marketing · Content Marketing · Digital Marketing · Positioning · Destination Brand · Destination Image · Visual Classification

1 Introduction

Destination marketing in the 21st century has been marked by the emergence of new digital channels, visual content overtaking text as the marketing medium, and the attention shift of the target audience from DMO's own content to user-generated content (UGC). Marketers, whose goals remain to develop a successful *brand identity* and differentiate themselves from their competitors through *positioning*, face an increasingly complex situation in determining the optimal content marketing strategy, because (a) the dominant image of a destination among consumers is being determined by UGC which is outside of their (direct) control, and (b) that destination image is being communicated through non-textual media such as visitor photos and videos which require a distinct analysis approach compared to text. Tourism marketing has always been highly visual since imagery can best invoke the experience of visiting the destination for consumers. First the Web and then social networks has increased the scale and the reach of visual marketing content, as well as introducing a new and more significant determinant of destination image for a global audience which is UGC – the photos and videos visitors themselves post online. Whereas stakeholders, e.g. DMOs, have long made use of textual analytics to understand how their destinations are being presented online (whether in the news, in reviews on travel websites or in posts on social networks), the content of purely visual media could not be easily included in marketing analysis as accurate descriptions were largely only feasible through manual, expert annotation which could not scale up.

K. Berezina et al. (Eds.): ENTER 2024, SPBE, pp. 16–28, 2024.
https://doi.org/10.1007/978-3-031-58839-6_2

Computer-assisted understanding of the content of images and videos has long been a challenging research area due to the complexity of defining to a computer what is "seen" in the image. However, in just the last few years, the combination of deep learning (complex neural network architectures) and huge scale media collections for training (e.g. crawled from the Web) has led to a paradigm shift in the capability of so-called *computer vision* systems, including (in our case) the field of *visual classification* (i.e. labelling a media item with the correct concept from some controlled vocabulary of concepts). Accuracy on the ImageNet dataset (a benchmark in the computer vision community, with 1000 visual concepts) has jumped from 63.3% (AlexNet in 2013) to 91.1% (BASIC-L in 2023) while Web platforms host models and make them accessible to anyone via APIs (HuggingFace.co reports 5270 models for image classification at the time of writing). The advances in computer vision mean that tourism marketers now have access to AI-based systems that can automatically classify tourist photography and use this classification in gaining a deeper understanding of what visitors give particular focus to when at their destination. Digital marketing online, especially on social networks, is highly competitive as consumers are overwhelmed by information and can switch easily between sources. Marketers could benefit from the new insights image classification can offer them, especially comparing how their destination and its competitors are being presented visually, how that user-driven presentation compares to their targeted content marketing, and where, if at all, their destination is differentiating itself from the others in the global online marketplace. However, this requires a visual classification which is provably accurate in the domain of destination image measurement, an approach to collect and classify large sets of images as well as a methodology to represent the resulting classification in a form for marketing analysis. The contribution of this paper is the visual classification model, evaluated against a specifically prepared ground truth data set and provably accurate for destination image, as well as the methodology for compositional data analysis (CoDa) of the resulting classifications as a representation of a destination's visual brand.

The rest of this paper continues with the current state of the art in the domain of tourism (marketing) and image classification (Sect. 2). We then present the concept of "visual destination brand", explain it in the context of destination marketing and how it can be measured through image classification (Sect. 3). Then we introduce our experiment for acquiring the visual destination brand of 9 European cities, both projected (DMO) and perceived (user) (Sect. 4). The extracted brands are compared in Sect. 5 with a focus on identifying significant variations within and between destinations. Finally, Sect. 6 concludes with lessons learnt for tourism marketing from our experiment.

2 State of the Art

There has been a lack of studies regarding the role of visual content in destination marketing [1], particularly with respect to branding and positioning, two key aspects of a marketing content strategy. While tourist photography has long been seen as a valuable source of insights into what visitors focus on at a destination (which in turn acts as an indicator of what is most appealing to visitors), researchers had to manually classify photos, following self-determined classification vocabularies, either alone (in the role of experts) or through solicitation from the people who took the photos. This method could not scale up to handle the amount of online visual content available for any destination. Past work focused on the use of photography in the measurement of *destination image*, which is defined as "beliefs, ideas and impressions that a person has of a destination" [2]. Researchers agree on one component of destination image being the *cognitive*, which relates to the attributes that the consumer thinks of (or visualises) when they think of the destination – those with external, tangible representations may also be called *functional* [3]. While there is discussion about the other parts such as *affective* and *conative*, and that the holistic measurement of destination image requires combining all of the components, it has been studied that the other components are themselves influenced from the cognitive component [4]. The use of (user and/or DMO) photography to determine destination image is seen as valid since "*both organic and induced secondary sources of information... significantly influences the cognitive component*" [4]. Destination image is increasingly being formed through online visuals [5], and photos on social media are a valid source of consumer's image [6]. UGC photos are the materialisation of what a visitor deems as important, even iconic, at a destination [7], and thus a means to reconstruct the destination image [8]. The cognitive component would be measured as a set of (visually identifiable) destination attributes and an individual destination represented by the analysis of the frequency, co-occurrence, clustering etc. of the aggregated attributes of a dataset [9].

The destination image is typically seen as synonymous with or similar to *destination brand*, which is the application of a branding strategy to market a tourism destination. Branding actions by the brand owner can be called brand identity, e.g. "a unique set of brand associations that the brand strategist aspires to create or maintain" [10]. On the other hand, brand image can be defined as "perceptions about a place as reflected by the brand associations held in tourist memory" [11]. The key characteristic of a successful branding is *uniqueness*, i.e. the branded concept, such as a tourism destination, is differentiated in the minds of consumers from competing concepts, which gives it an USP for consumers to choose it in place of any other option at the time of purchase. A key methodology for branding is *positioning*, which is about "*about identifying the key characteristics that visitors had in mind* [when choosing the destination] *and reinforcing these*" [12]. Positioning is seen as a source of competitive advantage [13]. For positioning to be effective, the range of differentiated characteristics should be limited [14]. Visual content forms part of the destination branding [15]. Perceptions of the destination brand value play a major role in boosting tourism to the destination [16].

With the emergence of deep learning-based advances in computer vision, e-tourism research has considered the use of pre-trained AI models in classifying larger scales of tourism photography and using this classification for analysis [1]. Generally, the same approaches have been followed, just with larger image sets, e.g. deriving the perceived destination image of a place through publicly available social media (e.g. Beijing [17]; Hong Kong [18]; Seoul [19]). Research has shifted from initially using Flickr to Instagram and TikTok, both highly visual social networks (e.g. [20, 21]).

Measurement of destination image and/or brand is significant for marketers as a favourable image or brand is seen as positively influencing intention to visit [22] and WoM recommendation [23]. Social networks are a valid source of data as they act as one of the major channels today to influence consumers' brand perceptions [23]. Studies have demonstrated a relationship between UGC and destination brand [24]. Both DMO and UGC communication were analysed, and the latter was found to have a stronger positive influence on the destination image [25]. In marketing, it is generally accepted that the closer the perceived and projected destination images are, the better. Therefore, marketers seek to match the images [26]. Destination marketers want to know if their projected brand has been incorporated into consumer's perceived images [27].

A major shortcoming of past tourism research using AI-based image classification for destination image measurement has been that the researchers have used the classifier directly in its available state rather than fine-tuning it for the tourism context. The model training has used broad, generic, large scale image datasets for classification into an equally broad, generic, object- or scene-focused classification scheme. For example, most off-the-shelf AI models for image classification are available pre-trained with ImageNet (1000 labels), as this dataset acts as the standard benchmark for accuracy in the computer vision community. However, the resulting models annotate photos just as the training data was annotated, which was not for the purpose of destination image measurement, and hence may focus on less relevant labels (e.g., a touristic photo in the Sahara is highlighting the presence of *desert*, but ImageNet models will label the *camel* which focuses rather on the attribute of *animals*. In fact, ImageNet has no label for desert so no desert photo would be labelled as such). Two studies on the accuracy of ImageNet-based classifiers showed that the results for destination image measurement were much less accurate than the reported benchmark [19, 28]. Off-the-shelf models are used to label thousands of photos, leading to a post-classification clustering step to reduce the broadly distributed results into a smaller number of categories, which however proves non-deterministic (changes in the clustering approach will lead to different clusters; data from other destinations will produce distinct clusters that can not be compared across destinations). As we will introduce in the next section, this is why we decided to fine tune a state of the art model specifically on destination visual attributes.

3   Visual Destination Brand

This paper makes use of the concept of *visual destination brand*. This term is coined by the authors to refer to the projected brand identity or the perceived brand image (depending on the source analysed), as a factor of the content of the photos posted online and shared publicly by visitors to a destination. Given the limitations in previous work discussed in the previous section, the authors have implemented their own visual classifier which has been demonstrated to be accurate in destination image measurement. The currently available model (bit.ly/destinationclassifier) uses the Vision Transformer architecture which is regarded as state of the art in computer vision. The model was fine tuned with a training dataset of 4,949 tourism photos found via Google Images. To independently test its accuracy without the risk of overfitting (reusing the data the model was trained on), the authors additionally created a "ground truth" dataset made up of 100 photos per attribute acquired via hashtags from the YFCC100M dataset (openly available photography from Flickr), scoring 94% for top-1 accuracy (bit.ly/visualdestination). Full details have been provided in [34]. As there is no single, unique correct list of destination attributes for analysis of destination image [29], we determined an appropriate classification scheme by surveying the attributes identified by the most cited (i.e. most authoritative) papers which developed lists through either expert interview or consumer surveys, particularly [4] who referred to the earlier works and aimed to list "*all factors influencing image assessments*", as well as [9] where the attribute list was specifically developed for the task of photo classification (so e.g. visually distinguishable attributes were important). Table 1 shows our attribute list (rightmost column) which are aligned with all attributes previously determined as relevant.

Table 1. Visual destination attributes of our classifier, aligned to past work.

(Echtner & Richie, 1993)	(Baloglu & McClearly, 1999)	(Beerli & Martin, 2004)	(Stepchenkova & Zhan, 2013)	The authors
Climate	Climate	Weather		
Scenery/nature	Scenery/nature	Countryside	Nature & landscape	Landscape
Tourist activities		Theme parks	Tourist facilities	
		Zoos	Animals, wildlife	Animals
Nightlife/entertainment	Nightlife/entertainment	Nightlife, Bars, discos and clubs		Entertainment
Fairs/exhibits/festivals		Festivals, concerts, Casinos		
Sport		Sports	Leisure activities	Sport
Parks/wilderness		Nature reserves	Country landscape	Trees
		Lakes, mountains, deserts	Outdoor/adventure	Water; mountains; desert
		Flora and fauna	Plants	Plants and flowers
Transportation	Infrastructure	Private and public transport	Transport/infrastructure	Roads and traffic
		Roads, airports, ports		
Architecture/buildings	Cultural attractions		Art object	Art and museums
			Archaeological site	Monument
Historical sites/museums	Historical attractions	Museums, hist. buildings, monum	Architecture/buildings	Historical building
Beaches	Beaches/water	Beaches		Beach
Shopping		Shopping		Shops and markets
Accommodation/restaurants	Accommodation	Accommodations		Accommodation
	Cuisine	Restaurants, gastronomy	Food	Gastronomy
Cities			Urban landscape	Modern building

The classification of an image dataset by the classifier results in a set of frequencies for each attribute and conversely a ratio of how present each attribute is in the dataset (i.e. frequency of occurrence/total number of images classified). A ratio is preferred to absolute frequency as results may be compared between classifications which were produced from a different number of input images. In our previous work, our intuition was to model the set of ratios as a *multidimensional vector,* as then we could analyse and visualise results in the same manner as "embeddings" are handled as outputs of AI models, e.g. cosine distance is used as the measure for closeness rather than Euclidean. In this work, we reflect that these vectors are also *compositional data* since they express information about the relative importance of many parts to a whole. The characteristic of compositional data is that it sums to a constant, and any change in any one value within the composition (the vector, in our case) must have an equal and opposite change on another value. As such, Compositional Data Analysis (CoDa) is the right statistical approach to this data [30]. The vectors are transformed to centered logarithms of ratios and then CoDa-specific approaches may be used to quantify differences between the compositions, e.g. between projected and perceived destination images [31]. In the rest of this paper, we extract visual destination brand vectors for 9 European capitals using our visual classifier and show how compositional data analysis can be employed to identify the relative differences between how those cities are presented visually online, both by content marketers (DMOs) as well as by visitors (UGC).

4 Experiment

Following the theory of destination positioning, destination marketers should identify the most significant attributes of the destination (as seen by potential visitors), compare these with their competitors, and focus only on those which genuinely distinguish them. Our experiment will show how this can be done using visual destination brand vectors and compositional data analysis. The vectors will be constructed from the classification of image datasets extracted from Instagram. We consider Instagram as a valid source since it is a leading visual-centric social network for destination marketing which contributes to the co-creation of destination brand [32]. It is more recently used in tourism research as a source of destination image measurement (e.g. [21]). Besides identification of differences between city images among DMO or UGC sources, we will also compare both (projected vs perceived image) as managers can use the incongruence between them to improve their promotion of the destination [31].

We identified the ten most visited European capital cities (based on Eurostat data for the year 2019 to exclude pandemic related outliers, number of nights spent in tourist accommodation): Paris, Budapest, Rome, Madrid, Berlin, Vienna, Stockholm, Prague, Lisbon and Athens. We believe it is valid to compare directly between these cities as they largely market to the same target audience: city travellers visiting or in Europe. As many of these travellers will plan travels between different cities in the same trip (or on different trips), the European cities compete directly with one another for traveller choice ("intention to visit"). We acknowledge that there are always other factors that influence the final destination selection (e.g. price and accessibility) but our choice of the most popular European cities means that costs both to get to the city and to be in the city can be very similar for tourists and all of our chosen destinations are similarly well connected internationally in transportation networks.

The resulting datasets are as follows, with an indication of which DMO account/UGC hashtag was used for collection (the official city tourism site was found via Google and the Instagram link followed; the recommended tourism hashtag is usually given in their Instagram account bio) and how many photos were acquired within the calendar year 2023 (we use the Python library *Instaloader*. Please note the image files were used exclusively for this research and deleted afterwards). We had to remove Prague from the list of cities for two reasons: the Prague DMO account @cityofprague posts content the least regularly of all the considered DMO accounts, meaning that the DMO photo dataset would have been smaller than the rest; also the Prague DMO is alone in our sample in not promoting a related destination tourism hashtag so we would have to choose from user's own selected hashtags, from which #cityofprague seemed to be popular for visitor photography but also lower scale than the hashtags of the other cities. So in the end we will compare these 9 popular European cities (Table 2).

We use the datasets to measure the respective visual destination brand by labelling each photo in the dataset with one of our 18 visual destination attributes (using our visual classifier implementation). For each dataset, a vector is constructed by taking for each attribute the number of photos in the dataset labelled by that attribute divided by the total number of photos in the dataset, then mapping each attribute value to one feature (or dimension) in the vector. Since these vectors represent compositional data (the sum of all of the values in the vector is constrained to a constant value - since they are ratios

Table 2. Photo datasets collected from Instagram.

Destination	DMO account	Photos	UGC hashtag	Photos
Athens	@thisisathens	329	#thisisathens	2070
Berlin	@visitberlin	334	#visitberlin	1187
Budapest	@visitbudapest_official	566	#visitbudapest	1594
Lisbon	@visit_lisboa	348	#visitlisboa	1260
Madrid	@visita_madrid	496	#visitmadrid	2791
Paris	@parisjetaime	140	#parisjetaime	1432
Rome	@turismoromaweb	467	#visitrome	623
Stockholm	@visitstockholm	232	#visitstockholm	717
Vienna	@viennatouristboard	565	#viennanow	684

in our case all vectors sum to 1), we follow the approach in compositional data analysis to convert them to *centred logarithms of ratios* [33], which has the effect of removing the sum constraint, introduces linearity in the differences between values, and makes the data applicable to standard statistical techniques. Once we have determined the centred log-ratio vectors for the visual destination brands, we can apply statistical methods and data visualisations to test for:

(a) *Destination positioning* – how distinct is the projected image by DMO marketing of each destination from the other European capital cities?
(b) *Alignment to perceived image* – how aligned is the projected image by DMO marketing of a destination to the perceived image of that destination as reflected in UGC photography by visitors?

5   Results and Interpretation

We cluster the DMO vectors according to cosine distance from one another, so that we can identify which cities position themselves through their DMO-driven marketing in a manner visually similar to others and, as the corollary, which cities if any already demonstrate successful destination positioning (offering a marketed image of the city which is distinct from the others). Cosine distance is used instead of Euclidean as we want to consider similarly significant attributes as closer than similarly insignificant attributes (i.e. (3.2, 3.5) should be closer than (0.9, 1.2) whereas it would be the same in Euclidean distance). We use k-means clustering, normalise the vectors and choose the optimal number of clusters using the Calinski index (a metric which is optimal for compositional data) for values between 2 and 6 (we do not want to spread clusters too thin, so use 2/3 of the total number of data points as a max value). The Calinski index value indicates optimally 6 clusters for 9 cities, suggesting that the DMO's do distinguish their destinations visually in their content marketing. Budapest and Rome are clustered together (cluster 0), Athens and Paris as well (cluster 2), and a third cluster pairs Berlin and Stockholm (cluster 3). Madrid (cluster 1), Lisbon (cluster 4) and Vienna (cluster 5) are all individual clusters, suggesting greater distinctiveness in the distribution of visual attributes in their (Instagram) content marketing.

We compare the geometric means of the values of the attributes for all the cities' visual destination brands in each cluster in order to interpret the visual meaning of each cluster (which attributes are relatively more present in each). Figure 1 shows a geometric bar plot for the six clusters, which highlights the relative differences between them across the 18 attributes. It visualises the variation of the attribute values from the geometric mean for the attribute values over all of the data therefore highlighting those values which are relatively higher or lower than the rest. We include in our calculation a weighted mean, which reduces the variation calculated for attributes which are overall less significant as part of the branding (e.g. while 10% is double 5% and 30% is equally double 15%, the latter is clearly more significant for the branding). Cluster 0 cities (Budapest, Rome) show relatively more entertainment and monument content. Cluster 1 (Madrid) has relatively much more shops & markets content and much less water content (i.e. lakes, seas) than the others. Cluster 2 (Athens, Paris) proves to be the brands which are closest to the overall mean, suggesting they may not stick out from the other destination marketing. Cluster 3 (Berlin, Stockholm) are brands which show relatively more modern buildings and trees. Cluster 4 (Lisbon) and cluster 5 (Vienna) show the most relative variation in attributes in their marketing. Lisbon highlights more than other destinations animals, beach, landscape and water; Vienna is highlighting more its historical buildings, gastronomy and museums.

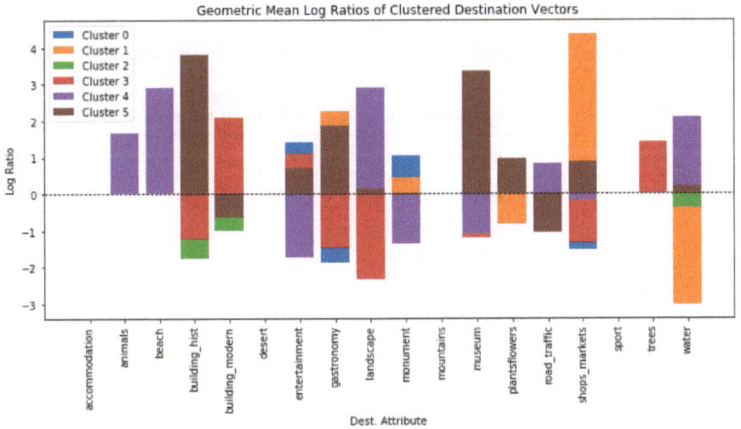

Fig. 1. Geometric bar plot of the 6 city clusters comparing the visual attributes.

We have noted that how the DMO markets the city may not align with what visitors actually attach importance to in their visit. We make the informal assumption that the photos visitors choose to post to a social network such as Instagram are knowingly selected out of a much larger set of options, where the purpose of selection may be to show the destination to their friends and followers, but also there can be the intention that their public photos will be seen broadly and globally. The latter is much more the case with those who deliberately use the tourism-related hashtag to acquire more visibility, as is the case with our UGC datasets. This assumption is based on our own usage of Instagram while travelling as well as observation of friends and family. As a result, we may assume that the set of UGC photos posted of the city by visitors using the tourism hashtag reflect a curated set of visual attributes of the city that they have deemed of significance (for themselves, and to others). Through the centring of the log-ratios in the visual destination brand vectors, which means subtracting the geometric mean of the vector values (as a measure of central tendency) from each individual value, positive values already indicate the attributes which are relatively more present in the visual destination brand than the others and as a logarithmic function, the extent of positive value does correlate with relatively more significance of the attribute in the photos over the dataset. Therefore, we can compare the DMO and UGC vectors of each city to identify where incongruence occurs, which can indicate where DMOs overemphasize an attribute which is comparably less significant to visitors or where DMOs need to emphasize more strongly an attribute which is found to have greater significance among visitors to that destination. We measure the Aitchison distance between both vectors to assess the similarity in direction (distribution of features), Fisher's exact test pairwise on the features of both vectors (to find significance in variation between the same feature) and a geometric mean bar plot of both vectors to visualise where the vectors vary most from each other. Due to space, Table 3 is restricted to reporting for each city the Aitchison distance between the vectors, and the visual attributes which show significance in difference, as indicated by the centred log-ratio value – the higher the positive value, the more significantly present:

Table 3. Attributes with significant differences between DMO and UGC branding.

City	Distance	Significant att.	DMO log-ratio	UGC log-ratio
Athens	0.78	shops markets	1.9	0.77
Berlin	1.53	Gastronomy	0.75	2.12
		plants flowers	2.7	0.8
		shops markets	−0.62	1.27
Budapest	2.1	Entertainment	1.62	0.27
		plants flowers	1.29	0.02
Lisbon	2.07	landscape	2.98	1.47
Madrid	1.14	shops markets	3.35	1.38
Paris	2.82	Accommodation	−7.39	0.08
		entertainment	2.35	−0.2
Rome	2.72	Gastronomy	0.84	2.64
		museum	1.76	3.1
Stockholm	2.1	Accommodation	−1.62	0.87
		entertainment	1.46	−0.29
Vienna	1.34	Museum	3.19	1.07
		roads traffic	0.6	1.48

Athens' DMO marketing aligns closest to the UGC photography from the destination, whereas it is Paris and Rome which show the most incongruence between projected and perceived images. Focusing on attributes which show relatively more importance to visitors in UGC content than in the DMO marketing (i.e. higher positive value), we can identify "gastronomy" and "shops markets" in Berlin, "gastronomy" and "museum" in Rome as well as "roads traffic" in Vienna as attributes DMOs should focus more strongly on presenting in their content marketing as they resonate with visitors.

Finally, we provide an interpretation of this data for the purposes of destination brand management. DMOs want to provide a consistently distinct visual communication about their destination through the strategy of positioning to successfully form a destination brand with the consumers. We have seen that European city marketing does lead to distinct positioning of their destinations as a visual brand, with Madrid promoting comparatively more its shopping offer, Berlin and Stockholm modern buildings and trees, Lisbon shows more animals, beach, landscape and water, and Vienna focuses on historical buildings, gastronomy and museums. In as far as this branding is aligned with what visitors find to be significant to visit at the destination, marketers believe this branding activity maximises consumer intention to visit as well as other success metrics like intention to recommend (including eWOM). We found that DMO and UGC visual destination brands were often aligned, which is perhaps to be expected (DMOs repost some of the UGC content and visitors photograph aspects they consider significant, which also may come from the projected image by the DMO). However, some attributes were more strongly present in UGC content which suggests that DMOs could incorporate more of those visual aspects in their content marketing strategy, such as the gastronomic offer in Berlin and Rome, shopping in Berlin, museums in Rome and roads/traffic (i.e. street scenes, the red and white trams) in Vienna.

6 Conclusions

In this paper, we have shown how a *visual destination brand* can be extracted and analysed to better understand how destinations are being presented in terms of their visual attributes. While studies have shown that images and videos is increasingly becoming more determinant for consumer's image of a destination, tourism research lacks shared methodologies and approaches for measuring and processing those inputs as part of a destination branding strategy. We presented our approach which is based on an image classifier specifically fine tuned for destination visual attributes to measure the destination brand, the brand representation as a multidimensional vector and the use of compositional data analysis to cluster and compare vectors. Unlike previous work where we had looked at very distinct destinations (e.g. Maldives and New York), this time we chose 9 European cities which market themselves to a similar target audience. We found that their DMO marketing does position each destination differently, with Madrid, Lisbon and Vienna being the most distinct due to relatively more content highlighting different attributes of each destination. DMOs also seek to align projected with perceived image, with a number of cities (Berlin, Rome and Vienna) having opportunities to still strengthen their branding with attributes that are found to be significant to their visitors. The same approach may be applied to any destination(s). Future work would be to validate the set of visual attributes with visitors (do they align with how people make mental associations with a destination), compare the automatic labelling of the classifier with human annotators' decisions, as well as correlate the extracted vectors with quantifiable destination metrics which, at the end, is the most important outcome for any destination marketer: e.g., which visual destination brand leads to more visitors? Such experiments are much more difficult as one can not easily separate out all the other factors which might influence a dependent variable such as visitor numbers. However, the means to (accurately) extract a visual destination brand and represent it in a manner viable for statistical analysis is an important first step and will hopefully support further research on understanding visual brand and its relevance to tourism research and marketing.

References

1. Picazo, P., Moreno-Gil, S.: Analysis of the projected image of tourism destinations on photographs: a literature review to prepare for the future. J. Vacat. Mark., 1–22 (2017)
2. Crompton, J.L.: Motivations for pleasure vacation. Ann. Tour. Res. 6(4), 408–424 (1979)
3. Gallarza, M., Saura, I., García, H.: Destination image. Ann. Tour. Res. 29(1), 56–78 (2002). https://doi.org/10.1016/s0160-7383(01)00031-7
4. Beerli, A., Martín, J.D.: Factors influencing destination image. Ann. Tour. Res. 31(3), 657–681 (2004)
5. Kim, S.B., Kim, D.Y., Wise, K.: The effect of searching and surfing on recognition of destination images on Facebook pages. Comput. Hum. Behav. 30, 813–823 (2014)
6. Liu, L., Zhou, B., Zhao, J., Ryan, B.D.: C-IMAGE: city cognitive mapping through geo-tagged photos. GeoJournal 81(6), 817–861 (2016)
7. Pan, S., Lee, J., Tsai, H.: Travel photos: motivations, image dimensions, and affective qualities of places. Tour. Manage. 40, 59–69 (2014)
8. Hunter, W.C.: The social construction of tourism online destination image: a comparative semiotic analysis of the visual representation of Seoul. Tour. Manage. 54, 221–229 (2016)
9. Stepchenkova, S., Zhan, F.: Visual destination images of Peru: comparative content analysis of DMO and user-generated photography. Tour. Manage. 36, 590–601 (2013)
10. Aaker, D.A.: Managing Brand Equity. Free Press, New York (1991)
11. Keller, K.L.: Conceptualizing, measuring, and managing consumer-based brand equity. J. Mark. 57(1), 1–22 (1993)
12. Botha, C., Crompton, J.L., Kim, S.S.: Developing a revised competitive position for Sun/Lost city, South Africa. J. Travel Res. 37(4), 341–352 (1999)
13. Greenley, G., Hooley, G., Saunders, J.: Management processes in marketing planning. Eur. J. Mark. 38(8), 933–955 (2004)
14. Crompton, J.L., Fakeye, P.C., Lue, C.C.: Positioning: the example of the Lower Rio Grande Valley in the winter long stay destination market. J. Travel Res. 31(2), 20–26 (1992)
15. Blain, C., Levy, S.E., Ritchie, J.B.: Destination branding: insights and practices from destination management organizations. J. Travel Res. 43(4), 328–338 (2005)
16. Horng, et al.: Developing a novel hybrid model for industrial environment analysis: a study of the gourmet and tourism industry in Taiwan. Asia Pac. J. Tour. Res. 19(9), 1044–1069 (2013)
17. Zhang, K., Chen, Y., Li, C.: Discovering the tourists' behaviors and perceptions in a tourism destination by analyzing photos' visual content with a computer deep learning model: the case of Beijing. Tour. Manage. 75, 595–608 (2019)

18. Zhang, K., Chen, Y., Lin, Z.: Mapping destination images and behavioral patterns from user-generated photos: a computer vision approach. Asia Pac. J. Tour. Res. **25**(11), 1199–1214 (2020)
19. Kim, D., Kang, Y., Park, Y., Kim, N., Lee, J.: Understanding tourists' urban images with geotagged photos using convolutional neural networks. Spat. Inf. Res. **28**, 241–255 (2020)
20. Shao, T., Wang, R., Hao, J.-X.: Visual destination images in user-generated short videos: an exploratory study on Douyin. In: 16th International Conference on Service Systems and Service Management (ICSSSM), pp. 1–5 (2019)
21. Arefieva, V., Egger, R., Yu, J.: A machine learning approach to cluster destination image on Instagram. Tour. Manage. **85**, 104318 (2021)
22. Tigre Moura, F., Gnoth, J., Deans, K.R.: Localizing cultural values on tourism destination websites: the effects on users' willingness to travel and destination image. J. Travel Res. **54**(4), 528–542 (2015)
23. Hudson, S., Huang, L., Roth, M.S., Madden, T.J.: The influence of social media interactions on consumer–brand relationships: a three-country study of brand perceptions and marketing behaviors. Int. J. Res. Mark. **33**(1), 27–41 (2016). https://doi.org/10.1016/j.ijresmar.2015.06.004
24. Dedeoglu, B.B., Taheri, B., Okumus, F., Gannon, M.: Understanding the importance that consumers attach to social media sharing (ISMS): scale development and validation. Tour. Manage. **76**, 103954 (2020). https://doi.org/10.1016/j.tourman.2019.103954
25. Huerta-Álvarez, R., Cambra-Fierro, J.J., Fuentes-Blasco, M.: The interplay between social media communication, brand equity and brand engagement in tourist destinations: an analysis in an emerging economy. Destin. Mark. Manag. **16**, 100413 (2020)
26. MacKay, K.J., Fesenmaier, D.R.: Pictorial element of destination in image formation. Ann. Tour. Res. **24**(3), 537–565 (1997)
27. Ji, S., Wall, G.: Understanding supply-and demand-side destination image relationships: the case of Qingdao, China. J. Vacat. Mark. **21**(2), 205–222 (2015)
28. Nixon, L.: Assessing the usefulness of online image annotation services for destination image measurement. In: ENTER 2018, January 2018 (2018)
29. Stepchenkova, S., Mills, J.E.: Destination image: a meta-analysis of 2000–2007 research. J. Hosp. Market. Manag. **19**(6), 575–609 (2010)
30. Coenders, G., Ferrer-Rosell, B.: Compositional data analysis in tourism. Review and future directions. Tour. Anal. **25**(1), 153–168 (2020)
31. Marine-Roig, E., Ferrer-Rosell, B.: Measuring the gap between projected and perceived destination images of Catalonia using compositional analysis. Tour. Manag. **68**, 236–249 (2018)
32. Fatanti, M.N., Suyadnya, I.W.: Beyond user gaze: how Instagram creates tourism destination brand? Procedia Soc. Behav. Sci. **211**, 1089–1095 (2015)
33. Aitchison, J.: The Statistical Analysis of Compositional Data: Chapman and Hall, London (1986). Reprinted in 2003 with additional material by The Blackburn Press
34. Nixon, L.: Do DMOs promote the right aspects of the destination? A study of Instagram photography with a visual classifier. In: ENTER 2022, January 2022 (2022)

Automated Topic Analysis with Large Language Models

Andrei Kirilenko$^{(\boxtimes)}$ (iD) and Svetlana Stepchenkova (iD)

University of Florida, Gainesville, FL 32611-8209, USA
andrei.kirilenko@ufl.edu

Abstract. Topic modeling is a popular method in tourism data analysis. Many authors have applied various approaches to summarize the main themes of travel blogs, reviews, video diaries, and similar media. One common shortcoming of these methods is their severe limitation in working with short documents, such as blog readers' feedback (reactions). In the past few years, a new crop of large language models (LLMs), such as ChatGPT, has become available for researchers. We investigate LLM capability in extracting the main themes of viewers' reactions to popular videos of a rural China destination that explores the cultural, technological, and natural heritage of the countryside. We compare the extracted topics and model accuracy with the results of the traditional Latent Dirichlet Allocation approach. Overall, LLM results are more accurate, specific, and better at separating discussion topics.

Keywords: Large Language Model (LLM) · GPT-3 · topic modeling · social media

1 Introduction

The history of automated annotation of textual documents starts from the 1960s when Borko and Bernick [1] applied exploratory factor analysis to unsupervised classification of scientific publication abstracts. Nowadays, dozens of models have been developed and applied to extract topics from a texts [2, 3]. In tourism and social sciences in general, the most popular approach [4] is Latent Dirichlet Allocation (LDA) developed by Blei [5]. Meanwhile, LDA has important restrictions, which are usually ignored by authors. First, LDA relies on discerning parameters of the document-topic and topic-word distributions, which necessitates the presence of documents of ample length to effectively encapsulate a diversified amalgamation of topics. Second, the LDA algorithm mandates a substantial corpus of textual data to ensure precise estimation of the underlying topic distributions. Lastly, the discordant or extraneous documents within the corpus, which are common in social media, negatively impact the quality of the inferred topics. Even when all these assumptions are met, LDA topic models are criticized for inherent instability and challenges in defining the "optimal" number of target topics.

In the past few years, a new crop of large language model (LLM) such as Google's BERT [6] has become increasingly popular, owing the success to their ability to capture the context instead of considering document words in isolation. In tourism domain,

© The Author(s) 2024
K. Berezina et al. (Eds.): ENTER 2024, SPBE, pp. 29–34, 2024.
https://doi.org/10.1007/978-3-031-58839-6_3

TourBERT topic model was pre-trained on tourist reviews, descriptions of tourist services, attractions and sights [7], though we are not aware of any publication in tourism journals that would utilize it.

The explosive development of the LLM field, which drew public attention after a ChatGPT became freely available over a web-based interface, has led to exploration of LLM topic extraction capabilities following a set of instructions (prompts). A new discipline known as prompt engineering explores LLM ability to learn new tasks from examples provided as an input (prompts). The key concepts of prompt engineering are the precise setting of the context such as providing relevant facts; providing elaborate instructions; conditioning LLM behavior by, e.g., providing examples; controlling for data biases; iterative refinement of LLM responses; and, finally, result validating [8, 9].

Emerging studies hint at ability of using LLM prompt engineering for topic modeling [10–12]. In this respect, LLMs have numerous advantages over previous generation of topic models such as leveraging general knowledge obtained in the pre-training process to infer the comments' topics, even when the data is incomplete or ambiguous; ability to infer the topic of short comments by transferring knowledge from similar domains; and robustness to noise in the data. They can handle misspellings, grammatical errors, and inconsistent punctuation, which are common in noisy documents, by capitalizing on the surrounding context and their understanding of language patterns [8, 9].

This paper is the first to the best of our knowledge attempt to apply an LLM (GPT-3) to extraction of topics from a set of online feedbacks (reactions) of blog readers. A typical reaction is short (one sentence) and noisy (contains cultural references, slang, and typos), which makes topic extractions with traditional methods challenging. We compare extracted topics with results of traditional LDA model trained on the same dataset.

2 Data and Methodology

The specific setting are online reviews of a famous Chinese social media influencer Li Ziqi who holds a Guinness World Record for the "most subscribers for a Chinese language channel on YouTube". The focus of Li Ziqi's videos is on rural China; their depiction of simple yet beautiful traditional way of life evidently impacts potential tourists wishing to "visit LIZIQI'S world". We collected all Weibo and Youtube reactions to four most popular Li Ziqi's videos reflective of her area of interest: Rural way of life; Traditional self-made culture; Food and cooking; and Input of China to the world civilization. The collected data was cleaned, and short reactions (lesser than three words) were removed. In total, 1,852 reactions in English language were collected on Youtube. On Weibo, 2,980 reactions in simplified Chinese were collected and translated to English with Google translate. The quality of translation was verified by a native speaker.

Collected data was then processed in batches of circa 2,000 words to fit GPT-3 limits using the following prompt: "Find the most common and prominent topics covered in the {text}. For each topic that you find print the number of occurrences of this topic." Here, {text} represents a block of reactions. Identified topics were then merged using GPT-3, resulting in 18 major topics. Finally, the reactions were mapped back to the topics following prompt engineering best practices (abridged):

- goal = "match review to the best fitting review topic from a list of topics"
- steps = "1. Break the list of reviews onto separate reviews; 2. For each review find two best matching review topics from the list of review topics separated by the ';' sign; 3. When there are no well-matching topics, assume that the topic is 'Other'; 4. Print the review followed by the best matching topics"
- actAs = "a classifier assigning a class label to a data input"
- format = "a table with reviews in the first column ..."
- prompt = "Your goal is to {goal}, acting as {actAs}. To achieve this, take a systematic approach by: {steps}. Present your response in markdown format, following the structure: {format}. The list of review topics are as follows: {topics_str}".
- The list of reviews is as follows: {text}

For comparison, we used identical set of reactions to extract their topic with LDA. Data was pre-processed following the best practices of topic modeling: stop word removal, bigram tokenization, and lemmatization. Then, LDA topic modeling was completed for the number of topics varying from 5 to 25. A 13-topic solution was selected for its best interpretability.

3 Results

Table 1 presents LLM topics, together with validation outcomes. The quality of topic modeling was validated by bilingual expert on a stratified random sample consisting of 360 reactions (20 per topic). The overall accuracy of topic modeling, as conducted by LLM, was found to be 97.7%. The most important reason for the high accuracy is improved recognition of short texts. Note that 30% of reviews were classified into "Other" category and were not rated. In a similar way, we performed validation of LDA topics (Table 2). For each document, LDA returns a mix of topics; we validated the topic with the highest probability and only this probability exceeded 0.5. One can interpret this decision as assigning documents not related to any high probability topic to the category "Other" (42% of dataset) and removing them from validation process. Overall accuracy of topic assignment was 58%.

Table 1. Topic validation outcomes, LLM.

Topics	Weibo	YT	Overall
Admiration & praise for Li Ziqi	86%	100%	93%
Curiosity about Li Ziqi background	100%	100%	100%
Desire to learn from Li Ziqi & replicate her creations	92%	91%	92%
Enthusiasm and support as a fan	100%	100%	100%
Li Ziqi beauty & resemblance to a princess	92%	88%	90%
Li Ziqi's genuineness, sincerity, & trustworthiness	100%	100%	100%
Li Ziqi's impact on viewers	100%	100%	100%
Li Ziqi's role model status	100%	100%	100%
Animals (specifically dogs & sheep)	100%	100%	100%
Beauty and aesthetics of traditional life & products	92%	100%	96%
Desire to live a peaceful, natural, simple, self-sufficient life	100%	100%	100%
Nature & rural life	100%	100%	100%
Nostalgia & childhood memories	100%	100%	100%
Li Ziqi's connection with her grandmother	100%	92%	96%
Chinese traditional crafts & skills	100%	92%	96%
Chinese traditional culture & heritage	100%	91%	96%
Art of calligraphy	100%	100%	100%
Food & cooking	100%	100%	100%

Table 2. Topic validation accuracy, LDA.

Topic words	Topic name	Acc.
chinese; little; culture; admire; chinese culture; need; inherit; ability; music; inherit chinese	Chinese traditional culture & heritage	35%
life; live; place; wish; thank; beauty; nature; love; perfect; start	Beauty of living with nature	55%
love; cute; like; feel; sheep; lamb; follow; powerful; puppy; skill	Cute dogs & sheep	40%
girl; amazing; treasure; china; miss; think; home; sister; life; make	L. is amazing, treasure	50%
know; sister; happy; want; marry; fairy; snack; qiqi; good; want know	L. is fairy like, I want to marry her	65%
work; great; hard; lady; young; quot; malaysia; hard work; young lady; share	L is hard working	40%
want; house; make; time; fruit; grow; live; tree; build; candied	Interest in grounds, visiting, marriage	60%
look; paper; make; traditional; popcorn; chinese; brush; super; inkstone; wonderful	Traditional culture, craft, and cooking	75%
woman; make; awesome; world; best; mother; real; cook; amazing; feel	Admiration & praise for L	65%
good; thing; amaze; person; good good; heart; life; hungry; make; mickey	Expressions of enthusiasm	65%
beautiful; talented; strong; woman; make; people; wool; amazing; ancient; process	L. is beautiful, talented, and strong	75%
bamboo; time; grandma; make; hand; long; wear; glove; child; sofa	Traditional crafts, wear gloves!	55%
come; fairy; people; kind; update; kind fairy; mango; dislike; help; night	General support from fans	75%

4 Discussion

Given that the social media reactions tend to be short, it is not surprising that LDA topic modeling accuracy was moderate (58%); in comparison, LLM accuracy was excellent (98%). Meanwhile, even though LDA performance in terms of assigning the documents to specific topics was unimpressive, the overall set of topics is similar between LDA and LLM. It includes themes related to Chinese culture, crafts, beauty of living with nature, pets, and variations of expressions of praise towards the influencer. Note that LLM derived topics are much more specific, easy to comprehend, and did not require tedious interpretation process.

To our best knowledge, this is the first attempt to use LLM in tourism domain, a much wider effort is needed to make solid conclusions about the best practices and limitations of the methodology. The field of prompt engineering has existed for only one year. However, in our view application of LLM to topic modeling in tourism domain seems to have a very high potential. Our next plans are exploration of LLM capabilities in analysis of textual and pictorial tourism data with goals of understanding limitations and formulation of the best practices.

References

1. Borko, H., Bernick, M.: Automatic document classification. J. ACM JACM **10**, 151–162 (1963)
2. Churchill, R., Singh, L.: The evolution of topic modeling. ACM Comput. Surv. **54**, 1–35 (2022)
3. Vayansky, I., Kumar, S.A.: A review of topic modeling methods. Inf. Syst. **94**, 101582 (2020)
4. Egger, R., Yu, J.: A topic modeling comparison between LDA, NMF, Top2Vec, and BERTopic to demystify twitter posts. Front. Sociol. **7**, 886498 (2022)
5. Blei, D.M., Ng, A.Y., Jordan, M.I.: Latent dirichlet allocation. J. Mach. Learn. Res. **3**, 993–1022 (2003)
6. Devlin, J., Chang, M.-W., Lee, K., Toutanova, K.: BERT: pre-training of deep bidirectional transformers for language understanding. ArXiv Prepr. arXiv:1810.04805 (2018)
7. Arefieva, V., Egger, R.: TourBERT: a pretrained language model for the tourism industry. ArXiv Prepr. arXiv:2201.07449 (2022)
8. Ekin, S.: Prompt Engineering for ChatGPT: A Quick Guide to Techniques, Tips, and Best Practices (2023)
9. White, J., et al.: A prompt pattern catalog to enhance prompt engineering with chatgpt. ArXiv Prepr. arXiv:2302.11382 (2023)
10. Bhaskar, A., Fabbri, A.R., Durrett, G.: Zero-shot opinion summarization with GPT-3. ArXiv Prepr. arXiv:2211.15914 (2022)
11. Kublik, S., Saboo, S.: GPT-3. O'Reilly Media, Incorporated, Sebastopol (2022)
12. Rijcken, E., Scheepers, F., Zervanou, K., Spruit, M., Mosteiro, P., Kaymak, U.: Towards interpreting topic models with ChatGPT. Presented at the The 20th World Congress of the International Fuzzy Systems Association (2023)

AI-Generated Future: What Awaits Tourism and Hospitality with AI-Based Deep Learning Technologies?

Ayşe Collins[1], Seyid Amjad Ali[2], and Semih Yılmaz[1(✉)]

[1] Department of Tourism and Hotel Management, Bilkent University, 06800 Ankara, Turkey
{collins,semihsaityilmaz}@bilkent.edu.tr
[2] Department of Information Systems and Technologies, Bilkent University, 06800 Ankara, Turkey

Abstract. AI-based technologies are taking the world by storm – rapidly changing the course of many industries from arts to education, healthcare to entertainment, and even areas of life we are yet to discover [1–4]. The application of AI-based technologies is also emerging in travel and tourism industries [5, 6], but remains underexplored as a research area [7–9] when specific and feasible AI applications are considered. This study describes and appraises several emerging AI-based deep learning technologies that are un(der)utilized in tourism fields but promise high utility in the future. Furthermore, potential application areas of these technologies within the context of tourism are detailed. Possible research routes and methodologies to investigate the functionality of AI-based applications are also outlined.

Keywords: Artificial Intelligence · Deep Learning · Tourism · Hospitality

1 Background

While studies are proliferating on how AI may change the face of tourism [6, 10, 11], there's an obvious lack of describing which specific AI technologies are in question and how they particularly relate to tourism. This situation risks the use of AI as yet another hollow 'buzzword'. AI is indeed a game changer for tourism [7] – but we need to specify which technologies we mean by AI, how they work and what they mean for tourism. There are many sub-branches of AI, such as machine learning and deep learning, and delineating them is necessary for maximum utility [12, 13].

While all technologies that aim to mimic human intelligence in non-human platforms can be labeled as Artificial Intelligence (AI) [14, 15], machine learning (ML) refers to a subset of these technologies which comprises software applications that are able to learn to predict outcomes of actions or inputs without human intervention [11]. Machine learning can broadly be categorized into three subsections: supervised, unsupervised, and reinforced learning [16]. Among these categories, multi-layered algorithms that are modeled after the neurons in human brain (artificial neural networks) to make more complex decisions collectively make up the deep learning subfield [17, 18]. Deep learning

K. Berezina et al. (Eds.): ENTER 2024, SPBE, pp. 35–39, 2024.
https://doi.org/10.1007/978-3-031-58839-6_4

Table 1. AI-based DL technologies and potential application areas in tourism

AI-based DL Technology	Type	Generic Application Areas	Application to Tourism
Convolutional Neural Network *An algorithm specifically designed for image processing and recognition tasks*	Computer Vision	Image & facial recognition; medical image analysis; voice recognition; automatic sign language recognition	Secure registration at borders and check-ins, temporary ownership, purchase authorizations
Style Transfer *A computer vision and graphics technique to combine the content of one image with the visual style of another*	Computer vision, graphics	Transferring or superimposing famous artistic styles to user-supplied images	Deep localization in marketing communications
Deep Learning Based Recommender System *An application that is based on multiple DL technologies, and uses an algorithm to suggest choices of interest based on Big Data*	Ranking	Suggesting consumer products based on past purchases or browsing histories; personalized list of choices; preference predictions (Amazon, Spotify, etc.)	Personalized itineraries, authenticated reviews
Generative Adversarial Network *A type of learning architecture that pits two neural networks against each other to generate new synthetic data in close resemblance to an existing data distribution*	Generative AI	Generating examples for image datasets, such as human faces or realistic photographs, image-to-image, text-to-image, or semantic-image-to-photo translations, video prediction (such as Memoji creation in iPhones)	Personalized interactive ads; tangibilization of future experiences

(continued)

Table 1. (*continued*)

AI-based DL Technology	Type	Generic Application Areas	Application to Tourism
Variational Autoencoder *An algorithm to generate new content while detecting & removing noise*	Generative AI	Image morphing; image reconstruction; outlier detection	Event simulations, accuracy in recreational programming
Recurrent Neural Network *An algorithm that operates on sequential data to predict new outcomes*	Sequential data processing	Language translation; natural language processing (NLP); speech recognition & image captioning; (e.g., Alexa, Google Translate)	Polylingual tour guiding; universal translators; accessible, anti-ableist visitor experiences
Graph Neural Networks (GNN)	Solve problems related to graph-structured data	Networks that can be represented via graph. Some examples are social networks, molecular structures, and transportation networks	Tourist flow prediction

(DL) is believed to embody the farthest advancement in AI technologies as it creates models that are able to learn from complex environments and make optimal decisions without the need of human input [19, 20]. Therefore, this study focuses on emerging AI-based technologies rooted in deep learning where potential breakthroughs in service provision and customer satisfaction exist.

2 Purpose of the Study

The purpose of this propositional study is to a) identify and review emerging AI-based technologies, chiefly rooted in deep learning, that have a high potential of operational utility for tourism industries, b) propose specific application areas for each identified deep learning technologies within the context of tourism and hospitality.

3 Review of AI-Based Technologies and Application Areas

Upon review of AI, ML and DL literature as well as industry reports, seven AI-based deep learning technologies identified and reviewed in this study were *Convolutional Neural Network* [20], *Style Transfer, Deep Learning Based Recommendation System* [21, 22], *Generative Adversarial Network, Variational Autoencoder, Recurrent Neural Network and Graph Neural Networks (GNN)* [23, 24]. Definition, function, and potential application areas of each technology are summarized in the Table 1.

4   Conclusion and Future Implications

This review appraises the most prominent deep learning technologies with applicability to tourism and hospitality industries. Two important highlights of this review were 1) the indispensability of interdisciplinary frameworks to study the utility of AI-based technologies in tourism, and 2) the challenge of reliable data in tourism and hospitality domains. A crucial aspect of AI-based technologies is that they are highly data-dependent. This is a challenge for potential AI applications as sustainable solutions to adequate and accurate data collection are lacking in many tourism sectors. Therefore, it might be necessary to prioritize operational areas that are more conducive to reliable data collection than others such as international border crossings, hotel customer registrations, ticket sales for attractions, etc. AI-based applications may be more likely to succeed if they are first applied in these areas and then expand into other contact areas as reliable data linkages are established.

References

1. Zhang, K., Aslan, A.B.: AI technologies for education: recent research & future directions. Comput. Educ. Artif. Intell. **2**, 100025 (2021). https://doi.org/10.1016/j.caeai.2021.100025
2. Li, B.H., Hou, B.C., Yu, W.T., Lu, X.B., Yang, C.W.: Applications of artificial intelligence in intelligent manufacturing: a review. Front. Inf. Technol. Electron. Eng. **18**, 86–96 (2017)
3. Lee, D., Yoon, S.N.: Application of artificial intelligence-based technologies in the healthcare industry: opportunities and challenges. Int. J. Environ. Res. Public Health **18**(1), 271 (2021)
4. Plastino, E., Purdy, M.: Game changing value from Artificial Intelligence: eight strategies. Strategy Leadersh. **46**(1), 16–22 (2018)
5. Weed, J.: Can ChatGPT plan your vacation? Here's what to know about A.I. and travel. The New York Times, 16 March 2023. https://www.nytimes.com/2023/03/16/travel/chatgpt-artificial-intelligence-travel-vacation.html
6. Martiny, J.: How AI is changing the world of travel – DW – 04/12/2023. dw.com, 13 April 2023. https://www.dw.com/en/how-ai-is-changing-the-world-of-travel/a-65283176
7. Li, M., Yin, D., Qiu, H., Bai, B.: A systematic review of AI technology-based service encounters: implications for hospitality and tourism operations. Int. J. Hosp. Manag. **95**, 102930 (2021). https://doi.org/10.1016/j.ijhm.2021.102930
8. Huang, A., Chao, Y., de la Mora Velasco, E., Bilgihan, A., Wei, W.: When artificial intelligence meets the hospitality and tourism industry: an assessment framework to inform theory and management. J. Hosp. Tour. Insights **5**(5), 1080–1100 (2022)
9. Bulchand-Gidumal, J., William Secin, E., O'Connor, P., Buhalis, D.: Artificial intelligence's impact on hospitality and tourism marketing: exploring key themes and addressing challenges. Curr. Issue Tour. (2023). https://doi.org/10.1080/13683500.2023.2229480
10. Gursoy, D., Li, Y., Song, H.: ChatGPT and the hospitality and tourism industry: an overview of current trends and future research directions. J. Hosp. Market. Manag. **32**(5), 579–592 (2023)
11. Manyika, J., Sneader, K.: AI, Automation, and the Future of Work: Ten Things to Solve For. McKinsey & Company, 1 June 2018. https://www.mckinsey.com/featured-insights/future-of-work/ai-automation-and-the-future-of-work-ten-things-to-solve-for
12. Corea, F.: AI knowledge map: How to classify AI technologies. In: Corea, F. (ed.) An Introduction to Data: Everything You Need to Know About AI, Big Data and Data Science, pp. 25–29. Springer, Cham (2019). https://doi.org/10.1007/978-3-030-04468-8

13. Press, G.: Forrester predicts investment in artificial intelligence will grow 300% in 2017. Forbes, 1 November 2016. https://www.forbes.com/sites/gilpress/2016/11/01/forrester-pre dicts-investment-in-artificial-intelligence-will-grow-300-in-2017/?sh=6fd1caf55509

14. Gasser, U., Almeida, V.A.: A layered model for AI governance. IEEE Internet Comput. **21**(6), 58–62 (2017)

15. Long, D., Magerko, B.: What is AI literacy? Competencies and design considerations. In: Proceedings of the 2020 CHI Conference on Human Factors in Computing Systems, pp. 1–16, April 2020

16. Aggarwal, K., et al.: Has the future started? The current growth of artificial intelligence, machine learning, and deep learning. Iraqi J. Comput. Sci. Math. **3**(1), 115–123 (2022)

17. Ongsulee, P.: Artificial intelligence, machine learning and deep learning. In: 2017 15th International Conference on ICT and Knowledge Engineering (ICT&KE), pp. 1–6. IEEE, November 2017

18. Alom, M.Z., et al.: A state-of-the-art survey on deep learning theory and architectures. Electronics **8**(3), 292 (2019). MDPI AG. https://doi.org/10.3390/electronics8030292

19. Campesato, O.: Artificial Intelligence, Machine Learning, and Deep Learning. Mercury Learning and Information, Virginia (2020)

20. Shinde, P.P., Shah, S.: A review of machine learning and deep learning applications. In: 2018 Fourth International Conference on Computing Communication Control and Automation (ICCUBEA), pp. 1–6. IEEE, August 2018

21. Zhang, S., Yao, L., Sun, A., Tay, Y.: Deep learning-based recommender system: a survey and new perspectives. ACM Comput. Surv. (CSUR) **52**(1), 1–38 (2019)

22. Ko, H., Lee, S., Park, Y., Choi, A.: A survey of recommendation systems: recommendation models, techniques, and application fields. Electronics **11**(1), 141 (2022). MDPI AG. https://doi.org/10.3390/electronics11010141

23. Sáenz, F.T., Arcas-Tunez, F., Muñoz, A.: Nation-wide touristic flow prediction with graph neural networks and heterogeneous open data. Inf. Fusion **91**, 582–597 (2023)

24. Zhou, J., et al.: Graph neural networks: a review of methods and applications. AI Open **1**, 57–81 (2020)

Innovations in Destination Marketing and Management

Cross-Cultural Differences in Emotional Response to Destination Commercials

Christian Weismayer[1]([⊠]) [iD] and Ilona Pezenka[2] [iD]

[1] Department of Sustainability, Governance, and Methods, Modul University Vienna, Am Kahlenberg 1, 1190 Vienna, Austria
christian.weismayer@modul.ac.at
[2] Department of Communication, FH Wien der WKW University of Applied Sciences for Management and Communication, Währinger Gürtel 97, 1180 Vienna, Austria
ilona.pezenka@fh-wien.ac.at

Abstract. In this paper we examine whether cultural characteristics lead to different emotion expressions whilst watching tourist destination ads via digital media, and thus, ads might be perceived differently depending on the country of origin of the viewer. To test this assumption, participants from two different countries, located on two different continents, Austria/Europe, and Colombia/South America, are exposed to a destination ad. Their faces are recorded and post-processing analysis on the recorded videos using the AFFDEX algorithm, that is capable of inferring emotions based on the facial action coding system (FACS), is conducted. Valence scores are compared among the viewers of the two countries over the time span of the whole commercial, and subpopulation differences of basic emotions (joy, surprise, anger, sadness, disgust, fear, and contempt) are explored using time series clustering along with optimizations for the dynamic time warping (DTW) distance. Screening sequences in this way reveals insight on the emotional reactions of different viewer groups. The findings instruct tourism marketers on how to fit the targeted emotions elicited by tourist destination advertising with various cultural settings.

Keywords: Commercial · Cultural Difference · Facial Action Coding · Emotions · Dynamic Time Warping

1 Introduction

Destination image videos are strong instruments that influence people's perceptions of locations. Their purpose is to convey a certain image and to arouse the interest of both nationals and foreigners in a target destination and ultimately to persuade them to visit the destination. However, cultural differences have an impact on the perception and subsequently the effectiveness of advertising campaigns [1–3].

As a result, investigating cultural differences in emotional responses to advertisements is supposed to shed light on the complex interplay between marketing communication and cultural contexts. Thus, this paper presents a methodology to explore how

K. Berezina et al. (Eds.): ENTER 2024, SPBE, pp. 43–54, 2024.
https://doi.org/10.1007/978-3-031-58839-6_5

cultural factors contribute to the variation in emotional responses to advertisements. By examining the emotional dimensions that advertisements evoke in distinct cultural groups, we seek to uncover diverse affective responses, highlight key differences, and offer insights into the necessity of crafting culturally sensitive advertising campaigns. We answer the question if customers in various countries react differently to the same advertising appeal.

By considering affective responses as culturally constructed, this study contributes to the existing literature in three ways: First, this study responds to the demand of more emotion-based research [4] in tourism by measuring emotional reactions to tourism ads. However, in contrast to most previous studies in a tourism context, we do not rely on self-reported measures of emotions, which have inherent shortcomings [5]. Rather, we contribute to the short list of recent studies that employ psycho-physiological methods instead of, or in addition to, self-reporting measures by employing automatic facial expression analysis. Furthermore, our study goes beyond prior attempts, which have always assessed the effectiveness of the advertisement as a whole by examining responses on a frame-by-frame basis. Third, we employ time series clustering and dynamic time warping (DTW), which are new in this context and have not been applied before using such data. Thus, we analyse emotional responses in an objective, automated, and more detailed way than previous research has. The present study underpins and explains the results by employing a benchmark approach grounded on Hofstede's national culture scores. The results finally allow us to offer valuable implications for practitioners seeking to engage diverse audiences effectively.

2 Literature Review

2.1 Cultural Aspects in Tourism Destination Promotion

According to Hofstede et al. [6], culture is the "collective programming" that distinguishes societies from one another. Minkov and Hofstede [7] demonstrate that at the national level, cultures can be evaluated and contrasted along four cultural dimensions, namely power distance, individualism-collectivism, masculinity-femininity, and uncertainty avoidance. Power distance describes the importance of individual hierarchy, the individualism-collectivism dimension indicates the level of interdependence among persons, masculinity-femininity the extent of stereotypical masculine or feminine characteristics, and uncertainty avoidance the degree of rule orientation [6].

These cultural dimensions reflect the value systems of a society, which influence lifestyle, employment, leisure, and consumer behaviour patterns [8]. These values are also crucial in explaining why attitudes toward advertising are not universal [3]. Thus, Hofstede's typology was adopted by scholars to explore cross-cultural differences in advertising in general [2, 9] and in tourism destination promotion in particular [10–12].

Moura, Gnoth, and Deans [11] adapted Hofstede's cultural framework [6] for the evaluation of cultural values on tourism destination websites. Following this framework and applying it to destination commercials, individualism focuses on the uniqueness of the destination and therefore a commercial should contain images of solitude and self-fulfilment, whereas collectivism should be represented on the basis of the availability of activities related to interaction with the local community and depictions of families or teams. Power distance centred images contain prominent individuals in society and celebrities, as well as statements regarding the destination from people with societal power. To avoid uncertainty, facts about the destination and tourist services, contact information, maps, and so forth are recommended. Because tourism products are generally intangible, these visual aspects are especially important for destination advertising. Summarized, it is critical to pay particular attention to the visual appeals and to examine the emotional reactions to advertising in depth. For instance, Mele and Lobinger [10] argue that the representation of cultural values in tourist visuals is heavily connected to visual style parameters such as colours, lightning, scene composition, and the arrangement of actors.

However, in addition to cultural differences, novelty-seeking plays a crucial role in the selection of a destination [13]. Mitas and Bastiaansen [14] explore effects of novelty on positive emotions and find that the influence of tourism experience on happy emotions is mediated in part by novelty. As tourism commercials are designed to inspire and motivate people to explore new destinations and experiences, novelty-seeking also plays an important part when people watch tourism advertising. Thus, this aspect must be taken into account when analysing tourism ads.

Therefore, considering the novelty-seeking aspect, this study shows how to explore whether cultural differences are reflected in the emotional response to a tourism ad.

3   Data Collection and Pre-processing

A comparison of Hofstede's national culture scores for Colombia and Austria shows that the two countries differ most significantly in terms of power distance (Austria/Colombia: 11/67) and individualism (55/13) [15]. To allow for comparison between the two countries, located on different continents with innate cultural idiosyncrasies due to their geographical locations, histories, traditions, and societal norms, 15 participants from Austria/Europe, and 34 from Colombia/South America were asked to watch an Austrian tourist destination commercial online. The study uses a convenience sample composed of personal contacts of the authors as well as students. Participants' faces were recorded while watching the commercial using face detection.

The AFFDEX algorithm was used to post-process 18 facial expressions based on 34 facial landmarks using the facial action coding system (FACS) developed by Ekman & Friesen [16]. In the subsequent emotion expression modelling task, these facial expressions were used as input to estimate the likelihood for an emotion to occur. The resulting emotion predictors either have a positive or a negative effect on the likelihood of an emotion (e.g., nose wrinkle and upper lip raise increases the likelihood of disgust, lip suck and smile decreases the likelihood of disgust). Seven emotions (anger, contempt, disgust, fear, joy, sadness, and surprise) and valence (overall positive or negative emotion) were traced [17]. Interpolation was used to rescale varying time intervals to 40 ms.

4 Methodology

4.1 Smoothing

To stress long-lasting emotional reactions that occurred due to the influence of the promotional video (e.g., smiling), and flatten short lasting facial expressions other than emotional ones (e.g., sneezing), the raw time series scores were smoothed using rolling means with a time window of $n = 50$. . This data preparation step, so-called simple moving average (SMA), shortens each time series by two seconds.

$$\text{SMA} = \frac{X_1 + X_2 + X_3 + \cdots + X_n}{n} \tag{1}$$

4.2 Normalization

Due to different facial expression intensities across the 49 study participants, the smoothed emotion scores were normalized onto a scale ranging from 0 to 1.

$$x_{normalized} = \frac{x - \min(x)}{\max(x) - \min(x)} \tag{2}$$

4.3 Group Means

Mean aggregation of the smoothed normalized emotion scores was conducted at the country level. The resulting group means are displayed together with their 95%-confidence intervals (CI).

$$\bar{x} = \frac{\sum_{i=1}^{n} x_i}{n} \text{ and } \text{CI} = \bar{x} \pm 1.96 \frac{\sigma}{\sqrt{n}} \tag{3}$$

4.4 (Cumulative) Differences and Ratio

Country comparisons are presented by means of three different indicators, differences (4), ratios (5), and cumulative scores (6).

$$\bar{x}_{difference_t} = \bar{x}_{Austria_t} - \bar{x}_{Colombia_t} \tag{4}$$

$$\bar{x}_{ratio_t} = \frac{\bar{x}_{Austria_t}}{\bar{x}_{Colombia_t}} \tag{5}$$

$$\bar{x}_{cumulative_t} = \sum_{i=1}^{t} x_i \tag{6}$$

4.5   Time Series Clustering

In the literature, it has been shown that only about 50% of study participants express emotions with observable facial features [18]. As a result, comparisons across the entire samples are not well suited to reveal cultural differences in response to the commercial as not all sample members disclose visually observable reactions. Therefore, time series clustering is used to group respondents according to facial expression similarities. This fulfils the need of disclosing subpopulations with time-variant but synchronous facial expressions to discrete scenes. Time series clustering is split into three categories, whole time series clustering, subsequence time series clustering, and time point clustering [19]. The first group of this taxonomy is used here to classify individuals based on time series of a selected emotion and video sequence.

4.6   Dynamic Time Warping (DTW)

When it comes to the selection of a dissimilarity measure for the clustering procedure, 'structure-based' concepts focus on underlying correlational structures, whereby 'shape-based' concepts stress proximities [20]. As 'shape-based' concepts can fail if there is a lot of noise or anomalous records, which is the case for short-lasting facial expressions not based on emotional grounds (e.g., itchiness), prior normalization is required (see Sect. 4.2). In combination with time series clustering along with optimizations for the DTW distance, this is the method of choice due to its insensitiveness to local compression and stretches [21].

For DTW, the elements of two time series are aligned with the purpose of determining an optimal path through their cross-distance matrix. The warping functions, $\varnothing_x$ and $\varnothing_y$, optimize the average accumulated distortion, d, of two time series, $X = x_1, \ldots, x_N$ and $Y = y_1, \ldots, y_M$, by locally remapping their time point indices to the warping curve elements $\varnothing(k)$.

$$d_\varnothing(X, Y) = \sum_{k=1}^{T} d(\varnothing_x(k), \varnothing_y(k))m_\varnothing(k)/M_\varnothing \tag{7}$$

Instead of skipping time series elements while aligning X and Y to each other, duplication allows a single time point of X to match multiple consecutive time points of Y. The symmetric multiplicative weight of such transitions, $m_\varnothing(k)$, is 1, whereby direct transitions take on the value 2. These weights can be set differently. No limit was specified for the number of time expansions or compressions, i.e., a time point of X might be matched with an unlimited number of Y elements. The optional boundary constraint ensures that the warping path starts and terminates at the starting and ending points of X and Y. To preserve time order, monotonicity is imposed, and the continuity condition limits transitions to adjacent points in time. Figure 1 exemplifies two study participants. The solid line represents the reference time series, the dashed line the query time series, and the dotted lines the match guidelines. Irrelevant whether respondents are smiling longer or shorter, or start smiling earlier or later, shape similarities are identified.

The resulting minimum cumulative Euclidean distances are divided by $M_\varnothing$, the sum of time points $N + M$, to allow for comparison between different time series pairs. Finally, the global dissimilarity matrix, containing distances between all respondents'

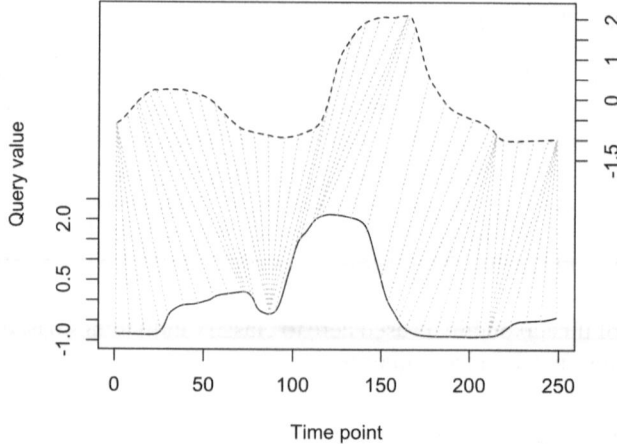

Fig. 1. DTW alignment example between two study participants.

time series, is handed over to an agglomerative hierarchical clustering algorithm using average linkage, whereby Ward.D2 and centroid linkage led to comparable results.

5   Results

The results section is split into two parts. First, valence scores are presented to explore the likelihood to perceive overall positive or negative emotions as well as country variations. Second, a selected basic emotion is examined for a particular sequence to exemplify differences between the study participants of the two countries.

5.1   Valence – Whole Commercial

Figure 2 contrasts the absolute smoothed normalized mean-aggregated valence scores along the time span of the Austrian commercial, 1 min 41.2 s, between Austrian and Colombian participants. Emotion scores run synchronously for the two countries after the introductory section of the commercial. Colombians show higher overall valence intensity levels compared with Austrians. The wider confidence interval of the Austrian sample is partly due to the smaller sample size of 15 participants, compared with 34 Colombians. But there are no striking differences, in the sense of non-overlapping confidence intervals, detected at the coarse level of overall valence.

Other possibilities to stress these differences are presented in Fig. 3. Absolute (thick line) and relative (thin line) valence differences between the Austrian and Colombian sample, based on their smoothed normalized likelihood to experience overall positive or negative emotions, underline the higher intensity levels of Colombian participants. Negative differences and ratios less than one are black coloured if Colombians showed higher valence levels, in the opposite case coloured differently. The valence likelihood is higher for Colombian participants through a major part of the Austrian commercial.

As Colombian study participants watched a commercial that presents a country located at a different continent with possibly lots of new and inspiring content, compared

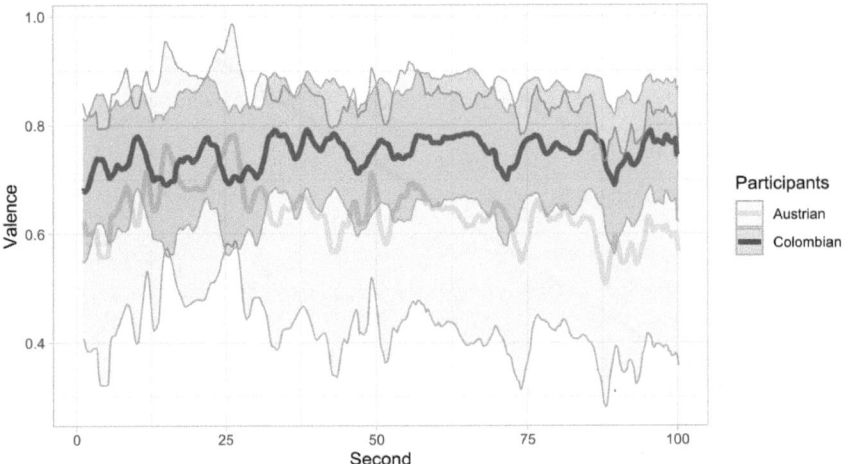

Fig. 2. Valence score means and 95%-CIs.

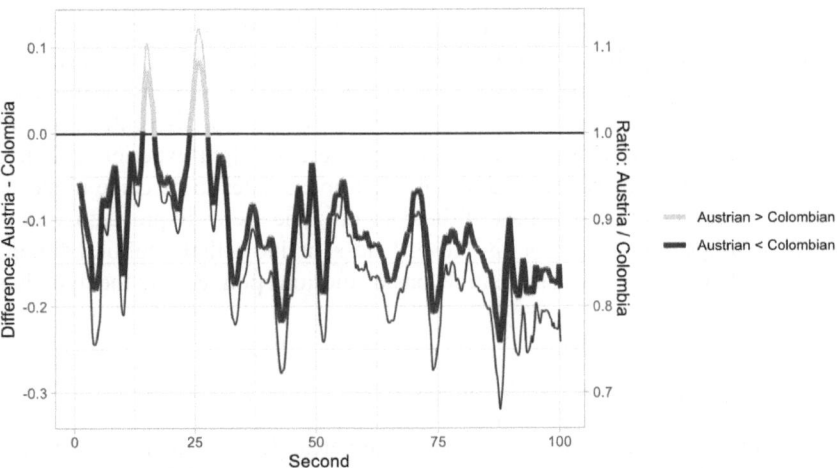

Fig. 3. Austrians and Colombians valence differences (thick line) and ratios (thin line).

with Austrians who watched a commercial about their home country in which not too much new impressions might be presented, likewise the cumulative overall valence score reaches a higher level throughout the whole commercial for Colombians (Fig. 4).

In general, as exemplified in Fig. 4, the cumulative valence scores point into the expected direction through the time span of the Austrian commercial. On closer inspection, at the level of basic emotions, negative emotions like anger, contempt, disgust, or sadness sum up to lower levels for Colombians watching the Austrian commercial. On the contrary, surprise closes at higher levels. Fascinating content of promotional campaigns seem to affect emotions in a positive way.

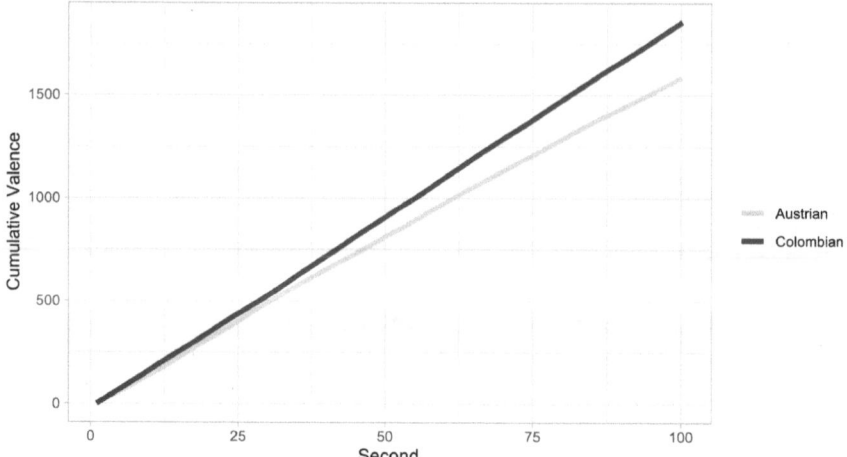

Fig. 4. Valence for Austrian and Colombian participants.

Unexpectedly, Austrian study participants reached higher cumulative likelihood levels for the emotion joy. But this might be related to the findings for the basic emotion fear, since Colombian participants perceived higher levels of fear. Reasons might lie in a lot of new, unfamiliar, and unexpected content raising emotional discomfort. As a result, Austrian participants watching the Austrian commercial might experience their usual safety in their known environment, and only that opens gates to perceive higher levels of joy. Consequently, the dominance of the comfort zone seems to prevent Colombians from experiencing higher levels of joy. Nevertheless, in line with the cultural dimensions and the novelty arguments, all other single basic emotions pointed into the hypothesized direction.

5.2   Basic Emotions – Selected Sequence

Figure 2, 3 and 4 reveal differences between the participants of the two countries with respect to overall positive and negative emotions, i.e., valence. The following chapter presents an example at the differentiated level of single basic emotions. A remarkable difference between the two groups along the timeline of the whole commercial was identified between the 65th and 73rd second for the basic emotion surprise, depicted with dashed vertical lines (Fig. 5). The level of surprise is lower for the Austrian study participants. Whether all within group members behave in the same way, the home country group, and the foreign group respectively, a fine-grained analysis is needed.

As stated in the methodology section, only about 50% of the participants show feelings with facial expressions [18]. Therefore, time-series clustering along with optimizations for the DTW distance was used to identify clusters with similar patterns. As DTW is computationally burdensome for large datasets [20], instead of the whole standardized time series only the highlighted scene (Fig. 5) is used to identify four clusters with comparable behaviour patterns (Fig. 6).

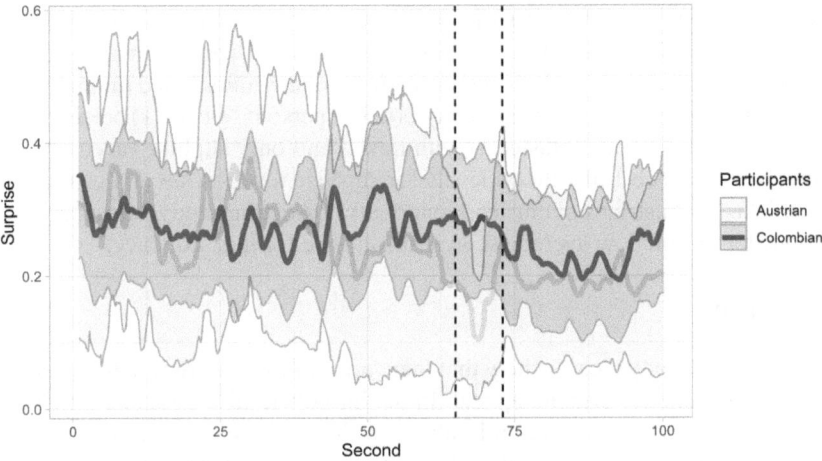

Fig. 5. Surprise score means and 95%-CIs.

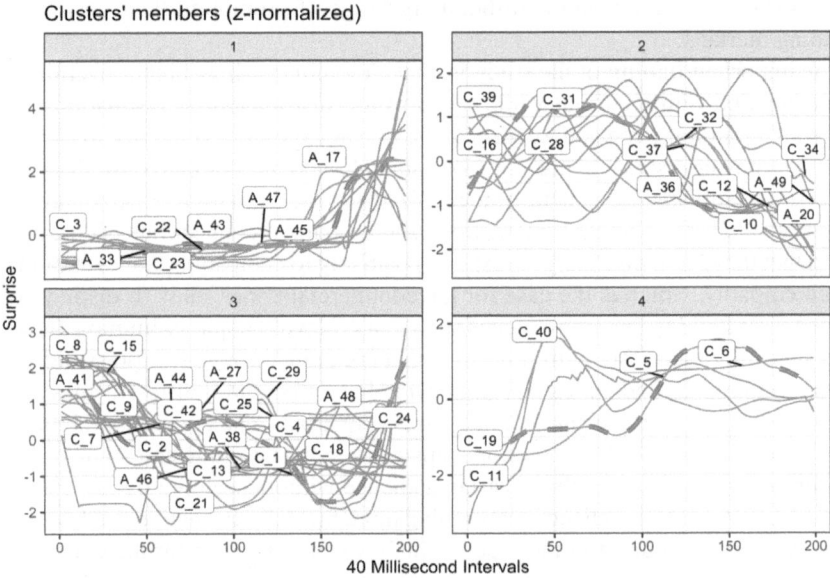

Fig. 6. Surprise time series cluster 65th to 73rd second (individuals = solid; centroids = dashed).

Study participants with strong emotional face expressions in the middle of the scene are separated from the rest of the sample, cluster 2 (12 pax) and cluster 4 (5 pax), see bold dashed centroids. This peak seems to be responsible for the slight increase in surprise for Colombians. The two clusters together represent 35% of all study participants, being close to the theoretically established and empirically validated 50% [18]. As Colombian participants are confronted with new content (novelty) and behave differently for the two Hofstede's cultural dimensions (power distance and individualism/collectivism), they should also show a peak of surprise. In line with these arguments, 14 out of 17 pax (82%) who belong to these two groups are Colombian participants, but only 3 are Austrian (Note: Individuals are indicated with their country initials and running number).

The resulting cluster solution further assorted 12 persons (cluster 1) presenting rather flat patters, and 20 persons (cluster 3) with mixed and only slightly varying reactions. The latter has the lowest likelihood levels for surprise towards the end of the selected sequence. The six Austrians of cluster 3, out of all 12 Austrian study participants (50%), are responsible for the low average scores for surprise for this sequence.

6 Discussion

The results of this study clearly show that there are cultural differences in the emotional response to the same advertising appeal. In the introduction, we assume that these differences are due to different cultural values on the one hand, and to novelty-seeking aspects on the other. Although cultural effects cannot be empirically separated from novelty effects here, we discuss the country-specific differences based on Hofstede's dimensions [6], as this is of particular importance to destination management organizations (DMOs) who have the difficult challenge of promoting their destinations in expanding markets.

One important finding of the study is, that Colombians show higher overall valence levels compared with Austrians while watching an Austrian tourist destination commercial. From a cultural perspective, this can be explained by the generally lower individualism and power distance values of Colombia (13 and 11, compared to 55 and 67 for Austria). Colombians are generally recognized for their passionate personalities who frequently value interpersonal interactions and emotional connections. Thus, it can be derived that they are more likely to respond positively to campaigns that evoke emotions or elicit empathy, which is the case for the commercial under study. It displays people enjoying their holiday including scenes such as a group of people swimming and having fun by splashing each other with water, a woman running through the forest and smiling, two boys running around with a kite and having fun, or people at different ages enjoying traditional food at an alpine pasture. In contrast, Austrians tend to prefer straightforward factual communication. Thus, emotional appeals need to be subtle and aligned with cultural norms to resonate with the Austrian audience without seeming overly dramatic or insincere. This could be realized by providing more factual information, such as entitling the areas/locations courted in the video, which was not the case for the commercial at hand.

In conclusion, the findings of this exploratory research indicate that there are cross-cultural differences in advertising perception which can be explained by Hofstede's cultural dimensions. Thus, successful advertising campaigns need a thorough awareness of these distinctions as well as a specialized approach to resonate with each group. Therefore, destination marketers are highly recommended to use A/B testing that features cultural differences, such as collectivist cues (vs. individualist cues). Alternatively, marketers should take care to make advertising as neutral as possible in terms of cultural cues to outweigh any potential cultural differences. In any case, they must be culturally aware, use suitable imagery, and emotional signals. Advertisers may build compelling ads that effectively engage both Colombians and Austrians by considering these distinctions.

This study has also important implications for academia and future research. In terms of methodology, the problem of delays in the emotional reactions among multiple sequences must be mentioned. In this regard, future research should weaken the boundary constraint of the DTW optimization and free the ending parameter to allow for unconstrained endpoints, i.e., partial mapping. But the exclusion of overlaps in the identification of emotions belonging to one single sequence requires its separate presentation, and associated therewith, a modified face recording attempt, that does not allow for conclusions at the cumulative level as drawn for the present study.

An important limitation is the selection of an Austrian destination commercial. Thus, in addition to cultural differences, the analysis is based on different tourist segments (inbound vs outbound). This entails a different familiarity with the destination that could influence emotional reactions to the ad due to, e.g., novelty aspects. Although we controlled for destination familiarity, this could threaten the validity of the study.

Secondly, there should be a qualitative analysis of the scenes. For example, Mele and Lobinger [10] found that the representation of cultural values in visuals is connected to parameters such as shot composition (number of people in an image). A prototypical example of individualism consists of a picture showing a single subject positioned far from the viewer (long shot), as it reinforces the idea of independence, whereas increased proximity (e.g., close-up shot) with multiple persons (e.g., a family) can emphasize closeness and togetherness – which relate to collectivism. Detailed sequential analyses are needed to theoretically support the detected differences.

References

1. Mele, E., Kerkhof, P., Cantoni, L.: Analyzing cultural tourism promotion on Instagram: a cross-cultural perspective. J. Travel Tour. Mark. **38**(3), 326–340 (2021)
2. De Mooij, M.: Global Marketing and Advertising: Understanding Cultural Paradoxes, 6th edn. SAGE Publications Ltd, Thousand Oaks (2022)
3. Martín-Santana, J.D., Beerli-Palacio, A.: Why attitudes toward advertising are not universal: cultural explanations. J. Euromark. **17**(3/4), 159–181 (2008)
4. Volo, S.: The experience of emotion: directions for tourism design. Ann. Tour. Res. **86**, 103097 (2021)
5. Poels, K., Dewitte, S.: How to capture the heart? Reviewing 20 years of emotion measurement in advertising. J. Advert. Res. **46**(1), 18–37 (2006)
6. Hofstede, G., Hofstede, G.J., Minkov, M.: Cultures and Organizations: Software of the Mind, 3rd edn. McGraw Hill, New York (2010)
7. Minkov, M., Hofstede, G.: Is national culture a meaningful concept? Cultural values delineate homogeneous national clusters of in-country regions. Cross-Cult. Res. **46**(2), 133–159 (2012)
8. Richardson, S.L., Crompton, J.L.: Cultural variations in perceptions of vacation attributes. Tour. Manage. **9**, 128–136 (1988)
9. Albers-Miller, N.D., Gelb, B.D.: Business advertising appeals as a mirror of cultural dimensions: a study of eleven countries. J. Advert. **25**(4), 57–70 (1996)
10. Mele, E., Lobinger, K.: A framework to analyze cultural values in online tourism visuals of European destinations. In: Information Resources Management Association (ed.) Destination Management and Marketing: Breakthroughs in Research and Practice, pp. 204–220. IGI Global, Hershey (2020)

11. Moura, F.T., Gnoth, J., Deans, K.R.: Localizing cultural values on tourism destination websites: the effects on users' willingness to travel and destination image. J. Travel Res. **54**(4), 528–542 (2015)
12. Pan, S.: Tourism slogans–towards a conceptual framework. Tour. Manage. **72**, 180–191 (2019)
13. Lee, T.-H., Crompton, J.: Measuring novelty seeking in tourism. Ann. Tour. Res. **19**(4), 732–751 (1992)
14. Mitas, O., Bastiaansen, M.: Novelty: a mechanism of tourists' enjoyment. Ann. Tour. Res. **72**, 98–108 (2018)
15. Hofstede Insights. https://www.hofstede-insights.com/country-comparison-tool. Accessed 24 Aug 2023
16. Ekman, P., Friesen, W.V.: Facial Action Coding System. Environmental Psychology & Nonverbal Behavior (1978)
17. iMotions. https://imotions.com/products/imotions-lab/modules/fea-facial-expression-analysis/. Accessed 10 July 2023
18. McDuff, D., El Kaliouby, R., Cohn, J.F., Picard, R.W.: Predicting ad liking and purchase intent: large-scale analysis of facial responses to ads. IEEE Trans. Affect. Comput. **6**(3), 223–235 (2014)
19. Zolhavarieh, S., Aghabozorgi, S., Teh, Y.W.: A review of subsequence time series clustering. Sci. World J. **2014**, 312521 (2014)
20. Montero, P., Vilar, J.A.: TSclust: an R package for time series clustering. J. Stat. Softw. **62**(1), 1–43 (2015)
21. Sardá-Espinosa, A.: Time-series clustering in R using the dtwclust package. R J. **11**, 1–22 (2019)

Authentication of SMIs by Culturally Different Audiences: Investigation with Chat GPT-3 Prompt Engineering

Svetlana Stepchenkova[1]([✉]) [iD], Andrei Kirilenko[1] [iD], and Jing Yang[2]

[1] University of Florida, Gainesville, FL 32611-8209, USA
svetlana.step@ufl.edu
[2] Guizhou Vocational College of Culture and Tourism, Qingzhen, Guiyang 551499, China

Abstract. This study investigates how online users from culturally different audiences authenticate social media influencers (SMIs) and their creative products which promote destination culture, traditions, and heritage. We specifically examined the theme of existential authenticity focusing on an elevated sense of being, self-reflection, personal discovery, and a sense of community. The context of the study was Chinese influencer Li Ziqi and her videos that depict domestic, day-to-day life in rural areas of the Sichuan province of China. The videos indirectly and organically promote tourism by contributing to more developed perceptions of China's destinations, people, and the country's brand through building positive associations, which potentially can be leveraged by the DMOs in their marketing efforts.

Keywords: Authentication · Large Language Model · Social Media Influencers

1 Introduction

Travel restrictions during the Covid-19 pandemic resulted in a substantial increase in "home, daily life scenes, and intimate content" [1], with YouTube (YT) seeing the most significant growth of any social media app among American adults, with usage jumping from 73% in 2019 to 81% in 2021 [2]. The popularity of domestic, culture-related content, even if it does not promote travel directly, indicates that destinations can benefit from the public's interest in the day-to-day lives of the destination's people as increased familiarity and positive associations provided by SMIs contribute to a more favorable attitude toward the country's brand. However, the SMI's influence is conditioned on followers' perceptions of SMI authenticity including such factors as sincerity, trustworthiness, originality, spontaneity, and a noncommercial orientation [3, 4]. In this study, we investigate how viewers authenticate SMIs and their content and whether the strategies they employ vary between culturally different audiences such as domestic vs. international. We specifically examine the authentication aspect called existential authenticity [5].

K. Berezina et al. (Eds.): ENTER 2024, SPBE, pp. 55–60, 2024.
https://doi.org/10.1007/978-3-031-58839-6_6

We use online discussions of video content created by Li Ziqi (Ziqi), an SMI from Sichuan province, China, who has millions of followers around the globe. Ziqi synchronously posts her videos on YT and Weibo (WB) focusing on Chinese cultural tradition, rural way of life, handicrafts, and cooking [6]. She has over 128 videos with a total view count exceeding 2.92 billion and an average view count per video of over 29 million [6]. We examine the topics of online discussions and provide quantitative comparisons of domestic (WB) and international (YT) audiences using the interpretive capabilities of artificial intelligence, namely, Large Language Model (LLM) prompt engineering [7, 8].

2 Study Background

In this study, we posit that the moments of existential authenticity expressed in online comments signify acceptance of SMIs as authentic. Existential authenticity is an activity-related state [5, 9] that is primarily focused on "emotions, sensations, relationships, and a sense of self" [10:680]. It acts as a "counterdose to the loss of true self" in everyday life [5:358] that is typically associated with the commercialization of mainstream Western culture [11]. Despite the argument that the sense of self is not attainable in modern society as the various roles that individuals play pull them in various directions [12], a positive aspect of the pandemic, if there was one, is that it provided ample opportunities for self-reflection [13]. Existential authenticity includes intra-personal authenticity via sensory organs as well as self-making, and social bonding with SMIs and other followers [5, 14]. Increased cultural awareness and understanding of how similar or different we are from other people and cultures are valuable learning moments and an element of existential authenticity as well. We tentatively propose that authentication via moments of self-reflection, self-discovery, and cultural comparisons will have a greater presence in the discussions on YT as the videos present a stronger "otherizing" element for international audiences, which is one of the ways people authenticate [15].

3 Method

Four videos that represent the main themes of Ziqi's videography with the largest number of comments on YT and WB were selected: (1) Using Bamboo to Make a Sofa; (2) The Life of Cotton; (3) Snacks for Spring Festival; and (4) The Scholar's Four Jewels of China. The data was collected in April 2021. English language users on YT represented international audiences (1,852 messages) while WB users of simplified Chinese language represented the domestic audience of Mainland China (2,980 comments).

LLMs, such as GPT-3 used in this study, can leverage their general knowledge obtained in the pre-training process to infer the comments' topics, even when the data is incomplete or ambiguous. LLMs can also infer the topic of short comments by transferring knowledge from similar domains and are robust to noise in the data. The effective implementation of LLMs relies on the process of designing and formulating effective prompts or instructions to elicit desired output from LLMs (prompt engineering) [8, 9]. The key concepts of prompt engineering are the precise setting of the context such as providing relevant facts; providing elaborate instructions; conditioning LLM behavior by providing examples; controlling for data biases; iterative refinement of LLM responses; and, finally, result validating. For example, the comments were mapped into the topics using the prompt (only the first 3 points are provided):

"goal = match YouTube review to the best fitting review topic from a list of topics"

steps = "1. Break the list of reviews onto separate reviews using the '\n' symbol as a separator";

2. For each review find two best matching review topics from the list of review topics separated by the ';' sign;

3. When there are no well-matching topics, assume that the topic is 'Other';

We obtained 18 topics of online discussions which were further classified into four larger groups (Table 1): Admiration and a role model (8 categories), Beauty of simple life (6), China's traditions (3), and Food and cooking (1). Validation was conducted using a stratified random sample of 360 messages; the accuracy was 97.7%. We also tracked the most endorsed comments as they indicated the shared sentiment.

Table 1. Distribution of topics in YouTube and Weibo comments to Ziqi's videos.

Combined categories	YT (1,852)	WB (2,980)	% YT	% WB	DIF
Admiration and role model	1257	1768	54.5%	49.1%	−0.10
Beauty of simple life	588	867	25.5%	24.1%	−0.06
Chinese traditions	321	559	13.9%	15.5%	0.11
Food and cooking	141	407	6.1%	11.3%	0.61
TOTAL	2307	3601	100.0%	100.0%	

*DIF - each message is coded into one or two topics. The difference in the topic presence is expressed as $Ln(count_{WB}/count_{YT})$. It is positive when a topic is more present on WB and negative when a topic is more present on YT [16]

4   Results

Each original category was examined for the presence of themes indicating existential authenticity experienced by online users, that is, moments of self-reflection, self-discovery, personal and cultural comparisons, and social bonding. For interpretation, we select the comments with the largest number of upvotes as they indicate shared sentiment from the YT and WB audiences and minimize researchers' bias.

On YT, original categories ##1, 3, 8, 10, and 11 (Table 2) were identified as carrying existential authenticity sentiment (we do not include the names of original categories to save space):

o *Deep down, I know this is how life is actually supposed to be* (25,000)
o *You inspired me to clean my room today... i've been depressed for 5 years now... I cleaned, threw away a lot... and took a shower...thank you!* (16,000)

o *I didn't know I needed this in my life* (9,800)
o *Honestly what even is my life compared to this... I've done nothing and learned nothing...* (9,200)
o *I feel at peace with myself while watching these videos* (8,000)
o *I suddenly feel the urge to turn my life 180° and become the best version of myself* (6,500)
o *Not to sound dramatic but being an artist and seeing her work until the sun came down, I cried, I love how art can make us forget* (1,300)

On WB, existential authenticity sentiment was most often expressed in categories ##3, 10, 12, and 13:

o *I suddenly feel very sad, this is the bamboo art of my hometown. Seventh sister, thank you for this video to let everyone know about this craft [hug]* (16,171)
o *The bamboo pavilion in our yard has just been done according to your previous steps* (4,418)
o *Ziqi, I'm working hard to practice calligraphy!* (610)
o *Why is there everything in this place where gods live! Every time I watch the video, I sigh* (17)
o *It is really very powerful... I feel that there will be strands of fragrance when I sit on it* (6)
o *Watching really makes me feel calm, this is probably the life I yearn for* (4)

Next, we calculated the upvotes per comment ratio for each identified category (Table 2). We adjusted the YT ratio for fair comparisons, as the international audience provided considerably more comments. Following [16], we expressed the difference in sentiment as $Ln(ratio_{WB}/Adj. Ratio_{YT})$. Large negative numbers indicate that YT audiences reflect substantially more on a non-commercialized way of Ziqi's life and on their own character and abilities in comparison to her skillset. Moderately high positive numbers show that WB users expressed existential authenticity mostly through nostalgia and childhood memories. They are also inspired by the videos to replicate Ziqi's creations of traditional Chinese objects. We consider this result to support our proposition that authentication via moments of self-reflection, self-discovery, and cultural comparisons has a greater presence on YT. Instances of social bonding were limited and entirely on the WB side.

Further Research
At the time of doing the study, the publicly available LLM GPT-3 limit was 4,096 tokens (approximately 3,000 words) while the limits for the invitation-only GPT-4 and GPT-4-32k were 8,192 and 32,768 tokens respectively. More powerful and sophisticated tools would allow a more refined analysis. LLMs are also sensitive to the phrasing of input queries, which underscores the need for precisely constructed input formulations, especially when researchers are dealing with abstract constructs and notions.

Table 2. Existential authenticity: Comparisons of YT and WB audiences.

Identified comment categories in which existential authenticity is expressed	Upvotes per comment			Ln
	WB	YT	Adj. YT	(WB/Adj. YT)
11. Desire to live a peaceful, natural, simple, & self-sufficient life	0.7	575.4	187.8	−5.56
8. Ziqi's role model status (disciplined, focused, hardworking, & skilled)	0.9	262.6	85.7	−4.57
12. Nature & rural life	1.5	241.2	78.7	−3.94
1. Admiration & praise for Ziqi	10.6	268.1	87.5	−2.12
13. Nostalgia & childhood memories	149.3	117.8	38.4	1.36
3. Desire to learn from Ziqi & replicate her creations	281.5	409.8	133.7	0.74
10. Beauty and aesthetics of traditional life & products	184.5	292.0	95.3	0.66

References

1. Femenia-Serra, F., Gretzel, U., Alzua-Sorzabal, A.: Instagram travel influencers in# quarantine: communicative practices and roles during COVID-19. Tour. Manage. **89**, 104454 (2022)
2. Pew Research Center: Social Media Use in 2021, 7 April 2021. https://www.pewresearch.org/internet/2021/04/07/social-media-use-in-2021. Accessed 19 Aug 2023
3. Balaban, D.C., Szambolics, J.: A proposed model of self-perceived authenticity of social media influencers. Media Commun. **10**(1), 235–246 (2022)
4. Audrezet, et al.: Authenticity under threat: when social media influencers need to go beyond self-presentation. J. Bus. Res. **117**, 557–569 (2020)
5. Wang, N.: Rethinking authenticity in tourism experience. Ann. Tour. Res. **26**(2), 249–370 (1999)
6. Liang, L.: Consuming the Pastoral Desire: Li Ziqi, Food Vlogging and the structure of feeling in the era of microcelebrity. Global Storytelling J. Digi. Moving Images **1**(2) (2022)
7. Ekin, S.: Prompt engineering for ChatGPT: a quick guide to techniques, tips, and best practices. TechRxiv. Preprint. https://doi.org/10.36227/techrxiv.22683919.v2 (2023)
8. White, et al.: A prompt pattern catalog to enhance prompt engineering with ChatGPT. arXiv preprint arXiv:2302.11382 (2023)
9. Kim, H., Jamal, T.: Touristic quest for existential authenticity. Ann. Tour. Res. **34**(1), 181–201 (2007)
10. Rickly-Boyd, J.M.: Existential authenticity: place matters. Tour. Geogr. **15**(4), 680–686 (2013)
11. Cohen, E.: A phenomenology of tourist experiences. Sociology **13**(2), 179–201 (1979)

12. Cohen, S.: Searching for escape, authenticity and identity: experiences of lifestyle travellers. In: The Tourism and Leisure Experience: Consumer and Managerial Perspectives, vol. 44, p. 27 (2010)
13. Roy, R., Uekusa, S.: Collaborative autoethnography: "Self-reflection" as a timely alternative research approach during the global pandemic. Qual. Res. J. **20**(4), 383–392 (2020)
14. Brown, et al.: From headliners to hangovers: digital media communication in the British rock music festival experience. Tour. Stud. **20**(1), 75–95 (2020)
15. Koontz, A.: Constructing authenticity: a review of trends and influences in the process of authentication in consumption. Sociol. Compass **4**(11), 977–988 (2010)
16. Törnqvist, et al.: How should relative changes be measured? Am. Stat. **39**(1), 43–46 (1985). https://doi.org/10.1080/00031305.1985.10479385

Varying Roles of Destination Management Organizations in the Digital Business Ecosystem of Tourist Destinations

Volha Herasimovich[1]([⊠]) [iD], Aurkene Alzua-Sorzabal[1,2] [iD],
Basagaitz Guereño-Omil[2] [iD], and Daniela Thiel-Ellul[1] [iD]

[1] Nebrija University, Sta. Cruz de Marcenado 27, 28015 Madrid, Spain
vherasimovich@nebrija.es
[2] University of Deusto, Mundaiz Kalea, 50, 20012 Donostia-San Sebastián Gipuzkoa, Spain

Abstract. Understanding the varying roles of Destination Management Organizations (DMOs) in shaping the digital ecosystem is needed in the management and governance of tourist destinations. However, the evaluation is intricate, needing extensive resources to analyze data from numerous stakeholders. This research uses the Digital Business Ecosystem (DBE) framework, hyperlink network analysis, and webometrics to address the complexities. The study examines DMOs' roles in Gipuzkoa province, Spain, spotlighting its capital San Sebastian recognized as a Smart Destination. It scrutinizes connections of DMOs' websites alongside websites of other tourism actors (N = 670) and more than 36,000 websites connected to the destination stakeholders' network. DMOs have distinct roles in the DBE compared to other tourism sectors, with differences evident among DMO types. DMOs play connecting and mediating roles in destination, strengthening network ties and bridging various stakeholders. The study emphasizes the value of varying DMO connections for attracting website visitors. Future research should explore destinations with diverse tech adoption levels and digital transition strategies, while further categorizing stakeholders in the DBE and identifying various ICT actors and their network ties.

Keywords: DMO · tourist destination · digital business ecosystem · hyperlink network

1 Introduction

Destination Management Organizations (DMOs) play varying roles in shaping the digital ecosystem of tourist destinations, influenced by their surrounding economic, social, and cultural settings and different ways of adopting information and communication technologies (ICTs). Their interaction with the digital environment alters their roles in information dissemination, networking, and marketing, impacting destination technology adoption and reshaping business strategies. Understanding the diverse DMOs' roles is needed for destination management and governance of digital transition. However, it is complex due to the need for multiple resources to gather and assess data from multiple stakeholders. This study seeks to explore these challenges using the Digital Business Ecosystem (DBE) framework, hyperlink network analysis, and webometrics.

© The Author(s) 2024
K. Berezina et al. (Eds.): ENTER 2024, SPBE, pp. 61–66, 2024.
https://doi.org/10.1007/978-3-031-58839-6_7

2 Theoretical Framework

2.1 DMOs Within the Digital Business Ecosystem

Conceptualizing a tourist destination as an ecosystem facilitates a holistic approach to the analysis of DMOs' roles, going beyond industry-specific insights and positioning them within a complex system of interconnected and interdependent actors. Like in a natural ecosystem, tourism "species" are embedded into the environment that is being shaped by the community of actors and shapes it (e.g., geographic, economic, cultural, political, and technological environments).

A tourist destination is a business ecosystem, or an economic community of inter-related and interacting organizations and individuals who create valuable goods and services [1, 2]. This system encompasses diverse entities such as suppliers, customers, competitors, and other stakeholders interacting to provide value, among which DMOs are the key players facilitating connections within and between destinations [3].

With ICTs becoming more central to tourism operations, the digital environment has taken on greater significance in the tourism ecosystem, what got reflected in the term "Digital Business Ecosystem" (DBE) [1]. According to Baggio [1] and Nachira et al. [4], a DBE is a business ecosystem enhanced by a technological infrastructure that provides a digital environment for varying interconnected tourism stakeholders and houses diverse digital objects. These entities, termed "digital species," range from software and services to knowledge and are decipherable by humans (e.g., software, services, knowledge). A DBE denotes a blend of socio-economic and technical elements which include real-world participants, digital entities, and underlying technology. In a DBE, tourism stakeholders have both a physical component and a technological representation, such as websites. These two facets co-evolve and merge, resulting in a unified complex entity [1, 4]. Thus, examining digital representations of tourism stakeholders provides insight into both a dimension of the digital ecosystem and the online-offline processes of tourist destinations' digital transformation.

2.2 Interorganizational Hyperlink Networks

Being pivotal tools for conducting business in the tourism industry, organizational web-sites stand out as digital representations. Specifically, DMO websites serve as central points for sharing information with tourists and discovering destination actors [5]. As key digital representations coupled with the economic entities they stand for, organi-zational websites serve as a proxy for DMOs as complex online-offline entities in the DBE. Hyperlinks connecting interorganizational websites are valuable proxies for offline relations and essential tools of digital networks, facilitating online visibility [6, 7].

Past tourism research has observed differences in link intensities and preferences across tourism sectors [7, 8]. In particular, DMOs' linking strategies differ based on cultural variations between societies [5]. Most studies analyze the general hyperlink structure of online tourism networks, overlooking specific focus on DMOs and their ties to the broader Web. Given the diverse online embeddedness of tourism actors in different settings, DMOs may have varying roles in tourist destinations undergoing distinct digital transitions.

3 Methodology

This study examines the roles of DMOs in Gipuzkoa province, Spain, where the capital, Donostia/San Sebastian, is recognized as a Smart Destination. A convenience sample was used due to the difficulties of acquiring a random sample. The initial entities were chosen based on their accessibility, which facilitated an exploratory study. DMOs were analyzed within the ecosystem of other tourism sectors: accommodations (57%), public bodies (13.3%), travel agencies (10%), sports and recreational activities (9.3%), nature and cultural resources (7.6%), and DMOs (2.8%) (N = 670). Organizational websites of tourism actors were analyzed as the online destination network (ODN), utilizing the web crawler Hyphe [9] in April 2023. This revealed over 36,000 websites linked to the ODN via over 47,000 connections, termed the discovered digital ecosystem (DDE). Further ODN connectivity data was sourced from Ahrefs.com. Key players in the DDE (those with 5+ connections from the ODN, n = 447) were categorized to identify ICT actors (n = 101, e.g., Google.com, Apple.com, Instagram.com). Additionally, DMOs based in Donostia were classified as central, while those outside the Smart Destination were labelled as peripheral. The study used hyperlink network analysis, webometric techniques, and statistical evaluations.

4 Results

Table 1. Connecting activity of DMOs compared to other stakeholders of the tourist destination and between varying types of DMOs

Industries	Average numbers							
	N	1	2	3	4	5	6	7	8
DMOs	19	158	139	34	105	19	11	6	0.030
Public bodies	89	96	91	5	86	5	10	5	0.002
Nature and cultural resources	51	59	50	5	45	9	8	4	0.002
Accommodations	382	89	87	2	86	1	4	3	0.000
Sports and recreational activities	62	16	13	1	12	3	4	3	0.000
Travel agencies	67	31	30	1	30	1	6	3	0.000
Peripheral DMOs	16	97	84	22	62	13	10	6	0.014
Central DMOs	3	484	434	104	330	50	19	7	0.111

Note. 1 – Total connections (degree). 2 – Total of placed links (outdegree). 3 – Placed links to ODN. 4 – Placed links to DDE. 5 – Received links within ODN (indegree). 6 – Links to ICT actors. 7 – Linked ICT types. 8 – Betweenness centrality.

DMOs were highly active in establishing connections, having a significantly higher average number of connections than other tourism sectors and leading in both incoming and outgoing links in the ODN (Table 1, Fig. 1). First, on average, DMOs placed more links within and outside the ODN, behaving as connectors of digital ecosystem objects. Notably, they bridged actors otherwise unconnected to the ODN. Second, DMOs had the highest average number of links from other network stakeholders, indicating their visibility, recognition, and authority within the ODN. Only public bodies neared their link-attracting power. Importantly, central DMOs were notably more active connectors than peripheral ones (Table 1).

For DMOs, more links placed within the ODN correlated with more links received from the ODN members (r = .959, p < 0.01), meaning that their connecting activity was associated with recognition by other tourism actors. In contrast, other sectors showed only a moderate correlation between placing and receiving links (r = .461, p < 0.01). Moreover, a strong correlation existed between DMOs' links placed outside the ODN and those received within it (r = .817, p < 0.01). This indicates that DMOs' linking both within and outside the ODN was related to the recognition from the network members.

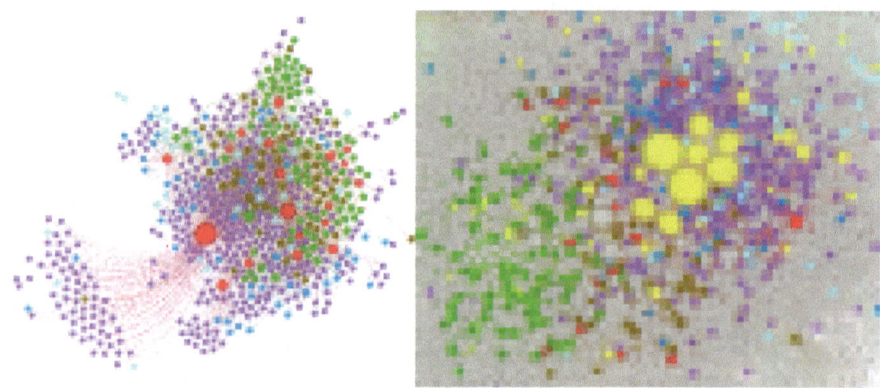

Fig. 1. DMOs in the Digital Business Ecosystem. **Left:** The ODN of tourism actors (n = 579) without isolated nodes (n = 91, 14%). The size of nodes is proportional to the number of connections within the network (in- and out-links). **Right:** The core of a tourist destination ecosystem. The size of nodes is proportional to the number of in-links (significance for tourism actors). **Colors:** ■ DMOs; ■ public bodies; ■ nature and cultural resources; ■ accommodations; ■ sports and recreational activities; ■ travel agencies; ■ ICTs; ■ unidentified. Visualized in Gephi 0.10.1.

DMOs recognition within the ODN was closely tied to their estimated monthly web traffic (r = .819, p < 0.01), meaning that having links from other network members was associated with more visitors to their websites. Moreover, any DMOs link-placing – within and outside the network – was strongly positively associated with the web traffic (r = .879, p < 0.01; r = .970, p < 0.01, correspondingly). Neither of these relations was true for other tourism actors. Likely, the quality of DMOs' connections influenced this higher traffic, as their traffic was closely related to Domain Rating – a measure that considers the quality, not just quantity, of links (r = .671, p < 0.01 for DMOs; r = .302,

$p < 0.01$ for others). Importantly, DMOs were also notable by the average number of links to ICT actors and the variety of ICT actors they connect to (Table 1).

DMOs were distributed around the network's core, dominated by diverse ICT actors (Fig. 1). DMOs were placed in between businesses (accommodations, sports and recreational activities, and travel agencies) and public bodies. Their location was akin to nature and cultural resources, also related to the public domain. DMOs occupied the position of mediators, being on the path connecting varying tourism sectors, further underscored by their high betweenness centrality (Table 1). Notably, central DMOs surpassed peripheral DMOs in average betweenness centrality (Table 1).

5   Conclusions

The study provides a fresh perspective on DMOs' roles in tourist destinations by integrating the DBE framework, hyperlink network analysis, and webometrics. DMOs have distinct roles in shaping and maintaining the DBE compared to other tourism sectors. Also, the roles vary between different DMOs with different proximity to the Smart Destination. DMOs act as key connectors and mediators in destinations, increasing link density, integrating actors into the stakeholder network, and facilitating connections among diverse stakeholders. The study indicates the importance of DMOs' links to other tourism actors, their incorporation into the broader Web, and the quantity and variety of connections with ICT actors in attracting visitors to their websites.

While the study is not representative of the broader population and only partially depicts the multi-dimensional online-offline roles of DMOs, it still enriches our grasp of DMOs' contributions within the complex system of a tourist destination. However, further comparative research is needed to provide more insights for digital transition and destination management. This entails evaluating destinations with diverse technology adoption levels, various digital transition strategies, and distinct socio-economic contexts. Continued categorization of stakeholders in the digital ecosystem is essential, as is the identification of diverse ICT actors and their ties to the ODN.

References

1. Baggio, R.: Digital ecosystems, complexity, and tourism networks. In: Xiang, Z., Fuchs, M., Gretzel, U., Höpken, W. (eds.) Handbook of e-Tourism, pp. 1545–1564. Springer, Cham (2022). https://doi.org/10.1007/978-3-030-48652-5_91
2. Moore, J.F.: The Death of Competition: Leadership and Strategy in the Age of Business Ecosystems. Wiley, New York (1996)
3. Gretzel, U.: The Smart DMO: a new step in the digital transformation of destination management organizations. Eur. J. Tour. Res. **30**, 3002 (2022)
4. Nachira, F., Dini, P., Nicolai, A.: A network of digital business ecosystems for Europe: roots, processes and perspectives. In: Nachira F., Nicolai, A., Dini, P., Louarn M. L., Rivera Leon, L. (eds.) European Commission, Directorate-General for the Information Society and Media. Digital Business Ecosystems. Publications Office, pp. 1–20 (2007)
5. Park, H., Stepchenkova, S.: Invisible power of culture: mapping tourist information flow of national DMO websites. J. Travel Res. **62**(4), 753–767 (2023)

6. Baggio, R., Del Chiappa, G.: Real and virtual relationships in tourism digital ecosystems. Inf. Technol. Tour. **14**(1), 3–19 (2014)
7. Raisi, H., Baggio, R., Barratt-Pugh, L., Willson, G.: Hyperlink network analysis of a tourism destination. J. Travel Res. **57**(5), 671–686 (2018)
8. Ying, T., Norman, W.C., Zhou, Y.: Online networking in the tourism industry: a webometrics and hyperlink network analysis. J. Travel Res. **55**(1), 16–33 (2016)
9. Jacomy, M., Girard, P., Ooghe-Tabanou, B., Venturini, T.: Hyphe, a curation-oriented approach to web crawling for the social sciences. In: Gummadi, K. P., Strohmaier M. (eds.) Proceedings of the Tenth International AAAI Conference on Web and Social Media, vol. 10, no. 1, pp. 595–598. Cologne (2016)

Does More Data Create Better Strategies for Destinations?

Anne-Maria Moilanen[1]($\boxtimes$), Juho Pesonen[2] (iD), and Johanna Heinonen[3] (iD)

[1] Savonia University of Applied Sciences and University of Eastern Finland, Kuopio, Finland
anne-maria.moilanen@savonia.fi
[2] University of Eastern Finland, Joensuu, Finland
[3] LAB University of Applied Sciences, Lappeenranta, Finland and University of Eastern
Finland, Joensuu, Finland

Abstract. This research provides insight into the current knowledge management position in Destination Marketing Organizations (DMOs). We explore what kind of tourism data is utilized in the strategy process and how. The main challenges and issues of big data management are addressed. Destinations and tourism businesses need to have a clearly defined strategy on what kind of value they provide and for whom and understand how this strategy leads to a competitive advantage. Access to data and formulation of knowledge for the strategy process is critical. We interviewed 9 Finnish DMO representatives using semi-structured interviews. We identify that enhanced knowledge management skills, resources and successful stakeholder collaboration are needed to enable business strategies based on data and knowledge. The crucial strategy development process still requires an improved understanding of tourism and destination management research.

Keywords: knowledge management · big data · destination management · strategy

1 Introduction

Digital technologies have much potential for businesses but also many pitfalls. Business managers have never had as much data as they do now. Data allows, at least in theory, more informed decision-making in businesses. This should lead to competitive advantage and improved management [1]. However, adoption of digital technologies is always challenging. According to research conducted by Deloitte, around 70% of digital transformation projects fail [2].

The digital era challenges the tourism industry and destinations. Tourism is one of the biggest industries in the world, corresponding to around 10% of global GDP [20]. This means that the competition in the field is fierce, and novel approaches are needed for competitive advantage. Digital technologies might provide this edge, but only if correctly utilised.

Tourism organizations such as Destination Management Organizations (DMOs) have more and more data at their disposal. Big data analytics allow destinations to understand

© The Author(s) 2024
K. Berezina et al. (Eds.): ENTER 2024, SPBE, pp. 67–71, 2024.
https://doi.org/10.1007/978-3-031-58839-6_8

the marketplace and business environment better than before, at least in theory. These data sources should improve decision-making processes in organizations. We focus on one of the most important decision-making processes, namely how DMOs formulate their strategies and identify competitive advantage.

2   Research Problem

There is a lack of research regarding tourism data utilisation when developing strategies. Strategies can be considered the cornerstone of competitive advantage, e.g. [3, 4]. Destinations and tourism businesses need to have a clearly defined strategy on what kind of value they provide and for whom and understand how this strategy leads to competitive advantage. This strategy planning process requires many decisions to be made. Thus, data is needed to support managers and organisations in making the right decisions.

Numerous researchers have studied how tourism data can improve tourism destinations' competitive advantage [5–9]. These studies typically examine the customer experience of a specific hotel or restaurant using big data from online sources such as social media. However, the crucial strategy development process has not been examined previously in tourism and destination management research. Tourism destinations should develop a knowledge-based approach using various data sources to support decision-making.

This research is based on strategic management and knowledge management theories. Strategy can be described as an insight into long-term goals with choices, actions and allocated resources to develop a competitive advantage in an organisation [10, 11]. Pechlaner and Sauerwein [12] defined the role of strategic management as interpreting essential knowledge provided by the environment into a form that supports future-oriented organisation structuring. Strategic management's primary goal is to ensure the strategy is accomplished effectively [13] by planning, organising, leading and coordinating the whole strategy process [10]. This process includes managing strategy planning, implementation, and analysing performance. [13]; [11] This research considers these three stages of strategy to understand strategic management as a process and how novel data sources are influencing it.

Knowledge management is about how an organisation transforms data into information and information into knowledge and how that knowledge is utilised in managing the organisation [14]. Big Data is crucial in knowledge management, mainly when producing new knowledge [9]. It has been defined in multiple ways, emphasising the difference from traditional data. Big data can be described as a considerable amount of data gathered from various sources [15]. From a business point of view, big data is a significant factor in improving operations and supporting decision-making processes [14]; [9]. However, the issue of using big data is not the availability of data anymore but how that data is used [16].

3   Methodology

The research method of this study is qualitative. Qualitative research enables one to find interpretations based on collected data by exploring social phenomena. It provides an in-depth understanding of the phenomenon and supports or argues for it and supports or argues with previous theories. [17]. This research and its structure are supported by earlier studies related to the phenomenon of this study.

This research was conducted in the context of Finnish DMOs. Qualitative research was conducted with nine semi-structured interviews in May 2023. The researchers contacted through telephone Finnish DMOs identified through Google search and the VisitFinland website. We used purposive sampling to interview different kinds of DMOs from all of the four major tourism regions (Lapland, Capital Region, Coast Archipelago, Lakeland). Interviews were conducted in Finnish online using Microsoft Teams. All interviews were recorded and transcribed.

The interview was divided into themes such as knowledge management and strategic management based on the literature. The core questions were structured beforehand to ensure that the interviews followed the same line and produced proper data related to the research topic. Even though there might come new perspectives or considerable issue issues to add to the interview, it remained the same and, thus, guaranteed the trustworthiness of the study as well [18]. The core of the interview is built based on previous studies and the research questions.

The data is analyzed using thematic analysis, widely used in semi-structured interviews. As the interview method of this study, thematical analysis can also be described as a flexible method as it provides also be described as flexible as providing rich and accurate data to analyze. Braun & Clarke [19] presented how to process thematic analysis within six stages, which are utilized in this research.

4 The Results

The findings show that the current position of knowledge management in DMOs in Finland is yet in the development stage. A lot of data is already available, but there is a lack of understanding of how to turn that data into knowledge that would lead to a competitive advantage. Utilizing tourism data effectively in tourism strategy requires enhanced knowledge management skills, resources and successful stakeholder collaboration. It is crucial to identify the relevant data and the purpose for its use. Additionally, further developing tourism data platforms would support DMOs and tourism companies as well as tourism strategies to collect data, analyze it and share it in the form of knowledge and interpretations.

The role of knowledge management could be divided into three themes: current strategy, updating strategies, and engaging stakeholders. DMOs were the hub for knowledge management in the destination, often responsible for using available data, procuring new data, and sharing the data to engage stakeholders.

DMOs acknowledge that big data from various sources can provide possibilities for competitive advantage and enable better strategies, but the current data use methods have not achieved that. This would suggest that there is a danger that big data-based strategy processes do not significantly improve destination strategies for competitive advantage.

5 Conclusions

This study elaborates on how destinations perceive the influence of big data and other novel data sources on destination strategies. Destinations are building capabilities in the field but are seeing limited results so far. There is little understanding of how big data can be turned into a competitive advantage through strategic decision-making processes. This study suggests that strategic management knowledge and expertise can enhance the possibilities to utilize data in DMOs. With novel data sources and possibilities to utilize data, destinations need to continuously evaluate current strategies and modify them if needed. Data enables better decision-making when comparing strategic possibilities. Thus, knowledge management and strategic management practices need to be implemented together [5]. Even though destinations are utilizing various novel data sources for benchmarking and customer understanding, they struggle with converting that data into knowledge that benefits the organization because they lack expertise in strategic management. More data does not automatically lead to better strategies, but efficient strategic management requires the implementation of knowledge management practices.

Acknowledgements. This research is based on the master's thesis written by Anne-Maria Moilanen and published by University of Eastern Finland.

References

1. Guo, Y., Wu, Y.: Research on the improvement strategy of "Sound Taishan" tourism destination brand construction based on big data analysis. In: Proceedings - 2021 7th Annual International Conference on Network and Information Systems for Computers, ICNISC 2021 (2021)
2. Bottke, T., Manolatos, D., Troilo, G.: Do you really know the financial impacts of your digital transformation?, 1 January 2023. https://hbr.org/sponsored/2023/04/do-you-really-know-the-financial-impacts-of-your-digital-transformation. Accessed 15 August 2023
3. Lim, C., Kim, M.J., Kim, K.H., Kim, K.J., Maglio, P.P.: Using Data to Advance Service: Managerial Issues and Theoretical Implications from Action Research. J. Serv. Theory Pract. **28**(1), 99–128 (2018)
4. Urbinati, A., Bogers, M., Chiesa, V., Frattini, F.: Creating and Capturing Value from Big Data: A Multiple-Case Study Analysis of Provider Companies. Technovation **84–85**, 21–36 (2019)
5. Almeida, F., Calistru, C.: The main challenges and issues of big data management. International Journal of Research Studies in Computing **2**(1), 11–20 (2013)
6. Fuchs, M., Höpken, W., Lexhagen, M.: Big data analytics for knowledge generation in tourism destinations – a case from Sweden. J. Destin. Mark. Manag. **3**(4), 198–209 (2014)
7. Sheehan, L., Vargas-Sánchez, A., Presenza, A., Abbate, T.: The use of intelligence in tourism destination management: an emerging role for DMOs. Int. J. Tourism Res. **18**(6), 549–557 (2016)
8. Bowen, J., Whalen, E.: Trends that are changing travel and tourism. Worldwide Hospitality Tourism Themes **9**(6), 592–602 (2017)
9. Pahus, H.S., Sunesen, L.: Working strategically with big data in the tourism sector: a qualitative study of twelve European destination management organisations. Res. Hospitality Manage. **12**(1), 81–83 (2022)

10. Bolland, E. J.: Strategizing: New Thinking about Strategy, Planning, and Management. Emerald Publishing Limited, Bingley (2020)
11. Whittington, R., Regnér, P., Angwin, D., Johnson, G., Scholes, K.: Exploring Strategy: Text and Cases, 12th edn ed., Pearson, London (2020)
12. Pechlaner, H., Sauerwein, E.: Strategy implementation in the Alpine tourism industry. Int. J. Contemp. Hosp. Manag. **14**(4), 157–168 (2002)
13. Kools, M., George, B.: Debate: The learning organization-a key construct linking strategic planning and strategic management. Public Money Manage. **40**(4), 262–264 (2020)
14. Iorio, C., Pandolfo, G., D'Ambrosio, A., Siciliano, R.: Mining big data in tourism. Qual. Quant. **54**(5–6), 1655–1669 (2019). https://doi.org/10.1007/s11135-019-00927-0
15. Hamid, R., et al.: How smart is e-tourism? A systematic review of smart tourism recommendation system applying data management. Comp. Comput. Sci. Rev. **39**, 100337 (2021)
16. Pesonen, J.: Management and leadership for digital transformation in tourism. In : Handbook of e-Tourism, pp. 1–34 (2020)
17. Ragab, M., Arisha, A.: Research Methodology in Business: A Starter's Guide. Research Gate., (2018)
18. Brinkmann, S.: Qualitative Interviewing. Oxford University Press, Oxford (2013)
19. Braun, V., Clarke, V.: Using thematic analysis in psychology. Qual. Res. Psychol. **3**(2), 77–101 (2006)
20. WTTC. Total contribution of travel and tourism to gross domestic product (GDP) worldwide in 2019 and 2022, with a forecast for 2023 (in trillion U.S. dollars) [Graph]. In Statista. Retrieved October 26, 2023, 9 May 2023

Emerging Technologies in Tourism Education

Can ChatGPT Inspire Me? Evaluate Students' Questioning Techniques on AI Tool for Overcoming Fixation

Rosanna Leung[1]([✉]) [iD] and Iris Sheungting Lo[2]

[1] National Kaohsiung University of Hospitality and Tourism, Kaohsiung, Taiwan
rosannaleung@mail.nkuht.edu.tw
[2] University of Chester, Chester, UK
iris@montaie.org

Abstract. AI-powered large language models are shaping a new era of learning. Students use AI chatbots for information search and idea inspiration. However, are students' questioning skills effective enough to interact with an AI Chatbot? This study explores the interaction between students and ChatGPT on idea generation and identifies whether participants can effectively use AI chatbots to simulate creativity for idea generation. The results indicated that, rather than discussing their idea with AI Chatbot for suggestions and recommendations to enhance the existing ideas, many students ask AI to generate more ideas without providing directions. Participants reflected that ChatGPT provided generic ideas and were unsatisfied with its creativity. They are more positive towards using the question guide, developed using SCAMPER questioning technique combined with a narrative approach by the researcher, compared to ChatGPT because the question guide enables perspective-shifting to generate ideas from a new perspective.

Keywords: ChatGPT · questioning technique · creativity · idea generation · fixation

1 Introduction

The introduction of the Chat Generative Pre-trained Transformer (ChatGPT) in November 2022 dramatically revolutionised education. This AI-driven conversation platform, developed under the idea of a chatbot, mimics human conversation; therefore, the user does not need any training before interacting with it. ChatGPT has the learning ability that allows its database to grow while conversing with the user, and users can obtain almost everything from its enriched database. Result searching on Google is a one-off, while the interaction with ChatGPT is continuous, so users can fine-tune their criteria without repeating them. Its ability to answer open-ended questions and generate texts has made ChatGPT a popular topic in universities and schools [1, 2].

As the text generated by AI is often indistinguishable from the recent plagiarism tools, academia is concerned with its impact on their ability to evaluate students' works fairly since students can use ChatGPT as a tool to complete their homework, and it is

K. Berezina et al. (Eds.): ENTER 2024, SPBE, pp. 75–86, 2024.
https://doi.org/10.1007/978-3-031-58839-6_9

challenging for teachers to verify the originality of the work. Many educators have raised concerns about academic integrity and plagiarism [3, 4]. However, we lack insights on whether and under what circumstances ChatGPT has the potential to enhance students' creativity if the attention is merely given to the impact it has on academic integrity.

Powerful questioning is said to help overcome fixation [5], which is a mental blockage caused by past experience, prior knowledge, or prior learning that constrain our creative minds to think of the best alternatives to solve a problem [6, 7]. Yet, the effectiveness of questioning in triggering creative thoughts depends on how questioning as a whole process is conducted to facilitate thinking [5]. In the context of AI Chatbot, particularly large language models (LLM) like ChatGPT, one can get immediate responses to their questions. One can simply ask the AI Chatbot directly to seek ideas. It is uncertain whether questioning in the context of AI Chatbot helps trigger creativity, as suggested by previous studies of questioning for creativity in other contexts [5, 8].

This paper evaluates the perceived usefulness of AI chatbots like ChatGPT as a creativity tool for idea generation and students' questioning techniques for idea generation. A pre-post experiment was conducted to examine students' creativity in three different settings (i.e., no tool, with an AI Chatbot as a creativity tool, with a structured question guide as a creativity tool). A creativity challenge was designed and assigned to ten master students studying hospitality management in Taiwan for the study.

To address the research question, "Is an AI Chatbot an effective tool for overcoming fixation in idea generation?" four objectives have been identified:

1. To assess the perception of using an AI chatbot for idea generation compared to not using any tool and using a structured question guide to overcome fixation.
2. To analyse the questioning behaviours while utilising the AI chatbot for idea generation.
3. To evaluate the self-perception of creativity when using the AI chatbot, in contrast to not using any tool and a structured question guide for idea generation.
4. To compare students' self-assessed creativity with their perception of using the AI chatbot for idea generation.

This study can comprehensively explore students' use of ChatGPT, questioning techniques, and the overall impact on creative idea generation across different experiment stages by addressing these research objectives.

2   Theoretical Background

2.1   Idea Generation and Fixation

All innovation starts with an idea. In business settings, an idea can be a partial or complete thought of a solution, method, or simply a concept in response to an identified problem [6, 7]. In idea generation, a major obstacle to overcome is fixation. Fixation is a form of cognitive bias that restricts one's creative thinking [9]. What contributes to forming such a mental barrier to creativity can often be imperceptible. Even as tedious as how instruction is given for problem-solving can lead to fixation [10]. For example, offering samples or detailed description to students of how the outputs could look can lead to conformity effects, meaning that ideas being generated are already fixated or shaped to a certain type of output, even though one were instructed to develop ideas that are completely different from the samples given [6] One way to help overcome fixation is to ask questions that help challenge the status quo [11].

2.2 Fixation and Questioning

Questioning is argued to be an effective method in triggering creativity as it helps facilitate divergent and convergent thinking [5, 8]. While the former involves a mindset to come up with alternatives to conventional thinking, the latter necessitates the ability to associate remote concepts with creativity. By observing and analysing the idea-generation process of undergraduate students working on a product design project, [5] notices that different types of questions can help guide one to switch thinking modes; in particular, more divergent thinking should be encouraged through generative design questions during idea-generation to allow possibility thinking and more convergent thinking should be encouraged through deep reasoning questions during idea selection to reduce ambiguity [5]. However, formulating questions itself is already a creative act. What makes it even more challenging is that questioning is found to be more effective when it is conducted as a thinking process.

SCAMPER questioning technique has been adopted widely for idea generation, primarily through a perspective-switch of products with ten elements: Substitute, Combine, Adapt, Modify, Magnify, Minimise, Put to other use, Eliminate, Reverse, and Rearrange products [12]. Previous studies suggest that SCAMPER can improve both the quantity and quality of ideas during the divergent thinking process [13]. Yet, the development of questioning as a flow with SCAMPER is still challenging as there is no guideline on how this can be achieved. Its product-oriented nature also limits the perspective-shifting encouraged by SCAMPER. It misses the importance of perspective-shifting in terms of a person's questioning development.

2.3 Narrative Approach for Fixation

Currently, idea generation is largely dominated by divergent thinking tools, which only rely on generating a large number of alternatives for creative problem-solving. It is said that it is best to avoid logical thinking during divergent thinking. [14] argue that existing creativity tools are created based on the assumption that our divergent thinking and convergent thinking for creativity can be completely separated, just like how a computer works. Without associative thinking, the alternatives' quality and practicality are in question even though the quantity is there. Hence, they propose using a narrative approach to stimulate associative thinking as a flow during idea generation without having logical thinking stepped in. A narrative approach uses storytelling and creation to promote associative creative thinking. In particular, perspective-switching is effective in helping one see from a different person's perspective for idea generation. Such a perspective switch does not only focus on viewing the product differently. Rather, it is to see the world of the users differently or to encourage one to play a different role through storytelling.

2.4 Creative Self Concept and Creativity

The role that one's creative self-concept plays in idea generation [15, 16], their creative behaviours [17] and their creative performance [18] have been essential to creativity research. Previous studies suggest that one's creative potential can be elevated by one's creative self-concept, which is formed by self-belief in one's creative ability and the importance of creativity in shaping self [19]. It is also said to be positively related to creative motivation [20]. However, to the authors' knowledge, no research has been conducted to examine how one's self-concept is related to the perceived usefulness of a creativity tool.

3 Methodology

3.1 Experiment and Questionnaire Design

A pre-post experiment with a post-activity survey was conducted to examine the perceived usefulness of AI Chatbot in enhancing student's creativity when compared to two other scenarios: 1) no tool at all, and 2) with a question guide. ChatGPT was chosen for the study as it has recently become the most popular AI Chatbot among students.

At the beginning of the experiment, students were presented with a scenario sheet for participants to envision themselves in. This sheet is bilingual, containing both English and Chinese and is related to proposing creative ideas for using hotel waste towels to craft gifts to delight hotel guests. The scenario comprises four different market segments, allowing students the flexibility to propose ideas tailored to their target group(s). This experiment consists of three rounds. In the first round, students are required to propose three creative ideas without using any tools within a 10-min time frame. In the second round, they have 10 min to interact with ChatGPT before presenting three distinct creative ideas, which should differ from those in the first round. In the third round, conducted one week later, students are allocated 10 min to utilise a question guide prepared by the researchers, based on the SCAMPER technique [12] combined with a narrative-based approach for enhancing creativity [14]. Subsequently, they are expected to propose another three creative ideas that differ from the ones presented in the first two rounds. Figure 1 illustrates the research framework of this study.

At the end of the experiment, participants were asked to save the whole conversation with ChatGPT to a file and send it to the researcher for analysis. Participants were then required to fill in three questionnaires, including two post-experiment questionnaires and one creative self-concept profile. The key purpose of the post-experiment questionnaire was to obtain their perspectives on the three different creative processes: 1) No tool, 2) With ChatGPT, and 3) With a question guide. To ensure that participants' motivation for the challenge does not influence their creative outputs in the three rounds of the challenge, post-activity questionnaires included questions regarding outcome-focused and process-focused motivation. These questions were adapted and modified from [21] to improve the validity of the findings. Creative self-concept questions were asked after all three rounds of challenge were taken. The six questions were adopted from [19, 20] to evaluate one's self-creative concept (see Appendix A).

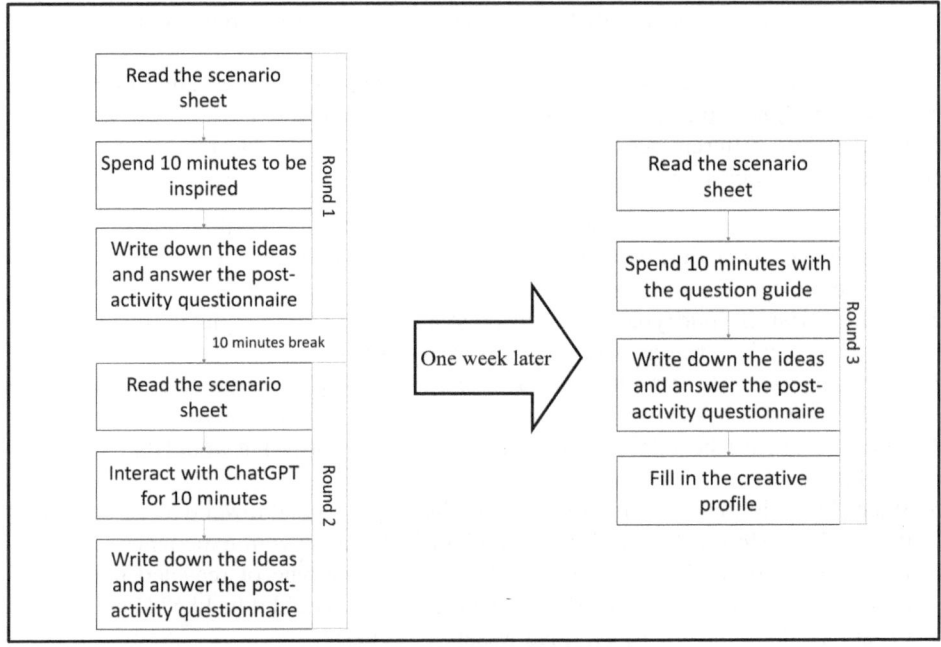

Fig. 1. The Research Framework

3.2 Question Guide Design

A question guide was devised to assess the effectiveness of questioning in two distinct contexts: questioning with immediate responses (e.g., ChatGPT) and questioning without immediate responses (e.g., self-questioning). This guide was constructed utilising the SCAMPER technique as its foundation. A narrative approach was employed to adapt and enhance the technique to address the potential limitation of the SCAMPER technique, which may not naturally incorporate questioning. Its perspective-shifting that focuses on the product can also be overcome by instilling a guest-focused narrative while using SCAMPER to help develop a question guide. In other words, the question guide was developed based on SCAMPER with a narrative approach to guide students to imagine themselves as if they were the guests and how their "products" interplay with guests' needs and guest experience as a whole.

During the development of the question guide, several rules were applied, drawing from the work of [5, 10]. First, the questions were designed to encompass both divergent and convergent elements to enhance the originality and relevance of generated ideas. Divergent questions were predominantly used at the outset, followed by an increased emphasis on convergent questions later in the process. Second, the questions were structured to build upon one another, creating a coherent narrative for idea generation. This approach ensured that the questions were not treated as isolated entities but integral parts of a continuous thought process. Third, more abstract categories were employed in the questions to avoid prematurely narrowing down possibilities. For instance, the initial questions encouraged students to contemplate the overall "experience" of the guests rather than focusing narrowly on the old towel at the beginning of the questioning process.

After incorporating the perspective-shifting and guest-focused narrative, the question guide was designed to inspire participants to think from different perspectives and put themselves into different scenarios. The finalised question guide for this experiment consists of eight questions:

1. Think of a typical guest staying at this hotel. Think of what this person has been through and the environment the person is in. If you were this guest, what frustrates you the most at this moment?
2. As this guest, if your typical experience at a hotel can be completely rearranged to delight you, what arrangement do you want it to be like?
3. If someone were to suddenly take away an essential part of the new arrangement, what would that be? How will the whole experience become for you?
4. If you were to use the old towels to replace the missing part, what would the experience be like for you?
5. What if the old towels do not look or feel the way a typical towel does, what would they be like? How will their different look or feel change your experience?
6. If you were to combine the old towels with another type of recycled item to re-create the missing part of the new arrangement, what would it be like? How will you experience these newly transformed wastes as a guest?
7. Where else can you use these newly transformed wastes as a guest?
8. Think of what hotels and cities would be like in 30 years. How will this new arrangement made possible with the transformed wastes adapt to your changing needs and the changing environment you are in?

3.3 Data Collection

Invitation emails were sent to all master's level students in the researchers' department. Ten students agreed to participate. The experiments were conducted on May 18 and 25, 2023, with four second year and June 7 and 15, 2023, with six first-year Master level students. At stage one, students were asked to propose three ideas without tools. At Stage Two, they were asked to propose three new ideas with the assistance of ChatGPT. After that, they fill out the post-experiment questionnaire. One week later, students were invited to participate in round three. They were given a guide with 15 questions designed to inspire them to think of three more new ideas. After the experiment, participants were asked to complete post-experiment questionnaires and a creative profile survey.

3.4 Data Analysis

Content analysis was carried out to analyse the conversation between participants and ChatGPT. A total of 81 questions were asked. One participant only asked ChatGPT one question. The highest number of questions asked was 13. These questions are further analysed into five categories (Table 1).

Table 2 illustrates the demographics of the participants. All of them have prior experience with ChatGPT, but two mentioned that they only created an account and used it once. Meanwhile, two participants claimed they have extensive experience and

Table 1. Categorisation of Conversation with ChatGPT

Categories	No. of questions
1. Questions purely ask ChatGPT to provide suggestions	20 (24.7%)
2. Assign role to ChatGPT and/or focus on a target user	25 (30.9%)
3. Discuss with ChatGPT for comments or advice	5 (6.2%)
4. Ask ChatGPT for more ideas	27 (33.3%)
5. Others	4 (4.9%)

Table 2. Demographics of the Participants

ID	Master level	Gender	Self-reflect ChatGPT experience	CS Score (6 to 30)	Relative Creativity*
S1	Year 2	M	Beginner	17	Low
S2	Year 2	F	Beginner	26	High
S3	Year 2	F	Just once	19	Low
S4	Year 2	M	Advance	26	High
S5	Year 1	M	Beginner	23	Middle
S6	Year 1	M	Beginner	23	Middle
S7	Year 1	F	Beginner	23	Middle
S8	Year 1	M	Beginner	21	Middle
S9	Year 1	F	Advance	24	High
S10	Year 1	F	Just once	17	Low

* *Relative creativity among the participants*

use it frequently. The Creative Self-Concept score (CS score) was generated by summing up the responses to six creative self-concept questions from the creative profile. Based on their CS scores, participants were further divided into three groups to indicate their relative creativity among all participants. The relative creativity group were classified by distribute evenly based on the difference between the lowest and the highest score. Therefore, a CS score between 17 and 19 indicated relatively low creativity, while a score between 20 and 23 indicated relatively moderate creativity, and a score between 24 and 26 indicated relatively high creativity.

4 Findings and Discussions

4.1 Questioning ChatGPT

Within the 10 min, participants can interact with ChatGPT in any form and language they prefer until they get satisfactory results. At the beginning of the conversation, half of the students directly asked ChatGPT to propose ideas. "How to reuse waste towels"

[S1]; "Help me to find 3 ways to reuse waste towels" [S3]; "Please help me to use waste towels to make different products" [S5]; "…using towel to reuse and transform, give examples" [S6] and "What creative product can be made by waste towels" [S10]. From the results generated by ChatGPT according to these five questions, we found that without specifying "the purpose" (for hotel to delight guests) and target users, ChatGPT provided many ideas that do not match the purpose stated in the scenario sheet. For example, cleaning cloth, wipes, kitchen towels, construction bricks, and gift wrap.

The most frequently asked question was "more ideas." One-third of the questions belonged to this category, such as "any newer ideas" [S5], "I need something more creative" [S6], and "Can you provide me with more ideas?" [S8], among others.

Two participants were assigned roles for ChatGPT. S4 instructed the chatbot, saying, "Your role is a fashion designer" [S9]. S4 even assigned six different roles, including recycle product designer, artist, designer, engineer, Nobel Prize winner, and Elon Musk, so that the chatbot could provide a variety of ideas. However, these questions also did not specify the purpose and the target users, resulting in generated results (e.g., biodegradable towels, recycled fibre, and garments) that did not align with the intended purpose.

S7 and S8 began their conversations by providing all the required criteria, including competition, waste towels, four market segments, and delighting the customers to Chat-GPT. After the chatbot provided suggestions such as shopping bags, slippers, toiletry bags, facial cotton pads, and yoga mats, both asked the chatbot for more ideas four times before ending the conversation.

Only three participants sought advice from ChatGPT, asking questions like "Do you think… is suitable for hotel guests?" [S3], "What is the meaning of having…" [S4], and "Do you think… is feasible?" [S9]. Moreover, S9 was the only participant who engaged in humanised conversations with the chatbot. However, rather than discussing idea generation, she pressured the chatbot for more useful ideas.

Most participants were primarily focused on the outcome, a creative idea for repurposing waste towels into a product. They often overlooked the importance of considering the target market and its needs. Of the 90 ideas generated, only 13 (14%) mentioned the target users or their specific needs, while the rest focused solely on the product.

In conclusion, throughout their conversations with ChatGPT, most participants did not engage in in-depth discussions to explore their ideas further. None of them sought advice from the chatbot to refine their ideas or overcome creative fixation. Instead, they were eager to obtain creative outputs directly from ChatGPT.

4.2 Perceived Usefulness of Idea Inspiration Tools

In this study, students perceived ChatGPT as a fast and efficient tool [S10] that inspire them to think in different dimensions and discipline [S3, S6], simplify the convergent thinking process among different ideas [S7], and remind them of the discipline that was outlooked [S5]. Interestingly, some participants did not think AI Chatbot is a good tool for idea inspiration. Three of them feel that the ideas provided by ChatGPT were direct [S2], standard, generic [S5] and non-creative [S8]. S9 point out that whenever similar question and request were inputted, ChatGPT provided similar answers. Therefore, the answers were not creative at all.

For the perceived usefulness of the question guide, all Year 2 students indicated it restricted their imagination and exploration of new ideas [S1, S2, S3]. S4 agreed that the question guide "can alter thinking logic but did not strongly impact the final outcome". On the other hand, Year 1 students have completely different perspectives. They feel that the question guide can guide them to think in different dimensions [S6] and lead to a creative direction [S8]. The question guide offered a story set so S5 could understand the target user's needs and have a clear direction to think of good ideas. S9 pointed out that the question guide helped her to explore more ideas without barriers and "visualise" the situation [S10].

4.3 The Proposed Creative Ideas

Participants were asked to self-evaluate the creativity of the ideas they proposed in each round using a 5-point Likert scale, where 1 indicated "strongly disagree" and 5 indicated "strongly agree." The ANOVA test results showed that individuals with high self-creative concept scores felt significantly more creative (mean = 5.0; STD = 0; F = 13.3; p = 0.004) when suggesting ideas in Round 1 compared to those with medium (mean = 3.75, STD = 0.5) and low creative profile scores (mean = 4.0, STD = 0). However, participants with high self-creative concept scores perceived that the ideas they proposed in Round 3, after using the inspiration tools (ChatGPT [F = 0.7; p = 0.528] and question guide [F = 0.122; p = 0.887]), were not as creative as those in Round 1.

At the end of the second questionnaire, participants were asked to select the three best ideas from the nine they had proposed and express their perceived usefulness of the two inspiration tools. Eleven ideas were from both Round 1 (no tool) and Round 3 (question guide), while six ideas were from Round 2 (ChatGPT).

The results revealed two intriguing phenomena. Firstly, participants favoured the ideas they had generated over those AI recommended. Secondly, despite the expectation that ChatGPT would outperform other tools, participants did not consider the ideas proposed by the chatbot to be creative enough to make them the top three choices.

5   Conclusions

Students admire the capabilities of ChatGPT and find it interesting, motivating, and helpful for study and work [22]. However, when it comes to idea generation, does it have the same effect? The paper starts by asking, "Can AI chatbots help overcome fixation for better idea generation?". The findings suggest that AI Chatbot has the potential to help expand one's thinking and knowledge for creative problem-solving. However, its evocativeness, which refers to the capacity of a learning activity or material to give rise to "personal thought" [23], is not fully realised. When one focuses on the creative outputs instead of the creative process, AI Chatbot becomes an ineffective tool for idea generation. When it is seen as a tool to help expand one's thinking and knowledge as a part of a creative thinking process, it is perceived as fast and effective. Hence, the perceived usefulness of AI Chatbot depends largely on the student's capability and knowledge in asking questions that help them overcome fixation. Instead of asking divergent and convergent questions in a flow, as suggested by [5], participants of this study focus on gaining creative outputs from ChatGPT by giving orders or requests. When they were not satisfied with the creative outputs offered by ChatGPT, they simply requested "more ideas" instead of asking various questions. Students were found to be fixated on their own questions while using ChatGPT for idea generation.

Asking questions as a form of interactive learning has a long history, dating back to the teachings of Socrates. Interacting with AI chatbots is made easy and engaging through its natural language conversations. Through conversation, questions scaffold learning and promote awareness and thought. AI chatbots' conversational format enables students to exchange questions and answers, leading to deeper personal reflection. Sadly, students cannot take full advantage of technological advancement as they are rarely taught how to ask questions or even given a chance to ask questions in the classrooms.

This study also finds that the creative self-concept of the students has an impact on the perceived usefulness of ChatGPT in idea generation. Those more confident in their creative ability tend to see ChatGPT as less useful. They prefer generating ideas on their own or with a question guide. Instead of seeing ChatGPT as a tool to help modify or expand their original ideas, they simply prefer not to use it at all. This seems to suggest that those with higher creative self-concept do not see AI chatbots as what helps overcome fixation. Rather, it creates fixation by offering non-creative and similar answers.

The theoretical contribution of this study is twofold. While most studies adopt an outcome-based approach in the evaluation of the effectiveness of an intervention, this study also takes into consideration the user's perspective as well as their creative concept as an indicator of the effectiveness of a creativity intervention [24]. This study is also among the very few studies to examine the impact of AI Chatbot technology on one's creativity and questioning technique. In terms of practical contribution, this study sheds light on whether and how AI chatbots and large language models can be adopted to enhance students' creativity.

Creativity has become one of the most sought-after skills. Nevertheless, schools have not effectively cultivated their students' creative potential [25]. Students are often expected to apply their creativity skills for idea generation and selection in project-based learning, but they are rarely taught how to do so in the classrooms. Students are often left alone and feel most anxious about generating ideas for creative problem-solving [26]. Now, with the popularisation of AI chatbots, it is unavoidable that students will rely on AI chatbots to help generate ideas to solve problems. Therefore, it is of foremost urgency for educators to explore how students can take full advantage of the technology instead of restricting its usage.

This study has two major limitations. First, the sample size is notably small, with participants from the same university with similar educational backgrounds. Consequently, the findings may not be generalisable to contexts outside this demographic. Second, data collection occurred approximately two months after the launch of ChatGPT in Taiwan with Chinese large language model. Given this relatively short time frame, most participants were still relatively new to ChatGPT, which could have impacted their familiarity and comfort with the tool. Therefore, they may not have been fully adept at utilising the chatbot to its fullest potential during the study.

Appendix A –Creative Self-concept Questions – Bilingual in Chinese and English

1) I think I am a creative person.
2) My creativity is important to who I am.
3) I trust my creative abilities.
4) I am sure I can deal with problems requiring creative thinking.
5) I am good at proposing original solutions to problems.
6) Ingenuity is a characteristic which is important to me.

References

1. Baidoo-Anu, D., Owusu Ansah, L.: Education in the era of generative artificial intelligence (AI): understanding the potential benefits of ChatGPT in promoting teaching and learning (2023). https://papers.ssrn.com/abstract=4337484. https://doi.org/10.2139/ssrn.4337484
2. Kasneci, E., et al.: ChatGPT for good? On opportunities and challenges of large language models for education. Learn. Individ. Differ. **103**, 102274 (2023). https://doi.org/10.1016/j.lindif.2023.102274
3. Cotton, D.R.E., Cotton, P.A., Shipway, J.R.: Chatting and cheating: ensuring academic integrity in the era of ChatGPT. Innov. Educ. Teach. Int. 1–12 (2023). https://doi.org/10.1080/14703297.2023.2190148
4. Skavronskaya, L., Hadinejad, A. (Hana), Cotterell, D.: Reversing the threat of artificial intelligence to opportunity: a discussion of ChatGPT in tourism education. J. Teach. Travel Tour. **23**, 253–258 (2023). https://doi.org/10.1080/15313220.2023.2196658
5. Eris, O.: Effective Inquiry for Innovative Engineering Design. Springer, Boston (2004). https://doi.org/10.1007/978-1-4419-8943-7
6. Beda, Z., Smith, S.M.: Unfixate your creative mind: forgetting fixation and its applications. Transl. Issues Psychol. Sci. **8**, 66–78 (2022). https://doi.org/10.1037/tps0000290
7. Kornish, L.J., Hutchison-Krupat, J.: Research on idea generation and selection: implications for management of technology. Prod. Oper. Manag. **26**, 633–651 (2017)
8. Royo, M., Mulet, E., Chulvi, V., Felip, F.: Guiding questions for increasing the generation of product ideas to meet changing needs (QuChaNe). Res. Eng. Des. **32**, 411–430 (2021). https://doi.org/10.1007/s00163-021-00364-x
9. Crilly, N., Cardoso, C.: Where next for research on fixation, inspiration and creativity in design? Des. Stud. **50**, 1–38 (2017). https://doi.org/10.1016/j.destud.2017.02.001
10. Ward, T., Kolomyts, Y.: Creative cognition. In: Kaufman, J.C., Sternberg, R.J. (eds.) The Cambridge Handbook of Creativity. Cambridge University Press, New York (2010)
11. Marquardt, M.J.: Leading with Questions: How Leaders Find the Right Solutions by Knowing What to Ask. Wiley, Hoboken (2014)
12. Boonpracha, J.: SCAMPER for creativity of students' creative idea creation in product design. Think. Ski. Creat. **48**, 101282 (2023). https://doi.org/10.1016/j.tsc.2023.101282
13. Vernon, D., Hocking, I., Tyler, T.C.: An evidence-based review of creative problem solving tools: a practitioner's resource. Hum. Resour. Dev. Rev. **15**, 230–259 (2016). https://doi.org/10.1177/1534484316641512
14. Fletcher, A., Benveniste, M.: A new method for training creativity: narrative as an alternative to divergent thinking. Ann. N. Y. Acad. Sci. **1512**, 29–45 (2022). https://doi.org/10.1111/nyas.14763

15. Madrid, H.P., Patterson, M.G.: An examination of the relationship between idea generation versus idea implementation and subsequent self-efficacy and positive affect. J. Bus. Psychol. **38**, 529–537 (2023). https://doi.org/10.1007/s10869-022-09820-4

16. Ng, T.W.H., Shao, Y., Koopmann, J., Wang, M., Hsu, D.Y., Yim, F.H.K.: The effects of idea rejection on creative self-efficacy and idea generation: intention to remain and perceived innovation importance as moderators. J. Organ. Behav. **43**, 146–163 (2022). https://doi.org/10.1002/job.2567

17. Kumar, D., Upadhyay, Y., Yadav, R., Goyal, A.K.: Psychological capital and innovative work behaviour: the role of mastery orientation and creative self-efficacy. Int. J. Hosp. Manag. **102**, 103157 (2022). https://doi.org/10.1016/j.ijhm.2022.103157

18. Huang, N., Chang, Y., Chou, C.: Effects of creative thinking, psychomotor skills, and creative self-efficacy on engineering design creativity. Think. Ski. Creat. **37**, 100695 (2020). https://doi.org/10.1016/j.tsc.2020.100695

19. Karwowski, M.: The dynamics of creative self-concept: changes and reciprocal relations between creative self-efficacy and creative personal identity. Creat. Res. J. **28**, 99–104 (2016). https://doi.org/10.1080/10400419.2016.1125254

20. Goulet-Pelletier, J.-C., Cousineau, D.: The profiles of creative students. Think. Ski. Creat. **44**, 101007 (2022). https://doi.org/10.1016/j.tsc.2022.101007

21. Touré-Tillery, M., Fishbach, A.: How to measure motivation: a guide for the experimental social psychologist. Soc. Personal. Psychol. Compass. **8**, 328–341 (2014). https://doi.org/10.1111/spc3.12110

22. Shoufan, A.: Exploring students' perceptions of ChatGPT: thematic analysis and follow-up survey. IEEE Access. **11**, 38805–38818 (2023). https://doi.org/10.1109/ACCESS.2023.3268224

23. Harel, I., Papert, S.: Software design as a learning environment. Interact. Learn. Environ. **1**, 1–32 (1990). https://doi.org/10.1080/1049482900010102

24. Wöhler, J., Reinhardt, R.: The users' perspective on how creativity techniques help in the idea generation process—a repertory grid study. Creat. Innov. Manag. **30**, 144–163 (2021). https://doi.org/10.1111/caim.12424

25. Runco, M.A., Acar, S., Cayirdag, N.: A closer look at the creativity gap and why students are less creative at school than outside of school. Think. Ski. Creat. **24**, 242–249 (2017). https://doi.org/10.1016/j.tsc.2017.04.003

26. Heong, Y.M., Yunos, J.M., Othman, W., Hassan, R., Kiong, T.T., Mohamad, M.M.: The needs analysis of learning higher order thinking skills for generating ideas. Procedia - Soc. Behav. Sci. **59**, 197–203 (2012). https://doi.org/10.1016/j.sbspro.2012.09.265

Applying Design Thinking to Improve Students' Experience in Online Hospitality Courses

Katerina Berezina(✉) ⒾⒹ, Rasoul Mahdavi ⒾⒹ, and Mahsa Talebi ⒾⒹ

University of Mississippi, University, MS 38677, USA
eberezin@olemiss.edu

Abstract. The purpose of this article is to introduce the design thinking approach and illustrate how it may be used to facilitate an online course redesign by providing a specific example. This article builds on the theoretical foundation of the design thinking literature. It reviews the stages of the design thinking process, namely empathize, define, ideate, prototype, and test. The paper also presents an example of design thinking steps being applied to a graduate online hospitality course. The paper used a survey with both qualitative and quantitative questions to understand student experiences in this course, to identify students' goals and challenges, and to build student personas. This research presents one of the personas developed for the redesigned course and offers an approach to redesigning the class to improve the learning experience for this persona. The approach presented in this paper may be useful to other instructors, program directors, hospitality and tourism training professionals, and instructional designers.

Keywords: User Experience · Course Design · Learner Experience · Design Thinking

1 Introduction

The COVID-19 pandemic led to a rapid increase in the availability of online education within higher education in 2020. According to the National Center for Education Statistics, more than 14 million postsecondary students in the United States, constituting 75% of the total, engaged in online coursework during the fall of 2020 [1]. Online learning offers students several advantages, such as flexibility in terms of location and pace of study and access to a diverse array of educational options and resources [2, 3]. On the other hand, online learning may be criticized for lack of interaction and social engagement, feelings of isolation, and reduced motivation [4]. Questions emerge regarding whether students participate in courses as educators envision and which aspects of online courses effectively involve students to improve the learning experience. The purposeful design of online courses can maximize the potential for student engagement and consequent learning [5].

Design thinking is an approach that has been used in technology design for years. Educators can learn from the principles of the design thinking approach to build better online educational experiences. The topic of design thinking in education has been

K. Berezina et al. (Eds.): ENTER 2024, SPBE, pp. 87–99, 2024.
https://doi.org/10.1007/978-3-031-58839-6_10

presented in the literature from two major perspectives: teaching design thinking as a part of the curriculum to develop innovation and critical thinking skills [6–8] and applying the design thinking process to instructional design [9]. It is important to note that while both perspectives have been documented in the literature, the first one seems to have higher coverage and attention than the second one.

In hospitality and tourism education literature, design thinking has been mainly introduced from the skill-development perspective. There is an emerging stream of literature that looks at the development of higher-order thinking skills in hospitality and tourism students, including creativity, critical thinking, teamwork, and problem-solving [10–12]. Such skills may be applied to creating innovation in the hospitality industry, e.g., by developing future hospitality concepts [13] or envisioning smart hotel concepts and guest experiences [14]. However, the hospitality and tourism education literature lacks the instructional design view on design thinking in hospitality education. The review of relevant literature demonstrated a gap in explaining the specific steps of applying design thinking to hospitality course design.

Given the literature gaps presented above, the purpose of this article is to introduce the design thinking approach to hospitality instructional design and illustrate how it may be used to facilitate a course redesign by providing a specific example. This article builds and contributes to the theoretical foundation of design thinking and e-learning in hospitality and tourism education literature, reviews the stages of the design thinking process, and presents an example of design thinking steps being applied to an online hospitality course.

2 Literature Review

2.1 E-Learning in Tourism

With the utilization of Information and Communication Technology (ICT), higher education has transitioned to online platforms in order to connect with students and implement virtual instructional methods for the delivery of courses via the Internet [15]. Electronic learning (e-learning) can be incorporated into the tourism and hospitality sector by means of creating and executing online training programs and modules [16]. Sigala [17] suggests that the development and implementation of technologically and pedagogically effective e-learning platforms are important for enhancing e-learning effectiveness. E-learning offers several key benefits, including flexible access to course materials [18], a vast array of multimedia resources, and the promotion of self-directed learning and critical thinking skills. It also facilitates collaboration among students and instructors via online platforms, reduces costs associated with physical classrooms and travel, and enables personalized learning experiences [19].

The pandemic, while having a detrimental effect on tourism and hospitality education, has spurred researchers to investigate innovative approaches to teaching and learning and students have enthusiastically embraced novel modes of instruction, encompassing virtual lectures, discussion forums, virtual group assignments, augmented/virtual reality-based learning, simulations, and gamification [20]. While e-learning offers flexibility and accessibility, it also presents challenges as well. The transition to e-learning has created a need for educational institutions to equip themselves with online learning tools and techniques. Instructors should continuously adapt and improve their online teaching strategies based on student feedback and evaluation to enhance the effectiveness of e-learning experiences [15]. The next sections of the paper explain the concept of design thinking and illustrate how it may be used to take a user-centric approach to course design.

2.2 Design Thinking

Design thinking may be defined as an analytic and creative process that involves an individual in opportunities to experiment, generate and develop prototype models, collect input, and revise designs [21]. It involves a human-centered and iterative process of understanding users' needs, defining problems, ideating solutions, prototyping, and testing [22]. Design thinking is significant because it offers a systematic approach to problem-solving and innovation that can be implemented in various contexts [23].

Design thinking evolved into pedagogy in the 1950s when John E. Arnold collaborated with psychologists, designers, and industrial researchers to develop a creative and human-centered design approach. In the 1970s, the design pedagogy developed creative and humanistic designers with aesthetic and technical knowledge, resulting in inventions and entrepreneurship [24]. Design thinking has several uses in education, including developing students' creativity, problem-solving, and critical thinking skills, fostering a culture of innovation and entrepreneurship, enhancing the quality and relevance of academic programs, improving the learning experience and engagement of students, addressing complex educational challenges, and preparing students for the demands of the 21st-century workforce [22].

Watson [25] acknowledges that there are many variations of design thinking models and he believes that having a model like the Stanford design thinking model is valuable because it provides educators with a guiding approach and tools to overcome creative blocks, generate creative insights, and develop more and better ideas. The Stanford model encompasses five phases or stages of design thinking, often referred to as modes, that are progressed through in order to arrive at solutions or resolutions for problems. Stages in design thinking include: empathize, define, ideate, prototype, and test. It is an iterative process that fits the nature of education where it is expected that instructors improve and refine their courses based on students' feedback [26]. The following sections elaborate further on the stages of the design thinking process.

Empathize. Empathy, as the first mode, serves as the cornerstone of human-centered design, serving as a crucial initial step for all design work. During this phase, designers closely observe user actions and behaviors, engage in interactions and interviews with them, and deeply involve themselves in comprehending the user's experiences and viewpoints [9, 26]. These insights empower designers to tackle the subsequent phases of the process with a more profound grasp of the surrounding context and the issue at hand [26].

Personas might be highly appropriate for describing various categories of students, each with occasionally distinct needs, preferences, and anxieties related to their learning process [27]. Personas encompass brief descriptions of potential users, serving as aids for system developers in acknowledging the characteristics, needs, and concerns of potential users. Initially formulated in user experience (UX) research, personas' utility could extend to the realm of education, contributing to the enhancement of teaching and learning experiences [27, 28]. Personas are used to induce and promote empathy with users [29]. By empathizing with the learners, educators can gain a deeper understanding of their needs and tailor the redesign efforts to meet those needs effectively.

Define. In the second phase, known as the Define mode, designers leverage the insights garnered during the empathizing stage to concentrate on the problem. Their objective is to go beyond a basic definition as they elaborate on the complexities of the user, the problem, and the surrounding context. During this phase, designers formulate a problem statement grounded in the specifics and insights they previously acquired. They narrow down and define the problem, providing a framework to steer design endeavors in the subsequent stages [9, 26].

In the context of education and course redesign, the define stage helps educators and instructional designers to identify the specific areas that need improvement or modification in the existing curriculum or teaching methods. It allows them to clearly articulate the problem statement and set clear objectives for the redesign process. By clearly defining the problem and setting goals, the define stage ensures that the redesign efforts are focused and purposeful, leading to more effective and meaningful educational experiences for the learners [22].

Ideate. In the Ideate phase, the objective is to delve into various solutions and concepts. The aim is to surpass the evident and engage in brainstorming, nurturing, and producing a broad spectrum of ideas, solutions, and strategies pertinent to the issue at hand. Designers are encouraged to generate a wide range of ideas while maintaining the problem's focus and to also let their imagination explore unexplored, innovative concepts. With the aim of unfettered idea generation, postponing judgment on idea assessment permits unhampered creativity [26].

In the context of education and course redesign, this stage encourages educators and instructional designers to think outside of the box and explore innovative approaches to improve the curriculum and teaching methods. This stage emphasizes brainstorming and idea generation, where diverse perspectives and viewpoints are encouraged to foster creativity and generate a multitude of ideas [22]. This stage involves encouraging educators and instructional designers to think creatively, brainstorm ideas, and explore different possibilities for addressing the problem at hand [9, 21, 30].

Prototype. The prototype stage involves creating tangible representations or models of the ideas generated during the ideation stage to test and gather feedback from users [22]. Prototypes can take various forms, such as physical models, digital simulations, or even sketches, depending on the nature of the problem and the available resources. The purpose of prototyping is to bring ideas to life and make them more tangible, allowing designers to evaluate their feasibility, functionality, and user experience [21]. This is not an attempt to reach a definitive solution, but rather a chance to experiment with rendering ideas tangible [26].

The prototype stage in design thinking for education and course redesign involves creating tangible representations of the proposed solution [30]. It can allow educators and instructional designers to develop and test prototypes of new teaching methods, learning activities, or curriculum components. This stage helps with evaluating the feasibility, effectiveness, and user experience of proposed changes before implementing them on a larger scale [22].

Test. In the Test stage, designers evaluate the prototype by involving real users or representative stakeholders. This can involve user interviews, observing interactions with prototypes, or employing other techniques to collect feedback for enhancing the solution(s). Testing might reveal the necessity to fine-tune the prototype or even reassess and reevaluate the initial perspective. It might prompt a return to the empathize phase for a deeper understanding of users, or a revisit to the ideate phase to explore alternative solutions [26].

In the context of education and course redesign, the test stage allows educators to pilot the proposed changes in a controlled environment, such as a small group of students or a specific course module, to observe how well they work in practice. Testing in education involves collecting data and feedback from students, teachers, and other stakeholders to assess the impact of the redesigned elements on learning outcomes, engagement, and overall satisfaction [22].

Although we depict them in a sequential manner, design thinking is inherently an iterative procedure. Designers, educators, and individuals in other roles can go through the process repeatedly or reengage with different phases as necessary, aiming to comprehend and explore issues and potential solutions [26]. This paper continues to demonstrate how the design thinking approach may be applied to designing online courses in hospitality and programs.

3   Methods

The design thinking approach was applied to a graduate-level online course in the Hospitality Management program at a university in the United States. This course was taken by both master's and Ph.D. students. While the Ph.D. program offers a mix of face-to-face and online courses, the master's program is delivered asynchronously online. Therefore, it was deemed important to understand the user experience of this student group with online courses and redesign the course in response to that.

3.1   Data Collection

The first stage in the design thinking approach is Empathize. This step relies on data collected from the users (learners in the case of this project). All the following design thinking steps (define, ideate, prototype, test) are grounded in the understanding of user goals, interactions with the technology, and frustrations and developed based on the authors' thinking. Therefore, the Methods section of this study describes the approaches to data collection and analysis for the empathize stage.

To better understand student experiences in the online courses, the course instructor conducted an online survey. Students were informed that participation in the survey was anonymous and voluntary. The survey was available to students for one full week via the Blackboard course website. Also, they were offered bonus points for participating in this survey resulting in a 100% response rate.

The first item on the survey explained to students the purpose of the questionnaire. It was shared with the students that the instructor is trying to understand how they engage with the course and provided materials. The opening statements stated that the instructor is looking to understand what is important for students in an online course, their goals and frustrations, how they interact with the course, and how the instructor can improve the experience for the current and future cohorts of students. Following the opening statement, the survey instrument used a mix of multiple-choice and essay questions. While multiple-choice questions were used to collect quantitative data about students' behavior on consistent scales, essay questions were used to collect qualitative data to yield deeper understanding and insights into learner experience with the course.

Multiple-choice questions were used to collect data about the overall rating of the course experience, technology tools used to access the course (e.g., laptop, tablet, smartphone; personal or shared device), time spent going through the course resources and completing assignments, as well as identifying the key features of the course website that students used frequently (e.g., announcements, to-do lists, assignments, etc.). The essay questions were designed to understand the story of every learner. Students were encouraged to express their thoughts in full sentences and write from a couple of sentences to a paragraph. The essay questions asked students to describe their goals, how they use the Blackboard course website (e.g., which sections they visit and in which order), their frustrations with the online course, and how they would make it a "perfect" course.

3.2 Data Analysis

The data analysis for this project included descriptive statistics that summarized the technologies used for accessing the course website, time spent on materials and assignments, and most frequently used features. Thematic analysis was applied to qualitative data collected via essay questions. The analysis of goals, frustrations, and uses of the Blackboard website were used to generate learner personas.

Personas are fictional characters that are built to represent groups of users who exhibit similar behaviors. Persona templates are widely available online as a part of resources for UX research, for example, through professional associations, such as Interaction Design Foundation [31]. User personas may include different types of information, such as the name of the persona, a catchphrase, demographic characteristics, a description of the persona, goals, frustrations, personality traits, brands that the persona uses, and other categories based on the needs of a specific project. The following section presents the results of the study, including the sample description, a persona example, and further considerations for all stages of the design thinking process.

4   Results

4.1   Sample Profile

All 14 students enrolled in the course in the Fall of 2022 participated in the course experience survey. An average overall evaluation of the course experience was 4.5. The course experience was measured on a 5-point scale anchored at 1 - poor to 5 - excellent. Only one student rated the course experience as average (3 points). All other students evaluated their course experience as good (5 students) or excellent (8 students). All students accessed the course content on their personal laptop/desktop computers.

Most frequently (42.9%) students reported spending three or more hours going through the course resources (e.g., reading announcements, watching video lectures, etc.) on an average week. The next two categories were reported equally frequently: 1.5 h and 2 h (21.4% for each category). A similar pattern was observed on the next question asking students how much time per week they spent completing assignments. The majority of students answered 3 or more hours (57.1%), followed by 2 h (21.4%), and 1.5 h (14.3%).

To understand students' circumstances outside of the learning environment, they were also asked about their work status and other personal commitments that they had during the semester. Half of the students (50%) worked full time and another 28.6% worked half-time. Work responsibilities were the most frequently reported commitment outside of school (64.3%), followed by personal relationships (e.g., significant other/spouse; 50%), friends (50%), sport (28.6%), and children (21.4%).

4.2   Developing Personas

The next step in developing empathy with learners involved reading the essay answers along with the responses to quantitative questions, finding the key themes, and identifying similarities in user goals, interactions with the Blackboard website, and frustrations. The main goal of this activity is to identify the key personas that are present in the class and think about the course redesign from the perspective of that persona. To meet the publication length requirements, this paper further presents one of the personas developed for the subject course. Please see Fig. 1 for the persona profile.

Please review the card to meet Angelica who is a 35-year-old female student, who balances a full-time job, busy personal schedule, raising two kids, and working towards her online master's degree in Hospitality Management. Angelica says: "I work full time and make progress on my online courses whenever I have free time". Her goals are to balance school, work, and personal life, to learn effectively from her classmates and the course professor, and to submit all assignments on time. Angelica tried to use the mobile app and was frustrated by that experience. She is also looking for ways to get hands-on experience with the content she is learning and increase her real-time interactions with the course participants.

Creating personas like Angelica helps instructors of online courses better understand their students, "hear" their stories, goals, and struggles, and put themselves in students' shoes when thinking about course redesign as suggested by Rapanta and Cantoni [32] to empathize with the end-users more. The next steps in the design thinking process

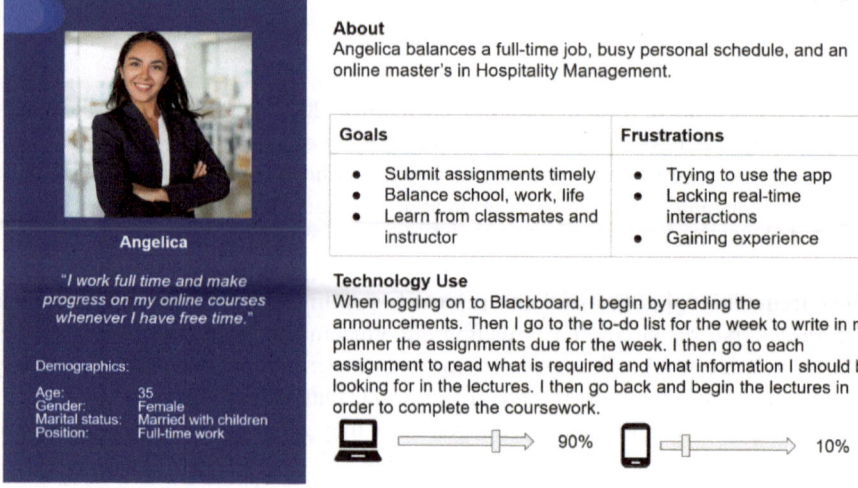

About
Angelica balances a full-time job, busy personal schedule, and an online master's in Hospitality Management.

Goals	Frustrations
• Submit assignments timely • Balance school, work, life • Learn from classmates and instructor	• Trying to use the app • Lacking real-time interactions • Gaining experience

Angelica

"I work full time and make progress on my online courses whenever I have free time."

Demographics:

Age: 35
Gender: Female
Marital status: Married with children
Position: Full-time work

Technology Use
When logging on to Blackboard, I begin by reading the announcements. Then I go to the to-do list for the week to write in my planner the assignments due for the week. I then go to each assignment to read what is required and what information I should be looking for in the lectures. I then go back and begin the lectures in order to complete the coursework.

90%   10%

Fig. 1. Learner persona example. Photo credit:katemangosta on Freepik.

include defining the problem, ideating potential solutions, prototyping, and testing. This paper continues to demonstrate how the developed persona of Angelica may be used to complete this process.

4.3 Using Personas to Improve Online Courses

Define. Using the insights from students like Angelica, the project progresses to identifying the problems in the course design that need to be solved to improve the learning experience for this user group. When working on this step, it is important to consider the frustrations that the learner persona expressed explicitly, but also it is valuable to look at the overall context and to make conclusions about how the goals and frustrations of the user interact with the broader circumstances of their lives. If we try to put ourselves in Angelica's shoes, we may identify the following areas that she is struggling with:

- Timely submission of assignments. It is easy to miss a deadline when juggling work, school, and personal responsibilities. Angelica mentioned that she moves the to-dos and deadlines of each module to her personal planner to keep track of all the work that she needs to complete.
- Extracting the key material from the video lectures that are essential for learning and completing the assignments. Angelica may have a lot of interruptions in her learning schedule. She acknowledged that she makes progress on her online classes whenever she has time. Therefore, she may be trying to learn at various opportunities, such as short breaks at work, waiting for a meeting, or interrupted circumstances.
- Lacking real-time interactions. Angelica is taking an asynchronous class online. The course does offer interactive elements, such as the kick-off meeting at the start of the semester and discussion boards for the students to interact and exchange ideas. However, the discussion boards may take time for students to respond to as everyone

learns on their own schedule. Therefore, Angelica is looking for ways to increase her interactions with other learners and the professor.

- Gaining experience. Overall Angelica enjoys her learning experience and values the material that she has been exposed to. However, she does not feel confident yet applying this content to real-life problems and situations (Table 1).

Table 1. Generating course redesign ideas at the ideate stage.

	Calendar/Announcements	Video Lectures/Resources	Assignments/Projects
Timely submission of assignments	Create a shareable course calendar that students can import and receive reminders Send out weekly announcements describing the scope of work Send a reminder to students without submissions 2 days before the due date	Add timestamps to video lectures to facilitate navigation to the right content needed for the assignments Provide students with useful methods and apps that help them manage their time Provide learning materials in advance to allow flexibility in working through them	Break down complex assignments into smaller, scaffolded tasks Scaffolding of term projects Provide rubrics to clearly indicate the key concepts and skills students need to develop Provide an estimated time of completion Choice-based projects: Provide students an option to choose a project that aligns with their interests and time availability
Extracting key material from video lectures		Add a label for essential and supporting video lectures Include instructions on the elements to pay attention to when studying a particular resource (e.g., articles, reports)	Include links to relevant video lectures in the description of the assignment Encourage students to create visual aids like concept maps or diagrams to represent key concepts and relationships within the video lecture

(*continued*)

Table 1. (*continued*)

	Calendar/Announcements	Video Lectures/Resources	Assignments/Projects
Lacking real-time interactions	Periodically schedule live question-and-answer sessions	Enable the web conferencing feature in LMS so that students can organize meetings without the instructor	Ask students to collaborate on small projects in teams for certain weeks Use peer review assignments where students provide feedback to their classmates
Gaining experience		Give real-life examples and case studies Record interviews with guest speakers Organize online guest lectures Use virtual tours (e.g., Hyatt in virtual reality)	Assign students to keep reflective journals or blogs where they document instances where they've applied class knowledge in their daily lives Partner with a local hospitality/tourism business for projects Use role-playing exercises

Ideate. After meeting Angelica and defining her learning problems, the next step is to create ideas for how these problems may be solved for the group of users represented by the persona of Angelica. There are many ways to generate ideas. Such approaches may include asking students for suggestions, e.g., the survey described in this study asked students to indicate how they would make the course a "perfect" course. Additionally, ideas may be generated by working in groups with other professors or with students who took or are taking the subject course. For this project, the instructor worked with two students who had taken the subject course previously. Therefore, these students were familiar with the content and structure of the course, and after familiarizing themselves with personas, could offer ideas for improving experiences for those students.

As a team, the authors brainstormed ways of solving Angelica's problems across different elements of the course, such as the course calendar, announcements, video lectures, resources, assignments, and projects. The team followed the structured approach of thinking about the problem and different course elements but also left room for exploring solutions that were outside of the box. Table 1 presents a summary of various modifications that may be applied to the course based on the persona created for this project and the challenges that this persona experienced in the online hospitality marketing course.

Prototype and Test. Following the design thinking approach, the next two steps of the process would be to prioritize the solutions to the identified problems that would be the most impactful for the student experience, prototype them, and test them with students. The presentation of the current project stops here with all the considerations that have been outlined above. It is important to note that usually the student body in any program would host at least two or more personas. It is important to consider how the changes proposed for one learner persona may affect other personas. From this point forward the judgment of each individual instructor should be used to select the elements that best fit the personas of their students and the content of the course.

5   Conclusions

This paper introduced the readers to the design thinking process and illustrated how such a process may be applied to a redesign of an online course. This approach presents a critical, data-driven, and creative framework for thinking about a course redesign and identifying the right changes to be made. The design thinking is a user-centric approach, which in this case learner-centric. It shifts the focus from the educator's perspective to the student's perspective as quite often the way a professor envisions the course may differ from the way students experience the course.

As online learning continues to grow [1], it becomes highly important for educators to understand the goals and challenges that their students are having in online courses. This commonly presents a challenge in online education as professors do not see their students in class on a weekly basis, have a harder time connecting to students, lack instant feedback, and have fewer opportunities to receive comments from students. One of the major benefits of applying the design thinking approach is being intentional in learning about the students and their experiences. When adopting such an approach, educators are asked to get to know their students, collect data, empathize, build personas, and redesign the course keeping the behavior of those personas at the center of the redesign.

While this paper brings value by demonstrating an application of the design thinking approach to redesigning an online course, it also has certain limitations. The design thinking and user experience fields have created other methods, such as empathy maps and user journey maps, that may be helpful for better understanding the students and developing empathy with them. Future research may look at the use of other user experience research tools and evaluate their value for course redesign. This study was built based on one hospitality course. Further research at a larger scale may provide deeper and more generalizable results for broader populations of online students.

References

1. Forbes.: The rise of online learning in the U.S. – Forbes Advisor. https://www.forbes.com/advisor/education/online-learning-stats/ (2023)
2. Adedoyin, O.B., Soykan, E.: Covid-19 pandemic and online learning: the challenges and opportunities. Interact. Learn. Environ. **31**(2), 863–875 (2023)
3. Greenhow, C., Graham, C.R., Koehler, M.J.: Foundations of online learning: challenges and opportunities. Educ. Psychol. **57**(3), 131–147 (2022)

4. Besser, A., Flett, G.L., Zeigler-Hill, V.: Adaptability to a sudden transition to online learning during the COVID-19 pandemic: understanding the challenges for students. Scholarsh. Teach. Learn. Psychol. **8**(2), 85–105 (2020)
5. Tualaulelei, E., Burke, K., Fanshawe, M., Cameron, C.: Mapping pedagogical touchpoints: exploring online student engagement and course design. Act. Learn. High. Educ. **23**(3), 189–203 (2022)
6. Novak, E., Mulvey, B.K.: Enhancing design thinking in instructional technology students. J. Comput. Assist. Learn. **37**(1), 80–90 (2021)
7. Taheri, M., Unterholzer, T., Meinel, C.: Design thinking at scale: a report on best practices of online courses. Design Thinking Research: Taking Breakthrough Innovation Home, pp. 217–235 (2016)
8. Wrigley, C., Straker, K.: Design thinking pedagogy: the educational design ladder. Innov. Educ. Teach. Int. **54**(4), 374–385 (2017)
9. Shé, C.N., Farrell, O., Brunton, J., Costello, E.: Integrating design thinking into instructional design: the #OpenTeach case study. Austral. J. Educ. Technol. **38**(1), 1 (2022)
10. Assen, H., Benhadda, L., Losekoot, E., van Diggelen, M.: Design thinking in hospitality education: lessons learned and future opportunities. J. Hosp. Leis. Sport Tour. Educ. **32**, 100439 (2023)
11. Sándorová, Z., Repáňová, T., Palenčíková, Z., Beták, N.: Design thinking-A revolutionary new approach in tourism education? J. Hosp. Leis. Sport Tour. Educ. **26**, 100238 (2020)
12. Wang, M.J.S., Munoz, K.E., Tham, A.: Enhancing industry-ready competence and skills through design thinking integration: evidence from a CLIL-based hospitality course. Consum. Behav. Tourism Hospitality **17**(3), 326–337 (2022)
13. Lub, X.D., Rijnders, R., Caceres, L.N., Bosman, J.: The future of hotels: the lifestyle hub. A design-thinking approach for developing future hospitality concepts. J. Vacation Marketing **22**(3), 249–264 (2016)
14. Wan, C. B., Lee, K. S., Leung, D., Park, S.: Using design thinking as an educational tool for conceptualizing future smart hotel guest experiences. e-Review Tourism Res. **17**(3), 349–367 (2019)
15. Amin, I., Yousaf, A., Walia, S., Bashir, M.: What shapes E-Learning effectiveness among tourism education students? An empirical assessment during COVID19. J. Hosp. Leis. Sport Tour. Educ. **30**, 100337 (2022)
16. Cantoni, L., Kalbaska, N., Inversini, A.: ELearning in tourism and hospitality: a map. J. Hosp. Leis. Sport Tour. Educ. **8**(2), 148–156 (2009)
17. Sigala, M.: Investigating the factors determining e-learning effectiveness in tourism and hospitality education. J. Hosp. Tour. Educ. **16**(2), 11–21 (2004)
18. King, C., So, K.K.F.: Creating a virtual learning community to engage international students. J. Hosp. Tour. Educ. **26**(3), 136–146 (2014)
19. Abbas, T.M., Jones, E., Hussien, F.M.: Technological factors influencing university tourism and hospitality students' intention to use e-learning: a comparative analysis of Egypt and the United Kingdom. J. Hosp. Tour. Educ. **28**(4), 189–201 (2016)
20. Nair, B.B.: Endorsing gamification pedagogy as a helpful strategy to offset the COVID-19 induced disruptions in tourism education. J. Hosp. Leis. Sport Tour. Educ. **30**, 100362 (2022)
21. Razzouk, R., Shute, V.: What is design thinking and why is it important? Rev. Educ. Res. **82**(3), 330–348 (2012)
22. Panke, S.: Design thinking in education: perspectives, opportunities and challenges. Open Educ. Stud. **1**(1), 281–306 (2019)
23. Dorst, K.: The core of design thinking and its application. Des. Stud. **32**(6), 521–532 (2011)
24. Auernhammer, J., Roth, B.: The origin and evolution of Stanford University's design thinking: from product design to design thinking in innovation management. J. Prod. Innov. Manage **38**(6), 623–644 (2021)

25. Watson, A.D.: Design thinking for life. Art Educ. (Reston) **68**(3), 12–18 (2015)
26. Henriksen, D., Richardson, C., Mehta, R.: Design thinking: a creative approach to educational problems of practice. Thinking Skills Creativity **26**, 140–153 (2017)
27. Weinhandl, R., Mayerhofer, M., Houghton, T., Lavicza, Z., Eichmair, M., Hohenwarter, M.: Personas characterising secondary school mathematics students: Development and applications to educational technology. Educ. Sci. **12**(7), 7 (2022)
28. Rooij, V., Williams, S.: Research-based personas: teaching empathy in professional education. J. Effect. Teach. **12**(3), 77–86 (2012)
29. Haag, M., Marsden, N.: Exploring personas as a method to foster empathy in student IT design teams. Int. J. Technol. Des. Educ. **29**, 565–582 (2019)
30. Lugmayr, A., Stockleben, B., Zou, Y., Anzenhofer, S., Jalonen, M.: Applying design thinking in the context of media management education. Multimedia Tools Appl. **71**(1), 119–157 (2014)
31. Friis Dam, R., Siang, T.Y.: Personas – a simple introduction. The interaction design foundation, 23 February 2022. https://www.interaction-design.org/literature/article/personas-why-and-how-you-should-use-them
32. Rapanta, C., Cantoni, L.: Being in the users' shoes: Anticipating experience while designing online courses. Br. J. Edu. Technol. **45**(5), 765–777 (2014)

Escaping the Routine: Virtual Escape Rooms in Online Hospitality Courses

Katerina Berezina[1]([✉]) [iD], Olena Ciftci[2] [iD], Mahsa Talebi[1] [iD], and Rasoul Mahdavi[1] [iD]

[1] University of Mississippi, University, MS 38677, USA
eberezin@olemiss.edu
[2] New York University, New York, NY 10003, USA

Abstract. Virtual escape rooms (VER) are online educational games that place learners in the scenario of being locked in a specified environment and require them to collect clues, answer questions, or solve puzzles in exchange for an escape code. This paper documents the process of designing a VER for an online hospitality course using Google Workspace tools (i.e., Google Sites, Slides, and Forms). The paper walks the readers through the VER design process, which includes identifying the purpose of creating a VER, creating a storyline, preparing clues (e.g., puzzles and activities for students to solve), setting up an escape code, and collecting student feedback. This process may be followed by online instructors to create VERs that will meet the needs of their courses. The same process may be applied when developing VERs in other environments (e.g., Microsoft products, mobile apps, or metaverse). Based on the feedback of 21 students who participated in the VER described in this paper, the experience was engaging, fun, enjoyable, and helped them learn and understand the class material. This paper may be useful for hospitality and tourism instructors, industry training professionals, and instructional designers.

Keywords: Learner Experience · Online Education · Gamification

1 Introduction

Online learning has been growing rapidly in recent years, especially due to the COVID-19 pandemic, which forced many universities to shift to online modes of teaching and learning. This educational trend of remote learning continues to grow in post-pandemic times, with an annual growth rate of approximately 7% in 2025. The popularity of online learning is motivated by remote and flexible learning options as well as personalized and engaging learning experiences supported by advancements in technology [1]. Student expectations of online education raise a need for online teaching techniques and tools to facilitate student engagement and stimulate involvement in the learning process.

One of the approaches to engaging students in an active learning process is gamification. Gamification in education requires adding elements and mechanisms of games in the educational process [2]. This paper focuses on designing virtual escape rooms (VER) as one of the popular gamification tools in online education [3–5]. The carefully

K. Berezina et al. (Eds.): ENTER 2024, SPBE, pp. 100–112, 2024.
https://doi.org/10.1007/978-3-031-58839-6_11

designed VER can create an immersive and engaging learning experience to increase student involvement and motivation [3, 6–9]. Despite its advantages of enhancing educational experience, there is a research and utilization gap in incorporating VER into hospitality and tourism education. The extant academic literature documents a few studies investigating tourist experience at escape rooms (ER) [10–12]. While the industry applications of ERs have received some attention in research, there is a lack of research and guidance on creating ER and VER in hospitality and tourism education.

Therefore, this study aims to illustrate how a VER may be built using widely accessible tools (i.e., Google Sites, Google Forms, and Google Slides). The proposed VER design in this project includes various activities that not only entertain and engage students but also allow them to learn, test their knowledge, and apply what they have learned. In addition, this paper discusses possible implementations of the proposed VER design in the educational process. The contribution of this study is in documenting the method for designing and building a VER for a hospitality course. The goal of this paper was reached by illustrating how a VER was implemented in one of the courses in the hospitality curriculum. The approach documented in this paper may be used to expand the idea to other hospitality- and tourism-related courses.

2   Escape Rooms

The contemporary landscape of educational methodologies encompasses both teacher-centered and student-centered approaches. A discernible trend is emerging, marked by student inclination toward active engagement and participation in their educational experiences, in contrast to the traditional passive listening paradigm [5, 13, 14]. Active learning entails a teaching method where learners are actively involved in interacting with the material and putting their knowledge into practical use, as opposed to merely receiving information passively. Research has shown that Escape Rooms (ERs) can be an effective tool for facilitating active learning outcomes, such as critical thinking, problem-solving, and teamwork skills [3–5, 7, 8, 15].

ERs are live-action team-based games where players must solve challenges to complete a mission within a limited time frame. Originally, the mission was to escape from a room, but now, the missions can vary [16]. ERs have become very popular in the entertainment industry and are now being used as learning environments in various educational settings [9, 17]. They offer an enjoyable and efficient method for captivating students in the learning process while fostering the growth of problem-solving abilities and teamwork skills [9].

ERs have found utility across a range of educational applications, such as student recruiting [18], introducing students to institutional services [19, 20], facilitating learning processes within student teams [21], or promoting the utilization of teamwork and leadership skills among students [22]. Veldkamp and colleagues [9] present studies of ERs crafted to cultivate domain-specific skills and knowledge, spanning fields, such as nursing, medicine, pharmacy, physiotherapy, chemistry, physics, computer science, mathematics, history, and English. Furthermore, they are also employed to bolster the acquisition of generic skills.

ERs represent innovative, active, collaborative, and constructivist instructional methods that have the potential to influence learning more profoundly than traditional teaching approaches. These immersive experiences enable learners to grasp the importance of examining challenges from diverse angles, immerse themselves in collaborative teamwork, foster engagement and perseverance, fortify social connections, kindle team cohesion, and catalyze the advantages of deep learning through group discussions [7].

2.1 Key Elements of Virtual Escape Rooms

Virtual escape rooms (VERs) are digital versions of physical escape rooms that can be accessed remotely. They are designed to provide an immersive and engaging experience for learners and can be used to teach a variety of subjects. VERs have become increasingly popular in recent years due to their accessibility and flexibility [3]. The VERs rose to prominence in recent years, particularly during the COVID-19 pandemic when physical escape room visits were constrained. Although the precise origins of VERs lack comprehensive documentation, they are likely to have evolved organically as an extension of the popularity of physical escape rooms, propelled by the growing accessibility of digital technologies [3, 15].

These escape room experiences often incorporate thematic elements and storylines to enrich the overall player engagement. These themes span diverse settings, from historical settings to fantastical worlds, and narratives may encompass mystery-solving or mission completion. Developing a storyline for a VER involves the creation of an interactive experience where participants' decisions shape the route they follow to achieve specific educational goals [23]. This can be accomplished by utilizing a branching storyline approach within a platform such as Google Forms, where the answers selected by participants lead to different outcomes and scenarios [24]. The objective is to engage participants and offer them chances to tackle challenges and make choices within the VER setting [25]. The storyline should involve puzzles, clues, and riddles that the learner can interact with and solve to unlock doors and advance through the room [25, 26].

As participants explore VERs, they find clues that will help them to escape the room. Such clues usually include puzzles for participants to solve and at the end provide them with the escape code or parts of it to escape. Escape rooms employ various puzzle structuring techniques. The most prevalent approach is path-based, wherein participants encounter multiple puzzle pathways leading to a final resolution as an escape code. Another organizing strategy is sequential, wherein participants solve one puzzle sequentially, with each solved puzzle unlocking the subsequent one in a linear progression as a cue [16].

Different tools can be used to create VERs. Google Apps and Microsoft Office serve as valuable tools for both planning the learning objectives and designing the escape room. Google Drawing, Google Slides, and Microsoft PowerPoint are instrumental in crafting puzzles and concealing links to each puzzle within the room or environment's imagery. Additionally, a form can be established for students to submit their puzzle solutions, allowing them to unlock each of the locks. This setup can include response validation to ensure the submission of the correct response before advancing to the subsequent lock. Synchronous and asynchronous approaches can be applied to perform VER [27, 28].

Accordingly, students may be asked to either work through a VER on their own or in teams on their own time or at a class online meeting.

2.2 Benefits and Challenges of Using Escape Rooms

VERs can be an effective tool for incorporating gamification elements in education. They provide an immersive and engaging way for learners to develop critical thinking, problem-solving, and teamwork skills while also incorporating game-like elements to increase engagement and motivation [3]. Zhanni [2] provides a comprehensive definition of gamification in education, elucidating it as the strategic incorporation of game-design elements and mechanisms into non-gaming contexts to incentivize desired behaviors. VERs are a popular tool for gamifying instruction and engaging students in a variety of educational contexts [3–5]. VERs can use gamification elements such as points, badges, and leaderboards to increase engagement and motivation among students. These elements provide students with a sense of achievement and progress, which can help to increase their motivation and engagement. Moreover, it can incorporate gamification elements, such as storytelling, feedback, and rewards to create an engaging and immersive learning experience [3].

Adams and colleagues [6] created a VER as a teaching tool to facilitate active learning in nursing education. The VER was designed to help students develop critical thinking, problem-solving, and teamwork skills. The authors found that the VER was an effective tool for facilitating active learning outcomes. Students reported that the VER was engaging and helped them to apply their knowledge practically. The authors also noted that the VERs provided an opportunity for students to work collaboratively and develop communication and leadership skills. Pozo-Sánchez and colleagues [5] found that physical ER was more effective in terms of enjoyment, while VERs were more effective in terms of autonomy and creative thinking. Teachers need to consider an appropriate learning environment and gamification approach when planning their teaching and learning activities, while also taking into consideration students' specific needs and the dimensions that should be cultivated [5].

While VERs offer advantages, they also pose challenges. Designing VERs requires meticulous attention to user interface and experience, ensuring seamless communication and collaboration among learners. VERs may lack the physicality and tactile experiences of traditional ERs. A significant challenge lies in ensuring the accessibility and availability of necessary technology and equipment, particularly in educational settings [29]. Fotaris and Mastoras [7] conducted a systematic review of ER challenges, identifying issues such as deficient evaluation methods, substantial time and resource investment, limited facilitator availability, poor design, and limited playtesting, occasionally yielding games with imbalanced difficulty levels and a sensation of being either too brief or overly protracted.

Furthermore, designing VERs presents challenges in creating immersive gameplay experiences and maintaining consistent game contexts [9]. The absence of physical interaction, difficulty in generating a sense of urgency, and challenges in implementing complex puzzles in a digital format are additional hurdles. Technical issues or glitches can disrupt gameplay, and fostering teamwork and collaboration in a virtual environment is challenging. Potential distractions and a lack of focus due to the digital format also complicate adapting educational objectives to a virtual setting [30].

3 Methods and Results

This paper documents an approach to building a virtual escape room using Google Workspace products, including Google Sites, Forms, and Slides. The process presented below was used for building a VER for a research methods course delivered to social sciences students (e.g., hospitality management, sport management, food and nutrition, and political sciences).

3.1 Purpose

The goals of incorporating this VER were:

- Engaging students with the material using an innovative and different approach,
- Assisting students with learning the materials by providing them with feedback as they moved through the escape rooms,
- Providing students with the opportunity to practice course concepts (e.g., aligning research questions with questions included on the questionnaire), and
- Checking students' understanding of the learned material.

In line with the goals, the VER was administered to students in one of the modules of an online asynchronous course as the last element in the module. Students were instructed to attempt the VER after studying all the materials provided in the module. This room was used as an assessment instrument where clues were designed as various activities, including multiple-choice and matching questions, as well as questions allowing students to apply the learned concepts. The VER was assigned as an individual untimed project and graded based on students' performance in answering questions presented in each clue. Even students who did not escape the room received credit for their answers.

3.2 Storyline

The storyline designed for a VER sets the theme and complexity of the experience. The story of the VER created for this project was set in a library. Graduate students taking the course read the scenario of them studying late in the library and falling asleep. When they woke up, the library was closed and students needed to use the clues hidden around the library to collect the secret code and escape. The pictured room included bookcases along the walls and a study area in the middle with desks, coffee tables, and armchairs. The escape room consisted of one room only. This activity was the first VER that the students experienced, and, therefore, it was decided to keep it simple to avoid any confusion with the story or format and focus on student engagement and learning.

The virtual room experience was built using Google Sites, which offers a variety of templates that instructors may choose from to build their VERs. For this project, the course instructor entered the title that was shown at the top of the webpage, then edited the text fields to provide students with the scenario and basic instructions for navigating the escape room. Please refer to Fig. 1 to see the design of the website and the virtual escape room. Alternatively, instructors may choose to create two pages on their VER website: one for instructions and the call to action button to start the escape room experience and another one to host the VER itself.

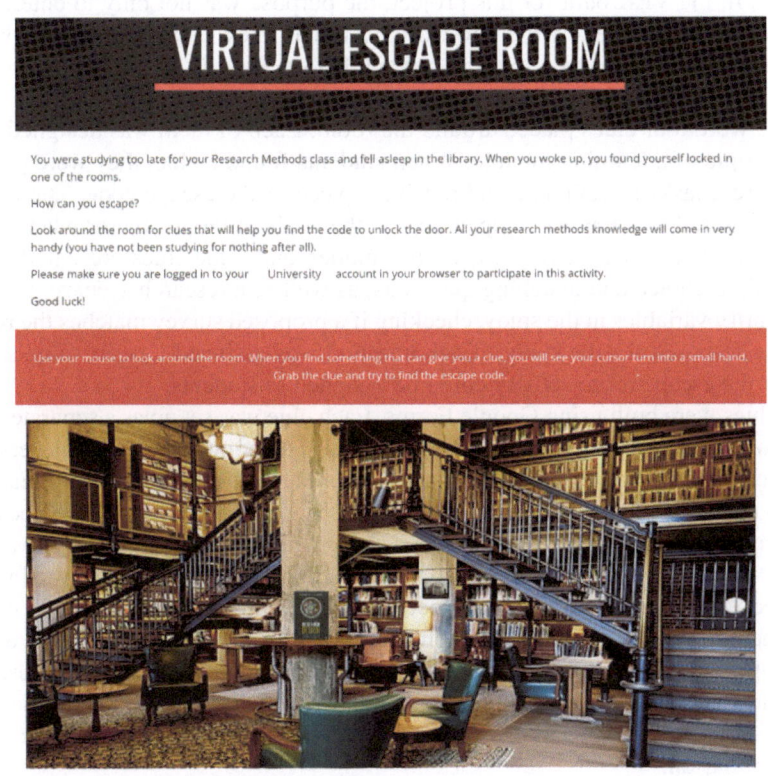

Fig. 1. Website hosting the virtual escape room.

If the university subscribes to Google services, the instructor may choose to limit access to the website and all elements of the VER only to those individuals who are affiliated with the university. This is the setting that was chosen for this project, therefore, the instructions instructed students that they need to be logged in to their university Google account to participate in this activity.

The VER itself was built using Google Slides and embedded on the webpage following the instructions. To create the virtual room, the instructor created a new Google Slides and selected a background that matched the theme, in this case, it was the library room. The background may be set using one picture that fits the theme of the VER or by changing the color of the background and placing different objects on the background. The background creates the overall atmosphere of the escape room. Once it is set, different clues may be added to it to send students on the hunt for an escape code.

3.3 Clues

In physical escape rooms, clues are different objects that are placed around the room and, when discovered, contribute to players' understanding of the secret code. When playing the game for entertainment, players may find some clues and still figure out the solution to escape. In the VER built for this project, the purpose was not only to entertain and engage students but to allow them to learn, test their knowledge, and apply what they have learned. For this reason, it was important that students discover and go through all the clues placed in the room.

There were four clues placed around the room. Each of them was designed around a certain topic of a learning module. When students found a clue, they were presented with different tasks to complete and receive a piece of the escape code. The activities presented to students may vary depending on the goals of the instructor when building a particular VER. In our case, the activities hidden under the clues presented students with multiple-choice and matching questions, as well as a research scenario to analyze (e.g., identify variables in the study, checking if a proposed survey matches the research questions proposed for the study). Each question was assigned a point value so that a grade for the escape room activity could be assigned to students.

All clues were built using Google Forms. Each clue was set up as a separate Google Form. To provide students with feedback and assign points for their answers to the challenges, the Google Form was set as a quiz (Settings → Make this a quiz). Each form was also restricted to the members of the university so that students would need to log in. Students' email addresses were recorded along with the accumulated point values for correctly answered questions, which allowed grading this activity. Also, the instructor set up feedback for correct and incorrect answers to all questions. Students were not shown the correct answer but were offered suggestions on how to think about a certain question/problem or which mini-lecture to watch to review the relevant material. The forms allowed students multiple attempts on each clue. This way, those students who were interested in retaking the quiz could do so after receiving the feedback on their initial submission.

Once each clue was created, it needed to be placed in the VER to be discovered by students. To do so, the form should be published first (Send → Link → Copy). After this, a special object should be placed on the slide with the virtual room. It may be a picture that matches the theme of the VER or an invisible shape that aligns with one of the objects on the background selected for the room. In this project, two clues were attached to added objects (i.e., the textbook used in the class and a picture of the university campus), and another two were attached to the images in the background. When students moved the mouse around the VER, the cursor would turn into a little hand when a clue was found indicating there was a link to click on.

The Google Forms may be set up with all questions being placed in one section. However, Google Forms also allows the creation of different sections. Such functionality may be used to send students on different routes depending on their answers. For example, Sect. 1 may contain a certain question that, once answered, creates branches. For the logic to work, this question should be marked as required in the settings. Then, those students who answered correctly may be directed to Sect. 2, and all others to Sect. 3. For example, in our project, such logic was used to make sure that the students correctly identified the number of variables involved in the study described in the scenario. Those students who answered correctly were invited to proceed to the following questions. Those students who did not give the right answer were offered an opportunity to go back to the scenario, read it carefully, and think about the question one more time. Making sure that students could identify the variables correctly was important for this escape room because the following questions asked students to identify the appropriate questions to be included in the survey, which cannot be done without knowing all the variables that the survey needs to measure. After completing all exercises under a certain clue, students received a piece of the escape code.

3.4 Escape Code

The escape code could be a phrase or alphanumeric string that would unlock the door and allow students to escape the room. This may be a string of random characters, a word, or a phrase that means something to the class. It may be something funny or serious depending on the tone that the instructor chooses to maintain. For this project, the instructor chose an escape code similar to "ResearchMethodsRock!" (the original escape phrase contained the course number and was modified for anonymity). This phrase was randomly split into four segments and provided to students one at a time as they solved each of the four clues. Such an approach was taken to ensure that students discovered all the clues and attempted all corresponding activities. Each piece of the code was presented with a sequence number (e.g., 2 out of 4) to indicate where that piece of the code should be placed in the entire string. It is important to direct students to write down the piece of the code along with the sequence number so that they can correctly assemble the escape code when they collect all parts.

A separate Google Form was set up for the escape door. The link to this form was placed over the door in the background of the virtual room. It is intuitive for students to think that the escape should be where the door is. Alternatively, the escape could be set up through a window (if present) or any other object in the room that would serve as an escape portal. When students clicked on the door in the escape room, they were presented with a picture of the door lock and the following narrative:

"Oops! This door is locked. To open this door, please look around the room to collect the clues. The code has four parts. Once you find all of them, please come back here to unlock the door. If you do not have the code yet, please close this tab to return to the room."

The instructions served several purposes: they indicated to students that they found the escape door, informed them that they needed to find a code, and shared that the code has four parts. If the students did not have all parts of the code yet, they were asked to return to the room. Providing such instructions is important because the instructor cannot predict at which step students will find and click on the door. Therefore, guidance should be provided for all possible scenarios so that students do not feel lost. Those students who already have the code were invited to enter it in the next question. This question was set up to accept only one answer that matches the escape code exactly. If the code did not match, students were given an error message and asked to keep looking. If the code did match, the students were directed to the next section of the form with the picture of an open door and congratulations on their success. Once escaped, students were invited to submit their feedback on the VER activity.

3.5 Student Feedback

Graduate students in the research methods class provided feedback on the effectiveness of the VER assignment. A total of 21 students participated in the anonymous online survey. In line with the goals of this VER (engaging with the material, assisting students with learning, providing opportunities to practice, and checking students' understanding of the material), students were asked to indicate whether their experience in VER was interesting, fun, engaging, educations, and helpful for understanding the course material.

The scale for experience was a 5-point Likert scale from "1 - Strongly disagree" to "5 - Strongly agree." All respondents strongly agreed or agreed that their experience with the VER assignment was interesting (M = 4.76), fun (M = 4.76), engaging (M = 4.81), and helpful in understanding the material (M = 4.81). A total of 20 students strongly agreed or agreed that the experience was educational, and one student found the VER assignment "neutral" in this category (M = 4.81).

The majority of students indicated that they completed the VER assignment in 30 min to 1 h (71.4%), 23.8% completed the assignment in less than 30 min, and only one student completed the assignment in a time from 1 h to 2 h. Further, students were asked to describe the difficulty level of VER activity as "too easy," "as expected for homework," or "too difficult". All students described the difficulty of the activity as "as expected for homework." Also, all students, except one, recommended keeping the VER activity without changes in future classes.

The students also provided narrative comments about the VER assignment. The top five themes are summarized below.

- Engaging and Enjoyable Learning Experience: Students repeatedly expressed their enjoyment and engagement with the assignment. They found it fun and engaging, which helped them learn the course material better.
- Effectiveness in Learning: Students mentioned that the VER was a helpful way to learn the material in the course. They appreciated the hands-on approach and how it contributed to their understanding of the content.
- Feedback and Review: Students valued the feedback provided within the escape room. They appreciated the opportunity to review and correct their answers and the feedback given on questions they answered incorrectly.
- Desire for Future Use: Many students expressed a desire to see this assignment format used in future classes. They found it to be a creative and effective way to learn, indicating its potential for long-term use.
- Appreciation for Variety in Assignments: Several students mentioned that they enjoyed the change of pace from traditional assignments like writing papers. They appreciated the opportunity to engage in a hands-on activity that made the class more enjoyable.

3.6 Summary

This section showed an example of building a virtual escape room with Google Sites, Slides, and Forms. The authors hope that the presented process will assist other educators in making a decision whether they want to use escape rooms in their courses, and if so, provide relevant considerations for how to move through this process (Fig. 2). While the rooms built for different courses and different purposes may vary greatly, the questions to ask in the design process and the core elements will remain the same. Below is a diagram that summarizes the important considerations or helpful tools that may be used on the journey of building a virtual escape room.

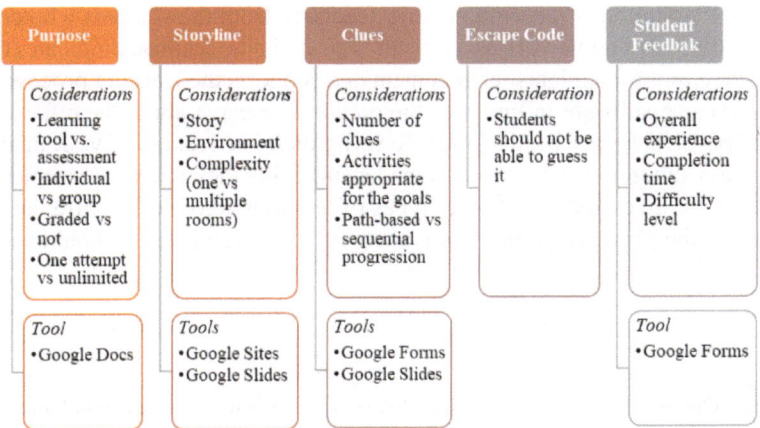

Fig. 2. Diagram describing the VER design process

4 Conclusions and Discussion

This paper documents an approach to building a virtual escape room (VER) using Google Workspace products, including Google Sites, Forms, and Slides. The Google Workspace tools are widely available and popular software that does not require additional knowledge or skills to work with it. Thus, the approach of building VER proposed in this paper is suitable for professors who do not have coding skills or access to specific software or applications.

However, the value of this project is not limited to those instructors using Google Workspace applications. Following the process and logic presented in this paper, instructors may use Microsoft products if their campuses provide access to these tools. Furthermore, the proposed approach for building VER may be used as a foundation for developing a VER in mobile applications or the metaverse. This paper proposes the logic for designing and creating a VER that can be used in different stages of teaching and learning processes, types of classes, and technology tools (See Fig. 2).

The proposed VER design incorporates gamification elements, such as storytelling, feedback, and rewards in the form of points for the answered questions to create an engaging and immersive learning experience [3]. VER assignments offer a lot of flexibility to the instructors: they may be timed or untimed, graded or ungraded, providing text or video feedback. Many variations of VER assignment design can be used based on the needs of the course and the instructors' ideas.

However, instructors who want to incorporate VER activities in their courses should be aware of some weaknesses of these learning tools. The VER assessment is more time-consuming to create compared to traditional quizzes or assignments. It also requires skills in creating Google Sites, Google Forms, and other elements mentioned earlier in this article that may be time-consuming to learn for some people. However, once the VER is created, it can be recycled in future semesters or used as a base for other VER assessments for other topics of other courses.

The VER assignment received positive feedback from the students who completed the VER activity as a homework assignment. The students' feedback indicates that VER is an effective tool for students' engagement and supports the learning process in active learning. These results are in line with the previous research about the effectiveness of VERs and physical escape rooms [3, 6]. To verify the effectiveness of VER in the educational process, other researchers may consider surveying their students completing VER assignments for assessment and other types of learning activities in different subjects. In the future, the year-over-year effectiveness of VER assignments should be assessed as well.

References

1. Statista: Online education – worldwide (2023). https://www.statista.com/outlook/dmo/eservices/online-education/worldwide
2. Zhanni, L.: Gamification for educational purposes: what are the factors contributing to varied effectiveness? Educ. Inf. Technol. **27**(1), 891–915 (2022)
3. Makri, A., Vlachopoulos, D., Martina, R.A.: Digital escape rooms as innovative pedagogical tools in education: a systematic literature review. Sustainability **13**(8), 4587 (2021)
4. O'Brien, K., Pitera, J.: Gamifying instruction and engaging students with breakout EDU. J. Educ. Technol. Syst. **48**(2), 192–212 (2019)
5. Pozo-Sánchez, S., Lampropoulos, G., López-Belmonte, J.: Comparing gamification models in higher education using face-to-face and virtual escape rooms. J. New Approaches Educ. Res. **11**(2), 307–322 (2022)
6. Adams, V., Burger, S., Crawford, K., Setter, R.: Can you escape? Creating an escape room to facilitate active learning. J. Nurses Prof. Dev. **34**(2), E1 (2018)
7. Fotaris, P., Mastoras, T.: Escape rooms for learning: a systematic review. In: European Conference on Games Based Learning, pp. 235–243, XII (2019)
8. López-Pernas, S., Gordillo, A., Barra, E., Quemada, J.: Comparing face-to-face and remote educational escape rooms for learning programming. IEEE Access **9**, 59270–59285 (2021)
9. Veldkamp, A., van de Grint, L., Knippels, M.-C.P.J., van Joolingen, W.R.: Escape education: a systematic review on escape rooms in education. Educ. Res. Rev. **31**, 100364 (2020)
10. Kolar, T.: Conceptualising tourist experiences with new attractions: the case of escape rooms. Int. J. Contemp. Hosp. Manag. **29**(5), 1322–1339 (2017)
11. Kolar, T., Čater, B.: Managing group flow experiences in escape rooms. Int. J. Contemp. Hosp. Manag. **30**(7), 2637–2661 (2018)
12. Villar, L.A., García, M.M.: Decoding escape rooms from a tourism perspective: a global scale analysis. Morav. Geogr. Rep. **29**(1), 2–14 (2021)

13. Anastasiadis, T., Lampropoulos, G., Kerstin, K.: Digital game-based learning and serious games in education. Int. J. Adv. Sci. Res. Eng. **4**(12), 139–144 (2018)
14. Pereira-Moliner, J., Molina-Azorín, J.F., Tarí, J.J., López-Gamero, M.D., Pertursa-Ortega, E.M.: How do dynamic capabilities explain hotel performance? Int. J. Hosp. Manag. **98**, 103023 (2021)
15. Cohen, T.N., et al.: Using escape rooms for conducting team research: understanding development, considerations, and challenges. Simul. Gaming **51**(4), 443–460 (2020)
16. Nicholson, S.: Peeking behind the locked door: A survey of escape room facilities (2015). http://scottnicholson.com/pubs/erfacwhite.pdf
17. Sanchez, E., lumettaz-Sieber, M.: Teaching and learning with escape games from debriefing to institutionalization of knowledge. In: Gentile, M., Allegra, M., Söbke, H. (eds.) GALA 2018. LNCS, vol. 11385, pp. 242–253. Springer, Cham (2019). https://doi.org/10.1007/978-3-030-11548-7_23
18. Connelly, L., Burbach, B.E., Kennedy, C., Walters, L.: Escape room recruitment event: description and lessons learned. J. Nurs. Educ. **57**(3), 184–187 (2018)
19. Guo, Y.R., Goh, D.H.-L.: Library escape: user-centered design of an information literacy game. Libr. Q. **86**(3), 330–355 (2016)
20. Wise, H., Lowe, J., Hill, A., Barnett, L., Barton, C.: Escape the welcome cliché: designing educational escape rooms to enhance students' learning experience. J. Inf. Literacy **12**(1), 86 (2018)
21. Järveläinen, J., Paavilainen - Mäntymäki, E.: Escape room as game-based learning process: causation - effectuation perspective. In: Proceedings of the 52nd Hawaii International Conference on System Sciences (2019)
22. Warmelink, H., et al.: AMELIO: evaluating the team-building potential of a mixed reality escape room game. In: Extended Abstracts Publication of the Annual Symposium on Computer-Human Interaction in Play, pp. 111–123 (2017)
23. Murphy, G., Slowinski, P.D., Sweeney, A.B., Morse, C.Y.: Escape the anxiety: an interactive dosage calculations escape room as a contextualized math review. Nurs. Educ. Perspect. (2023)
24. Cutler, L., Tucker, A., Schiewe, R., Fischer, J., Dirksen, N., Darnell, E.: Authoring interactive VR narratives on baba yaga and bonfire. In: ACM SIGGRAPH 2020 Talks, pp. 1–2 (2020)
25. Bucher, J.: Storytelling for Virtual Reality: Methods and Principles for Crafting Immersive Narratives. Routledge, New York (2017)
26. Greeff, M., Lalioti, V.: Interactive cultural experiences using virtual identities. In: Proceedings of International Cultural Heritage Informatics, pp. 455–465 (2001)
27. Neumann, K.L., Alvarado-Albertorio, F., Ramírez-Salgado, A.: Online approaches for implementing a digital escape room with preservice teachers. J. Technol. Teach. Educ. **28**(2), 415–424 (2021)
28. Smith, M.M., Davis, R.G.: Can you escape? The pharmacology review virtual escape room. Simul. Gaming **52**(1), 79–87 (2021)
29. Clarke, S.J., Peel, D.J., Arnab, S., Morini, L., Keegan, H., Wood, O.: EscapED: a framework for creating educational escape rooms and interactive games to for higher/further education. Int. J. Serious Games **4**(3) (2017)
30. Taraldsen, L.H., Haara, F.O., Lysne, M.S., Jensen, P.R., Jenssen, E.S.: A review on use of escape rooms in education – touching the void. Educ. Inq. **13**(2), 169–184 (2022)

Immersive Technologies in Tourism

Body and Mind in Virtual Dark Tourism Experiences and Artwork Creations: Embodied Cognition Reaction Perspectives

Halim Budi Santoso[1,2](✉) , Benjamin Quarshie[3](✉) , Dandison Ukpabi[4] ,
and Jyun-Cheng Wang[1]

[1] Institute of Service Science, National Tsing Hua University, Hsinchu, Taiwan
{halim.budi,jcwang}@iss.nthu.edu.tw

[2] Information System Department, Universitas Kristen Duta Wacana, Yogyakarta, Indonesia

[3] Mampong Technical College of Education, Mampong, Ghana
bquarshie@mtce.edu.gh

[4] School of Business, University of Jyväskylä, Jyväskylä, Finland
dandison.c.ukpabi@jyu.fi

Abstract. Dark tourism experiences visualized in destinations evoke diverse tourist experiences, triggering negative emotions and offering insights into historical events. Embodied cognition reactions prompt distinct expressions, reflections, and artwork creation, which can leverage Virtual Reality in tourism and augment dark experiences for distant tourists. This study examines embodied cognition reactions in virtual dark tourism with 32 participants, investigating their responses to narratives and auditory stimuli while impacting artwork. Results show amplified affective experiences via added auditory stimuli and cognitive experiences influenced by narratives. Post-experience, participants manifest their encounters in artworks, reflecting body-mind links.

Keywords: Artwork Creation · Dark Tourism · Embodied Cognition · Sensory Stimuli · Virtual Reality

1 Introduction

Sharpley and Stone [1] posit dark tourism as *a visit to sites, attractions, or events linked to adverse historical events where death, violence, suffering, or disaster played a significant role*. Dark tourism in tourism research has been studied for decades by bringing the tourism themes of a historical place with a sense of death, disaster, and horror.

Chornobyl in Ukraine and Ground Zero in New York offer different types of tourism experiences since these destinations present a *"dark history in human life"* to the visitors, help them to learn about those disasters, and evoke negative emotions [2, 3]. The concept of dark tourism is the most frequently used since this concept offers a basic continuum concept of "dark" and "light" in the unusual form of travel. Sharpley [4] discovered various *"shades of darkness"* of the behavior of the tourists while experiencing dark

K. Berezina et al. (Eds.): ENTER 2024, SPBE, pp. 115–127, 2024.
https://doi.org/10.1007/978-3-031-58839-6_12

tourism and visiting those sites. Further, the development of the dark tourism continuum has evolved from *"dark"* to *"pale"* and vice versa [1].

Despite the contradiction of dark tourism continuum, dark tourism seems interesting since it can connect visual stimulation with the tourism experience, covering cognitive and affective experiences [2, 3]. People see and learn to create connections between vision and experience, mainly mental experience [3, 5]. The physical sensation at the tourism site due to the activation of the human senses might influence the unconscious mind of the visitors [6]. During their visit, tourists are exposed to various sensory experiences, such as touching the museum collections, smelling authentic food aroma, or tasting local food. Sensory experiences trigger embodied cognitive reactions to how individuals perceive and respond to the surrounding environment [7–9].

The recent development of multisensory extended reality, including virtual reality (VR) in tourism, can impact destination image processing in different stages of tourism experiences [10], indicating the effect of sensory stimuli in the virtual environment. The emergence of VR in tourism can help people from far to enjoy destination in which tourists can have different reactions on certain digital stimuli from the embodied cognitive reactions perspective [2, 11], connecting body and mind in virtual dark tourism contexts.

We extend our study by understanding the effect of additional auditory experiences and narratives on embodied cognitive reactions of virtual dark tourism [11]. As a reaction, we asked participants to create a reflection and an abstract clay model after experiencing virtual dark tourism. Art creation can help to understand people cognitions, emotional states, and sensory engagements [12, 13] after exposing to certain stimuli. Hence, this study aims to answer the research question: *How do narratives and/or auditory stimuli in virtual dark tourism experiences influence individuals' cognitions and affections, considering the embodied cognitive reactions?* To provide a theoretical background for this research, we explain on virtual dark tourism. Then, we elaborate dark tourism and artwork creation that involves activation on certain reactions. Third section explains the research methodology and data collection procedures. Lastly, we provide a discussion on our findings.

2   Literature Review

2.1   Virtual Tour Experience: Influences of Sensory Stimuli and Narratives

VR can create an immersive multisensory environment by augmenting digital human senses, creating any sensations in the virtual environment [10, 14]. Sensory stimuli can facilitate individuals to create perceptions through cognitions and affections, enhancing user experiences in an immersive environment [10, 15]. When a stimulus impinges on the receptor cells of sensory organs, sensations aid in the perception of sensory stimuli [6]. The sensory experiences stimulated in the virtual environment can influence individuals' perceptions, such as human minds, mental imagery, or cognitive imagination.

Moreover, users can construct their storylines and imaginations while exploring virtual environments depicting places they have never been. A content stimulus like a narrative enables users to build original stories based on their experiences [15]. Content can transports people to another world and a transported individual can have emotional responses in which users are involved and interact [15, 16].

2.2 Embodied Cognition in Dark Tourism

Dark tourism is emotionally laden tourism that evokes tourist negative emotions [2] and simultaneously proceeds the cognitive experience [1]. Negative emotions, such as fear, sadness, or sorrow can influence psychological state of tourists, as described by embodied cognition theory [8, 9, 11]. This theory describes how people respond cognitively, affectively, and physically to an environment and some sensory stimuli. Cognitive processes necessitates comprehending their intimate relationship to the motor surfaces that may generate action and the sensory surfaces that offer sensory signals about the world. The embodiment implies the information processing, facilitating connection between cognitive processing and the sensorimotor systems happen [17, 18]. Experience in dark tourism can help tourists process information by activating sensory information processing, which is gained through sensations from predominant visual stimuli [2, 3, 11, 14]. Simply having people visualize physiological sensations and read verbal expressions associated with sensory-based metaphors can elicit embodied cognitive reactions [18], resulting in cognitive, affective, and behavioral states [7].

2.3 Art Creation as a Cognitive and Affective Effort

Art creation involves cognitive and affective, by involving cognitive intervention, critical engagement, positive challenge, physical and mental development [12, 13]. Further, art is a conduit for externalizing our inner cognitions, emotional states, and sensory engagements [12, 13]. The creative process and the resultant artistic product serve as conduits for innovation, fostering avenues for introspection and sociocultural influence [19]. Historical movements within the realm of art have consistently wielded significant agency in effecting shifts within the social fabric, with artistic endeavors frequently catalyzing transformative cognitive changes and engendering alterations in ideological inclinations. Creating artwork establishes a seamless synergy between the human apparatus (psychomotor faculties), mental, and affective through an interactive fusion of artistic elements and materials [13, 19]. However, creating artwork transcends just the chemistry between the body and mind. The process encompasses a plethora of multi-interactions with visual elements and materials. In other words, the interaction of artists with the features and materials significantly influences our aesthetic perception of the artwork, contributing to the establishment of the brain's state of consciousness [19, 20]. Visual elements and art materials becomes a vital conduit for an aesthetic analysis and appreciations of an artwork. Predominant visual stimuli can provide a connection between body and mind in the art creation through sensorial engagement.

Combining dark tourism and art creation can provide this study with an integrative body and mind through virtual dark tourism experiences. Figure 1 shows our conceptual framework, which we observe in this study. This framework posits experiencing virtual dark tourism through different stimuli triggers different sensations, and an individual can create any perception. The source, such as embodied experience, can generate more

abstract outcomes, often from the concrete sensory domain [18]. This sensory information processing might be enhanced with other sensory channels. Sensory information processing can start sensorimotor enactivism [17], a sensorimotor activity that can explain
the perceptual experience. Individuals create any possible perception to understand the
relationship in the sensory experience and perceptions.

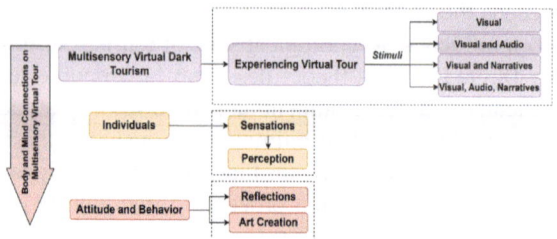

Fig. 1. Conceptual Framework

3 Research Methodology

3.1 Research Design

This study employs a qualitative vignette experiment design [21] as a direction to bridge
the quantitative experiment and qualitative research method. Qualitative Vignette experiment design denotes vignettes used in qualitative semistructured interviews to introduce
experimentally controlled variety in information and can be considered a mixed method.
This study started with creating a virtual tour as an experimental tool. We use one of the
dark tourism sites in Indonesia, "Museum Sisa Hartaku" (English: *Museum of the Rest of
My Treasure*). This museum is a museum to remember the volcanic eruption in Indonesia
in 2010 with 400 casualties and mass evacuations. Figure 2 shows the screenshot of two
scenes of Museum Sisa Hartaku.

Fig. 2. Virtual Tour of Museum Sisa Hartaku

3.2 Experimental Procedure and Data Analysis

This study involves Ghanaian college art students as voluntarily respondents by asking
their consent before their participation. Given the geographical distance between Ghana

and Indonesia, virtual tours offer a suitable means for potential tourists to explore museums. One of the research team members from Ghana helped with the data collection from May to June 2023. Initially, 41 students from the art department of two Ghanaian colleges of education expressed willingness to participate. The respondents (*named with RX with X: number sequence*) should complete two stages: (1) Experiencing the virtual tour and (2) Creating a colorful abstract artwork.. Ineligible participants failing to complete both stages are excluded. Nine participants didn't finish the two stages, resulting in a final count of 32 participants, who is randomly assigned in a non-immersive virtual dark tourism experience using desktop: (1) no sound and no narrative; (2) narrative and no sound; (3) sound and no narrative; (4) sound and narrative. Participants receive US$3 as an incentive. Each group consists of eight participants with a maximum time for a virtual tour is 15 min per person to experience virtual dark tourism.

Employing a vignette experiment design enables researchers to conduct experimental design and provide context-rich data with a mixed-method approach to understanding causal relationships [21]. In the first stage, each participant provided a written reflection on their virtual dark tourism encounters. Participants then create an abstract clay model representing their virtual tour experience, uploading three pictures of the artwork and writing an art appreciation. Table 1 shows the example of datasets. Then, the collected data underwent deductive content analysis [22], comprising reflections, artworks, and appreciations which prioritized the identification of patterns and themes [22], encompassing both negative and positive expressions of sentiment.

4 Findings

We extracted participants' responses, including virtual tour reflections, artwork pictures, and appreciation. First, one of the researchers, a lecturer from the art department, evaluated the artwork by providing some reviews according to the collected clay model pictures. Then, two researchers joined to conduct a deductive content analysis by analyzing the reflections and artwork appreciation. Figure 3 shows our content analysis approach that is applied to determine our findings. We analyzed the content of the users reflections and artwork appreciation by highlighting keywords that can illustrate their experiences.

4.1 Virtual Tour Reflections Among Individuals

- **Group 1: No audio and No narrative**

Participants in this group elicited various emotions, most telling the excitement of the virtual tour. They observed the museum collections virtually and used their artistic background to analyze the museum collections. For instance, R4 declared, "*In the Virtual Tour at Sisa Hartaku, I saw kinds of works made in different mediums.*" They just reacted naturally and expressed positive emotions, as written by R12 as follows: "*I saw a lot of artworks such as ceramics, wall hanging, painting works, am really happy to go through this tour.*" We also found a misinterpretation of the meaning of virtual tour, as declared by R5, "*Please, what I experienced was the old artworks.*" R5 understands that

Table 1. Sample of Virtual Tour Reflections, Artworks, and Appreciations

ID	Virtual Tour Reflections	Artwork	Appreciation
Group 1: No Narratives and No Sound			
R12	I saw a lot of artworks such as ceramics, wall hanging, and painting works, am really happy to go through this tour.		The artwork was produced by an artist called Dufie. The work is in three-dimensional form. It is assembled with clay I started modeling the clay to form a pot. After that, I painted it with colors. I used some elements and principles of design like shape, colors, and other designs in developing my cooking pot. The artwork serves as cooking material which we use in our various homes. It can be used to cook foods some of our parents even use it to boil traditional herbs. In virtual tourism, I saw some of the pot, which I think they were used for cooking foods
R19	It was very interesting and nice artwork and how they arranged things. And I felt emotional about how the room is very dark.		My work represents television at that time they use television to get information, or if something happens somewhere, they will get through the news or they will get what is going around all over the world.
Group 2: Narratives and No Sound			
R2	My experience of this observation was quite good, but what pains me most was the disaster because it killed living things and spoiled their habitats. I gained more knowledge about the museum, how the artifact was made, and how it was organized, This has given me an insight into artworks, and I appreciate it. Thank you for giving me this opportunity to go through your museum.		This is a work that was done on the 2nd of May, 2023, this work is a jewelry container that the victim uses in keeping jewelry, and it has been broken because of the disaster. The work was done using clay which I kneaded, and I used the three-dimensional technique, which is modeling in making the artifact. The color of the work shows newness because of the things stored in it and the natural environment. This work was done to show that disaster is a bad cause that leads to great loss of life and property. The artwork was built to show how disaster can destroy our items. Thank you
R25	Through my experience of viewing this museum collection about the disaster can also inspire empathy and compassion. Seeing the faces of survivors and the tireless efforts of rescue workers can remind us of the resilience of the human spirit and the importance of coming together in times of crisis. In this way, the museum's collection of disaster pictures can serve as a powerful tool for education, awareness, and empathy-building. By appreciating these images and the stories they tell, we become better-informed and more compassionate citizens of the world.		The story was a disaster that happened in one of the countries. The main motive behind this clay model is the properties that got burnt during the disaster. So I made this clay model to represent the houses that got burnt during that time. And I also painted with white, black, and dark reddish colors. I used white color for the wall, and I used dark reddish for the roofing, and black color was the burnt and the broking place in the house. Smoke in the house also represents how the house was burning during the disaster. So the meaning of this work is the properties that got burnt during the disaster in Indonesia.
Group 3: Sound and No Narratives			
R8	The experience I had in this video was very emotional because I was picturing the incident in my mind. Im worried about the victims of the incident, especially helpless women and children. This experience will be the first thing I will never wish for. May God protect us from such an experience. Thank you.		This art piece is a bone representing the poor victims who lost their lives during this natural disaster, especially women and children who were helpless at that moment, they had no strength to save themselves. The red pigment on the bone represents the blood of innocent people shared in the incident. imagine how sorrowful it will be. Lastly, the red band tied around the bone means danger. In conclusion, Natural disaster is nothing good to be prayed for. God is our protector.

(continued)

Table 1. (*continued*)

R16	The full awareness of passing the good quality of the artwork. In my experience, I saw many visual artworks, like textile works, in which I saw clothing being hanged on the wall. Then also I saw sculpture works and ceramic works in the museum. I noticed that our forefathers suffered a lot during this disaster. I felt worried and potty for the people who were there in that era. I saw the bones of human beings. I wish to join this museum live. Thank you.		The clay model is a clay pot, in my experience, I saw many clay pots of different kinds. Pottery works an important role in studying culture and reconstructing the past. Historically with distinct cultures, the style of pottery changed. It reflects the social, economic, and environmental conditions a culture thrived in, which helps archaeologists and historians understand our past.
Group 4: Narratives and Sound			
R24	The museum helps the victims to reflect on the incident that happened to serve as a remembrance, and also, the museum help as a collection and gathering of the materials that couldn't burn during the disaster. The museum can also help to generate money to support the victims financially. Thank you ❤️▢🖊😲 ⚒️⚒️😊🌸		The artwork is a burnt plastic plate that represents the cooking utensils that got burnt during the disaster and also tried to turn every opportunity I had to create this artwork as a reflection or remembrance of the properties that got burnt. I also came about a black color dominating my artwork that symbolizes sophistication, death, mourning, and depression about the disaster.
R30	I felt very sad seeing the leftover things in the museum left on the land of Yogyakarta. It was a nice experience, though, and it was my first time experiencing such things with background sound being so emotional 😲😲. I never want to be a victim of such an incident 😲♡.		It's a cup, and it reflects my experience on the tour because it was an object that was used to serve water, but afterward, it has now become a leftover thing after the disaster.

the artwork is a part of old collections. Some participants also have negative emotions by feeling dark and scared, as stated by R29, "*It was a little bit scary and interesting,*" and R23, "*And felt emotional about how the room is very dark.*"

- **Group 2: Narratives and No Audio**

Respondents of the second group felt the excitement of the virtual tour and wondered about the museum's creation. R31 stated, "*I was so excited to experience this tour as my first time seeing something like this.*" Narratives can evoke some negative emotions, such as sorrow. R6 reflected, "*I felt emotional watching these scenes because the place was dark. I have never seen broken arranged pots, old ragged bags, some cracked buildings with bushy areas.*" They also reflected on the event of the disaster and understood the story behind the Museum Sisa Hartaku. Based on their understanding and reflection, they can show empathy for the victims.

- **Group 3: Audio and No Narratives**

Audio can evoke more negative emotions, such as sadness, worry, and potty, as stated by most participants. R8 reflected, "*The experience I had in this video is very emotional because I was picturing the incident in my mind.*", whereas R18 said, "*I have not experienced anything like this one, but this museum exploitation with the sound made me kind of emotional, but I wanted to try without the sound.*" Participants observed that the several museum collections can make them feel emotionally involved, enhanced by the auditory stimuli. From the museum collections, participants learned about the museum, while auditory stimuli evoked negative emotions. R9 wrote in the reflection,

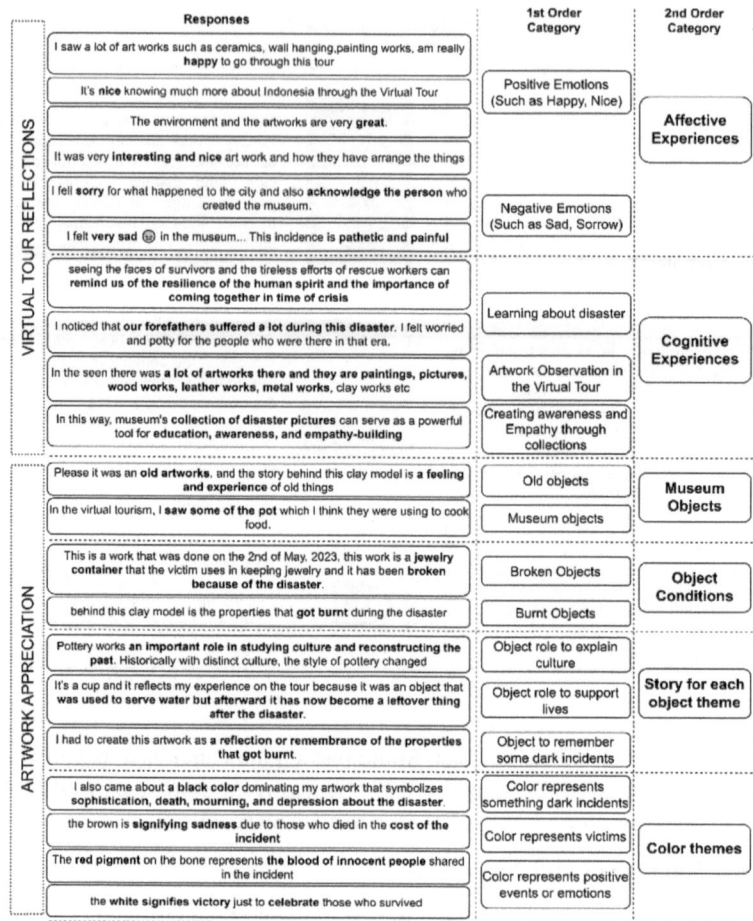

Fig. 3. Coding Scheme

"I observed many items that depicted the way the people live their lives,… they used before the disaster. I felt so emotional during the observation of the museum."

- **Group 4: Audio and Narratives**

We also found a similar mechanism within this group. Auditory stimuli evoke negative emotions, which appear during virtual dark tourism experiences. Participants reflected that they elicit sadness, pain, and pathetic in their reflections on virtual dark tourism experiences. R1 mentioned, *"I was very sad to see such a museum. I saw a designed art made with old metals and bags made with natural leather."* Other participants expressed their feelings using emoticons. Meanwhile, narratives influence their cognitions and help participants to have meaningful experiences. They can provide a deeper appreciation of the museum by understanding some museum collections.

4.2   Artwork Creation and Appreciation

- **Group 1: No audio and No narrative**

Participants harnessed artistic talents within this group to decode virtual tour visuals, yielding artworks that mirrored their experiences. Absent narrative or sound, they instinctively formed objects like televisions and household utensils. Participants found and observed these collections during the virtual tour experiences. R12 appreciated the cooking materials artwork, as described, *"The artwork serves as cooking material which we use in our various homes... In the virtual tourism, l saw some of the pot l think they were using it to cook food."* In terms of the object colors, these groups tend to use bright colors to project more positive emotions, which can be recognized as their excitement with the virtual tour, as mentioned in the virtual tour reflections.

- **Group 2: Narratives and No Audio**

The narrative significantly predominantly influenced cognitive encounters for this group of participants. In their artwork descriptions, some expressed condolences for victims. This group creates artworks that encompass the interpretation of the volcanic eruption. Participants highlight the effect of volcanic eruption by creating fragmented and burnt objects, such as shattered earthenware bowls, fragmented pots, and burnt houses. R17 reflects on the artwork by expressing, *"This work was done to show that disaster is a bad cause which leads to great loss of life and properties. The artwork was built to show how disaster can destroy our items."* The artworks created use dark hues to signify the conditions after the disaster, evoking adversity. Meanwhile, several participants used bright tones to project their sympathy and empathy.

- **Group 3: Audio and No Narratives**

Within this group, diverse thematic artworks emerged with a different range, such as museum-related objects, household objects, and museum collections, indicating various interpretations of the virtual tour. We posit that the mournful resonance of the sound likely influenced affective aspects, enabling the participants to link their creations to museum artifacts and ancient museum collections that appeared in the virtual tour. R9 expressed, *"The story behind this clay model represents the animals around the museum when the disaster took place and take their lives.".* Participants crafted artwork with a less bright color.

- **Group 4: Audio and Narratives**

The artworks of this group indicate both intact and damaged objects. Reading the narrative and listening to the audio stimuli predominantly influenced cognitive and affective virtual dark tourism experiences. Our analysis unveils that some pieces vividly depict their disaster experiences. For instance, participant R24 crafted a charred plastic plate to tribute destroyed properties, as stated, *"I had to create this artwork as a reflection or remembrance of the properties that got burnt. I also came about a black color dominating my artwork that symbolizes sophistication, death, mourning, and depression about the disaster."* Participants in this group primarily use a dark-theme color, reflecting their dark experience.

5   Discussion

This study highlights virtual dark tourism experiences from an embodied cognition reaction perspective. Without any auditory stimuli and narratives, predominant visual stimuli help participants to observe the museum collections, looking at some dark collections, such as broken housewares and animal bones. Dark collections shown in virtual dark tourism can help individuals recognize the purpose and meaning of the virtual tour experiences [2, 3]. Neglecting narratives and explanations to tourists can lead to misinterpretation of the virtual tour experiences, resulting in less meaningful experiences, as found in Group 1. Connecting their predominant cognitive experiences, participants remember some museum collections and try to recreate these collections in their artworks. However, providing individuals with a narrative can help participants reflect on virtual dark tourism more profoundly and meaningfully, resulting in dark hue artworks related to disasters. Participants tend to create artwork connecting to their mental consciousness and emotional states [19, 20]. This finding indicates the integration between cognitive and affective experiences [11], with cognition appearing and triggering affective experiences [2].

Adding auditory sensory stimuli into virtual dark tourism experiences enhances the affective experiences of participants. Predominant visual stimuli enriched by auditory can help to understand the experiences, creating any sensations that can trigger individual emotions [6, 14]. Individuals elicit slightly negative emotions to show sympathy and empathy for bad experiences without acknowledging the story behind the dark tourism. As a result of these experiences, individuals tend to create artworks to connect their sympathy to survival and encouragement in supporting the affected people.

Integrating narratives and audio stimuli into virtual dark tourism experiences can help people enhance the affective experience and recognize the meaning of the dark tourism experiences [2]. Individuals tend to have a darker and pale experience [1, 4] due to combining auditory and narratives, such as sadness and sorrow. Virtual tour dark tourism using auditory activates two human senses to facilitate sensory information processing and enhance individual emotional involvement [6, 14]. This emotional involvement becomes more engaging once the individuals activate the cognitions through narrative, bringing them to the another virtual dimensions. Following this deeper emotional engagement, participants try to reflect by creating artwork that portrays vary from before the incidents and after the disasters. Participants also use dark colors in their artwork to symbolize death and depression.

6   Conclusions

Our study uses embodied cognition perspectives to examine the connection between individual experiences and their perceptions of virtual dark tourism [8, 9] using narratives and auditory. Our investigation showed that respondents, categorized based on their respective research groups, generated reflections and artworks that intricately mirrored their encounters within dark virtual tours. Our analysis also unveiled a correlation and uniformity in applying cognitive semiotics [20], encompassing both color and form by participants to articulate their cognitive and affective experiences. Participants predominantly employed dark hues to symbolize negative sentiments while conversely utilizing vibrant shades to represent the persistence of life and optimism.

6.1 Limitations and Future Research Directions

Our study involved only 32 participants from Ghanaian undergraduate art students. We acknowledge our small sample size. However, we must be careful when we generalize the result to a more enormous population. Future studies can extend our research by exploring a larger sample size and comparing it within different countries. In addition, due to limited access to VR head-mounted devices, we only provide a non-immersive virtual tour experience with less technology embodiment. Technology embodiment influences emotions and engagement [16], and future research can understand the impact of technology embodiment on the embodied cognition of virtual tours.

6.2 Theoretical Contribution

This study provides a theoretical contribution by extending the embodied cognition reactions in virtual dark tourism by relating the virtual tour with artwork creation [8, 9, 11]. The finding reveals that participants are not only associated with the level of darkness of the colors but also reflect their clay models with different objects, choosing the suitable theme to express their experiences. In addition, we extend the current study by covering the other stimuli, such as content stimuli (narrative) and sensory stimuli (visual and auditory), in the virtual dark tourism experiences [10, 15].

6.3 Practical Contribution

The emergence of VR in tourism can benefit destination managers in expanding existing markets to different countries and lowering the cost of travel. Many destination managers already adopted the virtual tour; however, they do not capture what is precisely the tourist experience. This study's findings can help unbox online travelers' embodied virtual travel experiences and provide an understanding of the different effects of auditory and narratives in the virtual environment.

References

1. Sharpley, R., Stone, P.R.: The Darker Side of Travel: The Theory and Practice of Dark Tourism. Channel View Publications (2009)
2. Nawijn, J., Biran, A.: Negative emotions in tourism: a meaningful analysis. Curr. Issue Tour. **22**(19), 2386–2398 (2019)
3. Zhang, H., Yang, Y., Zheng, C., Zhang, J.: Too dark to revisit? The role of past experiences and intrapersonal constraints. Tour. Manage. **54**, 452–464 (2016). https://doi.org/10.1016/j.tourman.2016.01.002
4. Richard, S.: Travels to the edge of darkness: towards a typology of "dark tourism". In: Taking Tourism to the Limits: Issues, Concepts and Managerial Perspectives, pp. 215–226. Routledge (2006)

5. Dunkley, R., Morgan, N., Westwood, S.: Visiting the trenches: exploring meanings and motivations in battlefield tourism. Tour. Manage. **32**(4), 860–868 (2011). https://doi.org/10.1016/j.tourman.2010.07.011

6. Krishna, A.: An integrative review of sensory marketing: engaging the senses to affect perception, judgment and behavior. J. Consum. Psychol. **22**(3), 332–351 (2012)

7. Kock, F., Ringberg, T.: Embodied cognition effects on tourist behavior. Ann. Tour. Res. **78**, 102725 (2019). https://doi.org/10.1016/j.annals.2019.05.002

8. Barsalou, L.W.: Grounded cognition. Annu. Rev. Psychol. **59**(1), 617–645 (2008)

9. Barsalou, L.W.: Perceptual symbol systems. Behav. Brain Sci. **22**(4), 577–660 (1999). https://doi.org/10.1017/S0140525X99002149

10. Santoso, H.B., Wang, J.-C., Windasari, N.A.: Impact of multisensory extended reality on tourism experience journey. J. Hosp. Tour. Technol. **13**(3), 356–385 (2022). https://doi.org/10.1108/JHTT-01-2021-0036

11. Sun, J., Lv, X.: Feeling dark, seeing dark: mind–body in dark tourism. Ann. Tour. Res. **86**, 103087 (2021)

12. Brown, C.J., Chirino, A.F.C., Cortez, C.M., Gearhart, C., Urizar, G.G.: Conceptual art for the aging brain: piloting an art-based cognitive health intervention. Act. Adapt. Aging **45**(1), 39–69 (2021). https://doi.org/10.1080/01924788.2020.1719584

13. Saunders, R.J.: Creative and mental growth. Stud. Art Educ. **24**(2), 140–142 (1983). https://doi.org/10.2307/1319570

14. Agapito, D., Mendes, J., Valle, P.: Exploring the conceptualization of the sensory dimension of tourist experiences. J. Destin. Mark. Manag. **2**(2), 62–73 (2013)

15. Suh, A., Prophet, J.: The state of immersive technology research: a literature analysis. Comput. Hum. Behav. **86**, 77–90 (2018). https://doi.org/10.1016/j.chb.2018.04.019

16. Flavián, C., Ibáñez-Sánchez, S., Orús, C.: The impact of virtual, augmented and mixed reality technologies on the customer experience. J. Bus. Res. **100**, 547–560 (2019)

17. Regan, E.C., Price, K.R.: The frequency of occurrence and severity of side-effects of immersion virtual reality. Aviat. Space Environ. Med. (1994)

18. IJzerman, H., Semin, G.R.: The thermometer of social relations: mapping social proximity on temperature. Psychol. Sci. **20**(10), 1214–1220 (2009). https://doi.org/10.1111/j.1467-9280.2009.02434.x

19. Solso, R.L.: The Psychology of Art and the Evolution of the Conscious Brain (2003)

20. Bundgaard, P.F., Heath, J., Østergaard, S.: Aesthetic perception, attention, and non-genericity: how artists exploit the automatisms of perception to construct meaning in vision. Cogn. Semiot. **10**(2), 91–120 (2017). https://doi.org/10.1515/cogsem-2017-0011

21. Harrits, G.S., Møller, M.Ø.: Qualitative vignette experiments: a mixed methods design. J. Mixed Methods Res. **15**(4), 526–545 (2021). https://doi.org/10.1177/1558689820977607

22. Elo, S., Kyngäs, H.: The qualitative content analysis process. J. Adv. Nurs. **62**(1), 107–115 (2008). https://doi.org/10.1111/j.1365-2648.2007.04569.x

A Journey for All Senses: Multisensory VR for Pre-travel Destination Experiences

Jakob C Uhl[1]([✉]), Barbara Prodinger[2], Markus Murtinger[1], and Armin Brysch[3]

[1] AIT Austrian Institute of Technology GmbH, 1021 Vienna, Austria
{jakob.uhl,markus.murtinger}@ait.ac.at
[2] Austrian National Tourist Office, 1030 Vienna, Austria
barbara.prodinger@austria.info
[3] Kempten University of Applied Sciences, 87435 Kempten, Germany
armin.brysch@hs-kempten.de

Abstract. The rapid advancement of Virtual Reality (VR) technologies, bolstered by cutting-edge hardware, has ushered in a new era that blurs the lines between the physical and virtual realms. As opportunities for immersive information absorption in virtual worlds grow, the tourism industry faces escalating pressure to stay competitive. Although traditional VR mainly engages audio-visual senses, this study examines whether multisensory VR in the pre-travel phase enhances users' sense of presence and technology acceptance. Employing a mixed-methods, between-subjects design, we conducted an experiment with 103 participants divided into a multisensory VR group and an audio-visual VR group. Our aim was to investigate the impact on the sense of 'being there,' technology acceptance, and the relationship between increased presence and acceptance. Results from tourism professionals reveal no significant variation in physical presence between the two groups; however, the multisensory VR group showed a notable difference in self-presence. Our findings suggest that the inclusion of multisensory stimuli makes VR more approachable and user-friendly, leading to greater self-presence and technology acceptance.

Keywords: multisensory · virtual reality · technology acceptance · presence · tourism

1 Introduction

In 2023, the rapid development of VR was mirrored in the release and announcement of the latest VR hardware, such as the Meta Quest Pro and Apple Vision Pro. This ushered in an era of unprecedented possibilities by opening new avenues for integrating the physical and digital world. The tourism industry has been significantly impacted by these advances [1,2], as physical travel is becoming more exclusive, valuable and cost intensive compared to virtual experiences. In the future, successful organizations and brands need strategies for both the physical and virtual worlds [3], as well as for a mix of both - hybrid worlds. To

K. Berezina et al. (Eds.): ENTER 2024, SPBE, pp. 128–139, 2024.
https://doi.org/10.1007/978-3-031-58839-6_13

remain competitive tourist organizations are adopting their marketing strategies by delivering immersive virtual experiences to tourists [1, 2, 4, 5].

The engagement with cyber-worlds is rooted in people's desire to transcend the constraints of reality [6]. While physically exploring travel destinations offer a multisensory experience (such as the perception of heat or cold, distinctive scents or wind), reliance on images, videos or 360-degree-footage, falls short of capturing the sensory richness of a destination. This gap between the multisensory reality of a destination and the audio-visual pre-travel media constitutes an opportunity to enhance the pre-travel phase, enabling a greater sense of presence [1, 7, 8].

The salty scent of the sea, the brisk wind on a mountain peak, the warmth of the sun on your skin - multisensory stimuli like that add depth to the travel experience and often are the most memorable parts of a journey. Thus, in past research, multisensory components have been added to VR experiences, to allow a greater feeling of presence [8–10]–the 'sense of being there' [26]. The unique aspect of this work is the extended multisensory aspect, allowing the active tasting of regional products through the novel pass-through feature of the latest VR-glasses, the effect of mist, heat and wind as additional sensual components within a high-quality VR surrounding.

This work therefore aims to answer the following primary research question, with three subsidiary research questions:

RQ: Does the use of multisensory VR in the pre-travel phase enhance the sense of presence and technology acceptance compared to traditional VR?

- **RQ1:** Is there a difference in the sense of presence experienced by potential tourists in the pre-travel phase using multisensory VR compared to VR?
- **RQ2:** Is there a difference in technology acceptance among potential tourists in the pre-travel phase using multisensory VR compared to VR?
- **RQ3:** Is there a correlation between the enhanced sense of presence through multisensory stimuli and increased technology acceptance?

In response to these research questions, a novel multisensory VR experience for the pre-travel phase, incorporating olfactory, gustatory, and haptic stimuli (including heat, wind, and moisture) was tested. This was compared with a VR-only control group (without multisensory) in a user study, focusing on the user's technology acceptance and presence. The contribution is threefold: (1) The creation of a unique, multisensory VR experience for the pre-travel phase, integrating a range of sensory stimuli, (2) A comparative study investigating the potential benefits of multisensory VR over traditional VR in a tourism context and (3) Valuable insights for the future design of multisensory VR experiences in the pre-travel phase.

2   Related Works

2.1   Technology Acceptance Model (TAM)

The basis for the willingness to use new technologies can be traced back to the Technology Acceptance Model (TAM) of [11], which analyzed the acceptance of new information technologies by users in a professional context. The basic idea was the assumption that behavioral acceptance depends on the two central factors "perceived usefulness" (PU) and "perceived ease of use" (PEU). PU is understood as "the prospective user's subjective probability that using a specific application system will increase his or her job performance within an organizational context." (ibid., p. 985). PEU "refers to the degree to which the prospective user expects the target system to be free of effort." (ibid.). The core statement of the model is that the use of technology is positively influenced by simple or easy-to-use applications and by technological solutions with a high added value for the user.

The TAM has been empirically tested many times, validated [12] and further developed. First, the external factors influencing perceived usefulness were examined in more detail and five additional determinants (determinants of PU) and two moderators were integrated into the construct in TAM 2 [13]. Thus, stimuli were identified that explain social influence and cognitive instrumental processes [14]. The construct underwent further development as TAM 3 (ibid.) by integrating six factors as directly influencing PEU [15]. Venkatesh and Bala [14] indicate that the following factors are significant predictors of PEU: (1) Computer Self-Efficacy, (2) Perception of External Control, (3) Computer Anxiety, (4) Computer Playfulness, (5) Perceived Enjoyment and (6) Objective Usability.

In this paper, we examine the extent to which multisensory elements of VR technology in a travel context can enhance perceived ease of use. Disztinger et al. [16] highlight the potential of VR in tourism and emphasize its ability to provide additional sensory and visual information. Referring to the predictors 4 and 5 of the TAM3, it is conceivable that a playful interaction of the user with multisensory elements such as wind or warm/cold sensation or the perceived enjoyment can have positive effects. By including multisensory elements into VR, the immersion of the system is enhanced, which should also lead to a higher presence experienced by users [26]. We propose, that it is through the increased presence achieved by multisensory stimuli that PU and PEU rise in the context of pre-travel experiences, as the environment is easier to understand through contextual variables like wind or heat, and the experience should be more useful in terms of pre-experiencing a travel destination holistically (see Fig. 1 for our conceptual framework).

2.2   Multisensory VR and Presence in Tourism

VR can have a number of contributions on the tourism sector, including the fields of entertainment, education, management, planning, heritage conservation and accessibility at different stages of the customer journey [17,18]. By providing a 360-degree perspective, VR facilitates pre-trip exploration, a new form of information gathering as users can immerse themselves in destinations before their trip. This concept also applies within the destination [1]. Traditional methods of learning about new destinations, such as brochures, images or videos at information points, are evolving. VR experiences itself are now being offered and embraced as unique encounters [19]. In addition, tourists can share 360-degree videos with friends and family after their trip, which not only helps them relive their experience, but also inspires others in their travel planning [7,20].

Research showed that VR has a greater impact on creating a desire to visit a destination than traditional promotional materials [20]. The use of VR increases consumer confidence in the product and increases the likelihood of purchase, especially when the tourism product is complex [21]. This contradicts to findings arguing that fully immersive VR encounters are less influential than traditional travel guides [22]. People physically unable to take on climbs can now participate, by exploring a digital replication of a certain place. This illustrates the inclusive potential of VR in tourism [23]. Nevertheless, users interact differently.

Female participants manifest higher levels of spatial presence in an emotional domain. The feelings of enjoyment, satisfaction, involvement and virtual engagement with the destination is stronger [8].

A notable recent development is the evolution from audio-visual VR to multisensory VR experiences. Since the essence of tourism is intangible yet multisensory, it's recommended to engage all five human senses for a more authentic encounter. This includes sight, smell, hearing, taste and touch [1,7,24]. The inclusion of haptic and olfactory components has a positive impact on the audio-visual VR experience, especially in the domain of escapism. Meaning that multisensory components lead to a greater desire to escape the everyday surroundings in form of a mental or emotional getaway [7].

The integration of multisensory components within virtual contexts generates the feeling of presence which subsequently leads to positive emotional states and increased experiential satisfaction [2,8]. This phenomenon influences favorable consumer behavior towards tourism sector offerings and at the same time increases the willingness to adopt VR technologies [8]. Given the relevant literature, authors suggest the use of high-quality VR content [1], a controlled experimental setting for further investigations in the pre-travel and post-travel phase [7], as well as sample that extends beyond students [8] for further research.

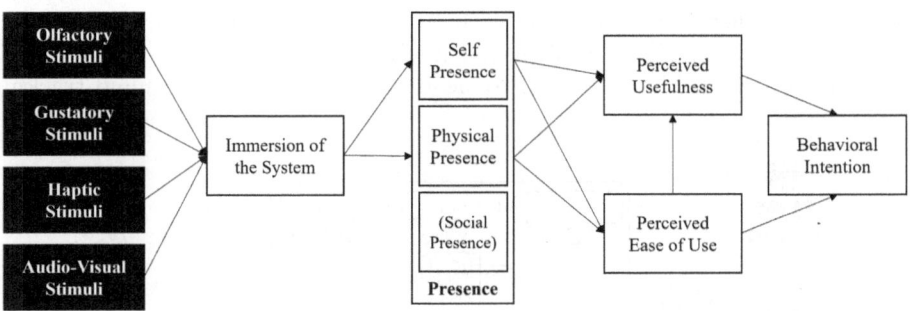

Fig. 1. Conceptual research framework. Social Presence is excluded, as there are no social encounters in the presented multisensory experience.

3   Methodology

3.1   Study Design and Procedure

To answer our research questions, we adopted a mixed-methods approach in our user-study, integrating qualitative and quantitative data. The strengths of both data types allow a more holistic understanding of the impact of multisensory VR compared to traditional VR in the context of tourism. For the study design we employed a between-subjects design with two conditions: participants experiencing (1) multisensory VR (MSVR) or (2) 'traditional', audio-visual VR (VR).

A total of 103 participants were recruited. The MSVR group consisted of 61 participants who experienced the virtual tourist destination environments during a trade fair in a separate booth. The VR group consisted of 42 volunteers of a tourism institution on their premises in a dedicated room.

In both scenarios, each participant was welcomed and briefed by the experimenter about participating in a scientific VR experiment, without revealing the study's specific goal. After signing a consent form and completing a sociodemographic questionnaire, the user was equipped with a Meta Quest Pro headset and instructed on the VR system. The participants familiarized themselves with the system in a habituation environment before starting the VR experience, which consisted of three scenes over three minutes each. After the experience, the equipment was removed, and participants completed the questionnaire. The qualitative data was gathered through open ended feedback from participants, providing rich insights into their subjective experiences. The entire procedure lasted approximately 15 min and the tests for both groups were conducted across August 2023. See Fig. 2 for an overview of the design and procedure.

3.2   Virtual Environment and Multisensory Enhancement

Three virtual environments were developed in the Unity engine, merging high-definition 360-degree photographs with 3D assets. The three virtual environments of Austrian sights are displayed in Fig. 3. The resulting virtual experience was run on a Meta Quest Pro headset and included the hand-tracking

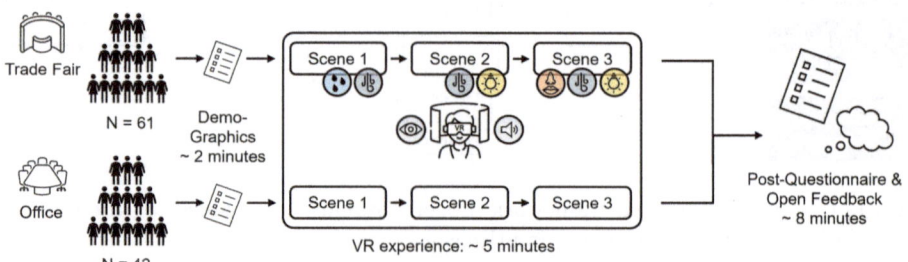

Fig. 2. Study design and procedure.

features in two variants: In scene one (mountain top) and two (pier by the lake), virtual hands controlled via hand-tracking were displayed. In scene three, the passthrough video feature of the Meta Quest Pro was used to cut out and display the participant's own hands.

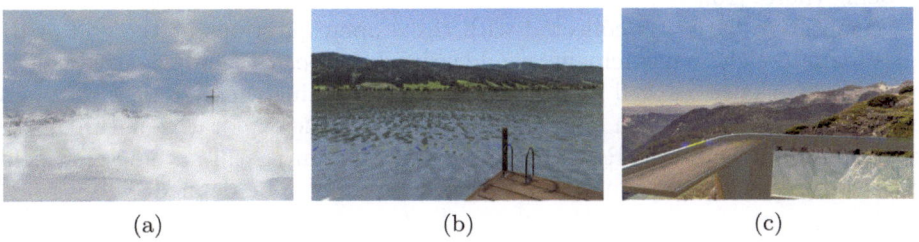

(a)   (b)   (c)

Fig. 3. The three virtual environments: (a) misty mountain top, (b) pier by the lake and (c) view platform in the mountains.

For the MSVR group, the three scenes were enhanced with multisensory stimuli. The setup consisted of four strong lamps placed above the user to induce heat, two fans for wind and one mist diffuser to cool down the wind and produce moisture. In scene (a), the snowy mountain top was enhanced with mist and wind, to create the feeling of standing on top of a misty mountain. In scene (b) and (c), the heat lamps simulated the sun on a summer day, mixed with warm wind. Scene (c) additionally included the senses of smell and taste. Herewith, on a table at the end of a viewing platform in the mountains, a 20 cm × 10 cm area was cut out of the virtual world to display the camera passthrough. In this spot, a table was placed in the physical environment, with a platter of local cheese, which participants could collect and consume, merging the physical and virtual environment.

3.3   Measurements and Procedure

To assess differences in technology acceptance between the MSVR and VR group, several items for the factors Perceived Usefulness (PU), Perceived Ease of Use (PEU) and Behavioral Intention (BI) of the TAM model were analyzed [16]. As the MSVR group experienced the scenes at a trade fair, the number of items per factor was shortened to two items each - meaning two excluded items for PU and PEU and one excluded item for BI.

For measuring the state of presence, the Multimodal Presence Scale (MPS) for virtual reality environments [25] was used, which consists of three scales: Physical Presence (i.e., the sense of being physically present in the virtual environment, 5 items), Social Presence (i.e., the sense of interacting with other entities or individuals in the virtual environment, 5 items), and Self-Presence (i.e., the sense of one's own virtual embodiment within the environment, 5 items). All items were rated on a 5-point Likert scale ranging from "Do not agree at all" to

"Agree Completely". Given that the virtual environments used in this study did not include any form of social interaction, solely the items for Physical Presence and Self-Presence were conducted. Self-Presence was of interest, as participants would interact with their hands (either virtual representations or pass-through video of their actual hands), while Physical Presence is aimed more at the 'sense of being there' [26].

Qualitative data was collected with three open questions at the end of the questionnaire, where participants would write down positive and negative aspects of their experience, as well as suggestions for improving the system. These were intentionally formulated in a broad way because of the explorative nature of this study. As multisensory VR in the context of tourism is still an emerging field, clear categories for assessing the experience are still to be defined.

4 Results

4.1 Empirical Results

A total of 103 participants were included in the analysis. 61 were part of the MSVR group (26 male, 35 female), with a mean age of 38.3 years (SD = 12.1), 42 were part of the VR group (19 male, 23 female), with a mean age of 32.7 years (SD = 9.4). In both samples 64% of participants were employees of tourism organizations and 7% were college students in the field of tourism. The remaining participants were a mix of researchers (2% MSVR, 5% VR), consultants (10% MSVR, 2% VR), and occupations with one occurrence like creators or marketing employees (13% MSVR, 21% VR). For the analysis of group differences for technology acceptance and presence, one-sided Mann-Whiteney-U-Tests (the non-parametric alternative to independent sample t-tests) were calculated for the 5 scales. One-sided testing was chosen as we hypothesize an improvement in the scales for the MSVR group. All p-values were corrected using the FalseDiscovery-Rate (FDR) [27]. For boxplots of the results, see Fig. 4.

The Mann-Whitney U test revealed no significant difference in the perceived usefulness between the MSVR and the VR group (U = 1120.5, p = 0.841). Both groups reported a median score of 4.5. A significant difference was observed between the two groups concerning their perceived ease of use (U = 1474, p = 0.039). While both groups had a median score of 5, the rank-based nature of the

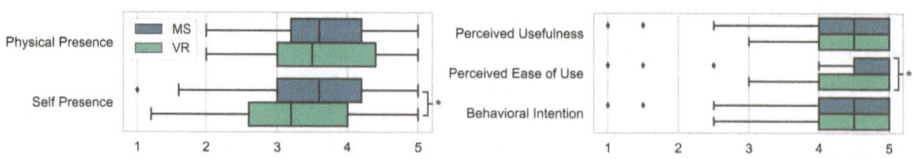

Fig. 4. Boxplots of Presence items (left) and Technology Acceptance Items (right). Items were answered on a 5-point Likert scale. Asterisks mark statistical significance of the paired t-test for $\alpha < 0.05$.

U test indicates that the distributions of scores in these groups were different, suggesting varying perceptions of ease of use between the groups. No significant difference was detected in the behavioral intention to use between the MS and VR groups (U = 1370.5, p = 0.213). The MS group reported a slightly higher median score (4.75) compared to the VR group (4.5).

While there was a noticeable difference in the median scores for physical presence between the MSVR (3.8) and VR (3.5) groups, this difference was not statistically significant (U = 1443, p = 0.106). A statistically significant difference was observed between the groups regarding their feelings of self-presence (U = 1542, p = 0.027). The MSVR group had a higher median score (3.6) compared to the VR group (3.2), suggesting that participants in the MSVR group felt a greater sense of self-presence than those in the VR group. In conclusion, among the TAM items, only the Perceived Ease of Use showed a significant difference between the two groups. For the presence items, the Self Presence stood out with a significant difference, with the MSVR group indicating a stronger feeling of Self Presence compared to the VR group. All results for the technology acceptance and presence scales are presented in Table 1.

Table 1. Means, Medians, U-values and p-values of the U-tests.

Variable	Group	N	Mean	Median	U	p
Perceived Usefulness	MS	61	4.4	4.5	1120.5	0.841
	VR	42	4.5	4.5		
Perceived Ease of Use	MS	61	4.8	5.0	1474.0	0.039*
	VR	42	4.6	5.0		
Behavioral Intention	MS	61	4.5	4.75	1370.5	0.213
	VR	42	4.4	4.5		
Physical Presence	MS	61	3.8	3.8	1443.0	0.106
	VR	42	3.6	3.5		
Self Presence	MS	61	3.6	3.6	1542.0	0.027*
	VR	42	3.3	3.2		

Looking at the correlations between presence and technology acceptance scales, medium correlations emerged between PEU and the two presence scales (r_{PP} = 0.37 (MSVR) and 0.41 (VR), r_{SP} = 0.33 (MSVR) and 0.30 (VR)) and between BI and the two presence scales (r_{PP} = 0.26 (MSVR) and 0.24 (VR), r_{SP} = 0.36 (MSVR) and 0.31 (VR)) in both groups. A notable difference between the groups could be observed for PU: Whereas the correlation with SP in the VR group is medium (r = 0.37) it was high in the MSVR group (r = 0.55). Similarily, the correlation between PU and PP was medium in the VR group (r = 0.40) and high in the MSVR group (0.53). The link between presence and perceived usefulness was thus stronger when the experience was enhanced with multisensory stimuli.

4.2 Qualitative Results

The answers to the open question for open feedback were coded using the software Atlas.ti. Using the AI-coding feature, thematic codes were found inductively and further combined. Regarding positive feedback on the experience, five main themes were identified: General positive comments regarding the (1) quality of the experience, comments highlighting the (2) multisensory aspects, comments regarding the felt (3) realim and presence, the (4) soundscape and the (5) visuals. Comments from all 103 participants of the quantitative analysis were included. On a descriptive level it can be observed, that quality of experience as well as realism & presence were mentioned similarly often in the MSVR and the VR group. A thematic shift in the comments became clear regarding which sensory elements were highlighted: Whereas the VR group often praised the graphics and the soundscape, the MSVR group explicitly highlighted the multisensory elements as a positive aspect of the experience (38%) and less the 'conventional' sensory elements such as visuals (16% vs. 42% in the VR group) or the soundscape (5% vs. 17% in the VR group).

5 Discussion

The study aimed to investigate the differential impacts of multisensory virtual reality (MSVR) and conventional virtual reality (VR) on the user's technology acceptance and state of presence in pre-travel experiences. While no statistically significant difference was found in terms of physical presence between the MSVR and VR groups, there was a notable divergence in self-presence (RQ1). Specifically, the MSVR group reported a significantly higher sense of self-presence compared to the VR group. This suggests that multisensory elements can effectively enhance the individual's sense of being within the virtual environment. Thus, the statements on the positive effects and promotion of authentic perceptions of tourist experiences through multisensory stimuli [1,7,17] can be confirmed. It lends credence to the notion that MSVR, by providing a richer, more immersive sensory experience, has the potential to increase the user's emotional and psychological engagement with the virtual destination.

Interestingly, no significant difference was found between the MSVR and VR groups in terms of perceived usefulness and behavioral intention to use the technology (RQ2), which contradicts some prior work [8]. This could be interpreted in several ways: it may be that the added sensory elements did not necessarily contribute to a perception of the technology as being more useful, or it could imply that other factors (e.g., personal affinity with the tourism industry) influenced these metrics. However, there was a significant difference in perceived ease of use, suggesting that the multisensory elements in MSVR might make the technology appear more accessible or intuitive to users, which is in line with prior work on accessibility of VR [22].

Data showed medium to high correlations between the presence scales and the perceived usefulness in the MSVR group (RQ3), indicating that an enhanced sense of presence through multisensory stimuli positively correlates with higher technology acceptance. This is an intriguing result and could suggest that there is an interactive effect between the enhanced sensory inputs in MSVR and its consequent impact on technology acceptance.

The study's limitations lead to suggestions for future research. First, the sample, including participants from mainly the tourism industry, restricts the generalizability of the findings due to a potential professional bias. Second, the lack of random sampling affects the study's external validity and risks introducing selection bias. Third, multisensory stimuli and the user's active interaction with the virtual environment were limited. This could lead to even more insights about MSVR. Future research should diversify the participant pool to include tourists, broaden the multisensory stimuli used, and employ randomization.

6   Conclusion and Implications

This study evaluated the efficacy of multisensory virtual reality (MSVR) against traditional audio-visual virtual reality (VR) in enhancing pre-travel experiences by the user's technology acceptance and state of presence. While no significant difference in the degree of PU was noted, differences emerged in PEU and self-presence, pointing to the unique benefits of MSVR. The findings offer partial support for the Technology Acceptance Model (TAM) in the MSVR context. This leads to a need for an extended TAM model that incorporates the factor of presence, especially given its stronger correlation with PU in the MSVR setting. Concerning our framework (Fig. 1), it could be noted that Physical presence is largely determined by the audio-visual fidelity (as there were no differences between the groups), whereas Self Presence could be heightened by the inclusion of multisensory stimuli, leading to an adapted model.

The study provides further managerial implications, recommending the use of multisensory virtual reality experiences to enhance pre-travel phase. Tactile and olfactory stimuli have a large role to play. Guests are given a sense of teleportation, a tantalizing preview within a sensual 360-degree perspective. The Meta Quest Pro headset with its advanced features is recommended. The high acceptance of VR technologies is evident. To effectively engage visitors, a trade fair-style approach to attracting attention and interest is recommended. Guided VR experiences by an experimenter are preferred to passive displays. A VR zone where visitors can capture photographs with VR headsets creates a form of virtual memorabilia.

This study demonstrates that both the straightforward use of VR technology and the incorporation of multisensory stimuli present new avenues for destination marketing. Multisensory VR addresses the dual nature of tourism as both a tactile and tech-driven industry.

References

1. Hopf, J., Scholl, M., Neuhofer, B. Egger, R.: Exploring the impact of multisensory VR on travel recommendation: A presence perspective. In: Information and Communication Technologies in Tourism 2020: Proceedings Of The International Conference In Surrey, United Kingdom, January 08–10, 2020, pp. 169–180 (2020)
2. Ijsselsteijn, W., Riva, G.: Being there: the experience of presence in mediated environments. Emerg. Commun. **5**, 3 (2003)
3. Prodinger, B., Neuhofer, B.: Never-Ending Tourism: Tourism Experience Scenarios for 2030. Inform. Commun. Technol. Tourism **2023**, 288–299 (2023)
4. Buhalis, D.: Technology in tourism-from information communication technologies to eTourism and smart tourism towards ambient intelligence tourism: a perspective article. Tourism Rev. **75**, 267–272 (2020)
5. Flavián, C., Ibáñez-Sánchez, S., Orús, C.: The impact of virtual, augmented and mixed reality technologies on the customer experience. J. Bus. Res. **100**, 547-560 (2019)
6. Manis, K., Choi, D.: The virtual reality hardware acceptance model (VR-HAM): extending and individuating the technology acceptance model (TAM) for virtual reality hardware. J. Bus. Res. **100**, 503–513 (2019)
7. Prodinger, B., Neuhofer, B.: Multisensory VR experiences in destination management. In: Information And Communication Technologies In Tourism 2022: Proceedings of The ENTER 2022 ETourism Conference, January 11–14, 2022, pp. 162–173 (2022)
8. Melo, M., et al.: Immersive multisensory virtual reality technologies for virtual tourism: a study of the user's sense of presence, satisfaction, emotions, and attitudes. Multimedia Syst. **28**, 1027–1037 (2022)
9. Uhl, J., Murtinger, M., Zechner, O., Tscheligi, M.: Threat assessment in Police VR training: multi-sensory cues for situation awareness. In: 2022 IEEE International Conference On Metrology For EXtended Reality, Artificial Intelligence, and Neural Engineering (2022)
10. Uhl, J., Schrom-Feiertag, H., Regal, G., Gallhuber, K., Tscheligi, M.: Tangible immersive trauma simulation: is mixed reality the next level of medical skills training?. In: ACM CHI Conference On Human Factors In Computing Systems 2023 (2023)
11. Davis, F., Bagozzi, R., Warshaw, P.: User acceptance of computer technology: a comparison of two theoretical models. Manage. Sci. **35**, 982–1003 (1989)
12. Sharp, J.: Development, extension, and application: a review of the technology acceptance model. Director **7**, 3–11 (2006)
13. Brysch, A.: Extended Reality (XR) im Tourismus - Erlebnisse durch Augmented Reality und Virtual Reality. Digital Leadership Im Tourismus: Digitalisierung Und Künstliche Intelligenz Als Wettbewerbsfaktoren Der Zukunft, pp. 461–475 (2023)
14. Venkatesh, V., Bala, H.: Technology acceptance model 3 and a research agenda on interventions. Decis. Sci. **39**, 273–315 (2008)
15. Jockisch, M.: Das Technologieakzeptanzmodell: die verhaltenswissenschaftliche Modellierung von Beziehungsstrukturen mit latenten Konstrukten am Beispiel von Benutzerakzeptanz. Das Ist Gar Kein Modell¡' Unterschiedliche Modelle Und Modellierungen In Betriebswirtschaftslehre Und Ingenieurwissenschaften, pp. 233–254 (2009)
16. Disztinger, P., Schlögl, S., Groth, A.: Technology acceptance of virtual reality for travel planning. In: Information And Communication Technologies In Tourism

2017: Proceedings Of The International Conference In Rome, Italy, January 24–26, 2017, pp. 255–268 (2017)

17. Wiltshier, P., Clarke, A.: Virtual cultural tourism: six pillars of VCT using co-creation, value exchange and exchange value. Tourism Hosp. Res. **17**, 372–383 (2017)

18. Han, D.-I.D., Weber, J., Bastiaansen, M., Mitas, O., Lub, X.: Virtual and augmented reality technologies to enhance the visitor experience in cultural tourism. In: tom Dieck, M.C., Jung, T. (eds.) Augmented Reality and Virtual Reality. PI, pp. 113–128. Springer, Cham (2019). https://doi.org/10.1007/978-3-030-06246-0_9

19. Beck, J., Rainoldi, M., Egger, R.: Virtual reality in tourism: a state-of-the-art review. Tourism Rev. **74**, 586–612 (2019)

20. Rainoldi, M., et al.: Virtual reality: an innovative tool in destinations' marketing. Gaze J. Tourism Hospital. **9**, 53–68 (2018)

21. Chan, C., Wong, K., Lui, T.: Marketing tourism products in virtual reality: moderating effect of product complexity. In: ENTER22 E-Tourism Conference, pp. 318–322 (2023)

22. Tussyadiah, I., Wang, D., Jia, C.: Virtual reality and attitudes toward tourism destinations. In: Information And Communication Technologies In Tourism 2017: Proceedings Of The International Conference In Rome, Italy, January 24–26, 2017, pp. 229–239 (2017)

23. Dick, E.: Principles and Policies to Unlock the Potential of AR/VR for Equity and Inclusion. Information Technology (2021)

24. Wiedmann, K., Labenz, F., Haase, J., Hennigs, N.: The power of experiential marketing: exploring the causal relationships among multisensory marketing, brand experience, customer perceived value and brand strength. J. Brand Manage. **25**, 101–118 (2018)

25. Makransky, G., Lilleholt, L., Aaby, A.: Development and validation of the Multimodal Presence Scale for virtual reality environments: a confirmatory factor analysis and item response theory approach. Comp. Hum. Behav. **72**, 276–285 (2017)

26. Slater, M.: Immersion and the illusion of presence in virtual reality. Br. J. Psychol. **109**, 431–433 (2018). https://onlinelibrary.wiley.com/doi/10.1111/bjop.12305

27. Benjamini, Y., Hochberg, Y.: Controlling the false discovery rate: a practical and powerful approach to multiple testing. J. R. Stat. Soc. Ser. B (Methodological). **57**, 289–300 (1995)

Hospitality in the Cyborg Age: The Power of Brain-Computer Interfaces in a Field-Experiment

Alexander Kiess[1] and Alexander Lennart Schmidt[2]([✉])

[1] RWTH Aachen University, Kackertstr. 7, 52070 Aachen, Germany
kies@time.rwth-aachen.de
[2] Research Centre, Hotelschool The Hague, Jan Evertsenstraat 171, 1057 BW Amsterdam, Netherlands
a.schmidt@hotelschool.nl

Abstract. This paper explores the emerging role of Brain-Computer Interfaces (BCI) in the hospitality industry. BCI technology allows users to control devices with their thoughts, potentially transforming guest experiences. The study investigates how guests perceive BCI-enhanced experiences compared to traditional ones. Drawing from service and human-computer interaction literature, the paper conducts a quasi-field pre-study, where participants interact with a BCI-equipped waitress. Surprisingly, participants perceived the BCI-equipped waitress as superior and warmer, resulting in an improved service experience.

The research contributes in two ways: it advances understanding of how people perceive BCI-augmented interactions in hospitality and explores the use of BCIs in addressing service failures, improving efficiency in handling customer complaints. The paper outlines plans for larger-scale field studies and online experiments across different hospitality contexts. This research offers insights into the evolving landscape of human-computer interaction in hospitality, with practical implications for the industry's future.

Keywords: Brain-Computer Interfaces · Digital Experiences · Field Study · Hospitality · Human Enhancement Technology · Service Recovery

1 Introduction

There is an ongoing debate on how hospitality businesses are impacted by emerging digital technologies [1]. In this regard, scholars put the design of technology-enhanced, digital guest experiences on the research agenda for hospitality scholars [2]. Next to studies discussing the impact of digital technologies such as service robots, virtual realities, or cryptocurrencies, brain-computer interfaces (BCI) have entered the scholarly debate [2]: Picture the ability to command your computer or smartphone solely through your thoughts. What was once considered a futuristic idea, often found in science fiction literature and films, is now on the verge of becoming reality thanks to the rapid advancements

© The Author(s) 2024
K. Berezina et al. (Eds.): ENTER 2024, SPBE, pp. 140–145, 2024.
https://doi.org/10.1007/978-3-031-58839-6_14

in consumer-grade BCI [3]. Recent advances in BCI technology have yielded remarkable results, one of which is the successful training of monkeys to play Pong wirelessly through mind control, a breakthrough achieved by Elon Musk's company Neuralink. Meanwhile, NextMind, a startup that was acquired by Snapchat's parent company Snap in 2022, has developed a BCI headset that allows users to interact with their smart home or control their TV [4]. Hence, by wearing a BCI device, humans turn into cyborgs, i.e., individuals whose physical abilities get enhanced by digital technology [5]. These consumer-grade devices hold tremendous potential to enhance the user experience by providing a more intuitive and seamless way of interacting with technology, both on a customer and service provider side. Based on forecasts, it is evident that BCI technology will play a significant role in shaping and transforming how users interact with technology, thereby redefining hospitality experiences [6]. For this study, BCI refers to an information technology that is placed on the outside of the brain that enables humans to interact with technology without any body movement, using only electrical signals generated in the brain to record activity [7]. BCIs have primarily been researched to provide communication abilities to disabled or "locked-in" patients [8]. Simultaneously, service researchers debate impacts of human-enhancement technologies, such as BCI, on customer experiences [5].

Clearly, the way guests perceive hospitality experiences, which are enhanced by BCI technology is relevant in determining BCI's future diffusion in the hospitality and tourism sector. However, despite the abundance of literature on the technical aspects of BCI, research on guests' perceptions is limited but much needed [5]. Recognizing this research gap, our study is directed towards addressing the research question: How do guests perceive BCI-enhanced experiences at the hospitality frontline compared to traditional, non-BCI-enhanced experiences?

By answering this research question, our study contributes to literature in both information systems and hospitality research, ultimately promoting interdisciplinary collaboration and knowledge exchange: (1) Our research is among the first to analyze the effects of BCI technology at the hospitality frontline. (2) We investigate the evaluative outcomes of BCI technology for service recovery through a real-life experiment.

2   Literature Review

We anchor our study in the ongoing debates surrounding the impact of digital technologies on the tourism and hospitality sector. Recent reviews underline the growing relevance of understanding the consequences of emerging technologies on guest experiences and guest-host interactions [9, 10]. Current advances in artificial intelligence have paved the way for precise and reliable Brain-Computer Interfaces (BCI) that will reimagine how Frontline-Employees (FLE) interact with customers. By just thinking about what a FLE wants to do, they can look up databases, transfer orders or make decisions using a BCI. These devices can be worn inconspicuously as headphones or glasses. Most existing research on BCI has primarily focused on extracting features from brain waves or developing medical applications to assist users with brain injuries or locked-in states to communicate or control robotic extensions [8]. Despite these efforts, there has been a lack of research on the acceptance of BCI and the impact on guest experience [2, 3, 11].

Limited studies have begun to investigate the implications of consumer-grade BCI for users in applications such as gaming, controlling Internet-of-Things (IoT) devices, and inferring user intentions from brain waves. In gaming, enabling consumers to interact with games through a BCI has been shown to enhance the experience by serving as both an active and passive controller, fostering higher engagement and introducing novel forms of interaction [3]. Improved signal detection and the ability to distinguish it from noise has shown to make it feasible to utilize BCI technology to control IoT devices, such as smart homes [4].

Moreover, research in the field of hospitality, tourism, and service marketing has begun to pay attention to human enhancement technologies (HET) and their implications for consumers and guests [5]. As part of HET, BCI are a central technology which could allow more advanced approaches to merge its users with artificial intelligence. This, in turn, could reshape the service experience, improving the well-being of guests and enhance their overall experience. However, there may also be drawbacks, such as financial inequality or ethical concerns related to the technology. Grewal et al. [5] have conceptualized the impact of HET on front-line employees, who may be perceived as robotic cyborgs, leading to potential dehumanization and negative perceptions of warmth and competence during service encounters. In this context, cyborgs are users who interact with BCI technology to augment their abilities.

3   Research Design and Methodology

This research suggests that implementing BCI technology in hospitality, specifically in dining contexts, can yield insights into service experience during service failure recovery. Our main goal is to explore BCI's practical application in real-world frontline scenarios and analyze the primary effects it produces in these interactions. We start our initial investigation with a pre-study where we showcase a genuine interaction between patrons and a frontline cyborg enhanced with BCI technology in a quasi-field setting. Following this, we'll briefly introduce study 1 (field experiment) and study 2 (online experiment), scheduled for late 2023 and early 2024.

The study design for the quasi-field pre-study utilized a 2 (waitress input type: BCI vs. Pen & Paper) x 1 between-subjects design. A total of 20 students at a major European hotel school participated in the study in exchange for a complimentary meal. Our dependent variable was the perceived service performance assessment and we additionally assessed warmth, responsibility for failure and employee superiority, among other measures. Participants received a paper briefing before the study, which outlined the study procedure and information about their waitress using either a BCI or pen & paper to aid in the service encounter and to provide a definition for the technology used. Additionally, they were asked to express their service expectations before the experiment.

Participants ordered food from a food truck, where they were intentionally served the wrong dish prepared in advance to create a service failure scenario. Next, participants were seated at assigned tables with instructions to alert the waitress if they had any problems. Because the food was served in a closed-lid container, individuals noticed the wrong dish only when they sat down. Once the employee was contacted by the individuals about their incorrect order, the guest was informed that handling the issue involves using either BCI or pen and paper. With a pre-programmed mental command (vs. written down information), the kitchen staff was alerted about the incorrect dish, allowing them to immediately start preparing the correct one upon receiving the information. After voicing their complaints, participants received the correct dish, finished their meals, and were then asked to take a survey about their dining experience.

In the BCI condition, we employed an Emotiv EPOC X headset and a programmed Python script to record all orders. We trained the waitress on a pre-programmed mental command on the Emotiv BCI software to signal when a served dish was incorrect. This information was then relayed to the kitchen via the script, allowing the food truck staff to promptly prepare the correct food. In the pen and paper condition, the waitress physically walked to the food truck to convey that an order was incorrect. After this information was transmitted to the staff, they began preparing the correct dish.

The planned experiment in Study 1 closely resembles the pre-study but with a larger sample size. In Study 2, we will conduct a pre-registered online experiment on Prolific to assess the strength of our observed effects in a different hospitality context.

4   Results of Pre-study 1

In a first step, we tested participants' perception of enhanced employee capabilities through the application of technology, serving as our manipulation check. As we had anticipated, the cyborg waitress was perceived as significantly more superior than the waitress using pen and paper ($M_{BCI} = 4.59$, SD $= 0.72$; $M_{Pen\&Paper} = 3.8$, SD $= 0.86$, $p = 0.049$). Therefore, the manipulation proved to be successful.

The presence of a cyborg waitress resulted in a perception of improved service performance compared to the use of pen and paper. Our findings indicate that customers who interacted with a BCI-equipped waitress experienced a notably improved service encounter following a failure, compared to those assisted by a waitress using pen and paper ($M_{BCI} = 5.14$, SD $= 1.68$; $M_{Pen\&Paper} = 2.5$, SD $= 0.84$, $p = 0.005$). Moreover, participants perceived the BCI waitress as weakly significantly warmer compared to control ($M_{BCI} = 4.56$, SD $= 1.1$; $M_{Pen\&Paper} = 3.6$, SD $= 1.17$, $p = 0.096$). The attribution of the cyborg waitress's performance outcome to the restaurant was lower compared to the control group. Patrons attributed less responsibility for the service failure to the restaurant in the BCI condition ($M_{BCI} = 3.79$, SD $= 1.1$; $M_{Pen\&Paper} = 2.75$, SD $= 1.17$, $p = 0.069$).

5   Discussion, Expected Contributions and Outlook

The study shows that participants perceived the service recovery experience to be better with a cyborg waitress compared to the control group. Customers also blamed the restaurant less for service issues in this scenario. Surprisingly, the enhanced waitress was seen as warmer than the control group. We plan to investigate these findings and interaction effects further in Studies 1 and 2 with a larger sample size to understand the interactions within the data and investigate possible confounding effects.

We expect this study to offer two major contributions. First, this study will advance the limited research on frontline cyborgs in service marketing and hospitality literature.

By addressing a gap in the literature, which primarily investigated observing users, this research takes a pioneering step towards understanding how individuals perceive interacting with individuals who are augmented with a BCI. We thus contribute to the research in hospitality and provide an additional perspective exploring the utilization of BCI by FLE in a restaurant setting. Our second contribution involves the application of BCI in addressing service failures. We propose that the enhanced efficiency offered by BCIs in promptly handling customer complaints can lead to more favorable customer outcomes. Based on the evidence from our pre-study, we were able to confirm this benefit and as a result we will present a further investigation into this potential to enhance the service recovery process. After a successful pre-study, we are now preparing a large-scale field study and subsequent pre-registered online studies to expand our investigation into various aspects of the hospitality industry. This dual approach will provide a comprehensive understanding of our research area and offer valuable field insights.

References

1. Tajeddini, K., Ratten, V., Merkle, T.: Tourism, Hospitality and Digital Transformation: Strategic Management Aspects, 1st. Routledge/Taylor & Francis Group, London; New York (2020)
2. Busulwa, R.: Digital transformation and hospitality management competencies: toward an integrative framework. Int. J. Hosp. Manag. **16** (2022)
3. Vasiljevic, G.A.M., de Miranda, L.C.: Brain-computer interface games based on consumer-grade EEG devices: a systematic literature review. Int. J. Hum.-Comput. Interact. **36**, 105–142 (2020). https://doi.org/10.1080/10447318.2019.1612213
4. Brown, D.: Your tech devices want to read your brain. What could go wrong? Washington Post 1 (2021)
5. Grewal, D., Kroschke, M., Mende, M., Roggeveen, A.L., Scott, M.L.: Frontline cyborgs at your service: how human enhancement technologies affect customer experiences in retail, sales, and service settings. J. Interact. Mark. **51**, 9–25 (2020)
6. Grand View Research: Brain Computer Interface Market Report, 2022–2030 (2023). https://www.grandviewresearch.com/industry-analysis/brain-computer-interfaces-market. Accessed 4 May 2023
7. Nicolas-Alonso, L.F., Gomez-Gil, J.: Brain computer interfaces, a review. Sensors **12**, 1211–1279 (2012). https://doi.org/10.3390/s120201211
8. Kawala-Sterniuk, A., et al.: Summary of over fifty years with brain-computer interfaces—a review. Brain Sci. **11**, 43 (2021). https://doi.org/10.3390/brainsci11010043
9. Gutierriz, I., Ferreira, J.J., Fernandes, P.O.: Digital transformation and the new combinations in tourism: a systematic literature review. Tour. Hosp. Res., 14673584231198414 (2023). https://doi.org/10.1177/14673584231198414
10. Kim, H., So, K.K.F.: Two decades of customer experience research in hospitality and tourism: a bibliometric analysis and thematic content analysis. Int. J. Hosp. Manag. **100**, 103082 (2022). https://doi.org/10.1016/j.ijhm.2021.103082
11. De Keyser, A., Bart, Y., Gu, X., Liu, S.Q., Robinson, S.G., Kannan, P.K.: Opportunities and challenges of using biometrics for business: developing a research agenda. J. Bus. Res. **136**, 52–62 (2021). https://doi.org/10.1016/j.jbusres.2021.07.028

Enhancing the Museum Experience on the Metaverse: The Blend of Technological Embodiment and Social Presence

Carlos Flavián[✉], Sergio Ibáñez-Sánchez, and Carlos Orús

Faculty of Economy and Business, University of Zaragoza, Gran Vía 2, 50005 Zaragoza, Spain
{cflavian,sergiois,corus}@unizar.es

Abstract. The metaverse is currently highlighted as one of the technologies with the greatest potential, particularly in the tourism industry. Despite this fact, most of the research on this topic has been of a conceptual nature. This research aims to contribute to this nascent research field by analyzing how the use of the metaverse for viewing a museum can influence the different dimensions of the customer experience. For this purpose, the degree of technological embodiment of the device, as well as the presence (or not) of other users in the digital environment, will be taken into account. Two focus groups were conducted to explore this matter. The results bring to light the importance of the affective and cognitive states that customers feel when they are in the museum through the metaverse. In addition, participants indicate that they prefer to experience the metaverse museum with other people, noting that this closeness to other users may be greater when embodied technologies are applied. This research contributes empirically to this field of research by trying to delineate how the museum experience should be constructed to offer value through the metaverse.

Keywords: Metaverse · Museum · Social Presence

1 Introduction

Recent years have seen a surge in the emergence of the metaverse, which is considered one of the technologies with greater prospects for the future [1]. The metaverse aims to be a more advanced form of virtual experience, facilitated by an amalgam of several cutting-edge innovations such as virtual reality (VR), augmented reality, artificial intelligence, or blockchain, among others [2, 3]. Its potential is highlighted in some reports noting that this platform can generate up to $5 trillion in value by 2030 [4].

Despite the potential of the metaverse, current literature is mainly of theoretical basis (e.g., [5, 6]), asking for empirical contributions on the use of the metaverse for tourism purposes. Considering the nascent nature of this research realm, this article conducts a qualitative study to explore how the use of a metaverse museum can influence the different dimensions of the customer experience [7, 8]. Based on its results, a subsequent study is proposed which aims to quantitatively analyze how social presence and the type of device used can affect the overall metaverse museum experience. This research aims to

K. Berezina et al. (Eds.): ENTER 2024, SPBE, pp. 146–150, 2024.
https://doi.org/10.1007/978-3-031-58839-6_15

contribute empirically to this field of research by trying to delineate how the museum experience should be constructed to offer value through the metaverse.

2   Theoretical Background

2.1   Theoretical Foundations: Social Presence Theory and the Theory of Technological Mediation

The social presence theory [9] and the theory of technological mediation [10] are the main theories on which this article is based. The social presence theory [9] explains how digital technologies influence the feeling of being with another in human-technology interactions. Social presence is defined as the "degree of salience of the other person in the interaction and the consequent salience of the interpersonal relationships" [9; p. 65]. Social presence is an inherent feature of any medium and the varying capabilities of the medium to transmit it are key to how individuals relate to others in online communications [12]. Thus, the ability of the technology to convey information related to facial expressions, eye gaze, body posture, attire, and nonverbal cues collectively contribute to the extent of social presence within a communication medium [12].

The theory of technological mediation [10] seeks to elucidate the processes through which humans interact with technology. This theory investigates how technology acts as an intermediary between individuals and the world around them. Among the different types of human-technology interactions, technological embodiment is considered as a situation in which the technology mediates the user experience and the device becomes an extension of the human senses [11]. According to the proposal of [11], technological devices can be divided into external and internal devices. External devices are not attached to the human body (e.g., from stationary devices like desktop PCs to portable external devices such as smartphones) and internal devices reach a higher level of fit into the human body (from wearables such as VR headsets to implanted devices) [11]. A great sense of technological embodiment of the device promotes the immersion, the sensory stimulation and the realism of the interaction in a digital experience [11].

The customer experience is composed of several dimensions: affective, cognitive, sensory, conative, social, and personal [7, 8]. The metaverse can generate superior experiences by driving all these components of experience. Particularly, based on the social presence theory [9, 12], we propose that as individuals feel connected and accompanied by others within the virtual museum environment, their overall perceptions about the experience will be improved. By being able to feel closer to others, this higher level of social presence can enrich their experience by allowing them to explore, discuss and interact in a natural way. This effect is proposed to be reinforced when embodied devices (e.g., VR headsets) are applied to the interaction in the metaverse, compared to low embodies ones (e.g., desktop PCs). Drawing from the theory of technological mediation [10], the heightened immersion and the provision of realistic and organic interactions through high embodied devices are expected to closely mimic real-world interactions [11]. This emulation will reinforce the effect of social presence on the dimensions of the customer experience in the metaverse. Thus, two proposals are presented:

P1: High levels of social presence will positively affect the perceptions about the different dimensions of the customer experience in the museum through the metaverse.

P2: High levels of technological embodiment of the employed device will strengthen the effect of social presence on the different dimensions of the customer experience in the museum through the metaverse.

3 Methodology

Considering the nascent nature of the research in this area, two focus groups (with 5 participants per session) were conducted to explore the users' experience in a museum held in the metaverse. The participants were recruited from a Spanish university (6 men and 4 women; aged between 21 and 28 years old). The participants reported having different levels of knowledge on the use of new technologies and low levels of use of the metaverse. The sessions lasted between 60 and 90 min and were audio-video recorded. Three experts in marketing and new technologies conducted the analysis.

The script of the focus groups follows two stages to explore the consumer experience in the metaverse, particularly in a museum. First, participants were asked to indicate the general characteristics they believe the metaverse has. In the second stage, participants were required to connect to the museum experience in the metaverse using a low embodiment device (computer [11]) and together with the other participants (high social presence). The metaverse platform that was employed was Spatial.io. This platform, with a structure similar to a museum, displayed different artworks shown in paintings. Once all the participants were on the platform, they had some time (10–15 min) to view all the artwork and interact/discuss with the other participants. After their experience, they were instructed to return to the video call, where they reflected and discussed various questions about the dimensions of the experience.

4 Results and Discussion

The results of the first stage of the focus groups show that participants consider the metaverse to be a virtual/digital/online space. Participants also acknowledge the multitude of opportunities offered by the metaverse considering it as creative/imaginative/fictitious. Finally, participants emphasize the social dimension of the metaverse (e.g., social/interactive), where people can connect, interact, and collaborate within a digital realm. Once they had the experience in the museum on the metaverse, the participants reported their perceptions of the dimensions of the customer experience. A summary of the results is displayed in Table 1.

Overall, participants note the potential of the metaverse for displaying museums, particularly regarding the affective and cognitive responses. As a result, they consider it as a platform that encourages the actual visitation of these tourism products and they may consider repeating this metaverse experience in the future. This aligns with the pattern observed in other technologies, such as VR [13]. The findings also highlight that users prefer having the metaverse experience with others, reinforcing the social nature of this platform. However, despite participants having the experience together, they feel that they were not close to the others. One reason pointed out is the lack of embodiment of the device they used (computer), believing that the use of highly embodied devices (e.g., VR headset) would increase their perception of being together with others.

Table 1. Summary of the results of the qualitative study.

Dimension	Explanation
Affective	Curiosity (e.g., P10) was the predominant emotion, mainly due to the novelty of the platform, along with laughter or joy (e.g., P3) (possibility of dancing, etc.). Negative emotions also were noted, as frustration and disorientation (e.g., P1) (lack of instructions or technical problems of the platform)
Cognitive	As it is immersive and realistic, participants consider it to be useful to transmit knowledge in an effective way (e.g., historical representations). Technical improvements are needed. *"For knowledge sharing, it is useful if you get people to mimic the environment visually and aurally, it can be close to reality"* P4
Personal	Some participants selected an avatar similar to themselves (feeling represented by their avatars), but many others chose their avatars without reflecting on it. *"The avatar I chose the first time, it is true that I looked for it to represent me, the only brunette girl there was, because it is important to feel represented"* P7
Social	Participants indicated that they prefer to use the metaverse with more users because it brings more immersiveness and fun. However, in general, they did not feel close to the rest of the users. A possible cause identified is the low embodiment of desktop computers. *"I would like to be able to interact with people, I think it's cool to share it, but there is a lack of tools to be able to feel the closeness of the users"* P8
Sensory	Some participants noted the vivid colors of the experience. Most, however, did not feel very sensorially stimulated and believe that the metaverse in the future will only be able to stimulate sight and sound, at least when using low embodied devices such as computers. *"Reaching the senses is very difficult through a PC screen, there is a long way to go"* P10
Conative	Participants reported that it is an interesting tool for having pre-experiences of museums and other tourism products. None would use it as an alternative to travel. *"I would find it useful, for example, as an experience prior to going, as an advertising tool, it would achieve that 'WOW' effect. I see it as a complementary element to travel"* P6

Based on these results and the importance given to the social experience in the metaverse, a subsequent experimental study will be conducted. In this experiment, participants will be required to experience the same museum on the metaverse, and it will be manipulated the level of social presence (having the experience alone vs. with another person) and the level of technological embodiment of the device employed to access the metaverse (desktop computers vs. VR headset). By conducting this study, it is expected to confirm the importance of the social dimension within the metaverse, particularly in museum experiences. This significance is expected to be amplified when embodied technologies are utilized to enhance the sense of proximity and connection among users.

References

1. Hennig-Thurau, T., Aliman, D.N., Herting, A.M., Cziehso, G.P., Linder, M., Kübler, R.V.: Social interactions in the metaverse: framework, initial evidence, and research roadmap. J. Acad. Mark. Sci. **51**(4), 889–913 (2023)
2. Ball, M.: The Metaverse: And How it Will Revolutionize Everything. Liveright Publishing (2022)
3. Richter, S., Richter, A.: What is a novel about the Metaverse? Int. J. Inf. Manage. **73**, 102684 (2023)
4. McKinsey & Company. Value creation in the metaverse goo.su/adiyUe. Accessed 08 Sept 2023
5. Buhalis, D., Leung, D., Lin, M.: Metaverse as a disruptive technology revolutionising tourism management and marketing. Tour. Manage. **97**, 104724 (2023)
6. Gursoy, D., Malodia, S., Dhir, A.: The metaverse in the hospitality and tourism industry: an overview of current trends and future research directions. J. Hosp. Market. Manag. **31**(5), 527–534 (2022)
7. Brakus, J.J., Schmitt, B.H., Zarantonello, L.: Brand experience: what is it? How is it measured? Does it affect loyalty? J. Mark. **73**(3), 52–68 (2009)
8. Ibáñez-Sánchez, S., Orus, C., Flavian, C.: Augmented reality filters on social media. Analyzing the drivers of playability based on uses and gratifications theory. Psychol. Market. **39**(3), 559–578 (2022)
9. Short, J., Williams, E., Christie, B.: The Social Psychology of Telecommunications. Wiley (1976)
10. Ihde, D.: Technology and the Lifeworld: From Garden to Earth. Indiana University Press, Indiana (1990)
11. Flavián, C., Ibáñez-Sánchez, S., Orús, C.: The impact of virtual, augmented and mixed reality technologies on the customer experience. J. Bus. Res. **100**, 547–560 (2019)
12. Gunawardena, C.: Social presence theory and implications for interaction and collaborative learning in computer conferences. Int. J. Educ. Telecommun. **1**(2), 147–166 (1995)
13. Kim, M.J., Lee, C.K., Jung, T.: Exploring consumer behavior in virtual reality tourism using an extended stimulus-organism-response model. J. Travel Res. **59**(1), 69–89 (2020)

Technology for Enhanced Experiences

Beyond Sensors: A Rule-Based Approach for Cost-Effective Visitor Guidance

Stefan Neubig[1,2]([⊠]) [iD], Markéta Bečevová[1] [iD], Fabian Brosda[1], Ronja Loges[1], Andreas Hein[2] [iD], Robert Keller[3] [iD], and Helmut Krcmar[2] [iD]

[1] Outdooractive AG, Missener Straße 18, 87509 Immenstadt, Germany
{stefan.neubig,marketa.becevova,fabian.brosda,
ronja.loges}@outdooractive.com
[2] Technical University of Munich, Boltzmannstraße 3, 85748 Garching b. München, Germany
{andreas.hein,helmut.krcmar}@tum.de
[3] Kempten University of Applied Sciences, Bahnhofstraße 61, 87435 Kempten, Germany
robert.keller@hs-kempten.de

Abstract. Tourism is an important economic driver for numerous regions, attracting more than one billion visitors annually. While economically significant, excessive numbers of visitors lead to local overcrowding, which negatively impacts visitors' experience and safety, and causes environmental harm. This paper proposes a practical approach to empowering destination management organizations (DMOs) to manage tourist flows. We advocate for a rule-based approach that models visitor occupancy based on easily understandable influence factors like weather and date. As a central component, an ontology-guided knowledge graph ensures compatibility with diverse touristic data models and allows seamless integration into existing infrastructures. By digitizing DMOs' experiential knowledge, we facilitate the implementation of lean and cost-effective visitor guidance. We demonstrate our approach by implementing two applications for two different use cases. The results of our qualitative evaluation reveal the compelling potential for rule-based occupancy modeling approaches serving as a baseline for future visitor management systems.

Keywords: Overcrowding · Rule-Based Occupancy · Knowledge Graphs · Ontologies · Visitor Guidance · Recommender Systems

1 Introduction

Tourism has long been a vital economic driver for numerous regions in the world, attracting visitors to explore inspiring landscapes and cultural offerings. Despite many benefits, the rapid growth of global tourism comes at the price of overcrowding, which is well-known in popular places such as Venice, Barcelona, and Dubrovnik [1] but also increasingly affects smaller rural areas [2]. Overcrowding not only leads to decreased visitor satisfaction [3] but also poses a higher risk to visitor safety and adversely impacts the surrounding landscape, nature protection efforts, and biodiversity [4, 5]. This raises the need for effective visitor management.

K. Berezina et al. (Eds.): ENTER 2024, SPBE, pp. 153–164, 2024.
https://doi.org/10.1007/978-3-031-58839-6_16

Data-driven methods hold potential for this task [6]. However, while advanced technologies enable the accurate tracking and forecasting of the expected visitor traffic [7], many destination management organizations (DMOs) still struggle with hurdles in implementing such measures, often caused by a lack of technical expertise and financial resources [8, 9], making widespread adoption of expensive technologies infeasible. Even without expensive technology, however, DMOs possess invaluable experience in their regions' high-traffic conditions and peak periods. Therefore, one viable option would be to digitize this knowledge as a digital asset and use it for visitor management.

This paper proposes a lean reference concept to empower DMOs to digitize their experiential insights on visitor traffic, making them available for various touchpoints. We advocate for a rule-based approach based on easy-to-grasp factors like weather, temperature, season, date, and holidays, which is cost-effective and accessible to DMOs with limited technical expertise and financial resources. Employing a knowledge graph as our central element fosters compatibility with a wide range of touristic data models and seamlessly integrates into existing infrastructure. We demonstrate how manually captured occupancy rules can be used on exemplary touchpoints to guide visitors with tailored recommendations.

2 Background

For DMOs, overcrowding of specific areas [4] is a well-known issue. Overcrowding can be described from two standpoints: the subjective visitor perception of the crowdedness of an area [10, 11] and the objective capacity of an area to offer hospitality services (i.e., parking lots, hotels, availability of adjacent free-time activities) [4, 12]. Besides nature protection agencies and emergency services that manage access to certain places due to specific situations, such as wildlife protection or natural events (e.g., avalanches and floods), DMOs manage visitor traffic, focusing on the visitors' experiences [13]. Considering multiple stakeholders, DMOs adopt a more holistic perspective and act on various aspects, including visitors' impact on the environment [14], visitor safety, and visitor satisfaction, all by guiding visitors to mitigate overcrowding [15, 16].

DMOs' visitor guidance varies from stricter closures [17] to nudging (i.e., a behavioral economics concept where subtle suggestions influence human decision-making) [18] by delivering recommendations to alternatives in order to distribute visitor traffic evenly [13]. Nudging is especially effective due to preserving visitors' feeling of agency and satisfaction while empowering the tourist to choose a more sustainable option [19, 20] and the higher willingness of today's tourists to actively search for better experiences using digital tourist solutions [21]. A delivery system for recommendation nudges can be a brochure, information board or a QR code, the latter having the advantage of delivering dynamic information, making it the optimal low-cost scalable solution [22].

Real-time and future occupancy estimates are key requirements for fast responses indispensable for managing overcrowding and ensuring the overall resilience of the destination [7, 23]. Highly dynamic data such as tourist arrivals, bookings, parking availability, weather, holidays, and web traffic have proven successful in measuring and predicting occupancy in real-time, even for areas only partly covered by sensors [7]. Nonetheless, many DMOs still struggle with implementing such measures due to a lack of technical and financial resources [8, 9] and data privacy concerns [21, 24, 25].

Our approach addresses several gaps left in the current literature. Past studies focus on the effectiveness and acceptance of visitor guidance practices and leveraging digital technologies for spatiotemporal occupancy prediction but fall short of exploring cost-effective, scalable methods. Installing sensors can be expensive [26], and the data architecture [27] and maintaining prediction models requires further financing. In the following sections, we introduce a cost-efficient approach based on digitizing DMO experiences concerning spatiotemporal occupancy that can be used out-of-the-box even by DMOs with a limited level of digitization. DMOs with a higher level of digitization can integrate our approach with existing sensors or other occupancy prediction systems, striking the perfect balance between accessible, accurate, and scalable.

3   Method

Our overall research process follows a design science paradigm [28] since it is an effective approach for generating and evaluating practical solutions. We implement the six-step framework of [29], comprising (i) motivation, (ii) solution objectives, (iii) conceptualization, (iv) demonstration, (v) evaluation, and (vi) communication (covered by this publication). Guided by the motivational scenario and solution objectives outlined above, we conceptualized our framework and developed prototypes in multiple iterations, incorporating continuous expert feedback.

Within the scope of four expert workshops with different German DMOs, ranging from alpine to seaside tourism, we determined key factors to be incorporated into a rule-based occupancy model. Considering the widespread adoption of knowledge graphs and ontologies in tourism (e.g., for cross-DMO data sharing) [30–32], we designed our approach to extend existing knowledge graphs by occupancy values (i.e., measurements, predictions, and rule-based occupancies). Based on the determined factors for occupancy rules, we developed the tourism occupancy ontology (TOO) following best practices, including the NeOn ontology engineering framework [33]. To demonstrate and evaluate our work, we identified two relevant use cases within the domain of German outdoor tourism. We developed two simple, easy-to-use prototypes: (i) a web-based user interface for DMOs to incorporate occupancy rules and (ii) a progressive web app (PWA) for on-site visitors that can be opened by scanning stationary-mounted QR codes. The choice of a QR-code-based application as an exemplary touchpoint resulted from the selected use cases. Our approach was evaluated as a workshop with each use-case-specific DMO, discussing our end-to-end solution in the context of the DMO's specific requirements.

4   From Rule-Based Occupancy to Visitor Guidance

Our proposed approach consists of different components. DMO representatives capture rules based on certain influence factors and describe different occupancy levels as a function of these factors (e.g., when it is sunny, beach A is crowded). The resulting rule sets are persisted in a knowledge graph alongside touristic entities (e.g., POIs and tours) and optionally other occupancy descriptions stemming from alternative sources (e.g., sensors, predictions). A rule inference component evaluates the captured occupancy rule sets based on a given context (e.g., sunny), turning them into realized occupancies relating to specific entities. The contextual data is gathered from local or third-party sources (e.g., weather API). Based on this information, recommendations (e.g., beach A is likely to be crowded, go to beach B) are generated and displayed to visitors using one or multiple touchpoints.

4.1 Overall Process

The end-to-end process, from capturing occupancy rules to deploying visitor guidance, is summarized in Fig. 1. Its components are outlined below.

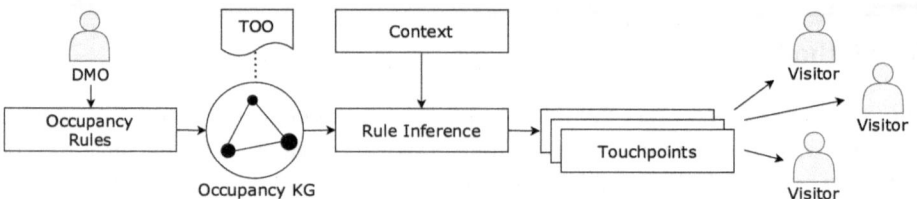

Fig. 1. Communicating occupancy rules to visitors (overall process). Solid arrows indicate the flow of data and information, the dashed line indicates the knowledge graph's data semantics.

Occupancy Rules. To turn their experiences into formal rules, DMO representatives leverage a set of pre-defined influence factors. During our expert workshops in the first step of our research, the most influential factors described comprised (i) weather conditions (e.g., cloudy, sunny, rainy), (ii) temperature ranges, (iii) temporal conditions including months and seasons, as well as (iv) public and school holidays. Notably, we found that offering additional influence factors would be counterproductive, as it contradicts the simplicity of the rule-based approach and complicates collaboration.

Occupancy Knowledge Graph. Knowledge graphs (KGs) [34] have evolved as a de facto standard for data management in tourism [31] and are used in a wide range of projects, including for open data sharing (e.g., [35, 36]). They offer a flexible data structure comprising nodes (i.e., instances) and edges (i.e., relationships) linking them. KGs are often guided by ontologies [37], formal conceptualizations of real-world entities that capture the semantics of entities in the graph and serve as the graphs' underlying schema [31]. The occupancy KG extends existing touristic KGs by incorporating occupancy as an additional concept, which can be linked to geographic objects, such as POIs, areas, or hiking tours. Its additional semantics are contained in the touristic occupancy ontology (TOO). The occupancy KG serves as an application-agnostic data source. Instead of being bound to one specific application, it can serve multiple applications that may realize different visitor touchpoints.

Rule Inference. The rule inference component evaluates formal rules given a specific context (e.g., current weather and time of the year). To determine the validity of configured rules, it acts on top of the attached TOO following the semantics described. As a result, it passes entities with their determined occupancies to different touchpoints that process these results and display them to visitors.

Touchpoints. Visitor touchpoints refer to any point of contact with current or potential visitors (e.g., destination websites, digital kiosks, flyers, tourist information points). In previous work [38], we identified high-impact touchpoints in collaboration with DMOs suitable for visitor guidance concerning the different stages of a visitor's travel. Within the scope of Fig. 1, touchpoints are standalone applications that realize services to visitors, including the recommendation of less-crowded touristic offerings. These applications act on top of the occupancy KG and the contextual occupancies inferred by the rule inference component and may further process this data.

4.2 Tourism Occupancy Ontology

The occupancy knowledge graph is a crucial component and contains formal rules to determine the crowdedness of geographic objects (e.g., POIs, hiking tours, and areas). While existing touristic ontologies offer a wide range of relatively static data types (e.g., POIs, events, hiking tours), they fall short of modeling dynamic context, such as spatiotemporal occupancy [31]. Therefore, we developed the tourism occupancy ontology (TOO) by following best practices of ontology engineering [33]. The TOO provides an abstraction of geographic entities, which makes it compatible with a wide range of existing related ontologies, including schema.org and its extensions [39], as well as the FIWARE Smart Data Models [40].

Figure 2 depicts an abstract overview of the TOO, including its mapping to schema.org. In its current version, the TOO comprises three components (i.e., geometry, occupancy, and occupancy rules) and supports modeling the occupancies of arbitrary geographic objects represented by the *GeoObject* class. Specifications of this class are basic geometric building blocks and include points (*GeoPoint*), lines (*GeoLineString*), and polygons (*GeoPolygon*), each of which can have arbitrary relationships to each other (e.g., polygon intersections and point containments). Geometric objects are identified by appropriate attributes (e.g., coordinates). Moreover, these objects serve as links to more concrete touristic entities, such as hiking tours or POIs, which can be imported using other well-established ontologies, as exemplarily shown for schema.org using the *owl : equivalentClass* axiom. An occupancy is characterized by different values, including a score between 0 and 1 and additional metadata (e.g., creation date). While the TOO aims at supporting different types of occupancies, namely measured occupancy (e.g., occupancy from sensors), predicted occupancy (e.g., occupancy derived from machine learning algorithms), and rule-based occupancy, the rest of this paper will only regard rule-based occupancies. Each occupancy type has conditions for when a given occupancy is considered valid. In rule-based occupancy, this validity is determined by whether its respective occupancy rule set matches a given context.

Occupancy rule sets are specifications of when instances of *RuleBasedOccupancy* apply. They are collections of logically conjunct conditions, that is, a specific occupancy is triggered if and only if all conditions hold. Following our expert workshops for rule-based occupancy modeling, we identified five specific condition categories: weather conditions, temperature, date and time, public holidays, and school holidays.

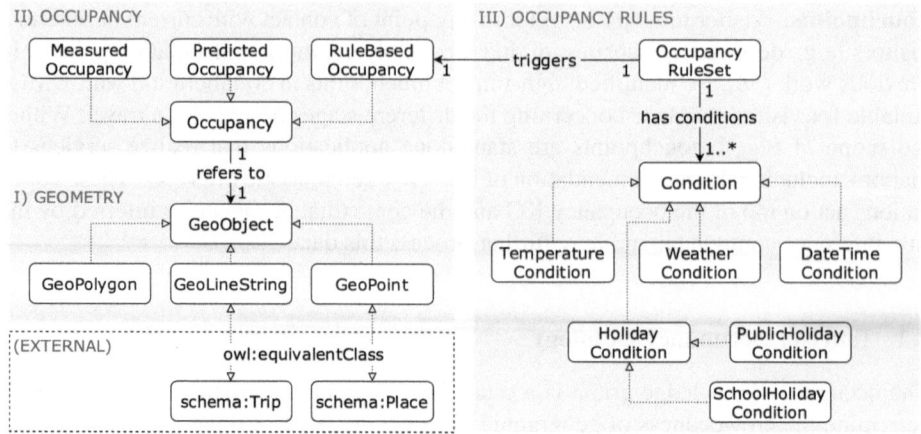

Fig. 2. Components of the TOO including an exemplary mapping to schema.org concepts. Dashed arrows denote sub-class relationships, solid arrows refer to non-taxonomic relations. Geometric relations and attributes are omitted to ensure better readability.

5   Visitor Guidance for German Outdoor Tourism

To showcase the efficiency of our concept, we developed a web-based prototype for applying visitor guidance to the exemplary domain of German outdoor tourism. We instantiate our solution on two specific use cases, namely (i) navigating visitors around a lake using a route as under-occupied as possible and (ii) recommending low-occupancy POIs and hiking tours nearby. We detail both use cases (UC) in the following.

UC1: UC1 relates to a popular bike trail in Germany. A notable hotspot along the trail is a lake, whose northern shore tends to suffer from severe overcrowding on certain days. Thus, the goal of UC1 is to recommend on-site visitors to opt for the southern shore on occupied days.

UC2: UC2 refers to one of Germany's most popular alpine tourist destinations, well-known for its famous castles. During the summer months (i.e., June to September), the destination becomes a significant hotspot with only a few less-occupied alternatives. Besides local POIs and hiking tours, overnight guests should partly be recommended less crowded places in a larger radius to relax local overcrowding while offering visitors the best memories possible.

In line with the overall data flow described in Fig. 1, our demonstration consists of three parts. First, occupancy rules are captured by DMO employees using a web-based application. Second, an inference API evaluates the pre-defined rules within a given context and returns the actual occupancy condition to the requesting client. Third, a mobile application with a UI configurable specific to the use case displays recommendations for less-crowded alternatives to on-site visitors.

Fig. 3. Occupancy rule management based on polygons. The map[1] shows the selection of an exemplary polygon with two rule sets attached (see right panel).

5.1 Occupancy Rule Management

The first application (Fig. 3) implements a simple web-based user interface (UI) for DMO employees. It covers all necessary aspects of the TOO. The rule-based occupancy configuration is based on visually drawn polygons $p \in GeoPolygon$, which can have attached multiple rule-based occupancies $rbo \in RuleBasedOccupancy$ with a rule set $rs \in OccupancyRuleSet$ that comprises logically conjunct conditions $c \in Condition$ (e.g., weather, time). Instead of a continuous value score $s \in [0, 1]$, the UI has been restricted to allow only a set of categorical occupancy values $v \in \{low, medium, high\}$, which map to 0, 0.5, and 1, respectively. This results from our initial expert workshops and the intention to keep the UI simple and tangible.

Polygons can receive different rule-based occupancies at once, each resulting from the applicability of different rules. To apply the specified rules to touristic objects, POIs, and hiking tours are identified within the polygon's boundary by evaluating the geometric relations specified by the TOO (e.g., point containment and intersection). Besides rules and conditions, a short description of each polygon's rule set can be attached for better collaboration of different co-workers of the same DMO.

5.2 QR Code Touchpoint for Local Visitor Guidance

In both use cases, we mainly plan to reach on-site visitors via stationary-mounted QR codes to keep the DMOs' efforts small and minimize the risk of vandalism. Scanning a QR code leads to a location-aware progressive web app (PWA), which can be configured to the use case's specifics. Figure 4 showcases the resulting PWAs.

For UC1, a QR code is intended to be installed on a physical sign on the inside wall of a ferry positioned shortly before the lake, which most visitors of the trail use. In line

---

[1] The map is based on Leaflet (leafletjs.com) and Outdooractive (outdooractive.com). Map data from OpenStreetMap (openstreetmap.org/copyright).

with the workshop key outcomes, the linked PWA highlights two alternative routes: one via the northern shore and the other along the southern shore. The occupancy of each route is modeled using a polygon surrounding the respective route and having a set of rules attached. After rule evaluation, routes are colored green, orange, or red, referring to a low, medium, or high occupancy, respectively. To nudge visitors, interesting POIs (defined by the DMO) are shown alongside the less crowded route. If the conditions of at least one occupancy rule set hold, a generated statement is shown that explains that overcrowding is expected.

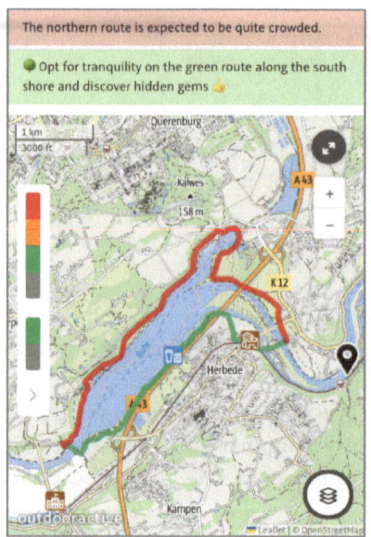 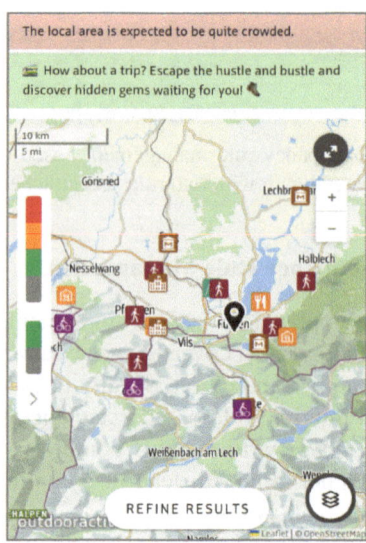

Fig. 4. PWA with maps[2] configured for UC1 (left) and UC2 (right).

Regarding UC2, QR codes are meant to be printed on flyers or displayed in the lobbies of local hotels. In contrast to UC1, where only two local route alternatives are shown, UC2 intends to guide visitors within a radius of 45 km. Thus, the occupancy is modeled in a much wider area. While the DMO decided not to directly display the determined occupancy polygons, the recommender only suggests POIs and hiking tours with low to medium occupancy while giving low-occupancy objects higher ranks. Moreover, due to the large number of possible recommendations, a recommendation dialog may be opened to answer questions regarding personal preferences, including favorite activities, fitness level, and cultural interest (the latter may lead to routes along castles or historical buildings).

---

[2] The maps are based on Leaflet (leafletjs.com) and Outdooractive (outdooractive.com). Map data from OpenStreetMap (openstreetmap.org/copyright).

6 Evaluation

Based on the two use cases outlined above, we evaluated our end-to-end solution in use-case-specific workshops with the respective DMOs, aiming to assess the feasibility and potential of our approach for managing tourist flows in overcrowded destinations. The workshops involved various experts and key stakeholders, including DMO representatives in leading positions and individuals from independent academic and research institutes. Each workshop consisted of two parts. First, to give participants a general understanding of our approach, we gave a complete overview of the use-case-specific instantiation of our concept, that is, the occupancy rule management UI and the accordingly configured PWA. Second, we processed a comprehensive catalog containing all built-in functionalities of our exemplary applications step-by-step, discussing the use-case-specific relevance of each functionality to map the collected feedback to our more general concept.

Despite demonstrating two very different instantiations of the same concept, the overall perception of our demonstrations across all workshops was remarkably positive, and our solution generated great interest among the involved DMOs. What participants found particularly insightful was the simplicity and scalability of the concept of digitizing DMOs' experiences for overcrowding. Also, the participants were convinced that the accuracy of a rule-based occupancy should be sufficient for most of their use cases concerning visitor guidance, which primarily requires rough occupancy estimates rather than concrete numbers.

While the experts of UC1 argued that a rule-based occupancy assessment is specifically helpful for them due to the occurrence of significant but relatively infrequent crowding events, where expensive sensors might not pay off, UC2 suffers from many high-traffic hotspots. It recognizes the usefulness of our approach, particularly in widespread adoption. Although the destination of UC2 already possesses a relatively large number of sensors at the most frequented spots, the intended area with a radius of 45 km cannot be covered by sensors alone; the DMO, therefore, strives for a rule-based solution stating, however, that other DMOs must be involved in the capturing process of relevant occupancy, as not every single part of this area falls under their responsibility. This underscores the need for decoupling information and data sharing, a key competency of knowledge graphs, which are an integral part of our approach.

Another aspect attracting considerable interest during the evaluation workshops was our PWA and the fact that it is activated using a stationary-mounted QR code. The participants agreed that QR codes are affordable, easy to maintain, and highly scalable. They are suitable for ad-hoc experiments while offering sufficient room for personalization. According to UC2, QR codes could be tailored to the hotels' needs by adding their design and related service offers (e.g., transportation to the recommended places and lunch packages), which may also increase the hotels' willingness to adopt such a measure. This finding confirms the necessity of decoupling individual touchpoints from the knowledge graph's data basis.

7 Conclusion, Limitations, and Future Research

In this paper, we proposed a theoretical concept and a practical solution for a lean, cost-effective, and privacy-preserving reference concept for multi-touchpoint visitor guidance with low onboarding requirements, delivering accessible solutions to DMOs in all stages of digitization. Our approach is based on digitizing DMO's experiences on the occupancy of different areas of their destination into rule-based descriptions, constituting a novel combination of experiential knowledge with data-driven methodologies, enriching traditional visitor management strategies [41] and serving as a baseline for occupancy-aware methods [13, 42]. Furthermore, we provide the TOO, a touristic ontology capable of modeling occupancy data, a known research gap [31]. Practically, we provide DMOs with a feasible and scalable solution for mitigating overcrowding situations cost-efficiently and two elaborated examples for a concrete implementation. Our approach is highly accessible, even for DMOs without technical expertise. DMOs with a higher level of digitization can incorporate our approach into their existing infrastructure without significant disruption.

Like other work, this work suffers from certain limitations. First, our initial workshops to determine occupancy influence factors, as well as the investigated use cases and their evaluation, are subject to the domain of German outdoor tourism and may miss out on other perspectives. Second, while valuable, our evaluation is based on qualitative workshops limited to two use cases and needs further investigation, including additional use cases and (quantitative) user studies.

For future research, we plan to strengthen our results by deploying our prototype at scale, incorporating real users, and measuring the deployed application's impact on visitors' (re-)distribution. Furthermore, since the occupancy of our rule-based approach only reflects the assessment of the capturing DMO, we aim at a more granular investigation of the trade-off between simplicity and factors that should be included to obtain a sufficiently accurate occupancy estimation. Moreover, we motivate future research to investigate multistakeholder occupancy calibration to collect the occupancy-related perceptions of visitors and further stakeholders to calibrate the possible thresholds of occupancy levels. Finally, future applications should incorporate values from different sources (e.g., sensors and predictions) to obtain a more diverse view of overcrowding.

Acknowledgements. This work is a result of a cooperation between Outdooractive AG, the Technical University of Munich, and the University of Applied Sciences Kempten. This study was supported by the AIR research project (67KI21005B), funded by the German federal ministry for the environment, nature conversation, nuclear safety, and consumer protection.

References

1. Capocchi, A., et al.: Correction: Capocchi, A., et al. Overtourism: a literature review to assess implications and future perspectives. Sustainability **11**, 3303 (2019). Sustainability **12**(4), 1541 (2020)

2. Krajickova, A., et al.: Visitors' perception of overtourism impacts in a small destination. Anatolia **33**(2), 236–246 (2022)
3. Jacobsen, J.Kr.S. et al.: Hotspot crowding and over-tourism: antecedents of destination attractiveness. Annal. Tourism Res. **76**, 53–66 (2019)
4. Vukadin, I.M.: Sustainability issues in management of tourism in protected areas: case study of Plitvice lakes national park. In: Dwyer, L., et al. (eds.) Evolution of Destination Planning and Strategy, pp. 201–219. Springer, Cham (2017). https://doi.org/10.1007/978-3-319-422 46-6
5. Hobbs, R.J., et al.: Guiding concepts for park and wilderness stewardship in an era of global environmental change. Front. Ecol. Environ. **8**(9), 483–490 (2010)
6. Neubig, S., et al.: Data-driven Initiatives of destinations supporting sustainable tourism. In: Americas Conference on Information Systems (AMCIS) (2022)
7. Bollenbach, J., et al.: Using machine learning to predict POI occupancy to reduce overcrowding. In: INFORMATIK 2023. Gesellschaft für Informatik, Bonn (2022)
8. Martins, C.A., et al.: Key factors for implementation and success of destination management systems. Empirical evidence from European countries. Indust. Manag. Data Syst. **121**(6), 1287–1324 (2021)
9. Pike, S., Page, S.J.: Destination marketing organizations and destination marketing: a narrative analysis of the literature. Tour. Manage. **41**, 202–227 (2014)
10. Neuts, B., Nijkamp, P.: Tourist crowding perception and acceptability in cities. Ann. Tour. Res. **39**(4), 2133–2153 (2012)
11. Neuts, B., Vanneste, D.: Contextual effects on crowding perception: an analysis of Antwerp and Amsterdam. Tijdschrift Voor Econ. Soc. Geog. **109**(3), 402–419 (2018)
12. Filingeri, V., et al.: Factors influencing experience in crowds – the organiser perspective. Appl. Ergon. **68**, 18–27 (2018)
13. Schmücker, D., et al.: The INPReS intervention escalation framework for avoiding overcrowding in tourism destinations. Tourism Hosp. **4**(2), 282–292 (2023)
14. Alexander, M.: Management Planning for Nature Conservation. Springer, Dordrecht (2008). https://doi.org/10.1007/978-1-4020-6581-1
15. Butler, R.W.: Tourism carrying capacity research: a perspective article. Tourism Rev. **75**(1), 207–211 (2020)
16. Hartman, S., et al.: The future of tourism destination management: building productive coalitions of actor networks for complex destination development. J. Tourism Futures **6**(3), 213–218 (2020)
17. Glasson, J., et al.: Towards visitor impact management: visitor impacts, carrying capacity, and management responses in Europe's historic towns and cities. Avebury (1995)
18. Thaler, R.H., Sunstein, C.R.: Nudge: The Final Edition. Penguin Books Limited (2012)
19. Souza-Neto, V., et al.: Lowering the harm of tourist activities: a systematic literature review on nudges. J. Sustain. Tourism 1–22 (2022)
20. Evjemo, B., et al.: User acceptance of digital tourist guides lessons learnt from two field studies. In: Jacko, J.A. (ed.) Human-Computer Interaction. Interaction Design and Usability, vol. 4550, pp. 746–755. Springer, Heidelberg (2007)
21. Femenia-Serra, F., Ivars-Baidal, J.A.: Do smart tourism destinations really work? The case of Benidorm. Asia Pacific J. Tourism Res. **26**(4), 365–384 (2021)
22. Tan, W.-K., Chang, Y.-C.: QR code as an on-site tourism information source. Inf. Technol. Tourism **13**(2), 75–91 (2011)
23. Bethune, E., et al.: Real time response (RTR): Conceptualizing a smart systems approach to destination resilience. J. Destin. Mark. Manag. **23**, 100687 (2022)
24. Boes, K., et al.: Smart tourism destinations: ecosystems for tourism destination competitiveness. Int. J. Tourism Cities **2**(2), 108–124 (2016)

25. Gretzel, U.: The Smart DMO: a new step in the digital transformation of destination management organizations. Eur. J. Tourism Res. **30**, 3002 (2021)
26. Duives, D.C., et al.: Enhancing crowd monitoring system functionality through data fusion: estimating flow rate from Wi-Fi traces and automated counting system data. Sensors **20**(21), 6032 (2020)
27. Mariani, M., Baggio, R.: Big data and analytics in hospitality and tourism: a systematic literature review. Int. J. Contemp. Hosp. Manag. **34**(1), 231–278 (2022)
28. Hevner, A., et al.: Design Science in Information Systems Research. MIS Quarterly **28**(1), 75 (2004)
29. Peffers, K., et al.: A design science research methodology for information systems research. J. Manag. Inf. Syst. **24**(3), 45–77 (2007)
30. Deutsche Zentrale für Tourismus e.V. Domain Specifications Browser. https://open-data-germany.org/domain-specifications-browser/. Accessed 03 Oct 2022
31. Neubig, S., et al.: To graph or not to graph: the missing pieces for knowledge graphs in sustainable tourism. In: INFORMATIK 2023. Gesellschaft für Informatik, Bonn (2023)
32. Şimşek, U., et al.: Towards a knowledge graph lifecycle: a pipeline for the population of a commercial knowledge graph. In: Conference on Digital Curation Technologies (2020)
33. Suárez de Figueroa, M. del C.: Neon Methodology for Building Ontology Networks: Specification, Scheduling and Reuse. Universidad Politécnica de Madrid (2010)
34. Ehrlinger, L., Wöß, W.: Towards a definition of knowledge graphs. In: SEMANTiCS (Posters, Demos, SuCCESS) (2016)
35. Bayern Tourismus Marketing GmbH. BayernCloud Tourismus – BayernCloud Tourismus by BayTM. https://bayerncloud.digital/. Accessed 27 Feb 2022
36. Open Data Destination Germany. https://open-data-germany.org. Accessed 03 Sept 2023
37. Guarino, N., et al.: What is an ontology? In: Staab, S., Studer, R. (eds.) Handbook on Ontologies, pp. 1–17. Springer, Heidelberg (2009). https://doi.org/10.1007/978-3-540-92673-3
38. Huber, D., Neubig, S.: Touchpoints in der Besucherlenkung. https://zenodo.org/record/8098662. Accessed 03 Sept 2023
39. Schema.org Community Group. Schema.org. https://schema.org/. Accessed 03 Oct 2022
40. FIWARE Foundation. Smart Data Models. https://www.fiware.org/smart-data-models/. Accessed 03 Oct 2022
41. Kuo, I.-L.: The effectiveness of environmental interpretation at resource-sensitive tourism destinations. Int. J. Tour. Res. **4**(2), 87–101 (2002)
42. Zubiaga, M., et al.: Towards smarter management of overtourism in historic centres through visitor-flow monitoring. Sustainability **11**(24), 7254 (2019)

Glamping as a Bourgeoisie Fantasy: The Symbolic Meaning Behind Ritualized Scenes

Qin Li and Shihan (David) Ma[✉]

School of Management, Zhejiang University, Hangzhou, China
mashihan@zju.edu.cn

Abstract. Cultivating a luxurious ambiance and kindling a bourgeois fantasy of a high-quality lifestyle, glamping has increasingly been viewed a consumption ritual. The purpose of this study is to dig deeper into the composition of ritual scenes in glamping and the symbolic meaning behind them. We obtained 3,176 text reviews and 22,379 photos from Ctrip. Utilizing visual identification and textual mining, this study revealed three categories of ritual scenes in glamping (environmental, activity, and equipment), and four types of ritual symbolism (self-renewal, self-participation, self-presentation, and social connection). The findings highlight that glamping goes beyond simple enjoyment and becomes a way for customers to build social networks and claim a bourgeoisie-lifestyle identity.

Keywords: glamping · consumption ritual · bourgeoisie

1 Introduction

As a safe, socially distanced choice that limits exposure to others while simultaneously facilitating some ritual sense of travel [1], camping, particularly glamping, has garnered the upmost popularity in China in the past three years. Camping, once viewed as a cost-saving activity [2, 3], is seemingly "upgraded" to glamping as a fashionable demonstration of a bourgeois lifestyle, which has been primarily appealed to the middle class [4]. Glamping have offered more than just a leisure option during the pandemic, but a symbolic consumption cultivating a luxurious ambiance and kindling a bourgeois fantasy of a refined, high-quality lifestyle [5]. The bourgeois lifestyle in glamping allows participants to flaunt their wealth, culture, aesthetics, and social status, viewing it as a lifestyle choice that is intertwined with their identities [6]. Glamping, therefore, could be considered as a consumption ritual, given the symbolism and status it represents.

However, the extant studies have predominantly emphasized the leisure needs of campers. Although acknowledging luxury experience and aesthetic enjoyment as additional motivations for glampers [5, 7, 8], the ritual-related motivations that underpin glamping have been largely overlooked. This oversight leads to an incomplete understanding of why glamping is popular among the consumers as a manifestation of social ascent. To our knowledge, no studies have analyzed glamping from the perspective of consumption rituals.

© The Author(s) 2024
K. Berezina et al. (Eds.): ENTER 2024, SPBE, pp. 165–170, 2024.
https://doi.org/10.1007/978-3-031-58839-6_17

To address the gap, this study aims to explore the ritual scenes and symbolic meanings in glamping. The study contributes to the overarching literature on tourism and leisure by examining glamping as a consumption practice, with an aim to unearth the deep-rooted motivations behind such engagement. Utilizing large-scale user-generated-contents and automatic data mining techniques, it offers valid and valuable insights for marketing professionals and campsite operators. By interpreting the ritualistic and symbolic significance of glamping activities, tourism operators can leverage our findings to design glamping programs that transcend the provision of luxury amenities, and instead, provide transformative experiences imbued with profound meaning for their guests.

2   Data and Method

This study selected Ctrip (https://www.ctrip.com/), the largest online travel agency (OTA) in China, as the data source. We collected user comment data posted from October 2015 through October 2022, totaling 3,176 text reviews and 22,379 photos. Prior to analysis, the DeepL translation API was employed to convert Chinese text comments into English.

This paper seeks to investigate the rituals associated with glamping through a multifaceted approach that incorporates both textual and image data mining. Firstly, we used Google Vision API for image recognition and identified ritualistic scenes with a confidence score above 0.5, resulting in 703 image tags. Word Mover's Distance (WMD) was followed to measure tag similarity, and agglomerative clustering grouped these tags into 50 categories. Principal Component Analysis (PCA) further reduced these categories into 16 ritual scenes. Secondly, Latent Dirichlet Allocation (LDA) topic modeling was adopted to extract and elucidate the glampers' ritual symbolism inherent in textual data. We finalized nine topics to achieve optimal interpretability. Lastly, an exploration of the interplay between ritualistic scenes and ritual symbolism in the realm of glamping is undertaken.

3   Result

3.1   Ritual Scenes

Sixteen distinct ritual scenes were extracted and grouped based on image identification labeling and similarity clustering. We subsequently categorized these scenes into three overarching types: environmental, activity-related, and equipment-related (See Fig. 1).

Environmental scenes are the most frequent scenes in glamping. Drawing from the insights of servicescape research [9, 10], we have identified seven distinctive scenes related to the environment of campground. Among these, six pertain to ambient attributes, including *landforms and architecture, bodies of water, flora, natural surroundings, fauna,* and *public facilities*, while the seventh is design factor, namely *decorative aesthetics*. Not only the natural environment and decorative aesthetics are important, but campers also value the activities in glamping. Based on image recognition and classification, we extract seven types of activity-related scenes, *namely outdoor recreations, take photos with others, food and beverage, road transportation, barbecue, music performance, and aero adventure.* Equipment-related scenes encompass *furnishings* and *outdoor apparatus* tailored for glamping. At times, individuals pursue a sense of ritual through the details of the surrounding items to reflect the meaning of life.

3.2   Ritual Symbolism

We discerned nine topic themes from online comments, which we subsequently distilled into four symbolic representations of ritual, specifically self-renewal, self-participation, self-presentation, and social connections.

Self-renewal: The concept of self-renewal finds expression across three distinct topics. The pivotal terms of Topic 1, "refresh" and "escape," underscore glamping's role as an escape from the rigors of daily work and a means to slow down, thereby affording respite to the mind. Topic 9 accentuates the concepts of "recreation" and "relaxation". Glamping, as a micro-vacation retreat, negates the need for elaborate getaways and instead enables individuals to bask in relaxation and unfettered freedom. The crux of Topic 3 hinges upon "convenience" and "enjoyment," indicating that many visitors enjoying the services offered by the campsite.

Self-Participation: There are four topics are included. Topic 2 Fireside night talk relates to people's longing for an idyllic pastoral life. Topic 4 spotlights "climb" and "ropeway" as high-frequency terms, indicative of the penchant among outdoor enthusiasts for mountain climbing and hiking coupled with camping. Topic 7 accentuates the thrill and distinctive encounters associated with glamping. Several campsites offer activities like desert motorcycling, desert skiing, and off-road vehicles. Topic 8 is centered around the core concept of being "close to nature."

Self-Presentation: The facet of self-presentation within camping aligns with Topic 5, underscored by keywords like "photo-taking". A subset of campers aspires to project an image of "refined living" on social platforms. The core of Topic 5 revolves around capturing striking views. For these campers, the essence lies not in the camping experience itself but rather in the ambiance and opulence that their photos convey to their online audiences.

Social Connections: Topic 6, encompassing the largest proportion among all topics, encapsulates the symbolism of social connections within the realm of glamping. This topic is characterized by keywords associated with vacationing alongside family and friends.

3.3   Integration of Ritual Scenes and Ritual Symbolism

As delineated in Fig. 1, the analysis reveals distinctive associations between ritual symbolism and ritual scenes. Firstly, the ritual symbolism of **self-renewal** finds most resonance in *environmental ritual scenes*, including bodies of water, public facilities, decorative aesthetics, and outdoor apparatus. Secondly, the ritual symbolisms of **self-participation** and **self-presentation** are depicted through an integration of both *environmental* and *activity scenes*, with unique landscapes alongside a medley of activities such as barbecues and music performance. Thirdly, the ritual symbolism of **social connections** primarily harmonizes with visual depictions of *equipment scene* and *activities* reflecting personal interactions, including food preparation, photo-taking, and musical performance activities.

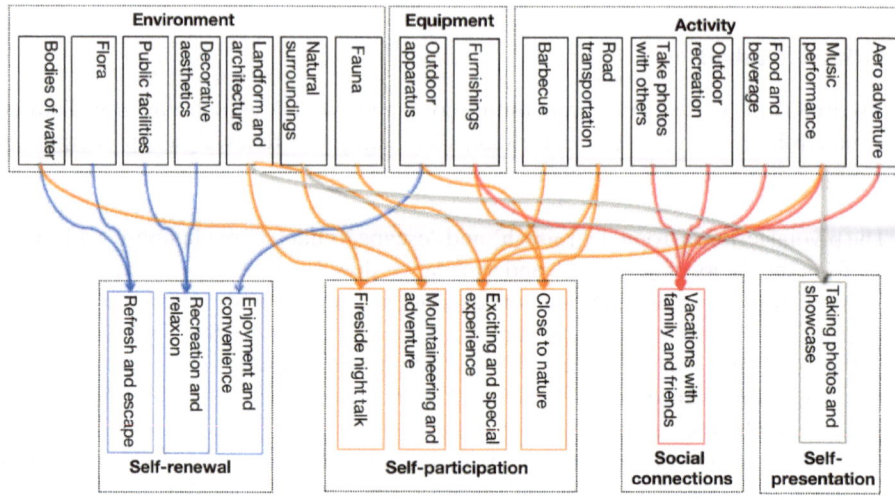

Fig. 1. Integration of ritual scenes and ritual symbolism

4 Discussion and Conclusion

Our study sheds light on glamping's consumption rituals and the hidden symbolism behind them. Current studies, despite examining glamping from a ritual perspective, overlook the potential connection between glamping and conspicuous consumption. For instances, the latest study by Xiang identifies glamping as a form of ritual interaction; yet still focuses on the positive emotions and flow experiences brought about by glamping [11]. Another study highlights the role of group interactions and social identity construction in achieving this sense of communitas but ignored the self-presentation motivation in social interaction [12]. Our research provides a deeper understanding of glamping motivations compared to existing studies. It suggests that self-presentation is an additional reason for glamping; people aim to enhance their image through conspicuous consumption. Additionally, our study uncovers that bourgeois consumption rituals do not solely hinge upon the display of economic capital; cultural capital, such as aesthetics and taste, equally functions as a conduit for self-expression.

Our research holds significant implications for tourism operators and destination management organizations to incorporate well-designed ritualistic elements within glamping experiences. With the middle class more keenly recognizing the intertwined extrinsic and intrinsic value of glamping, it emerges as both a rite of intensification and a rite of passage. The former revolves around the divergence between the experience and environment of glamping and the mundane everyday life. The latter signifies the perspective that glamping serves as a means of elevating one's bourgeois status. Consequently, there exist two avenues for shaping glamping products: one entails enriching the visitor's experiential journey and fostering spiritual enrichment, while the other involves offering avenues for identity cultivation through rituals.

Though novel, the study has limitations. It doesn't entirely rule out the pandemic's impact, leaving questions about whether its popularity stems from short-term stimulus or long-standing societal demands. Additionally, the absence of demographic data in social media necessitates further research to determine if identity-seeking is influenced by social media or indicative of middle-class identity concerns. Moreover, future research can explore how various social media platforms influence the expression of glamping consumption rituals.

References

1. Craig, C.A.: Camping, glamping, and coronavirus in the United States. Ann. Touris. Res. (2020)
2. Brooker, E., Joppe, M.: Trends in camping and outdoor hospitality—an international review. J. Outdoor Recreat. Tour. **3–4**, 1–6 (2013)
3. Bell, S., Tyrväinen, L., Sievänen, T., Pröbstl, U., Simpson, M.: Outdoor recreation and nature tourism: a European perspective. Living Rev. Landsc. Res. **1** (2007). https://doi.org/10.12942/lrlr-2007-2
4. Budiasa, I.M., Suparta, I.K., Nurjaya, I.W.: Implementation of green tourism concept on glamping tourism in Bali. In: Proceedings of the International Conference on Applied Science and Technology 2019 - Social Sciences Track (iCASTSS 2019), pp. 191–195. Atlantis Press, Paris (2019)
5. Sun, T., Huang, T.: Research of glamping tourism based on the aesthetics of atmosphere. Sustain. Sci. Pract. Policy **15**, 581 (2022)
6. Rocha, A.R.C., da Rocha, A., Rocha, E.: Rituals of cruise consumption and the "new" middle class: desiring and "devouring" maritime cruises. Leis. Stud. **36**, 468–480 (2017)
7. Cvelić-Bonifačić, J., Milohnić, I., Cerović, Z.: Glamping–creative accommodation in camping resorts: insights and opportunities. Tourism Southern Eastern Europe **4**, 101–114 (2017)
8. Lopes, D., Brandão, F., Breda, Z., Costa, R.: The four dimensions of tourist experience: a comparative analysis between camping and glamping. In: Advances in Tourism, Technology and Systems, pp. 385–395. Springer, Singapore (2021). https://doi.org/10.1007/978-981-33-4256-9_35
9. Min, D.: Servicescape, perceived value, flow and behavioral intention among participants of international outdoor camping exhibition. Korean J. Sports Sci. **33**, 125–139 (2022)
10. Bitner, M.J.: The servicescape. In: Handbook of Services Marketing and Management, pp. 37–50 (2000)
11. Xiang, K., Cao, Y., Qiao, G., Li, W.: Glamping: an exploration of emotional energy and flow experiences in interaction rituals. Tour. Manag. Perspect. **48**, 101149 (2023)
12. Xiang, K., Cao, Y., Qiao, G., Zhang, H.: Mechanisms of communitas experience generation in glampers: an interactive ritual perspective. J. Hosp. Tour. Manag. **55**, 355–367 (2023)

Coming to Terms with the Digital Natives: Understanding the Marketing Sensitivities of GenZers as Hospitality Consumers

Semih Yılmaz[1][(✉)], Ayşe Collins[1], and Seyid Amjad Ali[2]

[1] Department of Tourism and Hotel Management, Bilkent University, Ankara 06800, Turkey
`semihsaityilmaz@bilkent.edu.tr`

[2] Department of Information Systems and Technologies, Bilkent University, Ankara 06800, Turkey

Abstract. As "digital natives", GenZ is set apart from previous generations in terms of its online connectedness. Even though this generation is expected to be the prevailing customer base around the world by 2026, there is a noticeable lack of studies on GenZ's consumer characteristics within the hospitality context. This study investigates the marketing-related factors affecting GenZ's accommodation decisions as well as their consumer sensitivities to contemporary constructs such as brand uniqueness, social media presentability, sustainability consciousness, and cancel culture.

Keywords: GenZ · Social Media · Marketing · Consumer Behavior · Hospitality · Cancel Culture

1 Background

Even though the share of Gen Z in consumer markets is rising to the top [1, 2] studies on their consumer behavior are still lacking [3]. The dearth of research is even more noticeable in the field of hospitality [4–8]. While sharing certain characteristics with millennials, such as internet savviness and a need to be connected [9], as "digital natives" [10] their consumer experiences are not simply extended or enhanced by digital connectivity, but mostly born of it [2, 11]. Therefore, the role mobile internet technologies and social media play in the consumer decisions and choices reaches a new level in Gen Z's status-seeking, diversity-driven, and community-oriented search for brands [12, 13].

As Gen Z is expected to dominate both consumer and labor markets by 2026, it is imperative to conduct research on Gen Z as hospitality consumers for a better appraisal of their marketing sensitivities and responses to brand communications, especially on online platforms. Few recent studies suggest that overall brand uniqueness [11] social media presentability and sustainability-consciousness [12, 14] might be useful constructs in understanding brand responses of Gen Z to hotel and restaurants services. As another distinct characteristic, Gen Z does not shy away from cutting ties with a brand permanently [3] – or "canceling" it due to perceived corporate wrongdoings or

© The Author(s) 2024
K. Berezina et al. (Eds.): ENTER 2024, SPBE, pp. 171–174, 2024.
https://doi.org/10.1007/978-3-031-58839-6_18

shortcomings. However, no known scholarly research evaluates the impact of cancel culture – a prominent component of contemporary public discourse – on Gen Z's hospitality decisions, let alone accommodation choices. Therefore, building upon these constructs conjointly, this study focuses on understanding the preferences, digital priorities, and marketing-related sensitivities of Gen Z as accommodation consumers.

2   Purpose of the Study

The purpose of this study is threefold: i) what factors are influential in Gen Z's online search for accommodation options, ii) what accommodation attributes are important for Gen Z, and iii) how contemporary constructs such as brand uniqueness, social media presentability, sustainability consciousness, and cancel culture impact Gen Z's brand perceptions in accommodation.

3   Methodology

As an exploratory study, both qualitative and quantitative (mixed) methods are employed. First, a survey was conducted with students at a private university in Türkiye. Qualitative parts of the study (focus group interviews with Gen Z students and semi-structured interviews with hotels, and intermediaries such as tour operators and travel agencies) are currently in progress following the conclusion of the survey. Interviews are designed to investigate the impact of brand uniqueness, social media presentability and cancel culture on Gen Z's accommodation-based consumer decisions. Innovative visualizations for explanatory data analyses were created with the use of custom R code by utilizing the 'ggplot2' package.

4   Findings

Results from the initial part of the study (survey in progress, current $N = 394$) reveal that social media and mobile friendliness of accommodation choices are important factors in how favorably Gen Z responds to marketing communications. Furthermore, preference for a desirable location close to entertainment options, as well as internet access and high service quality signify the utilitarian and social dimension of their hospitality choices (see graphics below). These findings attest to the "digital native" dimension of the Gen Z population. All results from currently conducted survey as well as future parts of the study (interviews with hotels, intermediaries, and Gen Z students) will be shared at the presentation.

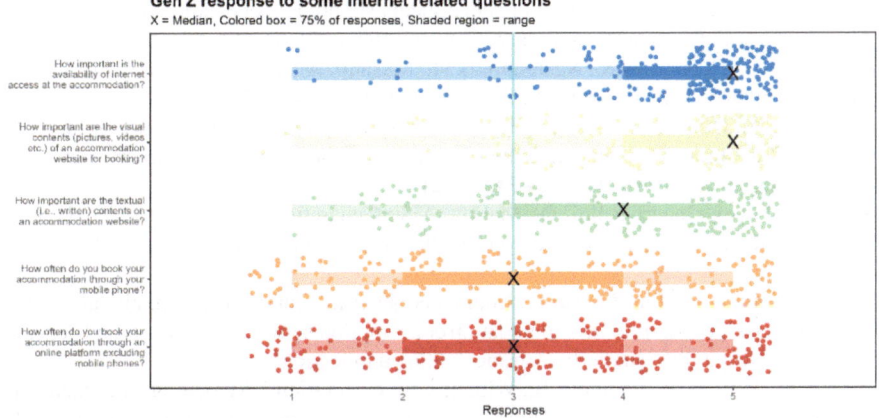

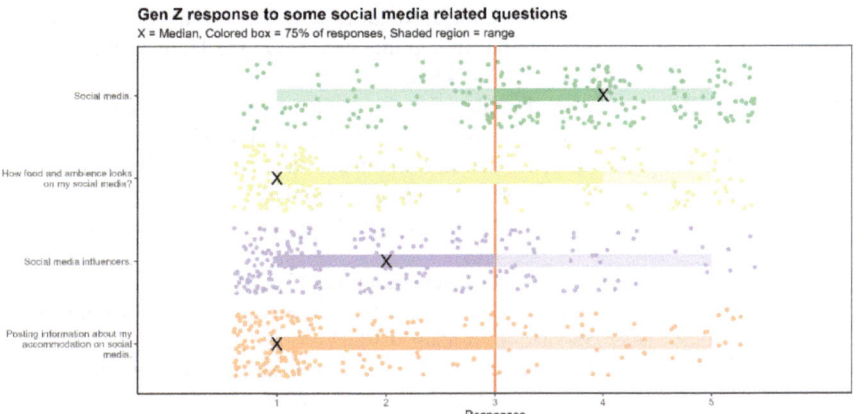

5   Limitations

This study focuses on accommodation-related preferences and choices of Gen Z in a specific country culture. However, authors believe the implications can resonate with global audiences in this understudied area of hospitality consumption by arguably the most-globally connected generation.

References

1. Fromm, J.: As Gen Z's Buying Power Grows, Businesses Must Adapt Their Marketing. Forbes (2022, October 12). https://www.forbes.com/sites/jefffromm/2022/07/20/as-gen-zs-buying-power-grows-businesses-must-adapt-their-marketing/?sh=5b6a8142533c
2. Francis, T., Hoefel, F.: 'True Gen': Generation Z and its implications for companies. McKinsey & Company (2018, November 18). https://www.mckinsey.com/industries/consumer-packaged-goods/our-insights/true-gen-generation-z-and-its-implications-for-companies

3. Goldring, D., Azab, C.: New rules of social media shopping: personality differences of U.S. Gen Z versus Gen X market mavens. J. Consum. Behav. **20**(4), 884–897 (2021)
4. Wiastuti, R.D., Lestari, N.S., Ngatemin, B.M., Masatip, A.: The generation Z characteristics and hotel choices. Afr. J. Hosp. Tourism Leisure **9**(1), 1–14 (2020)
5. Ramgade, A., Kumar, A.: Changing trends of hospitality industry: emergence of millennials and gen Z as future customers and their influence on the hospitality industry. Vidyabharati Int. Interdiscip. Res. J. **12**(01), 336–342 (2021)
6. Chen, F. (Faye), Quadri-Felitti, D., Mattila, A.S.: Generation influences perceived coolness but not favorable attitudes toward cool hotel brands. Cornell Hosp. Quart. **64**(1), 95–103 (2023)
7. Fan, A., Shin, H.W., Shi, J., Wu, L.: Young people share, but do so differently: an empirical comparison of peer-to-peer accommodation consumption between millennials and generation z. Cornell Hospitality Quarterly. Advance online publication
8. Stylos, N., Rahimi, R., Okumus, B., Williams, S.: Generation Z Marketing and Management in Tourism and Hospitality: The Future of the Industry, 1st edn. Palgrave Macmillan (2021)
9. Hall, A., Towers, N., Shaw, D.R.: Understanding how Millennial shoppers decide what to buy: digitally connected unseen journeys. Int. J. Retail Distrib. Manag. **45**(5), 498–517 (2017)
10. Prensky, M.: Digital natives, digital immigrants part 1. On the Horizon **9**(5), 1–6 (2001). https://doi.org/10.1108/10748120110424816
11. Smaliukiene, R., Kocai, E., Tamuleviciute, A.: Generation Z and consumption: how communication environment shapes youth choices. Media Stud. **11**(22), 24–45 (2020)
12. Tyson, A., Kennedy, B., Funk, C.: Gen Z, Millennials stand out for climate change activism, social media engagement with issue. Pew Research Center (2021). https://www.pewresearch.org/science/wp-content/uploads/sites/16/2021/05/PS_2021.05.26_climate-and-generations_REPORT.pdf
13. Hill Holliday. Meet gen z: The social generation (2017). https://thinking.hhcc.com/hubfs/Gen%20Z%20-%20The%20Social%20Generation%20%7C%20Hill%20Holliday-4.pdf?submissionGuid=e1937055-9a4a-400f-a5ab-f910a8b6fdbb
14. Apaolaza, V., Paredes, M.R., Hartmann, P., D'Souza, C.: How does restaurant's symbolic design affect photo-posting on Instagram? The moderating role of community commitment and coolness. J. Hosp. Market. Manag. **30**(1), 21–37 (2021)

Customer-to-Customer Real-Time Value Co-creation in Tourism Live Streaming: A Live Streamer Perspective

Kaiti Shang[(✉)] [iD], Dimitrios Buhalis [iD], Daisy X. F. Fan [iD], and Marcjanna Augustyn [iD]

Bournemouth University, Poole BH12 5BB, Dorset, UK
{kshang,dbuhalis,dfan,maugustyn}@bournemouth.ac.uk

Abstract. Live streaming has emerged as a new medium for the creation and dissemination of travel experiences, product marketing and destination promotion. Empirical studies on live streamers' motivations and travel behavior in tourism live streaming are currently under-explored. This study adopted a live streamer perspective and followed a qualitative approach to 1) explore the motivations and travel behaviour of live streamers in tourism, and 2) investigate the process of customer-to-customer real-time value co-creation of the live streamer with other stakeholders by drawing on the Porter-Lawler model. Findings provide in-depth understanding of live streamers' motivations for engaging in tourism live streaming and the influence of viewers on live streamers. Recommendations are also offered to tourism live streaming platforms regarding how to develop a better incentive strategy for live streamers.

Keywords: Live streamer · Travel behavior · Co-creation · Value · Customer to customer

1 Introduction

Live streaming has been increasingly used by online influencers, travel bloggers, travel agencies and tourism destination marketing organisations [1]. This is becoming an emerging channel for creating and disseminating travel experiences, selling products and promoting destinations [2]. Through live streaming platforms, anyone can live stream self-created content (i.e., become a streamer) or watch other people's live streams (i.e., become a viewer) in real time. Live streaming is becoming a new tool for content creators to share the scenery of the destination, interact with viewers and enrich their travel experiences in real time [3]. The integration of live streaming technology into the tourism sector is a major advancement in tourism experience development. Previous studies indicated that live streaming can provide the public with immediacy, intimacy, authenticity and interactivity by sharing online tourism experience [4]. However, empirical studies on live streamers' motivations and travel behavior are currently under-explored. This study

---

This paper is an adaptation of the lead author's thesis.

K. Berezina et al. (Eds.): ENTER 2024, SPBE, pp. 175–179, 2024.
https://doi.org/10.1007/978-3-031-58839-6_19

adopted a live streamer perspective and followed a qualitative approach to 1) explore the motivations and travel behaviour of live streamers in tourism, and 2) investigate the process of customer-to-customer real-time value co-creation of the live streamer with other stakeholders by drawing on the Porter-Lawler model.

2   Literature Review

Social media has significantly transformed the way people interact and communicate with each other [5]. Social media can be seen as an extension of Web 2.0 concepts and technologies, facilitating the creation and distribution of user-generated content [5]. Traditional social media plays its part in the pre-travel, during-travel and post-travel stages of the traveler's journey [6]. For example, when travelers make pre-trip decisions, online information search channels consist of search engines such as Google, independent websites of tourism stakeholders, OTA websites such as Ctrip and travel user generated content (UGC) platforms such as TripAdvisor [6]. During and after the trip, individuals share their experiences through social media in the form of pictures and text descriptions [7].

Driven by 5G technology, travelers are beginning to flock to new media platforms that are more vivid, instant, shared and interactive, such as short video platforms and tourism live streaming platforms [8]. Tourism live streaming accompanies travelers throughout their whole travelling experience with its timely dissemination and real-time interaction [9]. The unanticipated pandemic became a booster for the growth of live streaming in the tourism industry [1]. Live streaming bridges the gap between on-the-go travelers and their family members and friends who are still quarantine at home to deliver virtual travel experiences in real time [3]. The unique and immersive scene in live streaming allows even non-travelers to follow the camera changes from the first-angle of view, as if they were visiting the destination themselves [4]. The subject of tourism live streaming is also becoming abundant, including but not limited to ordinary residents, tourists, key opinion leaders, tour guides, travel agencies, online travel companies and tourism destination governments. In response to the motivation and intention to share travel experiences in the form of texts and photos on social media, scholars have conducted studies using various theories, such as theory of reasoned action [10], self-determination theory [11], social influence theory [7], flow theory [12] and interaction ritual chain theory [9]. Existing research has been started shifting the focus from social media in general towards live streaming. The research is mainly concerned with three aspects of live streaming, live streamers and viewers. In terms of live streaming, existing research has mainly discussed the definition [4], characteristics [12], types [13], and stakeholders of live streaming [3]. In terms of viewers, scholars have mainly examined viewers' stickiness of live streaming platforms [12], motivations to watch [14] and shop [15], the influence of tourism live streaming on viewers' travel intention [16], psychological well-being [17] and trust and incentives of e-commerce live streaming platforms [18]. For live streamers, related studies have discussed the definition [2], motivations of live streamers [19], and sustainability of live streamers [20]. In the tourism sector, research on understanding the live streamers is still in its infancy. As a representative real-time value co-creation activity, the specific process of tourism live streaming has not yet been fully revealed. Hence, the motivation of live-streamers to engage in tourism live-streaming activities and the process of customer-to-customer real-time value co-creation in tourism live streaming needs to be studied.

3 Methodology

This study aims to understand live streamers' travel behaviour and explore the customer-to-customer real-time value co-creation process in tourism live streaming. The current study followed a qualitative research approach, using a semi-structured interview to explore an in-depth individual experience. China is the pioneer of the live streaming industry [1]. All informants were recruited through purposive sampling method from Wechat Live Streaming, Douyin, Ctrip.com, and Mafengwo.com which are the leading and well-established tourism live streaming platforms in China. An inclusion criterion was set that informants had done tourism live streaming at least once in the past two years to ensure the depth of their experience. Data collection was undertaken between March 2023 and August 2023. In total, 36 semi-structured interviews were conducted. The average length of interviews was 50 min. The informants included 20 females and 16 males, aged between 20 and 50 years. On average, all informants did tourism live streaming twice a year. The interview protocol mainly comprised four parts: the motivation of doing tourism live streaming; the process of tourism live streaming; the experience of interacting with viewers during live streaming; and the differences in travel behaviour between do tourism live streaming and don't do tourism live streaming. The data were analyzed using thematic analysis.

4 Preliminary Results

The process of customer-to-customer real-time value co-creation in tourism live streaming is shown in Fig. 1. Tourism live streamers make live streaming preparations based on their own motivations, such as selecting a live streaming location and creating a live streaming script. Viewers interact with the live streamer by sending real-time comments based on the scene, content and voice presented in the live streaming. At the same time, based on real-time feedback from viewers, the live streamer senses whether the pre-live expectations are being met. If viewers send positive real-time comments to the live streamer and the live streaming statistics, such as the number of current viewers, minutes watched and total number of likes, meet the live streamer's expectations, the positive value is co-created through the real-time interaction between the tourism live streamer and the viewers. The tourism live streamer would do the enhancement for the live streaming according to the viewers' real-time positive comments. The positive value would contribute to the motivation of the live streamers for the next tourism live streaming. If viewers send negative real-time comments to the live streamer and the live streaming statistics don't meet the live streamer's expectations, the negative value is co-created through the real-time interaction. Some tourism live streamers have been able to reflect on negative comments from viewers in order to improve their live streaming. There are also some live streamers whose motivation to live streaming may be influenced by negative values, thus causing them to stop live streaming.

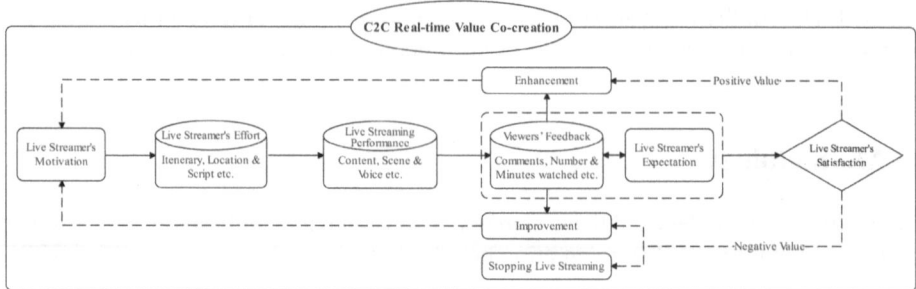

Fig. 1. Customer-to-customer real-time value co-creation in tourism live streaming

5 Discussion and Conclusion

This study explored live streamers' travel behaviour and delineated the process of customer-to-customer real-time value co-creation in tourism live streaming from the perspective of live streamer. Theoretically, this study extended the knowledge of live streamers' motivations for engaging in tourism live streaming. It not only demonstrates the real-time interactions between live streamers and viewers, but also reveals the influence of viewers on live streamers' travel behaviour. Previous research has only explored the motivations of live streamers to share their travel experiences on live streaming platforms [19]. This study further depicts the live streamers' motivation to engage in tourism live streaming as a dynamic, developing and flexible orientation or disposition, which is responsive to the inputs of viewer feedback. Practically, this study provided suggestions for tourism live streaming platform, which can develop a better incentive strategy for live streamers. For example, tourism live streaming platforms can offer virtual medals to be worn while live streaming for live streamers who interact positively with their viewers. The limitation of this study is that it only explores the process of customer-to-customer real-time value co-creation in tourism live streaming from the perspective of live streamers. Future research could consider exploring this phenomenon from the viewers' perspective, or from both live streamers' and viewers' perspectives.

References

1. Liu, X., Yuan, Y., He, J., Li, Z.: Framing the travel livestreaming in China: a new star rising under the COVID-19. Curr. Issu. Tourism 1–20 (2022)
2. Xie, C., Yu, J., Huang, S. (Sam), Zhang, J.: Tourism e-commerce live streaming: Identifying and testing a value-based marketing framework from the live streamer perspective. Tourism Manag. **91**, 104513 (2022)
3. Deng, Z., Benckendorff, P., Wang, J.: Travel live streaming: an affordance perspective. Inf. Technol. Tourism **23**(2), 189–207 (2021)
4. Lin, K., Fong, L.H.N., Law, R.: Live streaming in tourism and hospitality: a literature review. Asia Pacific J. Tourism Res. **27**(3), 290–304 (2022)
5. Buhalis, D., Sinarta, Y.: Real-time co-creation and nowness service: lessons from tourism and hospitality. J. Travel Tour. Mark. **36**(5), 563–582 (2019)

6. Amaro, S., Duarte, P., Henriques, C.: Travelers' use of social media: a clustering approach. Ann. Tour. Res. **59**, 1–15 (2016)
7. Oliveira, T., Araujo, B., Tam, C.: Why do people share their travel experiences on social media? Tour. Manage. **78**, 104041 (2020)
8. Clement Addo, P., Fang, J., Asare, A.O., Kulbo, N.B.: Customer engagement and purchase intention in live-streaming digital marketing platforms. Serv. Ind. J. **41**(11–12), 767–786 (2021)
9. Li, X., Xie, J., Chen, S.X.: Cannot wait to share? An exploration of tourists' sharing behavior during the 'traveling to the site' stage. Curr. Issue Tour. **25**(22), 3640–3656 (2022)
10. Bigne, E., Andreu, L., Hernandez, B., Ruiz, C.: The impact of social media and offline influences on consumer behaviour. An analysis of the low-cost airline industry. Curr. Issues Tourism **21**(9), 1014–1032 (2018)
11. Medeiros, M., Ozturk, A., Hancer, M., Weinland, J., Okumus, B.: Understanding travel tracking mobile application usage: an integration of self-determination theory and UTAUT2. Tourism Manag. Perspect. **42**, 100949 (2022)
12. Liao, J., Chen, K., Qi, J., Li, J., Yu, I.Y.: Creating immersive and parasocial live shopping experience for viewers: the role of streamers' interactional communication style. J. Res. Interact. Mark. **17**(1), 140–155 (2022)
13. Li, Y., Li, X., Cai, J.: How attachment affects user stickiness on live streaming platforms: a socio-technical approach perspective. J. Retail. Consum. Serv. **60**, 102478 (2021)
14. Long, Q., Tefertiller, A.C.: China's new mania for live streaming: gender differences in motives and uses of social live streaming services. Int. J. Hum. Comput. Interact. **36**(14), 1314–1324 (2020)
15. Ma, Y.: To shop or not: Understanding Chinese consumers' live-stream shopping intentions from the perspectives of uses and gratifications, perceived network size, perceptions of digital celebrities, and shopping orientations. Telematics Inform. **59**, 101562 (2021)
16. Zheng, S., Wu, M., Liao, J.: The impact of destination live streaming on viewers' travel intention. Curr. Issue Tour. **26**(2), 184–198 (2023)
17. Zhang, A., Xiao, H.: Psychological well-being in tourism live streaming: a grounded theory. J. Hosp. Tourism Res.10963480221149595 (2023)
18. Wongkitrungrueng, A., Assarut, N.: The role of live streaming in building consumer trust and engagement with social commerce sellers. J. Bus. Res. **117**, 543–556 (2020)
19. Li, F. (Sam), Ma, J., Tong, Y.: Livestreaming in tourism: what drives tourism live streamers to share their travel experiences? Tourism Rev. (2022)
20. Heo, J., Kim, Y., Yan, J.: Sustainability of live video streamer's strategies: live streaming video platform and audience's social capital in South Korea. Sustainability **12**(5), 1–13 (2020)

Technology for Marketing, Business Growth, and Development

A Service Ecosystem Perspective on Building a Cultural Tourism Co-creation Platform

Baolin Deng[1] and IpKin Anthony Wong[2]([envelope])

[1] Sun Yat-Sen University, Tang Jia Wang, Xiangzhou, Zhuhai, China
dengblin@mail2.sysu.edu.cn
[2] University of Macau, Avenida da Universidade, Taipa, Macau, China
anthonywong@um.edu.mo

Abstract. The aim of the paper is to provide practical insights into a cultural tourism co-creation platform for building a service platform ecosystem from multiple stakeholders' perspectives. Drawing on the service dominant logic and service ecosystem literature, the paper provides a comprehensive literature review and multiple stakeholder perspectives on the construction of a cultural tourism co-creation platform for the digital practice of Mogao Grottos. Four key actors of cultural tourism co-creation platforms from a service ecosystem perspective are identified, including platform owners, platform partners, technological providers, and platform customers, and the paper explores the actions and strengths of these actors. To the authors' knowledge, this study represents one of the early attempts to investigate the possible consequences of building a cultural tourism co-creation platform for destination organization management.

Keywords: Digital technologies · Service platform ecosystem · Mogao Grottos · Value creation

1 Introduction

A service ecosystem refers to "…a relatively self-contained, self-adjusting system of resource-integrating actors connected by shared institutional arrangements and mutual value creation through exchange" [1]. Economic sociology and institutional economics offer a theoretical lens, this definition emphasizes the significance of the institution in value creation. Other literature has considered the platform ecosystem as a connected, and creative network, and mainly concerns multiple stakeholders, including platform providers, customers, and technological stakeholders [2]. An ecosystem perspective inspires our research priorities should adhere to "… long-term large problems that go beyond individual customer satisfaction and short-term financial performance to encompass the total value creation system" [3].

Practitioners from the tourism and hospitality industries have stepped into a way of building digital services. For example, managers and frontline workers employ digital tools to improve their customer experience management [4–6], such as ordering meals using a smartphone and purchasing tickets via apps, and also employ digital-twin

K. Berezina et al. (Eds.): ENTER 2024, SPBE, pp. 183–194, 2024.
https://doi.org/10.1007/978-3-031-58839-6_20

technology to monitor the automation process [7]. Such digital service practices are identified as the early stage of digitalization services [8]. Moreover, the extant research mainly focuses on these digital applications on customers' responses [9–11]. Although the extant research has examined the multiple stakeholders' perspectives on the service robot's adoption [12], limited research has focused on more than two stakeholders' perspectives on digital services in the tourism and hospitality industries from a service ecosystem perspective. Hence, guided by the service ecosystems perspectives, this research elucidates a pathway for building a cultural tourism co-creation platform. The cultural-co-creation platform in the study is defined as the network of actors in an ecosystem that co-created digital experiences for customers through all actors' strengths and actions.

Guided by the available literature on the service platform ecosystem, this study proposes a framework for designing a tourism co-creation platform for tourism destinations from a service platform ecosystem perspective. We propose that a co-creation platform has three important research questions: 1) What are the diverse types of actors? 2) What are the roles and actions of multiple actors in building the cultural tourism co-creation platform? 3) What are the kinds of values co-created from the cultural tourism co-creation platform?

2   Literature Review

2.1   Service-Dominant Logic and Co-creation Platform

From the standpoint of service logic perspectives, the concept of co-creation processes entails the active involvement of the customer as a co-creator of value, while the provider assumes the role of a facilitator in enabling the production and delivery of claimed value [13, 14]. Following this logic, tech companies should embrace the value of co-creation in service innovation like the cultural tourism co-creation platform [15], thus means understanding the customers' practices and how customers perceive the multiple customer contact points in the platform [16, 17]. There are several co-creation values (e.g., unitarian value, emotional value, and social value) to identify in the interactions between suppliers and customers [18].

Co-creation platform refers to the formation of multiple actors' interactions [15]. For example, platform owner's and platform customer processes combine into a collaborative process and all actors can actively impact each other's procedures and results. Guided by a co-creation platform, destination management organizations (DMOs) can have a chance to chance to interact with the value creation of customers through direct interactions. DMOs can have the power to actively and immediately impact value accomplishment, keeping their word [15, 19].

2.2   Service Ecosystem Perspective

The value-creation process has been considered a dynamic and interactive process through multiple actors' actions in the tourism and hospitality discipline [20]. Unlike a firm-centered focus that emphasizes value exchange as the major type of value, the customer-centered view focuses on value in use during consumer-firm interactions and common actors' actions [21]. In accordance with the principles of service-dominant logic, the value co-creation process incorporates the service ecosystem perspective, wherein different stakeholders actively participate and contribute to the process [22].

The existing body of research has utilized the service ecosystem approach to examine the dynamic process of value co-creation from the standpoint of service design and service innovation. Baron, and Patterson [23] explored innovation practices for less food waste from a service ecosystem perspective. Brodie, Fehrer [24] defined actor engagement in networks of multiple actors and clarified the concept's future research direction. Shin [20] reviewed the service robot research from a service ecosystem perspective and analyzed the relationships between service robots and different actors. Specifically, four actors are identified in building a cultural tourism co-creation platform: platform owners, platformer partners, technological providers, and platform customers. Taking a case study of Moga Grottoes, the research is among the first studies to empirically explore the multiple actors' actors' roles and actions through their co-creation interactions from the destination level.

3   Methodology

Qualitative research methodology was employed in order to address the research questions. In-depth interviews were conducted to collect data from stakeholders. Purposive sampling, which refers to the selection of participants who are most likely to access appropriate and useful information [25], was used in selecting the target participants. The target interview participants were recruited from Dunhuang Cultural and Creative Company, Dunhuang Mogao Grottos Management, Tencent, and customers, which are multiple stakeholders responsible for the digital Dunhuang project. Table 1 states the characteristics of all participants.

The interview was conducted in August 2023, both offline and online in Dunhuang, China. The audio was recorded upon consent from the participants. The data was analyzed using content analysis. The data was coded following the systematic classification process recommended by Hsieh and Shannon [26]. Our research focuses on the exploration of types of practitioners, which are identified through a multi-round coding method. Our primary focus was on employing open coding methodology to generate codes throughout the initial phase of coding, whereby researchers carefully reviewed each review. Abstract codes are derived through iterative analysis of the reviews. Next, we proceeded to engage in axial coding within the framework of the second-cycle method. The focus of this cycle revolved around the consolidation of comparable codes into categories, wherein the coders "fit the piece of the data puzzle together" [27]. The entirety of the procedure was completed by two coders. In conclusion, we employed selective coding [27] to establish connections between categories in order to identify a central concept: a cultural tourism co-creation platform. To instill credibility and trustworthiness in the research, We established a distinct connection by utilizing Homburg, Xu, Hazée's [2] dynamic service ecosystem system while modifying the research framework among actors, actions, and strengths. In order to enhance the reliability and integrity of the findings of the research, different techniques were employed, such as triangulation and peer debriefing. The improvement of researcher triangulation was achieved through the involvement of two separate researchers (the primary author and secondary coders), with the aim of ensuring the coding results' reliability and consistency [28]. The examination of the study outcomes involved the inclusion of two peer debriefers. The data analysis and results were evaluated by the second author, who offered assistance and critical suggestions.

Table 1. Characteristic of participants

ID	Participant Background	Working time (years)	Affiliation
P1	Associate Head of Department	14	Dunhuang Mogao Grottos Management
P2	Associate Head of Department	18	Dunhuang Mogao Grottos Management
P3	Department Manager	10	Dunhuang Mogao Grottos Management
P4	Project Manager	5	Tencent
P5	Associate Head	14	Dunhuang Mogao Grottos Management
P6	Staff	2	Cultural and Creative Company
P7	Customer	1	Student
P8	Customer	0.5	Student
P9	Customer	0.5	Self-employed
P10	Customer	0.5	Self-employed

4   Findings and Discussion

Four actors and their roles in building a cultural tourism co-creation platform were identified: 1) platform owner: collect image data and shares resources with other actors, 2) platform partners: co-create the cultural products through user-centered design thinking, 3) technological provider: empowers the digital platform construction through technology compacity, 4) platform customers: engage actively in co-creation platforms through phygital experience. Table 2 states the different actors and their roles and actions in building a cultural tourism co-creation platform.

4.1   Platform Owner: Collect Image Data and Share Resources with Other Actors

Dunhuang Mogao Grottos Management is the owner of the platform and is open to obtaining resources, including digital images of grottoes, architecture, and murals. In

2006, Dunhuang Mogao Grottos Management established the digital center which was renamed the Institute for the Digitization of Cultural Relics in 2014. The institute is in charge of digitizing information regarding both fixed and movable cultural treasures so that it may be collected, processed, stored, transmitted, exchanged, and shown. As of 2023, data collection for more than 255 caves has been completed.

> "We established the Digital Center in 2006 and then devoted ourselves to the preservation of grottoes, in which digitalization is the direction of our efforts, after more than 10 years of development, our Dunhuang Mogao Grottos Management has been in the advanced stage of digitalization, during this period, we have maintained an open mind and sought external cooperation to promote the sustainable use of Dunhuang culture" from P2.

The interviewees state that Dunhuang Mogao Grottos Management continues to open digital cultural resources for society, calling on various stakeholders to promote Mogao culture. Therefore, they created a collaborative platform to share our digital images of architecture for organizations and other people to use. For example, in the online channel, they developed the digital Dunhuang mini-programs and Dunhuang digital Dunhuang Hidden Scripture Cave with Tencent (one of the largest technology providers in China). In the offline channel, they authorized their digital cultural resources for Dunhuang Cultural and Creative Company, then the designer from the company develops creative souvenirs based on these digital images, meanwhile, Respondents state that Dunhuang Mogao Grottos Management also engages in the design process because they have expertized in Dunhuang element. Except for this, Dunhuang Mogao Grottos Management also independently designs its own cultural products. The priority in designing cultural products for Dunhuang Mogao Grottos Management is to promote the Dunhuang culture by developing its own cultural products but considering the customers' needs.

> "We first have to screen what things and elements in our Dunhuang Grottoes, not only an element, not only the image, but also the cultural meaning of the meaning, we want to make a thing that can be promoted, and then we combine with the third party, let the third party develop, at the same time, we also have a part of our own design, because we have our own brand." from P5

> "As a cultural institution, Dunhuang Mogao Grottos Management is a unit carrying this mission of the state, so our primary purpose in making cultural and creative products is definitely not to make money, we cannot do this kind of thing that loses money, because after all, the design of cultural and creative products needs to be combined with the local society, so our primary consideration is culture, and culture is the inheritance and transformation and collision of culture and art." from P5

> "When we design cultural and creative products, we don't want Dunhuang to always be the kind of high-minded, difficult to approach, or very obscure in the hearts of young people, but still consider the aesthetics and needs of young people." from P6.

4.2   Platform Partners: Co-create the Cultural Products Through User-Centered Design Thinking

The company, social organization, and art creator are the platform partners. The role of these organizations is to design a creative product. Huawei is one of the key partners in cocreate with Dunhuang Mogao Grottos Management, designing a three-dimensional nine-colored deer, which accesses platform customers. Also, individuals can apply for Dunhuang Mogao Grottos Management to use these digital images, and they can design art products using these images. More importantly, they can post these works on the platform through the Dunhuang Mogao Grottos Management verification. Besides, social organizations, such as universities, and schools, can use these images to teach students. Therefore, the platform partners are multiple, which helps with diversified cultural product co-creation based on the Dunhuang Culture.

> "In 2020, we partnered with Huawei group to create a Huawei AR map, visitors can use the mobile phones we provide to look outside the grotto to see some mural images in the grotto, including nine-colored deer, flying sky, etc., to provide visitors with an immersive technology experience" from P1.

> "We can license to different groups, such as schools, and art creation institutions about Dunhuang murals and other materials, they can create their own, and after completing the creation, they can freely choose to upload to the platform, to give more consumers choices, but also to get benefits." From P2.

4.3   Technological Provider: Empower the Platform Construction and Operation Through Technology Compacity

Tencent is the platform technological provider, the role of the organization is to provide technological support. For example, with the help of Dunhuang providing a solution for the digitization of Dunhuang assets, Tencent used blockchain technology to provide a reliable base for creating, purchasing, and verifying digital products.

> "The project of the material library, you can understand the product that we jointly created with the Dunhuang Mogao Grottos Management, it does not mean that I may only be involved in a part, but that we have created a new industry solution from scratch. At that time, we discussed with the institute that the cultural museum industry is the digitization of cultural relics assets, and where its pain points are, they told us that the pain point was that they wanted to open up, but they did not know how to protect it, the first pain point." from P4

Besides, Tencent is Dunhuang Mogao Grottos Management's strategic partner with the Cultural Heritage Digital Creative Technology joint lab. In the past two years, the lab has created key cultural platforms and products. For example, an avatar named Jiayao is used for tourism live streaming, etc., now the avatar can be used as an online television program.

Moreover, Tencent employed gaming technology to design the digital Dunhuang Hidden Scripture Cave, which is among the first business actions to use gaming technology for cultural service innovation.

"The project of the material library, you can understand the product that we jointly created with the Dunhuang Mogao Grottos Management, it does not mean that I may only be involved in a part, but that we have created a new industry solution from scratch. At that time, we discussed with the institute that the cultural museum industry is the digitization of cultural relics assets, and where its pain points are, they told us that the pain point was that they wanted to open up, but they did not know how to protect it, the first pain point." from P4

"We just happened to have a strategic cooperation between the Dunhuang Mogao Grottos Management and our Tencent to set up a joint technology laboratory, so we used the ability of Tencent Interactive Entertainment of our game group to create this virtual human to help the researchers of the branch to create this virtual human." from P4

4.4 Platform Customers: Engage Actively in Co-creation Platforms Through Pygital Experiences

Tourists and people interested in Mogao Grottos culture are platform customers, they are active users of the co-creation platforms, Meanwhile, they can purchase items from the Dunhuang digital material library for personal use, also engage with platforms to experience virtual caves accessed through personalized avatars (e.g., Dunhuang Digital Hidden Scripture Cave project), and these platforms provide new touchpoints for the customer. Hence, such endeavors can inspire customers to explore Dunhuang Mago Grottos physically. Take the Dunhuang Digital Hidden Scripture Cave project as an example, The respondents perceived a higher level of personalization when they accessed the platform [29], which improved their immersive digital experience. Moreover, in the pre-trip stage, such a digital platform is considered a virtual product for people who can't physically visit Dunhuang Mago Grottos, offering knowledge introduction. During the trip, respondents stated that some touchpoints or context from the platform can be cued when they physically see Mago Grottos, and they have an emotional connection with these touchpoints, such as murals, which have a positive impact on their physical experience, even if they have a phygital experience [30].

"The design of this digital Hidden Gold Cave project is very interesting, through the design of this gamification, we can understand the history of the Hidden Gold Cave, we see the cave on the ground to provide a very good knowledge of the pavement, and then in this space, I can freely choose the items we want to see, and we are able to choose our personalized avatars to enter the virtual space, which greatly enriches our experience"-from P7.

"When I visit the cave, I think of the scene where I traveled to that place in the game, and it makes me feel as if the artifact is not just an object in front of you, it seems to talk and tell me some story."-from P8.

Table 2. A overview of actors' roles and actions on service ecosystem properties

Actors	Main activities	Example
Platform owner	Data collection and research on caves, Open for resources for actors, build a loyal relationship with customers and technological providers	Institute for the Digitization of Cultural Relics
Platform partners	Provide creative design services	Huawei, Dunhuang cultural and Creative company or social organizations
Technological provider	Provide technological support, such as virtual reality, augmented reality, blockchain, and avatar	Tencent culture and tourism
Platform Customers	Purchase products and behave in the virtual world	Mogao tourists or people interested in Mogao culture

4.5 Searching for Cultural Tourism Co-creation Ecosystem with Chinese Characteristics: A Mogao Grotto's Example

While actors and roles of cultural tourism co-creation platforms from a service ecosystem perspective have been explored, their interaction and the effect of such actors on value co-creation are not enough to understand these practices. The introduction of modern western-constructed co-creation practices links with the service ecosystem, essentially exploring new forms of destination practices and behaviors that modify China's co-creation platform construction from a service ecosystem perspective. Thus, guided by the third-order emergence approach [32], we proposed a new service ecosystem framework (Fig. 1). In general, there are two main characteristics that the cultural tourism co-creation ecosystem in China should draw much attention. One of those is the emergence of new value cocreation through the ecosystem is a goal-directed behavior [32]. The main goal of building the cultural tourism co-creation p is to promote the Dunhuang culture and its motivations to influence multiple actors' actions. Achieving the goal is not simple, since values of emergence are diverse through the service ecosystem properties, including cultural value, technological value, educational value, creative value, and emotional value.

Although these values exchanged from multiple actors of Mogao grottos are not inclusive of all the cultural tourism destination practices, they present actions of China's destination management organization to boost the emergence of these values through the ecosystems, these values are worth exploring because China's DMO's efforts can provide a guideline to search for new cultural tourism co-creation ecosystem.

1) Cultural value. The findings reveal that the new service innovations (e.g., digital hidden scriptures) and cultural products have boosted the cultural value of Dunhuang Mogao. For example, consumers who experienced these services expressed their positive attitudes toward their cultural values. Also, Mogao Grottos management states

that such innovative practices promote the Dunhuang culture for tourists through these new touchpoints.

2) Technological value. As a technological provider, Tencent is striving for an emerging area to exert its technological value. Moreover, Tencent's vision is to help with the revival of traditional Chinese culture through its technological capacity. Hence, respondents stated that Mogao grottos provide a testing area for Tencent's technological capacity. In addition, the management of the Mogao grottos has also made efforts to enhance their data collection practices pertaining to the digital imaging of the grottos.

3) Educational value. The opening of digital images to the faculty at the university can provide a vivid aspect of the art in Dunhuang, such as the nine-colored deer. These public resources offer a genuine representation complete with scientific facts gleaned from the experts at Mogao Grottos. These academics are able to give lectures in which they elaborate on aspects of the Magao. Students find themselves motivated as a result to either visit the Dunhuang Grottos in person or investigate them electronically. Even yet, a few of them have been inspired to play a part in the administration of the Mogao grottos.

4) Creative value. The symbolic significance of new cultural product design was highlighted. Cultural Creative Center respondents said we stressed the importance of our cultural products' creative value. The different phases of the cocreation process gave rise to every aspect of the final product, from the selection of Dunhuang materials to the debate over rough sketches. We also consult with Dunhuang culture specialists to acquire insight into the meaning of elements during the product design stage, according to respondents from a cultural and creative company.

5) Emotional value. The introduction of novel service innovations, such as digital hidden scripture, has the potential to enhance the emotional value experienced by customers. According to the respondents, gamification offers a means through which individuals may engage with and explore narratives and historical events from the past. This interactive approach is perceived as both entertaining and enjoyable. Furthermore, we have the option to select our genuine Dunhuang elements at no cost, thereby facilitating the process of designing our artwork. The scientific explanations behind these elements may evoke a sense of curiosity regarding the Mogao grottos.

5   Conclusion, Limitation, and Further Research

In the past twenty years, the extant research in value creation has emphasized the customers' focus on customer-firm interactions to advance our understanding of customer's roles and actions in this experience economy [14, 16, 31]. A common limitation of service-dominant logic arises from a lack of role of the institution in the value co-creation process [1]. Hence, A service ecosystem perspective should be paid more academic attention to clearly understand the mechanism of actors' coordination and cooperation [1, 32]. This study contributes to answering the research direction not only to empirically investigate actors' roles and actions from a service ecosystem perspective, as responding to the call for research in the literature [2] but to consider the service ecosystem through a case study of destination. To this end, we propose the framework for the ecosystem in regard

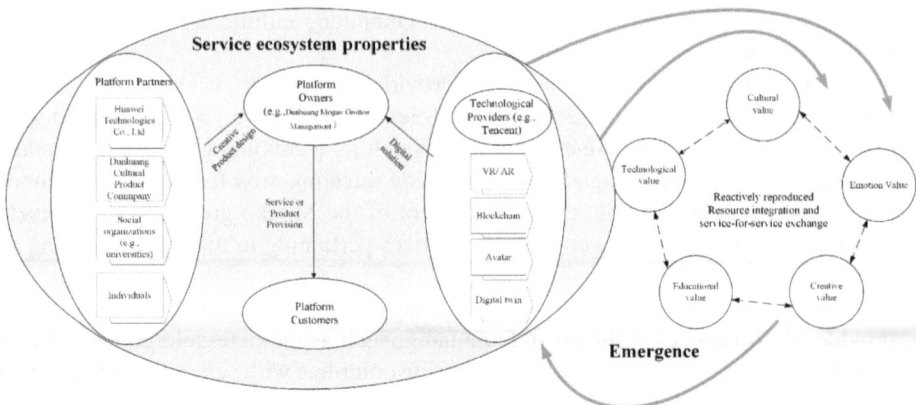

Fig. 1. The framework of the cultural co-creation ecosystem of Dunhuang Mogao Grottos

to the cultural tourism co-creation platform. The novel framework emphasizes the role of digital technologies in empowering the digitalization of destinations, hence linking the connection between technology and DMOs' service innovation. Also, the framework is based on a cultural tourism cocreation ecosystem with Chinese characteristics, and scant research attention has been paid to this.

In previous studies on the value creation of digital services in the context of tourism and hospitality [33, 34], we can provide new insight into several grounds. Firstly, this study adopts a comprehensive framework that includes all four actors and their activities within a service ecosystem, in contrast to earlier studies that only focus on the customer's perspective or the perspectives of related stakeholders such as employees, while examining the value co-creation process. Specifically, this study further sheds new insight to center on DMO's service innovation and answers questions about how a destination without technology compacity steps into a road of digitalization service through coordination and cooperation with actors. With the popularity of digitalization toward the goal of being a smart destination for DMOs, we believe that DMOs will seek more digital service innovation that could benefit their future actions. This research thus provides a novel research initiative for future service provisions. The emergence of five values from the service ecosystem has been identified, including cultural value, technological value, educational value, creative value, and emotional value. These values that are derived from the properties of the service ecosystem should serve as a source of inspiration for the future practices of destination management organizations.

Several limitations should be acknowledged for future research. First, the interview data were collected from Dunhuang Mogao Grottos in China, Hence, the findings lack other populations of interest. Therefore, findings should be expanded on other nations, which improve the generosity of the research. Second, the research is among the first studies on the multiple actors' actors' roles and actions from one case of destination, future research should be considered in other destinations even hospitality services.

References

1. Vargo, S.L., Lusch, R.F.: Institutions and axioms: an extension and update of service-dominant logic. J. Acad. Mark. Sci. **44**(1), 5–23 (2016)
2. Xu, Y., Hazée, S., So, K.K.F., Li, K.D., Malthouse, E.C.: An evolutionary perspective on the dynamics of service platform ecosystems for the sharing economy. J. Bus. Res. **135**, 127–136 (2021)
3. Webster, F.E., Lusch, R.F.: Elevating marketing: marketing is dead! Long live marketing! J. Acad. Mark. Sci. **41**, 389–399 (2013)
4. Okumus, B., Bilgihan, A.: Proposing a model to test smartphone users' intention to use smart applications when ordering food in restaurants. J. Hosp. Tour. Technol. **5**(1), 31–49 (2014)
5. Prentice, C., Weaven, S., Wong, I.A.: Linking AI quality performance and customer engagement: the moderating effect of AI preference. Int. J. Hosp. Manag. **90**, 102629 (2020)
6. Wong, I.A., Huang, J., Lin, Z., Jiao, H.: Smart dining, smart restaurant, and smart service quality (SSQ). Int. J. Contemp. Hosp. M. **34**(6), 2272–2297 (2022)
7. Lu, Q., Xie, X., Parlikad, A.K., Schooling, J.M.: Digital twin-enabled anomaly detection for built asset monitoring in operation and maintenance. Automat. Constr. **118**, 103277 (2020)
8. Tussyadiah, I.: A review of research into automation in tourism: launching the annals of tourism research curated collection on artificial intelligence and robotics in tourism. Ann. Tour. Res. **81**, 102883 (2020)
9. Beck, J., Rainoldi, M., Egger, R.: Virtual reality in tourism: a state-of-the-art review. Tour. Rev. **74**(3), 586–612 (2019)
10. Flavián, C., Ibáñez-Sánchez, S., Orús, C.: The impact of virtual, augmented and mixed reality technologies on the customer experience. J. Bus. Res. **100**, 547–560 (2019)
11. Hollebeek, L.D., Clark, M.K., Andreassen, T.W., Sigurdsson, V., Smith, D.: Virtual reality through the customer journey: framework and propositions. J. Retail. Consum. Serv. **55**, 102056 (2020)
12. Zhong, L., Verma, R., Wei, W., Morrsion, A.M., Yang, L.: Multi-stakeholder perspectives on the impacts of service robots in urban hotel rooms. Technol. Soc. **68**, 101846 (2022)
13. Vargo, S.L., Lusch, R.F.: Service-dominant logic: continuing the evolution. J. Acad. Mark. Sci. **36**(1), 1–10 (2008)
14. Vargo, S.L., Lusch, R.F.: Evolving to a new dominant logic for marketing. J. Mark. **68**(1), 1–17 (2004)
15. Grönroos, C., Gummerus, J.: The service revolution and its marketing implications: service logic vs service-dominant logic. J. Serv. Theor. Pract. **24**(3), 206–229 (2014)
16. Lemon, K.N., Verhoef, P.C.: Understanding customer experience throughout the customer journey. J. Mark. **80**(6), 69–96 (2016)
17. Homburg, C., Jozić, D., Kuehnl, C.: Customer experience management: toward implementing an evolving marketing concept. J. Acad. Mark. Sci. **45**(3), 377–401 (2017)
18. Prebensen, N.K., Rosengren, S.: Experience value as a function of hedonic and utilitarian dominant services. Int. J. Contemp. Hosp. M. **28**(1), 113–135 (2016)
19. Frías Jamilena, D.M., Polo Peña, A.I., Rodríguez Molina, M.Á.: The effect of value-creation on consumer-based destination brand equity. J. Travel Res. **56**(8), 1011–1031 (2016)
20. Shin, H.: A critical review of robot research and future research opportunities: adopting a service ecosystem perspective. Int. J. Contemp. Hosp. M. **34**(6), 2337–2358 (2022)
21. Prahalad, C.K., Ramaswamy, V.: Co-creation experiences: the next practice in value creation. J. Interact. Mark. **18**(3), 5–14 (2004)
22. Vargo, S.L., Akaka, M.A., Vaughan, C.M.: Conceptualizing value: a service-ecosystem view. J. Creat. Val. **3**(2), 117–124 (2017)

23. Baron, S., Patterson, A., Maull, R., Warnaby, G.: Feed people first: a service eco system perspective on innovative food waste reduction. J. Serv. Res. **21**(1), 135–150 (2017)
24. Brodie, R.J., Fehrer, J.A., Jaakkola, E., Conduit, J.: Actor engagement in networks: defining the conceptual domain. J. Serv. Res. **22**(2), 173–188 (2019)
25. Kelly, S.E., Bourgeault, I., Dingwall, R.: Qualitative interviewing techniques and styles. SAGE Handb. Qualit. Methods Health Res. **19**, 307–326 (2010)
26. Hsieh, H.F., Shannon, S.E.: Three approaches to qualitative content analysis. Qual. Health Res. **15**, 1277–1288 (2005)
27. Strauss, A., Corbin, J.: Basics of qualitative research techniques (1998)
28. Campbell, J.L., Quincy, C., Osserman, J., Pedersen, O.K.: Coding in-depth semistruc tured interviews: problems of unitization and intercoder reliability and agreement. Sociol. Methods. Res. **42**(3), 294–320 (2013)
29. Jaakkola, E., Terho, H.: Service journey quality: conceptualization, measurement and customer outcomes. J. Serv. Manag. **32**(6), 1–27 (2021)
30. Batat, W., Hammedi, W.: The extended reality technology (ERT) framework for designing customer and service experiences in phygital settings: a service research agenda. J. Serv. Manag. **34**(1), 10–33 (2023)
31. Pine, B.J., Gilmore, J.H.: The Experience Economy. Harvard Business Press (2011)
32. Vargo, S.L., Peters, L., Kjellberg, H., Koskela-Huotari, K., Nenonen, S., Polese, F., et al.: Emergence in marketing: an institutional and ecosystem framework. J. Acad. Mark. Sci. **51**(1), 2–22 (2023)
33. Zhong, L., Coca-Stefaniak, J.A., Morrison, A.M., Yang, L., Deng, B.: Technology acceptance before and after COVID-19: no-touch service from hotel robots. Tour. Rev. **77**(4), 1062–1080 (2022)
34. Xiong, X., Wong, I.A., Yang, F.X.: Are we behaviorally immune to COVID-19 through robots? Ann. Tour. Res. **91**, 103312 (2021)

Hot Topics in Travel Digital Transformation: A Swiss Perspective

Alessandro Inversini[1](✉), Meng-Mei Chen[1], Amélie Keller[1], and Roland Schegg[2]

[1] EHL Hospitality Business School, HES-SO, University of Applied Sciences and Arts Western Switzerland, Lausanne, Switzerland
{alessandro.inversini,maggie.chen-holleran,amelie.keller}@ehl.ch
[2] Institute of Tourism, University of Applied Sciences and Arts Western Switzerland, Sierre, Switzerland
roland.schegg@hevs.ch

Abstract. The advance of technologies has profoundly changed customers' expectation and behaviors, as well as companies' business processes and business models. Given the critical importance of digital transformation, surprisingly, there is scarce research documenting and sharing the knowledge, experience, and insights from digital transformation practitioners, especially in the tourism domain. This research aims to understand the perspectives and actions of Swiss tourism stakeholders in pursuing the digital transformation process. The research data was collected through interviews with tourism stakeholders. The interviews were analyzed through both theme identification and human synthesis. The findings are tourism stakeholders conduct digital transformation for better customer experiences, operation efficiency and profitability, and data collection for better management. Digital transformation needs technology as the tool and data as input and output while keeping in mind that all decisions should be customer-centric. The challenges include data ownership, various data formats, data analysis, and data sharing. Yet, stakeholders are optimistic about the future of digital transformation and willing to collaborate. Both technology and the right digital mindset are required to succeed in digital transformation. Technology can be used to save employees from repetitive tasks and focus on human interactions to create customer-centric experiences. Nevertheless, technology should never replace the human aspect of hospitality.

Keywords: digital transformation · resilient tourism · Switzerland · human interaction · customer centricity

1 Introduction

The advance of technologies has profoundly changed customers' expectation and behaviors, as well as companies' business processes and business models. Customers are empowered with technologies to search for endless information from a myriad of information sources, compare products and experiences based on other users' experiences and reviews, and finally purchase from the most familiar or cheapest channel. Companies

© The Author(s) 2024
K. Berezina et al. (Eds.): ENTER 2024, SPBE, pp. 195–206, 2024.
https://doi.org/10.1007/978-3-031-58839-6_21

face the challenges of acquiring and retaining these most informed customers in the history. Furthermore, companies must adopt their business processes and even their value propositions to stay competitive in the market. Hence, leveraging digital transformation to optimize the business process and serving customers better is one of the most critical challenges facing most companies.

Researchers have advocated the importance of digital transformation, identified critical success factors to ensure the success of the transformation, and measured the benefits of digital transformation. On top of this, tourism research has predicted the heavy transformation of travel related organization by adopting real-time consumer intelligence, artificial intelligence, real-time contextualization and personalization and dynamic business analytics [1]. Existing literature, mainly focus on the development and deployment of digital technology in the wider travel field to collect data and optimize back end functions towards enhancing competitive advantage [2]; even if this is an important avenue of research, the human-side of smart destinations and digital transformation should be taken into account [3].

A series of semi-structured interviews have been conducted with 15 practitioners to gain insights on the state-of-the-art of digital transformation processes, especially in the wider tourism domain. Among the other thing, each practitioner was asked to describe and comment a successful case of digital transformation in their practices. The paper documents digital transformation through real cases, providing practitioners' points of view with respect to the pure operational point of view but also from a customer experience perspective.

2   Literature Review

2.1 Digital Transformation

The transformation brought about by digital advancements and the resulting innovation in business models has significantly changed consumer expectations and actions. This has created pressure on traditional companies and caused disruptions across various markets [4]. The digitalization of the customer experience, particularly in the tourism sector, is not only reshaping competition but also altering the influence of different industries and enterprises [1]. The widespread utilization of big data and the emergence of novel digital technologies like artificial intelligence (AI), blockchain, internet-of-things (IoT), and robotics are predicted to have extensive consequences for businesses [5]. While not all of these technologies might meet their expected potential, their collective introduction underscores the necessity for companies to undergo digital transformation.

Consumer behavior is undergoing shifts in response to the digital revolution [4]. Market data demonstrates a move towards online purchases, with digital interactions playing a crucial role in shaping the customer journey and impacting both online and offline sales [6]. New digital (social) tools have enabled consumers to be more interconnected, knowledgeable, empowered, and engaged [7], empowering consumers to participate in value creation by personalizing products, engaging in last-mile distribution tasks, and aiding other consumers through sharing product reviews [8].

Furthermore, the introduction of the latest digital technologies (such as AI, Blockchain, IoT and Robots) is anticipated to fundamentally transform consumers' expectations [9]. Consequently, the adoption of these technologies could easily become the new standard and challenge traditional business norms.

Firms that fail to adapt to these shifts risk losing appeal with customers and may be replaced by competitors who effectively leverage such technologies. Therefore, firms need to undergo a process of digital transformation. Digital transformation can be described as a company-wide digital shift that leads to the development of new business models [e.g. 10]. The advent of digital transformation brings forward novel business models, introducing fresh business logic to create and capture value [11]. Digital transformation affects the entirety of a company and its operational methods [11], going beyond mere digitalization. It restructures processes to alter a firm's business logic (or its approach to value creation [12]. Furthermore, digital transformation leverages digital technologies to facilitate cross-border interactions with suppliers, customers, and competitors [4]. Consequently, digital technologies can confer a competitive advantage by transforming the organization, either by enhancing established core competences or fostering new ones. Hence, digital transformation is intrinsically tied to strategic modifications in the business model due to the integration of digital technologies [4].

2.2 Digital Transformation in Travel

The field of travel and tourism has always been prone to heavy use of digital technologies [13] due to its information-intensive nature; over the years, researchers and practitioners have discussed the impact of digital technology on business models [14] and travel experience [15]. Gretzel et al. (2015) highlighted how the integration of these technologies has led to the creation of more personalized and seamless travel experiences, where travelers can access real-time information, make informed decisions, and engage with travel providers through multiple digital touchpoints [16]. Moreover, the digital landscape has catalyzed the rise of online travel agencies, peer-to-peer accommodation platforms, and other novel business models, altering traditional industry structures and challenging established players [14].

The impact of digital transformation on traveler behaviors and expectations has also garnered significant attention. With the proliferation of social media platforms and user-generated content, travelers are increasingly relying on digital channels to seek inspiration, gather insights, and share their experiences [17]. Additionally, the advent of mobile applications and location-based services has empowered travelers to access on-the-go information, enhance navigation, and engage in location-specific activities [18].

Moreover, the field of travel has been witnessing the rise of multi-sided platforms [19] and the shift towards a travel digital ecosystem (already predicted in 2008 by [20]); this has not only provided convenience but has also presented challenges related to data privacy, security, and the digital divide [21]. Scholars have emphasized the need for travel organizations to navigate these complexities while harnessing the potential of digital technologies to meet evolving customer demands and maintain competitive relevance.

One other prominent concept that has emerged over the years in the field of tourism is the one of smart destinations [2]; this has emerged as a novel notion in the realm of tourism and urban planning, propelled by the integration of cutting-edge technologies and data-driven strategies [16]. Smart destinations harness extensive data derived from sensors and smartphones to enable technology-mediated value co-creation in real-time [3]. Notably, information and communication technologies continue to generate both fresh opportunities and new challenges for businesses in the tourism sector. Emerging technologies such as real-time consumer intelligence, artificial intelligence, real-time contextualization, personalization, and dynamic business analytics are currently focal points in tourism research, instigating transformative changes within the industry [22].

Destinations are here seen as ecosystems leveraging advanced digital infrastructure, such as the internet-of-things (IoT), artificial intelligence (AI), and data analytics, to enhance the overall tourist experience and optimize the management of resources and services [3]. Researchers emphasize that smart destinations aim to provide travelers with seamless, personalized, and context-aware experiences [2]. Nonetheless, as travel is both 'information intensive' and 'relationship intensive', researchers are also claiming a central role of the 'human factor' within the digital technology landscape [3].

Therefore, moving from this landscape, this research aimed at understanding the most relevant topics in the field of digital transformation in travel. Exploratory in nature, the research will focus on a specific country, Switzerland, and the broader travel field.

3   Methodology

3.1   Data Collection

In order to generate a better understanding of digital transformation happening in the broad Swiss travel field, a series of exploratory interviews have been conducted. The aim of the research was to understand the most relevant topics in the field of digital transformation in travel with a particular focus on the Swiss market.

Through purposeful sampling, 15 interviewees were identified; those belong to (i) tourism technology providers, (ii) DMOs, (iii) trade associations, (iv) consultants, and (v) academics (Table 1). The interviews took place between November 2022 and May 2023. The structured interview was conducted in different languages (German, French, Italian, and English). Interviews were then transcribed and translated into English for analysis purposes. Translation and meaning consistency was ensured by multilingual researchers on the project.

3.2   Data Analysis

The process of analysis involved two stages.

[Stage 1] Data Exploration and Theme Identification. The raw transcribed text collected from interviews was cleaned to allow for uniform processing. The cleaning process involved homogenizing formats (e.g., different capitalizations and inconsistent paragraphing). Unnecessary titles were also removed under the condition that they were not embedded in relevant sections of the text. The output was formatted in sentence case, with one paragraph corresponding to one interview. Interviewee names were also added at the beginning of each paragraph for the analysis software to identify different speakers. Then, the cleaned data were analyzed using Leximancer software (leximancer.com, edition 5).

Table 1. List of interviews

ID	Organization Type	Language
1	Digital Technology Solution Provider	English
2	World Heritage Site Association	French
3	Destination Marketing and Management Organization	Italian
4	Digital Technology Solution Provider	German
5	Digital Technology Solution Provider	French
6	Research Institution	English
7	Destination Marketing and Management Organization	French
8	Research Institution	German
9	Consultant & Digital Technology Solution Provider	French
10	Hotel Owner	German
11	Research Institution	French
12	Consultant and Research Institution	German
13	Event Organization	Italian
14	Research Institution	English
15	Destination Marketing and Management Organization	German

Leximancer [15] is a text-mining software that analyzes text content and presents findings in a bubble map. Leximancer adopts a two-stage approach for semantic extraction and relational extraction, respectively. Leximancer first conducts relative co-occurrence of words, names these first-level findings as *concepts*, then uses these *concepts* to reclassify text again, names these high-level findings as *themes*, and presents *concepts* and *themes* findings in visuals (bubble maps). Leximancer has been widely used in tourism and business research [16, 17]. The default settings of Leximancer were used, except manipulating Concept Seed Editor - merged concepts including customer-customers, guest-guests, hotel-hotels, project-projects, tourism-tourists-tourist, worked-work; Concept Coding Settings - hidden concepts including able, certain, course, examples, try; Concept Map - % theme size: 35%; and Concept Map - % of Concepts Shown: 100%.

[Stage 2] Inductive Coding and Synthesis. Although Leximancer's theme identification reveals the emerging themes, to gain granular insights further, transcripts were also independently analyzed with an inductive coding strategy to identify the key insights. The objective of this inductive coding analysis was to cluster the main categories of interest for digital transformation in Switzerland, thus informing the aim of this research.

4   Results and Discussions

4.1   Data Exploration: Themes Identification

Figure 1 presents the frequencies of the most popular words, while Fig. 2 presents the visualization of Theme Identification from Leximancer. In terms of frequency (Fig. 1) 'data' and 'digital' appear on top of the list, while 'information' and 'system' have less frequency. This can be an indication of the data-driven digital transformation that is happening in the travel field.

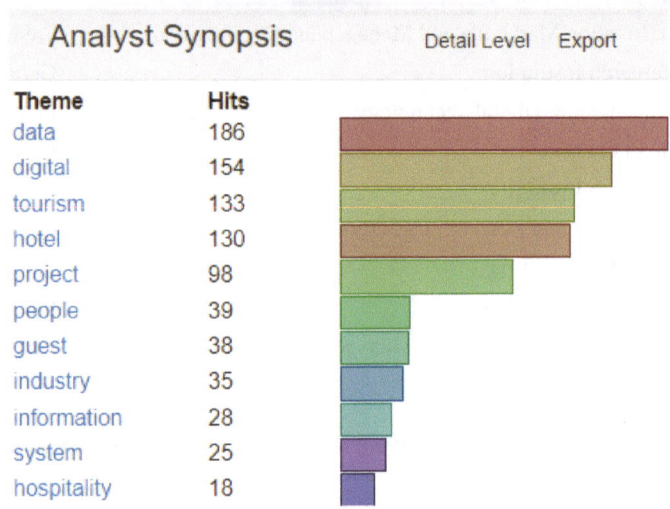

Fig. 1. Words Frequency

Looking at Fig. 2, the warm color bubbles (orange and yellow) are hot topics, while the cold color bubbles (blue and purple) are less discussed topics. The relative positions of bubbles indicate the relatedness between *themes*. As shown in Fig. 1, themes that emerged from the interview transcripts are data, digital, tourism, and hotels. Given that the interviewees speak about how tourism can benefit and be more resilient thanks to a digital transformation, it makes sense that data, digital, tourism, and hotel are the largest and most important themes. The two themes at the top (industry and hospitality) reflect that the hospitality industry started by doing everything by hand. There was a need for transformation regarding marketing and management (hotel theme), which is heavily linked to data and digitalization.

What seems to be important in this data exploration stage is the nature of the digital transformation happening in travel that is clearly data-driven [5] and project based; it is interesting how both 'people' and 'guest' appear in the external part of the figure but are connected with the 'hotel' and 'digital' respectively; this seems connected with a possibility of working with digital transformation to customer experience [15] also from a host (i.e. people) point of view. Lastly, digital transformation is connected with

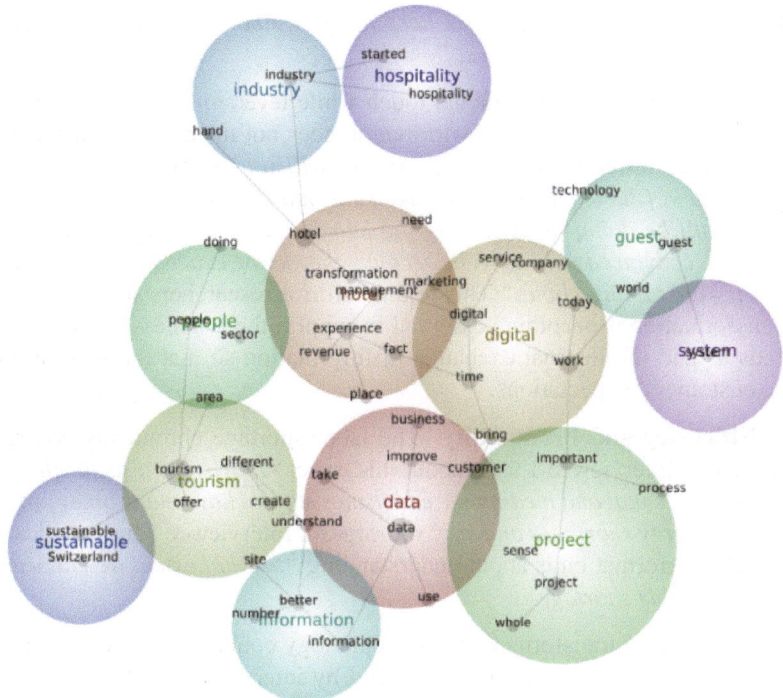

Fig. 2. All concepts

creativity and understanding of data; it is sustainable "done by the people" with inward and outward looking components [3].

Surprisingly enough, in this first data exploration analysis, there are not keyword connected with keywords clusters related concepts such as competitiveness and efficiency [2].

4.2 Hot Topics in Travel Digital Transformation

Our inductive coding analysis revealed that digital transformation can be conducted for three distinct purposes: (i) to enhance the guest experience, (ii) to improve efficiency and profitability, and (iii) to collect data for better management. If those are the streamlined themes, there is an emergent topic that is transversal to the whole interviews which can be summarized as (iv) human-centered digital transformation.

Enhance the Guest Experience. As underlined by interviewee 15, digital transformation in travel "*should simplify the internal processes, and increase the guest experience, and always have in mind the tourism stakeholders of the destination. Only in such a trio we can be successful*". This, as maintained by several interviewees, is the essence of travel, as interviewee 7 stated, "*[we should] not forget that tourism is made to travel. It's about having an experience; it's about making people dream. Don't forget to be customer-centric. That's the key in the end, it's to talk to people and make them dream.*"

Similarly, as put by interviewee 1 *"[in hospitality] we have the passion to deliver the best possible experience for our guests"*.

Therefore, maintaining the personal touch while leveraging digital technologies is essential and accelerating digital transformation does not intend to replace this human interaction as interviewee 1 stated: *"Digitalization will not take away the personal touch, [it] will help them [the employees] to make sure that they know what they are doing, but they will still be doing or delivering the human part of it in a more safe or more secure or more convinced way as well, because they know exactly what they are doing and what they are talking about."* This finding affirms researchers suggestion [16] that digital transformation is becoming essential to support the seamless communication of these needs as and the internal exchange of information so that the service provided meets the customers' expectations.

Improve Efficiency and Profitability. The labor shortage chronically confronts the tourism industry. Interviewee 1 talks about this issue: *"Tourism is a sector that is characterized by many small and medium-sized businesses that have many other problems to solve, such as energy shortages and staff shortages"*. Interviewee 1 further adds that the travel digital transformation is about understanding *"to what extent we can use digital tools to alleviate this shortage"*.

In addition, digital transformation and technology could provide feasible relief and attract young talents to this industry, as shared by interviewee 1: *"I see again young people being extremely passionate about this hospitality universe that we all live in, and I know for a fact that hospitality is something you do by passion and because you love being there and taking care of people. So, I'm very much looking forward to giving a little bit of help to this industry by digitalizing a bit more and making it interesting also for the younger generations."*

Automating recurrent tasks will help employees use their time more efficiently and improve performance. This will also affect operations as interviewee 9 stated, *"[digital transformation will allow] to take advantage of the number of resources that we are lucky enough to have available in our territories in Switzerland [...] to propose high-value-added offers for visitors, which can strengthen the attractiveness of the territory"*.

The above opinions are examples of digitalization can change business process and business logic as identified by researchers [10, 11]. However, digital transformation is mostly about optimizing processes to achieve desired outcomes [10–12]; as stated by interviewee 6, *"it's not really about the technology, it's more about 'what process are you fixing."*

One opinion which emerged frequently is related to the benefits of data: to fully unlock the power of data-driven digital transformation, stakeholders need to break down the boundaries of organizations and share information and knowledge and engage in cross-fertilization. As shared by interviewees 5 and 13: *"I strongly encourage [people] to share this data anonymously of course, but to share this data within a destination, within a group, at least to help each other. That's it, because we all live in the same industry. And if the industry is doing well, we are all doing well."* (interviewee 5).

This collaboration is even more crucial at the present time, *"I find that more and more it will be necessary to collaborate between players, not necessarily from the same sector, but also from complementary sectors. This dialogue can have to do either with know-how, so how we are addressing, for example, ticketing or digital transformation, or trivially, even simply change management within the company. How this can help other industries or other companies that potentially will then find themselves part of the same ecosystem, [...] to be more and more competitive together and move into the future?"* (interviewee 13).

Collecting Data for Better Management. Often, travel organizations struggle to align the interests of the various stakeholders, leading to unsustainable management and conflicts between parties. As stated by interviewee 2, *"We cannot put in place correct and adapted measures if we do not have a sufficiently precise vision of what is happening in the perimeter."* Therefore, some interviewees mentioned that the knowledge collected from these digital technologies enables better monitoring, management, and coordination among various stakeholders in the tourism industry (interviewees 2, 3 12 and 15).

Data can provide knowledge and information on visitor numbers, behaviors, trends, and many other elements. Having access to extensive knowledge of an organization's operations is essential for smart decision-making and strategic management, considering and involving all stakeholders' interests. Data also allows for elaborate efficient, targeted marketing through creative product offerings or real-time promotion specifically customized for the customer along the journey. In this context, while data serves as an input, technology is the medium that allows the tourism stakeholders to make better decisions and put in place efficient strategies. Interviewee 2 explains: *"once we have a better idea of their behavior and the sources of these people, we may be able to treat or offer qualitative tourist experiences, which will allow us to generate more money in the area and preserve the place better. [...].The data is extremely beneficial to bring, to support our arguments and our popularization"*. It's interesting to note the similarity between the interviewees' observations and smart destination discussion, even though interviewees did not mention smart destination [2, 3, 22].

Interviewees nevertheless identified challenges associated with data ownership, comparable to researchers' concern in data security and data privacy [21]. Both interviewees 12 and 7 provided examples of these challenges: *"Tourism needs a great deal in the way of digital tools, apps and websites and so on. But everything is held and managed separately, so to say in the form of silos. So, for every topic, for every organization and for every company there is a nice website, a nice app, whatever makes sense for them. And very often, the data that is needed for this is collected repeatedly. And that, fundamentally, is not very efficient. And it is, above all, not beneficial for the quality of the data that is being collected. You must put a lot of effort into such data collection."* (interviewee 12); this was echoed also by interviewee 7 who maintained: *"There is still some way to go to know our customers better because DMOs [...] is an intermediary, so all the transactions are not going through us. So, we still have this difficulty in recovering the data and then consolidating them."* (interview 7).

Human-Centered Digital Transformation. What transversely emerged is also a profound understanding of the field of travel and tourism, where the human-to-human interaction is still crucial for the success of the travel businesses. This finding echoes with researchers' advocate that travel is both "information intensive" and "relationship intensive" [3]. As interviewees 1 and 2 maintained, customer experience should be enhanced by digital transformation. Interviewee 14 introduced the topic in this way: *"digital transformation is no longer an option. It is really a necessity - but then it is important to understand that digital transformation should not be just to improve efficiency: in the end, they should focus on catering to customers' experience."*

This becomes really operational in the example of interviewee 1: *"[the technology artifact] will help [staff] to make sure that they know what they're doing, and they will still be doing or delivering the human part of [the experience] it in a more safe or more secure or more convinced way as well."* This point of view is complemented by interviewee 2 who stated: "we can totally guarantee a human experience that is completed based on data."

5 Conclusions

This research investigates shed light on the hot topics in digital transformation as portrayed by 15 Swiss digital technology experts. There are a few emerging trends to be highlighted.

The nature of digital transformation is directly linked with data. For our experts, it is crucial to access different types of data to create a more precise picture of the travel field at destination and business level. Three emerging trends related to digital transformation, which echoed the literature in the field, are (i) the importance of enhancing guest experience, (ii) the imperative of improving efficiency and profitability, and (iii) the need to collect data for better management. These three main directions are shaping the approach of Swiss travel organizations to digital transformation.

Last but not least, one emerging theme is about the human-centered nature of travel digital transformation: the travel field should not neglect its founding strength that is the one of 'human touch'. Therefore, digital transformation should cater to enhancing human relationships in the wider travel arena. Optimization of profitability and efficiency through data should lead to improved human-centered management and experiences to foster co-creative processes (BOES).

Nevertheless, the tourism sector still faces numerous challenges related to digital transformation, including the complexity of data ownership, the heterogeneity of data formats, the difficulty in data analysis, and the openness and possibility of data sharing. Both technology and the right digital mindset are required to succeed in digital transformation. Yet, Swiss stakeholders are optimistic about the future of digital transformation and willing to collaborate because of the possible mutualization of costs and exchange of data, and to learn from each other.

5.1 Limitation and Future Work

This research is exploratory in nature and based on semi-structured interviews to Swiss travel experts. Although it sheds lights on the state of the art of digital transformation in a given country, it comes with structural limitations: (i) the purposeful sample selection does not cater for a proper representation of the industry; rather it mixes the points of view of private and public organizations working in the field of tourism and other actors such as technology providers; (ii) the geographical scope of the research is limited due to the nature of the digital transformation phenomenon. Therefore, future work should focus in minimizing these two limitations by fostering industry representativeness on an international scale.

References

1. Pesonen, J.: Management and leadership for digital transformation in tourism. In: Handbook of e-Tourism, pp. 1–34 (2020)
2. Buhalis, D., Amaranggana, A.: Smart tourism destinations enhancing tourism experience through personalisation of services. In: Tussyadiah, I., Inversini, A. (eds.) Information and Communication Technologies in Tourism 2015, pp. 377–389. Springer, Cham (2015). https://doi.org/10.1007/978-3-319-14343-9_28
3. Boes, K., Buhalis, D., Inversini, A.: Smart tourism destinations: ecosystems for tourism destination competitiveness. Int. J. Tour. Cities **2**(2), 108–124 (2016)
4. Verhoef, P.C., et al.: Digital transformation: a multidisciplinary reflection and research agenda. J. Bus. Res. **122**, 889–901 (2021)
5. Ng, I.C., Wakenshaw, S.Y.: The Internet-of-Things: review and research directions. Int. J. Res. Mark. **34**(1), 3–21 (2017)
6. Kannan, P.K.: Digital marketing: a framework, review and research agenda. Int. J. Res. Mark. **34**(1), 22–45 (2017)
7. Lamberton, C., Stephen, A.T.: A thematic exploration of digital, social media, and mobile marketing: research evolution from 2000 to 2015 and an agenda for future inquiry. J. Mark. **80**(6), 146–172 (2016)
8. Beckers, S.F., Van Doorn, J., Verhoef, P.C.: Good, better, engaged? the effect of company-initiated customer engagement behavior on shareholder value. J. Acad. Mark. Sci. **46**, 366–383 (2018)
9. Hoffman, D.L., Novak, T.P.: Consumer and object experience in the internet of things: an assemblage theory approach. J. Consum. Res. **44**(6), 1178–1204 (2018)
10. Pagani, M., Pardo, C.: The impact of digital technology on relationships in a business network. Ind. Mark. Manag. **67**, 185–192 (2017)
11. Zott, C., Amit, R.: The fit between product market strategy and business model: implications for firm performance. Strateg. Manag. J. **29**(1), 1–26 (2008)
12. Li, L., Su, F., Zhang, W., Mao, J.Y.: Digital transformation by SME entrepreneurs: a capability perspective. Inf. Syst. J. **28**(6), 1129–1157 (2018)
13. Buhalis, D., Law, R.: Progress in information technology and tourism management: 20 years on and 10 years after the Internet—the state of eTourism research. Tour. Manag. **29**(4), 609–623 (2008)
14. Perelygina, M., Kucukusta, D., Law, R.: Digital business model configurations in the travel industry. Tour. Manag. **88**, 104408 (2022)
15. Neuhofer, B., Buhalis, D., Ladkin, A.: Conceptualising technology enhanced destination experiences. J. Destin. Mark. Manag. **1**(1–2), 36–46 (2012)
16. Gretzel, U., Sigala, M., Xiang, Z., Koo, C.: Smart tourism: foundations and developments. Electron. Mark. **25**, 179–188 (2015)
17. Sigala, M., Gretzel, U. (eds.): Advances in Social Media for Travel, Tourism and Hospitality: New Perspectives, Practice and Cases. Routledge, Abingdon (2017)
18. Im, J.Y., Hancer, M.: Shaping travelers' attitude toward travel mobile applications. J. Hosp. Tour. Technol. **5**(2), 177–193 (2014)

19. Abdelkafi, N., Raasch, C., Roth, A., Srinivasan, R.: Multi-sided platforms. Electron. Mark. **29**, 553–559 (2019)
20. Xiang, Z., Wöber, K., Fesenmaier, D.R.: Representation of the online tourism domain in search engines. J. Travel Res. **47**(2), 137–150 (2008)
21. Tussyadiah, I., Li, S., Miller, G.: Privacy protection in tourism: where we are and where we should be heading for. In: Pesonen, J., Neidhardt, J. (eds.) Information and Communication Technologies in Tourism 2019, pp. 278–290. Springer, Cham (2019). https://doi.org/10.1007/978-3-030-05940-8_22
22. Gretzel, U., et al.: E-Tourism beyond COVID-19: a call for transformative research. Inf. Technol. Tour. **22**, 187–203 (2020)

Transformative Communication on Webpages from the Eudaimonic Perspective

Johanna Heinonen[1,2]($\boxtimes$) (iD), Jade Myburgh[3], and Maria Murto[3] (iD)

[1] University of Eastern Finland, Yliopistokatu 2, 80101 Joensuu, Finland
johanna.heinonen@lab.fi
[2] LAB University of Applied Sciences, Lappeenranta, Finland
[3] LAB University of Applied Sciences, Mukkulankatu 19, 15120 Lahti, Finland

Abstract. The key to creating genuinely transformative travel experiences lies in effective communication strategies. By engaging with an audience through meaningful and thought-provoking content, tourism organisations can inspire them to fulfil their life's purpose and embark on a journey of personal growth and discovery. Whether through inspiring stories, beautiful imagery, or practical tips and advice, the right content can help connect with an audience on a deeper level and create unforgettable travel experiences. This study reviewed the literature on eudaimonic communication and analysed the textual content on selected companies' web pages. By identifying specific elements and their absence, the study aimed to enhance the effectiveness of webpage communication, ultimately leading to a transformative response in the end-user. As a result, it was clear that elements of transformative and eudaimonic communication appeared on web pages, but the way they were used did not support transformation.

Keywords: transformation · communication eudaimonia · webpages · word frequency analysis

1 Introduction

The landscape of tourism has undergone a significant transformation. Previously perceived merely as a means of relaxation and leisure, it has metamorphosed into a powerful instrument for personal enlightenment and self-evolution. The emergence of transformative tourism underscores the profound capacity of travel to metamorphose individuals. This transformation is achieved by immersing individuals in foreign cultures, novel ideas, and diverse lifestyles [1]. When executed proficiently, communication lays the groundwork for genuine and transformative travel encounters, paving the way for individual advancement, unity, and a heightened commitment to preserving our environment. In this digital age, advanced technologies amplify the scope of interactive multi-channel communication, ushering in profound transformation [2]. However, further in-depth studies are imperative to tap into the vast potential of communication within transformative tourism and devise efficacious strategies that propagate sustainable and equitable tourism, e.g. Waisbord [3] and Teoh et al. [4].

K. Berezina et al. (Eds.): ENTER 2024, SPBE, pp. 207–217, 2024.
https://doi.org/10.1007/978-3-031-58839-6_22

Eudaimonic communication, which emphasises genuine well-being and human flourishing, has been identified as pivotal in advancing transformative tourism experiences and championing sustainable tourism initiatives. By acting as a bridge between tourists and indigenous communities, eudaimonic communication catalyses personal development and cross-cultural appreciation while underscoring the importance of environmental and societal responsibility [5].

This study aims to comprehend how businesses offering transformative tourism experiences harness communication from a eudaimonic standpoint. The text on company websites is scrutinised by establishing a criterion derived from extensive literature. This study is piloting the webpage analysis in more extensive research of transformative travel implemented in a project by LAB University of Applied Sciences, Jyväskylä University of Applied Sciences and the University of Eastern Finland. It not only seeks to bolster the efficacy of online communication but also intends to offer tools for corporate strategy. Furthermore, it strives to plug the existing gap in research concerning transformative, eudaimonic communication on digital platforms.

2 Communication in Transformative Tourism

Communication in Transformative Tourism is essential in creating travel experiences that change and transform people [6]. In an era dominated by digital platforms, tourism marketing and communication strategies must place paramount importance on the online realm, given its demonstrable influence on tourist behaviour [7]. Authentic communication is the linchpin in curating transformative experiences, crafting interactions that resonate with tourists and immerse them in their environment. This involves fostering a culture of transparency, inclusivity, tolerance, and synergy among locals and entities involved in tourism [8].

Lengieza et al. [22] point out that across the literature, two of the top elements of eudaimonia are self-reflection and personal meaning within the context of a travel experience. Tourists seeking eudaimonic travel would, therefore, seek out activities that would contribute to personal growth, be personally meaningful and serve as potential motivators for more expansive pro-social or pro-environmental long-term outcomes. Focusing on eudaimonia and eudaimonic communication, tourism organisations can differentiate themselves and provide a truly unique and fulfilling customer experience.

Moreover, transformative tourism supports experiences that challenge individuals, pushing them to transcend their boundaries. Activities that throw down the gauntlet, like adventure sports or philanthropic endeavours, often propel tourists beyond their comfort zones. This confrontation with their perceived limitations can catalyse a surge in self-esteem and personal evolution, transforming the fabric of their existence, as Teoh et al. [4] echoed.

Narratives have emerged as potent instruments in transformative tourism. Storytelling resonates deeply with human emotions, facilitating profound connections and enabling tourists to engage with their environment intimately. Sheldon [9] propounds that tales woven around local traditions and history can accentuate tourists' bond with their destination.

Research endeavours, like those undertaken by Soulard et al. [10] and Pung et al. [11], shed light on the quintessential role of communication in transformative tourism. They advocate for a dialogue characterised by mutual reverence and a zest for mutual learning. Proficiency in language and cultural astuteness, enriched by a profound understanding of local customs and ethos, emerge as the cornerstones of effective communication [12]. This bridge of understanding fosters a deeper engagement with local communities and advances environmental conservation, as delineated by Krizanova et al. [13].

Further, technology has carved a niche in shaping transformative tourism experiences in this digital age. Cutting-edge digital innovations like virtual reality, augmented reality, and bespoke mobile applications curate holistic experiences that captivate tourists on diverse levels, rendering their journey profound and transformative [14]. Neuhofer et al. [15] opine that such digital tools, when wielded aptly, can conjure experiences that challenge the tourists' convictions and principles, steering them towards introspection and self-evolution.

3   Eudaimonic Communication

The philosophical concept of Eudaimonia, anchored in meaningful existence and self-actualisation, views well-being as an individual's potential being realised to its fullest [16]. Eudaimonia can be defined as ultimate happiness, psychological well-being or –success in life [17, 18]. Eudaimonia is not just about feeling good or enjoying life; it is connected to being inspired, fulfilled, and resulting in personal growth [19]. When translated to communication, eudaimonic communication emerges as a paradigm that fosters individual and societal well-being [20]. Eudaimonic communication has been spotlighted in transformative tourism as an integral element in crafting transformative experiences. This ethos is underlined by studies such as those by Zhang [21] and Ryu et al. [22], highlighting the profundity of experiences and the cultural pride engendered by eudaimonic communication. Contemporary research by Ko and Cho [23] also underscores its significance in fostering sustainable tourism.

Memorable messages have the potential to influence individuals significantly. Creating communication moments that lead to reflection and memorability could profoundly impact consumers. As Mirivel [24] suggests, communication methods that create meaningful and memorable connections can be a game-changer. This could be transmitted with content utilising nostalgia [25], perseverance or human connections [20]. The ability to incorporate memorable messages into communication strategies can be an essential tool for businesses to engage with their consumers effectively.

4   Method

The paper presents a pilot study related to a larger research project implemented by LAB University of Applied Sciences, Jyväskylä University of Applied Sciences and the University of Eastern Finland to improve and understand the business opportunities that transformational experiences and eudaimonic communication strategies provide in the tourism industry. Conducting a pilot study before commencing the larger-scale project is essential as it can help determine the feasibility of the research design [26]. The preliminary study will assist in testing the research methods planned for the project and will produce results that can guide the methodology of the larger-scale investigation.

The research method used in the paper includes two approaches. Firstly, it employs a web content analysis technique that turns text on web pages into valuable, structured data for research purposes [27]. This technique offers a detailed view of the words used on web pages. Secondly, the context in which these words are used to communicate with customers establishes current communication strategies employed by the organisations, which can shed light on opportunities for improvement towards the movement of eudaimonic communication.

First, a criteria table was developed based on the literature to identify transformative eudaimonic expressions. The table yielded 21 words, which are listed in Table 2 and which have their basis in individual and societal well-being [20] like *relaxation, yoga, fulfilment* etc., cultural pride [22] like *tradition, cultural*, meaningful and memorable connections [24] like memorable, fulfilment, knowledge and sustainability [23] like *nature*.

The selected companies' web pages were analysed using this criteria table to determine the presence or absence of these expressions. By discovering the elements used on current webpages of the selected companies – and also the lack of them – the study seeks to improve the effectiveness of webpage communication to achieve a transformative reaction and cognitive memory imprint.

The web content analysis uses a text mining tool to concentrate on the words on selected Finnish companies' web pages. We conducted a deductive content analysis, drawing inspiration from Crabtree and Miller's [28] template methodology. This technique relies on theoretical criteria, which are employed for the iterative assessment of the data.

The method chosen to collect the quantitative web content data in Table 2 was a Search Engine Optimiser (SEO) spider, also known as a website crawler. The crawler searches a website and its relevant Uniform Resource Locator (URLs) for the selected keyword input, resulting in pages that contain the chosen input, the frequency of the selected keyword and its dispersion rate across the entire website. The dispersion percentage indicates how many different URLs the searched word appears compared to the total number of URLs of the website. For example, a specific word on a website containing 50 URLs could appear 20 times on one URL, equating to 2% dispersion. Another word could appear once over 20 URLS, equating to 40% dispersion. The word frequency is the same; however, the dispersion rate differs.

The qualitative data collected from the web content will provide valuable insights into how these organisations use the criteria words in their promotional and marketing materials. We can determine how these organisations communicate with customers by analysing the word frequencies and dispersion rates. Moreover, examining the word context will help us understand if these organisations use the criteria words in descriptive or promotional ways on their web pages or if they showcase eudaimonic and transformative characteristics of co-creative and collaborative communication. We must collect sentence samples from each organisation's website to achieve this.

4.1 Target Group and Sample Size

The research concentrated on Finnish organisations as part of a transformative travel project. Two organisations were chosen, namely Amazing City and Golden Sun Golf, due to their relatively small number of URLs compared to the other organisations. Amazing City had 51 URLs, while Golden Sun Golf had 114 URLs. Table 1 provides an overview of both organisations and their current offerings. Also, these two companies have similar business elements, and both publicly strive for sustainable, even transformational, experiences.

Table 1. Participating Finnish organisations (*Follower and subscriber count as of 15 August 2023)

Company	Description	Social media platforms
Amazing City https://amazingcity.fi	Offers experience and program services, which include tailor-made packages and itineraries for unique experiences, such as outdoor activities, adventure walks, escape room-style adventure games and food and drink tastings. These activities can be customised to suit the needs of individual travellers, small groups or corporate gatherings and team-building exercises.	1,300 followers 1,448 followers
Golden Sun Golf https://www.goldensungolf.fi	A tour operator that offers golf trips and packages globally. As their website states, they are a golf tour travel organiser that can arrange individual and group tours with standard or tailor-made packages to suit the traveller's needs.	1,000 followers

4.2 Implementation of the Analysis

The site crawler tool came back with inconclusive results if a website's original language is Finnish with no English language option. Therefore, to maintain consistency throughout the word searches, the Finnish words were used to search the websites for the word frequency. Data integrity was improved by only using Finnish words and not switching between English and Finnish across the various organisations' websites.

In order to identify and analyse the transformative tourism experiences offered by Finnish organisations, this study investigated their websites. The data collection categories selected for this study reflected the various dimensions of transformation and incorporated elements of the transformation process previously identified in relevant research [22]. The triggers and components of transformation discovered included cultural activities, self-care activities, challenging activities, nature-based activities, and skill-acquisition opportunities. Based on the transformation categories and the literature on eudaimonic communication, 21 words were chosen for the quantitative data collection to reflect those that form part of the eudaimonic communication concept, e.g. kokemu*(experience), onnelli* (happiness) as seen in (Table 2). Translating the English words into Finnish allowed for a more comprehensive word search as most of the Finnish organisation's websites were in the Finnish language. Given the complex nature of the Finnish language, the base of the word was used with no suffixes to yield the most accurate results when searching for specific words and their derivatives.

The results obtained from each search were then sporadically cross-checked with the website to ensure the word appeared within the correct context. This is due to the possibility of a deviation in meaning for certain words in Finnish. For example, the Finnish word for 'skill" used within this study was 'taito'. While searching for words related to developing or improving a skill, all Finnish words containing 'taito' appear, resulting in the word 'ammattitaitoinen'. This word translates to 'professional' in English and, therefore, does not fit in the concept of the English word for 'skill' in this context. These results were subsequently removed from the word count.

5 Findings

One could find apparent differences by analysing the words on web pages (Table 2). Amazing City's vocabulary was more versatile than the one from the web pages of Golden Sun Golf. For instance, Amazing City uses 16 of the 21 words set throughout their website from the word criteria, compared to Golden Sun Golf, which only uses 13 of the 21 words.

The word *Nature* appeared most frequently on Amazing City's pages (26 times) and *Challenge* (75 times) on Golden Sun Golf's pages. Second place was held by *Experience* (19 times) on Amazing City and *Nature* (65 times) on Golden Sun Golf.

However, it is essential to note that each word should be viewed within the context of the service offerings the organisation promotes. When comparing the frequency of the word *Nature* on Amazing City's and Golden Sun Golf's pages, it is clear that the latter mentions it more often. While Amazing City does offer some activities within nature, it is not their primary focus. On the other hand, golfing is enjoyed in natural settings, which is likely why Golden Sun Golf talks about *Nature* more frequently.

Another aspect of the data to consider is the dispersion rate of a word. The figures may seem vastly different at first glance; for instance, the word *Experience* appears 19 times (21.57%) across Amazing City's website and 37 times (18.42%) across Golden Sun Golf's website. However, when analysing the dispersion rates against the total number of URLs for each organisation, the overall word frequency for *Experience* is approximately 1.7 per URL due to Golden Sun Golf having 114 URLS compared to Amazing City's 51 URLs. This means that the word *Experience* is distributed across both organisation's websites equally.

The study found that certain expected eudaimonic words were missing from the websites. This is significant because it suggests a need for more focus on elements that promote personal growth, purpose, and self-actualisation for the intended audience. Both organisations had null results. The Amazing City website missed five eudaimonic words: 'Enriching', 'Happiness', 'Knowledge', 'Transformative' and 'Yoga'. Similarly, Golden

Sun Golf's website did not include eight criteria words, including 'Digital', 'Engaging', 'Enriching', 'Happiness', 'Knowledge', 'Skill', 'Sustainable', and 'Transformative'. These findings are significant because they highlight areas where organisations can improve their communication strategies.

Table 2. Word frequency and dispersion rate

Criteria word *(in English)*	Amazing City		Golden Sun Golf	
	Frequency	Dispersion	Frequency	Dispersion
Haaste* *(Challenge)*	10	7.84%	75	21.05%
Kulttuuri* *(Cultural)*	7	5.88%	26	19.30%
Digitaali* *(Digital)*	8	3.92%	0	0%
Mukaansatempaava* *(Engaging)*	1	1.96%	0	0%
Rikastutta* *(Enriching)*	0	0%	0	0%
Kokemu* *(Experience)*	19	21.57%	37	18.42%
Täytty* *(Fulfilment)*	2	2.00%	1	0.88%
Onnelli* *(Happiness)*	0	0%	0	0%
Tuntemu* *(Knowledge)*	0	0%	0	0%
Tarkoitu* *(Meaning)*	6	9.80%	3	0.88%
Medit* *(Meditation)*	4	3.92%	4	2.63%
Unohtumat* *(Memorable)*	7	5.88%	14	8.77%
Luon* *(Nature)*	26	17.65%	65	27.19%
Rentout* *(Relaxation)*	14	3.92%	34	19.30%
Taito *(Skill)*	18	19.61%	0	0%
Kestäv* *(Sustainable)*	7	1.96%	0	0%
Perin* *(Tradition)*	5	7.84%	25	13.16%
Transformatiivi* *(Transformative)*	0	0%	0	0%
Ainut* *(Unique)*	12	9.80%	25	14.91%
Hyvinvoint* *(Wellness)*	2	1.96%	32	13.16%
Jooga* *(Yoga)*	0	0%	25	1.75%

The next critical step in the research process was to analyse how organisations use the words from the criteria list in Table 2 on their websites. By examining the language used, we aim to determine whether the communication style is more promotional or offers a personal and interactive conversation with the customer. This analysis will provide valuable insights into how these organisations engage with their target audience and help us better understand their effective strategies.

The eudaimonic and transformative words are used primarily in descriptive or promotional ways on the pages. They talk about the company's services and the skills one can learn.

Golfing taught by professionals

We organise educational trips for golf enthusiasts. During the trip, you get to practice under the guidance of real professionals. The trip appropriately includes training and playing as well as rest and relaxation. The courses are located a stone's throw from the hotel, and there is plenty of time for things other than golfing. You can get competent golf lessons from us...

They emphasised togetherness and individuality.

An upscale and personal experience service, for any caliber of needs!

Amazing city offers experience and program services to be experienced alone, as pairs or in groups of up to hundreds of people.

For companies, communities, travelers and locals – Tampere is an experience for everyone!

They mentioned that their services were meaningful.

We'll provide you with an entertaining experience program with a meaning.

Upon conducting a thorough analysis of both organisations' websites, it is apparent that they have skillfully integrated customer feedback and review mechanisms into their platforms. This highly advantageous approach enables organisations to capture their customers' genuine opinions through natural conversations.

However, a more comprehensive evaluation of each organisation reveals gaps in their use of eudaimonic communication to co-create transformative experiences with their customers, despite both companies utilising transformative language to some extent. For instance, both organisations could benefit from utilising more nuanced language that promotes personal growth and meaningful experiences. Additionally, the companies could consider adopting more collaborative approaches to customer engagement, facilitating a sense of community and shared values between the organisation and its customers.

6   Conclusions and Discussion

When looking at the results from a eudaimonic perspective, it can be said there is an effort for transformative communication. However, the communication style should be altered into a more personal, interactive conversation with the customer than traditional promotional text. This kind of discussion supports the transformation in an individual, as stated by Soulard et al. [10] and Pung et al. [11].

On the other hand, if a company wants to keep the one-sided, descriptive form in its communication, storytelling and narratives would work better as transformative elements [9] than basic promotion.

The contents on the pages emphasised the experiences with transformative elements, as Teoh et al. [4] mentioned; they challenge individuals to step out of their comfort zone, learn new things, increase self-esteem, etc.

From the eudaimonic perspective, elements of cultural pride [21] and sustainability [23] were present on the pages. However, the way they were communicated was again one-sided promotion.

So, the answer to the research question *"How businesses offering transformative tourism experiences harness communication from a eudaimonic standpoint?"* based on this pilot study is: "Quite poorly". The contents and the companies chosen for this case study were acceptable and suitable, but how they were communicated did not pay attention to the customer and their emotions or attitudes, and thus the transformation and transformational elements. The communication method seeks to share information more than create transformation and imprint a memory in the customer's mind.

From a *theoretical perspective,* this pilot study increases the knowledge of eudaimonic communication and its elements as well as their use of them. It supports the earlier findings and brings them together in the website context, which is still less studied.

When analysing the quantitative data obtained from the SEO tool, it is imperative to look at the word frequency or dispersion rate holistically. High word frequencies and dispersion rates indicate the use of eudaimonic communication in creating meaning for customers. However, looking at those results containing "0" values is equally important to improve communication strategies. This can be considered as the *managerial implication* of this study; being a company offering transformational experiences means that a mere statement of that is not enough; it has to be shown by the choice of words and expressions and in the way of communication, and even co-creation can be taken into consideration.

Furthermore, conducting additional research into these organisations' existing digital tools, marketing strategies, and social media communication tactics would be beneficial. This would provide a comprehensive understanding of the organisations and their methods of communication.

Since this was only a pilot study to find out what kind of results we would get from the pages and the material, it is clear that more research is needed to make the results generalisable. Also, a deeper analysis of the contents in different languages and more versatile companies would provide a deeper understanding of the issue. Thirdly, research on customer reactions and emotions towards the contents is needed in different research settings, e.g. laboratory experiments.

References

1. Egger, I., Lei, S.I., Wassler, P.: Digital free tourism–an exploratory study of tourist motivations. Tour. Manag. **79**, 104098 (2020)
2. Camilleri, M.: The promotion of responsible tourism management through digital media. Tour. Plan. Dev. **15**, 653–671 (2018)
3. Waisbord, S.: Translations|communication studies without frontiers? translation and cosmopolitanism across academic cultures. Int. J. Commun. **10**, 19 (2016)
4. Teoh, M., Wang, Y., Kwek, A.: Conceptualising co-created transformative tourism experiences: a systematic narrative review. J. Hosp. Tour. Manag. **47**, 176–189 (2021)

5. Pomfret, G.: Family adventure tourism: towards hedonic and eudaimonic wellbeing. Tour. Manag. Perspect. **39**, 100852 (2021)
6. Soulard, J., McGehee, N.G., Stern, M.: Transformative tourism organizations and glocalization. Ann. Tour. Res. **76**, 91–104 (2019)
7. Hua, L.Y., Ramayah, T., Ping, T.A., Jun-Hwa, C.: Social media as a tool to help select tourism destinations: the case of Malaysia. Inf. Syst. Manag. **34**(3), 265–279 (2017)
8. Matarrita-Cascante, D.: Beyond growth: reaching tourism-led development. Ann. Tour. Res. **37**(4), 1141–1163 (2010)
9. Sheldon, P.J.: Designing tourism experiences for inner transformation. Ann. Tour. Res. **83**, 102935 (2020)
10. Soulard, J., McGehee, N., Knollenberg, W.: Developing and testing the transformative travel experience scale (TTES). J. Travel Res. **60**(5), 923–946 (2021)
11. Pung, J., Chiappa, G.: An exploratory and qualitative study on the meaning of transformative tourism and its facilitators and inhibitors. Eur. J. Tour. Res. **24**, 2404 (2020)
12. Tsaur, S.H., Tu, J.H.: Cultural competence for tour leaders: scale development and validation. Tour. Manag. **71**, 9–17 (2019)
13. Krizanova, A., Lăzăroiu, G., Gajanova, L., Kliestikova, J., Nadanyiova, M., Moravcikova, D.: The effectiveness of marketing communication and importance of its evaluation in an online environment. Sustainability **11**(24), 7016 (2019)
14. Prandi, C., Nisi, V., Ceccarini, C., Nunes, N.: Augmenting emerging hospitality services: a playful immersive experience to foster interactions among locals and visitors. Int. J. Human-Comput. Interact. **39**(2), 363–377 (2023)
15. Neuhofer, B., Buhalis, D., Ladkin, A.: A typology of technology-enhanced tourism experiences. Int. J. Tour. Res. **16**(4), 340–350 (2014)
16. Ryan, R.M., Deci, E.L.: On happiness and human potentials: a review of research on hedonic and eudaimonic well-being. Ann. Rev. Psychol. **52**(1), 141–166 (2001)
17. Moran, J.: Aristotle on Eudaimonia ('Happiness'). Think: Phil. Everyone **17**(48), 91–99 (2018)
18. Deci, E.L., Ryan, R.M.: Hedonia, eudaimonia, and well-being: an introduction. J. Happiness Stud. **9**(1), 1–11 (2008)
19. Knobloch, U., Robertson, K., Aitken, R.: Experience, emotion, and eudaimonia: a consideration of tourist experiences and well-being. J. Travel Res. **56**(5), 651–662 (2017)
20. Rieger, D., Klimmt, C.: The daily dose of digital inspiration: a multi-method exploration of meaningful communication in social media. New Media Soc. **21**(1), 97–118 (2019)
21. Zhang, Y.: Tourism: a unique character strengths incubator. Tour. Anal. **28**(2), 163–186 (2023)
22. Ryu, J., Heo, J., Ellis, G., Widmer, M.A.: Leisure, eudaimonic behavior, physical activity and well-being of older adults. J. Leis. Res. **53**(4), 595–614 (2022)
23. Ko, E.E., Cho, M.: Exploring determinants of tourists' ethical behavior intention for sustainable tourism: the role of both pursuit of happiness and normative goal framing. Sustainability **14**(15), 9384 (2022)
24. Mirivel, J.: On the nature of peak communication. In: The Routledge Handbook of Positive Communication, pp. 50–59 (2018)
25. Watts, J., Bonus, J., Wing, H.: Celebrating your circle of life: eudaimonic responses to nostalgic entertainment experiences. J. Commun. **70**(6), 794–818 (2020)
26. Beets, M., von Klinggraeff, L., Weaver, R., Armstrong, B., Burkart, S.: Small studies, big decisions: the role of pilot/feasibility studies in incremental science and premature scale-up of behavioral interventions. Pilot Feasibil. Stud. **7**(1), 1–9 (2021)
27. Héroux-Vaillancourt, M., Beaudry, C., Rietsch, C.: Using web content analysis to create innovation indicators—what do we really measure? Quant. Sci. Stud. **1**(4), 1601–1637 (2020)
28. Crabtree, B.F., Miller, W.L.: Using codes and code manuals: a template organizing style of interpretation. Doing Qual. Res. **2**, 163–177 (1999)

The Growing Popularity of eSports Events: Insights from Parents

Nosiphiwo Mahlangu[1]([⌧]) [iD] and Rosa Naudé-Potgieter[2] [iD]

[1] University of South Africa (UNISA), Preller Street, Muckleneuk, Pretoria, South Africa
Mahlan1@unisa.ac.za
[2] Centre for Sustainable Tourism, Department of Tourism Management, Tshwane University of Technology, Pretoria, South Africa
naude-potgieterra@tut.ac.za

Abstract. The article discusses the growing popularity of eSports events and aims to understand the parents' perspective towards eSports and eSports events. As the growth of eSport events presents an opportunity of the tourism industry. The study used a qualitative approach utilising a semi-structured interview. The discussion of this semi-structured interviews forms part of a greater research study on eSports in South Africa, and these results are just preliminary results from an eSport event held high school in May 2023. The study found that parents have a positive perspective towards eSports events and are supportive of their children participating in them. The study also found that eSports events are relatively new and that there is a lack of research on parents' perspective of eSports tournaments. The study recommends further research to understand the motivations of participants and spectators to attend on-site eSports events, the expenses of children participating in eSports, and the benefits of eSports as an event. The article also defines eSports and the different types of eSports games, and discusses the adoption of eSports as a sport. The study provides valuable insights into the growing popularity of eSports events and the need for further research in this area.

Keywords: eSports · parents' perspective · eSports tournaments · motivation · expenses · eSports tourism · adoption of eSports

1 Introduction and Background

eSports also known as competitive gaming is a rapidly growing industry which has gained immense popularity in recent years, with the global eSports market being valued at over $ 1.38 billion dollars and estimated to be valued at $ 1.87 billion in 2025 [24]. The growth of eSport is a global phenomenon with the largest markets being in Asia and North America [24]. The growth in the eSports industry has presented an opportunity for eSports tourism and eSports events [11]. eSports events are being hosted all over the world although these events are particularly hosted in Europe, Asia, and the United States [12]. However, the expansion of eSports is not restricted to the northern hemisphere, with Games Industry Africa (GIA) predicting that Sub-Saharan Africa will experience

K. Berezina et al. (Eds.): ENTER 2024, SPBE, pp. 218–227, 2024.
https://doi.org/10.1007/978-3-031-58839-6_23

the world's fastest gaming growth [17]. eSports event which fall under the category of eSports tourism, according to Ioannis & Ioulia [11], shares multiple similarities with conventional sports tourism, with the key difference being that fans watch video game players rather than athletes competing in "traditional" team or individual sports.

A study conducted by Hamari and Sjöblom [10], stated that most participants are males below the age of 25. This is evident with Anderson et al.[3] stating that eSports has been growing in high schools around the world as eSports provides opportunities for students to develop skills as well as offer a platform for competition and personal development. Evidence of growth in the Southern hemisphere, is with the largest eSports arena of its sort has been developed at a high school in Johannesburg [6] further a well-known media outlet (Broad Media) has expanded its editorial staff by creating a post for an online gaming journalist [21].

There has been an increase of eSports, leagues, and competitions. The basic objective of eSports competitions, which are organised and held as either tournaments or leagues with players who compete against one another as either professional teams or as individuals, is to win [3].eSports was viewed as a substantive hobby in which one pursues to master games which require special skills, perseverance and knowledge towards eSports being viewed as a professional pursuit rooted in a hierarchal, competitive, and regulated global environment [25].

It is evident there has been a growth of eSport tournament, leagues, and competitions. This growth can be seen in schools with Cho, Tsaasan et al. [7] stating that collegiate esports leagues are growing rapidly with school eSports sports leagues particularly in high school emerging worldwide. The expectations of the participants and viewers, as well as what drives them to support this kind of event, are mostly unknown for this sort of sport. Anderson [3], who called eSports an emerging trend and noted the lack of research on this kind of event, supports this. Additionally, as this phenomenon has grown, there have been more eSports competitions, eSports leagues, and eSports tourism [19]. This growth of eSport events, competitions and leagues offer a modern, technological web-oriented trend which not only has the potential for the destinations to create new tourism products but also the promising opportunity to for alternative tourism offering [11, 16]. eSports competitions are becoming more popular, especially among schoolchildren and college students, and if this activity were to be practiced professionally, it may result in substantial rewards. This growth of leagues in school requires the understanding of parents' perspective towards eSports and eSports events, especially as eSport is still viewed as a new phenomenon which can grow into a new tourism sub-sector [25]. Students participating in school leagues require parental support by approving for the school to participate in the eSport league, financially as well as ability to participate in the event. Therefore, the study aimed to understand the parents' perspective by understanding 1] the view of eSports as a form of sports, 2] To conclude the motivational elements of participants and spectators to attend on-site eSports events 3] To determine the expenses of children participating in eSports 4] Benefits of eSport as event. The main objective of this article is to determine this shift of eSport being viewed from just a leisure activity toward a more professional activity (i.e. a sport) an adoption from early adopters in regards to the diffusion of innovation by parents of children who participate in eSports events. As understanding this shift with according to

Leon, Hinojosa-Ramos et al. [16] allow the event's atmosphere, staff, hospitality as well as good feelings about the live attendee and participants be considered when designing a satisfactory experience.

This article will define eSport and the different type of eSports games as well as discuss the adopters of eSports as a sport with regards to the diffusion of innovation the methodology used in the study and the findings that emerged during the provisional semi-structured interviews with the parents of the eSports players. The discussion of this semi-structured interviews forms part of a great research study on eSports in South Africa, and these results are just preliminary results from an eSport event held high school in May 2023.

2 Literature Review

2.1 Defining eSports and the Different Type of eSports Games

eSports (Electronic Sports) as "a form of sports where the primary aspects of the sport are facilitated by electronic systems; the input of players and teams as well as the output of the eSports system are mediated by human-computer interfaces" [15]. In more simpler terms, eSports refer to competitive video gaming (broadcasted on the internet).

eSports is unlike traditional major sports where the gamer/athletes play a single type of game, gamers/athletes in eSports compete in a wide range of games, each with its own set of nuances and target audiences [1]. All professionally played games are included in eSports, which also includes mobile games that cater to younger audiences and first-person shooter games that have a more adult-skewing audience [1].

eSports is made up of a variety of various and distinctive video games [15]. Even though FIFA (Fédération Internationale de Football Association) video games simulate 'conventional' sports like football, eSports is not often considered as the 'electronic' equivalent of a 'traditional' sport like athletics, soccer, or basketball [15]. As seen in Fig. 1: Snapshot of eSport games, eSports are frequently divided into distinct game genres.

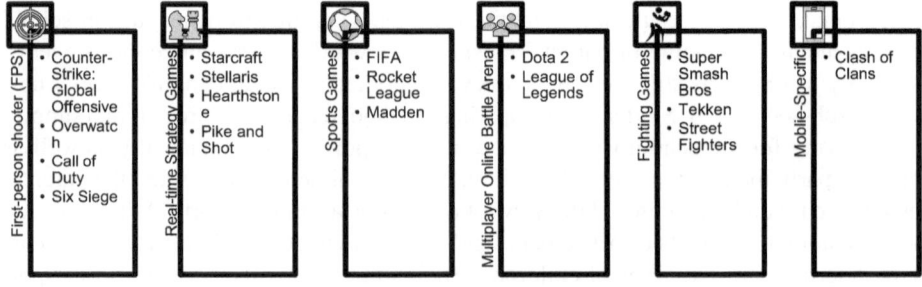

Fig. 1. Snapshot of eSport games.[18]

Games like FIFA 20, Tekken 7, Fortnite, Overwatch, PubG Rainbow Six Siege, Call of Duty, Hearthstone, Dota 2, CS:GO, League of Legends, CS:GO, Pike and Shot, and

Street Fighter are examples of eSports games [5, 14, 22, 27, 28]. First-person shooter (FPS), real-time strategy (RTS), sports, multiplayer online battle arena (MOBA), fighting games, and mobile-specific games are the six genres that can be used to categorize the games shown in Fig. 1. The two most popular eSports genres are "First-Person Shooter" and "Multiplayer Online Battle Arena" (MOBA) [5]. Regardless, of which eSports genre, eSports encompasses tournaments, leagues, prize winnings, player/team organisations genres, games, management structures and sponsorship agreements [3]. Therefore, it can be said that eSports involves a number of different games genres including first person shooters, racing game, and sports games amongst other. These games are played competitively in either a small team or as one-on-one, with the two most popular genres of eSports being "First-Person Shooter" and "Multi-player Online Battle Arena" (MOBA). Games are normally accepted as 'eSports' once they have been selected for official inclusion into an international eSports competition [3].

2.2 Adoption of eSports as a Sports

Despite the fact that eSports, or competitive video gaming, has been around for more than 20 years, it is still relatively young in terms of business and is not yet considered to be a mainstream sector [15]. As a result, there is currently no widely agreed-upon definition of eSports. This is due to its recent global adoption as well as general opposition (especially from fans of traditional sports) that eSports cannot be referred to as a sport because the players'/gamers' competence is not measured by either physical finesse or prowess as an eSports athlete is seen to be sitting down [15]. However, it has been stated that "professional gaming," a competitive kind of computer gaming carried out in a professional setting, is sometimes compared to eSports [27]. As seen in Fig. 2: Conceptualising contemporary sport, Guttman's methodology for conceptualizing model sports outlines sports as follows and may also be used to eSports.

Play, games, competitions, and sports are the four evolving transitional stages of the conceptualizing contemporary sports model shown in Fig. 2. All sports begin with play, a world of freedom where play means completely non-utilitarian physical or mental activity with the only goal of enjoying the "doing" process. The first level includes all sports, and all sports begin with play. The second stage of play, which is divided into organized play and spontaneous play, is where the play's substance can progress. This level denotes that every play has a set of guidelines that each player must abide by. Participants in this second level of the game agree to abide by the modified game rules and to forego their purely instinctual behaviour. An organized game's rules are primarily intended to make the game more challenging to play, with the major goal of establishing such regulations being to eliminate inefficiencies. The third stage consists of competitions, where most games can be played either competitively or non-competitively; sports at this level must have a win-lose result. However, competitions can go further and be divided into two groups, namely intellectual competitions and athletic competitions [13]. According to Greenhill & Houghton [9], while eSports may need less physical effort than sports like basketball, football, and tennis, they nonetheless require as much physical effort as shooting, pool/snooker, and bowling. eSports have a high intellectual demand since they call for highly focused, polished motor skills, as well as quick and accurate hand-eye

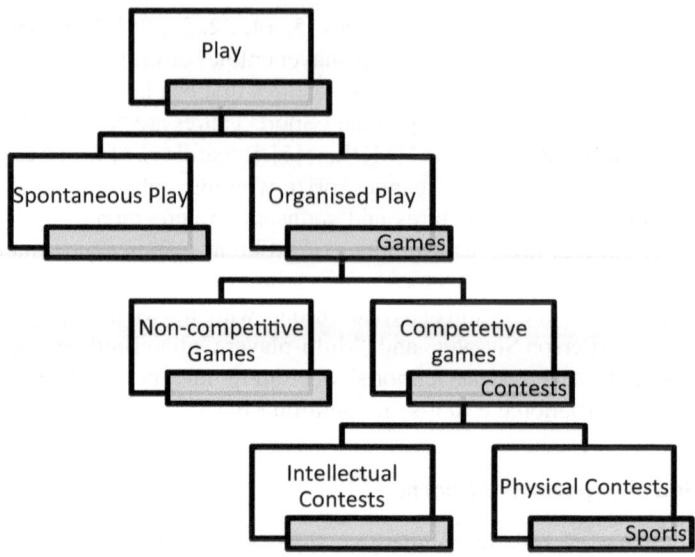

Fig. 2. Conceptualising contemporary sport [18]

coordination [9]. It may therefore be claimed that eSports is comparable to the preliminary paradigm, as mentioned in Jia [13] and Greenhill & Houghton [9]. The fundamental content of sports is play, and the basic content of eSports is play as well. Wagner [27] used terms like "training," "cyber fitness," "high performing teams," "strategy," and "cyber-sports" to try to qualify eSports as a sort of sport. Similar to conventional sports, teams will often be accompanied by experienced coaches, dieticians, mental health specialists, and physical fitness trainers when competing in the elite leagues [22]. Because of this, the definition of eSports can help distinguish between what is generally regarded as sports and what is particularly regarded as eSports [15].

eSports has been previously marginalized as a niche or fringe activity with eSports and eSports events being regarded as new [8]. However, despite that establishments of international and national bodies, the creation of teams with uniform, coaches, management, competitions, leagues, marquee evens, endorsement deals, scholarships as well as issues such as doping and gender-related issues eSports increasing similarity and legitimacy to traditional sports events and competition is still under debate [8]. With Tjønndal & Skauge [26] adding that the thought of considering eSports as a 'real sport' is still being met with significant resistance from some athletes, scholars, sport leaders and sports fans.

The adoption of eSport as a sport, especially eSports tournaments can be viewed through the lens of diffusion of innovation model. Innovation is defined as a change made to an existing idea, product, or field [20]. It can therefore be argued that eSports as a sport is an innovative concept. The diffusion of innovation is depicted with a normal distribution which illustrates how fast people adapt to innovations is depicted below (Fig. 3).

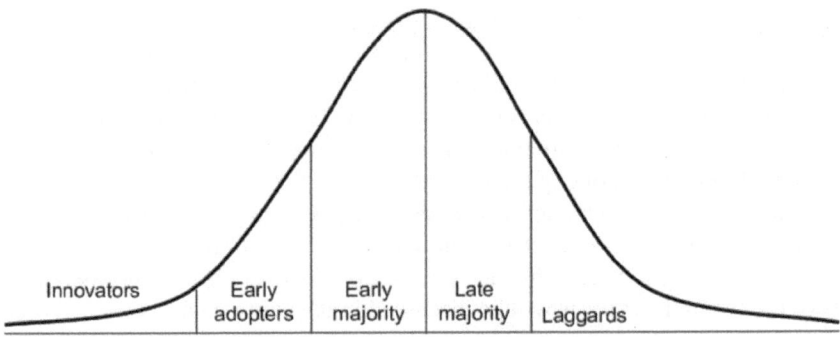

Fig. 3. Normal Distribution for diffusion of innovation.

According to Ahlsten et al. [2], innovators are brave, eager people who like trying out new ideas and are aware that there will be uncertainty, whereas early adopters have the power to pressure others into adopting and hasten the adoption process. With Pannekeet [23] confirming that the eSports market is on a fast track that consists of continual growth in the years to come due to its ability to be innovative as well as interest from especially sponsors and broadcasters for investment There are indications that there is a greater acceptance of eSports as a sports with Intentional Olympic Committee (IOC) considering the inclusion of eSports in the Olympic games with an announcement being made that eSports will be organized along with the traditional sporting competitions at the Olympic Games in Paris in 2024, with the Paris 2024 hosts expressing the possibility of adding eSports to the 2024 Olympic programme [26].

South Africa is still in the early stages of fully embracing eSports as a new form of sport and events within the tourism industry. According to Mahlangu and Naudé-Potgieter [18] a greater adoption and marketing of eSports, however, happened during COVID-19 when an article YOU Digital [27] was published in June 2020 promoting eSports to kids in the Generation Z demographic. In order to provide parents with pertinent information about eSports, including its benefits, regulations, and key players, BOO Games [5] put up a pamphlet titled "Parents Guide to eSports." The benefits of eSports are emphasized, and these include increasing brainpower, occupying kids and keeping them out of trouble, fostering self-esteem and a sense of belonging, and teaching kids valuable life lessons like compromise, decision-making, empathy, independence, leadership, problem-solving, social skills, teamwork, and respect for others [5]. There is however a lack of research on parents' perspective of eSport tournaments as well as have how the perceive eSport.

3   Methodology

The study used a qualitative approach utilizing a semi-structured interview. The interview method has been deemed the most useful method for this study an interview method has the potential to provide elicit rich and thick descriptions. This method furthermore gives the researchers an opportunity to clarify statements, as well as probe for additional information. A large benefit of collecting data through semi-structured interviews is that this allows potential to capture a person's perspective of an experience or event [4]. An eSports event was held at high school in May 2023, during which this study was undertaken. It is estimated that approximately 20 parents attended the event, with six parents that agreed to participate in the interview. Each parent had a child who was participating in the eSports tournament. The eSport event was a tournament which was held against different school eSports teams.

The interviews were recorded and transcribed after the event. Thematic analysis was conducted with codes extracted from the various transcribed interviews. The two researchers further observed each other's transcriptions to confirm codes assigned. The results of the thematic analysis will be discussed in the subsequent section.

4 Findings and Discussion

Parents were asked how many eSports events their child/ren (also known as participants) participate annually and whether they travel for these eSports events.

All parents stated that participants in eSport events (tournaments) are relatively new players, as well as being a part of an official eSports team. All the participants have been practicing participating in tournaments for 1 to 2 years. All participants who competed has competed in 1 to 3 eSports events so far. All event that they have participated in has been their home province of Gauteng and they haven't travelled outside the province requiring them to travel far or require accommodation in order to participate in the various tournaments.

This illustrates that's eSports tournaments and eSports teams are still in their foundation phase with children participating in 3 or less events. The tournaments is also limited to the participants home province. It is evident that there is an emerging area of interest for young players. As more players become more experienced in eSport the industry is more likely to continue to grow. According to Leon, Hinojosa-Ramos et al. [16] and Ioannis, Ioulia [11], the development of eSport events, competitions, and leagues presents a cutting-edge, technological web-oriented trend that not only presents a promising opportunity for destinations to develop new tourism products, but also presents a promising opportunity for alternative tourism offerings. Consequently, this offers Gauteng province the chance to develop tourist goods for both players and fans.

Parents were asked how much do they spend in year on eSports equipment, software, hardware games etc.

Parents stated that they currently are not spending a lot of money on eSports equipment or eSport event registration. This can be ascribed to various reasons such as a) the school supplied them with the eSports games and licensing for all the software b) the parent is still waiting to see if the eSports participant is going show a continued interest in eSports, before any further investment. One parent mentioned that they will look for a sponsorship if their child seeks to become an eSports professional. They also did not view eSports as an expensive form of sport. One specific parent, who had spent R20 000 in the year 2023 on eSports equipment, stated "spending money on eSports is a once-off thing, you buy the laptop and the software. If my child were to play soccer, I would have to buy him a new kit every year." c) They view the registration fee for the event reasonable for what the eSport participant is getting out of it.

According to the normal diffusion of innovation the are parents who are early adopters and scribe to eSports being a Sport. They also don't deem eSport any more expensive than other sports in which their children participate in. The low cost of entry can also see a greater adoption of eSports which will result in the eSports moving from early adopter to early majority in the coming years. This will also then result in the increase in revenue for the eSport event through registration.

Parents were asked if they will be staying at the eSports events itself or whether they make a whole trip of an eSport event and visit other attractions.

Parents indicated that they would be staying at the event and were not interested in participating in any other activities, such as shopping during the event. They wanted to be present at the event and support their children. One parent did indicate that they would go and have celebratory lunch somewhere after the event. Another parent mentioned that they used these school events as a time to view schools as they are currently deciding which high school their child will attend. It was observed that the eSports participants and parents were purchasing food and drinks throughout the day at the school's catering facility.

The eSport arena benefits the most from hosting the eSports event, as parents and participants are buying food and drinks at the venue. As the event is being held in the participants home province the venue benefits the most, as other sporting event in which people purchase food and drinks at the venue.

Parents were asked whether they view eSports as a form of sport of as a form of entertainment.

A number of parents initially viewed eSports as a form of entertainment for their children. Now that the eSports participants are starting to participate in tournaments and playing it more seriously, parents are changing their stance and starting to view eSports as a form of sport. The reasons for this were the expected teamwork, the commitment to practice the game, and the analytical skills required.

According to parents' responses and normal diffusion of innovation, parents have shifted their belief that eSport is a substantive hobby as defined by Thompson, Taheri et al. [25] toward viewing eSports as sports. Various sources such as BOO Games [5] and YOU Digital [28] have mentioned benefits of eSports, parents have also mentioned the benefits that they have observed in their children. This aligns with the normal diffusion of innovation, with these parents being early adopters. The acknowledgement of eSports as a sports can also lead to more resources being allocated to school programs as well as professional eSports teams. This also imply that the benefits of that destination and tourism receive from 'traditional' sports can be experienced with the growth of eSport as stated by Ioannis & Ioulia [11], eSports tourism, according to shares multiple similarities with 'traditional' sports tourism.

Parents were asked if they are aware that eSports can be used for educational purposes?

Parents were very open to the notion that eSports can be used for educational purposes. Numerous parents commented, "this is the way the world is going, with technology".

According to Ahlsten et al. [2], innovators are brave, eager people who like trying out new ideas and are aware that there will be uncertainty. The parents have accepted that there as been a shift in the world and that eSports was viewed as a substantive hobby to a professional pursuit [25], which can have educational benefits for their children.

5 Conclusion

The study found that parents have a positive perspective towards eSports events and are supportive of their children participating in them. The study also found that eSports events are relatively new and that there is a lack of research on parents' perspective of eSports tournaments. However, with the growth of this industry, especially with the support of parents who fund and give children to participant in this new industry also presents an opportunity for tourism industry to tap into this new market. The tourism industry and the esports industry can work together to develop new tourism products and destinations that cater to esports fans and promote esports as a new trend in the tourism industry. The study recommends further research to understand the motivations of participants and spectators to attend on-site eSports events, the expenses of children participating in eSports, and the benefits of eSports as an event. Overall, the study provides valuable insights into the growing popularity of eSports events and the need for further research in this area.

References

1. Abby, L., Nick, D. Hayley, R.: The emergence of eSports and the advertising opportunities within the ecosystems. PMG (2018)
2. Ahlstén, M, Heinonen, J, Murto, M.: Gamification and Innovation Acceptance Among Finnish DMOs - Case King's Road. In: Ferrer-Rosell, B., et al. (eds.) ENTER 2023, pp. 275–287. Springer, Heidelburg (2023). https://doi.org/10.1007/978-3-031-25752-0_30
3. Anderson, D.J.-F.: Investigating Fandom, Motives, and Consumption Patterns of ESports Consumers. Master of Science (Sport Management), Texas: Sam Houston State University (2019)
4. Bloomberg, L.D., Volpe, M.: Completing your qualitative dissertation, a road map from beginning to end. Sage, California (2012)
5. BOO Games Parents' guide to eSports. https://boogames.club/3d-flip-book/parents-guide-to-eSports/. Accessed 27 June 2021
6. Centennial Schools Sunninghill has built the largest eSports Arena of its kind in Africa. https://centennialschools.co.za/sunninghill-campus/esports-arena/. Accessed 06 Feb 2023
7. Cho, A., Tsaasan, A., Steinkuehler, C.: The building blocks of an educational esports league, pp. 1–11. ACM (2019)
8. Funk, D.C., Pizzo, A.D., Baker, B.J.: Esport management: embracing esport education and research opportunities. Sport Manag. Rev. 21(1), 7–13 (2018)
9. Greenhill, A., Houghton, R.: eSports and Streaming in the UK in 2017. Current State of eSports in the UK, London (2017)
10. Hamari, J., Sjöblom, M.: What is eSports and why do people watch it? Internet Res. 27(2), 1066–2243 (2017)
11. Nikas, I.A., Poulaki, I.: ESports tourism: sports tourism in a modern tourism environment. In: Katsoni, V., van Zyl, C. (eds.) Culture and Tourism in a Smart, Globalized, and Sustainable World. SPBE, pp. 105–115. Springer, Cham (2021). https://doi.org/10.1007/978-3-030-724 69-6_7

12. Jenny, S.E., et al.: Esports venues: a new sport business opportunity. J. Appl. Sport Manag. **10**(1), 34–49 (2018)
13. Jia, M.: Mapping the contemporary eSports ecosystem. Abertay University (2019)
14. Johnson, K.: The Evolution of eSports – The Events That Have Shaped the eSports Industry. https://www.bestonlinecasino.com/blog/evolution-of-eSports.html. Accessed 09 July 2021
15. Juho, H., Max, S.: What is eSports and why do people watch it? Internet Res. **27**(2), 211–232 (2017)
16. Leon, M., Hinojosa-Ramos, M.V., León-Lopez, A., Belli, S., López-Raventós, C., Florez, H.: ESports events trend: a promising opportunity for tourism offerings. Sustainability (Basel, Switzerland) **14**(21), 13803 (2022)
17. Libera, M.: The Ultimate Guide to Esports In South Africa. https://Mygaming.co.za/News/Features/125033-The-Ultimate-Guide-To-Esports-In-South-Africa. Accessed 05 Oct 2023
18. Mahlangu, N., Naudé-Potgieter, R.: Let the eSports games begin: a new business opportunity. In: Tassiopoulos, D., Swart, M.P. & Tassiopoulos, I. (eds.). Events Management: a Development and Managerial Approach, Juta, 4th edn, pp. 461–485 (2022)
19. Maslowski, P., Karasiewicz, T.: ESports as a new trend in tourism industry. Geogr. Tour. **9**(1), 95–105 (2021)
20. Merriam-Webster Dictionary, 2023-Last Update, Merriam-Webster Dictionary. https://Www.Merriam-Webster.Com/Dictionary/Innovation. Accessed 05 Sept 2023
21. Mybroadband, Gaming journalist job opportunity – apply now. https://mybroadband.co.za/news/industrynews/432896-gaming-journalist-job-opportunity-apply-now.html. Accessed 06 Feb 2023
22. Online Casino Review. When video games become big money. https://onlinecasinoreview.co.za/eSports/. Accessed 28 June 2021
23. Pannekeet, J.: Newzoo: Global Esports Economy Will Top $1 Billion for the First Time in 2019 (2019). https://newzoo.com/insights/articles/newzoo-global-esports-economy-will-top-1-billion-for-the-first-time-in-2019/. Accessed 05 July 2021
24. Statistic, Statistic_Id490522_Revenue-Of-The-Global-Esports-Market-2020-2025. (2023)
25. Thompson, J., Taheri, B., Scheuring, F.: Developing esport tourism through fandom experience at in-person events. Tour. Manag. **91**, 104531 (2022)
26. Tjønndal, A., Skauge, M.: Social innovation and virtual sport: a case of esports in Norway. In: Social Innovation in Sports. Nord University, Switzerland, pp.135–168 (2021)
27. Wagner, M.G.: On the scientific relevance of eSports. In: International Conference on Internet Computing, pp. 437–442 (2006.)
28. YOU Digital News24. https://www.news24.com/you/PartnerContent/play-esport-and-win-money-for-your-school-20200330. Accessed 23 June 2021

Algorithmic Control Across the Employee Lifecycle

Aarni Tuomi[1,2(✉)] and Mário Passos Ascenção[1] (ID)

[1] Haaga-Helia University of Applied Sciences, Pajuniityntie 11, 00320 Helsinki, Finland
`{aarni.tuomi,mariopassos.ascencao}@haaga-helia.fi`
[2] Wakayama University, 930 Sakaedani, Wakayama 640-8441, Japan

Abstract. This paper examines the employee lifecycle, that is, HR managers' role in decision-making. In tourism, HR faces unique challenges, e.g. labor shortage, staff turnover, diversity management. Algorithmic management, driven by data, is introduced as significant but ethically complex management strategy. The uses LEGO Serious Play to gather insights from managers (n = 17) and identifies eight potential use-cases for algorithmic control along the employee lifecycle. Implications for tourism management and research are discussed.

Keywords: LEGO Serious Play · HRM · algorithmic control · AI

1 Introduction

The employee lifecycle, a fundamental concept in organizational management, encapsulates the entirety of an individual's journey within a company, encompassing a series of distinct stages from recruitment of new employees to termination of employment [1]. As discussed by [1] and [2], the employee lifecycle framework starts with the employee attraction and recruitment phase, involving sourcing, interviewing, and selecting candidates. Once selected, the onboarding process begins, facilitating the smooth integration of new hires into the company's culture and policies [3]. Subsequent stages encompass career development and performance management, ensuring employees are equipped with the necessary skills to thrive and contribute effectively to the company's goals. Finally, the lifecycle concludes with the offboarding or separation phase, which could be due to retirement, resignation, or termination of employment and involves knowledge transfer [2]. Critically, throughout the employee lifecycle, human resource (HR) managers monitor, evaluate and develop talent, making managerial decisions that impact the employee experience [3]. In terms of line management, common issues in hospitality and tourism include maintaining service quality during peak periods of demand, addressing high turnover rates, balancing cost control with guest satisfaction, and navigating cultural diversity [4]. These issues impact operational efficiency, customer experiences, and employee morale, requiring adept leadership and tailored strategies to harmonize customer expectations, employee engagement, and financial goals within the dynamic and diverse context of the tourism industry [5].

K. Berezina et al. (Eds.): ENTER 2024, SPBE, pp. 228–233, 2024.
https://doi.org/10.1007/978-3-031-58839-6_24

Within the context of HRM, the concept of algorithmic management, also known as algorithmic control, has emerged as a significant phenomenon, whereby AI algorithms are increasingly used to supervise, regulate, and optimize various facets of employee interactions and operations [6], both in general and in the context of tourism [7]. Employed across the employee lifecycle, this mode of organizational management capitalizes on data-driven mechanisms to enhance decision-making efficiency and operational efficacy. Notwithstanding its potential advantages, algorithmic management introduces intricate ethical considerations concerning employee autonomy, privacy, and the potential for reinforcing systemic biases [8]. Against this backdrop, this study seeks to better understand managers' views of the optimal application of algorithmic control practices in specific use-cases across the employee lifecycle. Leveraging a qualitative approach, the study seeks to address research questions (RQs): RQ1: When and in what situations should HRM decisions be made by an algorithm? RQ2: What kind(s) of HRM decisions should be left for human decision-makers? Implications for tourism management are discussed, along with avenues for future research.

2 Algorithmic Control Across the Employee Lifecycle

Algorithmic human resource management refers to "the use of software algorithms that operate on the basis of digital data to augment HR-related decisions and/or to automate HRM activities" [9]. For example, in the context of recruitment and selection, algorithmic management is illustrated by the automation of processes such as resume screening and video interview analysis in order to streamline candidate evaluation, thus expediting the initial stages of recruitment [10]. However, this efficiency must be weighed against concerns of algorithmic bias and the potential exclusion of candidates not conforming to e.g. predetermined keyword patterns. In their seminal work [6] argue that algorithms have become a central tool in managing and coordinating work processes, reshaping power dynamics between employers and employees. The authors highlight six different mechanisms of algorithmic control, i.e. directing employees by restricting and recommending, evaluating employees by recording and rating, and disciplining employees by rewarding and replacing. Effectively, the use of algorithms in HRM imposes performance metrics which can influence worker behavior and productivity. Critically, these metrics often prioritize efficiency over employee experience.

Indeed, [11] stress the importance of addressing algorithmic biases and developing more transparent and equitable AI-driven HR practices to ensure fairness and diversity across the employee lifecycle. The deployment of such systems necessitates a nuanced appraisal of employee consent, the ethical boundaries of surveillance, and the establishment of safeguards against unintended consequences. As discussed by [9], while algorithmic management bears the potential to optimize operational aspects of the employee lifecycle, its ethical and human-centric dimensions merit rigorous contemplation to harmonize the imperatives of efficiency and equitable treatment of employees.

3   Method

To address its research questions, this study used LEGO Serious Play (LSP) to collect qualitative data from service managers. LSP is a workshop facilitation technique that employs LEGO bricks as a tool for collaborative problem-solving and creative thinking, with the aim of facilitating deeper qualitative insights in the form of stories and metaphors. Participants construct physical models with LEGO bricks to externalize complex ideas, e.g. the use of AI in tourism [12]. In this study, two LSP workshops were conducted during spring 2023 with 4 (workshop 1) and 15 (workshop 2) managers, with a total n = 19 managers across the two workshops. The workshops were facilitated by two LSP certified facilitator-researchers. The workshops were conducted in English, and a workshop facilitation guide was prepared and tested beforehand in a pre-test with 17 managers. After the pre-test the facilitation guide was revised slightly, whereby one building exercise was split into two separate exercises. Overall, the workshops lasted for 2 h and consisted of three rounds of LEGO building, story sharing, reflection and discussion: 1) warm-up exercise (10 min), 2) exercise about participant's future orientation (20 min), and 3) three separate exercises about algorithmic management across the employee lifecycle (3x30 min). Following [1, 2], the employee lifecycle was seen to consist of three major stages: 1) Attracting suitable candidates, recruitment, onboarding, 2) line management, continuous learning, renumeration, 3) appraisals, promotion, termination of employment. Against this framework, the workshops challenged participants to build models and discuss changes to the employee lifecycle chronologically. The discussions after each building stage were audio recorded, automatically transcribed with Otter.ai and manually anonymized. The data was analyzed thematically, drawing on a priori themes established in [1, 2, 6].

4   Findings

4.1   Attracting Suitable Candidates, Recruitment, Onboarding

In terms of the first stage of the employee lifecycle, participants highlighted three potential use-cases for algorithmic HRM: 1) screening candidates to ensure fit, 2) automated progress notification and feedback, and 3) monitoring performance during probation. First, in terms of screening, participants suggested filtering CVs and cover letters using AI based on specific criteria, e.g. driver's license, hygiene certification, academic degree, specific IT skills, target salary, or more soft factors, e.g. benefits that the candidate proposes to bring to the company. Further, several participants suggested a tiered system for filtering candidates, e.g. according to low, medium or high fit with the position and company. Interestingly, participants also suggested that AI could help improve diversity in hiring: "*Not just demographic diversity, but diversity of ideas, values* [...] *Analyzing the bios or personal statements or open applications from this point of view*" (P9). Second, in terms of progress notifications and feedback, participants commented that AI could be used on one hand to give automated updates on how the recruitment process is progressing, and on another give personalized feedback for those who were not selected for the next part of the recruitment process, i.e. explaining why they were not selected or how they could improve. Third, in terms of probation monitoring, participants suggested that

AI could be used for identifying any gaps in employees' current skills and knowledge, in order to suggest personalized training for them, either internally or externally.

4.2   Line Management, Continuous Learning, Renumeration

For the second stage of the employee lifecycle, participants suggested using AI for 1) tracking KPIs and implementing reward systems, and 2) ensuring compliance with industry-specific legal requirements. In terms of tracking KPIs, participants noted that *"AI could monitor your daily tasks, and based on this give personalized suggestions for how you could improve, like a coach"* (P7) and *"there could be an automated bonus system, where you have pre-determined criteria, e.g. a certain average customer review rating, that could automatically trigger a bonus, making it more fair and efficient"* (P15). Interestingly, besides tracking KPIs and assigning bonuses, participants stressed that AI could be used to make suggestions for improving wellbeing to ensure that employees stay mentally and emotionally well. Finally, for ensuring continued compliance, participants suggested that AI could be used to make sure employees' certificates are up-to-date, e.g. regarding health & safety or hygiene, that need to be renewed but might be forgotten. AI could be used to send automated notifications for employees when their certificates are due for renewal.

4.3   Appraisals, Promotion, Termination of Employment

For the third stage of the employee lifecycle, participants suggested using AI for 1) providing promotion recommendations, 2) capturing leaving employees' tacit knowledge, and 3) facilitating difficult conversations. In terms of recommendations for promotion, participants saw that AI could be used for mapping the motivation and skills gaps of employees, including their goals for career development. Based on these, AI could be used to suggest development pathways for the employee, e.g. which promotion to go for, or perhaps which department to move to within the company for better long-term fit. However, participants also noted the difficulty of implementing a fully data-driven HR approach in tourism: *"In a world where everything could be measured and compared, this would make promotion by AI fairer. But creating a world where everything is measured, especially in the tourism industry, it's impossible"* (P12).

Participants also considered how AI could be used to proactively capture the tacit knowledge of employees who were leaving, e.g. retiring, or thinking of leaving. As put by participants: *"When people are retiring, AI can be used to check that everything has been done according to the law, and also for capturing the tacit knowledge"* (P10). Finally, participants noted how AI could be used for whistleblowing: *"AI could be used for getting people to talk about the negative feelings they have about their work. It's sometimes difficult to get to the truth, especially talking about difficult topics like abusive behavior or unfair treatment, face to face. So using AI as an interface for capturing these* (P8).

5 Discussion, Conclusion and Future Research

Algorithmic HRM offers potential advantages and challenges across the tourism employee lifecycle, characterized e.g. by high turnover, seasonality and temporary employment contracts [5]. In recruitment, AI could streamline candidate screening, thus reducing the workload of recruiting managers [10]. Automated progress updates and personalized feedback could also be used to enhance the candidate experience. For line management, AI could be used e.g. to track KPIs, automating rewards and offering development suggestions. For promotions, AI could recommend pathways based on motivation, skills gaps and career goals. AI could also be used to capture the tacit knowledge of e.g. retiring employees. However, while these benefits are promising, ethical concerns like data privacy and fairness require careful consideration and future research for the responsible integration of algorithmic HRM in tourism management [7, 8]. Future research should also consider human-AI collaboration in HRM.

Acknowledgment. This study was supported by the Finnish Work Environment Fund, grant no.210336.

References

1. Cattermole, G.: Developing the employee lifecycle to keep top talent. Strateg. HR Rev. **18**(6), 258–262 (2019)
2. Thompsen, J.: Achieving a Triple Win: Human Capital Management of the Employee Lifecycle. Routledge, London (2010)
3. Plaskoff, J.: Employee experience: the new human resource management approach. Strateg. HR Rev. **16**(3), 136–141 (2017)
4. Baum, T.: Human resources in tourism: still waiting for change. Tour. Manag. **28**(6), 1383–1399 (2007)
5. Baum, T.: Human resources in tourism: still waiting for change? – a 2015 reprise. Tour. Manag. **50**, 204–212 (2015)
6. Kellogg, K., Valentine, M., Christin, A.: Algorithms at work: the new contested terrain of control. Acad. Manag. Ann. **14**(1), 366–410 (2020)
7. Wu, X., Liu, Q., Qu, H., Wang, J.: The effect of algorithmic management and workers' coping behavior: an exploratory qualitative research of Chinese food-delivery platform. Tour. Manag. **96**, 104716 (2023)
8. Tuomi, A., Jianu, B., Roelofsen, M., Ascenção, M.P.: Riding against the algorithm: algorithmic management in on-demand food delivery. In: Ferrer-Rosell, B., Massimo, D., Berezina, K. (eds.) ENTER 2023, pp. 28–39. Springer, Cham (2023). https://doi.org/10.1007/978-3-031-25752-0_3
9. Meijerink, J., Boons, M., Keegan, A., Marler, J.: Algorithmic human resource management: synthesizing developments and cross-disciplinary insights on digital HRM. Int. J. Human Res. Manag. **32**(12), 2545–2562 (2021)
10. Li, L., Lassiter, T., Oh, J., Lee, M.: Algorithmic hiring in practice: recruiter and HR professional's perspectives on AI use in hiring. In: AIES 2021: Proceedings of the 2021 AAAI/ACM Conference on AI, Ethics, and Society, pp. 166–176 (2021)

11. Köchling, A., Wehner, M.: Discriminated by an algorithm: a systemic review of discrimination and fairness by algorithmic decision-making in the context of HR recruitment and HR development. Bus. Res. **13**, 795–848 (2020)
12. Tuomi, A., Tussyadiah, I., Stienmetz, J.: Leveraging LEGO® Serious Play® to embrace AI and robots in tourism. Ann. Tour. Res. **81**, 102736 (2019)

Workplace Transformation: Exploring the Impact of Digital Nomad-Inspired Travel Experiences

Ekaterina Chevtaeva(✉)

Zayed University, Dubai, UAE
ekaterina.chevtaeva@zu.ac.ae

Abstract. This short research paper explores the experiences and transformations of employed remote workers who engage in remote work trips, a type of digital nomad-inspired travel where individuals combine work and leisure while traveling. The study aims to understand the meaning of these experiences and their impact on participants' work practices. The methodology employed in this study is Heidegger's hermeneutical phenomenology, which focuses on subjective interpretations of experiences. Data was collected between 2022 and 2023 through prolonged engagement with seven participants who have work flexibility but do not identify as digital nomads. Semi-structured interviews were conducted to empathize with the participants' experiences. The study highlights that remote work travel is not perceived as a typical vacation experience and differs from digital nomadism. The dimension of self-awareness at work emerged, revealing a range of feelings toward work arrangements in new environments. Some participants felt balanced and healthier, while others felt a lack of motivation. Overall, the experiences made participants more aware of their work style preferences that potentially benefits enterprises as well.

Keywords: digital nomads · transformative experiences · remote work

1 Introduction

The ability to use technology to stay mobile is a fundamental aspect of the digital nomad phenomenon [1, 2]. Digital nomads have the freedom to work remotely while continuously traveling and temporarily residing in various distant locations worldwide, without having a strong attachment to a specific home [3]. The phenomenon of digital nomad travel has developed over time. Since the establishment of digital nomad travel at the beginning of the century, it has evolved from a location-independent lifestyle to a distinct type of travel. A growing number of companies now allow employees to work remotely for a period of time, opening up opportunities for a more diverse group of people, including corporate workers, to experience travel while maintaining their work responsibilities [4]. Short-term digital nomad-like travel, previously referred to as remote work trips [5], offers a new and unique experience, even for seasoned leisure tourists, due to the additional component of 'work from anywhere.' However, it remains to be

© The Author(s) 2024
K. Berezina et al. (Eds.): ENTER 2024, SPBE, pp. 234–238, 2024.
https://doi.org/10.1007/978-3-031-58839-6_25

determined how traditional workers are transformed by this experience in terms of how they perceive their work practices.

Digital nomad-inspired remote work travel experiences have a potential to influence phycological and social transformation of people through self-inquiry [6]. While travel experiences have been studied in the past from the perspective of how they transform life views and overall self-awareness [7], this study suggests examining remote work trip experiences as events that help individuals gain a deeper understanding of which work style suits them best. Specifically, it explores how traveling while working remotely provides a novel perspective and transforms the meaning of productivity, workplace attachment, work structure, and colleagues within personal work practices. Therefore, the research question is: "What does the experience of remote work trips mean to employed remote workers, and why?".

2 Methodology

This study follows the Heidegger's hermeneutical phenomenology [8], that focuses on interpretations on the experiences ("being in" the experience). This research paradigm helps to address the subjective interpretations of the experience and uncover it's meaning. Data was collected throughout 2022–2023 through prolonged engagement with seven participants who do not identify as digital nomads but have work flexibility in their corporate jobs to engage in remote work trips. The concept of prolonged engagement stems from anthropological fieldwork, in which researchers spend extensive time with their participants to increase rapport, leading participants to be more open in their interactions with the researcher [9]. Participants were approached before and after their remote work trips to evaluate the extent of transformation towards their preferred work style. Semi-structured interviews were employed, focusing on empathizing with the meaning of the participants' experiences.

3 Results

Participants of the study have experienced the nuances of remote work trips, as they had to experience work practices from a different environment. The dimension of nuance combined the feeling of imbalance about experiencing work from a vacation space and the difference from a vacation. These feelings demonstrate that participants did not perceive remote work travel as a vacation experience. Digital nomad literature suggests that digital nomads do not perceive themselves as tourists [2, 10]. While digital nomads are not tourists, employed workers that combine work and vacation also do not fall into the categorization of tourists as they are not vacationers.

The mix of vacation and work mode is new for the majority of employed workers. A sense of confusion due to cognitive disequilibrium of customary division of work and vacation spaces was found in some of the experiences. Participant 1 reported that he felt imbalanced about experiencing work from a vacation space,

I do not know. It felt weird. A bit work and not work. I was the first in my team to do that. To use the one-month policy. When I was on a call with them, they were "Oh, where are you now?" - "I am in Bali". People were like "Wow", as I was showing them

that I am in the resort here. They were happy for me. But it felt so weird. I am not even at work. It was imbalanced.

Remote knowledge workers that act as early adopters of travelling while working remotely movement evidently have mixed feelings about blending work and leisure in traditionally vacation settings. The vacations environment would prevent participant 4 from feeling motivated, as she reflected, that *"In Thailand it feels that no one is working, everyone is so relaxed. I start thinking different things and get in the zone where I walk around and cannot figure what to do (work)"*. The opposite feeling of work interfering with leisure was reported by participant 6, *"I am out cycling on a mountain somewhere in Spain, I am not relaxed and my mind thinks 'Oh, that deployment could work slightly better if I would just tweak that system a little bit differently'"*.

Work and leisure are perceived as separated life domains in contemporary society [11]. Issues with work-life were observed in working from home literature [12], freelancers [13], corporate work [14]. Certainly, vacation environments have more novel and leisure attributes, but digital nomads advance in managing the boundaries between work and life [15]. Acceptance of lifestyle and treating work as serious leisure are among the elements that help digital nomads to blur the boundaries and embrace travelling lifestyle [3]. While travelling is just an occasional arrangement for hybrid digital nomads and they do not belong to a wide online community of digital nomads, they might go through their own learning curve.

After returning home, participants not only experienced a mix of emotions but also developed a heightened awareness of their preferred work style for productivity. One participant expressed the need for an office environment, stating, *"It was great to travel, but I do need an office to feel productive. My coffee and people around."* On the other hand, some participants felt a strong attachment to the new work environment, with statements like, *"I love my work, I love what I do, and I can focus anywhere,"* or *"Believe it or not, but it is my most productive environment (by the pool)."* These reflections were embraced by the participants as positive self-discoveries facilitated by their novel remote work trip experiences.

4   Conclusion

The dimension of self-awareness at work reflected a range of feelings in regard to work arrangements in a new place. Some felt balanced, some felt healthier, and some felt a lack of motivation. Overall this experience made participants more aware of their work style preferences by showing them the other way of doing things. It is fair to suggest that remote work trip experiences transform the idea of work practices for participants. The transformative power of travel is a recognised phenomenon in tourism [16]. Meanwhile, digital nomadism as a lifestyle goes beyond individual transformations and is strongly connected with revolutionary changes in the norms of society. However, remote work trips did not evident the feeling of a fundamental change in the minds of participants in regards to life values overall.

This study provides an outlook on the growing lifestyle mobility of employed knowledge workers that got facilitated after the COVID-19 pandemic restrictions. Arguably this trend will remain due to a high demand of flexibility from the employee's side.

Nevertheless, the degree of development of the phenomenon may be different in a time of crisis, due to more expensive travel and increased power of employers' preferences in organizations. However, this study suggests that enabling employees to engage in remote work trips goes beyond simply increasing perceived employment benefits. It is an experience that allows employees to develop their awareness of productivity, which can ultimately benefit the enterprise as well.

References

1. Aroles, J., Bonneau, C., Bhankaraully, S.: Conceptualising 'meta-work'in the context of continuous, global mobility: the case of digital nomadism. In: Work, Employment and Society (2022). 09500170211069797
2. Bozzi, N.: #digitalnomads,#solotravellers,#remoteworkers: a cultural critique of the traveling entrepreneur on instagram. Social Media+ Soc. **6**(2), 2056305120926644 (2020)
3. Nash, C., Jarrahi, M.H., Sutherland, W.: Nomadic work and location independence: the role of space in shaping the work of digital nomads. Human Behav. Emerg. Technol. **3**(2), 271–282 (2021)
4. Chevtaeva, E., Neuhofer, B., Rainoldi, M.: The "next normal" of work: how tourism shapes the wellbeing of remote workers. In: CAUTHE 2022 Conference Online: Shaping the Next Normal in Tourism, Hospitality and Events: Handbook of Abstracts of the 32nd Annual Conference: Handbook of Abstracts of the 32nd Annual Conference, p. 33. Council for Australasian University Tourism and Hospitality Education (CAUTHE) (2022)
5. Chevtaeva, E., Neuhofer, B., Egger, R., Rainoldi, M.: Travel while working remotely: a topological data analysis of well-being in remote work trip experiences. J. Travel Res. 00472875231151923 (2023)
6. Sheldon, P.J.: Designing tourism experiences for inner transformation. Ann. Tour. Res. **83**, 102935 (2020)
7. Kirillova, K.: Phenomenology for hospitality: theoretical premises and practical applications. Int. J. Contemp. Hosp. Manag. **30**(11), 3326–3345 (2018). https://doi.org/10.1108/IJCHM-11-2017-0712/FULL/PDF
8. Heidegger, M.: Being and time. In: Routledge Philosophy Guidebook to Heidegger and Being and Time. SCM (1962). https://doi.org/10.4324/9780203003084
9. Lincoln, Y.S., Guba, E.G.: Naturalistic Inquiry. Sage (1985)
10. Cook, D.: The freedom trap: digital nomads and the use of disciplining practices to manage work/leisure boundaries. Inf. Technol. Tour. **22**(3), 355–390 (2020)
11. Stebbins, R.A.: The Serious Leisure perspective: A Synthesis. Springer, Heidelberg (2020). https://doi.org/10.1007/978-3-030-48036-3
12. Nakrošienė, A., Bučiūnienė, I., Goštautaitė, B.: Working from home: characteristics and outcomes of telework. Int. J. Manpow. **40**(1), 87–101 (2019)
13. Miller, P.: Freelance workers—experiencing a career outside an organization. Qual. Sociol. Rev. **16**(4), 90–104 (2020)
14. Adnan Bataineh, K.: Impact of work-life balance, happiness at work, on employee performance. Int. Bus. Res. **12**(2), 99–112 (2019)
15. Rainoldi, M., Ladkin, A., Buhalis, D.: Blending work and leisure: a future digital worker hybrid lifestyle perspective. Ann. Leisure Res. **27**, 215–235 (2022)
16. Teoh, M.W., Wang, Y., Kwek, A.: Deconstructing transformations: educational travellers' cross-cultural transformative experiences. J. Hosp. Tour. Manag. **58**, 506–515 (2023)

Unlocking the Potential of Content-Based Restaurant Recommender Systems

Dante Godolja, Thomas Elmar Kolb[(✉)], and Julia Neidhardt

Christian Doppler Laboratory for Recommender Systems, TU Wien, Vienna, Austria
e11929150@student.tuwien.ac.at,
{thomas.kolb,julia.neidhardt}@tuwien.ac.at

Abstract. Content-based restaurant recommender systems use features such as cuisine type, price range, and location to suggest dining options to users. Current research explores ways to improve their effectiveness. In this work, we explore different ideas on how to build a recommender system. We explore TF-IDF as a baseline and the state-of-the-art model SBERT. These ideas are tested on a real-world data-set of a digital restaurant guide. Evaluation involves both qualitative assessment by a domain expert and quantitative analysis. The results show that, with proper preprocessing, TF-IDF can achieve similar scores to SBERT and, depending on the scenario, even better results. However, SBERT still provides more novel recommendations than TF-IDF. Depending on the scenario, both models can be used to generate meaningful restaurant recommendations. However, more implicit aspects like a restaurant's atmosphere can hardly be captured by these models.

Keywords: content-based restaurant recommender systems ·
domain-expert interview · real-world data-set

1 Introduction

The food and dining industry has been revolutionized by the internet, providing customers with a wealth of information and tools to enhance their dining experiences [6]. The rise of social media, food blogs, and review websites has empowered customers to share their opinions and experiences with a vast online community, while also allowing restaurants to showcase their menus and services to a broader audience. The primary goal of this paper is to introduce and demonstrate the efficacy of a content-based recommender system (RS) for restaurants that harnesses textual data, while notably omitting the need for user-specific information. We leverage a compiled list in the German language of more than 6000 restaurants, bars and cafés in Austria grouped by categories from Falter Verlagsgesellschaft m.b.H.[1] (Falter) for their column "WIEN, WIE ES ISST"[2].

---

[1] https://www.falter.at/https://www.falterverlag.at.
[2] https://www.falter.at/lokalfuehrer.

K. Berezina et al. (Eds.): ENTER 2024, SPBE, pp. 239–244, 2024.
https://doi.org/10.1007/978-3-031-58839-6_26

This digital guide is well established and is utilized by both residents and tourists. Relevant research has explored various approaches to restaurant RS. Gupta et al. [5] leverage a user's geolocation and visit history to recommend similar restaurants, while another approach [1] involves sentiment analysis of user reviews to derive food preferences for personalized suggestions. Additionally, user-entered favorite amenities can be used to recommend restaurants based on their offerings [4], and restaurant descriptions and photos can be combined with user data to create a hybrid recommendation system [2]. These diverse strategies showcase the versatility of RSs for enhancing restaurant recommendations. In this work, we highlight the importance of domain expert interviews for revealing crucial aspects that need to be incorporated into a content-based RS which can compensate for the lack of user reviews. Additionally, we demonstrate that baseline approaches can yield comparable, and sometimes even better, results in specific cases compared to state-of-the-art models.

1.1   Example of Falter's Recommendations

Falter's restaurant guide[3] lists restaurants by providing a description, metadata, as well as different tags to group restaurants by predefined properties, e.g., if a restaurant review is available or not (see example restaurant "Das Bootshaus"[4]). The restaurant recommender system currently in place works solely in a similar rule-based way by filtering tags and location. The problem with this basic approach becomes apparent when we see that "Das Bootshaus" offers seafood as a specialty, which is not indicated in the tags. There is thus a need for a recommender system that can utilize the restaurant's text to provide more meaningful recommendations.

2   Method

TF-IDF is used as a baseline method for textual recommendations. Reimers et al. [7] highlight in their work that Sentence-BERT (SBERT) can outperform previous approaches within this field. We used the T-Systems Roberta[5] model based on the publication of Reimers et al. [7] supporting both German and English words. For the evaluation of our text models, we executed qualitative and quantitative approaches. In the following two paragraphs, the results of both the TF-IDF and SBERT approaches are outlined. These recommendations are derived by using the restaurant discussed in Subsect. 1.1 as a reference point.

For the TF-IDF baseline, the text data was run through a preprocessing pipeline which first removes the prices from the description as they do not provide any contextual information, then we remove standard German stopwords and lemmatize the text by using the HannoverTagger lemmatizer [9]. Apart from

---

[3] https://www.falter.at/lokalfuehrer (01 Sep. 2023).

[4] https://www.falter.at/lokal/3239/das-bootshaus (01 Sep. 2023).

[5] https://huggingface.co/T-Systems-onsite/german-roberta-sentence-transformer-v2/tree/main (01 Sep. 2023).

these standard steps, we had a look at words that are used often in descriptions but do not provide meaningful information. Such words can be the German words for "Kitchen", "Dish", "Air Conditioning", "Sidewalk tables" (Schanigarten) etc. This was an important step that greatly improved the recommendations since it removes unnecessary noise from the data. The top-5 recommendations using cosine similarity are Ufertaverne, Pizzeria Adamo, Neuzeit, Gästhaus Käpt'n Otto, and Cafe Restaurant Denito.

SBERT is our state-of-the-art model of choice. The self-attention mechanism of the BERT architecture [3, 8] allows for improved performance and understanding of context, which in turn produces more novel recommendations when compared to the baseline. For this model, we decided to feed the text as-is (without preprocessing) as the preprocessing steps used for the baseline seemed to worsen the performance. The top-5 recommendations are Landtmann's Jausen Station, Mühlwasser Platz'l, Klyo, Zur Alten Kaisermühle, and propeller.

The novelty lies in the fact that SBERT was able to recommend restaurants that are near the Danube, like the restaurant from our example (see Subsect. 1.1), while also recommending restaurants from the same franchise like Landtmann's Jausen Station. This is a distinction which could not be achieved by simple word frequency calculation from our baseline. Further insights for both recommenders will be discussed in Sect. 3.

2.1 Evaluation

Quantitative Evaluation. We consider only 2300 restaurants with an existing kitchen in their given tags, meaning that not all venues have a food specialty (i.e. Viennese, Chinese etc.). We used the three biggest kitchen types and their subtypes: the Italian kitchen, Asian together with its subtypes Japanese, Chinese, Korean, Thai, Vietnamese; and lastly the Viennese kitchen. For the Viennese kitchen, we also include Austrian, Tyrolean, and Styrian cuisines as subtypes. While it might seem counter-intuitive to categorize Austrian cuisine as a subtype of Viennese, this was simply done for practicality purposes, since more restaurants have the tag Viennese rather than Austrian. All these listed cuisines cover more than 70% of all restaurants that have a kitchen attribute. To demonstrate the performance with restaurants from smaller kitchen groups, we chose the Indian kitchen. The evaluation metric used is the hit rate which is defined as the total number of recommendations (from a top-10 recommendation list) with the same kitchen type (or subtype) as the given restaurant divided by the total number of recommendations (ten).

Qualitative Evaluation (Domain Expert Interview). The qualitative evaluation was done in the form of an interview with the help of an expert from Falter. For the interview, we divided the restaurants into three categories: Restaurants with a given kitchen attribute; Restaurants with a focus on certain food but no specified kitchen tag in the data-set; Restaurants with no particular focus on any food and no specified kitchen tag in the data-set. For each of the first two categories we chose two restaurants and for the last category only one restaurant, for which recommendations were generated. For each of these restaurants, we had one top-5 list from TF-IDF and one from SBERT leading to a total of 50 recommendations. The interviewee did not know which model generated the recommendations until the interview had concluded and they were asked to rate the recommendations and give feedback based on their opinion.

3   Results

Table 1 shows the quantitative results from the hit rate metric. We observe TF-IDF outperforms its counterpart on Italian and Asian kitchens but greatly underperforms when it comes to the Viennese kitchen. A possible explanation for this could be the use of more common words for the first two cases (Italian: pizza, pasta etc.) (Asian: sushi, maki, bento etc.) whereas for the Viennese case, it could only be characterised by the adjective "Viennese" and less common food names giving it a lower similarity score for TF-IDF. SBERT however picks up semantic similarities and thus performs better in this case. When looking at the hit rate for Indian kitchen, we see a significant drop in accuracy. This could be due to the low number of Indian cuisine restaurants, which comprise only 78 out of 2300 restaurants with an existing kitchen attribute.

Table 1. Hit Rate of TF-IDF and SBERT

Kitchen	TF-IDF	SBERT
Italian	84.05%	81.35%
Asian	84.84%	77.66%
Viennese	68.20%	80.53%
Indian	49.49%	42.95%
Average	**71.65%**	**70.62%**

From the conducted domain expert interview we had the following qualitative key findings: TF-IDF tends to provide less diverse suggestions compared to SBERT due to SBERT's contextual understanding. While TF-IDF performs better when specific kitchen attributes are given, SBERT excels in general cases and offers more novel recommendations (see example from Sect. 2). Restaurant ratings are context-dependent, as a restaurant may receive a lower rating when surrounded by better suggestions. Additionally, the atmosphere of a restaurant significantly influences ratings, even when restaurant descriptions are similar. The previous point is very important as it can lead to recommendations from TF-IDF to perform worse than the ones from SBERT even if TF-IDF can find places that offer similar food but not the same atmosphere, which SBERT seems to perform better at. Lastly, the importance of considering price range and location in recommendations is emphasized, with the suggestion to recommend restaurants with similar price ranges.

4 Conclusion

In this work, we showed that baseline RS such as TF-IDF can outperform state-of-the art algorithms in special cases, whereas state-of-the-art algorithms offer more novel recommendations by using contextual understanding to their advantage. This leads to the practical advantage of cheaper and faster integration into the system architecture of an already running platform. Furthermore, we showed that domain expert interviews provide crucial insight to improve domain-dependent RS. During the interview, the expert highlighted the importance of grasping the atmosphere of a restaurant, which is not a metric that can be calculated out of the box. Especially, the knowledge gained during the qualitative evaluation leads to future work. Latent features, such as the atmosphere of a restaurant, should be incorporated into modern state-of-the-art restaurant recommender systems. In addition, the next step would be to conduct a user study to compare their perception and needs with the domain expert. Furthermore, the use of generative AI could be beneficial for improving recommendations within this domain.

Acknowledgments. This research is supported by the Christian Doppler Research Association (CDG).

References

1. Asani, E., Vahdat-Nejad, H., Sadri, J.: Restaurant recommender system based on sentiment analysis. Mach. Learn. Appl. **6**, 100114 (2021)
2. Chu, W.-T., Tsai, Y.-L.: A hybrid recommendation system considering visual information for predicting favorite restaurants. World Wide Web **20**(6), 1313–1331 (2017)
3. Devlin, J., Chang, M.W., Lee, K., Toutanova, K.: Bert: pre-training of deep bidirectional transformers for language understanding. arXiv preprint arXiv:1810.04805 (2018)
4. Gomathi, R.M., Ajitha, P., Krishna, G.H.S., Pranay, I.H.: Restaurant recommendation system for user preference and services based on rating and amenities. In: 2019 International Conference on Computational Intelligence in Data Science (ICCIDS), pp. 1–6 (2019)
5. Gupta, A., Singh, K.: Location based personalized restaurant recommendation system for mobile environments. In: 2013 International Conference on Advances in Computing, Communications and Informatics (ICACCI), pp. 507–511 (2013)
6. Kim, W.G., Li, J.J., Brymer, R.A.: The impact of social media reviews on restaurant performance: the moderating role of excellence certificate. Int. J. Hosp. Manag. **55**, 41–51 (2016)

7. Reimers, N., Gurevych, I.: Sentence-bert: sentence embeddings using siamese bert-networks. In: Proceedings of the 2019 Conference on Empirical Methods in Natural Language Processing. Association for Computational Linguistics (2019)
8. Vaswani, A., et al.: Attention is all you need. In: Advances in Neural Information Processing Systems, vol. 30 (2017)
9. Wartena, C.: A probabilistic morphology model for German lemmatization. In: Proceedings of the 15th Conference on Natural Language Processing (KONVENS 2019), pp. 40–49 (2019)

Technology for Smartness
and Disruption

Artificial Intelligence and Hospitality: A Challenging Relationship

Alesia Khlusevich[1], Alessandro Inversini[2(⊠)], and Roland Schegg[3]

[1] HES-SO, Lausanne, Switzerland
alesia.khlusevich@master.hes-so.ch
[2] EHL Hospitality Business School, HES-SO, University of Applied Sciences and Arts Western Switzerland, Lausanne, Switzerland
alesandro.inversini@ehl.ch
[3] Institute of Tourism, University of Applied Sciences and Arts Western Switzerland, Sierre, Switzerland
roland.schegg@hevs.ch

Abstract. The study employs a qualitative research methodology, involving interviews with experts and hoteliers to explore their understanding and adoption of artificial intelligence (AI) in the hospitality industry. The interviews focused on the participants' perception of IT adoption, the benefits and challenges of adopting AI technologies, and the factors influencing AI adoption. The data analysis was carried out with deductive coding following the literature review and interpreted using the Technology-Organization-Environment (TOE) framework. This framework helped classify the factors influencing AI adoption into technological, organizational, and environmental factors. The study reveals a mismatch between experts and hoteliers' understanding of AI and indicates a need for a comprehensive and targeted approach to educating hoteliers about AI's benefits, challenges, strategic and operational implications, and providing a clear roadmap for its integration into existing systems and processes. This study underscores the critical gap in the industry's ability to fully leverage available technologies without external assistance and the necessity to bridge this gap to facilitate AI adoption in the hospitality sector.

Keywords: Artificial Intelligence (AI) · Hospitality Industry · Digital Transformation · Technology Adoption · Small and Medium-sized Hotel Enterprises

1 Introduction

The hospitality industry has been slow to adopt artificial intelligence (AI) and digital technologies [1–3] despite their potential to revolutionize the sector by improving operational efficiency, enhancing customer experiences, and enabling strategic decision-making. This reluctance is particularly pronounced among small and medium-sized hotel enterprises (SMEs), which have been identified as late adopters of digital technology

© The Author(s) 2024
K. Berezina et al. (Eds.): ENTER 2024, SPBE, pp. 247–258, 2024.
https://doi.org/10.1007/978-3-031-58839-6_27

solutions [4, 5]. The COVID-19 pandemic accelerated the digital transformation of various aspects of the hospitality sector, from hotel websites and mobile applications to customer relationship management (CRM) systems and AI applications [2, 6]. However, despite this progress, the industry's interest in AI technologies remains relatively low, with a small percentage of companies actively using them [3, 6, 7]. Several factors contribute to the slow adoption rate of AI in the hospitality sector, including a lack of knowledge and understanding of AI's real benefits, insufficient human and financial resources, and the desire to maintain a human element in hotel operations [4, 5]. These challenges highlight the need for a more comprehensive approach to understanding the benefits and challenges of AI adoption. This approach should encompass not only the technological aspects but also the strategic, operational, and financial implications of AI integration. A thorough understanding of these factors is crucial for the successful integration and utilization of AI technologies in the hospitality industry. This study aims to illuminate these issues by examining the perceptions and attitudes of both experts and hoteliers towards AI adoption in the hospitality sector.

2 Literature Review

The term "Artificial Intelligence" officially appeared in 1956 at the Dartmouth College Conference where John McCarthy proposed the following definition [8]:

> *"AI is a multidisciplinary technology, which has the ability to integrate cognition, machine learning, emotion recognition, human-machine interaction, data storage, and decision making."*

As determined in the definition above, AI is multidisciplinary and includes scientific domains such as machine learning, text and speech synthesis, natural language processing, computer vision, planning, robotics and expert systems [9]. Most AI applications are built on the basis of machine learning, thus using different algorithms and methods to obtain the best results in the different scientific domains mentioned above [9]. AI can be divided into two categories: weak AI and strong AI. Weak AI focuses on performing specific tasks, such as voice control of virtual assistants like Apple's Siri or Amazon's Alexa. Strong AI is said to be capable of performing all the tasks that humans are capable of. However, despite significant advances in the field, strong AI is currently only a theory and its realisation remains hypothetical [10]. Nevertheless, thanks to the relatively advanced maturity of technical conditions, AI is currently undergoing rapid development and is being applied in many fields [11], as it is now capable of efficiently solving real-world problems and generating economic benefits.

2.1 Artificial Intelligence and the Travel Field

In June 2017, McKinsey Global Institute published a working paper presenting the level of adoption of AI in various industrial sectors, the common characteristics of companies that have adopted this technology faster, as well as the future demand for AI [1]. According to this paper, the level of adoption of AI in Travel and Tourism was low, as well as their digital maturity. Digital maturity is one of the six common characteristics of AI early adopters: several studies have demonstrated the beneficial impact of digital technologies on business operations and performance, as well as on customer and employee satisfaction, thereby contributing to customer loyalty [12]. In addition, digital transformation enables companies to grow their business and transform their business models [12].

The hospitality sector has also shown some reluctance to integrate and use digital technologies, and hotel SMEs were considered late adopters of digital technology solutions [2, 4, 12]. The study by Calvino et al. [13] analysing data from 2001–2003 and 2013–2015 shows that the digital intensity of sectors varies. The study examined various factors such as the technological components of digitisation, the human capital required and the technological impact on online sales. The result reveals that accommodation and catering activities are considered to have low digital intensity. However, digitalisation is now playing an important role in the hotel sector. For example, according to a quantitative study [12] of 110 small and medium-sized hotels (2–3 stars) in Poland, digitalisation has a significantly positive effect on hotel performance, growth and market performance. In addition, digitalisation plays an intermediary role in the impact of entrepreneurial behaviour on performance. In particular, digitalisation is a determining factor in the impact of proactivity on business growth and in the impact of innovation on market performance. The COVID-19 pandemic has accelerated the digital transformation of the hotel sector, particularly in the areas of websites, mobile applications, social networks, advanced software such as CRM, and AI [2]. Despite progress in digitisation, a study by Telekom and Techconsult in Germany [6] found that the level of digitisation has not changed significantly compared to 2020. Websites have become crucial for information, direct bookings and brand awareness. Digital solutions have enabled contactless check-in, bill payment and access to hotel information and services [2]. Social networks, chatbots and conversation centralisation applications have facilitated direct communication with customers, resulting in operational savings and improved loyalty. CRM is now essential for building lasting relationships and driving innovation. Ivanov [14] emphasises that AI and automation will bring significant changes, which require preparation from both managers and employees. Companies need to assess the costs and benefits of these technologies, provide the necessary training and overcome the knowledge gap, which is a major challenge for hotel SMEs in identifying opportunities to adopt digital technologies [4]. However, according to Telekom Deutschland & Techconsult [6] the hotel industry's interest in AI technologies is lagging behind. According to the study, 54% of companies consider AI applications to be relevant to their business. Of these companies, 7% are already using them, mainly for text (24%) and speech (16%) processing, while 21% have concrete plans to introduce AI-based technologies. Nevertheless, it is imperative for employees to be proactive in improving their skills, as the willingness to use technology in the hospitality and tourism sector is influenced by individual characteristics. As the study by Ciftci, Berezina & Kang [15] shows, the propensity to use technology is associated with personal characteristics such as innovativeness, which defines an individual's openness to new ideas and ability to make independent innovation decisions without relying on the experience of others.

2.2 Artificial Intelligence in the Hospitality Sector

The use of AI technologies in hotels, as detailed in a study by Nam & al. [3], was primarily informed by interviews with senior hotel asset managers overseeing more than 40 hotels in Dubai. The adoption of these technologies was aimed at improving customer experience, reducing costs, increasing revenue, personalising customer service and increasing productivity. The findings of this study identified 11 factors influencing the adoption of AI in the hotel sector and categorized AI applications into four groups based on their types and characteristics. Bulchand-Gidumal [16] categorised the impact of AI into two main areas: operations and marketing. Operationally, AI enables the automation and customisation of various hotel processes, such as room and resource allocation, preventative management, inventory optimisation and energy management. On the marketing front, AI improves forecasting, CRM systems and intelligent marketing strategies, including dynamic pricing, personalised services and experiences, predictive analytics and real-time offers. Additionnaly, according to Tuomi [17], generative AI for SMEs in the hospitality and tourism industry can offer an increased autonomy and more internal control over their creative initiatives in generating contents for social media, facilitating in-house project management. Nonetheless, according to one of the latest report from Skift and AWS [18], the use of data, automation, and AI has the potential to humanize hospitality both on the customer facing and operations side braking down departmental silos.

3 Research Objectives and Methodology

The hospitality sector appears to be a suitable and promising domain for the integration of AI, yet its adoption in the industry is notably lagging [2]. To understand the under-lying reasons for this discrepancy and to develop a critical perspective, this research involves two sets of interviews designed to illuminate the key issues at hand. Addition-ally, this study aims to bridge the gap between technology companies and hoteliers by identifying common ground that could facilitate the adoption of AI. By fostering a better understanding and collaboration between these two key stakeholders, it is hoped that the barriers to AI adoption in the hospitality sector can be overcome, ultimately leading to enhanced operational efficiency, customer satisfaction, and overall competitiveness in the industry. In order to reach this aim, hospitality technology consultants and hoteliers have been interviewed to tackle the following research objectives: (i) from the experts' point of view, the research aims at understanding the view on hotels' adoption on AI, the reason why adoption would be recommended and the main obstacles; (ii) from hote-liers' point of view, the research aims at understanding the importance of AI for hotels' operations and what are the factors facilitating adoption.

3.1 Data Collection

80 interview requests were sent, mostly via LinkedIn.com, using purposive and snowball sampling resulting in 7 positive responses from hotel managers in Switzerland and 6 positive responses from experts in the field of AI (Austria, Germany, Switzerland, France, Spain). The description of the participants is presented in the tables below.

Table 1. Description of experts interviewed

	Role/Position	Product/Experience
E1	CEO	Platform that integrates communications between hotels and customers from various sources and applications, and can respond through instant messaging (ChatBot)
E2	Senior Customer Success Manager	Real-time revenue management system
E3	Director of Client Services and Customer Success	Real-time revenue management system
E4	CTO	Customer relationship and hotel operations platform (CRM, GuestApp, messaging, operations)
E5	Consultant	Consultant in the hotel/technology industry (21 years of experience in technical, commercial, marketing, consulting, and business leadership roles)
E6	Co-Founder	AI based guest experience management solutions for hotels

Table 1 presents the experts who agreed in taking part to the study; while Table 2 presents the hospitality companies involved. In order to ensure that hotel managers had relevant experience with AI, all interviews started with a soft assessment of the hoteliers' understanding of AI and a brief discussion of the AI solutions used in their respective properties. All the interviews tool place between March 2023 and June 2023.

Table 2. Description of accommodations

#	Accommodation type	Location	Hotel type	Star-level	Number of staff	Number of rooms	Independent	AI usage
H1	Hotel	City	Business/Seminar	5	~70	60	Yes	No
H2	Small group of hotels	Multiple locations	Depends on hotel	Luxury segment	1400 permanent staff (~1800 in season)	From 14 to 200	No	**Yes**
H3	Tourist residence (apartment hotel)	Mountain	Leisure	3	4	85	No	No
H4	Hotel	Mountain	Leisure	3	9	60	Yes	No
H5	Hotel	City	Business	4	~30	136	No	**Yes**
H6	Hotel	City	Business/Leisure	3	~35	71	Yes	No
H7	Tourist residence	Mountain	Leisure	–	~8	200	Yes	No

3.2 Data Analysis

The analysis of the data was conducted using deductive coding, which was informed by the literature review. The analysis of the interviews was conducted using MAXQDA 2022 software, significantly enhancing the coding of text segments and their hierarchical organization. The results were categorized and interpreted using the Technology-Organization-Environment (TOE) framework. The TOE framework identifies three categories of factors that influence a company's ability and decision to adopt new technologies [3].

- **Technological factors** refer to all factors, both internal and external, that are relevant to the business. Internal factors include technologies that are already adopted by the business, and external factors include technologies that are available on the market [19]. This therefore allows us to consider and understand how the characteristics of the technology already adopted may impact on the adoption of new technologies.
- **Organizational factors** include organizational characteristics and available resources that can impact the adoption of new technologies. SMEs often lack the financial and human resources that can facilitate the adoption process. Financial, technical, and human resources are the key factors when we talk about the adoption of new technologies by SMEs and hotels. They refer to the availability of all these resources for use in integrating new technologies into business processes.
- **Environmental factors** refer to external elements that impact the company's business activities such as industry, competitors, customers, as well as the legal context, and which influence the decision to adopt new technologies. Competitive pressure has been extensively studied as a characteristic that has an impact on the adoption of new technologies, particularly in the hotel sector [3].

4   Results and Discussions

4.1   Expert Interviews

Initially – as a warm up question - the interviewees were asked about their perception of IT and AI adoption in small and medium-sized hotel enterprises (SMEs). Several respondents noted that that COVID-19 pandemic accelerated technology adoption especially for tools related to guest safety and compliance with new health requirements; however, hoteliers are increasingly aware of technology's importance and understand that they can't do without it as E5 maintains: *"Today's hoteliers are well aware that they can't do without technology. [...] Technology has become an inescapable subject for them, they may vary in their degree of adoption, but all of them have understood that they have no choice".*

Hotel groups and chains are generally more inclined to adopt technology, however E4 explained that high-end independent hotels, driven by a commitment to exceptional guest experiences, are often leaders in technology adoption, while, perceptions of AI adoption among SME hotels also vary based on owners, managers, and generations as described by E6: *"If you're considering small and medium-sized hotels, it depends a little bit on the owner and the manager. There's also likely to be a generational difference in their approach. [...] the younger generation recognizes the value of the data, but they struggle with managing it effectively because it's dispersed across multiple systems".*

The hotel sector faces challenges like fragmented technologies, hoteliers' lack of knowledge about market-available solutions, and integration of diverse data sources. E1, E2, E3 and E6 affirmed that many hotels store data in silos, hindering communication, global data analysis, and the use of outdated software like PMS because as E1 maintains: *"[in the hotel business] digitalization is not at the center of hoteliers' concern [...] you do not have specific training and the only way to get new technology is trade show or consultants".*

Advantages of Adopting AI Technologies in the Hotel Industry. The experts were asked about the benefits that small and medium-sized hotels could gain from adopting advanced technologies like AI. Here are the key points from their responses:

- *Replacement of Repetitive Tasks.* Experts E1, E2, E3, E4, E5 and E6 noted that AI technologies can reduce time spent on repetitive tasks, particularly administrative ones that consume time without adding value. This reduction allows hotel owners and staff to focus on more important tasks. Additionally, AI-based technologies enable hotels to handle huge amounts of data within a short timeframe, to remain competitive and react more quickly to market changes;
- *Operational Efficiency in Marketing and Maintenance.* AI can enhance operational efficiency by automating tasks such as marketing and predictive maintenance (E1, E2, E3, E4 and E6). AI techniques help personalize offers and rates based on user behavior on hotel websites, optimizing revenue streams (E1, E2). The creation of unified customer profiles means that communication can be based not only on customer profiles (E1, E3 E4, E6), but also on the most appropriate pricing policy. As a result, AI-powered Revenue Management Systems (RMS) can offer accurate demand forecasts, assist in setting optimal pricing strategies, and ensure quick reactions to market changes (E1, E2, E3).
- *Customer Experience Personalization:* AI enables hotels to better understand customer preferences and desires, offering more personalized experiences (E1, E3). AI-driven communication tools automate interactions, enhancing customer satisfaction (E3). AI can assist in analyzing data to provide personalized services, improving overall guest experience and fostering loyalty (E3 and E6).

Factors influencing AI adoption. When asked about the factors influencing the advantages of AI-based systems, experts mentioned the following one, which have been classified following the TOE framework:

- **Technological Factors.** (i) *Quality of integration with old – and still working technologies* (e.g. PMS) (E1, E4, E6). This can cause dissatisfaction which could eventually lead to a decrease in their collaboration with the system. (ii) *Quantity and quality of data* (E1, E3, E5, E6): data plays an essential role for systems based on artificial intelligence. The number of software applications adopted by a hotel can have a considerable impact, as they constitute a source of digital data.
- **Organizational Factors**: (i) *Willingness of managers or owners to invest the necessary extra effort* (E2, E6): Decision-makers must be willing to invest time and

resources to reap the medium- and long-term benefits offered by software and services, including in ongoing training. (ii) *Hotel strategy and goals* (E1, E3): Depending on the customer experience or staff experience hoteliers want to offer, they need to choose the software that matches the hotel's expectations. (iii) *Hotel typology* (E2, E4, E6): this is an important factor to consider because customers' expectations may differ depending on their travel purpose. For example, hotels geared towards business travel focus more on administrative efficiency than individualisation and may therefore be less demanding in terms of content quality. Furthermore, the requirements of various types of hotels can vary. Therefore, it is important to determine whether AI models can be adapted to meet specific requirements. (iv) *Hotel classification* (E1, E4, E6): according to E1, 5-star hotels prefer to build a relationship with their customers based on human contact. E6 maintained that personalisation is more significant in the luxury segment compared to lower category hotels. (v) *Hotel size* (E1, E2, E3, E5): hotel size can affect the benefits of products based on AI technologies. This is mainly linked to the amount of data held, which can influence the relevance and accuracy of the recommendations and forecasts generated by the software. The larger and more visited the hotel, the easier it is to optimise AI technologies. (vi) *Resilience and usability* (E1, E3, E6): AI-based software can perform different tasks, but the interaction is often hybrid and also involves a human factor. So, it's essential for employees using a system to have a good understanding of how it works and how it interacts with other systems. If employees are reluctant to try something new, implementing this software can be extremely difficult.

- **Environmental Factors**: (i) *Belonging to a group/network (small or large) or independent establishment* (E2, E6) influences the software's ability to meet the different expectations of hotels. Hotels that are part of a group or a network have more standardised processes, which makes it easier to implement the software. (ii) *Number of direct competitors* (E2, E3): the presence of several direct competitors can improve system performance. This allows a better comparison of prices and a more accurate adaptation to market conditions. Other mentioned factors can be linked to the environment, such as client preferences (E1), AI algorithms (E1), system capacity (E1 and E6), and installation moment (E6), as various establishments have specific needs, for example, those related to different seasons.

4.2   Hoteliers Interviews

The participants' understanding of AI varied: H2 and H4 summarize the current understanding of AI in the industry in the following way respectively: *"[AI] it's still something new […] well, we've been talking about it for quite some time, but it doesn't really affect our industry at the moment […]"*, and then H4: *"I don't know of any other hotels that have implemented it. Of all the contacts I've had through the [Local Hotel Association] and others, so far none have told me that they use these solutions".*

Most frequently mentioned ideas included (i) personalizing customer experiences, (ii) communication for commercial purposes (customer profiling, recommendations, personalized offers), (iii) revenue management in real-time, chatbots and ChatGPT.

Subsequently, H2 and H5 mentioned several solutions they are currently using or plan to integrate. These include an intelligent video surveillance system that records only upon motion detection (and also using object search), an energy optimization system, an AI-driven electrical backup system, predictive maintenance tools, and a table management system that automatically assigns seating to customers. Surprisingly, the participants did not perceive these solutions as AI-related, or some participants expressed uncertainty about the specific technologies used behind them.

However, what become apparent during the conversation was the need of hoteliers to maintain the 'human side of the business' as maintained by H5: *"In my opinion, it's still important to retain a human element in the hotel business. The human element remains crucial in this field. [...] Customers are often also looking for an exchange with someone who creates an experience, and not just pure technology [...]"*.

A significant aspect highlighted by hotel managers is the management and support associated with the use of external software and IT service providers. Participants expressed that the quality of support did not always meet their expectations, and some noted a transition from personalized support to automated systems. Several participants mentioned that they often had to complete system configurations themselves (H5) or assume the role of a project manager (H6). Ultimately, multiple participants indicated that while the hotel industry has access to numerous tools, hotels are not always equipped to develop, maintain, install, or configure these tools independently. This underscores a critical gap in the industry's ability to fully leverage available technologies without external assistance. When it comes to obstacles, and challenges in adopting AI, participants highlighted potential use cases for AI in hotel operations, such as reservation management, housekeeping planning, waste monitoring, personalized customer interactions, revenue management, and more. The personnel will be freed to do other tasks, however the current level of knowledge is insufficient, and the actual economic benefit is not clear: H7: *"[...] on the one hand, digitalisation [and AI] would free up our staff's time to carry out other tasks"*. H2: *"[...] in terms of productivity, but not just productivity in terms of quantity, but also productivity in terms of quality. How many distortions, how many values we can make up... Yes, a gain in time, a gain in strategy based on more relevant points, on information that is better analysed, better centralised"*. H4: *"We haven't taken any courses on this [AI]. Personally, I've never had any courses, so I don't know how it works... Yes, especially in terms of knowledge, and what I could gain from it, what advantages it could bring"*.

Hoteliers also called for a more detailed explanations of AI benefits, seeking advice and consultation, ensuring data protection, remaining open to new opportunities, finding reliable partners, and staying updated on evolving technology trends.

TOE factors and AI Adoption. The adoption of AI in hotels is influenced by a variety of factors including technological ease, client preferences, AI product development, competition, human and financial resources, company strategy, hotel characteristics, and accountability considerations. These collectively determine the integration and success of AI technologies in the hospitality industry. Specifically:

- **Technological factors**. Benefits include operational efficiency (H1, H2, H3, H6, H7), improved customer experience (H1, H2, H3, H5, H6), empowered employees (H1, H2, H6, H7), competitive advantage (H1, H2, H5, H6) and improved overall performance (H1, H2, H5, H6, H7). AI achieves this through automation, personalisation and strategic insight. Compatibility (H2, H3) and simplicity (H1, H2, H5, H7) are critical for successful integration.

- **Organizational Factors.** Challenges in terms of skills, technical knowledge and time hinder the readiness of human resources (H2, H3, H4, H6, H7). Adequate budgeting and accurate cost estimation are critical financial factors (H1, H2, H3, H5, H6, H7). Corporate strategy and management priorities determine the pace of implementation (H1, H2, H3, H4, H6). Hotel size and type dictate resource availability and requirements to be met (H1, H2, H6). In addition, star rating is important in determining whether or not to implement robotic technologies in luxury hotels, given the importance of providing customers with personalised service and human interaction (H2). In addition, H1 mentioned another factor during the interview, which is responsibility in terms of incorrect chatbot responses. Responsibility should be clearly defined between the service provider and the hotel.
- **Environmental Factors.** Different customer expectations drive adoption, with some prioritising human interaction and others seeking digital convenience (H1, H3, H4, H5). The development of AI products varies, with potential for different deployments (H1, H3, H4). Competition may drive uptake, particularly in city hotels (H3, H4, H5), but is not currently considered a significant factor influencing uptake (H1, H3, H4, H5, H7). However, it should be considered in relation to supply, higher visibility and pricing (H5). Other factors such as external support, risks, ethics and trust also play a role, but are not the key factors to consider when deciding to adopt AI technologies (H2, H3, H4, H5, H6, H7).

5   Discussion and Conclusions

This research has highlighted the nuanced differences in the understanding of AI between experts and hoteliers within the hospitality industry. While the adoption of standardized technology is more straightforward for chain hotels, the fragmented nature of the industry poses significant challenges to the integration of artificial intelligence. It is important to note that the current discourse on this topic is often framed within the broader context of digitisation and IT adoption. However, AI in the hospitality sector presents unique challenges and opportunities that go beyond general IT adoption.

Experts continue to highlight the multiple benefits of AI, ranging from automating mundane tasks and increasing operational efficiency to refining the guest experience. However, a deeper dive into our findings reveals that many hoteliers, especially those from older generations, are not simply reluctant to adopt the technology. Their reluctance stems from a lack of fundamental understanding of the tangible benefits of AI, which are specific to the hospitality industry. The challenges posed by the digital transformation of tourism, as highlighted in reports [4, 5], parallel the need for a specialised educational approach tailored to hoteliers. Hoteliers need a detailed understanding of the value proposition of AI, including its potential ROI, the impact on human resources and the technological infrastructure required. This education should not be a cursory overview, but a deep dive into the strategic and operational implications of AI specific to the hospitality industry. Equally important is the demystification of the costs associated with AI integration, accompanied by a pragmatic roadmap for integrating AI into existing frameworks. Humanizing the AI transition: The transition to AI is not just a technological change, it's a human one. Resistance to change, particularly among older hoteliers, isn't just about technology - it's about redefining age-old operational paradigms. Recognizing this, it is imperative to formulate change management strategies that are holistic. These should not only include training modules, but also address the innate human resistance to change to ensure a smoother AI integration journey. Forge collaborative pathways: There's an undeniable need for technology vendors to be more than just solution providers - they need to be partners. This research underscores the critical role of technology providers in understanding the complex challenges hoteliers face, which require bespoke AI solutions tailored to individual needs. Beyond the initial integration, ongoing support, training and iterative feedback mechanisms will be critical to the successful deployment and optimization of AI technologies. The intersection of AI and hospitality is full of potential, but realising this potential requires a multi-faceted approach. While the benefits of integrating AI are clear, the challenges, both techno-logical and human, are significant. To realise the full potential of AI in hospitality, a harmonised effort that includes targeted education, comprehensive change management and a symbiotic relationship between technology providers and hoteliers is paramount.

References

1. Bughin, J., et al.: Artificial intelligence: the next digital frontier? McKinsey Global Institute Discussion Paper (2017)
2. Nikopoulou, M., Kourouthanassis, P., Chasapi, G., Pateli, A., Mylonas, N.: Determinants of digital transformation in the hospitality industry: technological, organizational, and environmental drivers. Sustainability **15**, 2736 (2023). https://doi.org/10.3390/su15032736
3. Nam, K., Dutt, C.S., Chathoth, P., Daghfous, A., Khan, M.S.: The adoption of artificial intelligence and robotics in the hotel industry: prospects and challenges. Electron Mark. **31**, 553–574 (2021). https://doi.org/10.1007/s12525-020-00442-3
4. Dredge, D., Phi, G., Mahadevan, R., Meehan, E., Popescu, E.S.: Digitalisation in Tourism: In-depth analysis of challenges and opportunities. In: Low Value procedure GRO-SME-17-C-091-A for Executive Agency for Small and Medium-sized Enterprises (EASME) Virtual Tourism Observatory. Aalborg University, Copenhagen (2018). https://clustercollaboration.eu/sites/default/files/news_attachment/report_tourism_digitalisation_2018.pdf
5. OECD. Preparing the tourism workforce for the digital future. OECD Tourism Papers, No. 2021/02, OECD Publishing, Paris (2021). https://doi.org/10.1787/9258d999-en
6. Telekom Deutschland & Techconsult. Digitalisierungsindex Mittel-stand 2021/2022. Der digitale Status quo im deutschen Gast-gewerbe (2022). https://telekom-digitalx-content-develop.s3.eu-central1.amazonaws.com/Telekom_Digitalisierungsindex_Gastgewerbebericht_7c4971afcf.pdf
7. Benabed, A., Miksik, O., Baldissera, A. & Gruenbichler, R.: Small and medium-sized enterprises' status in the perspectives of internationalization, globalization and artificial intelligence. IBIMA Bus. Rev. Article ID 622251 (2022). https://doi.org/10.5171/2022.622251
8. Zhang, C., Lu, Y.: Study on artificial intelligence: the state of the art and future prospects. J. Ind. Inf. Integr. **23**, 100224 (2021). https://doi.org/10.1016/j.jii.2021.100224
9. Mukhamediev, R.I., et al.: Review of artificial intelligence and machine learning technologies: classification, restrictions. Opport. Chall. Math. **10**, 2552 (2022). https://doi.org/10.3390/math10152552

10. Ding, H., Wu, J., Zhao, W., Matinlinna, J.P., Burrow, M.F., Tsoi, J.K.H.: Artificial intelligence in dentistry—a review. Front. Dent. Med **4**, 1085251 (2023). https://doi.org/10.3389/fdmed. 2023.1085251
11. Kılıçhan, R., Yılmaz, M.: Artificial intelligence and robotic technologies in tourism and hospitality industry. Erciyes Üniversitesi Sosyal Bilimler Enstitüsü Dergisi **50**, 353–380 (2020). https://doi.org/10.48070/erusosbilder.838193
12. Suder, M., Duda, J., Kusa, R., Mora-Cruz, A.: At the crossroad of digital and tourism entrepreneurship: mediating effect of digitalization in hospitality industry. Eur. J. Innov. Manag. (2022). https://doi.org/10.1108/EJIM-08-2022-0422
13. Calvino, F., et al.: A taxonomy of digital intensive sectors. OECD Science, Technology and Industry Working Papers, 2018/14, OECD Publishing, Paris (2018). https://doi.org/10.1787/f404736a-en
14. Ivanov, S.: Ultimate transformation: How will automation technologies disrupt the travel, tourism and hospitality industries? Zeitschrift für Tourismuswissenschaft **11**(1), 25–43 (2019). https://doi.org/10.1515/tw-2019-0003
15. Ciftci, O., Berezina, K., Kang, M.: Effect of personal innovativeness on technology adoption in hospitality and tourism: meta-analysis. In: Wörndl, W., Koo, C., Stienmetz, J.L. (eds.) Information and Communication Technologies in Tourism 2021, pp. 162–174. Springer, Cham (2021). https://doi.org/10.1007/978-3-030-65785-7_14
16. Bulchand-Gidumal, J.: Impact of artificial intelligence in travel, tourism, and hospitality. In: Xiang, Z., Fuchs, M., Gretzel, U., Höpken, W. (eds.) Handbook of e-Tourism. Springer, Cham (2020). https://doi.org/10.1007/978-3-030-05324-6_110-1
17. Tuomi, A. (2023). AI-Generated Content, Creative Freelance Work and Hospitality and Tourism Marketing. In: Ferrer-Rosell, B., Massimo, D., Berezina, K. (eds.) Information and Communication Technologies in Tourism 2023. ENTER 2023. Springer Proceedings in Business and Economics. Springer, Cham. https://doi.org/10.1007/978-3-031-25752-0_3
18. Skift & AWS. The 2023 Digital Transformation Report (2023). https://skift.com/insight/the-2023-digital-transformation-report/
19. Leung, D., Lo, A., Fong, L.H.N., Law, R.: Applying the technology-organization-environment framework to explore ICT initial and continued adoption: an exploratory study of an independent hotel in Hong Kong. Tour. Recreat. Res. **40**(3), 391–406 (2015). https://doi.org/10.1080/02508281.2015.109015

Personalized Smart Travel with Identification and Payment

Şuayb Talha Özçelik[1]([✉])[iD], Meltem Turhan Yöndem[1][iD], Tunga Sayıcı[2][iD],
Emre Balcı[2][iD], Begüm Al[3][iD], and Oğuzhan Akkurt[3][iD]

[1] SeturTech, IT and R&D Center, İstanbul, Türkiye
{talha.ozcelik,meltem.yondem}@setur.com.tr
[2] Turkcell Technology, İstanbul, Türkiye
tunga.sayici@turkcell.com.tr, emre.balci@atmosware.turkcell.com.tr
[3] Paycell, İstanbul, Türkiye
begum.al@kent.edu.tr, akkurt.oguzhan@turkcell.com.tr

Abstract. Tourism is a sector that has a substantial economic impact on countries. With the advancement of technology, personalized solutions have become essential in the tourism sector. Building a user profile is the most common method to personalize a system. Personalization in the travel industry aims to provide travelers with the same level of support that they would receive from an assistant who knows them best. This can be achieved by analyzing the traveler's previous activities, demographic information, and characteristics as a traveler. Various new technologies have started to be used in tourism, and one of them is blockchain, which can be a critical element in the tourism industry in the following years. Travelers must present their identification at various points throughout their trip. Blockchain-based identification technology allows users to go paperless throughout their journey. Digital transactions can enhance the payment experience for visitors at tourism destinations. Destinations that offer digital payment services are viewed as smart tourist hotspots and tend to be more successful in attracting visitors. In this perspective, we added a digital payment system to our system. In this project, as a sub-part of the Celtics-Next project, SmarTravel, we planned to develop the personalized tourism system of the future, in which the customer is the focus, with three institutions: Setur Tourism Agency, Turkcell Technology, and Paycell. We hope that our project will set an example of how payment processes and blockchain-based identification can be integrated into customer-oriented smart systems.

Keywords: Personalization · Smart Travel · Identification · Payment · Blockchain

1 Introduction

Tourism is one of the largest industries in the world, accounting for almost 10% of global GDP in 2019, according to World Travel and Tourism Council [24]. It

© The Author(s) 2024
K. Berezina et al. (Eds.): ENTER 2024, SPBE, pp. 259–271, 2024.
https://doi.org/10.1007/978-3-031-58839-6_28

is a sector that has a substantial economic impact on countries [13]. In recent years, with the advancement of technology, personalized solutions have become essential in the tourism sector [8]. Personalization in the travel industry aims to provide travelers with the same level of support that they would receive from an assistant who knows them best. This can be achieved by analyzing the traveler's previous activities, demographic information, and characteristics as a traveler [23]. Building a user profile is the most common method to personalize a system [9]. User profiles have been created mainly by analyzing the items preferred by the users [3]. This information is then used to create personalized recommendations for tourists, such as where to travel and stay. Personalized smart tourism can offer benefits for both tourists and tourism destinations. For tourists, it can help them to have a more enjoyable and memorable travel experience. For tourism destinations, it can attract more tourists and increase tourism revenue.

The analysis of user actions enables the configuration of users' habits, subsequently facilitating the construction of a comprehensive user profile [6]. Sellers employ both implicit and explicit information extraction processes to acquire knowledge about users based on the known attributes of the items and the information users provide [7]. Primary data about users can be obtained from multiple sources, including user information, users' sales history, and their activities on the company website.

In recent years, various types of new technologies have started to be used in tourism, and one of them is blockchain, which can be a critical element in the tourism industry in the following years [22]. One of the primary advantages of blockchain technology is its ability to store data securely and transparently [26]. Travelers must present their identification at various points throughout their trip. Blockchain technology allows users to go paperless throughout their journey. Additionally, the elimination of identity-based checks for tourists ensures a smooth and hassle-free experience [2]. Another new technology in tourism is digital payment, which has been recognized for its potential to enhance the payment experience for visitors at various destinations [12]. Destinations offering digital payment services are often perceived as smart tourist hotspots, resulting in increased visitor attraction [19]. From these perspectives, we added a digital payment system and blockchain-based identification to our system.

In this project, as a sub-part of the Celtic-Next (C2020/2-3) and TUBITAK (9220043) project, we planned to achieve three main objectives: 1) Collaborating with Setur Tourism Agency, Turkcell Technology, and Paycell to design and develop the SmarTravel system, which incorporates digital payment and blockchain-based identification; 2) To develop a customer-centric personalized tourism system that utilizes the user's digital payment history, purchased product features, and travel personality; 3) To demonstrate the advantages of integrating blockchain-based identification and payment systems into customer-oriented smart tourism services. We will analyze user activity logs (views, clicks, add to cart, purchase) to evaluate the success of this system. We will try to show that analyzing users' traveler type, purchasing habits, and features of the purchased product is crucial in the personalization of tourism-specific systems.

2   Methodology

The methodology for profiling in tourism applications is a multi-step process that involves collecting, analyzing, and interpreting data from multiple sources. The methodology aims to create a comprehensive user profile that can be used to provide personalized recommendations and improve the user experience through the collaborative efforts of three distinct companies (Fig. 1).

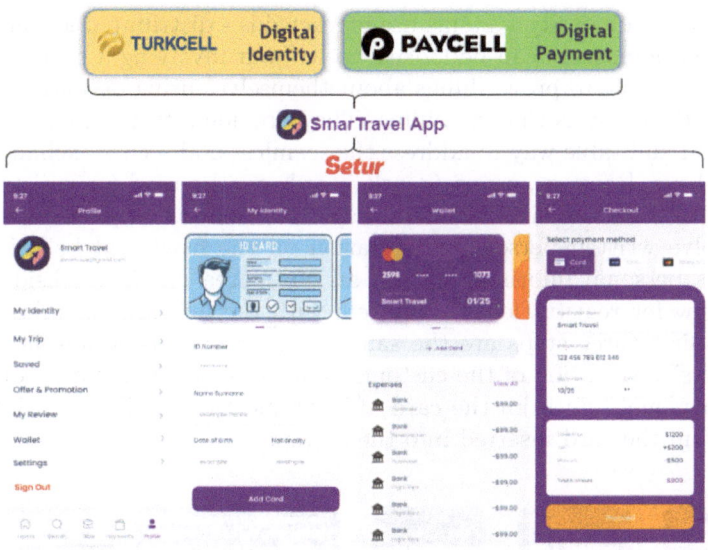

Fig. 1. Project structure

2.1   Identification

Travel industry increasingly relies on technology and digitization to create a safe and seamless passenger experience [17]. Passengers today can book their flights and check-in online, have their boarding passes on their smartphones, go through automated clearance gates, and even validate their boarding passes electronically to board planes [10]. As presented in the 2017 report on Digital Borders [21], enabling a secure, seamless, and personalized journey and incorporating new technologies into the process will dramatically reshape how the industry and governments manage the secure cross-border movement of people.

A digital identity that includes biometric and biographic data enables the traveler to authorize entities in their journey to access selected information about them to allow for risk-rating, verification, and access. Digital Identity App is a digital wallet that authenticates the user's own identity using the credentials that have been issued. Self-Sovereign Identity (SSI) solution enables people to manage all of their digital credentials from the safety of their own phone [18]. A self-sovereign identity is "owned" by the individual. As an owner, the individual has access to, can refer to, and share components of this identity at their discretion. While certain components of the identity are established by issuing authorities (passport number, bank details), the individual must consent to sharing their identities and any related data. This is achieved by individuals securely storing their own identity data on their own personal devices and providing it efficiently to those who need to validate it without relying on a central repository of identity data.

Self-sovereign identity systems use blockchains - distributed ledgers - so that decentralized identifiers can be looked up without involving a central directory. That allows people to prove things about themselves using decentralized, verifiable credentials just as they do offline. They provide a transparent, immutable, reliable, and auditable way to address the seamless and secure exchange of cryptographic keys. However, smart identity cards can be used for registration and validation in a secure and confident way instead of an application. These ID cards involve written personal information on the front and backside, a chip that stores personal information, and an NFC area on the backside. Figure 2 shows a flow for registration to a system with the information taken from the card. The first three steps are the same as the registration flow in the Smart card readers' verification of the customer's identity process, and it continues: 1) Reading personal info from the card after verification, 2) Personal information is taken from the card inserted into the system.

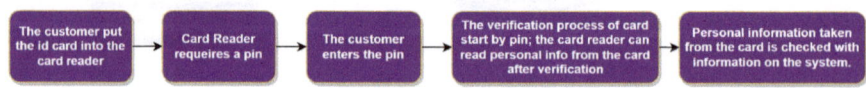

Fig. 2. SmartCard registration flow

NFC Technologies. There is an NFC area on the backside of ID cards. An NFC reader can scan the area to receive the information. The information is used for registration/validation similar to smart card reader processes. The customer chooses the identification types (Digital Identity App/ Smart Card Usage) before registration/verification processes, and which type preferred is asked to the customer by a dialog box on a system or SMS.

As the ecosystem evolves the number of parties grows, and the number of data sources, protocols/standards grow exponentially to create new value streams. The future connected ecosystem must be resilient to interoperability challenges facing data holders, consumers, and owners. This system will require an economical means to connect many organizations, services, and people together to create value - this will require a number of evolutions of authorization technologies to support data interoperability, identity interoperability, and local governance supporting connected communities that travelers will interact with. The future state of authorization will have some (but not limited to) of the following capabilities: 1) Interoperability with legacy and future identity paradigms (Traditional, federation, and SSI), 2) Ability to govern and interoperate with services and wallets authorized as agents in the ecosystem, 3) Integration pattern that supports non-direct, dynamically established connectivity between data holders and consumers, 4) Interoperability across regions/jurisdictions (locally relevant, internationally compatible), 5) Aligned to and supporting the internationally accredited trust frameworks.

Identification data with NFC is not stored in a static database. These data have been developed to be processed within the system by generating digital data created within the scope of General Data Protection Regulation (GDPR) [1]. The requirement for the use of NFC technology is aimed at the efficiency, accuracy, and speed brought by the technology. For this reason, it is ensured that the identities can be read quickly and their accuracy is determined. Information containing personal sensitive data (e.g., blood type and gender) that may be included in GDPR will be included in the blockchain system given below.

Blockchain. technology ensures the security and integrity of data through cryptographic techniques. Transactions are grouped into blocks and linked to previous blocks to form a blockchain. This connection is achieved through cryptographic hash functions that generate unique digital fingerprints for each block. Changing a block requires recalculating its hash and subsequent blocks, making it almost impossible to change [25].

The Camenisch-Lysyanskaya signature scheme enables secure and anonymous authentication. It allows users to prove their qualifications without revealing their true identity. These signatures securely encrypt identity data and store it on the blockchain. This method prevents the direct sharing of personal information, creating anonymous attributes that are verified against their peers in the blockchain [20]. Signatures are based on mathematical algorithms and cryptographic protocols and ensure user identity privacy. They offer authentication and authorization, preventing data breaches and unauthorized access [20]. Using blockchain and cryptographic methods such as Camenisch-Lysyanskaya signatures, the SmarTravel system provides a secure identification process. Users can interact with confidence knowing that their data is protected. In Fig. 3, the flow diagram shows how user information undergoes cryptographic transformation and how the corresponding signature equivalents are stored on the blockchain. This allows users to verify their credentials at any time, while preventing information from being stolen or copied.

The "Proof of Signature Submission" step is executed by the CL Signatures system to verify user identity, Fig. 3. "UTVerkey" refers to the Verification Key, which is part of the user's unique key pair. If there is a prior connection, the key is retrieved from the wallet; otherwise, new keys are generated. "keyValue Digital ID Attributes" contains the requested user credentials, where "key" refers to attributes such as first name, last name, and ID, while "value" represents the corresponding values. All this information forms the attributes of the credential.

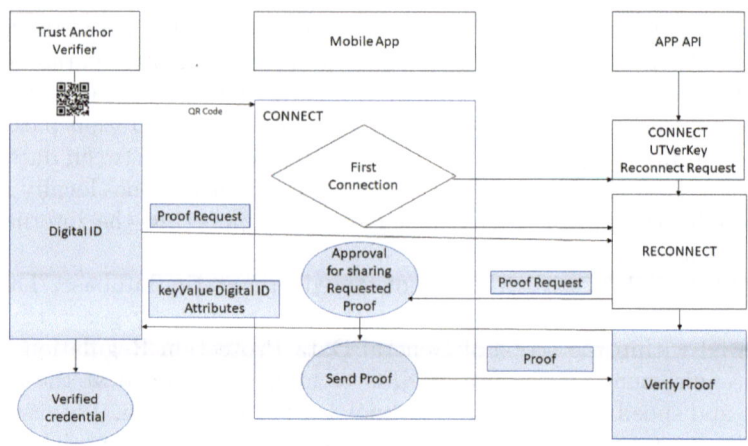

Fig. 3. Self-Identification architecture using cryptographic signatures

2.2   Payment

The SmarTravel app transcends traditional payment paradigms by implementing a digital wallet API. This visionary solution safeguards customers' card information with the utmost precision, simultaneously expediting transactions and enhancing the user experience. Powered by state-of-the-art card tokenization techniques, the digital wallet API replaces sensitive card data with impenetrable tokens. This approach mitigates data breach risks, rendering the tokens unusable to malicious actors. With this innovative layer of security, customers can confidently engage in seamless transactions, their private information shielded from harm.

The Paycell payment APIs integrate into various platforms (web, mobile applications) offered by member businesses, providing tourists with a frictionless payment experience through Paycell-defined mobile payment methods. These APIs empower member establishments to proficiently manage payment methods within Paycell, encompassing functionalities such as addition, update, mobile payment activation, and removal of payment methods. In this framework, member establishments ensure payment transactions through Paycell, leveraging Virtual POS information from banks tailored specifically for mobile payment methods. Furthermore, member businesses can incorporate mobile payment services, allowing travelers to conveniently make payments that effortlessly sync with their invoices. The payment process is simplified by selecting a Paycell-defined mobile payment method. Travelers can input their mobile payment phone number, followed by verifying the one-time password (OTP) sent to them. Notably, this integration design is exclusively dedicated to mobile payment methods, entirely excluding card-based transactions.

It is imperative to highlight that the functions do not incorporate a customer verification flow within their workflows. It is assumed that member establishments' applications consistently verify customers through the transmitted

MSISDN (phone number) during the integration process. Transactions encapsulated within the ambit of mobile payment method management include: 1) Payment Method Inquiry: Enabling the listing of customer mobile payment method information defined in Paycell; 2) Enabling Mobile Payment: Facilitating the activation of the mobile payment service for customers.

Transactions facilitated within the domain of mobile payment transactions encompass: 1) Payment: Seamlessly facilitating customers' payments by allowing them to enter their mobile payment phone number and verifying the OTP. This functionality is exclusively tailored to mobile payment methods; 2) Process Result Inquiry: Empowering the inquiry into the status of executed operations; 3) Cancellation: Enabling the cancellation of mobile payment transactions on the same day. 4) Refund: Providing the ability to initiate payment cancellations or partial refunds for mobile payment transactions from the subsequent day onwards; 5) Reconciliation: Ensuring the synchronization of transaction details between member establishments and Paycell, aligning quantities and amounts within the realm of mobile payment transactions.

The integrated SmarTravel and Paycell dataset offers valuable insights into tourist behavior and spending habits, enabling informed strategic decision-making. Key features include payment date/time, amount/category, payment type, location, demographics, and exchange rate/currency. This rich dataset allows for in-depth analysis of tourist activity, popular categories, payment methods, regional trends, and demographic-based preferences, making it an essential tool for understanding the tourism industry.

In the context of the SmarTravel project, an in-depth examination was conducted on the financial data sets collected under the name Paycell. Specifically, a segmentation study was carried out based on the payment behaviors of the customers and their levels of activity. The resultant segments obtained through the analysis are delineated as follows: 1) Highly Active Customers: Individuals within this segment have conducted more than ten payment transactions per week. Their transactions primarily consist of daily small-scale amounts and frequent purchasing tendencies. 2) Moderately Active Customers: Users within this group have engaged in 5 to 10 transactions per week. They exhibit a balanced payment pattern, encompassing both online and physical store transactions. 3) Low Activity Customers: Individuals within this segment have executed between 1 to 4 payment transactions per week. Notably, substantial-value purchases or monthly payments are distinct characteristics of this group. 4) Quiet Customers: Users within this segment have conducted sporadic transactions every few weeks, displaying low-frequency activity patterns. 5) Dormant Customers: Individuals in this group have refrained from any payment transactions within the past month. They potentially constitute a retrievable customer segment. Listed segmentation outcomes collectively provide an extensive overview of customers' payment tendencies.

The outcomes derived from our segmentation model provide a foundational basis for comprehending tourists' behaviors, preferences, and needs. Utilizing these results, Paycell possesses the potential to offer more personalized experiences for tourists, such as personalized marketing campaigns, product and service customization, strategic business decisions, and recommendation systems. In conclusion, the outcomes of the segmentation process are key to providing tourists with personalized, effective, and memorable experiences. This step is critical for enhancing tourist satisfaction and optimizing Paycell's business model and strategic approach.

Paycell implemented a different payment method called 'Charge to My Invoice,' enabling users to charge the cost of their desired product to their mobile phone bills. This option diverges among various mobile payment methods, particularly in permitting customers to opt for a card-independent payment approach. Lastly, Paycell's member businesses integrate with all the services within the payment infrastructure separately. The aim is to enhance this process through a plugin to achieve further efficiency.

2.3   Profile Card

We create the user's profile card with two main features: previous activities and demographic information. Previous activities have the following features:

- Purchasing: Paycell extracts segmentation of the users according to payment activities.
- Hotel: Setur extracts purchased hotel information of the user from previous activities, such as hotel type, hotel location, room count, and room type.
- Campaign: Setur extracts the campaign information that the user used.
- Holidays: Setur extracts which public holiday they purchased the hotel and stayed.

In marketing activities, business units utilize profile cards to send campaigns to customers. If users frequently make purchases on public holidays, targeted promotions are sent before these holidays. To retain regular customers, campaigns offer additional incentives on their preferred products. Furthermore, if users demonstrate specific hotel preferences, the campaign team suggests similar options from other regions.

The specifications extracted for the hotel were collected under four groups:

1. Hotel Type: Grown-Up, Family Friendly, Disabled Friendly, Pet Friendly, Luxury, Holiday Hotel, Town Hotel
2. Hotel Services: Room Service, Transfer Service, Tour Service, Cleaning
3. Hotel Features: Car Park, Restaurant, Bar, Shopping, TV, Internet, Night Club, Casino, Aqua Park, Indoor Pool, Public Beach, Outdoor Pool, SPA, Golf, Riding, Hobby, Adventure Sport, Sport, Activity
4. Hotel Location: Historical Destination, Nature, Seafront, Near the sea

The features extracted for the public holidays include public holiday names (such as Ramadan), preferences (1: if public holiday preferences exceed 30% of total purchases), and total count of purchases taken during public holidays. We extracted the features for the campaign that include the total count of early reservation discount usage and special discounts. In addition, Setur adds the average number of days a person stays, the average number of days in advance the purchase is made, the date of the last sale, the last check-out date, status ("Active" if the last release date is within the last two years, otherwise "Passive"), and frequency information (If the customer makes purchases within an average of 460 days (≈15 months), it is considered "Frequent", otherwise it is considered "Infrequent". If the customer has a total of one purchase, it is directly labeled as "Infrequent".).

2.4   Hybrid Personalization Model

The categorization of customers into distinct types is a crucial aspect of customer-oriented systems. This is particularly significant in the context of understanding traveler behaviors, where the classification of travelers in existing literature is taken into account. Researchers propose that a user's travel history can be perceived as a portfolio, which effectively portrays their travel persona [4,11,16]. Consequently, by examining the characteristics of their travels, it is possible to gain further insight into a user's travel behavior [5,14,16].

Based on the works of Park et al. published in 2008 [14] and 2010 [15], twenty travel personalities were identified, as depicted in Fig. 4. Participants were asked to select three of the twenty travel personalities listed in Fig. 4 in order to provide a more comprehensive understanding of their travel preferences and behaviors.

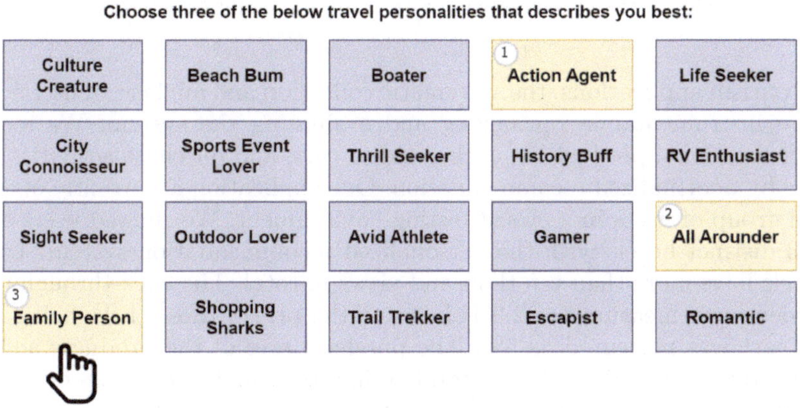

Choose three of the below travel personalities that describes you best:

Culture Creature	Beach Bum	Boater	Action Agent (1)	Life Seeker
City Connoisseur	Sports Event Lover	Thrill Seeker	History Buff	RV Enthusiast
Sight Seeker	Outdoor Lover	Avid Athlete	Gamer	All Arounder (2)
Family Person (3)	Shopping Sharks	Trail Trekker	Escapist	Romantic

Fig. 4. Travel personality question

We analyzed the user's purchase history with defining features of items (hotels). We extracted the features of the hotels from the provided information from the hotel owners, as mentioned in Sect. 2.3. We developed a hybrid model using the nomenclature in the literature and the user's previous purchase history. The system will feed and become more accurate as it is used.

Upon user registration for the application, a questionnaire is presented as an optional task. Users have the option to solve the questionnaire at any time, but they can win a discount for solving it, especially the users who have at least three purchase records. We pick their three most recent and most frequented sales records. We match the specifications of the hotel the user traveled to with the travel personalities we obtained from the questionnaire.

The hotel recommendation system takes the user's traveler type choices and its matched activities. The system selects the hotels with the relevant activity under the traveler types from the database; shared activities between traveler types will have priority. The system ranks the received hotels from most to least according to the total sales count. The recommendation system presents the top 5 hotels as suggestions to the user based on the latest ranking, as illustrated in Fig. 5.

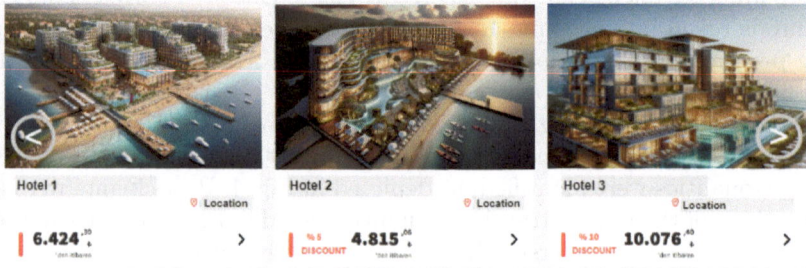

Fig. 5. Hotel recommendation example in sliding window

In tourism applications, the systematic collection and analysis of user activity logs are instrumental in optimizing and evaluating the system. We recorded product list views, product list clicks, add to cart, and purchase activities (logs) of users by personalized recommendation. Our application is currently open to a limited group of users in a closed testing environment. We showed users a total of 3253 distinct hotels with the personalized recommendation system. Twenty-six hotels have more than ten thousand views in total. The click-through rate of these views was measured as 2.3%. In total, the rate of these clicks being added to the cart was measured as 5%. The purchase rate of the products added to the cart was measured as 60% in total. While the number of views of the best-selling hotel list is 25.39% more than the number of views of the recommendation system, the number of clicks of the recommended hotels is 35.28% more than the number of clicks of the best-selling hotel list.

The platform of the SmarTravel project is used by all partners communicating via RESTful APIs, as illustrated in Fig. 6. Each partner processes the confidential information on their local servers and shares only algorithmically necessary information and algorithm results with other partners via APIs. Similarly, services such as payment infrastructure, user authorization, and customer segmentation will be used jointly by partners.

Fig. 6. SmarTravel SuperApp illustration

3   Conclusion and Future Work

Digitalization of identification systems, digital payment, and personalization can enhance tourist satisfaction and brand loyalty. Gaining insights into tourists' behaviors and preferences can provide a distinctive competitive advantage in the increasingly competitive tourism market. The segmentation results attained will open doors to providing personalized experiences that improve tourists' experience in countries. The segments generated from customer purchase history can serve as a robust foundation for augmenting the efficacy of marketing campaigns, pinpointing new product and service opportunities, and making informed strategic decisions based on customer preferences. This approach can contribute not only to short-term sales increases but also to strengthening long-term customer relationships.

In summary, this methodology revolves around the synergistic efforts of Setur, Turkcell, and Paycell, whose combined expertise enables us to create a highly customized and user-centric tourism application. Through the examination of user identification, payment history, and personal preferences, we seek to deliver the most relevant and appealing hotel recommendations to our users. User activity results showed that the personalized recommendation has a 35% higher click-through rate than the best-selling hotel listing.

References

1. General Data Protection Regulation. https://gdpr-info.eu/. Accessed 30 Sept 2023
2. Bodkhe, U., Bhattacharya, P., Tanwar, S., Tyagi, S., Kumar, N., Obaidat, M.S.: Blohost: blockchain enabled smart tourism and hospitality management. In: 2019 International Conference on Computer, Information and Telecommunication Systems (CITS), pp. 1–5. IEEE (2019)
3. Eke, C.I., Norman, A.A., Shuib, L., Nweke, H.F.: A survey of user profiling: state-of-the-art, challenges, and solutions. IEEE Access **7**, 144907–144924 (2019)
4. Fesenmaier, D.R., Johnson, B.: Involvement-based segmentation: implications for travel marketing in Texas. Tour. Manage. **10**(4), 293–300 (1989)

5. Gretzel, U., Mitsche, N., Hwang, Y.H., Fesenmaier, D.R.: Tell me who you are and i will tell you where to go: use of travel personalities in destination recommendation systems. Inf. Technol. Tourism **7**(1), 3–12 (2004)
6. Gulla, J.A., Fidjestøl, A.D., Su, X., Castejon, H.: Implicit user profiling in news recommender systems. In: International Conference on Web Information Systems and Technologies, vol. 2, pp. 185–192. Scitepress (2014)
7. Gupta, S., Dixit, V.S.: Scalable online product recommendation engine based on implicit feature extraction domain. J. Intell. Fuzzy Syst. **34**(3), 1503–1510 (2018)
8. Kabassi, K.: Personalizing recommendations for tourists. Telematics Inform. **27**(1), 51–66 (2010)
9. Kanoje, S., Girase, S., Mukhopadhyay, D.: User profiling trends, techniques and applications. arXiv preprint arXiv:1503.07474 (2015)
10. Khurramov, O.: The role of the tourism sector in the digitalization of the service economy. Econ. Innovative Technol. **2020**(1), 6 (2020)
11. Kim, S.I., Fesenmaier, D.R.: Evaluating spatial structure effects in recreation travel. Leis. Sci. **12**(4), 367–381 (1990)
12. Lou, L., Tian, Z., Koh, J.: Tourist satisfaction enhancement using mobile QR code payment: an empirical investigation. Sustainability **9**(7), 1186 (2017)
13. Mihalič, T.: Economic impacts of tourism, particularly its potential contribution to economic development. In: Handbook of Tourism Economics: Analysis, New Applications and Case Studies, pp. 645–682 (2013)
14. Park, S., Kim, H., Fesenmaier, D.: A revolutionary perspective on travel personality: implication for destination marketing. In: 39th TTRA International Annual Conference (2008)
15. Park, S., Tussyadiah, I.P., Mazanec, J.A., Fesenmaier, D.R.: Travel personae of American pleasure travelers: a network analysis. J. Travel Tourism Mark. **27**(8), 797–811 (2010)
16. Pearce, P.L.: Tourist Behaviour: Themes and Conceptual Schemes, vol. 27. Channel View Publications (2005)
17. Schnorr, C.P.: Efficient identification and signatures for smart cards. In: Brassard, G. (ed.) CRYPTO 1989. LNCS, vol. 435, pp. 239–252. Springer, New York (1990). https://doi.org/10.1007/0-387-34805-0_22
18. Shuaib, M., et al.: Land registry framework based on self-sovereign identity (SSI) for environmental sustainability. Sustainability **14**(9), 5400 (2022)
19. Susanto, E., Hendrayati, H., Rahtomo, R.W., Prawira, M.F.A.: Adoption of digital payments for travelers at tourism destinations. Afr. J. Hosp. Tour. Leis. **11**(2), 741–753 (2022)
20. Tezuka, M., Tanaka, K.: Improved security proof for the camenisch-lysyanskaya signature-based synchronized aggregate signature scheme. In: Liu, J., Cui, H. (eds.) ACISP 2020. LNCS, vol. 12248, pp. 225–243. Springer, Cham (2020). https://doi.org/10.1007/978-3-030-55304-3_12
21. Trauttmansdorff, P.: The politics of digital borders. In: Border Politics: Defining Spaces of Governance and Forms of Transgressions, pp. 107–126 (2017)
22. Valeri, M., Baggio, R.: A critical reflection on the adoption of blockchain in tourism. Inf. Technol. Tourism **23**, 121–132 (2021)
23. Völkel, S.T., et al.: Opportunities and challenges of utilizing personality traits for personalization in HCI. In: Personalized Human-Computer Interaction, vol. 31 (2019)
24. WTTC: Economic Impact. https://wttc.org/research/economic-impact. Accessed 30 Sept 2023

25. Zhai, S., Yang, Y., Li, J., Qiu, C., Zhao, J.: Research on the application of cryptography on the blockchain. In: Journal of Physics: Conference Series, vol. 1168, p. 032077. IOP Publishing (2019)
26. Zhang, R., Xue, R., Liu, L.: Security and privacy on blockchain. ACM Comput. Surv. (CSUR) **52**(3), 1–34 (2019)

Get Ready for the Future of Tourism and Hospitality with the Smart Hospitality Wheel

Nicolette Yvonne Bolté(✉), Ruth Pijls, and Sanne Ten Tije

Saxion University of Applied Sciences, Deventer, The Netherlands
n.y.bolte@saxion.nl

Abstract. Technologies have changed our world rapidly and have also reshaped the tourism and hospitality industry. Organizations need to innovate to fulfil their customers' changing needs and wishes. Students therefore need to be well prepared to enter the changing working field. Since innovation is a must, they need to learn how to use their creativity to design innovative concepts, making use of technology and data. This process can be stimulated and guided in a creativity process using the Smart Hospitality Wheel. This wheel has been developed for education, but the results in this study show its effectiveness in the industry as well. This paper introduces the development and use of the Smart Hospitality Wheel; a tool to come up with innovative ideas at the start of a design process. It stresses the importance of the use of the wheel in tourism and hospitality to design competitive and innovative concepts, describes the research method, shows some first results, and explores contributions and further research. The design and use of the wheel combined with the unique combination of theory linked to smartness and hospitality, creates a novel tool to use in the creativity process to design innovative and competitive concepts for the tourism and hospitality industry.

Keywords: innovation · technology · smart hospitality

1 Introduction

We are living in a smart world characterized by ubiquitous interconnection, intelligence, and computing, making our lives convenient, comfortable, and informed [1]. Smartness is the result of increased connectivity and data capabilities by technological advances [2]. It works to reengineer processes and data to support business information exchange and decision-making and to produce innovative services, products, and procedures ensuring stakeholder value maximization [3].

In the past decade, the rapid development of technology has also reshaped the tourism and hospitality industry [3, 4]. Technological innovations are a catalyst for developments and competitiveness in tourism and hospitality [3]. These firms need to embrace innovation and adopt the latest technologies to satisfy their customers and differentiate their products from competitors. After all, consumers want to interact in real time and

K. Berezina et al. (Eds.): ENTER 2024, SPBE, pp. 272–277, 2024.
https://doi.org/10.1007/978-3-031-58839-6_29

experience more personalized and contextualized services. Therefore, tourism destinations and service providers have already adopted various technologies to enhance the tourism experience [4]. Additionally, technologies are used by tourism and hospitality companies, affecting service advantage, value co-creation, employee job satisfaction, employees' perception of service cannibalization, and competitiveness [5].

The development of technologies and data within the tourism and hospitality industry has led to the development of Smart Hospitality Concepts (SHCs). SHCs are concepts, consisting of technology and/or data, that create added value for stakeholders within a tourism and hospitality ecosystem.

Both industry and educational institutions need to respond to the changing needs and wishes of organizations and consumers as well as technological developments. Ness [6] underscored the importance of cultivating students' creative and innovative skills during their studies to better prepare them for their future jobs, as they will need to deal with contemporary demands and disruptions in the world of tourism and hospitality.

This paper introduces the Smart Hospitality Wheel (SHW), a theory-based tool that enables education and practice to design SHCs to innovate in tourism and hospitality.

2 Smart Hospitality Wheel in Theory

The SHW is a tool to create innovative ideas for SHCs. The development of the SHW is based on theory on hospitality, customer journey, and business innovation, and has been tested in a number of practical settings in education and industry. The design of the wheel and the unique combination of theory linked to smartness and hospitality create a novel tool to use in the creativity process to design innovative SHCs. The novelty is the application, in combination with established approaches.

SHW consists of aspects visualized in 'rings' that can rotate independently. To create a concept, each ring is discussed within the team to see what aspect is included in the SHC. This paper introduces a basic set of rings. However, depending on the context, rings can be added or removed.

Hospitality Experience. The inner circle, the core, of a SHC is to enhance the hospitality experienced by its users. Based on Pijls et al. [7], the experience of hospitality consists of three different factors: inviting, care, and comfort.

Servicescape. A SHC can take place in the physical or virtual world. Hospitality is shifting to a hybrid service co-creation between tech and touch [8]. Customers can for example use an app using augmented reality in the physical environment of a location.

Effect. A SHC adds value. Based on Sigala [2], three types of value creators are distinguished: surprise, facilitate, and connect. SHCs are aimed at balancing the experience from the guest's point of view (surprise), creating an efficient and effective concept for the organization or user (facilitate), and promoting interconnectedness between stakeholders (connect).

Customer Journey. A visit in a service environment is a journey, consisting of a series of successive moments, the so-called 'touchpoints'. In the customer journey the phases of pre-arrival, arrival, stay, and departure can be discerned [9]. A SHC can be developed for a particular phase or combinations of phases within the customer journey.

Business case. A SHC may start from a particular business perspective. Van Wulfen [10] introduces four routes to a successful new business case. The chosen route depends on the starting point of the innovation: adopt a certain technology, solve an issue for customers, solve an economic issue in the organization, or adopt an idea like an opportunity found in the market.

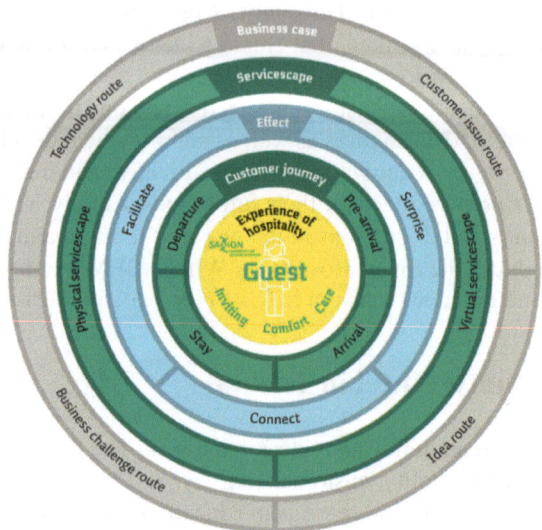

Fig. 1. The Smart Hospitality Wheel

3   Smart Hospitality Wheel in Practice

3.1   Procedure, Design and Settings

The SHW can be used both in practice and education. In practice, the wheel has been used in 12 workshops with about 140 participants in 2022 and 2023: a women's business network, a lustrum of the study Tourism Management (2×), an event of hotel schools (2×), a business event in tourism and hospitality in National Park Weerribben-Wieden (2×), a business event in tourism and hospitality in Zwolle (2×), a EuroCHRIE conference and an educational event (2×). The participants varied in professional background: 20 professionals in the tourism and hospitality business, 60 SME entrepreneurs in tourism and hospitality, and 60 educators in hospitality and tourism. In education, about 200 bachelor students used the wheel within various courses: Smart Tourism (n = 100), Minor Smart Events (n = 30), Hackathon Digital Workshop (n = 30), and Smart Solutions Semester (n = 40).

Two workshop leaders guided the design process. One was responsible for guiding the workshop, and the other observed the design process and took notes. Participants worked in groups of five to eight people. The input was either a current case created by the workshop leaders (i.e. staff shortage in restaurants, queues at security at airports) or a case suggested by the participants. After an introduction of the wheel and case, participants used a paper version of the wheel to take notes and guide ring by ring both the design process. At the end of the workshop, all groups presented their idea for a SHC and explained how the rings of the wheel were used to create the concept. Next, all participants evaluated the SHW by providing written feedback on the paper version of the wheel, and verbal feedback written down by workshop leaders and recorded in one workshop. In some workshops, the online feedback tool mentimeter or padlet was used to gather feedback. Feedback consisted of the usefulness and added value of the wheel.

3.2 Results

In both practice and education, the SHW appeared as a kickstarter in the process of designing innovative solutions. Practitioners indicated that the various rings offered support in making decisions and in getting the added value of hospitality concepts clear for both customers and the organization. The rings helped create new SHCs, for instance, a digital onboarding concept for staff in hospitality, an interactive table in restaurants, and a renewed body scan system for airports. As participants at EuroCHRIE illustrated: "The wheel was a great tool to bring an idea to life by outlining the key focus areas", and "the wheel has facilitated my ability to bring together all different perspectives and viewpoints". Entrepreneurs said: "Helpful to start looking from a certain angle" and "it encourages thinking about problems and solutions". Educators commented: "Very nice when you think about the effects, consequences, implementation. For things like that, it's very nice to keep going back to the wheel" and "It gives you a lot of grip and sense of purpose in the beginning. After that, it's nice for inspiration and check".

Furthermore, innovation and creativity in departments of large organizations were stimulated by using the SHW in brainstorming. Particularly SME business representatives tend to have a solution for their issue quite easily, so the use of the wheel helped them particularly in confirming the choices made. In addition, a logical order in the use of the rings appeared to depend on the case and personal preferences. A prescribed order does not seem to be useful. Finally, it was suggested to add other rings, such as a ring concerning stakeholders or sustainability. The workshop with business representatives additionally showed that the maximum number of rings should be five.

In education, the SHW helps students kick-start their creativity, make choices in this process by means of the rings, and finally come up with an innovative SHC. Students working with the SHW indicated that discussing each ring helped them in making choices and keeping their focus on the design of their SHC.

To illustrate, during the EuroCHRIE workshop, a group used the SHW to create a SHC to reduce long queues at airports. By using the rings (see Fig. 1) one by one they came up with ideas to solve this customer issue (ring 5 'business case') using technology. They proposed an app to reserve a particular timeslot and a smart corridor scanner. When travelers walk through the corridor, face recognition (passport control), and body and suitcase scan (security) automatically take place. This facilitates the organization and customer (rings 3 'effect' and 5 'business case') at arrival and departure at the airport (rings 2 'customer journey' and 4 servicescape') by reducing queues. Thereby it increases comfort for travelers (ring 1 'hospitality').

4 Conclusion and Future Directions

The SHW is of added value for the design process of creating smart hospitality concepts to boost innovation within the tourism and hospitality business and education. Business representatives primarily use the SHW to define the aim of innovation and justify design choices for a SHC. In education, the SHW appeared particularly useful for students to come up with innovative ideas for SHCs.

Up until now, the focus of the SHW was on the process of designing SHCs, less on the quality of the outcome itself. For future validation of the SHW, it is recommended to create a valid and reliable research design to thoroughly test the quality of the designed SHC; the product, and the role the SHW plays in the design process.

Although in this study the SHW was used in education and industry of tourism and hospitality, its effectiveness can also be used and further tested in other industries.

References

1. Liu, H., et al.: A review of the smart world. Futur. Gener. Comput. Syst. **96**, 678–691 (2019)
2. Sigala, M.: New technologies in tourism: From multi-disciplinary to anti-disciplinary advances and trajectories. Tour. Manag. Perspect. **25**, 151–155 (2018)
3. Buhalis, D.: Technology in tourism-from information communication technologies to eTourism and smart tourism towards ambient intelligence tourism: a perspective article. Tour. Rev. **75**(1), 267–272 (2020)
4. Buhalis, D., Sinarta, Y.: Real-time co-creation and nowness service: lessons from tourism and hospitality. J. Travel Tour. Mark. **36**(5), 563–582 (2019)
5. Diaz, E., Esteban, Á., Carranza, R., Sánchez-Camacho, C., Martín-Consuegra, D.: How do affect the infusion of smart technology and mindfulness of tourism SMEs on competitiveness? In: ENTER22 e-Tourism Conference, pp. 77–81. Springer, Cham (2023). https://doi.org/10.1007/978-3-031-25752-0_7
6. Ness, I.J.: Mind the gap: creative knowledge processes within interdisciplinary groups in organizations and higher education. In: Lemmetty, S., Collin, K., Glăveanu, V.P., Forsman, P. (eds.) Creativity and Learning. PSCC, pp. 195–217. Springer, Cham (2021). https://doi.org/10.1007/978-3-030-77066-2_9
7. Pijls, R., Groen, B.H., Galetzka, M., Pruyn, A.T.H.: Measuring the experience of hospitality: Scale development and validation. Int. J. Hosp. Manag. **67**, 125–133 (2017)
8. Buhalis, D., O'Connor, P., Leung, R.: Smart hospitality: from smart cities and smart tourism towards agile business ecosystems in networked destinations. Int. J. Contemp. Hosp. Manag. **35**(1), 369–393 (2023)
9. Lemon, K.N., Verhoef, P.C.: Understanding customer experience throughout the customer journey. J. Mark. **80**(6), 69–96 (2016)
10. Van Wulfen, G.: The Innovation Maze: 4 Routes to a Successful New Business Case. Bis Publishers, Amsterdam (2016)

Stakeholder Requirements and Governance for the European Data Space for Tourism

Jason Stienmetz[✉] and Yuliya Kolomoyets

Modul University Vienna, Am Kahlenberg, 1, 1190 Vienna, Austria
{jason.stienmetz,yuliya.kolomoyets}@modul.ac.at

Abstract. Data spaces enable public and private actors to connect and exchange their data assets, creating an environment for product and service innovations. This applied research provides insights into perceived values, necessary features, governance and business model requirements for designing the sustainable European Data Space for Tourism (ETDS) from the point of view of the European tourism experts. A two-round Delphi study revealed a moderate consensus around ETDS's data quality control measures, value creation, and key features. In contrast, the agreement regarding the governing body or business model was missing. Hence, no one-size-fit-all solution can meet the needs of all tourism stakeholders.

Keywords: data spaces · European Strategy for Data · Delphi · data sharing

1 Introduction

As a part of the 2020 European Strategy for Data, the European Commission has set into motion the creation of interoperable domain-specific data spaces that, in the future, will constitute a common European Data Space and realize the vision for single market for data within Europe. Given the significant impact of tourism on the European economy, the development of a European Tourism Data Space (ETDS) is an important part of this vision. Therefore, preparatory actions for the ETDS (a decentralized ecosystem for the secure exchange of data and data assets among public and non-public tourism actors and other industries) are underway. Digital transformation, seamless access to information, and network effects associated with the ETDS are expected to empower innovation, ensuring the European tourism industry's competitiveness in a global data-agile world.

To ensure that the ETDS meets the needs of European tourism stakeholders, this applied research employs a bottom-up approach to examine tourism experts' opinions regarding ETDS's perceived value, desirable features, governance approaches, and business models. Additionally, we explore the incentives for stimulating ETDS participation among public and private tourism actors.

K. Berezina et al. (Eds.): ENTER 2024, SPBE, pp. 278–283, 2024.
https://doi.org/10.1007/978-3-031-58839-6_30

2   Theoretical Background

A data space is "an infrastructure that enables data transactions between different data ecosystem parties based on the governance framework of the data space [1, p.5]. Development of a data space must balance the technical requirements (e.g., APIs, network protocols, hardware) with governance approaches (e.g., business, organizational, and operational agreements, and policies) [1, 2]. The ETDS' emphasis on data sovereignty and trust, decentralized architectures, and collaborative data space governance will be fundamental for inciting trust among participants, promoting cooperation, innovation, and fostering the development of new data-informed tourism policies, services and products that increase sustainability and competitiveness of the European tourism sector.

By maintaining control over their data assets, data space participants may decide when and what type of data assets to share, and under what terms. The data space governing body will provide the regulatory framework and guidance for these data exchanges. Since most public data spaces follow the decentralized multi-actor framework, the literature advocates for collaborative, alliance-based governance [3, 4]. The development, maintenance, and enforcement of interoperability principles, policies, and practices, as well as the coordination of the inter-stakeholder interaction is overseen by a collective body representing key stakeholder groups. In the European data space reality, the governing body typically consists of the boards (supervisory, advisory boards, and a council) in charge of the strategic and tactical level decisions, complemented by the working groups responsible for accession and certification, maintenance of innovations, technical implementation support, communication, and education [2]. The final composition of the governance framework must reflect the domain-specific aspects of a sectoral data space (such as the ETDS) and represent the interests and needs of both public and private sector actors. Therefore, the ETDS design must ensure a balanced representation of diverse tourism stakeholders' needs. This calls for a closer exploration and evaluation of those key governance features – a task undertaken by this study.

3   Methodology

A modified, two-round Delphi study was conducted from June 5–July 7, 2023, to identify consensus opinions among European tourism stakeholders about the critical success factors required for a sustainable ETDS. The sampling frame consisted of 261 tourism stakeholders of different operational scope (e.g., multinational, national, regional, local), organizational type (e.g., private enterprises, NGOs, DMOs, research institutes) and size, who previously declared interest in the research. During the first round of the Delphi study, tourism stakeholders were presented with open-ended questions soliciting their opinions about the following themes: 1) value creation, 2) key features of the ETDS, 3) motivations for participation in the ETDS, 4) EDTS governing body, 5) data quality control measures, and 6) ETDS business models. The expert (n = 77) responses to the open-ended questions were summarized by the research team into 120 statements. In the second round of the Delphi survey, the same European tourism experts (n = 55) were asked to indicate their level of agreement with each statement using five-point Likert scales. The agreement was used as the criteria for evaluating the Delphi survey results following Barnes and Mattson [5], where consensus for an item is indicated by 100 percent agreement among respondents, and majority agreement is characterized by at least 70 percent.

4   Results

Table 1 presents a summary of the number of unique statements corresponding to each EDTS governance theme, and the aggregate mean level of agreement for the statements for each theme. Results show that there was a moderate level of agreement among the sample of tourism experts with the statements regarding ETDS data quality control measures, value creation, and key features. There is weak agreement regarding statements concerning the governing body of the ETDS, the ideal business models, and how to incentivize participation in the ETDS.

Table 1. Number of unique statements and agreement per ETDS governance topic.

Theme	No. of Statements	Aggreg. Mean	Aggreg. SD
The ETDS will create value for by...	16	4.38	0.75
Important features of the ETDS should include...	41	4.23	0.84
The ETDS should motivate participation by...	15	3.97	1.03
The ETDS should be managed by...	19	3.17	1.16
The ETDS should ensure data quality by...	10	4.39	0.69
The ideal ETDS business model should...	19	3.58	1.03

Note: 1 = Strongly Disagree, 5 = Strongly Agree

Table 2 presents the four most agreed upon statements per above presented ETDS governance theme, as rated by the sample of tourism experts. These statements highlight the general attitudes, opinions, and priorities of European tourism experts. Importantly, there is strong evidence of a shared vision for an easy-to-use tourism data space that fosters data standardization, enables benchmarking, and evidence-based decision making

The results also confirm the ETDS's potential to create value for a variety of tourism stakeholders. However, accessibility of the data-based solutions (e.g., dashboards, visualizations, and analytics) will be crucial for conveying these advantages to broader tourism audience and engaging them in the data space. Data asset accessibility should be incentivized by ETDS business model(s) and facilitate a variety of transactions between participants, including both free and restricted (e.g., paid) access to data. However, results also indicate only mild agreement as to the ideal business model (freemium access).

Experts agree on the importance of open access data for the purpose of research. While indicating the need for European-level governance, there was no consensus on if an existing EU-level entity should be home for the ETDS.

Table 2. Most agreed upon statements per ETDS governance topic.

	Strongly disagree	Somewhat disagree	Neither agree nor disagree	Somewhat agree	Strongly agree
The ETDS will create value for tourism stakeholders and the tourism industry at large by...					
fostering collaboration & knowledge sharing among tourism stakeholders			9.6%	15.4%	75.0%
allowing for European-wide benchmarking			2.0%	29.4%	68.6%
improving decision-making and management			5.8%	26.9%	67.3%
fostering standardization of data formats and methodologies		1.9%	3.8%	28.8%	65.4%
Important features of an effective ETDS should include...					
access to up-to-date data			3.8%	11.5%	84.6%
ease-of-use				23.5%	76.5%
long-term commitment and support from EU			3.9%	21.6%	74.5%
political neutrality			11.3%	18.9%	69.8%
The ETDS should motivate participation by...					
providing dashboards and data visualizations	1.9%	9.4%		24.5%	64.2%
providing public access to the data space for tourism	5.8%		7.7%	32.7%	53.8%
providing license and policy templates for data sharing	2.0%		8.2%	40.8%	49.0%
providing a market analysis for data	1.9%	9.6%	9.6%	30.8%	48.1%
The ETDS should be managed by...					
the European Union	2.0%	8.2%	16.3%	38.8%	34.7%

(continued)

Table 2. (*continued*)

	Strongly disagree	Somewhat disagree	Neither agree nor disagree	Somewhat agree	Strongly agree
the European Travel Commission	10.4%	2.1%	29.2%	29.2%	29.2%
the Data Spaces Support Center	6.7%	2.2%	22.2%	40.0%	28.9%
Eurostat	6.3%	6.3%	25.0%	35.4%	27.1%
The ETDS should ensure data quality and promote interoperability by...					
maintaining transparency				15.4%	84.6%
setting data quality standards, methods, and guidelines			1.9%	17.0%	81.1%
publishing metadata			10.9%	23.9%	65.2%
utilizing APIs			3.9%	33.3%	62.7%
The ideal ETDS business model should...					
provide free data access for research and development		5.7%	15.1%	22.6%	56.6%
use a freemium model where some data are free, some paid	2.0%	3.9%	17.6%	35.3%	41.2%
offer cost reductions for organizations that share their data	2.0%		13.7%	43.1%	41.2%
facilitate data sharing based on data exchange/partnership agreements		6.0%	10.0%	48.0%	36.0%

5   Conclusion and Future Research

This study confirmed tourism stakeholders' interest in a common European data space for facilitating data exchange and promoting data-driven tourism solutions. While we identified potential governance and business models that would meet the diverse needs of European tourism stakeholders, it is also clear from the analysis that the ETDS is challenged with finding the ideal combination of solutions to create fair and equitable opportunities. Future research will investigate the ideal governance structure (e.g., private vs. non-profit) and roles of the ETDS governing body. The Delphi study has identified numerous potential business model options for the ETDS (including funding and revenue generation). However, it is apparent that there is not a one-size-fits-all option that can meet the needs of all tourism stakeholders. This suggests that in order to achieve adoption among European tourism stakeholders, the ETDS must employ a variety of mechanisms to incentivize and motivate stakeholder participation while ensuring inclusivity for a variety of tourism stakeholders based on both financial and accessibility by design.

References

1. Data Space Support Center: Starter Kit for Data Space Designers | Version 1.0 | (2023). https://dssc.eu/space/SK/29523973/Starter+Kit+for+Data+Space+Designers+%7C+Version+1.0+%7C+March+2023. Accessed 20 Oct 2023
2. Nagel L., Lycklama D.: Design Principles for Data Spaces. Position Paper| Version 1.0 | April 2021, Berlin, (2021). https://design-principles-for-data-spaces.org/. Accessed 19 Oct 2023
3. Tura, N., Kutvonen, A., Ritala, P.: Platform design framework: conceptualization and application. Technol. Anal. Strateg. Manag. **30**(8), 881–894 (2017)
4. De Reuver, M., Sørensen, C., Basole, R.C.: The digital platform: a research agenda. J. Inf. Technol. **33**(2), 124–135 (2018)
5. Barnes, S.J., Mattsson, J.: Understanding current and future issues in collaborative consumption: a four-stage Delphi study. Technol. Forecast. Soc. Chang. **104**, 200–211 (2016)

Technology for Sustainability, Health, and Well-being

Sustainability Nudges While Booking a Flight on an OTA Website

Jannina Maleika Stüben and Lorenzo Cantoni[(✉)] [iD]

USI – Università della Svizzera italiana, Lugano, Switzerland
{jannina.stueben,lorenzo.cantoni}@usi.ch

Abstract. In recent years the ecological impact of Tourism has been more and more considered, raising the issue of how to ensure higher levels of sustainability. Especially when it comes to flights, the issue of energy consumption and of exploring strategies to reduce the CO2 footprint of civil aviation has attracted a special attention, in particular while taking into account the so-called attitude-behavior gap, which describes major discrepancies between what people say about their commitment to sustainability and what they actually do when taking decisions. A possible strategy to address such issues is leveraging on "nudges" while persons are exploring available flights on an online travel agency's platform (OTA), ensuring that they are adequately informed and offered good – more sustainable – alternatives. Based on the current literature and on the analyzed cases, this study presents a first map of twelve possible types of nudges, organized in four main categories: CO2 emissions, transportation mode, CO2 compensation, and sustainability efforts. Moreover, it shows their actual, quite limited, presence on ten major OTAs.

Keywords: Sustainable Tourism · OTA · Online Booking · Nudges

1 Introduction

The worldwide increase of carbon dioxide (CO2) emissions goes along with the increase in global air traffic. Since the 1960s, it came to a seven-fold increase of aviation emissions [16]. The aviation industry is responsible for 2.5% of the world's CO2 emissions. If we take the whole tourism industry into account, it makes up already 8% of global greenhouse gas emissions [11]. Transportation is one of the significant contributors. An increase of demand in transportation and tourism does not align with the goal to adjust the industry to a more sustainable business.

To achieve the goal of reaching a higher consciousness of the environmental impact of tourism activities, another important aspect needs to be considered. At the same time as the air traffic and with it the CO2 emissions are increasing, also the number of online bookings is raising. In 2022 already 68% of all sales in travel and tourism have been made online with a projection to reach 74% by 2027 [23].

The digital world and the communication of the travel and tourism products play an important role in influencing people's travel choices. To get to the point where travelers take conscious decisions towards the environment, all players of the industry are

K. Berezina et al. (Eds.): ENTER 2024, SPBE, pp. 287–298, 2024.
https://doi.org/10.1007/978-3-031-58839-6_31

needed. The online travel market and online travel agencies (OTAs) are no exception to it. However, the possible role and actual efforts of OTAs in the sustainability domain are not yet sufficiently investigated.

The potential of nudging techniques through user interfaces is in the focus of this research. Nudging is a technique to not patronize the users but guide them in a direction that helps them to make decisions that are good according to certain criteria (in this case, for the environment). For people to act more sustainably, we encounter often the issue of the so-called "attitude-behavior gap": even though travelers want to contribute to a greener future, and declare their interest and commitment, their attitude is not represented in their actions [25]. By combining technology and sustainability in the context of tourism, a bridge can be built to spread more environmental consciousness and to overcome the attitude-behavior gap. Green nudges that are integrated in the flight booking process and in the interface design of OTAs can be used for it. Different nudging strategies and their current state of implementation by OTAs are introduced in this research.

2 Literature Review

2.1 eTourism

The advancement of Information and Communication Technologies (ICTs) has resulted in the accessibility of various products across several geographical regions, at any given time. It pushed the tourism industry to shift more and more to the online world. Tourists and businesses adopted the transformation of processes and value chains supported by ICTs. This development is called eTourism [12], which can be defined as: "the design, implementation and application of IT and ecommerce solutions in the travel and tourism industry as well as the analysis of the impact of the respective technical and economic processes and market structures on all the involved actors and especially on the traveler's experience" [29]. Increased accessibility, visibility of information and availability of products are some of the main benefits of the integration of ICTs in the tourism sector [10].

Travel agencies too, saw that its integration is inevitable for a successful business, hence online travel agencies have emerged, which serve as a database of travel providers and simplify the travel research for travelers. Online travel agencies achieve a more effective promotion and communication of their offers through ICTs while on the other hand also the travelers are empowered because their efficiency and competencies are improved by the use of information and booking systems [1]. Online communication is a crucial element in the sale of tourism products via OTAs, as ICTs are a driver of value co-creation [14]. Users are enabled to take part in the development of their experience. Against this background, OTAs have to adapt to the needs of users and try to reach their attention through digital communication and marketing.

In recent years, research and development in the field of eTourism has more and more integrated the issue of sustainability, underlying how digital tools and (big) data as well as physical processes, managerial practices and policies should be orchestrated in order to support a more sustainable tourism sector and more cautious and responsible tourism practices [7].

2.2 Sustainable Tourism

The topic of sustainability is an omnipresent topic both in praxis and in research. In the tourism research, the first scientific journal related to the topic was published in 1993 under the title "Journal of Sustainable Tourism" and the scientific interest in it has been growing ever since, exploring its many dimensions, encompassing economic, social, cultural and environmental sustainability [2], the one which is addressed in this paper. The online world of the sector is now also more in the focus. However, it is still a challenge to align the commercial interest of the industry with the principles of sustainability, not only from a business perspective but also from a traveler's view. The attitude behavior gap explains a typical phenomenon in the field, this gap can be best explained with the example of air travel. Most people are aware of the negative impact flying has on the environment, but such awareness that something needs to be changed towards a more sustainable future is not represented in the behavior of many travelers.

Research on how to make the aviation industry more sustainable is ongoing. Different scholars present approaches on how to reach a change. Guimarans et al. [8] for example places a lot of hope in a more effective air traffic management to avoid additional noise and greenhouse gas emissions. On the other hand, Qiu et al. [15] and Peeters et al. [13] do not see the problems of aviation independent of the whole business. Their main hope lies in the technological progress to avoid a restriction of flights in the future. The authors see that a step into the direction of more sustainability does not go without political innovation, financial instruments like taxes on international travel, and a change in tourism products.

Tiago et al. [24], Font et al. [5] and Tölkes [25] attribute the low number of sustainable tourism bookings not only to the lack of adequate products, but mainly to the lack of communication about it. They find that especially the research on the online communication of sustainable tourism products lacks behind.

2.3 Online Communication and Nudging

Online communication serves as a powerful tool for conveying information to customers. The digital communication sources are perceived as reliable and useful when it is used as a medium for marketing [17]. Through it, the customers are influenced in their buying decision. Hernández-Méndez and Muñoz-Leiva [9] find that optimizing the advertising campaigns of tourism businesses goes best when knowing the effectiveness of different online advertising strategies: it is getting more and more important to measure the effectiveness of web design and integrated advertising strategies.

Digital nudging harnesses this power to influence. Guiding people's behavior in digital choice environments with user interface design elements is the definition Schneider et al. [19] provide for digital nudging. The strategy of nudging is part of the behavioral economics, it addresses people's decision-making process [3]. However, they do not restrict the freedom of choice of the user. Different options get presented in a specific way, which influences the user to make a decision based on the given alternatives they have. The user is not able to make neutral decisions anymore because presenting options is never neutral [19]. Behavioral economics tries to look at the economic decisions of individuals by analyzing psychological, cultural, emotional, cognitive and social factors, and has offered a context within which nudging has been explored [21].

Websites and mobile apps serve as user interfaces, which are typical digital environments where nudges can be used. To promote more sustainable behavior, green nudges are designed [3]. Green nudging appears to offer a concrete possibility to overcome the attitude behavior gap in the sustainability topic: the research on green nudging in tourism is thus emerging. One of the main nudges that scholars investigate is providing information about CO_2 emissions when it comes to booking flights. Enste & Potthoff [4] find that the willingness to pay for flights with fewer emissions is higher if a label shows the flights with the least CO_2 emissions and a breakdown into more sustainable *vs.* less-sustainable flights is provided. It helps customers to make choices towards a greener flight. The authors conclude that websites that sell flights should include a nudge that promotes lower-emission flights in a non-freedom restricting way. Sanguinetti & Amenta [18] conducted a similar study where they prominently display the emissions of the flights next to cost, layovers, and airports. They found that participants in their study had an impressive rate of willingness to pay for lower-emission flights.

Wehrli et al. [27] tested another nudge where the CO_2 compensation of a flight is included in the price of the travel product, while an opt-out instead of an opt-in option is provided. Also, Weinmann et al. [28] concluded that changing the default to an opt-out option serves as a nudging technique with big potential.

While emerging, the current research in the field of green nudging in the tourism and especially aviation industry is however still very limited, in particular, the online communication of OTAs and different possible nudges are rarely tackled in research [20]. In this paper, we address this issue, in particular when it comes to the online booking of flights.

3   Methodology

OTAs play a crucial role in the communication of tourism products. They sell their products through web interfaces, by which they make their sales revenues [26]. OTAs are often used as search platforms by users to compare different flights. The platforms and their interfaces bear a huge potential to include nudges to make people opt for more sustainable tourism products. To find out about the current state of incorporation of nudges on the OTAs websites during a flight booking process, a content analysis has been conducted: information was collected on the presence of green nudging techniques.

Ten different OTAs have been chosen to conduct flight booking simulations. The selection of the OTAs is based on the statistics "most popular flight search engines online bookings by brand in Switzerland 2022" [22]. Billig-reise.ch is excluded from the analysis because the website did not show any results during the period of research from April to June 2023. The OTAs that were investigated were Booking, Ebookers, CheapTickets, Expedia, Fluege.de, Lastminute.de, Tripadvisor, Google Flights, Agoda, Skyscanner.

The investigation on the websites of those ten OTAs has been done on the desktop website and not via the mobile website or application.

On the 4th and 5th of June 2023, the content analysis was conducted. The simulation of two flights with the connection Zurich – Amsterdam on the 1st of August 2023 to the

8th of August 2023 and a long-distance connection Zurich – Bangkok in the same time period were performed. The flight booking process was executed as a guest user without logging into the OTAs user accounts. The English version of the website has been used, and the simulation was done with a MacBook Pro and the Incognito Mode of the Google Chrome Browser. Notes have been taken on the contents and functionalities that aim to encourage users to be more sustainable.

A list of categories of nudges has been developed in order to evaluate if they are present on the interface during the flight booking process through the OTAs website. The category-formation has been done descriptively by considering the current literature on the topic and cases from other OTAs and airline companies [20] as well as analyzing green nudges that are used in the web-design of OTAs that focus on sustainable travel like Fly Green (https://fly.green) or FlyGRN (https://flygrn.com). Additionally, by conducting flight booking simulations through the websites, each time an element was found, which was not yet present in the list, the list has been updated, and previously analyzed OTAs have been re-checked for consistency and completeness. By such recursive process, a list of twelve types of green nudges has been compiled.

By running the scenarios, notes were taken on the presence of the listed nudges. For a consistent analysis, the first flight option that was presented to the user on the search results page was chosen for continuing the process. The simulation stopped at the point of payment, and no information could be collected about the web design and the possible appearance of nudges during the payment process and afterward.

The results aim to answer the following research questions:

- Which nudges might be used by OTAs in their online communication in order to invite users to make more sustainable flight choices?
- Are such nudges extensively adopted in the online communication of OTAs and, if not, which ones are used and which ones are not?

4   Results

Hereafter, the results are presented as follows: first the list of identified types of nudges, then how they are actually implemented in the ten studied OTAs' platforms.

4.1   Towards a Taxonomy of Nudges

In Table 1, twelve types of nudges are listed, which could be integrated into the online communication of OTAs during the flight booking process. They have been organized according to four main categories, depending on their focus on (I) CO2 emissions; (II) Transportation mode; (III) CO2 compensation; and (IV) Sustainability efforts. While overall such twelve nudges can be considered – at the state of the art – collectively exhaustive, they are not mutually exclusive: more than one category can appear, and more than one nudge can be used belonging to the same category, even if this last case is very uncommon.

While it is not possible here to provide a detailed description of how each of those twelve nudges can be represented in the user-interface of OTAs, in Fig. 1 we provide just one example, taken from an OTA with a peculiar focus on sustainability. It represents a

Table 1. Identified types of nudges, and their categories.

Type/**Category**	Description
CO2 emissions	
1. Carbon emissions	Display the carbon emissions of the flights shown in the search result page
2. Ratio of emissions	Indicate the percentage of emissions of a specific flight compared to the average emissions of alternative flights on the same route shown in the search results
3. Emission comparison to everyday examples	Indicate the ratio of the emissions of a specific flight compared to the emissions of a more commonplace CO_2-emitting example like the carbon footprint of a steak or the annual CO_2 emissions of a person in Europe. This serves for a better understanding of the impact of the emissions of a specific flight
4. Sustainability filter	Present a filter function to indicate flights with lower CO_2 emissions than the average on top of the search results
5. Direct flights at the top	Present direct flights to the destination at the top of the search results, even if the departure airport changes, to get a direct connection
Transportation mode	
6. Alternative transportation mode	Show more sustainable transportation alternatives, like the train for a connection where possible, on top before displaying the flight results
7. Train connection to airport	Include the train connection to and from the airport in the ticket price and promote it
CO2 compensation	
8. Link to CO2 compensation payment	Provide a link to a provider where the user can offset the carbon emissions of the flight
9. Direct payment	Offer the option to pay CO_2 compensation directly in the flight booking process or via the website
10. Add offsetting to the price	Add the CO_2 compensation to the ticket price with the option to deselect the function (opt-out)

(*continued*)

Table 1. (*continued*)

Type/**Category**	Description
11. Different ticket options	Offer different ticket options in addition to economy, business, or first class, like economy green, where the CO2 compensation or SAF (Sustainable Aviation Fuel) is already included
Sustainability efforts	
12. Sustainability efforts of airline	Present the sustainability efforts of the airlines of the displayed flights in the search results

nudge under the category "Transportation mode": *Alternative transportation mode*. In this case, the platform suggests to travel by train, putting alternatives by train immediately above the flight ones (which are not visible in the screenshot). The example is given for the connection Zurich-Paris but can be applied to any connection where an alternative transportation mode is available.

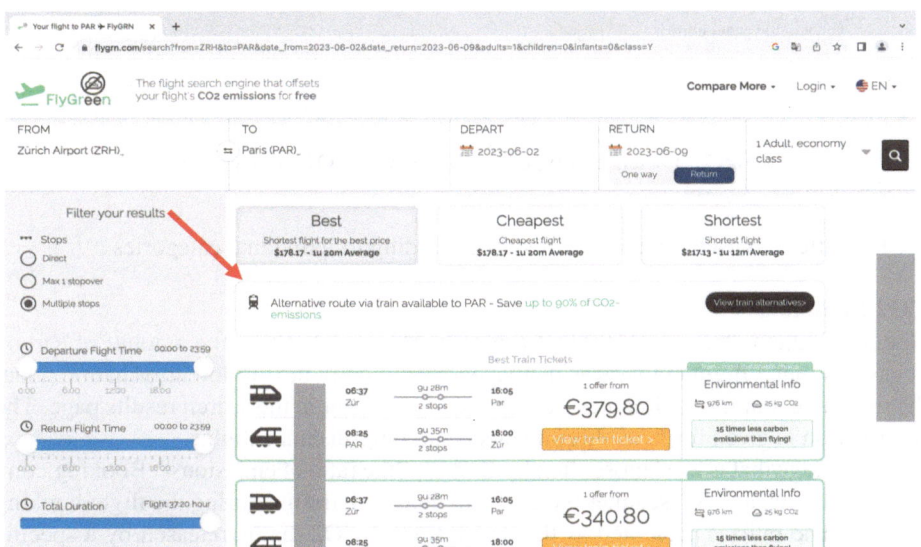

Fig. 1. Screenshot of FlyGRN with MacBook Pro via Google Chrome (the logos of the railway company and of social media channels have been covered in grey).

4.2 Presence Within OTAs Platforms

The results reveal the status quo of the presence of green nudges on the interfaces of OTAs' websites during the flight booking process. By evaluating the results, it can be concluded whether, which and how many of the green nudges are used by the ten analyzed OTAs and, in general, how many of the OTAs engage in green nudging at all.

From all the analyzed twelve nudges, five have been found in this study, and also five are the analyzed OTAs that engage in the implementation of any form of green nudging. Figure 2 provides an overview on the results.

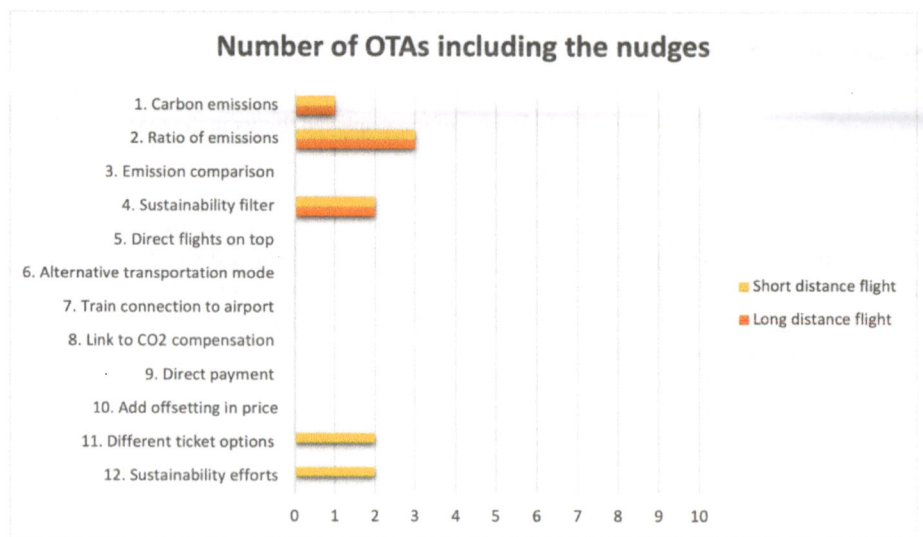

Fig. 2. Presence of types of nudges within OTAs' platforms.

Hereafter a presentation of the results according to individual categories.

CO2 Emissions

Google Flights is the only OTA that presents information about the amount of carbon emissions that a flight emits. It is displayed prominently next to the information about the timetable, duration, directness, and price of the flight in the search results page. The information is given for both short-distance and long-distance flights.

The nudge that is used most often by OTAs is "the ratio of emissions". Booking.com, Google Flights, and Skyscanner include it in their web design during the flight booking process. The ratio is presented as the proportion of CO2 that is released by a specific flight compared to an average flight on that route. It is interesting that more OTAs indicate the ratio of emissions than the exact amount of carbon dioxide.

None of the analyzed OTAs is comparing the emissions of the flight to a more day-to-day example that emits CO2 to create a greater consciousness about the negative impact of the emissions in the minds of the user choosing the flight. This would help the user to have a better comparison of the exact amount of emissions that are used for a flight on a specific route.

Two out of the three OTAs that present the ratio of emissions also include the option to filter after sustainability, namely Google Flights and Skyscanner. Because they already indicate the ratio of emissions, they provide the option to filter for the flights with fewer emissions than average.

Even though it is common for OTAs to display direct flights at the top of the search results, none of the OTAs presents it there because it has the lowest CO_2 emissions of all indicated flights, but because it has the "best value". Therefore, none of the OTAs explicitly state that the direct flights are prioritized due to their lower emissions compared to alternative flight connections.

Transportation Mode

Presenting alternative, more sustainable transportation modes at the top of the search results for connections where such an alternative is possible, is not done by the analyzed OTAs. From the html code of the website, it appeared that Google Flights was ready to include such a nudge, however, it seems that a certain threshold has not been met for it to be displayed for the analyzed connections.

Including the ticket for a train connection to the airport and from the airport to the city center of the destination, is not promoted by the analyzed OTAs. To reduce traffic congestion around airports, the inclusion of the public transportation tickets around the airport in the overall ticket price could be an approach.

CO2 Compensation

To compensate for the environmental impact of the chosen flights, the user could get a link presented, where the CO_2 offsetting can take place. However, none of the analyzed OTAs redirect their customers to websites that provide such a service.

Instead of providing a link, the OTA could include the CO_2 compensation in its booking procedure, where the user can add the extra payment to his/her flight. This saves the extra effort that the user has to do in order to redirect to another website for the compensation. The results show that none of the OTAs are offering the direct payment option.

A third nudge in the category "CO2 compensation" could be to already include the carbon offsetting into the ticket price with an opt-out instead of an opt-in option. The results of [27] and [28] show that offering an opt-out instead of opt-in option is more effective. However, none of the analyzed OTAs provided such a feature during the flight booking process.

The nudge "different ticket options" is only indicated by Ebookers and Expedia, and only for the short-distance flight.

Sustainability Efforts

As in the above-mentioned case of "different ticket options", also the nudge "sustainability efforts of the airline" is only adopted by Ebookers and Expedia. This has to do with the airline that is operating the flight. If the airline is providing the information to the OTA, the platform can display it. Because a different airline was chosen for the short-distance than for the long-distance flight, the nudges were not included for the long-distance flight even though it was the same OTA. If the other OTAs would include such a nudge if another airline than the ones indicated on top of the search results would have been chosen, cannot be concluded in this research. The different ticket options and sustainability efforts of the airline are no features of the OTAs, however if the information is available, the OTAs should include it in their web-design. However only two OTAs include such information.

5   Discussion and Conclusion

Our analysis has demonstrated that there is a major room for improvement when it comes to implement nudges toward more sustainable travelling practices within OTAs interfaces to select flights. In fact, according to the presented scenarios, only three out of four categories of nudges have been incorporated by just five OTAs out of the ten considered. The opportunity of action on the topic of sustainability in the tourism sector is evident, not only considering CO2 emissions, but also other polluting elements by airplanes, like nitrogen oxides (NOx).

This paper has provided a twofold contribution.

On the one side, at the academic level, it has provided a first taxonomy of green nudges that can be implemented by OTAs in order to raise awareness about sustainability issues and to promote more sustainable travelling practices. Moreover, it has contributed the current state of the art of ten major OTAs, those most used in Switzerland.

On the other side, from an industry perspective, the results can be used by OTAs – and at a large extent also by airline companies – in order to re-design their interface and to further embrace a sustainable travel "philosophy"; moreover, the studied nudges might contribute to bridge the attitude-behavior gap, which has been so frequently found when it comes to promoting sustainable and responsible travel practices.

While discussing the presented results, it is important to stress that the impact of air travelling is not evenly distributed among all travelers: according to a recent study, "The percentile of the most frequent fliers – at most 1% of the world population – likely accounts for more than half of the total emissions from passenger air travel. Individual users of private aircraft can contribute to emissions of up to 7,500 t CO2 per year" [6]; consequently, if possible, efforts should be mostly aimed at involving those specific publics. Moreover, further research from outside of the Tourism domain might in the future better specify the actual environmental impact of air travel or suggest further strategies to limit it.

This research has to be considered a preliminary one. Further follow-up studies might explore more OTAs and include also airline companies. Future research can furthermore take not only the point of view of the end user – like we did while executing the scenarios, searching for available flights to travel between two specific points in space – but also including the views of managers of OTAs.

A further perspective should focus on the actual effectiveness of such nudges. It might be implemented through digital analytics and A/B testing, answering such questions as *are those nudges effective? for whom? under which conditions?* Also a survey with end users might be done, assessing which nudges are perceived by them as the most convincing and effective ones.

Acknowledgements. This research is a development of a study started within the framework of the Master in International Tourism at USI – Università della Svizzera italiana (Lugano, Switzerland), as a Master thesis conducted by Jannina Maleika Stüben and supervised by Lorenzo Cantoni.

References

1. Buhalis, D., Jun, S.H.: E-Tourism, contemporary tourism reviews. International Centre for Tourism and Hospitality Research Tourism Management and Marketing School of Services Management (2011)
2. de Oliveira, R.A., Baracho, R.M.A., Cantoni, L.: The perception of UNESCO World Heritage Sites' managers about concepts and elements of cultural sustainability in tourism. J. Cult. Heritage Manage. Sustain. Dev. (2022). https://doi.org/10.1108/JCHMSD-03-2021-0058
3. Enste, D., Potthoff, J.: Behavioral Economics and Climate Protection. Better regulation and green nudges for more sustainability. IW-Analyse, p. 146 (2021)
4. Enste, D., Potthoff, J.: Klimaschonend Fliegen mit Green Nudging? IW-Kurzbericht, p. 12 (2022)
5. Font, X., English, R., Gkritzali, A., Tian, W.: Value co-creation in sustainable tourism. A service-dominant logic approach. Tourism Manage. **82**, 104200 (2021). https://doi.org/10.1016/j.tourman.2020.104200
6. Gössling, S., Humpe, A.: The global scale, distribution and growth of aviation: implications for climate change. Glob. Environ. Chang. **65**, 102194 (2020). https://doi.org/10.1016/j.gloenvcha.2020.102194
7. Gretzel, U., Werthner, H., Koo, C., Lamsfus, C.: Conceptual foundations for understanding smart tourism ecosystems. Comput. Hum. Behav. **50**, 558–563 (2015). https://doi.org/10.1016/j.chb.2015.03.043
8. Guimarans, D., Arias, P., Tomasella, M., Wu, C.: A review of sustainability in aviation: a multi-dimensional perspective. Sustain. Transp. Smart Logistics **2019**, 91–121 (2019). https://doi.org/10.1016/B978-0-12-814242-4.00004-1
9. Hernández-Méndez, J., Muñoz-Leiva, F.: What type of online advertising is most effective for eTourism 2.0? An eye tracking study based on characteristics of tourists. Comput. Hum. Behav. **50**, 618–625 (2015). https://doi.org/10.1016/j.chb.2015.03.017
10. Inversini, A., Xiang, Z., Fesenmaier, D.: New media in travel and tourism communication: toward a new paradigm. In: Cantoni, L., Danowski, J. (ed.) Communication and Technology, pp. 497–512. De Gruyter Mouton, Berlin, München, Boston (2015). https://doi.org/10.1515/9783110271355-029
11. Lenzen, M., Sun, Y., Faturay, F., Ting, Y., Geschke, A., Malik, A.: The carbon footprint of global tourism. Nature Clim. Change **8**, 522–528 (2018). https://doi.org/10.1038/s41558-018-0141-x
12. Pan, B.: eTourism. In: Jafari, J., Xiao, H. (eds) Encyclopedia of Tourism. Springer, Cham (2016). https://doi.org/10.1007/978-3-319-01384-8_77
13. Peeters, P., Gossling, S., Becken, S.: Innovation towards tourism sustainability: climate change and aviation. Int. J. Innov. Sustain. Dev. **1**(3), 184–200 (2007). https://doi.org/10.1504/IJISD.2006.012421
14. Polo Peña, A.I., Frías Jamilena, D.M., Rodríguez Molina, M.A.: Value co-creation via information and communications technology. Serv. Ind. J. **34**(13), 1043–1059 (2014). https://doi.org/10.1080/02642069.2014.939641
15. Qiu, R., Hou, S., Chen, X., Meng, Z.: Green aviation industry sustainable development towards an integrated support system. Bus. Strateg. Environ. **30**(5), 2441–2452 (2021). https://doi.org/10.1002/bse.2756
16. Ritschie, H.: Climate change and flying: what share of global CO2 emissions come from aviation (2020). https://ourworldindata.org/co2-emissions-from-aviation
17. Samson, R., Mehta, M., Chandani, A.: Impact of online digital communication on customer buying decision. Procedia Econ. Finance **11**, 872–880 (2014). https://doi.org/10.1016/S2212-5671(14)00251-2

18. Sanguinetti, A., Amenta, N.: Nudging consumers toward greener air travel by adding carbon to the equation in online flight search. Transp. Res. Rec. **2676**(2), 788–799 (2021). https://doi.org/10.1177/03611981211046924
19. Schneider, C., Weinmann, M., vom Brocke, J.: Digital nudging: guiding online users choices through interface design. Commun. ACM **61**(7), 67–73 (2016). https://doi.org/10.1145/3213765
20. Schories, F., Stüben, J., Hasenzahl, L., Strasdas, W., Cantoni, L.: Nachhaltigkeit bei Buchungsportalen und digitalen Reiseanbietern. Zentrum für nachhaltigen Tourismus & Institute of Digital Technologies for Communication (2023). https://www.zenat-tourismus.de/images/pdf/Report_HNEE-USI_Final_final%20002.pdf
21. Schubert, C.: Exploring the (behavioural) political economy of nudging. J. Inst. Econ. **13**(3), 499–522 (2017). https://doi.org/10.1017/S1744137416000448
22. Statista. Flight search engine online bookings by brand in Switzerland (2022). https://www.statista.com/forecasts/1348566/flight-search-engine-online-bookings-by-brand-in-switzerland
23. Statista. Travel & Tourism – Worldwide: Sales Channels (2023). https://www.statista.com/outlook/mmo/travel-tourism/worldwide?currency=usd%E2%80%8D#sales-channels
24. Tiago, F., Gil, A., Sternberger, S., Borges-Tiago, T.: Digital sustainability communication in tourism. J. Innov. Knowl. **6**(1), 27–34 (2021). https://www.elsevier.es/en-revista-journal-innovation-knowledge-376-articulo-digital-sustainability-communication-in-tourism-S2444569X19300617
25. Tölkes, C.: The role of sustainability communication in the attitude–behaviour gap of sustainable tourism. Tour. Hosp. Res. **20**(1), 117–128 (2020). https://doi.org/10.1177/1467358418820085
26. Tsang, N.K.F., Lai, M.T.H., Law, R.: Measuring e-service quality for online travel agencies. J. Travel Tour. Mark. **27**(3), 306–323 (2010). https://doi.org/10.1080/10548401003744743
27. Wehrli, R., et al.: How to Communicate Sustainable Tourism Products Effectively to Customers, Lucerne University of Applied Sciences and Arts (2013). https://www.hslu.ch/en/lucerne-university-of-applied-sciences-and-arts/research/projects/detail/?pid=84
28. Weinmann, M., Schneider, C., Brocke, J.V.: Digital nudging. Bus. Inf. Syst. Eng. **58**, 433–436 (2016). https://doi.org/10.1007/s12599-016-0453-1
29. Werthner, H., Alzua-Sorzabal, A., Cantoni, L., et al.: Future research issues in IT and tourism. Inf. Technol. Tourism **15**, 1–15 (2015). https://doi.org/10.1007/s40558-014-0021-9

Against Social Sustainability? Gender Role Models and Tourism Influencers' Success on Instagram

Irina V. Gewinner[✉] [iD]

Institute of Sociology, Leibniz Universität Hannover, Hanover, Germany
i.gewinner@ish.uni-hannover.de

Abstract. This paper examines the phenomenon of influencers with a special focus on the tourism industry. The question arises whether self-portrayal within a gender-stereotypical framework correlates positively with success and the number of followers. To this end, the profiles of twelve tourism influencers and their posted content in the first half of 2023 were analyzed. With the help of quantitative content analysis, we examined 427 photos of tourism influencers on the Instagram platform. The results show that while female tourism influencers more often present themselves in a sexualized way and focus on themselves and their bodies, male tourism influencers put their competencies in the foreground. In this way, both female and male influencers comply with their expected gender roles – in addition to the body, a presentation of socially expected actions and attributes is also in the foreground. The results are discussed against the background of social sustainability.

Keywords: Gender role models · tourism influencers · social sustainability · Instagram

1 Introduction

In today's digital landscape, social media users continually shape their identities by sharing videos, photos, and texts, blurring the line between active contributors and passive observers. The widespread use of social media has given rise to a growing number of influencers who document their daily lives, engage communities, and express opinions on various topics, brands, or products. In this era, individuals can independently create and influence their own communities, impacting follower numbers daily. Particularly among younger generations Y and Z (born between 1980 to the late 1990s and 1997 to approximately 2010, respectively), transparency and authenticity hold significant importance [2], qualities often conveyed by influencers to their communities.

This transformative shift positions the Internet not only as a replacement for traditional media like television and radio [1], but also as a force shaping social relations, cultural values, and communication methods. The study at hand explores the consequences of digitalization and influencer marketing on social sustainability. Here, social sustainability refers to a society's long-term capacity to challenge harmful cultural and societal

K. Berezina et al. (Eds.): ENTER 2024, SPBE, pp. 299–311, 2024.
https://doi.org/10.1007/978-3-031-58839-6_32

expectations that perpetuate discrimination and limit opportunities, with a specific focus on gender stereotypical representations and stereotypes among influencers.

The study deals with the consequences of digitalization and influencer marketing on social sustainability, the latter understood as a long-term capacity of a society to maintain and enhance the equity by challenging harmful cultural and societal expectations that limit opportunities and perpetuate (gender) discrimination. This research investigates the extent to which a gender stereotypical presentation is used in photos presented by tourism influencers. In a more focused approach, the study asks, to what extent do gender-stereotypical (self)presentations increase influencers' (self)marketing value? Are there gender differences in these representations?

2   Theoretical Underpinnings

2.1   Gender Stereotypes

Gender stereotypes are ingrained societal beliefs regarding the characteristics of women and men, shaping the attitudes, thoughts, and opinions of a community. This underscores gender as a social construct [3, 4]. These stereotypes exist in individual thinking and form the foundational understanding of typical characteristics of the sexes in a consensual, culturally shared manner. They encompass both descriptive aspects, defining what women and men are perceived to be, and prescriptive elements [5], outlining how they should behave. The consequence is a tendency toward generalizations and stigmatizations [3].

The endurance of gender stereotypes lies in their simplification of the multidimensional aspects of gender, providing a navigational tool for individuals within society. This classification often occurs automatically, with gender stereotypical ideas taking root in childhood. Typically, men are expected to embody competence and instrumentality, while women are associated with warmth and expressiveness. This is attributed to traditional roles in professional and family lives, as theorized by Alice Eagly [6, 7]. Social status, as introduced by Fiske et al. [8], further plays a role, highlighting the hierarchizing function of gender. In this framework, a group with high social status signifies competence, while low social status implies incompetence. The cooperative interdependence of women to men and the competitive orientation of men contribute to the persistence of behavioral rules that position women in a subordinate relationship to men, stabilizing the gender hierarchy [5]. This hierarchy is strongly supported by sexism, where women deviating from gender stereotypes face rejection, while those conforming enjoy positive connotations. Understanding and challenging these gender stereotypes is vital for fostering a socially sustainable society that acknowledges and addresses gender bias [3]. It involves dismantling entrenched beliefs, promoting inclusivity, and cultivating a society conscious of the impact of gender stereotypes on social hierarchies.

2.2 Gender Stereotypes and Social Media

The relationship between gender stereotypes and social media is intricate and interconnected. Social media platforms play a dual role in transmitting gender stereotypes, reflecting and perpetuating existing norms in society [3, 9, 10]. While some individuals and groups use these platforms to challenge traditional gender norms and advocate for equality and sustainability, others exploit social media to propagate harmful stereotypes and engage in online harassment.

Research indicates that social media often reinforces traditional gender stereotypes by promoting specific ideals of masculinity and femininity. Women are frequently depicted as focused on appearance and domestic roles, while men are portrayed as strong and assertive. Images, memes, videos, and targeted advertising contribute to the reinforcement of these stereotypes. Algorithmic bias exacerbates the issue, as social media platforms curate content based on users' existing beliefs, inadvertently amplifying gender bias. If users engage with content promoting traditional gender roles, they are more likely to be exposed to similar content, solidifying those stereotypes and hindering progress towards social sustainability [11, 12].

In essence, social media both mirrors and influences societal perceptions of gender. It has the potential to reinforce or challenge traditional stereotypes, providing a space for both inclusivity and regressive views. Ongoing efforts by various organizations, individuals, and platforms aim to combat gender stereotypes and harassment, striving for a more equitable digital world.

2.3 Gender Stereotypes and Instagram Tourism Influencers

Instagram, launched in 2010 for iOS and 2012 for Android operating system [13], has transformed social media by focusing on photos and videos. Users create profiles, deciding whether their contributions (photos or videos) are visible to the public or selected followers. The platform allows the addition of filters, text, hashtags, and the expression of approval through 'likes' and comments. The introduction of 'Stories' in 2016 enables users to share content that disappears after 24 h [13].

Influencers, arising from social media, possess the ability to shape opinions and purchasing behavior. Considered "grassroots influencers or micro-celebrities" [14, p. 148], they build strong connections with their followers, establishing themselves as brands and collaborating with companies. This collaboration offers brands a unique opportunity to directly engage with specific target audiences and thus to generate potential new customers [14].

The influencer phenomenon extends to the tourism industry, where influencers initially emerged from blogs and expanded to visual platforms like YouTube and Instagram. Successful campaigns showcase influencers sharing travel experiences, tips, and tricks, resonating with their followers. The modern influencer represents a digital lifestyle, influencing others through their appearance and behaviors shared on social media [1]. Influencers merge their private and public lives, taking their online community into their everyday experiences through photos, stories, and videos. Depending on their popularity, influencers become influential advertising representatives, appealing to advertising bodies [15].

Instagram, particularly popular among younger generations (Y&Z), occupies a significant space in daily life. Approximately 39% of users are under 24 years old, making it the most represented age group [17]. Influencers on Instagram become relatable figures for followers, addressing longings for vacation and leisure. Influencers, with their supposed closeness to followers, grow into influential role models, especially for adolescents.

Social media structures can mirror real-world social hierarchies, and influencers play a role in reinforcing these dynamics. They act as role models for adolescents, influencing perceptions of how women and men should look or behave. For instance, female influencers may focus on beauty and fashion, while male influencers may emphasize athleticism or entrepreneurship, reinforcing stereotypes about success and attractiveness [14]. Images, particularly in photography, hold significant power as socially constructed representations [13]. The perspective, focus, pose, and facial expressions in photographs influence the viewer's interpretation. 'Selfies,' a crucial aspect of visual communication, elevate the visibility of the human body on platforms like Instagram. The platform itself revolves around the constant optimization of body image, aligning with societal and community ideals [15].

It's essential to recognize that influencers only share a fraction of their lives, making it challenging to assess the extent to which gender-stereotypical actions are practiced in their everyday lives. Nevertheless, influencers have a profound impact on shaping ideas about gender norms and expectations. The representation of bodies on Instagram, particularly through the lens of influencers, contributes to the ongoing construction of societal ideals and expectations regarding appearance and behaviour [18].

3   State of the Art Discussion

For influencers, creating captivating content that appeals to a broad audience and is easily consumed by many potential followers is crucial. Self-presentation within established gender roles is significant, as deviation from these roles may lead to rejection [5]. Selfies, in particular, serve as a vital interface between the digital and real worlds, fostering a sense of closeness between influencers and their followers [18].

In the tourism industry, gender differences among influencers arise from prevailing stereotypes about vacations. Women are often associated with a focus on recreation and shopping [19, 20], emphasizing emotional warmth through eye contact or smiling in their social media presence. On the other hand, men are seen to prefer adventurous vacations [3] and tend to highlight their status by showcasing expensive clothing or special objects like cars [18].

The study by Döring et al. [18] explored the content of selfies on social media, with a focus on how these images either reinforce or challenge gender stereotypes. The study also aimed to compare gender representations in selfies with those in magazine advertisements. Analyzing 250 selfies, the authors found that women's selfies statistically featured more kissing mouths, while men's selfies emphasized muscles. Interestingly, the study revealed that gender stereotypes were more prevalent in selfies on Instagram compared to images in magazines, suggesting that Instagram selfies contribute to the propagation of gender stereotypes in the public sphere.

Butkowski et al. [21] delved into the relationship between Instagram usage and body image concerns among young adult women. The study sought to understand how the time and effort invested in seeking feedback on Instagram selfies might influence these concerns. Content analysis revealed traditional expressions of feminine gender presentation in selfies, including techniques like 'loss of control' (appearance of spontaneity or a lack of complete control over the image), 'body display' (emphasis a body in a flattering way), and 'leaning' (tilt of a body or head at an angle). Despite the prevalence of these stereotypical cues, the study observed a certain subtlety in the expression of gender poses. Notably, there were no statistically significant differences in factors such as race, sexuality, and political ideology.

Regarding the current state of research, existing studies do investigate gender stereotypical portrayal on social networks, however, there are research gaps in relation to tourism and marketing.

4 Method

The methodological approach is underpinned with quantitative content analysis using MAXQDA. Through content analysis, an effort was made to simplify a complex social phenomenon, which in turn raised questions about the way we perceive social reality [23]. In quantitative content analysis, measurement plays a major role, whereby a translation into numerical units is carried out [24], which in turn enable generalizable statements about the research topic [23]. At this point, the categories/concepts are numerical units, which can be found in quantitative content analysis, for example in frequency distributions [23]. Results are therefore often descriptive, showing how often a word appears, for example [23]. In this way, the focus is on the 'what' question and not the 'why' question [25].

The methodological approach combines several conceptual perspectives, integrating manifestations of emotional/body labor, (traditional) gender stereotypes, and tourism influencer marketing. It deploys visual material to facilitate analysis, since visual media are easily accessed, consumed, and shared by broad social groups without communication difficulties. The novelty of the approach lies in the attempt to decompose the complexity of the meanings pertinent to gender stereotypes, and demonstrate how single categories related to gender are mirrored explicitly by tourism influencers. Using this methodology, new insights with regard to effective methods in destination and influencer marketing, but also social sustainability, can be gained. Moreover, the approach considers both male and female travel influencers, and is thus able to elaborate a holistic view on the gender dimension related to social sustainability.

In order to move closer to answering the research question, twelve (travel) influencers (seven women and five men) were randomly selected on Instagram through a keywords based search. Instagram is suitable for this analysis because this platform is used internationally by people of all ages and backgrounds, especially by younger generations, with self-promotion and marketing playing a major role in its use. The data were collected in June 2023 and refer to all photos of each of the twelve influencers posted from January 2023 to May 2023, amounting to 427 pictures. We deliberately decided to exclude the Covid-19 years, since travel was restricted in many countries at that time, and analysis of that period would have been biased. Besides, while browsing through the profiles of prominent travel influencers of pre-Covid-19 years, we were surprised to detect that many were not as active as they used to be, which indicates a devastating effect of the pandemic, not only on travel, but also on influencer business. In total, the male influencers published 135 posts in the period under review, while the female influencers outnumbered this with 292 posts, which indicates an overrepresentation of female tourism influencers in the sample. This imbalance reflects gender representation within travel influencer marketing [14].

When selecting the influencers themselves, care was taken to ensure that the words "*travel*" or "*reisen*" could be found in each profile, which can be found using the search bar on Instagram. Reels, conventional videos, and storyposts were neglected, as the analysis of these contents cannot be realized within the scope of this project. Even with the so-called 'carousel posts', where several images can be published in a single post, only the cover image was considered, since this is also displayed in the feed of the influencers and thus creates the first impression for the entire post. In addition, care was taken of the frequency of influencer content during the study period, which meant that influencers with only up to ten photos were excluded. Furthermore, persons with less than 10,000 followers were excluded to foreclose micro-influencers.

Subsequently, we undertook the categorization of the photos. Categories for further analysis relating to gender representations were developed, which were then reflected and revised in order to secure the unambiguity of the terminology as well as to prevent measurement errors. The following categories were used: (1) Influencer's Name, (2) Gender, (3) Post text, (4) Hashtags, (5) Number of likes, (6) Date posted, (7) Date checked, (8) Number of comments, (9) Engagement rate [26], (10) Cooperation (link to other people or products), (11) Sum of product ads (definitely paid ads), (12) The way community is addressed, (13) Destination/location, (14) Destination description, (15) Activity type, (16) People (alone or with others), (17) Pose, (18) Muscles (yes/no), (19) Beard (yes/no), (20) Make up (yes/no), (21) Naked (1 = yes, 5 = desexualized), (22) Slim body (yes/no), and (23) Focus point of the camera.

These categories were deployed to find out how the influencers present themselves on Instagram, which poses are adopted, whether other people are pictured, to what extent make-up is visible and how much skin is shown. Furthermore, it is of interest how many likes and comments the individual photos received, how often influencers achieved collaborations, whether the community is addressed directly (e.g., through the text under the photo), and whether there are frequencies regarding the locations of the photos taken (Table 1).

Male influencers comprise albertvicente, andymtzurita, chrisburkard, lucafroehlings-dorf and mikelboisset. Together they have 6,746,000 followers. Anajohnson, cassidy.hornberger, liv.yah, nastjastasia, pilotmadeleine, sophiachiara__ and yvonnepferrer, on the other hand, are all female influencers who together have a reach of 4,983,200 followers.

Table 1. Considered tourism influencers with number of followers and posts, as well as their engagement rate; own representation.

Name (Instagram)	N of followers	N of posts	Engagement rate
albertvicente	256,000	24	7.77%
Anajohnson	1,300,000	42	6.18%
Andymtzurita	2,200,000	29	4.50%
cassidy.hornberger	17,200	39	13.25%
Chrisburkard	3,900,000	44	0.34%
liv.yah	301,000	48	4.13%
lucafroehlingsdorf	113,000	23	2.92%
Mikelboisset	277,000	14	5.51%
Nastjastasia	101,000	67	3.22%
Pilotmadeleine	1,400,000	23	1.10%
sophiachiara__	264,000	29	5.60%
Yvonnepferrer	1,600,000	45	0.88%

5   Findings

Dividing the variable likes by the gender of the influencers, we see that female influencers, with a mean of 30,826.64 likes, generated more likes than their male counterparts. The median here is 16,722 likes and this is also higher than the median of the entire group. The male influencers achieved an average of 27,670.63 likes with a median of 13,529.5 Likes. For the female influencers, there were 68 missing values, while among the men, only 12 posts had likes deactivated. It is striking that, despite their overall lower reach, the female influencers achieved more likes on average than the male tourism influencers.

Differences can also be found between the genders with regard to self-portrayal in their own photos. If we first look at the variable of physique, it is noticeable that all influencers in the sample were slim. A total of 28 posts were published by the male influencers in which they cannot be seen or in which their body shape cannot be clearly assigned. In the case of the female influencers, there is no such post – they were always themselves in one of the posted pictures. With regard to further categories, it can be observed that on 47.1% of the analysed photos, make-up could be seen visibly and 51.6% of the photos did not show any make-up, while 1.3% of the photos could not be assigned. In addition, in no photos of the men was make-up clearly visible. Moreover, a beard could be seen in 25 photos, which corresponds to 5.9% of all photos. The body of the influencers was often in the center of the photos (24.3%) (Fig. 1).

In the *pose* category, 60.1% are assigned to the term 'artificial' (unnatural) and 23.6% are assigned to the term 'natural'. 16.3% cannot be clearly determined. It is particularly noticeable here that the selected influencers predominantly adopted an unnatural pose in the photos. Moreover, muscles were visible in 42 photos (18.9%) of the women with none being visible in the remaining 180 (81.1%). For men, muscles were shown in 24

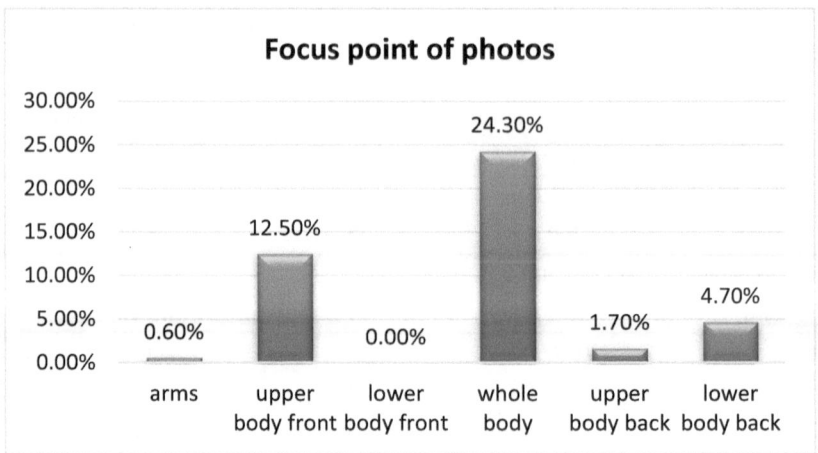

Fig. 1. Focus point of the tourism influencers' pictures on Instagram; own representation.

photos (22.0%) and none in 85 photos (78.0%). Additionally, influencers' own slim bodies were identified in 98.2% of the women's photos and 99.1% of the men's photos. The selected influencers present slim body figures in almost all photos. Furthermore, the category *naked* shows that 3.8% of the women's photos were assigned to number one on the scale (revealing e.g. underwear), with comparatively no photos being assigned to number one for the men. The photos of the women reach 28.3% for number two on the scale and 14.7% can be assigned to the photos of the men. Number three on the scale is assigned 15.5% to women and 9.2% to men, and number four is assigned 13.4% to women and 12.8% to men. On the other hand, number five on the scale (little to no skin is shown) is assigned 38.6% to women and 63.3% to men. With a value of 3.74, the mean value of the overall group shows the tendency to publish rather moderate to not at all sexualized pictures of themselves. The mean value for female influencers (3.55), however, is lower than that of their male counterparts (4.25). In comparison, male influencers dis not post any strongly sexualized posts. Among the posts of the female influencers, however, there are eleven posts in which the female influencer presented herself naked or strongly sexualized (Fig. 2).

In the category *collaborations*, men included links on 46.3% of their images. The women, on the other hand, included links on 16.1% of their images. Overall, there are no links on most of the photos, which is again strongly influenced at this point by the fact that the images of the women predominated. The correlation between the variables *naked* and *collaborations* indicates that regardless of the permissiveness, fewer influencers market collaborations on their posts. In percentage terms, however, we observed that 27.78% of the posts that are not permissive (Cat. 5 of the variable *naked*) are connected with a cooperation. In contrast, only 9.09% of the revealing pictures (Cat. 1 of the variable *naked*) were posted in connection with a cooperation. According to the category *Community addressed*, direct engagement with the community was observed 105 times, however, it was not clear in detail which type and manner of communication was meant. Furthermore, the community was addressed in 123 of the women's photos. In the case of

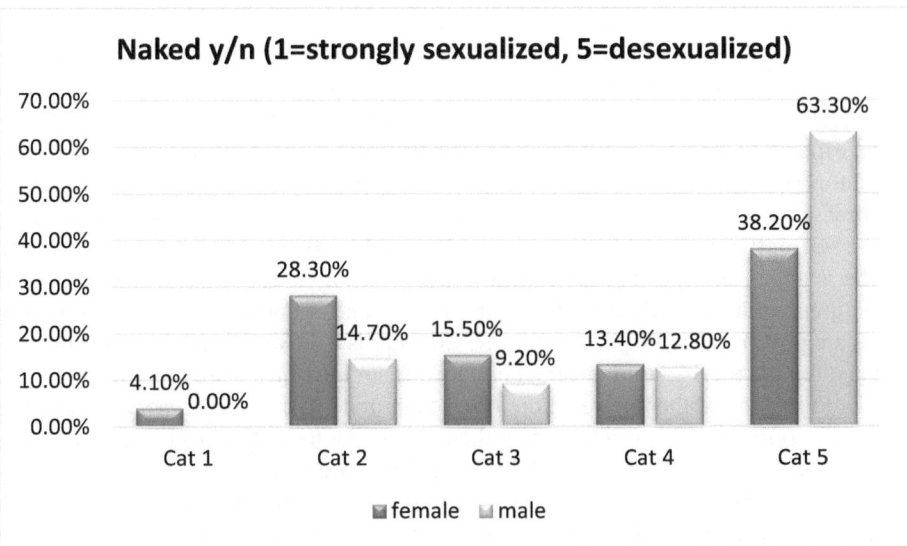

Fig. 2. Correlation between the categories *naked* and *gender*; own representation.

the men's photos, communication with the community could be observed in 61 photos, although not a single direct address could be found. This shows that the women addressed the community more frequently than men.

Among the female tourism influencers, it could be observed that they were more active on Instagram and posted more photos compared to the male influencers. Furthermore, they achieved more likes on average, while the engagement rate for both genders varied to a similar extent. With regard to the female tourism influencers, it was also noticeable that they more often disabled the viewing of likes; one female influencer had used this feature for her entire profile, an aspect that has not yet received attention in previous research. It can be assumed that the deactivation of the like insight is accompanied by a detachment from the metric evaluation of one's own content or serves to 'hide' less successful images. The deactivation thus offers users a possibility to publish content that also deviates from the expected gender role without being confronted with direct rejection.

6 Discussion

Tourism influencers have recognized the concept of 'travel' as a work opportunity and thus diligently share impressions of their vacations to the most diverse countries in social media. Not only does the place itself play an important role, but also how the influencers present themselves. Especially on visual platforms such as Instagram or TikTok, appearance plays a decisive role when it comes to attracting potential followers and retaining them in the long term. Thus, tourism influencers also orient themselves to the common ideals of beauty and reproduce them by sharing their content. In this respect, the digital world is a mirror of the real world.

Tourism influencers also have a stronger position in this respect than other influencer groups. By traveling to different tropical locations, they often show themselves lightly dressed or in swimwear, which means that their bodies are more often represented, which can cause followers' desire to establish a similar body. This can create a distorted body image, especially for adolescents in their formative years, in which an ideal of beauty is strived for, yet barely possible in real life. Conventional attractiveness seems to support this attraction factor, since not only the desire to travel, but also one's own ideal of beauty and the self-optimization of followers are addressed in such posts.

The analysis showed that the female influencers often adopt an unnatural pose in the pictures, with the body depicted in the foreground. In addition, mainly slim body figures are portrayed in the photos. In general, there is a difference between the posts of male and female tourism influencers. Female tourism influencers are more likely to post sexualized images of themselves more often than male tourism influencers. The latter, in contrast, post pictures in which they themselves are less likely to be seen, but only the nature and the surroundings of the visited places are in the foreground. For female influencers, on the other hand, their bodies and the representation of them seem to be an essential part of their content. While women are more often seen in bikinis or skimpy clothing compared to men, muscles are rarely presented in the photos, which is contrary to expectations. Furthermore, make-up is clearly visible on almost half of the women's photos, which is not the case on the men's photos.

The sexualization of one's own body on social media is a stylistic device often used to draw attention to one's own profile. This is primarily evident among female tourism influencers. In terms of gender-specific body features, female tourism influencers are distinctly more likely to present themselves according to the prevailing beauty ideals and also transfer this to their audience. For female influencers, gender stereotypical representation seems to be an important aspect of their content. These insights are in line with other findings documenting the power of scarce clothing, background settings, and physical postures in attracting attention [27–29] and redeeming it in the (self)marketing value, which often implies emotional or visible labor.

All in all, presentation within the gender-stereotypical framework contributes to the (self-)marketing of tourism influencers. This refers not only to body image, but also includes self-presentation in the gender-stereotypical roles, such as mother. Also, the assumption that female influencers post more sexualized images of themselves can be confirmed on the basis of the profiles studied. Thus, female tourism influencers are more likely to present themselves in their gender-stereotypical frame, while male tourism influencers sometimes even completely refrain from self-promotion on their profiles. One could argue at this point, however, that the distance between the influencer and the platform – or between the influencer and their following – is an aspect of male rationality and representation of their competence, which is also inscribed in the stereotypically male role image. Thus, this reproduction of the male gender role is subtler than that of the female, which may account for the overrepresentation of research regarding female social media use.

This has important implications for social reality and the public sphere, in general, and social sustainability, in particular. Influencers take advantageous poses, emphasize their bodies, show themselves in beautiful places, use make-up or even filters, which shifts the reality of their body and lives. At the same time, they perpetuate gendered ideas about how women or men should present themselves or how they should look. The visualization of gender stereotypes is significant against the background of current efforts towards a reduction of attributions and gender-based expectations as well as social sustainability. In the course of further research in the area of tourism influencers, the Instagram profiles of popular vacation providers should also be examined. It would be intriguing to investigate which influencer brands choose to collaborate directly as well as whether and to what extent an adaptation to gender roles is represented or how often people are revealed who do not conform to the Western ideal of beauty. Besides, investigating non-binary tourism influencers might be another research avenue, if such exist at all. Since the tourism influencers considered in this study act within the binary gender system, the question arises whether and how people succeed in establishing themselves in this field if they do not conform to heteronormativity.

Acknowledgement. The author very much appreciates the contribution of Jo-Lina W. and Melissa W. to the research project, as well as the generous support of Suzie M. and Jill M. in proofreading and editing the paper.

References

1. Jahnke, M.: Ist Influencer-Marketing wirklich neu? In: Jahnke, M. (ed.) Influencer Marketing. Für Unternehmen und Influencer: Strategien, Plattformen, Instrumente, rechtlicher Rahmen. Mit vielen Beispielen, pp. 1–12. Springer, Cham (2018). https://doi.org/10.1007/978-3-658-20854-7_1
2. Brix, R.: Wie sieht das Marketing im Influencer-Zeitalter aus? In: Jahnke, M. (ed.) Influencer Marketing. Für Unternehmen und Influencer: Strategien, Plattformen, Instrumente, rechtlicher Rahmen. Mit vielen Beispielen, pp. 15–51. Springer, Cham (2018). https://doi.org/10.1007/978-3-658-20854-7_2
3. Gewinner, I., Gretzel, U.: Gender stereotypes. In: Buhalis, D. (ed.) Encyclopedia of Tourism Management and Marketing, pp. 384–387. Edward Elgar Publishing, Cheltenham, UK (2022). https://doi.org/10.4337/9781800377486
4. Mooney, S., Gewinner, I.: Gender in marketing. In: Buhalis, D. (ed.) Encyclopedia of Tourism Management and Marketing, pp. 381–384. Edward Elgar Publishing, Cheltenham, UK (2022). https://doi.org/10.4337/9781800377486
5. Eckes, T.: Geschlechterstereotype: Von Rollen, Identitäten und Vorurteilen. In: Becker, R. (ed.) Kortendiek, Beate; Budrich, Barbara Handbuch: Frauen-und Geschlechterforschung. Theorie, Methoden, Empirie. VS, Verl. für Sozialwiss. Wiesbaden. 2. Auflage, pp. 171–182 (2008)
6. Eagly, A.H., Karau, S.J.: Role congruity theory of prejudice toward female leaders. Psychol. Rev. **109**(3), 573–598 (2002)
7. Koenig, A.M., Eagly, A.H.: Evidence for the social role theory of stereotype content: observations of groups' roles shape stereotypes. J. Pers. Soc. Psychol. **107**(3), 371–392 (2014)
8. Fiske, S.T., Cuddy, A.J., Glick, P., Xu, J.: A model of (often mixed) stereotype content: competence and warmth respectively follow from perceived status and competition. In: Fiske, S.T. (ed.) Social Cognition, pp. 162–214. Routledge (2018)
9. Kang, M.: The portrayal of women's images in magazine advertisements: Goffman's gender analysis revisited. Sex Roles **37**(11–12), 979–996 (1997)
10. Willem, C., Araüna, N., Crescenzi, L., et al.: Girls on fotolog: reproduction of gender stereotypes or identity play? Interact. Stud. Commun. Cult. **2**(3), 225–242 (2011)

11. Buolamwini, J., Gebru, T.: Gender shades: intersectional accuracy disparities in commercial gender classification. In: Conference on Fairness, Accountability and Transparency, pp. 77–91. PMLR (2018)
12. Broussard, M.: Artificial Unintelligence: How Computers Misunderstand the World. MIT Press, Cambridge (2018)
13. Schreiber, M.: Theoretische Konzepte. Bilder. In: Schreiber, M. (ed.) Digitale Bildpraktiken. Handlungsdimensionen visueller vernetzter Kommunikation. Springer, Cham (2020). https://doi.org/10.1007/978-3-658-30788-2
14. Gretzel, U.: Influencer marketing in travel and tourism. In: Sigala, M., Gretzel, U. (eds.) Advances in Social Media for Travel, Tourism and Hospitality: New Perspectives, Practice and Cases, pp. 147–156. Routledge, New York (2018)
15. Nymoen, O., Schmitt, W.M.: Die Entstehung der Werbekörper. In: Nymoen, O., Schmitt, W.M. (eds.) Influnecer. Die Ideologie der Werbekörper, pp. 45–59. Suhrkamp Verlag, Berlin. 4. Auflage (2021)
16. Google Play: Download Page Instagram. Google Play (2023). https://play.google.com/store/apps/details?id=com.instagram.android&hl=en_US&pli=1
17. Dixon, S.J.: Instagram: Distribution of global audiences 2023, by age group. Statista, 25 August 2023. https://www.statista.com/statistics/325587/instagram-global-agegroup/
18. Döring, N., Reif, A., Poeschl, S.: How gender-stereotypical are selfies? A content analysis and comparison with magazine adverts. Comput. Hum. Behav. 55, 955–962 (2016)
19. Slak Valek, N., Almuhrzi, H. (eds.): Women in Tourism in Asian Muslim Countries. PAT, Springer, Singapore (2021). https://doi.org/10.1007/978-981-33-4757-1
20. Oh, J.Y.J., Cheng, C.K., Lehto, X.Y., O'Leary, J.T.: Predictors of tourists' shopping behaviour: examination of socio-demographic characteristics and trip typologies. J. Vacat. Mark. 10(4), 308–319 (2004)
21. Butkowski, C.P., Dixon, T.L., Weeks, K.: Body surveillance on Instagram: examining the role of selfie feedback investment in young adult women's body image concerns. Sex Roles 81, 385–397 (2019)
22. Goffman, E.: Gender Advertisements. Harper & Row Publishers Inc., New York (1979)
23. Rössler, P.: Wozu quantitative, standardisierte Inhaltsanalysen? In: Rössler, P. (ed.) Inhaltsanalyse. UVK Verlagsgesellschaft mbH., pp. 13–25. Konstanz, München. 3. überarbeitete Auflage (2017)
24. Früh, W.: Einleitung. In: Rössler, P. (ed.) Inhaltsanalyse. UVK Verlagsgesellschaft mbH, Konstanz und München. 9. Auflage, pp. 11–15 (2017)
25. Schneijderberg, C., Steinhardt, I., Wieczorek, O.: Induktiv-quantitative Inhaltsanalyse und Auswertungstechniken am Beispiel der Kombination von AntConc und MAXQDA. In: Schneijderberg, C., Steinhardt, I., Wieczorek, O. (eds.) Qualitative und quantitative Inhaltsanalyse: digital und automatisiert. Eine anwendungsorientierte Einführung mit empirischen Beispielen und Softwareanwendungen, pp. 143–154. Beltz Juventa, Weinheim, Basel (2022)
26. Keyhole. How to Calculate Engagement Rate in 2023? Keyhole, 27 June 2023. https://keyhole.co/blog/calculate-engagement-rate/
27. Abidin, C.: Visibility labour: engaging with Influencers' fashion brands and #OOTD advertorial campaigns on Instagram. Media Int. Austral. 161(1), 86–100 (2016)
28. McFarlane, A., Samsioe, E.: #50+ fashion Instagram influencers: cognitive age and aesthetic digital labours. J. Fashion Mark. Manage. Int. J. 24(3), 399–413 (2020)
29. McFarlane, A., Hamilton, K., Hewer, P.: Putting passion to work: passionate labour in the fashion blogosphere. Eur. J. Mark. 56(4), 1210–1231 (2022)

A Closer Look of Revenge Travelers

Kyoungmin Lee[1] , Minsung Kim[2] , Qiuxia Chen[1] , and Jin-young Kim[2(✉)]

[1] Shandong University, Jinan, People's Republic of China
[2] Kyung Hee University, Seoul, Republic of Korea
{mikey1998,jk293}@khu.ac.kr

Abstract. This study investigated how three different types of revenge travel -
more expensive trips, longer stays, and more frequent travel - are affected by the
combination of consumers' perceived constraints, negotiation, and compromises.
Using fuzzy-set qualitative comparative analysis (fsQCA) on a sample of 500 survey responses, this study identified similar and distinctive patterns for each type of
the revenge travel. By enhancing our understanding of the revenge travelers across
different types, this study offers insights for industry managers and policymakers
in developing better strategies to facilitate recovery in tourism following a crisis.

Keywords: Constraint-negotiation · Revenge Travel · fsQCA

1 Introduction

Following the lifting of travel constraints, the recovery of tourism is becoming a reality.
Revenge travel, also described as compensatory travel, has been examined within the
constraint-negotiation framework [1], which explores the impact of consumers' negotiation on behavioral intentions in constrained situations. Prior research [2] has typically
conceptualized revenge travel intention as a single latent construct, manifested by travel
that is more expensive, more frequent, and longer in duration than before the crisis.

However, recent travel patterns challenges this conceptualization. For example,
Shum and Mak [3] highlighted that in China, despite a notable surge in travel following the easing of restrictions, consumers' spending on travel remained lower than
pre-pandemic levels. This observation indicates necessity to separately understand more
expensive, more frequent, and longer duration in travel rather than by the single construct of revenge travel. Moreover, given complex nature of economic and social shocks
during the crisis, combinations of constraints, negotiation, and compromising strategies
are likely to affect the types of revenge travel in the subsequent period.

From these, we recognize two points that warrant further investigation: i) It is necessary to analyze recent surge of travel by specific categories, such as more expensive,
more frequent, and longer-stay travel; ii) It is essential to comprehensively define the
factors that influence each type of revenge travel.

This work received grants from the Ministry of Education of the Republic of Korea and the National
Research Foundation of Korea (NRF-2021S1A5A03073227).

K. Berezina et al. (Eds.): ENTER 2024, SPBE, pp. 312–316, 2024.
https://doi.org/10.1007/978-3-031-58839-6_33

As such, this study utilizes fsQCA (fuzzy-set Qualitative Comparative Analysis), which allows for the identification of causal relationship in combinations of various factors, to examine revenge travel in more detail. Specifically, we establish the following two research questions: RQ1) How are each of the three types of revenge travel—namely, more expensive travel, more frequent trips, and longer stays—affected by combinations of prior constraints, negotiation strategies, and compromises? RQ2) How do these combinations differ or resemble each other?

This study provides useful implications for the travel-related industries enabling a more detailed understanding of revenge travelers. Since travel may be disrupted again by diseases, climate change, or other factors, this study aims to uncover lessons from the current experience that could prove useful in the future.

2 Literature

This study is related to the literature on revenge travel driven by pent-up demand, i.e., the desire to consume goods or services that have been suppressed due to constraints, such as a pandemic. In tourism, revenge travel refers to the disproportionate surge of travel after the release of the constraints placed under the travel restrictions; People want to spend more, stay longer and travel more often. Regarding this, Kim et al. [2] found perceived travel risk and financial constraints affected revenge travel while Yao et al. [4] found that boredom was a mediator between pent-up demand and revenge travel intention.

This current study is also related to the constraint-negotiation model, a framework that examines the impact of constraints on consumer behavior. According to the model, consumers negotiate with given constraints to achieve desired outcomes. In the tourism setting, constraints may arise in time, money, and health conditions. There have been studies that examined the role of constraints in travel decision-making. Karl et al. [5] explored travel constraints in cognitive (further by changing perception and aspiration) and behavioral aspects. Wang et al. [6] reported that constraints had a significant impact on travel frequency, travel duration, and travel destination. They also found that consumers used a variety of strategies to negotiate with constraints, such as saving money, planning ahead, and traveling with friends or family.

Building on the previous research on pent-up demand and the constraints-negotiation model, first, it separately modeled three types of revenge travel: more expensive travel, more frequent travel, and longer stays; Second, it uses fsQCA to identify the causal relationships between combinations of constraints, negotiation, and compromises; Third, it examines the differences and similarities between these combinations.

3 Methodology and Results

3.1 Data and Measurements

The data was collected through an online survey firm in Republic of Korea in April 2022. To ensure clarity and readability, pilot tests were conducted using 50 surveys. The survey included 6 constraints construct (intrapersonal, interpersonal, time, cost, place, subjective norm constraints) adapted from Boo et al. [7], 3 travel negotiation strategies (changing perception, aspiration, and behavior) adapted from Karl et al. [5] and Lyu and Oh [8], 1 compromise strategy (authors' own development based on the articles and media reports, e.g., Lannes and Xing [9]).

All of the constructs were measured by multiple survey items. Dependent variables are more-expensive, more frequent (each with 4 items, both from Park et al. [10]), and longer stay (3 item adapted from Amin et al. [11]) travel intention post-pandemic. The data were analyzed by fsQCA, which provides possible combinations of factors that are associated with a particular outcome, based on the set theoretic foundation. A total of 500 responses were collected and used in the analysis.

3.2 Results and Discussion

Table 1 presents the results. For common factors, behavioral negotiation was found across all three types of revenge travel. This result implies the concrete actions (such arranging travel schedule, budget, or travel companion) even under the constraints may result in any type of revenge travel later. Also, for each type, R4 appeared with a similar pattern; while the constraints are mostly present, absent social norm constraint with negotiation and compromise. These individuals are similar to "Invincible" travelers [13], who will take travel no matter what as long as it is perceived socially acceptable. R3, which shows the presence of constraints, the absence of cognitive negotiation, combined with the presence of behavioral negotiation and compromise, is similar for longer stays and more frequent travel.

As per each type of revenge travel, for more expensive travel intention, throughout R1 to R4, subjective norm appears as a core absent factor. The patterns unique to this type are R2 and R3, where constraints should be absent and either compromise strongly present with peripheral presence of behavioral negotiation and peripheral absence of changing aspiration (R2) or negotiation present (R3). Overall, for those who feel that travel is not against the social norm and low degree of perceived travel constraints over the pandemic are willing to take more expensive travel when the restriction is released.

For longer stays, R2 is highlighted with the absence of perceived constraints (time and cost-related constraints as core) with both negotiation *and* compromise present. This result can be interpreted that people who did not perceive strong cost and time constraints under the pandemic are likely to seek for compromise (e.g., luxury shopping compromising prohibited international travel). For the post-pandemic, these individuals may prefer longer stays (and not necessarily more expensive or frequent travel).

For more frequent travel, these travelers are likely to take a domestic trips to drive-to destinations while avoiding multi-stop travel as in 'Corona Light travelers' of Miao et al. [13]. R2 appears to be unique; among the constraints, only the interpersonal constraints are present while others are absent (with the cost constraint being core), with changing aspiration (core), behavioral negotiation, and compromise (both peripheral). These results suggest that during the pandemic, individuals who did not face economic constraints, but lacked travel companions resorted to compromising consumption while adjusting their aspiration for travel. When restrictions are lifted, they may opt for more frequent trips without necessarily increasing their expenses (possibly because there was a compromising alternative spending).

Table 1. fsQCA Results

Configuration Elements		Configurations for more expensive trip				Configurations for longer staying				Configurations for frequently traveling			
		R1.	R2.	R3.	R4.	R1.	R2.	R3.	R4.	R1.	R2.	R3.	R4.
Constraints	Intrapersonal constraints	⊗	⊗	⊗	●	⊗	⊗	●	●	⊗	⊗	●	●
	Interpersonal Constraints	⊗	⊗	⊗	●	⊗	⊗	●	●	⊗	●	●	●
	Time-related Constraints		⊗	⊗	●	⊗	⊗	●	●		⊗	●	●
	Cost-related Constraints		⊗	⊗	●	⊗	⊗	●	●		⊗	●	●
	Place-related Constraints	⊗	⊗	⊗	●	⊗	⊗	●	●	⊗	⊗	●	●
	Subjective norms constrains	⊗	⊗	⊗	⊗	⊗	⊗	●	⊗	⊗	⊗	●	⊗
Travel negotiations	Change perception	●		●	●	●	●	⊗	●	●		⊗	●
	Change aspiration	●	⊗	●	●	⊗	●	⊗	●	●	●	⊗	●
	Behavioral negotiation	●	●	●	●	●	●	●	●	●	●	●	●
Compromise	Compromising behaviors	●	●		●	⊗	●	●	●	●	●	●	●
	Consistency	0.817	0.883	0.829	0.830	0.890	0.889	0.877	0.861	0.882	0.890	0.872	0.899
	Raw Coverage	0.153	0.068	0.112	0.045	0.033	0.099	0.069	0.048	0.157	0.060	0.063	0.047
	Unique Coverage	0.051	0.038	0.019	0.026	0.011	0.074	0.045	0.021	0.115	0.028	0.042	0.018
	Overall Solution Consistency	0.817				0.911				0.871			
	Overall Solution Coverage	0.236				0.302				0.255			

●: presence of conditions, ⊗: absence of conditions (large symbols: core conditions, small circles: peripheral conditions); blank: irrelevant.

4 Implications

The current study contributes to the existing literature on travel constraints by investigating how combinations of the factors lead to different types of revenge travel. For theoretical contributions, this study refined the theory of constraints negotiation framework in the travel context by: i) analyzing specific categories of revenge travel and uncovering common as well as distinctive factors, ii) acknowledging the complexity in underlying factors through identifying causal relationships among combinations of constraints, negotiation, and compromising behavior. Overall, this study offers theoretical foundation for advancing knowledge in tourism recovery strategies following crises.

After a crisis, facilitating recovery is crucial, but without knowing which points to focus on, it is challenging to engage in effective marketing and communication plans. To this point, the results of this study can be utilized to design a customized approach targeting specific types of revenge travelers. For instance, if a local government or destination aims to attract travelers who will stay longer in the post-pandemic, their marketing campaigns may be built around R3 and R4, i.e., those who perceived constraints during the pandemic with particularly strong place-related constraints and actively engaged in behavioral negotiation. Therefore, promotions that highlight ease of restrictions *combined* with emotional appeal acknowledging individuals' behavioral negotiation efforts under the restriction may target the right segment.

Understanding consumers is a critical first step in developing any smart tourism system; findings from this study will also contribute to enhance the effectiveness of such systems. By analyzing and interpreting the unique travel behaviors identified in this study, smart tourism systems can be designed to cater more precisely to the needs and preferences of different traveler segments.

References

1. Crawford, D.W., Godbey, G.: Reconceptualizing barriers to family leisure. Leis. Sci. **9**(2), 119–127 (1987)
2. Kim, E.E.K., Seo, K., Choi, Y.: Compensatory travel post COVID-19: cognitive and emotional effects of risk perception. J. Travel Res. **61**(8), 1895–1909 (2022)
3. Shum, T., Mak, R.: Chinese tourists return with lighter wallets (2022). http://www.reuters.com. Accessed 10 Aug 2023
4. Yao, Y., Zhao, X., Ren, L., Jia, G.: Compensatory travel in the post COVID-19 pandemic era: how does boredom stimulate intentions? J. Hosp. Tour. Manag. **54**, 56–64 (2023)
5. Karl, M., Sie, L., Ritchie, B.W.: Expanding travel constraint negotiation theory: an exploration of cognitive and behavioral constraint negotiation relationships. J. Travel Res. **61**(4), 762–785 (2022)
6. Wang, F., Deng, Z., Petrick, J.F.: Exploring the formation mechanisms of urban residents' travel behaviour in China: perceptions of travel benefits and travel constraints. J. Travel Tour. Mark. **35**(7), 909–921 (2018)
7. Boo, S., Carruthers, C.P., Busser, J.A.: The constraints experienced and negotiation strategies attempted by nonparticipants of a festival event. J. Travel Tour. Mark. **31**(2), 269–285 (2014)
8. Lyu, S.O., Oh, C.O.: Recreationists' constraints negotiation process for continual leisure engagement. Leis. Sci. **36**(5), 479–497 (2014)
9. Lannes, B., Xing, W.: The luxury market in China: 2021 a year of contrasts (2022). https://www.bain.com/about/media-center/press-releases/2022/2021-china-luxury-report/. Accessed 12 Aug 2023
10. Park, I., Lee, J., Lee, D., Lee, C., Chung, W.Y.: Changes in consumption patterns during the COVID-19 pandemic: analyzing the revenge spending motivations of different emotional groups. J. Retail. Consum. Serv. **65**, 102874 (2022)
11. Amin, M., Ryu, K., Cobanoglu, C., Rezaei, S., Wulan, M.M.: Examining the effect of shopping mall attributes in predicting tourist shopping satisfaction and behavioral intentions: variation across generation X and Y. J. Qual. Assur. Hosp. Tour. **22**(3), 367–394 (2021)
12. Liu, J., Wang, R., Xu, S.: What academic mobility configurations contribute to high performance: an fsQCA analysis of CSC-funded visiting scholars. Scientometrics **126**, 1079–1100 (2021)
13. Miao, L., Im, J., Fu, X., Kim, H., Zhang, Y.E.: Proximal and distal post-COVID travel behavior. Ann. Tour. Res. **88**, 103159 (2021)

Senior Tourists' Digital Travel Experience: A Humanisation Perspective

Daisy X. F. Fan[1]([envelope]) [iD], Jiaying Lyu[2] [iD], Yi Huang[3] [iD], Kaiti Shang[1] [iD], and Dimitrios Buhalis[1] [iD]

[1] Bournemouth University Business School, Poole, UK
{dfan,kshang,dbuhalis}@bournemouth.ac.uk
[2] Hangzhou City University, Hangzhou, China
lvjy@hzcu.edu.cn
[3] Zhejiang University, Hangzhou, China
huang_yi@zju.edu.cn

Abstract. As with the development of digital technology, increasing older adults have used digital technologies in different stages of their travel. While advocating the positive aspects of digital usage among older adults, the downside has been largely neglected. Moreover, older adults vary in their backgrounds, lifestyles, digital competence and specific needs. When seeking appropriate solutions to enhance their digital travel experience, it is important to initially profile the diverse subgroups and delineate their specific preferences. This study adopted a humanisation perspective and a qualitative approach to 1) understand senior tourists' digital travel experience, 2) explore senior tourists' needs and requirements regarding digital travel, and 3) develop a senior tourists' digital travel experience typology. Findings provide rich contributions in understanding senior tourists' digital use and the humanised digital travel experience. Recommendations are also offered to destinations, tourism service providers and care providers regarding how to develop an age friendly destination digital environment.

Keywords: Senior Tourist · Digital Travel Experience · Humanisation

1 Introduction

Tourism plays an important role in supporting older adults' good quality of life. As with the development of digital technology, more and more older adults have used digital devices in different stages of their travel. Existing studies are mainly framed within seniors' digital stereotypes, lacking dynamic perspectives to understand this age group's changing needs in digital experience. While advocating the positive aspects of digital usage among older adults, the downside has been largely neglected. Moreover, senior people vary in their backgrounds, lifestyles, digital competence and specific needs. When seeking appropriate solutions to enhance their digital travel experience, it is important to initially profile the diverse subgroups and delineate their specific preferences and behaviours in terms of their travel motivation, digital competence, and digital adoption.

K. Berezina et al. (Eds.): ENTER 2024, SPBE, pp. 317–322, 2024.
https://doi.org/10.1007/978-3-031-58839-6_34

To bridge the aforementioned gaps, this study adopted a humanisation perspective and a qualitative approach, to 1) understand senior tourists' digital travel experience, 2) explore senior tourists' needs and requirements regarding digital travel, and 3) developing a senior tourists' digital travel experience typology. Findings provide rich contributions in further understanding senior tourists' digital use and the humanised digital travel experience. Recommendations are offered to destinations and service providers regarding how to develop an age friendly destination digital environment.

2 Literature Review

In the past decade, a shift from technology-centred digitalization to human-centred digitalization is evidenced in tourism business, academia and policy-making [1]. Humanising the digital tourism experience starts with acknowledging what it means to be human, to feel secure, respected, valued, and involved [2]. Originally aimed to challenge the public health field, Todres, Galvin and Holloway [3] developed a humanisation value framework to delineate core features to see the people they serve as humans rather than objects. Derived from the tradition of existential phenomenology, the framework is informed by Husserl's concept of lifeworld, Heidegger's thinking about being, and Merleau-Ponty's idea about body [4]. The framework consists eight dimensions of humanization and dehumanization, with each dimension considering as an emphasis along a continuum, rather than binary opposites [5]. They are insiderness-objectification, agency-passivity, uniqueness-homogenisation, togetherness-isolation, sense making-loss of meaning, personal journey-loss of personal journey, sense of place-dislocation, and embodiment-reductionist body. Extant research demonstrated that the framework has potential to bring together the subjective lifeworld of the person within the systems approach of health and social care institutions, and to inform and develop public policies and practices. By considering the inward human experience, the framework serves as a sounding board for making sense of older adults' experiences of living and ageing, which echoes to the current research.

Overall, prior studies of senior tourists as users of information technology are mainly based on the technology acceptance model, the motivation-opportunity-abilities model, the stimulus-organism-response theory, the leisure constraint theory, and the transaction cost theory. Exist research focuses on seniors' perceptions of the benefits and costs of the tourism information technology, and few studies examined their tourism experience through digital services.

3 Methodology

This study sought to understand senior tourists' digital tourism experience and establish a senior tourist typology through the humanising perspective. Therefore, the qualitative research method and interview design were chosen to achieve an in-depth investigation of the individual experience. The sampling frame consists of Chinese senior tourists who are 60 years or older, have travelled in the past two years, and have used digital technologies before, during, or after their trips. Data collection was carried out between April 2021 and June 2023. A total of 38 interviews were conducted, lasting between

20 and 80 min. Of the participants, 14 were female and 24 were male; the average age was 64 years. Additionally, 30 of the 38 participants held a high school diploma or higher. During the semi-structured interviews, the participants were first asked about their adoption of digital tools in general while traveling. Then, they were asked to recall their recent tourism experience related to digital technologies, including the details about their encounters with digital tools or digital services, and the positive and negative aspects of their digital experience. Moreover, they were invited to share their opinions on what humanization in digital tourism means to seniors and their attitudes, requirements or concerns about digital technology in tourism. Data analysis was conducted following a hybrid approach to thematic analysis [6] that combined inductive and deductive coding flexibly.

4 Findings

Seven types of senior tourists' digital travel experience have emerged from the interviews according to their travel motivation, digital device and technology usage and adoption, and their humanising travel experience.

4.1 Digital-Savvy Enjoyer

Digital-savvy enjoyers have an open and favourable attitude towards the digital transformation within the tourism sector. They possess a high level of digital literacy that facilitates their effective utilization of digital tools throughout each phase of tourism, thereby enjoying the tech-enhanced tourism experience. Such tourists represent the ideal tourist type in the digital age. With digital tools, digital-savvy enjoyers find their agency and uniqueness more profoundly respected and actualized during traveling. For digital-savvy enjoyers, digital interventions in areas such as payment, booking, identification, and content presentation are sense-making.

4.2 Collaborative Travellers

Collaborative travellers are older individuals who love traveling and prefer group journeys. With online platforms like WeChat, they set up group chats and exchange travel information, stay in touch, and share feelings and images before, during, and after the journey. Such digital platforms serve as a bridge, connecting them together throughout all times of the journey. Each members' roles and responsibilities within the travel group are allocated based on their specialties, particularly their varying proficiency with digital technology. *"We have a clear task division. Those who are good with digital technology are responsible for booking hotels and tickets and finding local delicacies according to online reviews from Meituan"* (S-003).

4.3 Active Learners

Active learners may not be experts in technology, however, often use digital devices with the assistance of others and recognize the significant improvements the technology brings to their tourism experience. *"These technologies truly bring a lot of conveniences for me. Although I'm still a beginner and often seek my children's help, I'm slowly but steadily learning how to use them"* (H-018). For active learners, the process of learning and adapting to these technologies is more than acquiring digital skills; it is a personal journey of aligning themselves— individuals of an older generation—with the rapidly updating modern age.

4.4 Digital Tourism Dependents

Digital tourism dependents typically have low digital literacy and limited willingness to learn. Often, they travel with companions who are proficient with digital tools. These companions handle common digital interactions like hotel bookings and accessing e-tickets for them. This assistance process fosters a deeper sense of togetherness among them. However, when they are along and have to deal with digital tools by themselves, their digital experience tends to be negative.

4.5 Life-Long Recorders

Life-long recorders cherish each moment of their journey, meticulously documenting what they see, feel, and experience for both sharing and remembrance. For them, travel is more than a vacation; it's an opportunity to engage deeply with the culture, history, and society of the destinations they visit. Digital technologies amplify this practice. Photos taken, digital introductions downloaded, and moments shared on social media are "digital footprints" that span their personal journey.

4.6 Digital-Ambivalent Traveller

Digital-ambivalent traveller, while possessing a commendable level of digital literacy and proficiency with digital tools, have mixed feelings toward the burgeoning digital revolution. On one hand, they acknowledge the enormous benefits digital technology brings, especially in supporting seniors' agency by empowering their travel engagements. On the other hand, they also have several concerns about the rapid transition from traditional face-to-face services to digital encounters. As more and more services are delivered through digital tools, seniors find themselves facing challenges in adapting, since their learning process usually demands considerable time and effort.

4.7 Digital-Wave Resister

Unlike other groups of seniors, digital-wave complainers have limited digital literacy and are alienated from digital technologies, resulting in their complain about the unsatisfactory digital tourism experience. They often find it difficult to understand or operate digital tools and might be unaware of certain functionalities such as online reservations, which makes them feel passive during traveling. *"Last Labor Day, we were told that online reservations were required for entering Zhuozheng Garden when we arrived there. But we hadn't seen any notice about this before and didn't know how to make the reservation"* (H-005).

5   Discussion and Conclusion

This study explored senior tourists' digital travel experience and developed a typology according to their travel motivation, digital usage and adaption from a humanisation perspective. Theoretically, this study extended the knowledge of seniors' digital experience by introducing the humanisation approach. It not only strengthens the human-centred digitalization progression for the ageing group, but also offers a new angle to understand this age group's travel experience, beyond the traditional technology acceptance and constraint approaches [7]. The established typology also corresponds to the literature that argued that digital divide exists especially by different age groups [8]. Compared with previous senior digital experience categorisation, this research takes humanisation and other travel and digital related preferences into consideration, offering a comprehensive perspective to understand the perceptional and behavioural differences in the ageing population. Results also shed lights to the destinations, attractions and relevant tourism service sectors regarding how to build an age friendly digital travel environment and eventually tackle the ageism in a broader society. Limitations of the current study relate to sample selection and the lasting effect of the pandemic on tourist behaviour.

References

1. Marini, C., Agostino, D.: Humanized museums? How digital technologies become relational tools. Museum Management and Curatorship **37**(6), 598–615 (2022)
2. Guest, D., Knox, A., Warhurst, C.: Humanizing work in the digital age: Lessons from socio-technical systems and quality of working life initiatives. Human Relations **75**(8), 1461–1482 (2022)
3. Todres, L., Galvin, K.T., Holloway, I.: The humanization of healthcare: A value framework for qualitative research. Int. J. Qual. Stud. Health Well Being **4**(2), 68–77 (2009)
4. Husserl, E.: The crisis of European sciences and transcendental phenomenology: An introduction to phenomenological philosophy. Northwestern University Press (1970)
5. Hemingway, A.: Can humanization theory contribute to the philosophical debate in public health? Public Health **126**(5), 448–453 (2012)
6. Braun, V., Clarke, V.: Using thematic analysis in psychology. Qual. Res. Psychol. **3**(2), 77–101 (2006)
7. Lyu, J., Wang, X., Fan, D. X.: Ageing in the context of accompanying migration: a leisure stress coping perspective. Leisure Studies, 1–16 (2023)
8. Minghetti, V., Buhalis, D.: Digital divide in tourism. J. Travel Res. **49**(3), 267–281 (2010)

Reimagining Travel Planning

An Empirical User Study on Congestion-Aware Route Recommendation

Kun Yi[1] , Xisha Jin[2], Zhengyang Bai[3] , Yuntao Kong[4] ,
and Qiang Ma[5] (✉)

[1] Institute of Economic Research, Kyoto University, Kyoto, Japan
[2] Graduate School of Management, Kyoto University, Kyoto, Japan
jin.xisha.87y@st.kyoto-u.ac.jp
[3] RIKEN Center for Computational Science, RIKEN, Tokyo, Japan
zhengyang.bai@riken.jp
[4] School of Information Science, Japan Advanced Institute of Science and
Technology, Ishikawa, Japan
[5] Department of Information Science, Kyoto Institute of Technology, Kyoto, Japan
qiang@kit.ac.jp

Abstract. Overtourism has become a significant concern in many popular travel destinations around the world. As one of considerable approaches to handle the overtourism issues, congestion-aware methods can be effective in mitigating overcrowding at popular attractions by spreading tourists to less-visited areas. However, they may lead to a potential Hawk-Dove game: tourists who share the same preference may have some of them assigned worse routes than others to avoid congestion, which raises a possibility that the tourists who are assigned to relatively unfavorable routes may feel dissatisfaction and unfairness. Most existing research focuses on alleviating congestion from an overall planner perspective through simulation studies, with little emphasis on actual user experience. In this study, we conducted a user survey on congestion-aware route recommendation in Kyoto, Japan, aiming to investigate the evaluation of congestion-aware route recommendation methods from each tourist's personal perspective and to clarify the development status and future research directions of congestion-aware route recommendation methods. We choose five congestion-aware route recommendation methods that vary in their consideration of congestion and multi-agent interactions. We reveal the strengths and weaknesses of these methods from multiple aspects. We cluster the respondents based on their text responses and explore the differences between these clusters. Furthermore, we investigate the factors affecting tourists' experience and compare the differences among groups of tourists.

Keywords: User Study · Congestion-aware Route Recommendation · Selfish Tourists · Sustainable Tourism

This work was partly supported by JSPS KAKENHI (23H03404, 22H03600), and MIC SCOPE 201607008.

K. Berezina et al. (Eds.): ENTER 2024, SPBE, pp. 325–338, 2024.
https://doi.org/10.1007/978-3-031-58839-6_35

1   Introduction

Tourism is a major industry in the world economy and plays an important role in our lives. While tourism can bring significant economic benefits to destinations, large numbers of visitors can cause overcrowded attractions and traffic congestion. Public facilities such as restrooms, parking areas, and visitor centers can become overwhelmed by the influx of tourists, which results in a negative impact on both tourists and local residents.

On one hand, for local governments, by adopting a holistic and sustainable approach to route recommendation, destinations can strike a balance between the economic benefits of tourism and mitigating the congestion problems associated with increased tourist numbers. On the other hand, for tourists, their primary focus is on finding a route that meets their individual conditions and maximizes their personal gains. The congestion-aware route recommendation can lead to a potential Hawk-Dove game [1]: If a sufficient number of tourists share the same preference, a portion of tourists has to be recommended relatively unfavorable routes to avoid excessive crowding at attractions. Taking tourists' selfishness into consideration, the tourists who are assigned to relatively unfavorable routes may feel dissatisfaction and unfairness.

However, most existing methods are designed from an overall planner's perspective, and their evaluations are primarily based on simulation data. There have been no studies that have investigated the actual personal experience of tourists regarding congestion-aware route recommendations. To investigate the evaluation of congestion-aware methods from tourists' personal perspectives, in this study, we conduct a user survey on congestion-aware route recommendations in Kyoto, Japan. We selected five state-of-the-art route recommendation methods with varying degrees of consideration for congestion and tourism diversification. While these methods have demonstrated promising results on their respective datasets, there have been no user studies that verify their performance from the perspective of actual users. Respondents evaluated routes recommended by these methods from various aspects in different scenarios and provided comments on each method within each scenario. We compared the methods using scores from different aspects to reveal their strengths and weaknesses. Furthermore, based on text comments from respondents, we conduct cluster analysis to uncover distinctions among various user types. Additionally, we use a series of regression to estimate the effects of scheduling, visiting order, distances between attractions, and travel comfort on the overall feelings of routes. We compare the coefficients for different groups and apply a bootstrapping method to determine the significance of differences observed between groups.

The contributions of this work are summarized as follows.

- We conducted a user study to investigate the evaluations of five route recommendation methods, with varying degrees of consideration for congestion and tourism diversification. To the best of our knowledge, this is the first study that compares congestion-aware route recommendation methods from tourists' personal perspectives.
- We examined the effect of scheduling, visiting order, distances between attractions, and comfort on the overall feeling of routes. Moreover, we compared

the effect of variables on overall feelings among groups and revealed that the sociodemographic factors exert a significant influence over the users' evaluation for each method.
– We applied clustering to identify patterns and similarities between users' responses. The demographic profiles and the effect of variables on overall feelings from each cluster are compared to reveal the differences in evaluation of route recommendation methods between clusters.

2 Related Work

Sustainability, green tourism, and ecotourism have attracted increasing attention in recent years [2,3]. With an increasing number of tourists flocking to particular popular attractions, congestion has emerged as a significant problem. Marsiglio [4] studied the determination of the optimal number of visitors in a tourism-based economy. Albaladejo et al. [5] conducted an emprical research on tourism demand of the most visited destinations in Spain, with special emphasis on the role of congestion. Takeuchi et al. [6] uses causal inference to estimate the effects of crowd movement guidance from a policy-making perspective.

To address overtourism issues, there has been a growing interest in congestion-aware route recommendation, a variant of the Orienteering Problem [7,8], while it is more challenging due to the potential congestion caused by multiple tourists arriving at the same attractions.

Cheng et al. [9] proposed a congestion-aware rescheduling method focusing on multigroup travelers with multiple destinations. Varakantham et al. [10] tackled the issue of crowd congestion at particular attractions by providing route guidance to multiple selfish users moving simultaneously. Kong et al. [11] proposed a multi-agent reinforcement learning approach with a dynamic reward mechanism to tackle multi-user route recommendation problem. Kong et al. [12] introduced a multi-agent reinforcement learning approach to address both traffic congestion and spot congestion. In [13], the Orienteering Problem with Time Windows is addressed by taking into account the reward and required stay duration at a spot, considering its congestion level.

However, most existing studies are conducted from an overall planner or policy-making perspective, and the evaluation of these methods is based on simulation data, leaving the actual experience of tourists hardly discussed. To bridge this gap, we conduct a user study to investigate the evaluation of the congestion-aware route recommendation method from the personal perspective of tourists.

3 Methodology

We conducted a user study in Kyoto, Japan, one of the world's most famous destinations. A screening questionnaire was distributed to 41 respondents. We investigated the following five route recommendation methods. These methods have varying degrees of consideration for congestion and tourism diversification. These methods are trained using the dataset of Kyoto Sightseeing Map 2.0 [14] and trajectory data provided by Yahoo Japan Corporation [15].

- **MARLRR**: An multi-agent reinforcement learning approach proposed in [11] for solving the congestion-aware route recommendation task. This method considers that several tourists groups are moving simultaneously, and a congestion penalty of reward function is introduced to avoid overconcentration at attractions.
- **RPMTD**: A multi-agent reinforcement learning based route recommendation method proposed in [12] that considers both multiple users accessing simultaneously and the congestion at attractions. This method introduces a dual-congestion mechanism, in which both the local congestion at visited spots and the global distribution of tourists affect tourists' satisfaction.
- **Non-Dual RPMTD**: An alternative version of RPMTD that does not consider the global distribution of tourists in the dual-congestion mechanism.
- **Pointer-NN**: A reinforcement learning approach to the Orienteering Problem with Time Windows proposed in [16], which considers neither multiple-agent nor congestion.
- **TRGCSC**: A reinforcement learning approach proposed in [13], which is based on [16] and introduces two novel concepts, "dynamic stay duration" and "environmental tax metaphor." The former concept estimates the necessary stay duration at a spot based on its congestion, and the latter concept assigns dynamic rewards depending on congestion at spots.

We investigated five different scenarios in the questionnaire.

- Start from Kyoto Tower and end at Kawaramachi, 4-hour time budget.
- Start from Kyoto Tower and end at Kawaramachi, 6-hour time budget.
- Start from Kyoto Tower and end at Kawaramachi, 8-hour time budget.
- Start from Kawaramachi and end at Arashiyama Station, 4-hour time budget.
- Start from Kawaramachi and end at Kinkakuji Temple, 6-hour time budget.

All participants were asked to evaluate routes from the following aspects for each method under each scenario.

- **Scheduling**: The evaluation of time scheduling that includes the time spent at attractions and the time spent moving between attractions.
- **Visiting Order**: Whether the visiting order of attractions in the recommended route is reasonable.
- **Distance**: Whether the distances between attractions in the recommended route are too far.
- **Comfort**: The evaluation of comfort with considering the congestion at spots and the traffic congestion during movement between spots.
- **Overall Feeling**: The overall evaluation for each route.

Moreover, all respondents were asked to provide comments on routes recommended by each method under each scenario.

To ensure that respondents are well-informed about the recommended route details, we have created a webpage displaying the information as illustrated in Fig. 1. The webpage consists of three parts from left to right: route information, map display, and spot information. In the route information section, respondents are able to see the designated visitation time for each spot. The map

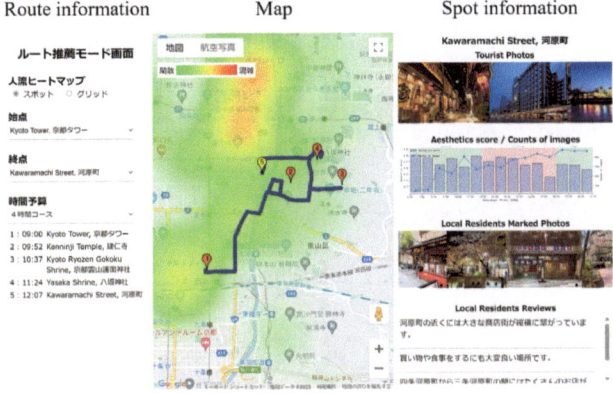

Fig. 1. The web page that displays the information about the recommended spots, distances between spots, and congestion levels.

Table 1. Demographic profile of respondents.

Characteristics		Percent		Percent
Gender	Male	39.02%	Female	60.98%
Frequency of travel	Once every few years	14.63%	Once a year	12.20%
	Twice a year	34.15%	Once every quarter	34.15%
	Once every two months	17.07%	Once a month	7.32%
	Twice a month	12.20%	Once a week	2.44%
Duration of travel	Daytrip	12.20%	2 days	4.88%
	3 days	19.51%	4 days	17.07%
	5 days	14.63%	6 days	0%
	7 days	14.63%	More than 7 days	17.07%
Factors of concern	Price	78.05%	Time cost	48.78%
	Scheduling	63.42%	Season	56.10%
	Popularity	48.78%	Congestion	80.49%
Popular or	Less-known places	63.42%	Neutral	7.32%
less-known spots	Popular places	29.27%		
Traffic congestion	Don't mind	9.76%	Care	43.90%
	Very care	46.34%		
Congestion at spots	Don't mind	2.44%	Care	36.59%
	Very care	60.98%		

display section illustrates the route and congestion level on a map, providing a visual representation of the journey. The spot information section displays photos, aesthetics scores of photos, congestion information, and reviews for each spot based on Kyoto Sightseeing Map 2.0 data [14].

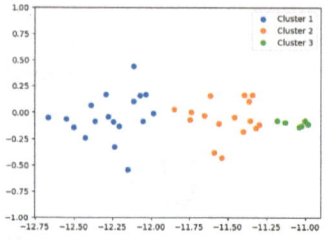

Fig. 2. Clustering of users.

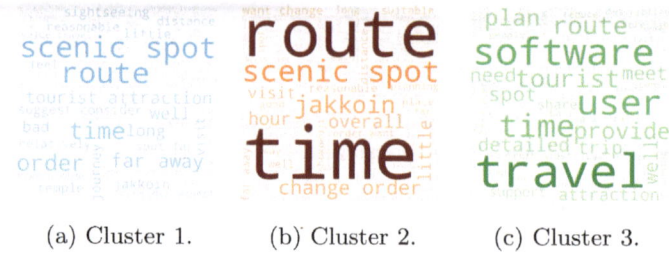

(a) Cluster 1.	(b) Cluster 2.	(c) Cluster 3.

Fig. 3. Word clouds of each cluster.

4 Characteristics of Respondents

4.1 Demographic Profile of Respondents

The respondents' demographic characteristics are listed in Table 1. There were approximately 20% more female (60.98%) than male respondents (39.02%). The frequency of travel varied from person to person, with 73.17% of the respondents traveling no less frequently than twice a year. The duration of travel also shows variability among individuals. We also asked about the factors that influence the selection of travel plans. Congestion is the most considered factor (80.49%), followed by price (78.05%), scheduling (63.42%), and season (56.10%). In the comparison of popular attractions and less-known places, 63.42% of the respondents preferred less-known spots, while 29.27% favored popular spots. Concerning congestion, 90.24% of the respondents expressed concern about traffic congestion, and 97.56% were concerned about congestion at spots.

4.2 Clustering Analysis

To explore the similarities and differences between respondents, we cluster the respondents using their text comments for routes under scenarios. We collected a total of 7,708 word comments from 41 users to route recommendation methods under five scenarios. We removed punctuation, convert case, reduce word forms and filter stop words by using Spacy [17].

We use Skip-Gram Word2Vec [18] to represent the words in vector embeddings. The vector representation of each comment is calculated by taking the mean of the words in the comment. Then the vector representation of each user is obtained by calculating the mean of the comments from that user.

We use the K-means method [19] to cluster the respondents, selecting $K = 3$ clusters based on the elbow method. Figure 2 shows the results of clustering after dimensionality reduction by t-SNE [20]. Furthermore, to gain insights into the features of each cluster, we create word clouds to visualize the most common words within each cluster, as illustrated in Fig. 3.

In Cluster 1 (26.8%), 73% of the respondents are female, and 27% are male. The respondents in Cluster 1 are the least frequent travelers but have the longest duration: 72.7% of them select "Twice a year" or less for the frequency, and 63.6% select "7 days" or "More than 7 days" for the duration. Respondents in Cluster 1 show a higher concern about time cost (54.5%), scheduling (72.7%), season (63.6%), and popularity (63.6%) compared to the other clusters. Respondents in Cluster 1 focus on "scenic spot," "route," and "order."

In Cluster 2 (41.5%), 18% of the respondents are female, and 82% are male. Cluster 2 respondents are more concerned about price (88.2%) and congestion (94.1%). Cluster 2 respondents focus on "time," "route," and "scenic spot."

In Cluster 3 (31.7%), 31% of the respondents are female, and 69% are male. Respondents in Cluster 3 are the most frequent travelers but have the shortest duration of travel. Specifically, 61.5% of them select "Once every quarter" or more for the "Frequency of travel," and 84.6% select "5 days" or less for the "Duration of travel," with 30.8% of them choosing "Daytrip." Additionally, they have a stronger preference for popular spots compared to the other clusters. Respondents in Cluster 3 focus on "travel," "software," and "time."

The differences among clusters demonstrate the respondents have varying points of emphasis and preferences which may influence the evaluation of route recommendation methods.

5   Comparison of Methods

5.1   Survey Results

Figure 4(a) demonstrates the evaluation of scheduling for each method. Pointer-NN receive a total of 63% "Very satisfied" or "Satisfied," followed by TRGCSC (60%), Non-Dual RPMTD (45%), RPMTD (33%), and MARLRR (32%).

Figure 4(b) illustrates the evaluation of the visiting order for each method. The routes recommended by TRGCSC are the most satisfactory on visiting order for respondents, with a total of 62% of the respondents selecting "Very satisfied" or "Satisfied," followed by Pointer-NN (60%), MARLRR (51%), Non-Dual RPMTD (41%), and RPMTD (40%).

Figure 4(c) shows the evaluation of distance for each method. TRGCSC received a total of 60% "Very satisfied" or "Satisfied," followed by Pointer-NN (53%), Non-Dual RPMTD (39%), RPMTD (32%), and MARLRR (30%).

Figure 4(d) displays the evaluation of comfort for each method. TRGCSC received the highest satisfaction, with a total of 65% of respondents selecting

"Very satisfied" or "Satisfied". Following closely were Pointer-NN (63%), Non-Dual RPMTD (44%), RPMTD (39%), and MARLRR (39%).

Figure 4(e) illustrates the overall feeling. Pointer-NN is the most satisfactory method for respondents, with a total of 67% of the respondents selecting "Very satisfied" or "Satisfied." This is followed by TRGCSC, with a total of 51% of the respondents selecting "Very satisfied" or "Satisfied." Non-Dual RPMTD (40%), RPMTD (41%), and MARLRR (40%) achieved similar performance.

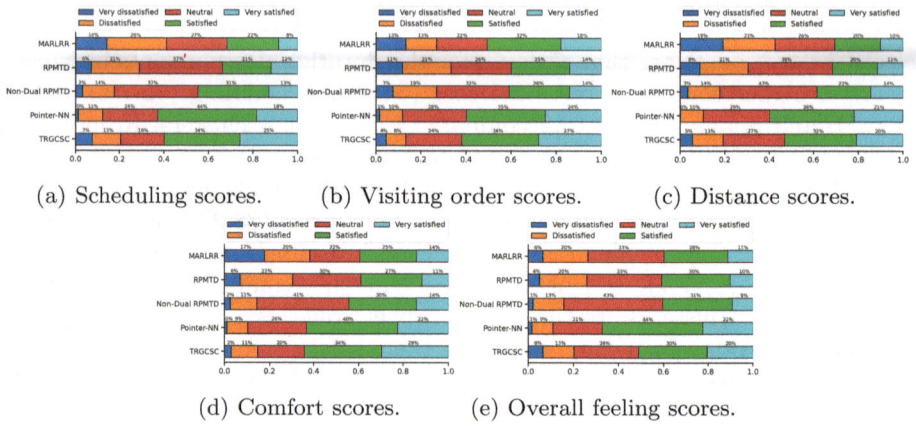

(a) Scheduling scores.   (b) Visiting order scores.   (c) Distance scores.

(d) Comfort scores.   (e) Overall feeling scores.

Fig. 4. Survey results for each method across scenarios.

5.2   Discussion

Compared to Pointer-NN, which does not consider congestion, the congestion-aware methods are outperformed in terms of overall feeling and distances between spots. This phenomenon supports the thought mentioned previously that the consideration of congestion could not always improve tourists' satisfaction. To avoid overcrowding, the congestion-aware methods are more likely to lead tourists to less-known spots rather than popular spots. Although local residents and local governments may benefit from it, the tourists might experience dissatisfaction with non-ordinary trajectories, particularly when the recommended less-known spots are far from other spots, resulting in low scores on distance and overall feeling.

Notably, the differences between Non-Dual RPMTD and RPMTD support the above opinion. With considering the places that no tourists visit, RPMTD tends to recommend more unpopular spots, compared to Non-Dual RPMTD. However, Non-Dual RPMTD outperforms RPMTD in all aspects, indicating that the consideration of the overall distribution of tourists actually makes the recommended routes worse. Hence, the consideration for congestion and tourism diversification is not a case of "the more, the better." Determining the level of consideration for congestion is a crucial concern for congestion-aware route recommendation methods.

6 Factors Influencing Overall Feeling

6.1 Regression Estimation Results for All Responses

In this section, we consider the effects of scheduling, visiting order, distance, and comfort on overall feeling. Coefficients of the following regression equation are obtained using ordinary least squares (OLS).

$$Feeling_i = \beta_0 + \beta_1 Scheduling_i + \beta_2 Order_i + \beta_3 Distances_i + \beta_4 Comfort_i + \varepsilon_i$$

Regression estimates for all responses are shown in Table 2. All of the variables are statistically significant, which indicates that the variables influence the overall feeling significantly. In terms of their impact on the final score, scheduling appears to have the greatest influence, followed by visiting order, and then distances between attractions. Comfort seems to be the least influential variable on the final score. We use Variance Inflation Factor (VIF) to detect multicollinearity. The VIFs of variables are smaller than 5, which suggests that the multicollinearity between variables is moderate.

With a decreasing order on importance, scheduling, visiting order, distance and comfort all have significantly positive effect on the overall feeling. These results support the previously mentioned opinion: the consideration of congestion and tourism diversification degrees should be balanced with other factors, especially when congestion consideration negatively impacts scheduling, visiting order, and distance between spots.

Table 2. Regression results for all responses. *** denotes $p < 0.01$.

Variables	Coefficients	Std. Err	Significant	VIF
Intecept	0.809	0.082	***	
Scheduling	0.273	0.030	***	2.2372
Visiting order	0.204	0.026	***	1.7676
Distance	0.188	0.032	***	2.5044
Comfort	0.107	0.031	***	2.4183
R^2	0.519			

6.2 Regression Estimation Results for Groups

As mentioned previously, differences in user demographics and preferences have been observed. We perform regressions to compare the effects of factors on overall feelings across user groups. The VIFs of variables for each regression, which are not reported here, are smaller than 5, suggesting moderate multicollinearity.

To determine the significance of observed differences in coefficient estimates, a bootstrapping method proposed in [21] is used to calculate empirical p-values

Table 3. Regression results for popular group and less-known group. Reported coefficients are estimated using OLS. Standard errors are in the parentheses. *** denotes $p < 0.01$, ** denotes $p < 0.05$, * denotes $p < 0.1$.

	Intercept	Scheduling	Visiting order	Distance	Comfort	R^2
Popular	0.821***	0.242***	0.270***	0.238***	0.011	0.504
	(0.134)	(0.048)	(0.041)	(0.052)	(0.053)	
Less-known	0.779***	0.296***	0.161***	0.166***	0.161***	0.533
	(0.104)	(0.039)	(0.033)	(0.040)	(0.039)	
Empirical p-values						
Popular vs. Less-known	0.6011	0.2249	0.9555	0.8293	0.0186	

that estimate the likelihood of obtaining the observed differences in coefficient estimates if the true coefficients are, in fact, equal. Observations are pooled from the two groups whose coefficient estimates are to be compared. Denoting the number of observations from each group as n_1 and n_2. For each simulation, n_1 and n_2 observations are randomly selected from the pooled $n_1 + n_2$ observations and assigned to group 1 and group 2, respectively. Coefficient estimates are then determined for each group using these observations, and this procedure is repeated 50000 times. The empirical p-value is the percentage of simulations where the difference between coefficient estimates exceeds the actual observed difference in coefficient estimates. For example, a p-value of 0.01 indicates that only 500 out of 50000 simulated outcomes exceeded the sample result, which implies the sample difference is significant.

Popular Group vs. Less-Known Group. We divided the respondents into a popular group and a less-known group based on their responses to the question "prefer to visit popular places or less-known places." Subsequently, we compared the effects of variables on overall feeling across the groups to explore the differences between different types of tourists.

Regression results for popular group and less-known group are presented in Table 3. As demonstrated by the empirical p-values, compared to respondents who prefer less-known spots, the popular group focuses more on visiting order (at a significance level of 95.55%) and distance between spots (at a significance level of 82.93%), and less on comfort (at a significance level of 1.86%) and scheduling (at a significance level of 22.49%).

Male Group vs. Female Group. Similarly, we compare the effects of variables on overall feeling between the male group and the female group (Table 4).

The 0.0254 p-value in the scheduling column suggests that the scheduling coefficient for the male group is smaller than the female group at a significance level of 2.54%, which indicates that the overall feeling score of female group is more sensitive to scheduling than the male group. In other words, the female respondents are more concerned about scheduling than the male respondents.

Table 4. Regression results for male group and female group. Reported coefficients are estimated using OLS. Standard errors are in the parentheses. *** denotes $p < 0.01$, ** denotes $p < 0.05$, * denotes $p < 0.1$.

	Intercept	Scheduling	Visiting order	Distance	Comfort	R^2
Male	0.989***	0.219***	0.228***	0.168***	0.106***	0.469
	(0.102)	(0.037)	(0.032)	(0.038)	(0.037)	
Female	0.436***	0.357***	0.179***	0.223***	0.103*	0.570
	(0.146)	(0.050)	(0.042)	(0.059)	(0.057)	
Empirical p-values						
Male vs. female	0.9996	0.0254	0.2306	0.5162	0.7788	

Regression Estimation Results for Clusters. Regression estimation results for the clusters are presented in Table 5. The respondents in Cluster 1 focus more on comfort (87.90%) and distance (83.50%), but less on scheduling (16.71%) and visiting order (0.88%) compared to Cluster 2. The respondents in Cluster 2 are more sensitive to scheduling (69.24%) and visiting order (87.65%) but less sensitive to comfort (25.73%) compared to Cluster 3. The 0.8512 p-value in the visiting order column for Cluster 3 vs. 1 suggests that the visiting order coefficient for Cluster 3 is greater than Cluster 1 at 85.12% level of significance.

Table 5. Regression results for each cluster. Reported coefficients are estimated using OLS. Standard errors are in the parentheses. *** denotes $p < 0.01$, ** denotes $p < 0.05$, * denotes $p < 0.1$.

	Intercept	Scheduling	Visiting order	Distance	Comfort	R^2
Cluster 1	0.944***	0.229***	0.100*	0.244***	0.165**	0.476
	(0.187)	(0.059)	(0.053)	(0.070)	(0.069)	
Cluster 2	0.716***	0.307***	0.273***	0.162***	0.062	0.580
	(0.113)	(0.044)	(0.037)	(0.045)	(0.046)	
Cluster 3	0.859***	0.265***	0.191***	0.178***	0.112**	0.446
	(0.159)	(0.059)	(0.047)	(0.059)	(0.054)	
Empirical p-values						
Cluster 1 vs. 2	0.8822	0.1671	0.0088	0.8350	0.8790	
Cluster 2 vs. 3	0.2196	0.6924	0.8765	0.4183	0.2573	
Cluster 3 vs. 1	0.3606	0.6474	0.8512	0.2673	0.2902	

Discussion. The comparison of user groups reveals that tourists have significantly varying concerns about comfort among different groups, indicating that their tolerance for congestion varies and could be inferred from their demographic profiles and historical records. Therefore, a further study with more focus on personalized congestion awareness is suggested. For instance, incorporating personalized congestion penalties into the reward function based on tourists' demographic profiles and preferences may yield better results than fixed penalties.

7   Conclusion

The purpose of this study is to determine the evaluation of congestion-aware route recommendation methods from tourists' personal perspective through an experimental questionnaire survey. We investigated respondents' evaluations of five route recommendation methods with varying degrees of consideration for congestion and tourism diversification. Respondents were asked to evaluate these methods based on five aspects. Moreover, we conducted a series of regression estimations to explore the differences among respondent groups.

Although congestion-aware methods are preferred in terms of visiting order scores and comfort scores, the method that does not consider multiple users or congestion tends to provide the highest overall feeling satisfaction for tourists. The results of regression estimation also support the notion that consideration for congestion is necessary but needs to be balanced with other factors. In decreasing order of importance, scheduling, visiting order, distance between spots, and comfort all exhibit a significantly positive effect on overall feeling.

Additionally, this study did not consider other stakeholders, such as local residents, travel agencies and local governments. These entities typically benefit more from congestion-aware route recommendation methods than tourists. To determine an appropriate degree of consideration for congestion and, consequently, sustainable tourism, the opinions of these stakeholders are also important. We are planning to conduct a survey that takes into account both tourists and local stakeholders in future work.

References

1. Osborne, M.J., Rubinstein, A.: A Course in Game Theory. MIT Press, Cambridge (1994)
2. Milano, C., Novelli, M., Cheer, J.M.: Overtourism and degrowth: a social movements perspective. In: Tourism and Degrowth, pp. 113–131. Routledge (2020)
3. Santos-Rojo, C., Llopis-Amorós, M., García-García, J.M.: Overtourism and sustainability: a bibliometric study (2018–2021). Technol. Forecast. Soc. Change **188**(C) (2023)

4. Marsiglio, S.: On the carrying capacity and the optimal number of visitors in tourism destinations. Tour. Econ. **23**(3), 632–646 (2017)
5. Albaladejo, I.P., González-Martínez, M.: Congestion affecting the dynamic of tourism demand: evidence from the most popular destinations in Spain. Curr. Issues Tourism **22**(13), 1638–1652 (2019)
6. Takeuchi, K., Nishida, R., Kashima, H., Onishi, M.: Grab the reins of crowds: estimating the effects of crowd movement guidance using causal inference. In: AAMAS 2021, pp. 1290–1298 (2021)
7. Chao, I.-M., Golden, B.L., Wasil, E.A.: The team orienteering problem. Eur. J. Oper. Res. **88**(3), 464–474 (1996)
8. Golden, B.L., Levy, L., Vohra, R.: The orienteering problem. Naval Res. Logist. (NRL) **34**(3), 307–318 (1987)
9. Cheng, S.-T., Horng, G.-J., Chou, C.-L.: The adaptive recommendation mechanism for distributed group in mobile environments. IEEE Trans. Syst. Man Cybern. Part C (Appl. Rev.) **42**(6), 1081–1092 (2012)
10. Varakantham, P., Mostafa, H., Fu, N., Lau, H.C.: Direct: a scalable approach for route guidance in selfish orienteering problems. In: AAMAS 2015, pp. 483–491 (2015)
11. Kong, W.K., Zheng, S., Nguyen, M.L., Ma, Q.: Diversity-oriented route planning for tourists. In: Strauss, C., Cuzzocrea, A., Kotsis, G., Tjoa, A.M., Khalil, I. (eds.) DEXA 2022. LNCS, vol. 13427, pp. 243–255. Springer, Cham (2022). https://doi. org/10.1007/978-3-031-12426-6_20
12. Yuntao, K., Chen, P., Le, N.M., Qiang, M.: Dual congestion-aware route planning for tourists by multi-agent reinforcement learning. In: Strauss, C., Amagasa, T., Kotsis, G., Tjoa, A.M., Khalil, I. (eds.) DEXA 2023. LNCS, vol. 14147, pp. 331–336. Springer, Cham (2023). https://doi.org/10.1007/978-3-031-39821-6_27
13. Maekawa, T., Kasahara, H., Ma, Q.: Tour route generation considering spot congestion. In: Strauss, C., Amagasa, T., Kotsis, G., Tjoa, A.M., Khalil, I. (eds.) DEXA 2023. LNCS, vol. 14146, pp. 478–492. Springer, Cham (2023). https://doi. org/10.1007/978-3-031-39847-6_38
14. Xu, J., Sun, J., Li, T., Ma, Q.: Kyoto sightseeing map 2.0 for user-experience oriented tourism. In: MIPR 2021, pp. 239–242 (2021)
15. Yahoo Japan Corporation. Yahoo! JAPAN
16. Gama, R., Fernandes, H.L.: A reinforcement learning approach to the orienteering problem with time windows. Comput. Oper. Res. **133**, 105357 (2021)
17. Honnibal, M., Montani, I.: spaCy 2: natural language understanding with Bloom embeddings, convolutional neural networks and incremental parsing. https://spacy. io/
18. Mikolov, T., Chen, K., Corrado, G., Dean, J.: Efficient estimation of word representations in vector space. arXiv:1301.3781 (2013)
19. MacQueen, J., et al.: Some methods for classification and analysis of multivariate observations. In: Proceedings of the Fifth Berkeley Symposium on Mathematical Statistics and Probability, Oakland, CA, USA, vol. 1, pp. 281–297 (1967)
20. Van der Maaten, L., Hinton, G.: Visualizing data using t-SNE. J. Mach. Learn. Res. **9**(11) (2008)
21. Cleary, S.: The relationship between firm investment and financial status. J. Financ. **54**(2), 673–692 (1999)

U-KyotoTrip: A Travel Planning System for User Experience Oriented Trips

Kun Yi[1], Takeyuki Maekawa[2], Yuntao Kong[3], Zhengyang Bai[4],
Xisha Jin[5], and Qiang Ma[6(✉)]

[1] Institute of Economic Research, Kyoto University, Kyoto, Japan
[2] Graduate School of Informatics, Kyoto University, Kyoto, Japan
[3] School of Information Science, Japan Advanced Institute of Science and
Technology, Ishikawa, Japan
[4] RIKEN Center for Computational Science, RIKEN, Tokyo, Japan
zhengyang.bai@riken.jp
[5] Graduate School of Management, Kyoto University, Kyoto, Japan
jin.xisha.87y@st.kyoto-u.ac.jp
[6] Department of Information Science, Kyoto Institute of Technology, Kyoto, Japan
qiang@kit.ac.jp

Abstract. We propose U-KyotoTrip, a travel planning system designed
for user-experience-oriented trips in Kyoto, Japan. U-KyotoTrip integrates extensive content analysis of user-generated content, Point-Of-
Interest (POI) recommendations, and route recommendations, with the
aim of assisting users in acquiring information and travel planning.
To capture new users' preferences, we propose user-friendly ask-to-rate
methods to handle cold-start user scenarios. Furthermore, we employ five
route recommendation methods that vary in their consideration for congestion and tourism diversification to address the overtourism problem.
An empirical user study was conducted to evaluate U-KyotoTrip, revealing that users are satisfied with the system, particularly the approach
that utilizes photos to present their preferences.

Keywords: Travel Planning · POI Recommendation · Route
Recommendation · User Study · Cold-start · Ask-to-rate

1 Introduction

Tourism is a major industry in the global economy and plays a significant role
in our lives. To create enjoyable and fulfilling travel experiences, it is crucial
for tourists to consider potential destination cities, local attractions, cultural
experiences, and route planning. However, much of the imagery and information
provided by travel enterprises and local governments may have been beautified
to attract tourists from a marketing and publicity perspective [1], potentially
leading to untrustworthy information. Therefore, information based on user-
generated content is necessary to assist tourists in deciding on destinations and
attractions to visit.

This work was partly supported by JSPS KAKENHI (23H03404, 22H03600), and MIC
SCOPE 201607008.

K. Berezina et al. (Eds.): ENTER 2024, SPBE, pp. 339–352, 2024.
https://doi.org/10.1007/978-3-031-58839-6_36

Moreover, personalized POI and route recommendations also face challenges when dealing with tourists who have little or no historical records (e.g., check-ins, tweets, images, etc.), which is known as cold-start user scenarios. To make personalized recommendations in cold-start user scenarios, extra user effort is required to learn user preferences [2]. One direct way to acquire information from a new user for personalized recommendation is to provide POIs for the user to rate or attributes to select [3]. However, this can pose a challenge for users who are unfamiliar with the destination city, as they tend to select only what is familiar to them or what they expect to enjoy, which leads to a lack of exploration in the destination city.

Another challenge that travel planning systems face is the overtourism problem: large numbers of visitors can cause overcrowded attractions and traffic congestion, which leads to diminished experiences for both tourists and local residents. Although there has been an increasing interest in congestion-aware route recommendations to handle this task, the application of these recommendations in travel planning systems remains limited.

In this paper, we propose U-KyotoTrip, a travel planning system designed to offer information and recommendations for spots and routes in Kyoto, Japan, renowned as one of the world's most famous destinations. We developed an iOS application to demonstrate how U-KyotoTrip assists users in information acquisition and generates recommendations for spots and routes. To supplement user-experience-based information in the information search process, we utilize spot information presented in Kyoto Sightseeing Map 2.0 [4]. In order to provide personalized recommendations, especially for users new to the application, we propose user-friendly methods for acquiring information and utilize the POI recommendation approach proposed in [5]. For new users, they can express their preferences by uploading their own photos or by rating several random images from the database. Their preferences are captured based on their responses, and the POI and route recommendations are generated based on the inferred preferences of the users. Moreover, to provide personalized congestion-aware route recommendations, we employed route recommendation methods that have varying degrees of consideration for congestion and tourism diversification. Users can choose from various route recommendation methods based on their preferences.

The contributions of this work are summarized as follows.

- We propose a travel planning system which integrates spot information based on user generated contents, POI recommendation and route suggestion.
- To address cold-start user scenarios, in Sect. 3.3, we introduce novel photo-based information acquisition methods, which are more user-friendly compared to existing approaches.
- To address the issue of overtourism, in Sect. 3.5, we utilize a variety of congestion-aware methods for route recommendations. Users can select routes with varying levels of congestion consideration based on their preferences.
- To evaluate the proposed U-KyotoTrip, we conducted an empirical user study. The results of the user study demonstrate that users are satisfied with U-KyotoTrip, the recommended spots and the approach that utilizes photos to present preferences.

2 Related Work

Numerous studies have focused on mining tourism spots based on user-generated content to discover attractions and provide information. Zhuang et al. [6] analyzed geotagged images and comments uploaded on social networking sites, discovering attractions through clustering. Katayama et al. [7] developed a system that identifies potential spots using location information from tourists' historical records. Xu et al. [4] introduced Kyoto Sightseeing Map 2.0, a web-based application that employs comprehensive content analysis of information from user-generated content to assist travelers in their information search process.

There has been a growing interest in designing mobile applications for POI or route recommendations [8]. Vansteenwegen et al. [9] introduced a city tour planner featuring a Greedy Randomised Adaptive Search Procedure (GRASP) [10] as its core planning engine. Brilhante et al. [11] presented TripBuilder, a web-based application that leverages POI collections from Wikipedia and albums of photos from Flickr to provide POI recommendations. Gavalas et al. [12] proposed eCOMPASS, a mobile application that integrates public transport options into recommended trips. Wang et al. [13] proposed a personalized crowd-aware trip recommendation algorithm that considers the most crowded times at tourist spots. Khodadadian et al. [14] addressed the time-dependent orienteering problem with time windows and service time-dependent profits. Herzog et al. [15] developed TourRec, a context-aware tourist trip recommender system capable of suggesting routes for both individual and group users.

However, most existing methods focus solely on providing spot information, recommending POIs, or recommending routes. In contrast, the proposed U-KyotoTrip offers spot information and recommendations for both POI and route, presenting users with a comprehensive solution for their travel planning needs. With U-KyotoTrip, users can complete their travel planning all at once. Furthermore, many existing methods require new users to select attributes at the start, which can be relatively challenging for those unfamiliar with the destination city. In comparison, our approach offers more user-friendly methods to learn user preferences, enhancing the usability of the proposed application. Moreover, the route recommendation module in U-KyotoTrip integrates route recommendation methods that consider varying levels of congestion. These congestion-aware methods can assist users in avoiding overcrowded attractions based on their tolerance for congestion.

3 System Overview

3.1 System Architecture

U-KyotoTrip, as a travel planning system, assists users in discovering tourism information and provides recommendations for POIs and routes. The foundational concepts of U-KyotoTrip are drawn from [4,5,16,17], and [18]. demonstrated in Fig. 1, U-KyotoTrip comprises four modules: information display, preference capture, POI reccommendation, and route recommendation. The iOS application of U-KyotoTrip is developed using Node.js.

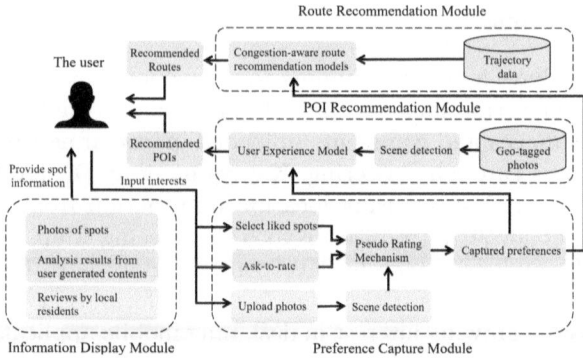

Fig. 1. System architecture.

3.2   Information Display Module

For each spot, U-KyotoTrip provides comprehensive information through user-generated content and analysis results presented in Kyoto Sightseeing Map 2.0 [4]. This information includes the pictures of spots uploaded by locals, statistical graphs showcasing aesthetic quality and image counts for each POI, congestion information, and reviews contributed by local residents. This wealth of information enables users to make well-informed judgments and establish reasonable expectations of tourist spots, aiding them in deciding whether to visit a particular destination.

3.3   Preference Capture Module

For users who have previously utilized U-KyotoTrip, POI and route recommendations can be generated based on their historical records. For new users who are unfamiliar with U-KyotoTrip, one of the following three approaches is required to understand their preferences.

- The new user can review spot information and mark certain spots as either "want to visit" or "do not want to visit".
- The new user is asked to rate several photos provided from the server. Based on the ratings of the photos, the user's preferences are inferred.
- Alternatively, the new user can upload photos to the server. Descriptive words for these photos are extracted using the scene detection method proposed by [19]. These extracted words are considered as keywords representing the user's preferences, which are then used to infer their preferences.

Based on the input, the Pseudo-Rating Mechanism (PRM) proposed in [5] is used to infer the user's preferences. We provide a detailed demonstration of the preference capture process for the approach of rating photos. As for the other two approaches, we can substitute the images with locations or extracted words.

Suppose n images from N ($n << N$) records of other users are randomly provided to a new user u' to capture this user's preference, and u' rates the images.

We denote the rating information by $R = \{(r_k, l_k, w_k, I_k)\}_{k=1}^n$, where r_k, l_k, w_k represent the rating, location and keywords of the image I_k, respectively. Under the assumption that every user's ratings of all images $\{r_k\}_{k=1}^N$ follow a known distribution F_{rating}, the ratings can be inferred and used to predict the spots and behaviors that u' may prefer. Denote the set of users, spots, and keywords in the database as U, L, and W, respectively. For arbitrary location $l_i \in L$ and keyword $w_j \in W$, the visit probability is

$$p(l_i, w_j | R) = \sum_{u \in U} p(l_i, w_j | u) p(u | R).$$

Applying Bayes' theorem,

$$p(u|R) \propto p(R|u)p(u) = \prod_{k=1}^n p(rating(l_k, w_k, I_k) = r_k | u)p(u).$$

Under our assumption of rating distribution,

$$p(rating(l_k, w_k, I_k) = r_k | u) = p\left(\frac{N + 1 - rank(l_k, w_k, I_k)}{N} = F_{rating}(r_k) \middle| u\right).$$

where, $rank(l_k, w_k, I_k)$ is the rank of (l_k, w_k, I_k) in N images. We approximate the distribution of $rank(l_k, w_k, I_k)$ using Monte Carlo sampling. The captured preferences are used for subsequent POI and route recommendations.

3.4 POI Recommendation Module

Based on the captured preferences, the User Experience Model (UEM) proposed in [5] is employed to recommend spots. The UEM considers not only "where to visit" but also "what to do" at attractions. The UEM used in U-KyotoTrip is trained using geo-tagged photos in YFCC100M Kyoto [20] as the data source. Descriptive words for the photos are extracted using the scene detection method proposed in [19]. Out of a total of 91 spots, the system recommends the top 10 spots that may interest the user.

3.5 Route Recommendation Module

If the user has decided and selected all the spots to visit, U-KyotoTrip could provide the shortest route based on the user's choices using GRASP [10].

If the user wants the recommended route to include spots that are not initially selected, the route recommendation module of U-KyotoTrip offers the option to provide routes using the following route recommendation methods. These methods have varying degrees of consideration for congestion and tourism diversification. These methods are trained using the dataset of Kyoto Sightseeing Map 2.0 [4] and trajectory data used in [18] and [17].

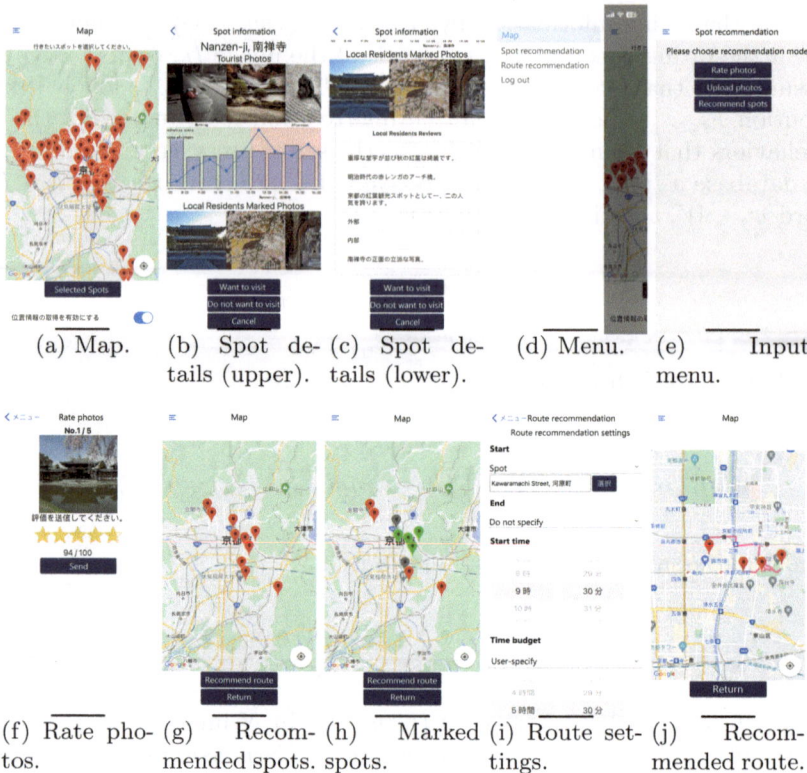

(a) Map.   (b) Spot details (upper).   (c) Spot details (lower).   (d) Menu.   (e) Input menu.

(f) Rate photos.   (g) Recommended spots.   (h) Marked spots.   (i) Route settings.   (j) Recommended route.

Fig. 2. The interface of U-KyotoTrip.

- **MARLRR**: An multi-agent reinforcement learning approach proposed in [16] for solving the congestion-aware route recommendation task. This method considers that several groups are moving simultaneously, and a congestion penalty of reward function is introduced to avoid overconcentration at spots.
- **RPMTD**: A multi-agent reinforcement learning based route recommendation method proposed in [17] that considers both multiple users accessing simultaneously and the congestion at attractions. This method introduces a dual-congestion mechanism, in which both the local congestion at visited spots and the global distribution of tourists affect tourists' satisfaction.
- **Non-Dual RPMTD**: An alternative version of RPMTD that does not consider the global distribution of tourists in the dual-congestion mechanism.
- **Pointer-NN**: A reinforcement learning approach to the Orienteering Problem with Time Windows proposed in [21], without considering congestion.
- **TRGCSC**: A reinforcement learning approach proposed in [18], which is based on [21] and introduces two novel concepts, "dynamic stay duration" and "environmental tax metaphor." The former concept estimates the necessary stay duration at a spot based on its congestion, and the latter concept assigns dynamic rewards depending on congestion at spots.

3.6   Interface and User Interaction

Figure 2 demonstrates the user interface of U-KyotoTrip. In Fig. 2(a), upon user login, the map displays a total of 91 spots in Kyoto. Clicking on a marker on the map leads the user to the corresponding spot's information page. The upper part of this page, as shown in Fig. 2(b), provides photos of spots uploaded by locals, statistical graphs presenting aesthetic quality and image counts for each spot, and congestion details. The lower part of this page, as shown in Fig. 2(c), provides reviews from local residents. Within the spot information page, users can select from three options: "want to visit," "do not want to visit," or "cancel."

The user can utilize the button located at the top left corner of the map display page to access the map view, perform POI recommendations, or route recommendations, as illustrated in Fig. 2(d). For new users who are using U-KyotoTrip for the first time, POI and route recommendations are not available until they complete the "ask-to-rate" step to capture their preferences. As depicted in Fig. 2(e), users can initiate a brief questionnaire by clicking the first button labeled "Rate photos," which presents several photos for rating. Figure 2(f) illustrates the presentation of photos for rating. These ratings contribute to capturing users' interests and preferences as described in Sect. 3.3. Alternatively, users can click the second button labeled "Upload photos" in Fig. 2(e) to express their preferences by uploading photos. Moreover, if the user has already marked certain spots as "want to visit" or "do not want to visit," the third button enables them to directly obtain recommendations.

Subsequently, as illustrated in Fig. 2(g), the recommended spots are shown on the map. Similar to the map page in Fig. 2(a), users can click on a marker to access spot information and mark it as "want to visit" or "do not want to visit." As shown in Fig. 2(h), the marker for the "want to visit" spot will turn green, while the marker for the "do not want to visit" spot will turn gray.

After the user has selected a few spots they wish to visit, they can click the "Recommend route" button. The system will return the shortest route using GRASP. Alternatively, the user can also utilize congetsion-aware route recommendation methods from the menu page. This action takes them to the route recommendation page, depicted in Fig. 2(i), where they can input the start location, end location, start time, and time budget. The user can select a spot or an arbitrary coordinate as the start or end point, thereby providing flexibility to the route recommendation system. Figure 2(j) illustrates the recommended route.

Table 1. Demographic profile of respondents.

Characteristics			Percent		Percent
Gender	Male		39.02%	Female	60.98%
Frequency of travel	Once every few years		14.63%	Once a year	12.20%
	Twice a year		34.15%	Once every quarter	34.15%
	Once every two months		17.07%	Once a month	7.32%
	Twice a month		12.20%	Once a week	2.44%
Duration of travel	Daytrip		12.20%	2 days	4.88%
	3 days		19.51%	4 days	17.07%
	5 days		14.63%	6 days	0%
	7 days		14.63%	More than 7 days	17.07%
Factors of concern	Price		78.05%	Time cost	48.78%
	Scheduling		63.42%	Season	56.10%
	Popularity		48.78%	Congestion	80.49%
Popular or	Less-known places		63.42%	Neutral	7.32%
less-known spots	Popular places		29.27%		

4   User Study

4.1   Participants and Setting

We conducted a user study in Kyoto, Japan to evaluate the proposed U-KyotoTrip. A screening questionnaire was distributed to 41 participants. The respondents' demographic characteristics are listed in Table 1. We had participants experience the tour planning process as new users. Each participant was provided with 10 random photos and asked to rate these photos, capturing their preferences. POI reccommendations and route suggestions were made based on the inferred preferences. Participants could explore spot information on the map, as shown in Sect. 3.6. After reviewing the recommendations, participants were asked to respond to the following questions:

- **Q1.** How many of the recommended spots did you like?
- **Q2.** Did you find the number of recommended spots too many or too few?
- **Q3.** Did you find the types of recommended spots too many or too few?
- **Q4.** Did you find the popular spots too many or too few?
- **Q5.** Did you find less-known spots too many or too few?
- **Q6.** How satisfied did you feel overall with U-KyotoTrip?
- **Q7.** Did the recommended spots meet your satisfaction?
- **Q8.** Did you find the use of photo ratings to express preferences satisfactory?
- **Q9.** How satisfied did you feel with the route recommendation methods?

Additionally, we asked respondents to provide written comments on the recommended spots, the use of photo ratings, and the overall feeling of U-KyotoTrip.

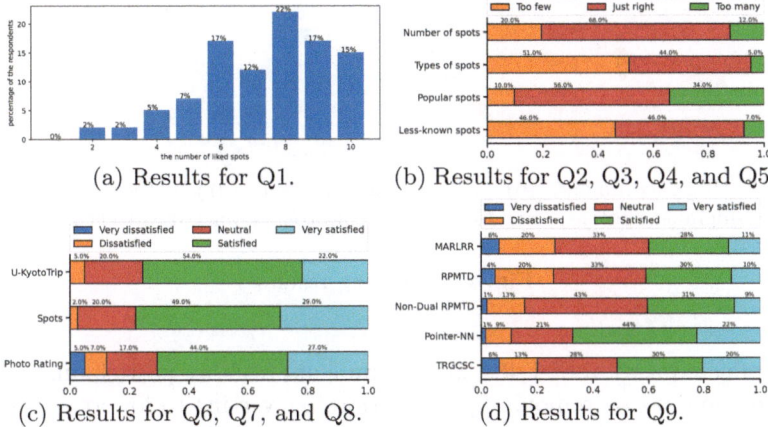

(a) Results for Q1.

(b) Results for Q2, Q3, Q4, and Q5.

(c) Results for Q6, Q7, and Q8.

(d) Results for Q9.

Fig. 3. Survey results.

4.2 Survey Results

Figure 3(a) illustrates the results for Q1, showing that 84% of the respondents liked 6 or more of the recommended spots, and 54% of the respondents liked 8 or more of the recommended spots. This suggests that the recommended spots are considered satisfactory for most respondents.

Figure 3(b) illustrates the results for Q2, Q3, Q4, and Q5. For the number of recommended spots, 68% of the respondents selected "just right," 20% chose "too few," and 12% opted for "Too many." As for the types of recommended spots, 51% noted "Too few," 44% selected "Just right," and 5% thought "Too many." Regarding popular spots and less-known spots, many respondents thought popular spots are "Too many," and less-known spots are "Too few."

Figure 3(c) displays the responses to Q6, Q7, and Q8. While a few respondents expressed dissatisfaction, the majority were "Satisfied" or "Very satisfied" with the application, the recommended spots, and rating photos.

Figure 3(d) illustrates the satisfaction with route recommendation methods. Pointer-NN is the most satisfactory method for respondents, with a total of 67% of the respondents selecting "Very satisfied" or "Satisfied." This is followed by TRGCSC, with a total of 51% of the respondents selecting "Very satisfied" or "Satisfied." Non-Dual RPMTD (40%), RPMTD (41%), and MARLRR (40%) achieved similar performance. More details concerning the evaluation of route recommendation methods can be found in [22].

4.3 Clustering Analysis

To explore further subjective satisfaction with the recommended spots, the approach of expressing preferences through photo ratings, and the overall feeling of U-KyotoTrip, we conducted a clustering analysis on the textual comments provided by respondents.

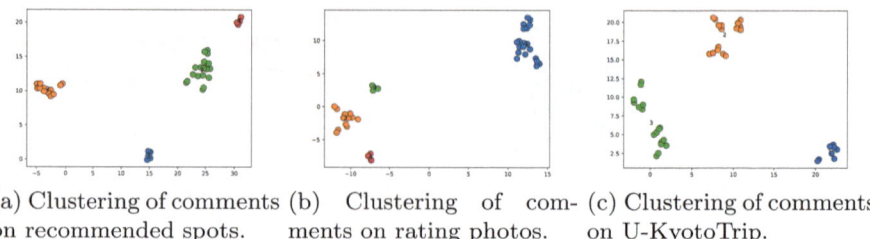

(a) Clustering of comments on recommended spots.

(b) Clustering of comments on rating photos.

(c) Clustering of comments on U-KyotoTrip.

Fig. 4. Clustering results.

We collected a total of 1,489 word comments from 41 participants. We preprocessed the data by removing punctuation, converting to lowercase, reducing word forms, and filtering stop words using Spacy [23]. The Skip-Gram model in Word2Vec [24] was utilized to embed words into high-dimensional vectors, capturing their semantic meanings. We employed DBSCAN [25] to cluster similar comments for each question, and UMAP [26] to reduce the comment vectors to two dimensions for visualization purposes. The results are presented in Fig. 4. Furthermore, to gain insights into the features of each respondents' cluster, we created word clouds to visualize the most common words in each cluster, as illustrated in Fig. 5, Fig. 6, and Fig. 7.

Regarding the recommended spots, the comments are divided into 4 clusters. As illustrated in Fig. 5, all clusters exhibit a significant proportion of positive sentiment, suggesting that respondents are satisfied with the recommended spots. Meanwhile, Cluster 1, Cluster 3, and Cluster 4 express concerns about potential overcrowding at these recommended spots.

The comments regarding the use of photo ratings are divided into 4 clusters, and the word clouds are shown in Fig. 6. On one hand, numerous respondents convey a positive sentiment, indicating that the utilization of photo ratings is a simple but effective way to capture users' preferences. On the other hand, a few respondents express that some provided photos may have been beautified for attractiveness, potentially leading to inaccurate preference capturing.

For the overall feeling of U-KyotoTrip, the comments are divided into 3 clusters. As demonstrated in Fig. 7, all the clusters agree that the application is easy to use and can assist users in travel planning. Respondents in Cluster 1 express satisfaction with U-KyotoTrip due to the high-quality recommendations it provides. Cluster 2 respondents emphasize that this application enables tourists to easily explore scenic spots, assisting users in making decisions about which attractions to visit. Clusters 3 respondents emphasize the term "convenient," "concise," "saving time," and "simple," indicating their high satisfaction with the user-friendly nature of U-KyotoTrip.

(a) Cluster 1.   (b) Cluster 2.   (c) Cluster 3.   (d) Cluster 4.

Fig. 5. Word clouds of comment clusters on recommended spots.

(a) Cluster 1.   (b) Cluster 2.   (c) Cluster 3.   (d) Cluster 4.

Fig. 6. Word clouds of comment clusters on rating photos.

(a) Cluster 1.   (b) Cluster 2.   (c) Cluster 3.

Fig. 7. Word clouds of comment clusters on U-KyotoTrip.

4.4   Discussion

As demonstrated in Sect. 4.2, most of the respondents are satisfied with the proposed U-KyotoTrip and the recommended spots. This indicates that the system effectively captures the preferences of most participants, resulting in a high level of satisfaction with the suggested spots. One limitation of the system is that many respondents found the variety of spot types to be insufficient. The POI recommendation module tends to recommend spots of similar types to users after capturing their preferences. Another limitation pertains to the number of less-known spots. The participants who favor less-known spots expressed that the quantity of such spots provided was inadequate. Therefore, future research on the inclusion of diversification and more less-known spots in POI recommendations is necessary to establish more satisfactory travel planning systems.

Regarding the approach of presenting preferences through photo ratings, the majority of respondents expressed that their preferences were satisfactorily captured. The comment analysis indicates that most participants appreciate the visual experience and find it intuitive. However, some participants express concerns that the provided photos may have been enhanced for attractiveness, potentially leading to inaccurate preference capturing. Incorporating 360-degree views or videos would further enhance the user experience.

Concerning the route recommendation methods, respondents show a tendency to favor Pointer-NN, which does not consider congestion, over the congestion-aware route recommendation methods. This phenomenon suggests that the consideration of congestion could not always improve tourists' satisfaction. Although local residents and governments may benefit from these methods, the tourists might experience dissatisfaction with non-ordinary trajectories, particularly when the recommended less-known spots are far from other spots.

5   Conclusion

In this paper, we propose U-KyotoTrip, a user experience-oriented travel planning system designed to assist users in planning their trips. U-KyotoTrip integrates spot information, POI recommendation, and route recommendation, offering users a comprehensive solution for their travel planning needs. We evaluated U-KyotoTrip using an empirical user study. Most participants expressed that U-KyotoTrip is enjoyable to use for information search and recommendations, and the utilization of rating photos effectively captures participants' preferences. Two major limitations are that the variety of recommended spot types tends to be too few, and the system tends to prioritize suggesting popular spots over less-known ones. Therefore, future studies on diversifying POI recommendations are needed to establish more satisfactory systems. Furthermore, the comparison of route recommendation methods reveals that the consideration of congestion may not always improve tourists' satisfaction. Further research should be undertaken to explore the balance between tourism diversification and satisfaction.

References

1. Ma, Q.: Forefront of sightseeing informatics-technologies of collective intelligence for promotion of personalized and distributed sightseeing. IPSJ Mag. **58**(3), 220–226 (2017)
2. Gope, J., Jain, S.K.: A survey on solving cold start problem in recommender systems. In: ICCCA 2017, pp. 133–138 (2017)
3. Rubens, N., Elahi, M., Sugiyama, M., Kaplan, D.: Active learning in recommender systems. In: Recommender Systems Handbook, pp. 809–846 (2015)
4. Xu, J., Sun, J., Li, T., Ma, Q.: Kyoto sightseeing map 2.0 for user-experience oriented tourism. In: MIPR 2021, pp. 239–242 (2021)
5. Yi, K., Yamagishi, R., Li, T., Bai, Z., Ma, Q.: Recommending POIs for tourists by user behavior modeling and pseudo-rating. arXiv:2110.06523 (2021)
6. Zhuang, C., Ma, Q., Yoshikawa, M.: SNS user classification and its application to obscure poi discovery. Multimedia Tools Appl. **76**, 5461–5487 (2017)
7. Katayama, S., Obuchi, M., Okoshi, T., Nakazawa, J.: Providing information of hidden spot for tourists to increase tourism satisfaction. In: UbiComp 2018, pp. 377–380 (2018)
8. Wörndl, W., Herzog, D.: Mobile applications for e-tourism. In: Handbook of e-Tourism, pp. 1–21 (2020)

9. Vansteenwegen, P., Souffriau, W., Berghe, G.V., Van Oudheusden, D.: The city trip planner: an expert system for tourists. Expert Syst. Appl. **38**(6), 6540–6546 (2011)
10. Feo, T.A., Resende, M.G.C.: A probabilistic heuristic for a computationally difficult set covering problem. Oper. Res. Lett. **8**(2), 67–71 (1989)
11. Brilhante, I.R., Macedo, J.A., Nardini, F.M., Perego, R., Renso, C.: On planning sightseeing tours with tripbuilder. Inf. Process. Manag. **51**(2), 1–15 (2015)
12. Gavalas, D., Kasapakis, V., Konstantopoulos, C., Pantziou, G., Vathis, N., Zaroliagis, C.: The ecompass multimodal tourist tour planner. Expert Syst. Appl. **42**(21), 7303–7316 (2015)
13. Wang, X., Leckie, C., Chan, J., Lim, K.H., Vaithianathan, T.: Improving personalized trip recommendation by avoiding crowds. In: CIKM 2016, pp. 25–34 (2016)
14. Khodadadian, M., Divsalar, A., Verbeeck, C., Gunawan, A., Vansteenwegen, P.: Time dependent orienteering problem with time windows and service time dependent profits. Comput. Oper. Res. **143**, 105794 (2022)
15. Herzog, D., Laß, C., Wörndl, W.: Tourrec: a tourist trip recommender system for individuals and groups. In: RecSys 2018, pp. 496–497 (2018)
16. Kong, W.K., Zheng, S., Nguyen, M.L., Ma, Q.: Diversity-oriented route planning for tourists. In: Strauss, C., Cuzzocrea, A., Kotsis, G., Tjoa, A.M., Khalil, I. (eds.) DEXA 2022. LNCS, vol. 13427, pp. 243–255. Springer, Cham (2022). https://doi.org/10.1007/978-3-031-12426-6_20
17. Yuntao, K., Chen, P., Le, N.M., Qiang, M.: Dual congestion-aware route planning for tourists by multi-agent reinforcement learning. In: Strauss, C., Amagasa, T., Kotsis, G., Tjoa, A.M., Khalil, I. (eds.) DEXA 2023. LNCS, vol. 14147, pp. 331–336. Springer, Cham (2023). https://doi.org/10.1007/978-3-031-39821-6_27
18. Maekawa, T., Kasahara, H., Ma, Q.: Tour route generation considering spot congestion. In: Strauss, C., Amagasa, T., Kotsis, G., Tjoa, A.M., Khalil, I. (eds.) DEXA 2023. LNCS, vol. 14146, pp. 478–492. Springer, Cham (2023). https://doi.org/10.1007/978-3-031-39847-6_38
19. Patterson, G., Chen, X., Hang, S., Hays, J.: The sun attribute database: beyond categories for deeper scene understanding. Int. J. Comput. Vision **108**(1–2), 59–81 (2014)
20. Sun, J., Kinoue, T., Ma, Q.: A city adaptive clustering framework for discovering POIs with different granularities. In: Hartmann, S., Küng, J., Kotsis, G., Tjoa, A.M., Khalil, I. (eds.) DEXA 2020. LNCS, vol. 12391, pp. 425–434. Springer, Cham (2020). https://doi.org/10.1007/978-3-030-59003-1_28
21. Gama, R., Fernandes, H.L.: A reinforcement learning approach to the orienteering problem with time windows. Comput. Oper. Res. **133**, 105357 (2021)
22. Yi, K., Jin, X., Bai, Z., Kong, Y., Ma, Q.: An empirical user study on congestion-aware route recommendation (2024, to appear)
23. Honnibal, M., Montani, I.: spaCy 2: natural language understanding with Bloom embeddings, convolutional neural networks and incremental parsing. https://spacy.io/
24. Mikolov, T., Chen, K., Corrado, G., Dean, J.: Efficient estimation of word representations in vector space. arXiv:1301.3781 (2013)
25. Ester, M., Kriegel, H.-P., Sander, J., Xiaowei, X.: A density-based algorithm for discovering clusters in large spatial databases with noise. In: KDD 1996, pp. 226–331 (1996)
26. McInnes, L., Healy, J., Melville, J.: Umap: uniform manifold approximation and projection for dimension reduction. arXiv:1802.03426 (2018)

Visualizing Explainable Touristic Recommendations: An Interactive Approach

Stefan Neubig[1,2]($\boxtimes$) (ID), Daria Cappey[1,2], Nicolas Gehring[2], Linus Göhl[1], Andreas Hein[2] (ID), and Helmut Krcmar[2] (ID)

[1] Outdooractive AG, Missener Str. 18, 87509 Immenstadt, Germany
{stefan.neubig,daria.cappey,linus.goehl}@outdooractive.com
[2] Technical University of Munich, Boltzmannstr. 3, 85748 Garching b. München, Germany
{n.j.gehring,andreas.hein,helmut.krcmar}@tum.de

Abstract. Personalized recommendations have played a vital role in tourism, serving various purposes, ranging from an improved visitor experience to addressing sustainability issues. However, research shows that recommendations are more likely to be accepted by visitors if they are comprehensible and appeal to the visitors' common sense. This highlights the importance of explainable recommendations that, according to a previously specified goal, explain an algorithm's inference process, generate trust among visitors, or educate visitors by making them aware of sustainability practices. Based on this motivation, our paper proposes a visual, interactive approach to exploring recommendation explanations tailored to tourism. Agnostic to the underlying recommendation algorithm and the defined explainability goal, our approach leverages knowledge graphs to generate model-specific and post-hoc explanations. We demonstrate and evaluate our approach based on a prototypical dashboard implementing our concept. Following the results of our evaluation, our dashboard helps explain recommendations of arbitrary models, even in complex scenarios.

Keywords: Tourism · Recommender Systems · Knowledge Graphs · Explainable Artificial Intelligence

1 Introduction

Recommender systems have been around for multiple decades. In tourism, they help visitors to identify, among others, worthwhile points of interest (POIs), hiking tours, or destinations. Compared to early, relatively simple approaches, state-of-the-art recommender systems achieve impressive results, often thanks to improved technologies, including matrix factorization, deep learning, and graph neural networks (GNNs) [1]. Recent use cases even go beyond recommender systems that "simply" identify suitable items but aim at generating multistakeholder recommendations [2], for example, to address sustainability goals [3, 4]. Such recommender systems consider multiple perspectives, including visitors' preferences, nature preservation, local inhabitants, and the spatiotemporal occupancy of specific places. Regarding visitors' acceptance of generated

K. Berezina et al. (Eds.): ENTER 2024, SPBE, pp. 353–364, 2024.
https://doi.org/10.1007/978-3-031-58839-6_37

recommendations, there is significant evidence that visitors tend to follow recommendations better if they understand the reasons behind them [5]. Moreover, recommender systems tackling sustainability issues (e.g., by guiding visitors to little-crowded places [4]) not only aim to recommend alternatives but include the critical aspect of visitor education, making them understand the implications of their actions [6].

This, however, reveals an essential shortcoming of many state-of-the-art recommender systems. Due to their complex underlying architecture, they are usually hard to understand and often referred to as (AI) black boxes [7]. Fortunately, not all use cases require opening these black boxes and hence do not require visitors to understand the actual recommender's (algorithmic) inference (i.e., the technical path the algorithm takes to derive a particular recommendation). In contrast, it is often sufficient to find approximate explanations, for instance, a comprehensible explanation of why a visitor should not visit a specific place for sustainability reasons and why a recommended (possibly similar) alternative may also appeal to the visitor's interests [8]. Developing such systems, even based on approximate explanations, is still challenging for developers. It requires considerable engineering effort and domain-specific knowledge, involves expensive trial and error, and demands sufficiently high accuracy.

In this paper, we introduce an approach for visually and interactively exploring the space of potential explanations for generated recommendations, showcasing how trustworthy explanations can be designed based on an interactive dashboard. We employ knowledge graphs (i.e., structural descriptions of real-world entities [9]) to incorporate domain-specific knowledge, allowing the systematic exploration of interrelationships within generated recommendations. Intended to be used by researchers and developers of touristic recommendation services, our dashboard helps find convincing reasoning paths suitable to simplify implementing a goal-oriented explanation logic. We evaluate our approach using a prototype to find explanations for two state-of-the-art recommender systems, including a knowledge-based system that exposes hints of its internal functionality and a deep-learning approach that we consider a complete black box.

2 Background

The most prominent distinction of recommender system categories comprises content-based (CB), collaborative-filtering-based (CFB), and hybrid methods. CB recommendation techniques aim to recommend items similar (i.e., with respect to item attributes) to those a user has interacted with in the past [10]. In contrast, CFB recommenders create recommendations based on the unseen items of similar users (i.e., users with a similar user-item interaction history) [10]. Hybrid recommender systems [11] combine different techniques to balance the disadvantages of specific methods and tend to score a higher precision than traditional algorithms [12]. More recent approaches to recommender systems leverage information beyond pure interaction data and item attributes. Context-aware recommender systems extend the generation of recommendations by incorporating additional context information about entities (e.g., users, items, additional objects) [11] comprising time, location, groups, and social context [13]. Similarly, knowledge-based recommender systems leverage side information, often contained in knowledge graphs (KGs) [9], to achieve better recommendation performance [7]. KGs capture entities in a structured way, presenting them as labeled nodes that are linked by labeled edges (representing relationships). Using formal semantics, KGs allow logical reasoning to capture information about subtle relationships (e.g., if A is related to B and B is related to C, A is also related to C) [14].

With the growing complexity of the underlying recommender algorithm, generating comprehensive yet understandable explanations of why an algorithm inferred a specific item internally becomes an increasingly difficult task. However, full transparency on how a recommender's inference internally works may be irrelevant and even overwhelm regular visitors. [8] identifies seven frequently used explanation goals in the literature: transparency, scrutability, trust, effectiveness, persuasiveness, efficiency, and satisfaction. Since achieving all goals in any use case is neither possible nor necessarily desirable, the authors highlight the importance of defining the individual goals before diving deeper into a specific implementation.

The specified explainability goal determines which information is required for the explanation task. Transparency, for example, where explanations should reason about an algorithm's inference process, requires a model-specific approach that reveals model internals (e.g., the structure of regression trees [15] or attention weights [16]). Otherwise, a post-hoc method with explanations generated by a separate model and thus independent of the selected recommender may be sufficient or even lead to more suitable explanations [7].

For conveying generated explanations to a user, researchers presented different types of explanation styles that may vary depending on the recommendation model, the explanation goal, the intended users, and the application domain [8]. Table 1 summarizes prominent examples of explanation styles.

Table 1. Overview of Explanation styles.

Explanation Style	Description
Relevant Users	Explains an item's relevance by emphasizing its (positive) ratings received from similar users [7]
Relevant Items	Explains an item's relevance by highlighting similar items the user has interacted with in the past. Studies suggest the superiority of "relevant items" over "relevant users" [7]
Feature-Based Explanations	An extension of "relevant items", additionally reasoning about what features make items similar [7, 17]
Opinion-Based Explanations	Employs user-generated content (e.g., reviews) that contain information about different aspects (e.g., breakfast quality in a hotel) to generate explanations [7]
Sentence-Based Explanations	Explanations in text form are created using templates (i.e., sentences with placeholders) or by a suitable model [7]

Despite the research progress in explainable recommendation systems, developing such systems remains challenging. Choosing suitable explanation techniques and communication styles requires comprehensive knowledge of the underlying domain and a thorough analysis of the particular use case [8]. This considerable engineering effort is complemented by expensive trial and error, regularly evaluating the effects of changes. A viable solution would allow researchers and developers to explore different explanation techniques and styles without needing constant re-development.

However, existing approaches in this regard are rare and bound to specific explanation styles and use cases [18], leaving tourism largely untouched. Furthermore, visualizing the data and internals of recommender systems for algorithmic improvement is an urgent yet underexplored field [19]. In the following, we propose a visual, interactive approach to explore different explanations tailored to the tourism domain, where location-based recommendations and geographic attributes are crucial [20]. Our approach is centered around KGs, which have proven successful not only for generating recommendations but also for generating related explanations [1]. Employing KGs, we allow incorporating tourism-specific knowledge to deep-dive into model internals or to support the creation of model-agnostic (i.e., post-hoc) explanations. Using our approach, researchers and developers can interactively evaluate different explanation styles (and configurations) to find the most effective approach for their use case.

3   Method

This paper adopts a design science paradigm (DSR) [21], an optimal fit for develop-ing and evaluating novel artifacts to solve real-world problems. To endow our research with the necessary rigor, we follow the framework of [22] using an objective-centered approach comprising the following steps: (i) definition of solution objectives, (ii) con-ceptualization, (iii) demonstration, (iv) evaluation, and (v) communication (covered by the publication of this work).

Our overall objective is to support researchers and developers in making decisions for implementing recommendation explainability in the scope of tourism. More precisely, we aim to provide them with an interactive, visual approach to experiment and explore various explanation styles and associated configurations to discover an appropriate solu-tion for their use case. Our objectives are based on the theoretical background outlined in the previous section and the specifics of the tourism domain, including the importance of geographic objects [20], touristic knowledge graphs [23], and the dynamic nature of data-driven tourism practices [24], making it necessary for explanations to specifically adapt to different use cases [8]. Considering the diversity of existing recommendation algorithms, we incorporate both model-specific and post-hoc explanation styles to keep our approach generalizable. In particular, we support side information from knowl-edge graphs, even for non-knowledge-graph-based models. Our concrete objectives are summarized in Table 2.

In line with the second DSR step, we developed a visual approach to realizing these objectives. For this purpose, we decided to conceptualize a dashboard, which contains interactive visualizations of different explainability methods. Following our objectives, our overall approach is heavily based on knowledge graphs, which allow highly dynamic data structures and enable modeling complex situations, which can be exploited for sophisticated explanations. Regarding DSR steps three (i.e., demonstration) and four (i.e., evaluation), we developed a prototypical implementation of our concept [26, 27]

Table 2. Determined solution objectives.

#	Solution Objective	Rationale
1	Support various explanation styles	Derived from the existence of a wide range of explanation styles, each of which is necessary for different use cases [7]
2	Allow post-hoc explanations	Derived from the existence of a wide range of complex models that do not expose specific data [7, 25]
3	Allow model-specific explanations	Derived from the possible use-case-specific explanation goals that may incorporate the need of full transparency [8]
4	Map-based visualization	Derived following the importance of geographic information in tourism recommender systems [20]
5	Deep KG support	Derived from the widespread adoption of KGs in the tourism domain and their valuable side information [23]
6	Tailored paths for KG navigation	Derived from the diversity of touristic knowledge graphs [23] and the need of use-case-specific explanation paths

and created an illustrative scenario [28] based on real-world objects and simulated user interactions to compare our solution objectives with the outputs of the developed prototype, a typical evaluation method in DSR for solutions to problems that are not yet sufficiently addressed [22]. In the following sections, we detail the conceptualization, demonstration, and evaluation steps, respectively.

4 Conceptualizing an Explainability Dashboard for Tourism

Our dashboard has been designed for explaining touristic objects (i.e., items), including POIs and tours. While bar charts and boxplot diagrams give detailed information about specific item features (e.g., tour lengths), a geographic map overviews the items' geographic properties. The interactive core visualization style of our dashboard is a graph-based approach that allows inferring relationships for the purpose of explainability.

Our explainability dashboard allows a deep dive into explanations for a configurable number of N recommendations of a selected model based on a selected user's profile and history. While the features of our dashboard can be used in any order, a typical analysis workflow (Fig. 1) starts with first inspecting item-based explanations before diving deeper into more complex explanations using graphs.

Fig. 1. Typical explainability analysis workflow using the explainability dashboard.

4.1 Item-Based Explanations

Item-based explanations refer to explanations generated based on item features. To emphasize the relevance of geographic properties in tourism [20], we further distinguish between feature-based and geographic-based explanations.

Feature-Based Explanations. Feature-based explanations provide insights into the distribution of feature values for recommended and interacted items. Boxplot diagrams visualize the distribution of numerical features (e.g., a tour's meters of altitude or steepness) and reflect their statistical properties (i.e., quartiles, minimum, and maximum). For categorical features (e.g., difficulty), we utilize bar charts to visualize the respective values' distribution. Feature-based visualization allows us to detect correlations and to understand which item properties may have been most influential to an underlying recommendation. Since preferred feature values may differ depending on item types (e.g., 30 km may be substantial for hiking but short for biking), we suggest creating several boxplot diagrams per item category, although this is a case-by-case consideration.

Geographic Explanations. Geographic explanations provide a more detailed overview of geographic features (e.g., the coordinates of a POI or the length and shape of a hiking tour). It helps identify interrelations between those items a user has interacted with and the items that have been recommended subsequently. This allows both a rough estimation of how well the underlying recommender works and what geographic similarities and proximities are important for a recommendation. Besides, the map should support visualizing the items' underlying regions. Regions may include political and touristic (marketing) regions and help visualize regional influence, including the effects of marketing campaigns by destination management organizations.

4.2 Graph-Based Explanations

Graph-based explanations exploit a knowledge graph's structure to find explanations based on paths. KGs often capture a wide range of domain knowledge, making them well-suited to interactively explore possible explanations. Note, however, that it is not necessary for a recommender to employ a graph-based model; KG-based explanations can be generated post-hoc without the involvement of the original recommender algorithm. On the other hand, if a graph-based model exposes internal knowledge about the algorithm's inference (e.g., attention weights), this information can be used to generate model-specific explanations. The following describes two approaches to generate explanations based on KG paths.

Shortest-Path Explanations. Shortest-path explanations aim to identify the closest connections between recommended and interacted items. Based on a shortest-path algorithm, the shortest paths from interacted to recommended items are identified and visualized as an interactive subgraph. For example, a recommended hiking tour A could be linked to an interacted hiking tour B via category or difficulty nodes, indicating that A and B belong to the same category and are similarly difficult. To compare different shortest paths interactively, filters can be applied to specify which intermediate nodes are allowed (e.g., to filter out less expressive nodes or such with a high node degree).

Score-Path Explanations. While shortest-path explanations may extract the most obvious connections and may be sufficient for a range of use cases, the result of this investigation largely depends on the knowledge graph's overall design. Score paths allow the definition of more sophisticated patterns (i.e., meta paths) to achieve precise results independent of the knowledge graph's structure. Meta paths are defined by specifying a sequence of allowed nodes and edges, each of which may be restricted to a subset of types (i.e., node types and edge types). Based on this specification, matching paths are retrieved from the knowledge graph and scored according to customizable scoring functions (e.g., page rank and centrality). While these graph metrics are independent of the underlying recommendation algorithm and, therefore, refer to a post-hoc explainability approach, model-specific explanations can be realized by simply adjusting the scoring function to incorporate information internal to the model's inference process (e.g., attention weights).

5   Demonstration and Evaluation

Following the DSR paradigm, we aim to compare our dashboard's functionality with the previously defined solution objectives [22]. To perform this comparison, we implemented a web-based prototype of our concept, a common evaluation technique in DSR [26], which aims to verify solutions based on artificial or naturalistic use cases [27]. We apply our prototype by adopting an illustrative scenario [28] serving the use case of explaining recommendations in outdoor tourism (i.e., a tour recommender). Based on real-world outdoor data and simulated user behavior, we showcase the creation of explanations for tour recommendations generated by two exemplary models.

5.1   Data and Model Generation

To initialize our illustrative scenario, we created a simple KG comprising 185,229 tours from Outdooractive [29], one of Europe's largest platforms for outdoor tourism. Our exemplary knowledge graph has been stored in a graph database. It includes three different types of entities: (i) tours, (ii) hierarchical tour categories, and (iii) touristic and political regions (which may overlap). Each tour has been connected to one category node (e.g., hiking, cycling) and multiple region nodes (i.e., all regions the tour intersects with). Furthermore, to simulate user interactions with tours, we generated 10,000 artificial users with random user preferences, including (i) preferred tour lengths and durations, (ii) a sub-selection between one and four favorite tour categories, and (iii) three to ten favorite regions. The preference distribution has been designed to be close to the real data in the Outdooractive platform. For each user, we generated five to 100 interactions (i.e., clicks) matching the specified preferences, resulting in 517,866 interactions.

To standardize the creation and training of our recommendation models, we used Recbole [30], a Python-based framework providing state-of-the-art recommendation models and a standardized training and evaluation process. We extended Recbole's ability to export model-internal data to evaluate model-specific explanations and chose two models, namely (i) KTUP [31], a knowledge-graph-based model that employs an attention mechanism allowing the use of attention weights for explainability, and (ii) MultiDAE [32], a general purpose, deep-learning-based recommender system that does not rely on a KG and is used for post-hoc explanations. Both models were trained for 100 epochs with a learning rate of 0.001 and a batch size of 2096.

5.2 Results

We verified the suitability of our approach by generating 50 recommendations for a randomly selected user using KTUP and MultiDAE. We map the dashboard's abilities to our objectives and discuss our solution's degree of support. In the following, we discuss the different explanation styles for the generated recommendations.

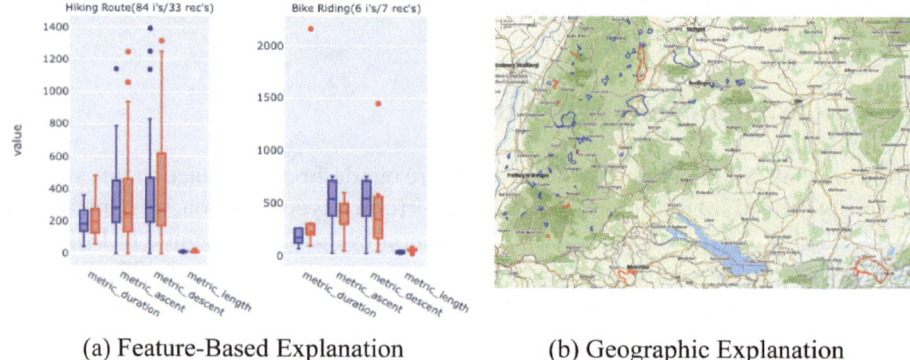

(a) Feature-Based Explanation   (b) Geographic Explanation

Fig. 2. Exemplary visualizations of interacted (blue) and KTUP-recommended (red) tours. Boxplots explain the distributions of numerical features, geographic features are shown in a map (The map is based on Leaflet (leafletjs.com). Map data from OpenStreetMap (openstreetmap.org/copyright)).

Feature-Based Explanation. To get an overview of the similarity between interacted and recommended tours, we first visualize their feature values using boxplot diagrams (Fig. 2. a) and recognize a correlation between interacted and recommended tours, showing that the applied KTUP recommender seems to respect such properties. For MultiDAE, we obtained a similar result (feature-based explanations are generated post-hoc).

Geographic Explanation. As a next step, we investigate the geographic properties of individual tours (Fig. 2. b). As with feature-based explanations, geographic explanations are generated post-hoc and lead to similar results for both models. Comparing the interacted with the recommended tours reveals one of the user's favorite regions (centered on the map) and their preference for round trips. Following this first impression of the map visualization, most recommendations seem to reflect these preferences, which allows inferring that tours are recommended based on their region and shape. However, contradicting examples exist. A red tour in the bottom right corner (i.e., "Drei Täler Runde", DTR) is in a different region and seems to exceed the user's preferred length. To explain this recommendation, a more sophisticated approach is necessary.

Graph-Based Explanation. To generate suitable explanations for more complex recommendations, we make use of a graph-based approach. For this, we navigate existing paths of the knowledge graph connecting users and tours using graph algorithms implemented in the underlying graph database. First, we apply the shortest-path explainability module to the DTR tour above and find that they share the same countries, categories, and provinces with many recommended tours. However, due to their size, countries may be insufficient for explaining a recommendation and should be excluded, while using the category seems to be a valid approach (Fig. 3).

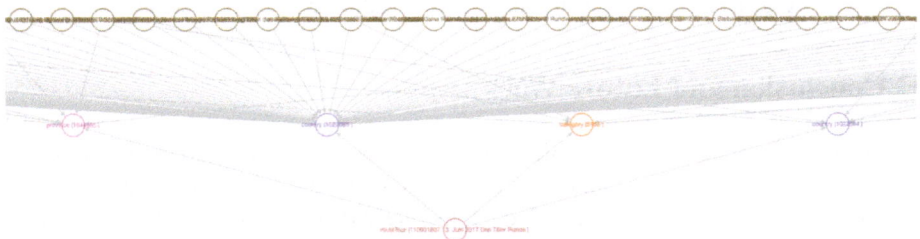

Fig. 3. Exemplary shortest-path explanation indicating (previously hidden) shortest relations between recommended (bottom) and interacted (top) tours according to the underlying KG.

Besides shortest paths, score paths allow fine-grained definitions of sub-graphs and meta paths. To investigate the DTR tour in more detail, we perform a model-specific explanation by scoring paths, which reveals the main differences between explanations with MultiDAE and KTUP. While MultiDAE is restricted to general graph metrics such as centrality and betweenness that do not capture any model internals, KTUP allows a model-specific exploration of why a specific recommendation has been inferred, as it exposes model-specific attention weights (Fig. 4). In the DTR case, the province seems to play the predominant role in the recommendation.

Next, we provide a mapping of the evaluation results to our initial solution objectives (SO). As the results show, our dashboard supports various explanation styles (SO #1), including the styles mentioned in the background section, except for opinion-based explanations. The latter was excluded from our evaluation due to the nature of the underlying data. However, we argue that opinion-based explanations can still be realized using our graph-based approach, provided that the KG includes the necessary opinions. Furthermore, we verified the support of both post-hoc and model-specific explanations (SO #2 and #3). Our map visualization module allows us to visually explore geographic properties (SO #4). Finally, our approach is centered around a touristic KG, exploiting arbitrary side information and allowing us to define (meta) paths for explanations tailored to the underlying use case (SO #5 and #6).

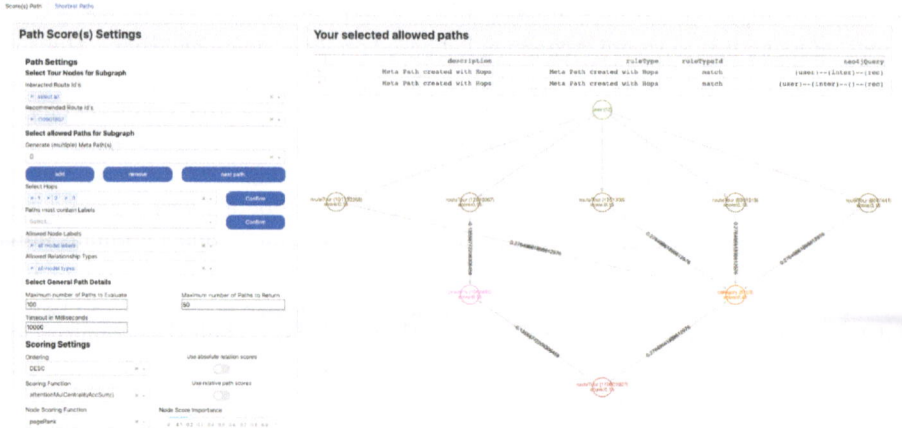

Fig. 4. Exemplary model-specific score path with attention weights.

6 Conclusion and Future Work

This paper introduced a visual, interactive approach to support the explainability of touristic recommendations, supporting both model-specific and post-hoc explanations, mainly based on knowledge graphs. To demonstrate and evaluate our approach, we developed a prototypical dashboard implementing our concept and evaluated it following an illustrative scenario. Our results show that our concept can explain recommendations, even in complex scenarios generated by state-of-the-art deep learning models. By providing a novel approach for interactively exploring recommendation explanations, our work contributes to theory and practice. Researchers may use our concept to study the feasibility of different explanations, especially when studying different explanation goals [8] in multistakeholder recommendation scenarios [2]. On the other hand, practitioners benefit from our dashboard by being provided a tool to develop tailored explanations for their specific real-world use cases.

Like other work, our work suffers from certain limitations. First, while supporting many of the most important recommendation explanation techniques mentioned in the literature, our approach does not consider opinion-based explanations. Moreover, our evaluation is based on an illustrative scenario and should be subject to further evaluation, especially with real user involvement. According to the results of this evaluation, our concept may have to be further adjusted.

For future work, we plan to use our dashboard more broadly, incorporating real-world user interactions and dashboard users to obtain more in-depth evaluation results. Furthermore, we will extend our dashboard to support even more types of explanation and model-specific parameters (e.g., integrated gradients). Moreover, we want to motivate other researchers to strengthen the investigation of visual recommendation evaluation tools in general, not limited to explainability. Finally, using our dashboard, we plan to develop an explainable, knowledge-graph-based recommendation model that captures the dimensions of multiple stakeholders and deploy it in the context of sustainable tourism.

Acknowledgements. This work is a result of a cooperation between Outdooractive AG and the Technical University of Munich. This study was supported by the AIR research project (67KI21005B), funded by the German federal ministry for the environment, nature conversation, nuclear safety, and consumer protection.

References

1. Sun, Z., et al.: Research commentary on recommendations with side information: a survey and research directions. Electron. Commer. Res. Appl. **37**, 100879 (2019)
2. Abdollahpouri, H., et al.: Multistakeholder recommendation: survey and research directions. User Model. User-Adap. Inter. **30**(1), 127–158 (2020)
3. Bollenbach, J., et al.: Using machine learning to predict POI occupancy to reduce overcrowding. In: INFORMATIK 2023. Gesellschaft für Informatik, Bonn (2022)
4. Schmücker, D., et al.: The INPReS intervention escalation framework for avoiding overcrowding in tourism destinations. Tourism Hospitality **4**(2), 282–292 (2023)
5. Nicholas, L., Thapa, B.: Visitor perspectives on sustainable tourism development in the Pitons Management Area World Heritage Site, St. Lucia. Environ. Dev. Sustain. **12**(5), 839–857 (2010)
6. Capocchi, A., et al.: Correction: Capocchi, A., et al. Overtourism: a literature review to assess implications and future perspectives. Sustainability 2019 **11**, 3303. Sustainability **12**(4), 1541 (2020)
7. Zhang, Y., Chen, X.: Explainable recommendation: a survey and new perspectives. Found. Trends® Inf. Retrieval **14**(1), 1–101 (2020)
8. Tintarev, N., Masthoff, J.: Beyond explaining single item recommendations. In: Ricci, F., et al. (eds.) Recommender Systems Handbook, pp. 711–756. Springer, Cham (2022). https://doi.org/10.1007/978-1-0716-2197-4_19
9. Ehrlinger, L., Wöß, W.: Towards a definition of knowledge graphs. In: SEMANTiCS (Posters, Demos, SuCCESS) (2016)
10. Beel, J., et al.: Research-paper recommender systems: a literature survey. Int. J. Digit. Libr. **17**(4), 305–338 (2016)
11. Dey, A.: Understanding and using context. Pers. Ubiquit. Comput. **5**, 4–7 (2001)
12. Chen, R., et al.: A survey of collaborative filtering-based recommender systems: from traditional methods to hybrid methods based on social networks. IEEE Access **6**, 64301–64320 (2018)
13. Meng, X., et al.: A survey of context-aware recommender systems: from an evaluation perspective. IEEE Trans. Knowl. Data Eng. **35**(7), 6575–6594 (2023)
14. Song, W., et al.: Ekar: An Explainable Method for Knowledge Aware Recommendation (2019). https://arxiv.org/abs/1906.09506
15. Tao, Y., et al.: The FacT: taming latent factor models for explainability with factorization trees. In: Proceedings of the 42nd International ACM SIGIR Conference on Research and Development in Information Retrieval, pp. 295–304. ACM, New York (2019)
16. Wang, X., et al.: KGAT: knowledge graph attention network for recommendation. In: Proceedings of the 25th ACM SIGKDD International Conference on Knowledge Discovery & Data Mining, pp. 950–958 (2019)
17. Zhang, Z., et al.: Effects of feature-based explanation and its output modality on user satisfaction with service recommender systems. Front. Big Data **5** (2022)
18. Richthammer, C., et al.: Interactive visualization of recommender systems data. In: Proceedings of the 4th Workshop on Security in Highly Connected IT Systems, pp. 19–24. ACM, Neuchâtel Switzerland (2017)

19. Wang, H.: Effective visualization and analysis of recommender systems. In: 2022 9th International Forum on Electrical Engineering and Automation (IFEEA), pp. 633–640. IEEE, Zhuhai, China (2022)
20. Chaudhari, K., Thakkar, A.: A comprehensive survey on travel recommender systems. Arch. Comput. Methods Eng. **27**(5), 1545–1571 (2020)
21. Hevner, A., et al.: Design science in information systems research. MIS Q. **28**(1), 75 (2004)
22. Peffers, K., et al.: A design science research methodology for information systems research. J. Manag. Inf. Syst. **24**(3), 45–77 (2007)
23. Neubig, S., et al.: To Graph or Not to Graph: the missing pieces for knowledge graphs in sustainable tourism. In: INFORMATIK 2023. Gesellschaft für Informatik, Bonn (2023)
24. Neubig, S., et al.: Data-driven initiatives of destinations supporting sustainable tourism. In: Americas Conference on Information Systems (AMCIS) (2022)
25. Gohel, P., et al.: Explainable AI: current status and future directions. IEEE Access (2021)
26. March, S., Storey, V.: Design science in the information systems discipline: an introduction to the special issue on design science research. MIS Q. **32**(4), 725 (2008)
27. Sonnenberg, C., Vom Brocke, J.: Evaluation patterns for design science research artefacts. In: Helfert, M., Donnellan, B. (eds.) Practical Aspects of Design Science. CCIS, vol. 286, pp. 71–83. Springer, Heidelberg (2012). https://doi.org/10.1007/978-3-642-33681-2_7
28. Peffers, K., et al.: Design science research evaluation. In: Peffers, K., et al. (eds.) Design Science Research in Information Systems. Advances in Theory and Practice. LNCS, vol. 7286, pp. 398–410. Springer, Heidelberg (2012)
29. Outdooractive. https://www.outdooractive.com. Accessed 20 May 2023
30. Zhao, W.X., et al.: RecBole: towards a unified, comprehensive and efficient framework for recommendation algorithms. In: Proceedings of the 30th ACM International Conference on Information & Knowledge Management. ACM (2021)
31. Cao, Y., et al.: Unifying knowledge graph learning and recommendation: towards a better understanding of user preferences. In: WWW 2019, pp. 151–161. ACM (2019)
32. Liang, D., et al.: Variational autoencoders for collaborative filtering. In: WWW 2018, pp. 689–698. ACM (2018)

ChatGPT as a Travel Itinerary Planner

Katerina Volchek[1] and Stanislav Ivanov[2,3]([✉])

[1] European Campus Rottal-Inn, Deggendorf Institute of Technology, Deggendorf, Germany
`katerina.volchek@th-deg.de`
[2] Varna University of Management, Varna, Bulgaria
[3] Zangador Research Institute, Varna, Bulgaria
`stanislav.ivanov@vumk.eu, info@zangador.institute`

Abstract. Generative AI has become a disruptive force for the Tourism industry. While its potential for generating unique content has been acknowledged, its feasibility for tourists remains unclear. This paper analyses ChatGPT as an itinerary planner. It compares ChatGPT-generated itineraries for 3 destinations with those developed by tourism experts. The evaluation of 11 quality criteria demonstrates that ChatGPT creates easy-to-understand and accessible but less accurate and less specific itineraries. It is a good starting point for travel inspiration. However, it currently cannot serve as an exclusive tool for trip planning.

Keywords: ChatGPT · generative AI · itinerary · e-tourism · service automation

1 Introduction

The contemporary travel industry offers tourists a range of options to acquire travel itineraries. The proliferation of Social Media has enabled tourists to use others' experience to develop their own itineraries [1]. The advancements of Smart Tourism and automation support them with apps that offer real-time customisation and personalisation [2]. However, these tools still require substantial time and effort to find a relevant itinerary, understand it and adapt it to individual needs. More recently, ChatGPT allows tourists to generate texts for various purposes, including for travel itineraries [3, 4]. While ChatGPT is a quick, easy-to-use, and innovative tool, the quality of the ChatGPT-generated content for travel itineraries remains unclear. This paper aims to provide a preliminary evaluation of the ChatGPT-generated travel itineraries quality compared to human-created itineraries offered by travel experts. The study suggests that ChatGPT can be used for efficiently drafting preliminary travel itineraries. Such itineraries need validation and further planning to ensure a positive travel experience.

K. Berezina et al. (Eds.): ENTER 2024, SPBE, pp. 365–370, 2024.
https://doi.org/10.1007/978-3-031-58839-6_38

2 Literature Review

2.1 The Value of a Travel Itinerary

A travel itinerary is a subset of points of interest (POI), organised sequentially to optimise travel experience within available tourist time [1]. Tourist experience from a destination is constructed as a sum of individual occurrences (aka "experiences") in specific contexts [5]. Thus, tourists are primarily interested in exploring attractions and engaging in other available activities at a chosen destination. A relevant choice of POIs and a convenient schedule would contribute to a positive tourist experience. Such factors as too many planned attractions, inadequate time dedicated to each of the POIs, and time and effort invested in commuting between them can prevent tourists from satisfying their needs while facing losses of time, energy, or money [1]. The tourist experience from a destination largely depends on the choice of the itinerary [6]. Tourists are in search of tools which can help them in optimising their travel experience.

2.2 The Quality of a Travel Itinerary

Planning a high-quality travel itinerary is a challenging task for tourists [7]. Initially, the quality of a travel itinerary was directly associated with the high density of attractions [1]. Taylor et al. [1] define a "good" travel itinerary as one that maximises the value of the POIs subset while being manageable within the available travel time and budget. An itinerary need to include useful planning information (e.g., locations, opening hours, distances, time for each POI, costs), which is conveniently presented to tourists. It should also be personalised, i.e., to be relevant to the tourists' individual needs [2]. The development a travel itinerary should take a holistic approach.

Wang & Strong [8] proposed a holistic framework for tourism content. An itinerary content should have high intrinsic quality. The POIs description, and the information required for planning, should be up-to-date, objective, reputable and believable [2]. The itinerary content should have high representational quality, i.e., to be consistent, concisely structured and presented to enable ease of use [9]. The itinerary should be adapted to real-time tourist context and to have exhaustive information for them [2]. Finally, the itinerary content should be accessible to all target tourists (Fig. 1).

2.3 ChatGPT for Travel Itinerary

ChatGPT can be used in all stages of the trip by both tourism managers and tourists. ChatGPT (Generative Pre-training Transformer) is a case of generative AI, which aims to predict the likelihood of typical human word sequences, thereby creating texts that resemble natural human speech [10]. It can generate ideas for a visit to a destination and outline the main attractions and activities by day based on a predetermined length of stay in the destination [3, 4]. It can also form a short description of the attraction/activity and the main reasons why it should be visited/performed. ChatGPT can used to automatically generate an itinerary-like text to substitute a multistage planning.

The quality of the ChatGPT-generated texts quality varies. The data ChatGPT used is until 2021, hence its itinerary might be outdated. Moreover, ChatGPT is known for

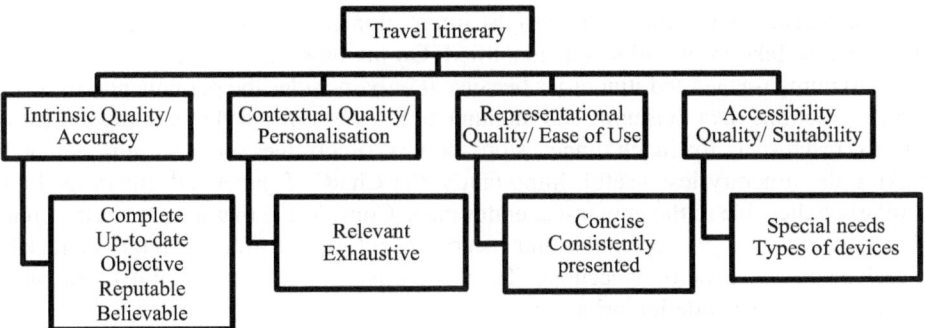

Fig. 1. Conceptual Framework for Travel Itinerary Quality

hallucination and invention of facts [10]; hence, its itinerary might not be factually correct. While ChatGPT has been tests for some tasks (e.g. passing exams, generating marketing text [10]), its potential for developing travel itineraries remains underexplored.

3 Methodology

To assess the quality of a ChatGPT-generated itinerary, the study compares the ChatGPT outcome quality towards expert-develop itineraries. The study analyses 3 different case studies: an iconic destination (Vienna, Austria), a secondary-level country destination (Plovdiv, Bulgaria), and a tertiary country-level destination (Spetses, Greece). First, the study created a baseline for comparison of the ChatGPT results with the information that is openly and easily available to tourists. The study collected travel itineraries from travel websites by using "3-day travel itinerary" + "*destination*" as search terms. Only the content published/updated at reputable website or a reputable author in 2023 was retained. 6 out of 17 Viennese itineraries and 3 out of 6 Plovdiv itineraries were selected as high-quality human-generated itineraries. For the case of Spetses, the search did not identify a published 3-days itinerary, which reflected a common trend of a single night stay at the island. Therefore, for Spetses, the study used the published suggestions for travel activities for this island. The content of itineraries was evaluated by the two researchers with the expertise in itinerary planning to ensure their quality. Second, ChatGPT-4 was used to generate 3-day itineraries for the abovenamed destinations: *Vienna* [11], *Plovdiv* [12], *Spetses* [13]. The quality of the ChatGPT texts was evaluated by the authors against the human-made itineraries.

4 Findings and Discussion

Table 1 present the evaluation of the human- and ChatGPT-generated itineraries. The intrinsic quality of the ChatGPT-generated itinerary can be characterised as question-able. ChatGPT generates objective facts about tourist attractions. ChatGPT officially acknowledges that its training data was until 2021. Its information might not reflect recent changes in a destination's offer. Nevertheless, the generated page includes the date of the text-generation, which creates a false impression of the itineraries being up to date. However, no fake information was identified. On the other hand, ChatGPT fails compared to human-generated itineraries because it only includes the permanently existing travel attractions (aka museums and monuments). Other types of POIs (temporal exhibitions, restaurants for lunch/dinner, stops, toilets, timeframes, etc.) are not included, making the itinerary less useful. Importantly, the ChatGPT-generated itineraries look similarly believable to the human-generates ones. Considering that in some cases ChatGPT positions itself as a reputable and accurate tool [10], the itinerary might be falsely perceived by non-experts as accurate. To ensure travel experience, ChatGPT-generated itinerary requires validation prior to usage.

Table 1. 3-days selected travel itineraries

Attributes of the travel itinerary	Human-generated			ChatGPT-generated		
	Vienna	Plovdiv	Spetses	Vienna	Plovdiv	Spetses
Reputable	✓	✓	*n/a*	*n/a*	*n/a*	*n/a*
Up to date	✓	✓	*n/a*	x	x	x
Believable	✓	✓	✓	✓	✓	✓
Objective	✓	✓	✓	✓	✓	x
Complete	✓	✓	✓	x	x	x
Relevant	✓	✓	x	✓	✓	✓
Exhaustive	✓	✓	✓	x	x	x
Concise	✓	✓	✓	✓	✓	✓
Consistent	✓	✓	✓	✓	✓	✓
Special needs	✓	✓	✓	✓	✓	✓
Different devices	✓	✓	✓	✓	✓	✓

The analysis of contextual quality of ChatGPT-generated itineraries provides contradicting results. ChatGPT can provide a personalised outcome. Thus, standardised expert-developed itineraries do not offer a 3-day itinerary for Spetses. ChatGPT produced a 3-day travel itinerary for this destination. This provides tourists with the response to their exact request. However, this outcome does not reflect optimal travel experience, taken into consideration by experts. Importantly, in comparison to human-made itineraries, ChatGPT fails to provide exhaustive content. It generates a minimalistic description of a POI, which limits the itinerary's usefulness and prevents tourists from making informed decisions. Tourists need to check the relevance of the whole itinerary and each POI to ensure positive travel experience.

The representational and accessibility quality of ChatGPT-generated itineraries is high. The POIs information is consistent and concise. The website is up-to-date and mobile-friendly, which makes it accessible from multiple devices and adjustable to individual needs. While this meets high usability standard, this might affect tourists' perceptions on believability of the content. The ease of use and the accessibility of ChatGPT-generated content can benefit in planning accurate and relevant itineraries.

5 Conclusion

ChatGPT demonstrates potential in generating relevant ideas for activities and attractions in a destination. For popular destinations, it can create factually correct and relatively feasible itineraries without "hallucinating". However, it only includes permanently available attractions and ignores other types of POIs, thereby, diminishing the usefulness of the itinerary. The itineraries also lack sufficient details to provide value. At the same time, for a small destination ChatGPT can create an itinerary that is not otherwise available from experts. ChatGPT can be used as a first rather than the last or the only point in the travel inspiration and planning stage.

The main limitation of the paper is the small sample size, although it focuses on three destinations with different characteristics. Future research may involve more destinations and validation of ChatGPT-generated itineraries by travel experts for more reliable results. Future research may focus on the practical challenges travel companies face in the implementation of ChatGPT and generative AI in their operations, and tourists' trust is AI-generated travel itineraries. Research can also shed light on the potential automatability of other tasks (beyond travel itinerary development) at travel agencies.

References

1. Taylor, K., Lim, K.H., Chan, J.: Travel itinerary recommendations with must-see points-of-interest. In: Companion Proceedings of the Web Conference 2018, pp. 1198–1205 (2018)
2. Sylejmani, K., Dorn, J., Musliu, N.: Planning the trip itinerary for tourist groups. Inf. Technol. Tourism **17**, 275–314 (2017)
3. Carvalho, I., Ivanov, S.: ChatGPT for tourism: applications, benefits and risks. Tourism Rev. **79**, 290–303 (2023). https://doi.org/10.1108/TR-02-2023-0088
4. Dogru, T., et al.: Generative artificial intelligence in the hospitality and tourism industry: developing a framework for future research. J. Hospitality Tourism Res. **2023**, 10963480231188663 (2023)
5. Neuhofer, B.: Innovation through co-creation: towards an understanding of technology-facilitated co-creation processes in tourism. In: Egger, R., Gula, I., Walcher, D. (eds.) Open tourism. TV, pp. 17–33. Springer, Heidelberg (2016). https://doi.org/10.1007/978-3-642-540 89-9_2
6. Wong, C.U.I., McKercher, B.: Day tour itineraries: searching for the balance between commercial needs and experiential desires. Tour. Manage. **33**(6), 1360–1372 (2012)
7. Tarantino, E., De Falco, I., Scafuri, U.: A mobile personalized tourist guide and its user evaluation. Inf. Technol. Tourism **21**, 413–455 (2019)
8. Wang, R.Y., Strong, D.M.: Beyond accuracy: what data quality means to data consumers. J. Manag. Inf. Syst. **12**(4), 5–33 (1996)
9. Kim, S.-E., Lee, K.Y., Shin, S.I., Yang, S.-B.: Effects of tourism information quality in social media on destination image formation: the case of Sina Weibo. Inf. Manage. **54**(6), 687–702 (2017)
10. Dwivedi, Y.K., et al.: "So what if ChatGPT wrote it?" Multidisciplinary perspectives on opportunities, challenges and implications of generative conversational AI for research, practice and policy. Int. J. Inf. Manage. **71**, 102642 (2023)
11. OpenAI.com: Vienna 3-Day Itinerary (2023). https://chat.openai.com/share/b4371ff8-159b-4c2d-bf98-29e9eb600473. Accessed 2 Aug 2023

12. OpenAI.com: Plovdid 3-day Itinerary (2023). https://chat.openai.com/share/9ff4cb07-ad2f-4a44-b3d9-49447103e857. Accessed 2 Aug 2023
13. OpenAI.com: Spetses 3-Day Itinerary (2023). https://chat.openai.com/share/28a46a82-20d5-4bd6-bc9e-babb4e4c900d. Accessed 2 Aug 2023

UGC and Social Media

UGC-Based Factors Influencing Customer Satisfaction Pre and Post COVID-19: The Case of Lake Constance

Dominic Regitz[1]([envelope]), Wolfram Höpken[1] [ORCID], and Matthias Fuchs[2] [ORCID]

[1] Ravensburg-Weingarten University of Applied Sciences, Institute for Digital Transformation, Weingarten, Germany
{dominic.regitz,wolfram.hoepken}@rwu.de
[2] Mid-Sweden University, The European Tourism Research Institute (ETOUR), Östersund, Sweden
matthias.fuchs@miun.se

Abstract. User-generated content (UGC) created and distributed through social media and tourism-related websites provides potential travelers the opportunity to gain first-hand experiences about destination products and services. UGC is also of great value to tourism service providers. Since UGC represents customers' opinions and experience outcomes, potential problems, but also drivers behind customer delight can be identified. In this regard, also temporal changes regarding customer requirements can be determined. The aim of this paper is to identify how certain topic areas mentioned in UGC affect customer satisfaction, exemplarily analyzed for the Lake of Constance Region. Furthermore, potential temporal changes regarding customer satisfaction since the outbreak of the COVID-19 pandemic will be examined. A sentiment analysis, topic detection and regression analysis are carried out on two datasets containing UGC before and after the outbreak of the pandemic. Findings show that the pandemic has changed customers' attitudes towards certain topic areas.

Keywords: Text Mining · Linear Regression · Sentiment Analysis · Topic Detection · User Generated Content · COVID-19

1 Introduction

The Internet has fundamentally changed the way tourism-related information is processed and distributed. Before the introduction of the Internet, experiences about products and services were not readily available. Such content however is now widely accessible in the form of user-generated content (UGC) through social media platforms or dedicated tourism websites [1]. Most importantly, such content enjoys higher credibility among customers due to the lack of commercial self-interest, compared to commercial sources like travel agencies or accommodation providers, and is therefore increasingly used in the planning of upcoming trips [2].

© The Author(s) 2024
K. Berezina et al. (Eds.): ENTER 2024, SPBE, pp. 373–384, 2024.
https://doi.org/10.1007/978-3-031-58839-6_39

Not only for end users, but also for providers of tourism services, such UGC is of immense value. Since UGC represents the opinions and experiences of customers, problem areas can be uncovered to make tourism planning activities and strategies more customer-oriented and thus effective [3]. More precisely, from 2014 to 2022, the total number of user reviews and opinions on Tripadvisor, one of the most renowned travel review websites, experienced a fivefold increase. Today, Tripadvisor encompasses over 1 billion online customer reviews just for the tourism business domain [4]. The fact that Tripadvisor was one of the most visited travel and tourism websites worldwide in January 2023 [5] undermines tourists' interest in posting and reading online travel tips and comments. Based on these facts it is of great importance to emphasize the significance of UGC for tourism service providers. In this paper, UGC is used to perform an analysis regarding potential temporal changes in customer satisfaction after the outbreak of the pandemic. Compared to other industries, tourism stands out as a highly volatile business [6]. Furthermore, crises such as SARS or COVID-19 lead to irregular and even dramatic fluctuations in tourism demand, as well as potential temporal changes in customer requirements and needs [7]. This greatly threatens the existence of companies in the tourism sector and challenges e-tourism science as whole [8, 9].

User-generated content (UGC), especially in the form of online reviews on platforms like Tripadvisor, is increasingly used by tourists to provide feedback during or shortly after their trip [10]. Since UGC represents the opinions and experiences of customers, it can be also used to identify specific factors describing how the fulfillment or non-fulfillment of certain topic areas affects customer satisfaction [11]. By analyzing UGC over specific time periods (e.g., before and after the outbreak of the COVID-19 pandemic), differences can be identified that represent changes of the drivers behind tourist satisfaction. Accordingly, the analysis process of this study, first, makes use of a topic detection and sentiment analysis to identify how often a certain topic is mentioned positively or negatively and, second, examines through linear regression which topic has a strong positive or negative influence on overall customer satisfaction. The following research questions are to be answered: (1) *can text mining techniques be used to uncover concrete factors affecting customer satisfaction* and (2) *are these factors showing changes since the outbreak of the COVID-19 pandemic?*

Our paper is structured as follows: First, a literature review is presented which shows general procedures for the implementation of topic detection and sentiment analyses for the analysis of UGC making use of text-mining methods in tourism. This is followed by a presentation of the methodology used to identify the positive and negative influences on customer satisfaction for a number of already pre-defined topic areas. Subsequently, these results are presented for both time periods and the differences between the two periods are highlighted. Finally, a discussion of future work and improvements to the methodological approach are presented.

2 Related Work

2.1 Topic Detection

Topic detection, i.e. the automated process of identifying and classifying themes or patterns in text, is widely used in tourism. Ahani et al. [12] evaluated medical travelers' satisfaction through the analysis of online reviews. By making use of Latent Dirichlet Allocation (LDA), main topic areas have been discovered from such medical tourism reviews. Menner et al. [13] presented an approach to extract topics from UGC. They used methods such as clustering, Latent Semantic Analysis (LSA) and Named-Entity-Recognition (NER) and compared these methods in terms of performance. They found out that NER performed best in identifying topics from UGC. Xiang et al. [14] conducted a comparative analysis of the online review platforms Tripadvisor, Expedia and Yelp. The main topics related to consumers experience have been discovered using LDA. Likewise, Schmunk et al. [15] conducted a topic detection based on online reviews from TripAdvisor, using Support Vector Machines (SVM), the Naive Bayes algorithm, k-NN, and lexicon-based methods. The best results could be achieved using SVM and lexicon-based approaches.

2.2 Sentiment Analysis

Sentiment analysis, i.e., the process of determining and categorizing opinions or emotions expressed in texts, is a well-known method for analyzing tourism reviews [3, 16]. Shi et al. [17] implemented a sentiment analysis for hotel reviews using SVM and achieved an accuracy of 85.2%. Sodanil [18] conducted a sentiment analysis for hotel reviews in various languages. For this purpose, both Thai and English reviews were extracted. Compared with Naïve Bayes and Decision Trees, SVM achieved most accurate sentiment results. In a sentiment analysis for online reviews conducted by Pang et al. [19], the Naive Bayes Classification yielded worst results, while SVM performed best. Garcia et al. [20] presented a lexicon-based approach to implement a sentiment analysis of online reviews for the tourism sector. Their approach uses a self-created annotated lexicon based on positive and negative words appearing within the reviews.

2.3 Comprehensive Analysis of User Generated Content

Finally, approaches that combine the above methods to comprehensively evaluate user-generated content are presented [2]. Ali et al. [21] developed a methodology that combines aspects of topic detection and sentiment analysis to extract valuable insights about the city of Marrakech. This approach ranges from the extraction of UGC to the identification of latent topics using LDA, as well as the application of sentiment analysis for each of these topics. Similarly, Garcia et al. [22] analyzed tweets related to content with the keyword COVID-19. For this purpose, topic detection and sentiment analysis methods were subsequently used in combination. It was found that most posts related to the pandemic are characterized with a negative sentiment. Schmunk et al. [15] presented an approach for extracting decision-relevant information from hotel reviews. These reviews were collected from websites such as TripAdvisor and subjected to the methods of topic detection, subjectivity classification and sentiment analysis. For this aim, a range of different methods were employed and compared in terms of their performance. It was concluded that both SVM and lexicon-based approaches achieved the best results in terms of accuracy.

While the aforementioned works mainly used methods of topic detection and sentiment analysis, this study will combine such methods with a consecutive regression analysis [11]. By doing so, concrete factors can be identified to explain how UGC-extracted topics affect customer satisfaction, both in case of fulfillment and non-fulfillment. Moreover, such compound analyses will be conducted on UGC data extracted for a time period before and after the outbreak of the COVD-19 pandemic, with the aim of highlighting major differences.

3   Method

3.1   Data Collection

This study is based on UGC that was extracted from the website TripAdvisor. By using a web crawler, hotel reviews were extracted during the period 2018–2023 and regarding the five city destinations Konstanz, Lindau, Friedrichshafen, St. Gallen, and Bregenz, all belonging to the Lake of Constance region located at the crossing borders of Germany, Austria, and Switzerland. The selection of these cities results from their importance as prominent tourist centers of the lake of constance region. The dataset consists of 989 reviews from 2018–2019 and 388 reviews from 2020–2023, extracted from 83 hotels in the aforementioned cities. Both datasets include 6 attributes, containing information regarding the hotel, the review title, the review text, the review date and, finally, the user rating on a scale from 1–5. The reduced number of reviews for the 2020–2023 period reflects the post-pandemic decrease of tourism demand.

3.2   Data Preparation

During data extraction, associated HTML-elements were removed and each hotel review has been split into its corresponding sentences since both the methods of topic detection and sentiment analysis are implemented at the sentence level in order to enable a more specific identification of topics. Further steps of data preparation included common tasks, such as tokenization, removal of stopwords and stemming. In numbers, the 989 reviews from 2018–2019 have been split into a total of 7,202 sentences and the 388 reviews from 2020–2023 into 2,712 sentences.

3.3   Topic Detection

After having prepared the extracted UGC data, each sentence is subject to a topic detection analysis. More concretely, this analysis step comprises the automated process of identifying and classifying topics or patterns in UGC-based texts. The topic detection was conducted by a lexicon-based approach. For this regard, wordlists were created that contain words that are typically associated with certain topic areas of the hotel by extending the wordlists used in previous studies [15, 16] and adding new topics such as *Booking & Check-In*. Using these word lists, each sentence can now be automatically examined to determine if it contains one or more words associated with these pre-defined topic areas. Obviously, the aim is to identify a specific topic area for each entry which best describes its content. There are five predefined topic areas: *'Location & Property'*, *'Food & Beverages'*, *'Room & Bathroom'*, *'Service & Staff'* and *'Booking & Check-In'*. Each topic area has its own set of words associated with it. If no such words could be identified within a sentence, it is assigned to the residual class N/A (not assignable). An example is the entry "I will definitely return!", which does not belong to one of the pre-defined topics and, thus, was assigned to the residual class N/A. Figure 1. Summarizes the sequence of steps performed during this process. By this topic detection process, each entry of both datasets is now classified as either one of the pre-defined topics or as the residual class N/A.

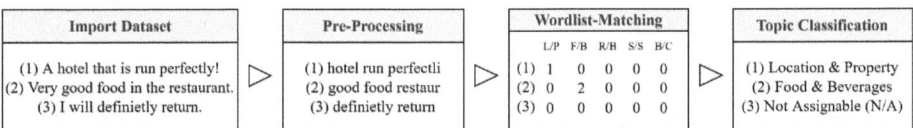

Fig. 1. Lexicon-based topic detection

3.4 Sentiment Analysis

The sentiment analysis is executed by a lexicon-based approach, as well. In this context, the wordlists by Hu and Liu [23] are used to categorize each sentence into the sentiment categories 'positive', 'negative' or 'neutral'. These wordlists comprise around 7,000 opinion words. Again, each sentence is automatically examined regarding its content to determine whether it contains one or more positive or negative words contained in the word list. More concrete, in case more positive than negative words could be identified within a sentence, it is assigned to the sentiment positive and vice versa. Instead, if an entry does not contain any of the 7,000 opinion words, it is classified as neutral. This lexicon-based sentiment analysis procedure is summarized in Fig. 2.

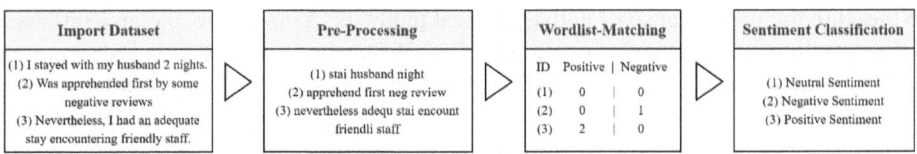

Fig. 2. Lexicon-based sentiment analysis

3.5 Regression Analysis

After assigning both a topic and a sentiment to each sentence, this information is now used to feed a linear regression in order to identify and quantify the effect of positive and negative feedback related to certain topic areas on overall customer satisfaction. In contrast to the previous procedures however, this analysis is carried out at the review-level, which is why each individual sentence is traced back to its original review. For each review, it is then counted how many positive or negative sentences for each topic are contained (see Fig. 3). This information is then used to be regressed on overall customer satisfaction.

ID	Title	Review Sentence	Sentence Original	Address	Date	Rating	Pred. Topic	Pred. Sentiment
5	Great hotel in..	spent night hotel	Spent 2 nights at this...	St. Gallen	2023	4	Location & Property	Neutral
5	Great hotel in..	room larg super clean	The room was very...	St. Gallen	2023	4	Room & Bathroom	Positive
5	Great hotel in..	spars furnish tast comfort	A bit to sparsely furnish...	St. Gallen	2023	4	N/A	Positive
5	Great hotel in..	front desk help	Front desk was very...	St. Gallen	2023	4	Service & Staff	Positive
5	Great hotel in..	locat superb	Location is superb...	St. Gallen	2023	4	Location & Property	Positive

ID	Rating	Location Pos	Location Neg	Food Pos	Food Neg	Service Pos	Service Neg	Room Pos	Room Neg	Booking Pos	Booking Neg	N/A Pos	N/A Neg
5	4	1	0	0	0	1	0	1	0	0	0	1	0

Fig. 3. Transformation of dataset for linear regression

Based on the above-described datasets, regression analyses were performed separately for both time periods, i.e., 2018–2019 and 2020–2023, respectively. By comparing these two regression models, interesting differences can be detected which describe changes in customers' preferences for each of these pre-defined topic areas.

4   Findings

In the following section, the findings from the regression models for both time periods are presented. A validation of the conducted topic detection and sentiment analysis was undergone by manually annotating 25% of the sentences in terms of their corresponding topic and sentiment as test dataset. In total, 2,478 sentences have been labeled, allowing to measure the performance of both analytical methods. As outcome, the lexicon-based topic detection could achieve an accuracy of 80.39%, while the lexicon-based sentiment analysis reached an accuracy of 77.28%, both constituting satisfactory results.

4.1   Regression Model for the 2018–2019 Dataset

Below, the regression model based on the dataset before the outbreak of the COVID-19 pandemic (i.e., 2018–2019) is presented (Fig. 4).

Notably, both the topic areas 'Room & Bathroom' and 'Booking & Check-In' are characterized as having a purely negative impact on customer satisfaction. The non-significant positive influence for both topics has been automatically removed during feature selection. This implies that a non-fulfillment of the quality expectations regarding

Linear Regression 989 Entries from 2018-2019			
Correlation: 0.542		RMSE: 0.938	
Attribute	Coefficient	P - Value	Code
Location_Property_Pos	0.099	<0.001	****
Location_Property_Neg	-0.105	0.066	*
Food_Beverages_Pos	0.187	<0.001	****
Food_Beverages_Neg	-0.147	0.030	**
Service_Staff_Pos	0.135	0.002	***
Service_Staff_Neg	-0.418	<0.001	***
Room_Bathroom_Neg	-0.448	<0.001	****
Booking_Check_Neg	-0,618	<0.001	****
NA_Pos	0.108	<0.001	****
NA_Neg	-0.407	<0.001	****
Intercept	4.076	<0.001	****

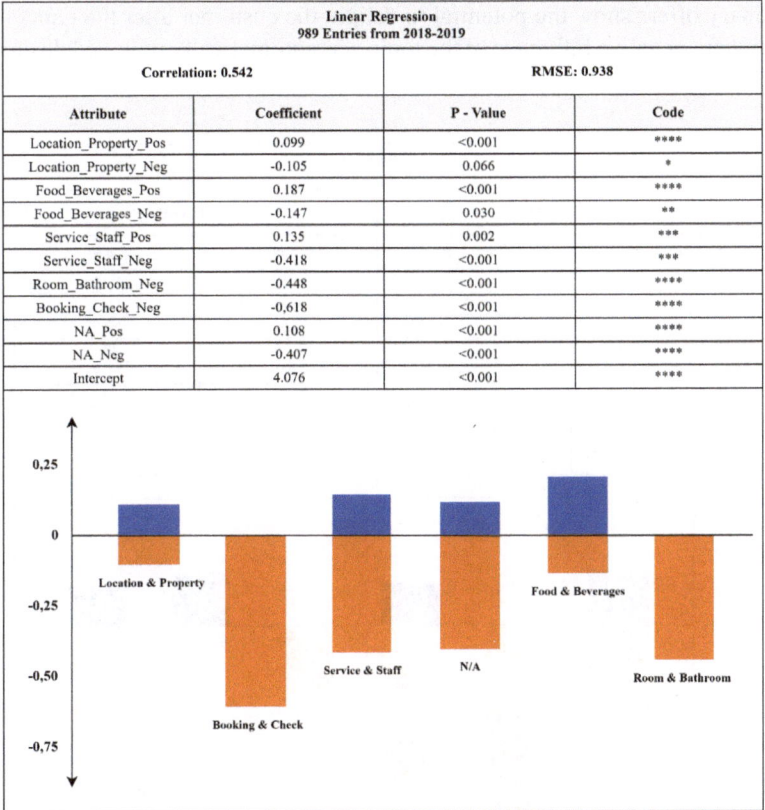

Fig. 4. Regression model pre-COVID

these topics reduces customer satisfaction significantly. However, at the same time, the respective quality fulfillment would not affect total customer satisfaction positively. Interestingly, the remaining topic areas show both positive and negative impacts on total satisfaction. The topic 'Food & Beverages' is the only topic with a dominance of the positive influence on customer satisfaction, hence this topic area shows potential to delight the customer.

4.2 Regression Model for the 2020–2023 Dataset

The regression model based on the dataset after the outbreak of the pandemic is presented in Fig. 5. The topic area 'Room & Bathroom' is now characterized by both a positive and negative influence on customer satisfaction. The topic area 'Booking & Check In' continues to show a purely negative influence, undermining the negative effect of a bad check-in or check-out procedure on customer satisfaction. The residual topic N/A is now characterized by a purely negative influence, whereas 'Location & Property' and 'Service & Staff' still show both a positive and negative impact on customer satisfaction. Interestingly, 'Food & Beverages' is now characterized by a purely positive influence, thus, culinary offers show the potential to delight the customer after the pandemic. The non-significant negative influence of the topic was automatically removed during feature selection.

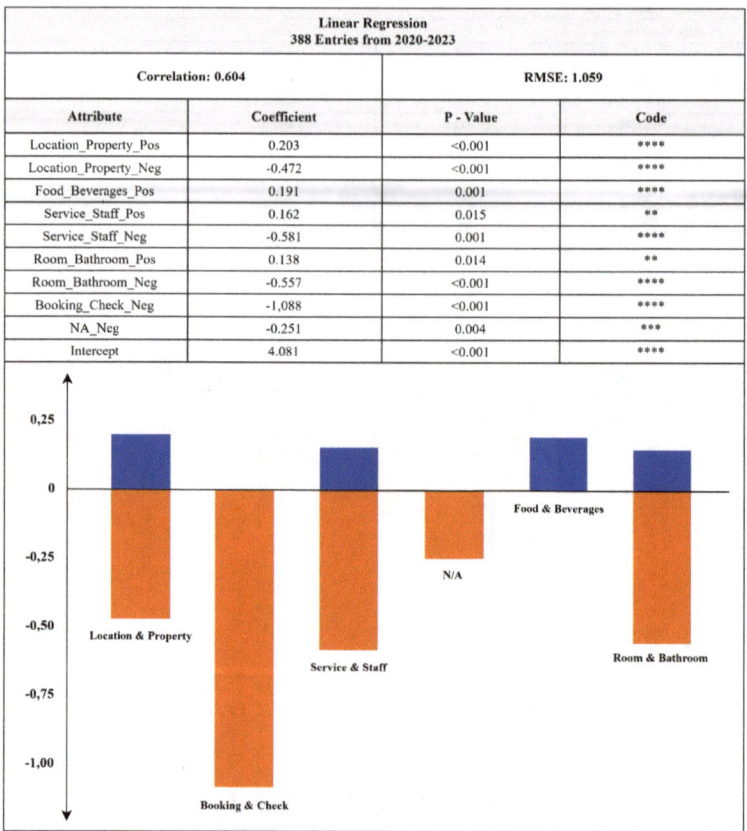

Linear Regression 388 Entries from 2020-2023			
Correlation: 0.604		RMSE: 1.059	
Attribute	Coefficient	P - Value	Code
Location_Property_Pos	0.203	<0.001	****
Location_Property_Neg	-0.472	<0.001	****
Food_Beverages_Pos	0.191	0.001	****
Service_Staff_Pos	0.162	0.015	**
Service_Staff_Neg	-0.581	0.001	****
Room_Bathroom_Pos	0.138	0.014	**
Room_Bathroom_Neg	-0.557	<0.001	****
Booking_Check_Neg	-1,088	<0.001	****
NA_Neg	-0.251	0.004	***
Intercept	4.081	<0.001	****

Fig. 5. Regression model post-COVID

4.3 Comparison of Results

In this section, we discuss differences between the two regression models, i.e., before and after the Covid-19 pandemic and highlight discrepancies and possible reasons for temporal changes. Figure 6 compares the outcomes of the two regression models.

Location and Property: This topic area is characterized by both a positive and negative influence on customer satisfaction. However, after the pandemic, these manifestations have intensified. Hence, fulfillment and non-fulfillment of quality expectations regarding this topic area now have a stronger effect on customer satisfaction. After extended periods of isolation or quarantine, individuals may place heightened emphasis on the value of

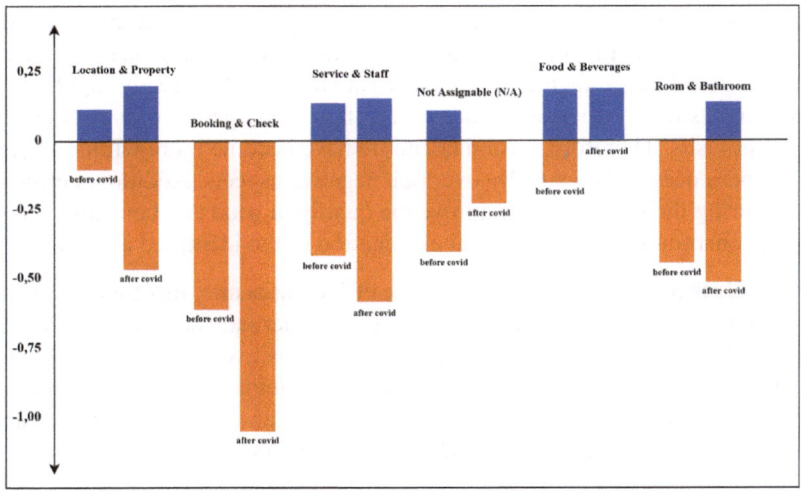

Fig. 6. Comparison of pre- and post-COVID regression models

their vacations or travels. Consequently, there could be an augmented focus on the quality of their surroundings, including the location of the hotel.

Booking and Check-In: Interestingly, this topic area is characterized by a purely negative influence on customer satisfaction, for both time periods. This most likely corroborates the negative effect a bad check-in or check-out process has on customer satisfaction. However, the negative impact of this topic area in case of non-fulfillment has intensified after the pandemic. Especially in times of increased uncertainty and potential health risks, customers seem to have developed a greater appreciation for processes that are simple, clear and safe. A cumbersome or confusing booking and check-in process could therefore be perceived as particularly disruptive, especially after a longer period of isolation.

Service and Staff: Interestingly, the topic area 'Service and Staff' is the only one that has remained largely unchanged in terms of its characteristic effect on total customer satisfaction. This indicates that the perception of service encounters has remained the same, even after the outbreak of the pandemic. While a good service increases customer satisfaction, a failure to address this important human-to-human interaction deeply worsens it.

N/A (not assignable): Before the outbreak of the pandemic, entries that could not be assigned to one of the pre-defined topic areas, were characterized by a mixed influence on customer satisfaction. Interestingly, after the outbreak of the pandemic, this topic area has developed into an exclusively negative influence regarding customer satisfaction. This can most likely be attributed to the fact, that the dataset collected after the outbreak of COVID-19 contains a large volume of entries regarding the pandemic itself. Such typically negative entries have been assigned to the residual class, presumably leading to its development into a strictly negative influence factor. In fact, Garcia et al. [22] have shown that such pandemic-related Twitter posts are mostly negative in nature.

Food and Beverages: This topic area was originally characterized by a mixed influence on customer satisfaction. After the pandemic, however, this has changed into a purely positive influence factor on customer satisfaction. As already highlighted, this suggests that customer expectations decreased after a long period of isolations and lack of restaurant visits. Therefore, customers might have become more willing to highlight positive experiences and eventually overlook negative aspects. Additional efforts made by hotels during the pandemic to improve the quality of food and beverages and regain customers constitutes another potential explanation of the identified changes.

Room and Bathroom: Before the outbreak of the pandemic, this topic area was perceived as a purely negative impact factor on total customer satisfaction. After the outbreak of the pandemic however, this has changed into both positive and negative influences on customer satisfaction. This could suggest that the Pandemic has heightened customers' awareness of cleanliness and hygiene, which is why an appropriate and clean room condition is no longer taken for granted, but instead appreciated.

5 Discussion of Results

Today's era has witnessed a large surge in UGC [4, 5]. This provides rich data for businesses to better understand their customers' needs and behaviour [2]. Especially after global challenges like the COVID-19 pandemic, it becomes essential for tourism businesses to delve into UGC, allowing them to better understand the evolving needs of their customers [8]. For tourism practitioners, especially hoteliers and destination managers, our proposed methods and findings may offer new insights and managerial implications. Based on the positive and negative impacts identified in the course of the analysis of UGC, businesses can determine which areas demand more attention and additional resources to further reach high levels of overall customer satisfaction. Other than that, it is crucial for hoteliers and destination managers to keep in mind that customer needs and expectations can change, especially during global challenges such as the pandemic. In this context, this study sheds light on how such quality factors may have shifted in the face of the COVID-19 crisis. This offers insights for businesses to adapt their services and strategies, allowing them to respond to such changing demands.

While the concept of analysing UGC to better understand customer needs is not entirely novel [2, 15, 16, 21, 22] this study provides a refined methodology that focuses on identifying possible shifts in customer satisfaction brought about by the pandemic. For this, UGC from TripAdvisor was extracted and analysed. While other research in this area strictly pre-classifies such topic areas as either positive or negative, this work aims to identify concrete factors that describe their positive or negative impact on customer satisfaction in case of fulfilment or non-fulfilment [11] to detect possible differences from before and after the pandemic.

To conclude, this study underlines the significance of UGC as a reflection of changes in societal tastes, needs and sentiments, especially during times of crisis, like the pandemic. In this context, it becomes evident that such shifts can indeed be tracked and better understood through a multi-method analysis of UGC.

6 Conclusion and Outlook

As the landscape of customer satisfaction evolves, especially in challenging times after the COVID-19 pandemic, businesses and researchers alike need robust and reliable methods to analyse online customer feedback. Through the application of text-mining techniques, it is not only possible to better understand the current sentiments of users towards certain topics, but also to keep track of possible changes regarding sentiments and topics. For future research, we recommend applying this proposed methodological procedure to destination regions with predominantly English UGC. UGC on TripAdvisor from the Lake of Constance region is predominantly written in German, which has limited the volume of information extractable, especially since the outbreak of the pandemic. Although the data basis was fairly limited, significant results could be achieved. Nevertheless, choosing a more suitable region with predominantly English UGC constitutes a natural next research activity. Additionally, this study employed a lexicon-based approach to identify pre-defined topics. Employing unsupervised learning techniques, such as clustering or Latent Dirichlet Allocation (LDA), could further facilitate the identification of such topics without prior classification [16]. This may yield more representative and unbiased topic areas suitable for this type of UGC analysis.

References

1. Zheng, X., Gretzel, U.: Role of social media in online travel information search. Tour. Manage. **31**(2), 179–188 (2010)
2. Marine-Roig, E.: Content analysis of online travel reviews. Handbook of e-Tourism, pp. 1–26. Springer International Publishing, Cham (2022). https://doi.org/10.1007/978-3-030-05324-6_31-1
3. Mehraliyev, F., Chan, I.C.C., Kirilenko, A.P.: Sentiment analysis in hospitality and tourism: a thematic and methodological review. Int. J. Contemp. Hosp. Manag. **34**(1), 46–77 (2022)
4. PRNewswire: Travelers Push Tripadvisor Past 1 Billion Reviews & Opinions! (2022). https://www.prnewswire.com/news-releases/travelers-push-tripadvisor-past-1-billion-reviews--opinions-301472329.html. Accessed 08 Sept 2022
5. Statista: Digitalization of the travel industry: Statistics & facts (2022). https://www.statista.com/topics/7589/digitalization-of-the-travel-industry/. Accessed 02 Aug 2023
6. Chen, J.L., Gang, L., Wu, D., Shen, S.: Forecasting seasonal tourism demand using a multiseries structural time series method. J. Travel Res. **58**(1), 92–103 (2019)
7. Höpken, W., Regitz, D., Liedtke, N., Fuchs, M.: Estimating tourist arrivals by user generated content volume in periods of extraordinary demand fluctuations. In: Ferrer-Rosell, B., Massimo, D., Berezina, K. (eds.) Information and Communication Technologies in Tourism 2023: Proceedings of the ENTER 2023 eTourism Conference, January 18-20, 2023, pp. 231–242. Springer Nature Switzerland, Cham (2023). https://doi.org/10.1007/978-3-031-25752-0_25
8. Gretzel, U., et al.: E-Tourism beyond Covid-19: a call for transformative research. Inf. Technol. Tourism **22**, 187–203 (2020)
9. UNWTO: Key tourism statistics (2022). https://www.unwto.org/tourism-statistics/key-tourism-statistics. Accessed 03 Aug 2023
10. Dedeoğlu, B.B., Taheri, B., Okumus, F., Gannon, M.: Understanding the importance that consumers attach to social media sharing: scale development and validation. Tour. Manage. **76**, 103954 (2020)

11. Jannach, D., Zanker, M., Fuchs, M.: Leveraging multi-criteria customer feedback for satisfaction analysis and improved recommendations. Inf. Technol. Tourism **14**, 119–149 (2014)

12. Ahani, A., et al.: Evaluating medical travelers' satisfaction through online review analysis. J. Hospital. Tourism Manage. **48**, 519–537 (2021). https://doi.org/10.1016/j.jhtm.2021.08.005

13. Menner, T., Höpken, W., Fuchs, M., Lexhagen, M.: Topic detection: identifying relevant topics in tourism reviews. In: Inversini, A., Schegg, R. (eds.) Information and Communication Technologies in Tourism 2016, pp. 411–423. Springer International Publishing, Cham (2016). https://doi.org/10.1007/978-3-319-28231-2_30

14. Xiang, Z., Du, Q., Ma, Y., Fan, W.: A comparative analysis of major online review platforms. Tour. Manage. **58**, 51–65 (2017)

15. Schmunk, S., Höpken, W., Fuchs, M., Lexhagen, M.: Sentiment analysis: extracting decision-relevant knowledge from UGC. In: Xiang, Z., Tussyadiah, I. (eds.) Information and Communication Technologies in Tourism 2014: Proceedings of the International Conference in Dublin, Ireland, January 21-24, 2014, pp. 253–265. Springer International Publishing, Cham (2013). https://doi.org/10.1007/978-3-319-03973-2_19

16. Höpken, W., Matthias Fuchs, T., Menner, M.L.: Sensing the online social sphere using a sentiment analytical approach. In: Xiang, Z., Fesenmaier, D.R. (eds.) Analytics in Smart Tourism Design, pp. 129–146. Springer International Publishing, Cham (2017). https://doi.org/10.1007/978-3-319-44263-1_8

17. Shi, H.X., Li, X.J.: A sentiment analysis model for hotel reviews based on supervised learning. Int. Conf. Mach. Learn. Cybernet. **3**, 950–954 (2011)

18. Sodanil, M.: Multi-language sentiment analysis for hotel reviews. In: 2016 International Conference on Measurement Instrumentation and Electronics, vol. 75 (2016)

19. Pang, B., Lee, L., Vaithyanathan, S.: Thumbs up? Sentiment classification using machine learning techniques. arXiv preprint cs/0205070 (2002)

20. García, A., Gaines, S., Linaza, M.T.: A lexicon-based sentiment analysis retrieval system for tourism domain. Expert Syst. Appl. Int. J. **39**, 9166–9180 (2012)

21. Ali, T., Omar, B., Soulaimane, K.: Analyzing tourism reviews using an LDA topic- based sentiment analysis approach. MethodsX **9**, 101894 (2022)

22. Garcia, K., Berton, L.: Topic detection and sentiment analysis in Twitter content related to COVID-19 from Brazil and the USA. Appl. Soft Comput. **101**, 107057 (2021)

23. Hu, M., Liu, B.: Mining and summarizing customer reviews. In: Proceedings of the tenth ACM SIGKDD International Conference on Knowledge Discovery & Data Mining, pp. 168–177 (2004)

I Know What You Think About Your Last Vacation: A Topic Modelling Approach for Destination Online Reviews

Benjamin Quarshie[1]([✉]) [iD], Halim Budi Santoso[2] [iD],
Antonius Rachmat Chrismanto[3] [iD], Paulina Ngubeni[4] [iD], and Dandison Ukpabi[5] [iD]

[1] Mampong Technical College of Education, Mampong District, Ghana
bquarshie@mtce.edu.gh
[2] Information System Department, Universitas Kristen Duta Wacana, Yogyakarta, Indonesia
hbudi@staff.ukdw.ac.id
[3] Informatics Department, Universitas Kristen Duta Wacana, Yogyakarta, Indonesia
anton@staff.ukdw.ac.id
[4] Department of Tourism Management, Tshwane University of Technology,
Pretoria, South Africa
ngubenipm@tut.ac.za
[5] School of Business, University of Jyväskylä, Jyväskylä, Finland
dandison.c.ukpabi@jyu.fi

Abstract. Online reviews (ORs) have garnered interdisciplinary attention, notably in hospitality and tourism. Despite their significance, concerns about OR credibility persist. Destination Management Organizations increasingly recognize ORs as valuable sources of firsthand, authentic feedback from consumers. However, there remains a dearth of cross-continental investigations into ORs, particularly concerning themes discussed by local and international travelers across various destinations. To address this gap, we employ Latent Dirichlet Analysis—a probabilistic technique to extract topics from a given corpus—to examine 10350 TripAdvisor reviews from 12 destinations in Ghana and Indonesia. Our analysis reveals shared concerns among domestic and international travelers regarding activities, destination attractions, local staff attitudes, and positive visitor experiences. This study advances insights, highlights limitations, and lays the groundwork for future research.

Keywords: Destination · Latent Dirichlet Analysis · Online Review · Topic Modelling

1 Introduction

The Online Review (OR) phenomenon has globally surged in the realm of consumer services due to technological advancements. This impact aligns with research by [1], indicating OR's influence on supply chains and consumer behaviors. ORs encompass consumer opinions about products or services, often on third-party websites. Despite

© The Author(s) 2024
K. Berezina et al. (Eds.): ENTER 2024, SPBE, pp. 385–397, 2024.
https://doi.org/10.1007/978-3-031-58839-6_40

their prevalence, OR credibility is intensely debated, as explored by [2]. Recent research applies ORs across diverse commerce domains, particularly in hospitality and tourism, where tourists' sentiments [3, 4] influence potential travelers. Instagram, X (Twitter), YouTube, TikTok, and TripAdvisor serve as platforms for sharing destination-related ORs, and transcending boundaries. These shared experiences play a pivotal role in travelers' decision-making [5]. These narratives are essential resources that shape the preferences of potential travelers by providing firsthand insights from previous explorers. Understanding tourists' sentiments and impressions across destinations is crucial for robust quality assurance in Destination Management Organizations (DMOs), as demonstrated in previous studies [1, 2, 4]. The impact of these ORs on brand images remains significant, even considering social media's rapid information spread [6]. DMOs monitor tourist ORs due to their influence on rankings and traveler choices. Recent research shows consumers prioritize aesthetic attributes and accommodation quality for perceived value [7]. Our study examines tourist sentiments in selected destinations in Indonesia and Ghana, focusing on emotional responses, activities, and sociocultural interactions.

Existing research ORs in tourism have gaps in comprehensively analyzing experiential narratives, especially among domestic and international travelers in specific cross-continental destinations. This study employs topic modeling [8] to address: *What are the primary travel concerns for domestic and international travelers in ORs?* Analyzing TripAdvisor ORs via text-mining, we focus on cross-continental destinations, extracting topics to reveal traveler experiences and emotions using Latent Dirichlet Analysis (LDA), with six destinations from Indonesia and Ghana. Findings, discussions, contributions, limitations, and future research directions follow.

2   Literature Review

The tourism industry, mainly service-oriented, relies on intangible experiences, and customer loyalty is crucial, influenced by quality and satisfaction [9:46]. Customer satisfaction in tourism significantly influences retention and word-of-mouth marketing [10]. To nurture loyalty, DMOs should focus on infrastructure, safety, service quality, and marketing to create a positive destination image [10]. The rise of online social media platforms has transformed tourism marketing, enabling consumers to review and assess services, affecting their purchasing decisions [12, 13]. Information technology advancements have revolutionized communication and destinations, fostering transformation [12]. Post-consumption customers increasingly provide feedback, with ORs becoming a prominent form of digitized word-of-mouth, shifting from traditional oral exchanges to platforms like TripAdvisor [16]. Recognizing the importance, marketers leverage ORs for their trustworthiness [15]. Similarly, [14] emphasizes the rise of electronic word of mouth (eWOM), propelled by electronic media. ORs are powerful marketing tools, impacting the trustworthiness of offerings [16]. To wit, [16] defines OR marketing as unpaid promotion based on customer feedback. Digitization has shifted customer reviews from personal conversations to online platforms like TripAdvisor, sharing experiences with a digital community. ORs potentially furnish consumers with credible and persuasive commercial information [14]. As this study delineates, Exploring ORs becomes imperative to impact the total growth of tourism destinations, especially in Africa and Asia.

2.1 Online Reviews and Customer Perceptions

The fourth industrial revolution (4IR) has significantly transformed the operations and marketing strategies of tourism and hospitality businesses. As the eWOM, commonly known as ORs, increases due to 4IR, web-based technologies have enabled extensive OR communication, directly impacting consumer purchase intentions and brand perceptions [17]. ORs are accessible globally regardless of location and play a pivotal role in e-commerce, influencing online and offline purchase decisions [18]. Some consumers find ORs more credible than conventional marketing campaigns, considering them unbiased and devoid of monetary influence [19]. However, this credibility is contested among researchers [2]. Sentiment analysis explores customer sentiments in Online Reviews (ORs) by identifying expressions as positive or negative opinions about the subject. It involves assessing sentiment expressions, their polarity, intensity, and their relation to the subject [20]. Sentiment analysis uses text mining and natural language processing to identify and extract subjective information from the text [21]. Mining consumer's emotions from online reviews is significant due to its ability to attract potential consumers by influencing their decisions, additionally, it enables organizations to get product feedback [22]. Yu et al. [23] argue that mining the online reviews on travel websites can help potential visitors better understand tourist attractions, choose their favorite scenic spots and avoid or reduce trouble throughout the planning of the tour or visit. Through ORs, consumers evaluate service risks and quality potential, while service providers gain insights to tailor their services to customer needs and expectations [18]. Consumers have the potential to make personal choices based on the perceptions gathered from the various OR platforms. ORs are vital in marketing tourism and hospitality, mitigate perceived risks and influence purchases, with platforms like TripAdvisor when engaged further through sentiment analysis [1]. Reviews assess risks, especially in foreign purchases. Positive reviews reduce perceived risks and enhance confidence [24]. Online platforms redefine consumer decision-making, transforming tourism communication [12, 13], allowing consumers to review, compare, and evaluate services, gauging value. Despite substantial research on online reviews, there is a noticeable dearth of studies pertaining to online reviews in Ghana and Indonesia, despite the vibrant tourism industries in these nations.

In this current study, we adopted Latent analysis as it aimed to identify underlying themes, attitudes, or patterns in text-based customer reviews posted on TripAdvisor [25]. This was necessary as this approach would assist in extracting important insights from customer reviews. [26] postulates that a tourist attraction with a high occurrence of reviews has a stronger perceived popularity and importance among tourists. For Ghanaian and Indonesian destinations, the situation differs as they do not yield a high volume of reviews. Popularity should not be solely gauged by review quantity; the relatively lower number still reflects their appeal. Therefore, our focus shifts to analyzing reviewer sentiment using LDA, as outlined in the methodology section.

3   Research Methodology

3.1   Data Collection

This research employs TripAdvisor online reviews for twelve destinations in Ghana and Indonesia, sourced using the third-party API platform APIFY (www.apify.com). Selection includes six destinations per country, encompassing cultural heritage, national parks, and natural attractions (beaches, volcanoes). Indonesian sites are drawn from the New Bali Projects list by the Ministry of Tourism, while well-known Ghana destinations are chosen. The ORs were downloaded via the API platform, with review counts detailed in Table 1. The research methodology, depicted in Fig. 1, employs LDA to extract topics from destination reviews.

Table 1.   Lists of Destinations and Number of Reviews

Country	Tourism Object	Total Review	Excluded Review	Final Review	
				Domestic traveler	International traveler
Ghana	Cape Coast Castle	701	238	45	418
	Kakum	716	211	53	452
	Kintampo Falls	36	13	3	20
	Mole	716	220	50	446
	Nzulezu	716	229	56	431
	Tafi Atome	716	225	49	442
Indonesia	Borobudur Temple	7593	3100	1364	3129
	Bromo Tengger	2565	1030	602	933
	Lake Toba	853	195	324	334
	Tanjung Lesung	119	32	82	5
	Thousand Islands	921	228	508	185
	Wakatobi	519	100	12	407

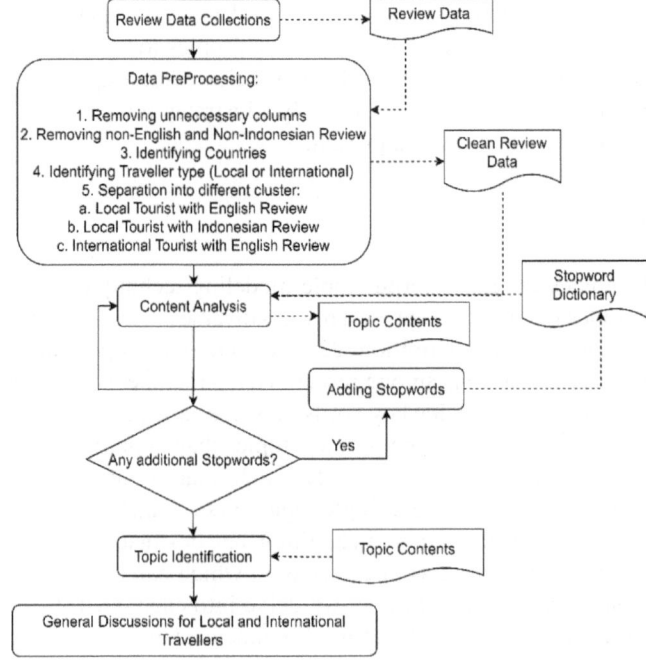

Fig. 1. Research Methodology

3.2 Data Preprocessing

From the acquired reviews, we extracted additional details like review title, publication date, username, location (city and country), language, helpful votes, user's review count, attraction review count, and attached images. Six columns (review ID, title, comments, city, country, and username) were retained after removing unnecessary columns. Non-English and non-Indonesian reviews were excluded, and a "Traveler Type" column was added, classifying reviewers as "Domestic" or "International" based on their origin. Review counts for each destination categorized by traveler type are provided in Table 1.

3.3 Data Analysis

Our analysis commenced by categorizing reviews based on language and traveler type, leading to distinct clusters. Given that two authors are Indonesians we conveniently formed three clusters for Indonesian destinations: domestic travelers with Indonesian reviews, domestic travelers with English reviews, and international travelers with English reviews. Ghana destinations yielded two clusters: domestic travelers with English reviews and international travelers with English reviews. We segmented words, removed punctuation and stopword, and aligned reviews with the required formats by applying a standard stopword dictionary. Topic modeling using LDA followed, with an initial five topics [25]. LDA is employed for information retrieval and analyzing document corpus content like patents or news. Python tool pyLDAvis aided topic extraction from online reviews. We tried a different number of topics for each analysis and then compared them. We agreed to use five topics as the initial number of topics to have a diverse number of topics that we could identify. We refined keyword clusters through iterative processes, enhancing topic justification. Figure 1 visually illustrates our research methodology, offering an overview of our study's approach.

4 Findings

This section elucidates the LDA corpus topic modeling technique [8, 21]. Employing LDA to discern topics from ORs is apt, as it reveals diverse attributes within reviews. The number of topics needs manual definition [22]; we set it to five topics and identify underlying themes through discussions among research team members. Actual review content aids context identification alongside keywords. In some cases, overlapping topics render certain themes indiscernible, resulting in fewer topics than anticipated, especially fewer than five for each destination by tourist type. Due to limitations in the number of reviews, there are two reviews that only have a single topic: First, Wakatobi (Indonesian Tourist, Indonesian Language) only has a topic. In addition, one destination in Ghana (Kintampo Falls, Domestic Travelers) only has three reviews, which can only be categorized into a single topic. Once topics are identified, we delve into each cluster's broader context (Fig. 2), aiding the grouping of similar topics for enhanced explanations. Understanding the higher context aids in delivering comprehensive insights.

4.1 Topic Modelling for Ghanaian Tourist Destination

Domestic Travelers

- *Positive Visitor Experience*: Ghanaian tourists expressed positive sentiments using terms like thrilling, attractive, amazing, fun, good, beautiful, and great during their visits. They also emphasized the sites' significance, considering them worthwhile and intriguing. Cape Coast Castle was particularly valued for its educational aspects, while other destinations were seen as sources of enjoyment and excitement.
- *Negative Visitor Experience*: Domestic visitors conveyed negative emotions, particularly related to Cape Coast Castle. Terms like dehumanizing, awkward, sobering, and horrific were used in reference to its slave history, reflecting their sentiment. Additionally, fear was expressed, particularly regarding the canopy walk at Kakum. Concerns about the littered state of Kintampo Falls were also raised.
- *Destination Attraction*: Ghanaian tourists exhibited contentment with their visited destinations, particularly highlighting the allure of natural landscapes and wildlife. These aspects were frequently described as amazing and integral to their great adventure. Historic education at Cape Coast Castle resonated positively. Floral and arboreal elements, wildlife encounters, and canoe cruises were also captivating features.
- *Activities:* Activities encompassed heritage education and dungeon exploration at Cape Coast, safari drives at Mole, hikes at Atome and Kakum, and canopy walks at Kakum. Canoe cruises (Nzulenzu), picnics, swimming at Kintampo Falls, and interactions with monkeys at Atome formed memorable experiences for many.

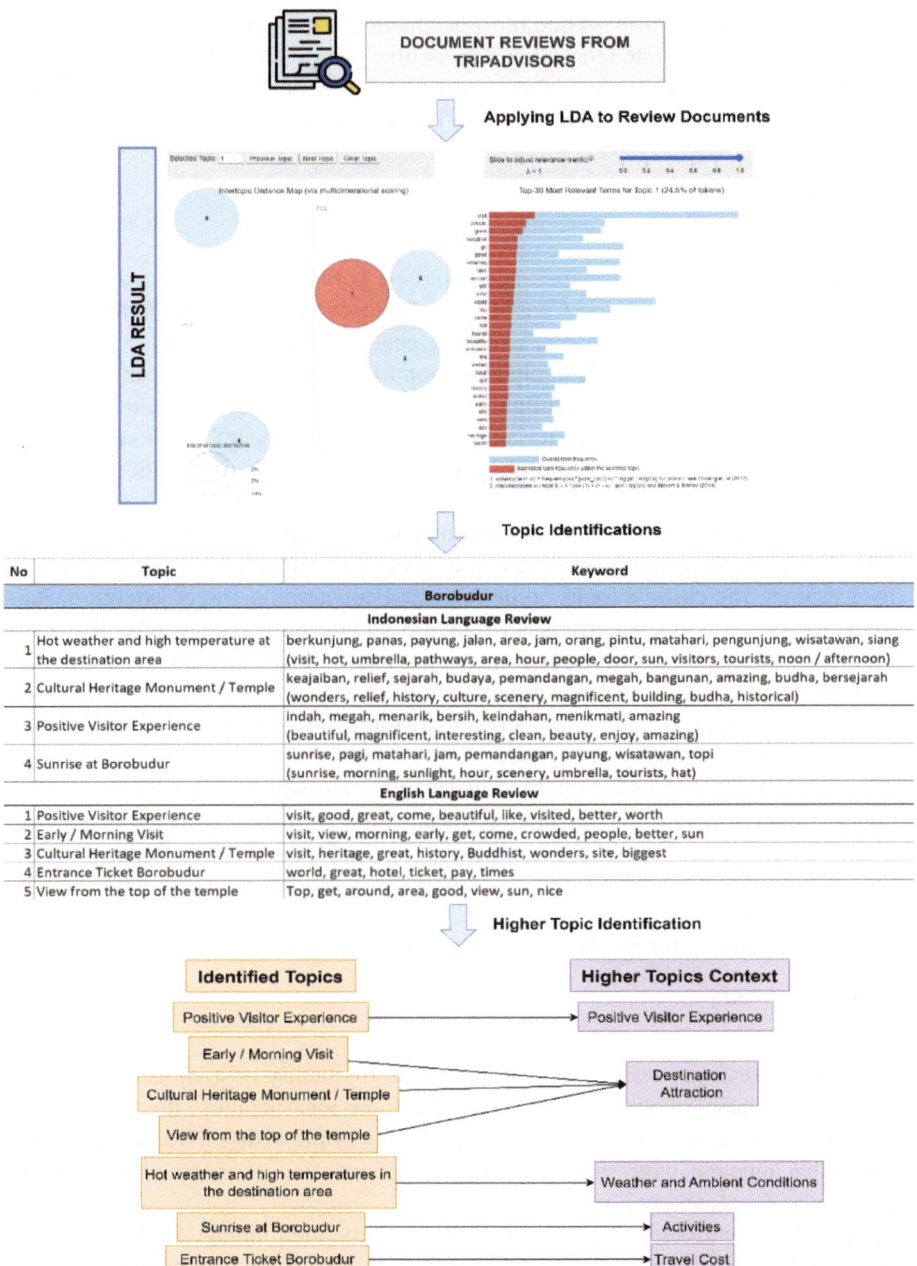

Fig. 2. Methodology on LDA, Topic, and Higher Context Identification

- *The Attitude of Staff and Local Guides:* Ghanaian visitors praised the knowledge of Cape Coast Castle's tour guide while expressing dissatisfaction with the Kakum guide for not accompanying them on the shaky canopy walk.

- *Accessibility/Affordability:* While most destinations were described as easily accessible with the appropriate fees, Ghanaian visitors perceived Mole Park as expensive. Cape Coast Castle was deemed inexpensive, and the encounter with friendly monkeys at Atome was c onsidered attainable with just a banana.

International Travelers

- *Activities:* Predominant activities encompassed heritage education and immersive dungeon exploration at Cape Coast Castle, hiking ventures at Atome and Kakum, game drives and safaris at Mole, engaging canopy walks at Kakum, and leisurely canoe cruises at Nzulenzu. Notably, Kintampo Falls entailed significant picnic and swimming endeavors. Also, highlights included close monkey encounters at Atome and unique lodging experiences at Kakum, such as sleeping near the monkey sanctuary or in tree houses. ORs indicate highly positive experiences for international travelers at these destinations.
- *Destination Attraction*: Certain international visitors were captivated by the vistas of Cape Coast Castle, often describing it as a "must-see" and a significant historical site for learning. The castle's focus on heritage and education garnered attention. Rainforest views at Kakum, waterfalls at Kintampo, and the unique Lake at Nzulenzu also drew admiration. Notably, discussions among international visitors about Ghanaian destinations frequently revolved around wildlife encounters. Monkeys (Atome), elephants, warthogs, crocodiles, and leopards (Mole) were encountered and described as thrilling, epic, amazing, and great.
- *The Attitude of Local Guides*: International visitors also expressed satisfaction with the quality of service. Travelers greatly appreciated the knowledgeable and experienced tour guides at Cape Coast Castle, while some raised concerns about guides leaving the group during the tour at Kakum.

4.2   Topic Modelling for Indonesian Tourist Destination

Domestic Travelers

- *Positive visitor experience:* Indonesian tourists frequently post about their positive experiences during their visits, and from the topic identification, this study cannot find any negative reviews or negative experiences of the visitors. The most frequent words that appear to express their positive visitor experiences are beautiful, amazing, good, nice, great, and enjoy.
- *Activities:* Indonesian travelers extensively describe their engaged activities during their journeys. Each destination provides unique experiences tied to their geographical advantages and natural surroundings. Frequently highlighted activities in ORs include watching sunrise from elevated points (Borobudur and Bromo), visiting cultural heritage temples (Borobudur), early morning jeep trips (Bromo), group excursions (Tanjung Lesung), swimming (Tanjung Lesung and Thousand Islands), snorkeling (Thousand Islands and Wakatobi), guided diving (Wakatobi), savoring local cuisine (Lake Toba), island-hopping by boat (Thousand Islands), and horseback riding (Bromo).

Furthermore, interactions with local inhabitants are cherished, particularly in Lake Toba, where discussions center around Batak culture and cultural immersion.

- *Weather and ambient conditions:* Indonesian travelers are concerned about the weather near their destination, such as hot temperatures and bringing an umbrella during a visit to Borobudur at noon, cold breeze while visiting Bromo in the early morning, and enjoying Lake Toba at night.
- *Destination attraction:* Indonesian tourists frequently mention nearby attractions that enhance their visits, such as the local Buddha temple at Borobudur, the Savana, caldera, mountain, and crater at Bromo, the Sea view at Tanjung Lesung, visiting various islands at Thousand Islands, Samosir and Parapat at Lake Toba, and luxurious villas and resorts at Wakatobi. Many reviews are positive and praise the attractions, but discussions also raise environmental concerns, particularly regarding issues like trash, especially in natural attractions like Tanjung Lesung.
- *Travel accompaniment:* Travel accompaniment is necessary, especially when the local people have collectivist cultures, such as Indonesia and other Asian countries. Indonesian tourists mention their companions when visiting destinations, such as traveling with friends at Tanjung Lesung, with working colleagues on weekends at Thousand Islands, and with family at Tanjung Lesung or Wakatobi.
- *Travel cost:* Traveling cost is the next topic domestic travelers least confer. They discuss the unaffordable luxurious Wakatobi vacation, which most Indonesians may not afford. Another review can be found on how they explain some accommodation prices at Tanjung Lesung and entrance tickets at Borobudur.
- *The attitude of staff and local guides:* Lastly, Indonesian travelers rarely mention the staff or local guides' attitudes. Only one topic was found, specifically about the positive attitude (friendly and kind) of resort staff at Wakatobi.

International Travelers

- *Attraction:* International travelers visit Indonesia to see and experience tropical nature and learn from historical sites like Borobudur. Indeed, they enjoyed different attractions, such as small islands at thousand islands, sand and mountains at Bromo, and the natural lake at Toba.
- *Positive Visitor Experience*: International visitors also write their positive visitor experience while enjoying Indonesian tourist destinations, such as the beautiful temple and historical significance at Borobudur, the Trip at Bromo, the beautiful scenery at Thousand Islands and Lake Toba, and the excellent resort at Wakatobi.
- *Activities:* Domestic travelers emphasize activities more than international travelers. Topics related to activities include admiration for Borobudur's ancient artwork, guided tours and horseback riding at Bromo, boat experiences and local cuisine at Thousand Islands, and relaxation at Lake Toba. Domestic travelers focus on swimming, diving and snorkeling activities and interactions with locals, while international travelers prioritize art appreciation and destination relaxation
- *Negative Visitor Experience:* International travelers also shared their negative experiences and dissatisfaction with certain destinations. A specific topic surfaced concerning international travelers' dissatisfaction with their visits to Tanjung Lesung.

Intriguingly, these travelers not only voice their negative experiences but also propose potential solutions to improve services.

- *The attitude of staff and local guides:* Similar to domestic travelers, international visitors are also concerned about the attitude of staff and local guides. We discovered one topic related to the attitude of staff at Wakatobi Resort, but we did not find one about Wakatobi diving guides.
- *The quality of services:* International travelers are also concerned about the quality of the service offered. We examined one topic discussion about the quality of the services of Wakatobi Resorts.

5   Discussion

Our findings reveal similarities in ORs from domestic travelers in Indonesia and Ghana. Four specific topics were highlighted, either in Ghanaian or Indonesian contexts. These topics predominantly encompass positive visitor experiences, destination attractions, activities, and the demeanor of staff and local guides (refer to Fig. 3). [27] notes that consumers find extreme ratings (positive or negative) more useful and enjoyable than moderate ones, significantly influencing their decision-making process. Domestic travelers' emphasis on positive visitor experiences contributes to a positive destination image for both domestic and international travelers. The role of staff and tour guides notably impacts these experiences, with positive attitudes enhancing visitor satisfaction [10, 16]. Therefore, domestic travelers emphasize staff and tour guide attitudes in their reviews. Positive reviews on reputable platforms can attract more travelers due to perceived reliability and reduced risk [1]. Local travelers also discuss potential activities and attractions, promoting the destination and forming a positive image. Activities and attractions contribute to conative experiences, pivotal for holistic customer satisfaction [10, 16]. Conversely, three topics are more prominent among international travelers, influencing their online reviews (Fig. 3). Unique destination attractions like the ancient artworks at Borobudur in Indonesia and the wild experiences with monkeys in Ghana, draw international tourists. Well-trained frontline staff and guides are vital for enhancing destination impressions and impacting tourist satisfaction [10, 16]. Hence, international travelers prioritize this aspect and share reviews regarding local staff or guides' attitudes.

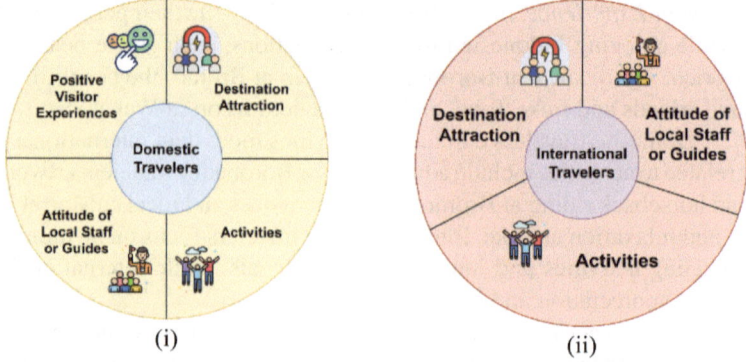

(i)   (ii)

Fig. 3. Top of Minds of (i) Domestic and (ii) International Travelers Online Reviews

6   Conclusions

This study investigates customer destination perceptions from ORs across 12 destinations in Ghana and Indonesia. Empirical results validate the significance of ORs in reflecting customer sentiments about the explored destinations. Both domestic and international travelers prominently discuss destination activities and experiences. Wang et al. [28] found that respondents valued the credibility and informativeness of travel post reviews, as well as their style and length, which enhanced trust in tourism offerings and influenced their decision-making. We herein posit that the experiences shared by TripAdvisor reviewers on the Ghanaian and Indonesian destinations could potentially increase attractions of tourists. Noteworthy is the recurring theme of excellent customer service in ORs, underscoring the influence of front-line staff in shaping lasting impressions across markets. The study also encompasses a review of existing research, underscoring the potent impact of positive ORs on customer perceptions of brands, albeit with potentially contrasting effects of negative ORs. The research underlines the pivotal role of ORs for tourism and hospitality businesses. Recognizing and comprehending ORs' role in assessing customer satisfaction is vital for sustaining and perpetuating the success of destinations.

6.1   Theoretical and Practical Contributions

Our study explores TripAdvisor ORs through the LDA topic modeling approach, hence contributing to existing literature on ORs. Our study is unique in the sense that we explored domestic and international travelers' thoughts from two developing countries in two continents. Our methodological approach has great potentials of guiding other scholars and researchers in similar future inquiries. Again, our study analyzes ORs to uncover experiential activities and sentiments of domestic and international travelers, potentially impacting DMOs' service quality and marketing strategies highlighted in the selected destinations.

6.2   Limitations and Future Research Agenda

We acknowledge three study limitations. Firstly, we focused on 12 popular destinations in Ghana and Indonesia due to their high comment volumes. Therefore, caution is required when generalizing findings beyond these destinations to the wider tourism industry in both countries. Second, our data collection centered exclusively on TripAdvisor, an interactive but not real-time platform [5]. Platforms like X (Twitter) and Facebook offer real-time dynamics that could yield distinct results, warranting future exploration of potential divergences. Lastly, Our study solely uses customer ORs, but future research could explore individual review histories in specific countries, establishing reviewer recognition programs on OR platforms to enhance OR credibility.

References

1. Schuckert, M., Liu, X., Law, R.: Hospitality and tourism online reviews: recent trends and future directions. J. Travel Tour. Mark. **32**(5), 608–621 (2015). https://doi.org/10.1080/105 48408.2014.933154

2. Pooja, K., Upadhyaya, P.: What makes an online review credible? A systematic review of the literature and future research directions. Manage. Rev. Q. (2022). https://doi.org/10.1007/s11 301-022-00312-6

3. Xiang, Z., Du, Q., Ma, Y., Fan, W.: A comparative analysis of major online review platforms: implications for social media analytics in hospitality and tourism. Tour. Manage. **58**, 51–65 (2017). https://doi.org/10.1016/j.tourman.2016.10.001

4. Qin, Y., Wang, X., Zhang, X.: Ranking tourist attractions through online reviews: a novel method with intuitionistic and hesitant fuzzy information based on sentiment analysis. Int. J. Fuzzy Syst. **24**(2), 755–777 (2021). https://doi.org/10.1007/s40815-021-01131-9

5. Nasution, R.A., Windasari, N.A., Mayangsari, L., Arnita, D.: Travellers' online sharing across different platforms: what and why? J. Hosp. Tour. Technol. **14**(2), 295–308 (2023). https://doi.org/10.1108/jhtt-02-2021-0040

6. Guo, X., Pesonen, J.: The role of online travel reviews in evolving tourists' perceived destination image. Scand. J. Hosp. Tour. **22**(4–5), 372–392 (2022). https://doi.org/10.1080/150 22250.2022.2112414

7. Zhuo, X., Wang, W.: Value for money? Exploring the consumer experience on shared accommodation platforms: evidence from online reviews in China. J. Hosp. Tour. Technol. **13**(3), 542–558 (2022). https://doi.org/10.1108/jhtt-03-2021-0087

8. Asmussen, C.B., Møller, C.: Smart literature review: a practical topic modelling approach to exploratory literature review. J. Big Data, **6**(1) (2019) https://doi.org/10.1186/s40537-019-0255-7

9. Corte, V., Sciarelli, M., Cascella, C., Gaudio, G.: Customer satisfaction in tourist destination: the case of tourism offer in the city of naples. J. Invest. Manage. **4**(1), 39–50 (2015)

10. Surahman, I.G.N., Yasa, P.N.S., Wahyuni, N.M.: The effect of service quality on customer loyalty mediated by customer satisfaction in tourism villages in Badung Regency. Jurnal Ekonomi dan Bisnis Jagaditha **7**(1), 46–52 (2020)

11. Adinegara, G.N.J., Suprapti, N.W.S., Yasa, N.N.K., Sukaatmadja, I.P.G.: Factors that influences tourist's satisfaction and its consequences. Eur. J. Bus. Manage. **8**(9), 39–50 (2017)

12. Sotiriadis, M.D., van Zyl, C.: Electronic word-of-mouth and online reviews in tourism services: the use of Twitter by tourists. Electron. Commer. Res. **13**(1), 103–124 (2013). https://doi.org/10.1007/s10660-013-9108-1

13. Popa, R.A., Săplăcana, Z., Dabija, D.C., Alt, M.A.: The impact of social media influencers on travel decisions: the role of trust in consumer decision journey. Curr. Issue Tour. **25**(5), 823–843 (2022). https://doi.org/10.1080/13683500.2021.1895729

14. López, M., Sicilia, M.: EWOM as source of influence: the impact of participation in eWOM and perceived source trustworthiness on decision making. J. Interact. Advert. **14**(2), 86–97 (2014). https://doi.org/10.1080/15252019.2014.944288

15. Nuseir, M.T.: The impact of electronic word of mouth (eWOM) on the online purchase intention of consumers in the Islamic countries – a case of (UAE). J. Islamic Market. **10**(3), 759–767 (2019). https://doi.org/10.1108/JIMA-03-2018-0059

16. Naylor, G.S.: Complaining, complementing, and word-of-mouth in the digital age: typology and terms. J. Cons. Satisfaction, Dissatisfaction Complain. Behav. **29**, 131–142 (2016)

17. Cheung, C.M.K., Lee, M.K.O., Rabjohn, N.: The impact of electronic word-of-mouth: the adoption of online opinions in online customer communities. Internet Res. **18**(3), 229–247 (2008). https://doi.org/10.1108/10662240810883290

18. Wan, Y., Ma, B., Pan, Y.: Opinion evolution of online consumer reviews in the e-commerce environment. Electron. Commer. Res. **18**, 291–311 (2018). https://doi.org/10.1007/s10660-017-9258-7

19. Kurdia, B., Alshurideh, M., Akour, I., Tariq, E., AlHamad, A., Alzoubi, H.: The effect of social media influencers' characteristics on consumer intention and attitude toward Keto products purchase intention. Int. J Data Netw. Sci. **6**(4), 1135–1146 (2022)

20. Nasukawa, T., Yi, J.: Sentiment analysis: capturing favorability using natural language processing. In: Proceedings of the Second International Conference on Knowledge Capture (pp. 70–77). ACM (2003)
21. Wankhade, M., Rao, A.C.S., Kulkarni, C.: A survey on sentiment analysis methods, applications, and challenges. Artif. Intell. Rev. **55**, 5731–5780 (2022). https://doi.org/10.1007/s10 462-022-10144-1
22. Xia, H., Yang, Y., Pan, X., Zhang, Z., An, W.: Sentiment analysis for online reviews using conditional random fields and support vector machines. Electron. Commer. Res. **20**(2), 343–360 (2020)
23. Yu, C., Zhu, X., Feng, B., Cai, L., An, L.: Sentiment analysis of Japanese tourism online reviews. J. Data Inf. Sci. **4**(1), 89–113 (2019). https://doi.org/10.2478/jdis-2019-0005
24. Stein, N., Spinler, S., Vanthournout, H., Blass, V.: Consumer perception of online attributes in circular economy activities. Sustainability **12**(5), 1–16 (2020)
25. Govindarajan, U.H., Trappey, C.V.: Intelligent collaborative patent mining using excessive topic generation. Adv. Eng. Inform. **42**, 100955 (2019). https://doi.org/10.1016/j.aei.2019. 100955
26. Yang, Y.: Understanding tourist attraction cooperation: An application of network analysis to the case of Shanghai, China. J. Destination Market. Manage. (2017). https://doi.org/10.1016/ j.jdmm.2017.08.003
27. Park, S., Nicolau, J.L.: Asymmetric effects of online consumer reviews. Ann. Tour. Res. **50**, 67–83 (2015)
28. Wang, Z., Huang, W.-J., Liu-Lastres, B.: Impact of user-generated travel posts on travel decisions: a comparative study on Weibo and Xiaohongshu. Ann. Tour. Res. Empirical Insights **3**, 100064 (2022)

Unveiling Destination Perceptions: A Machine Learning Study on Instagram Influencers' Cognitive Images

Roman Egger[1,2]([⊠]) [iD] and Veronika Surkic[1]

[1] Salzburg University of Applied Sciences, Urstein Süd 1, 5412 Puch Bei Salzburg, Austria
roman.egger@fh-salzburg.ac.at
[2] Modul University, Am Kahlenberg 1, 1190 Vienna, Austria

Abstract. This study examines the cognitive image of Austria as a travel destination through Instagram content posted by travel influencers. The study also investigates how the account type, influencer type, and posting frequency affect user engagement. Machine learning techniques and statistical analysis are used to analyze the data. The study found that influencers contribute to Austria's destination image mainly through content about the Alps, Vienna, and cycling. The study provides insights into successful destination promotion on Instagram through influencer marketing. Micro-influencers who post regularly with relevant content are ideal for DMOs. Meso-influencers and verified accounts receive more likes for less popular themes, while micro-influencers are sufficient for more popular themes. It is also disadvantageous for meso-influencers to be perceived as commercial accounts and not to post as often as emerging influencers.

Keywords: influencers · influencer marketing · destination image · destination marketing · Instagram · machine learning

1 Introduction

Social media are extensively studied in the tourism literature as they provide consumers with a wealth of information for purchase decisions [1] and have become a more important source of information in terms of brand image. User-generated content (UGC) can shape destination image [2, 3] a role previously reserved for traditional channels [4]. It is difficult for destinations to control UGC, which is why influencers act as intermediaries in their social media communications. [5]. Influencers' testimonials based on personal experiences are perceived as a strong eWOM, leading to increased demand and positive attitudes towards the brand [6].

As travel influencers have the power to shape the image of a destination and influence the experience of a destination and its future development [7, 8] this study 1) analyses the image of Austria as a travel destination and examines it through the content posted by travel influencers on Instagram, and 2) assesses how the account type (business account or verified account), influencer type (micro or meso influencer, depending on the number of followers) and posting frequency (number of posts) influence user engagement.

K. Berezina et al. (Eds.): ENTER 2024, SPBE, pp. 398–409, 2024.
https://doi.org/10.1007/978-3-031-58839-6_41

This study uses data collected on Instagram and applies a mixed methods approach using machine learning techniques and statistical analysis. The methodology includes computer vision analysis using a convolutional neural network (CNN) and multilevel cluster analysis to answer the following three research questions:

(1) What kind of content was posted by influencers on Instagram about Austria as a travel destination?
(2) What content is most attractive to users in terms of likes and comments?
(3) How do the influencers' profile characteristics (number of followers, number of posts, type of profile account) affect user engagement (likes and comments)?

From an industry perspective, the results should provide valuable insights into how successful promotion of a destination on Instagram by an influencer can be achieved. In addition, the study makes a methodological contribution by demonstrating the benefits of machine learning-assisted image content analysis.

2 Literature Review

Destination image is described as a tourist's collection of ideas, impressions and thoughts about a particular destination [9]. This image is built on the basis of the knowledge a person has about the destination and the emotions that the destination evokes [10–12]. Visitors nowadays have the possibility to create and spread their own impressions [8, 13, 14]. The image of a destination is thus shaped by the official channels and the tourists [8] which is why some DMOs turn to influencers to shape the destination's image through the influencer [4, 15]. Influencers provide content based on personal experiences, reflecting stories from their daily lives. [1, 6, 8, 16] and thus increase their popularity and influence, which is reflected in the number of likes, shares and comments [6, 8, 17]. According to Veirman et al. [1], the number of followers of influencers has a positive effect on perceived popularity and thus on likeability, while a positive effect on attributed opinion leadership is present but weak. In other words, a high number of likes is not always an indicator of their influencing power. Several studies [8, 16, 18] assume that the perceived match between the influencer and the brand they support plays a crucial role in the credibility and success of the advertising campaign [19]. These studies emphasise the importance of matching the influencer's lifestyle and published content with the brand's image and the brand's target audience with the influencer's target audience for successful advertising and promotion.

Other studies in the tourism industry have focused on the impact of social media influencers on the travel-related behavioural intentions of their followers [20]. Magno and Cassia [20] showed that the influence of travel bloggers on the travel intentions of their followers is highly dependent on the perceived trustworthiness [21] of the blogger and the perceived quality of the information they provide.

Taking into account these previous findings, this article aims to further contribute to the knowledge of how destination endorsement by influencers on Instagram affects destination image and user engagement.

3   Methodology

In this study, a mixed methods approach was used to identify quantitative relationships between user engagement and influencer profile characteristics and to conduct a qualitative content analysis of influencers' cognitive image of travel destinations. Instagram, the most popular social media platform among influencers and particularly suitable for promoting travel destinations [6, 8, 22] served as the online data source.

The entire research process was divided into three steps: (1) data collection, (2) machine learning model with content analysis and (3) statistical analysis.

3.1   Data Collection

The data collection process was based on the data mining tool PhantomBuster, which imitates human navigation on social media to respect anonymity and the general terms of service [23]. The travel influencer profiles were identified using the influencer marketing platform StarNgage and PhantomBuster. Only profiles with at least 1,000 followers were used, based on the observation of Femenia-Serra and Gretzel [4] regarding trending collaborations of DMOs and micro-influencers (1K-3K followers). The sample was narrowed down to 50 influencer profiles that included both verified (public figures or celebrities) and unverified users, and their profile information and posts were extracted using PhantomBuster. The data included the type of user account (e.g. number of followers, verified/unverified) and post information (e.g. number of likes, number of comments, location). Only those posts that included Austria as a location were used, resulting in 5,522 posts. Finally, for the content analysis, the images were extracted from the posts.

3.2   Data Analysis

In the first phase, image embedding was performed using Google's deep learning model Inception v3 to compute the feature vectors for each image [24–26]. Then, a hierarchical clustering of the high-dimensional image vectors was performed using the cosine distance and Ward's method to identify content-based clusters [27]. The number of clusters was determined in an iterative process. In each iteration step, cluster content analysis was performed until the maximum number of clusters with a satisfactory categorisation result was reached. Next, t-SNE dimensionality reduction technique was adopted to visualize the clusters in a scatter plot [28].

The second phase involved a statistical analysis using stepwise linear regression to determine whether the account type (business, verified), the total number of posts a user makes and the number of followers a user has have an impact on engagement (likes and comments).

Furthermore, an ANOVA with a Bonferroni Post-hoc test was performed to see, if the clusters differ significantly from each other.

4   Results

4.1   Analysis of the Image Content

The preliminary analysis of the clusters showed that 19% of the images could be very homogeneously characterised as "alpine landscape" (see Fig. 1).

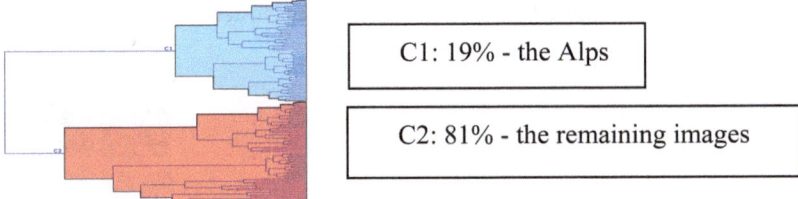

Fig. 1. Preliminary clustering from the dendrogram

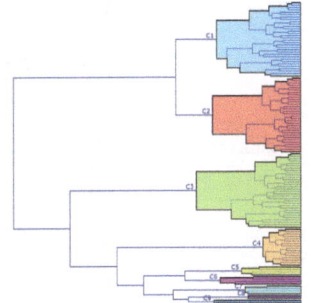

	Cluster name	N images	% of total images
C1	summer Alps	701	13%
C2	winter Alps	369	7%
C3	Urban	776	14%
C4	Bicycling	300	5%
C5	Parks	268	5%
C6	Lakes	474	9%
C7	Humans	757	14%
C8	Products	412	7%
C9	Diverse	1465	27%

Fig. 2. The nine final clusters

To gain deeper insights, a further second-level analysis was conducted, which resulted in a total of nine clusters (see Fig. 2). The description of the clusters is shown in Table 1.

4.2 Statistical Analysis

In the second phase of the analysis, descriptive data was created for the influencers' Instagram accounts (see Table 2). Of the 50 influencers included in the study, half (n = 25) were labelled as business accounts and six accounts were verified.

When looking at the influencer classification according to the number of their followers [15] 32% of micro-influencers (up to 10K followers) and 68% of meso-influencers (10k-1M followers) were included in the sample (see Table 3).

A stepwise linear regression analysis was performed to investigate the impact of account type (business, verified), total number of posts and number of followers on engagement (likes and comments). In our analysis, we checked for the assumptions of multiple regression and no violations were identified. First, the impact on the *number of likes* as the dependent variable was measured with two regression models (see Table 4). The first model included the independent variables *business account* and *number of posts*. For the second model, additional variables *verified account* and *number of followers* were added. Both models were significant ($p = 0.000$), explaining only 4% of the variance in the first model (adjusted $R^2 = 0.040$) but 54% of the variance in the second model (adjusted $R^2 = 0.542$). The second model shows that the *number of followers* had a strong positive effect (beta coefficient = 0.705), the *verified profile had* a weak positive

Table 1. Content analysis of the clusters.

	Cluster	Description	Example
C1	Summer Alps	Mountain and lake landscape in the warmer months	
C2	Winter Alps	Winter mountain panorama	
C3	Urban	Buildings (inside and outside), architecture and landmarks (Schönbrunn Palace, the Vienna Opera, etc.)	
C4	Cycling	Bicycles or people cycling	
C5	Parks	Trees, leaves, flowers, tree-lined streets or paths, flowering branch	
C6	Lakes	Heterogeneous; lakescapes and riverscapes (both in urban and natural contexts), some urban images from a bird's eye view and rooftops	
C7	People	Individuals and groups in different forms (face, partial view, back view, etc.) and environments (in nature or in urban settings)	
C8	Products	Promotional images of products, e.g. a backdrop of cosmetics	
C9	Diverse	Heterogeneous images without a common theme, e.g. animals, food, people, urban motifs, landmarks, interiors, everyday life, etc.	

Table 2. Influencer sample

Influencer accounts in total	50
Verified accounts	6
Accounts not verified	44
Business accounts	25
Non-business accounts	25

effect (beta coefficient = 0.228), the *number of posts had a* weak negative effect (beta coefficient = − 0.124) and the *business account had* a weak negative effect (beta coefficient = − 0.042).

A second stepwise regression was then performed with the same independent variables, using the *number of comments* as the dependent variable (see Table 5). Both models were significant ($p = 0.000$); however, only 1.3% of the variance was explained

Table 3. Influencers by number of followers

Number of followers	Frequency	Percentage
1K - 9K	16	32
10K - 999K	34	68
Total	50	100

Table 4. Regression model for the number of likes

Model		Non-standardised coefficients		Std. Coeff	t	**Sig**
		B	Std. Error	Beta		
Model 1 (adj. r^2) = .040 Model 2 (adj. r^2) = .542						
1	(Constant)	542.964	83.771		6.482	
	BusinessAccount	−121.586	79.958	−.020	−1.521	
	postsCount	.821	.057	.195	14.476	
2	(Constant)	956.560	61.416		15.575	.000
	BusinessAccount	−248.850	56.429	−.042	−4.410	.000
	postsCount	−.521	.045	−.124	−11.542	.000
	followersCount	.014	.000	.705	66.462	.000
	VerifiedAccount	2165.770	90.294	.228	23.986	.000

in the first model (adjusted R^2 = 0.013) and only 3.8% of the variance in the second model (adjusted R^2 = 0.038). The second model shows that the *number of followers* had *a* significant, weak positive effect (beta coefficient = 0.184; p = 0.000), while the *number of posts* (beta coefficient = − 0.130; p = 0.000) and the *business account* (beta coefficient = − 0.1374; p = 0.000) *had* a significant but weak negative effect on the *number of comments*. The variable *Verified Account* had no significant effect on the number of *comments* (*p* = 0.175).

Next, the standardised mean values of the likes and comments of each cluster were compared to see if a significant difference could be found between the clusters[1].

The t-SNE projection of the high dimensional image vectors indicates an acceptable overall cluster segmentation (Fig. 3).

The mean values for likes and comments per cluster are presented in Table 6.

Looking at the mean standardised likes, it can be assumed that the content of the *Summer Alps* and *Winter Alps* clusters appealed to users the most. On the other hand,

---

[1] The comparison of each cluster's mean values of the standardized number of likes and comments (the Kruskal – Wallis and the Post-hoc tests) can be seen here: https://tinyurl.com/ANOVA-Appendix.

Table 5. Regression model for the number of comments

Model		Non-standardised coefficients		Std. Coeff.	t	Sig
		B	Std. Error	Beta		
Model 1 (adj. r^2) = .013 Model 2 (adj. r^2) = .038						
1	(Constant)	124.134	9.562		12.982	
	BusinessAccount	− 79.224	9.127	− .118	− 8.680	
	postsCount	− .019	.006	− .040	− 2.928	
2	(Constant)	149.828	10.017		14.958	2
	BusinessAccount	−91.424	9.203	− .137	− 9.934	.000
	postsCount	− .061	.007	− .130	− 8.357	.000
	followersCount	.000	.000	.184	11.991	.000
	VerifiedAccount	− 19.959	14.727	− .019	− 1.355	.175

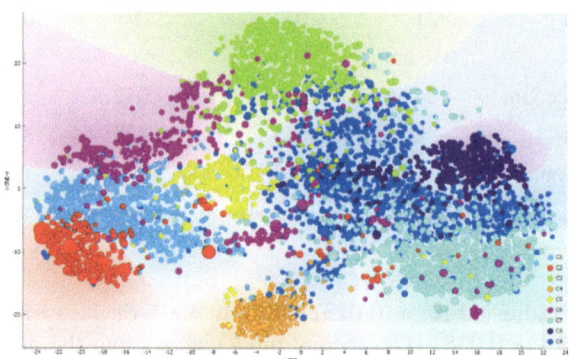

Fig. 3. Scatter plot of the nine clusters

the content in the *Bicycle* and *Products* clusters seemed to be the least appealing, with the lowest mean standardised likes. Looking at the mean standardised comments, the content in *Products* generated the most comments, while the content in the *Parks* and *Cycling* clusters generated the least comments.

5   Discussion of the Results

The aim of this study was to examine the cognitive image of Destination Austria based on the content posted by influencers and to assess how different content is received by Instagram users. Furthermore, while this study provides insights based on engagement metrics, it is understood that selecting the most suitable influencer from a destination

Table 6. Clusters by mean standardised likes and comments

	Cluster name	Mean std. Likes		Cluster name	Mean std. Comments
C1	Summer Alps	0,068	C8	Products	0,0048
C2	Winter Alps	0,066	C1	Summer Alps	0,0026
C6	Lakes	0,052	C7	People	0,0024
C3	Urban	0,047	C6	Lakes	0,0020
C9	Diverse	0,035	C3	Urban	0,0016
C7	People	0,034	C9	Diverse	0,0016
C5	Parks	0,033	C2	Winter Alps	0,0016
C4	Cycling	0,025	C5	Parks	0,0011
C8	Products	0,022	C4	Cycling	0,0009

marketing perspective involves a comprehensive evaluation, including factors like image congruency, target audience, and past collaboration successes.

The content analysis revealed that the most prominent cluster was the mountain landscape, making the Alps the most well-known cognitive image of the Austrian destination as conveyed by influencers. The Alps are more strongly positioned not only as a ski destination in winter, but also as a cycling and hiking destination [29]. The distinction between alpine summer and winter landscapes is clearly visible in the clustering.

The *Cycling* cluster can be interpreted as the sport most represented by influencers in creating a destination image of Austria. Another cluster that contributes to the destination image of Austria is the *Urban* cluster, which promotes the sights and attractions of the capital Vienna, such as Schönbrunn Palace, the Vienna State Opera etc.

It can be concluded that influencers contribute to the cognitive image of Austria as a destination mainly through content about the Alps, the capital Vienna and cycling, which seems to be in line with the current marketing objectives. The remaining five clusters contribute rather little to the image of the destination. The most promising among them is the *Lakes* cluster. Although this cluster contains quite heterogeneous content, the promotion of lake destinations such as Hallstadt and Salzkammergut, Neusiedler See, Wörthersee, Zell am See, etc. could potentially benefit from further influencer marketing campaigns. As mentioned above, travel influencers are very successful in convincing tourists about their choice of destination [8].

5.1 Effects on the Engagement Rate

With regard to the selection of suitable influencers for destination marketing campaigns, the following recommendation can be derived. If DMOs opt for micro-influencers with fewer followers, they should choose active influencers who regularly post relevant content. Regarding meso-influencers, a business account will not receive more likes. DMOs should therefore not perceive a business account label as an advantage when opting for a meso-influencer.

For comments, the situation is more complex, as a higher number of followers does not lead to a higher number of comments. It can be assumed that it takes more effort to achieve a higher level of engagement, e.g. through comments, than just having a wider follower base. This also means that the difference between micro and meso influencers in achieving higher levels of engagement in the form of comments is insignificant. These findings are consistent with some previous studies showing that both meso and micro-influencers seem to be as successful as their prominent online counterparts when it comes to brand promotion [30].

When comparing the clusters based on the standardised number of likes, it can be seen that users like the pictures of the Alps best. In contrast, the lowest number of likes was achieved in the *"bicycle"* and *"products"* clusters. Some previous studies have shown that posts with a face or physical representation of an influencer increase user engagement [16, 31]. However, in this case, the cluster *"people"* that only showed pictures of people did not result in a higher number of likes or comments compared to other clusters. According to a study by Silva et al. [16] influencers try to engage users by seeking direct interaction with their posts by asking questions, inviting comments, etc. It can be concluded that the inclusion of product images in a destination marketing campaign, along with direct invitations to comment, can be beneficial even if the product images appear less visually appealing to users.

According to the standardized number of likes analysis combined with the regression analysis, it can be assumed that when promoting a destination with a more appealing theme and a higher number of likes, such as the Alps and Lake destinations, the use of a micro-influencer would be sufficient. On the other hand, destinations in this case study with themes belonging to the less popular clusters would rather benefit from a meso-influencer or a verified Instagram account as they seem to receive more likes.

6   Conclusion and Implications for Future Research

This research contributes to the current literature by expanding the knowledge base of influencer marketing in the context of the tourism industry. The study provides a deeper understanding of how users are influenced by an influencer's number of follow-ers, account type and posted content. However, it's important to emphasize that while engagement metrics like likes and comments provide valuable data, they are just one facet of influencer suitability. The alignment between marketing objectives, selected content, and influencers who authentically represent this content is crucial. Other factors, such as image congruency between destination and influencer and the influencer's broader brand and audience, also play a pivotal role in determining the success of an influencer marketing campaign. In addition, the study offers a methodological contribution by demonstrating the benefits of machine learning and data mining models in the increasing analysis of social media data.

The results of this study have practical implications for the tourism industry as they provide guidance on what type of influencer would be suitable for a destination marketing campaign. This study clearly shows that the content itself influences the number of likes and comments and should therefore be taken into account when deciding on the optimal influencer type. The alignment between marketing objectives, selected content and influencers who authentically represent this content is of great importance. The business implications of this study show how DMOs can reduce the cost of an influencer campaign by actively using both meso and micro influencers, taking into account the impact of the content on engagement.

One of the limitations of this study is that it was not possible to distinguish between generic posts and paid sponsorships. Therefore, it is unclear whether the results of the clustering are biased. Furthermore, the cognitive image of the destination was analysed solely on the basis of influencer posts, without reference to the image of the destination among tourists. A comparative content analysis of UCG posts and influencer posts could provide additional insights into whether a certain aspect of the destination image is missing or could be improved through an influencer marketing campaign. Furthermore, due to the large scale of the destination under study and the large number of contributing influencer accounts, only a limited number of influencer accounts were included in the research.

References

1. de Veirman, M., Cauberghe, V., Hudders, L.: Marketing through Instagram influencers: the impact of number of followers and product divergence on brand attitudes. Int. J. Advert. **36**(5), 798–828 (2017)
2. Acuti, D., Mazzoli, V., Donvito, R., Chan, P.: An Instagram content analysis for city branding in London and Florence. J. Glob. Fash. Market. **9**(3), 185–204 (2018)
3. Huertas, A., Marine-Roig, E.: User responses to destination brand content on social media. Information Technology & Tourism **15**(4), 291–315 (2016)
4. Femenia-Serra, F., Gretzel, U.: Influencer Marketing for Tourism Destinations: Lessons from a Mature Destination. In: Neidhardt, J., Wörndl, W. (eds.) Information- und Kommunikationstechnologien im Tourismus 2020, pp. 65–78. Springer International Publishing, Cham (2020)
5. Uzunoğlu, E., Misci Kip, S.: Brand communication through digital influencers: leveraging blogger engagement. Int. J. Inf. Manage. **34**(5), 592–602 (2014)
6. Valderrama-Santomé, M., Fernández-Souto, A.-B., & Vázquez-Gestal, M. (2019). Travel Igers: innovation, influence and persuasion through a photo gallery. In M. Túñez-López, V.-A. Martínez-Fernández, X. López-García, X. Rúas-Araújo, & F. Campos-Freire (Eds.), Studies in Systems, Decision and Control. Communication: Innovation & Quality (Vol. 154, pp. 447–461). Cham: Springer International Publishing
7. Molinillo, S., Anaya-Sánchez, R., Morrison, A.M., Coca-Stefaniak, J.A.: Smart city communication via social media: Analysing residents' and visitors' engagement. Cities **94**, 247–255 (2019)
8. Palazzo, M., Vollero, A., Vitale, P., Siano, A.: Urban and rural destinations on Instagram: Exploring the influencers' role in #sustainabletourism. Land Use Policy **100**, 104915 (2021)
9. Bigné, J., Sánchez, M., Sánchez, J.: Tourism image, evaluation variables and post-purchase behaviour: interrelation. Tour. Manage. **22**(6), 607–616 (2001)
10. Ashkezari-Toussi, S., Kamel, M., Sadoghi-Yazdi, H.: Emotional maps based on social network data to analyse the emotional structure of cities and measure their emotional similarity. Cities **86**, 113–124 (2019)
11. Galí, N., Donaire, J.A.: Tourists taking pictures: the long tail in tourists' perceived image of Barcelona. Curr. Issue Tour. **18**(9), 893–902 (2015)

12. Ryan, C., Cave, J.: Structuring destination image: A Qualitative Approach. J. Travel Res. **44**(2), 143–150 (2005)
13. Fatanti, M.N., Suyadnya, I.W.: Beyond User Gaze: How Instagram Creates Tourism Destination Brand? Procedia Soc. Behav. Sci. **211**, 1089–1095 (2015)
14. Munar, A.M., Jacobsen, J.K.S.: Motivations for sharing tourism experiences via social media. Tour. Manage. **43**, 46–54 (2014)
15. Gholamhosseinzadeh, M.S., Chapuis, J.M., Lehu, J.M.: Tourism netnography: How travel bloggers influence destination image. Tour. Recreat. Res. **48**(2), 188–204 (2023)
16. Silva, M.J.D.B., Farias, S.A., Grigg, M.K., Barbosa, M.D.L.D.A.: Online engagement and the role of digital influencers in product advocacy on Instagram. J. Relationship Market. **19**(2), 133-163 (2020)
17. Lorgeoux, C., Divakaran, P.K.: How Foreign Social Media Influencers Help Shape Destination Country's Tourism Image: The Case of South Korea's Tourism Image in France. Tour. Anal. **28**(2), 337–347 (2023)
18. Casaló, L.V., Flavián, C., Ibáñez-Sánchez, S.: Influencers on Instagram: Antecedents and consequences of opinion leadership. J. Bus. Res. **117**, 510–519 (2020)
19. Xu, X., Pratt, S.: Social media influencers as endorsers to promote travel destinations: an application of self-congruity theory to Chinese Generation Y. J. Travel Tour. Mark. **35**(7), 958–972 (2018)
20. Magno, F., Cassia, F.: The influence of social media influencers in tourism. Anatolia **29**(2), 288–290 (2018)
21. Hofstaetter, C., & Egger, R. (2009). The importance and use of weblogs for backpackers. In Information and communication technologies in tourism 2009 (pp. 99–110). Springer, Vienna
22. Breves, P.L., Liebers, N., Abt, M., Kunze, A.: The Perceived Fit between Instagram Influencers and the Endorsed Brand. J. Advert. Res. **59**(4), 440–454 (2019)
23. Egger R., Gumus O., Kaiumova E., Mükisch R., Surkic V. (2022) Destination Image of DMO and UGC on Instagram: A Machine-Learning Approach. In: Stienmetz J.L., Ferrer-Rosell B., Massimo D. (eds) Information and Communication Technologies in Tourism 2022. ENTER 2022. Springer, Cham
24. Wai Ng, F. (2019). Data Science Made Easy: Image Analytics using Orange. Towards data science. Retrieved from https://towardsdatascience.com/data-science-made-easy-image-analytics-using-orange-ad4af375ca7a
25. Gupta, S. (2020). Classification of arbitrary objects with a pre-trained CNN model. Towards data science. Retrieved from https://towardsdatascience.com/classify-any-object-using-pre-trained-cnn-model-77437d61e05f
26. Arefieva, V., Egger, R., Yu, J.: A machine learning approach to clustering destination images on Instagram. Tour. Manage. **85**, 104318 (2021)
27. Popat, S. K., Deshmukh P. B., & Metre, V. A. (2017). Hierarchical document clustering based on cosine similarity measure. 1st International Conference on Intelligent Systems and Information Management (ICISIM), pp. 153–159
28. Egger, R. (2022). Machine Learning in Tourism: A Brief Overview. Applied Data Science in Tourism, 85–107
29. Egger, R., Novak, J., Taurer, W.: Austria: Where tourism has tradition. Europea n Tourism Planning and Organisation Systems: The EU Member States **61**, 163–182 (2014)
30. Boerman, S.C.: The impact of standardized Instagram disclosure for micro- and meso-influencers. Comput. Hum. Behav. **103**, 199–207 (2020)
31. Rietveld, R., van Dolen, W., Mazloom, M., Worring, M.: What You Feel, Is What You Like Influence of Message Appeals on Customer Engagement on Instagram. J. Interact. Mark. **49**, 20–53 (2020)

Understanding Users' Perceptions of Travel Accounts on Instagram: Comparing DMO and Travel Influencer Accounts

Larissa Neuburger[1]([⊠]) [iD], Danielle Barbe[2] [iD], and Giancarlo Fedeli[1] [iD]

[1] IMC University of Applied Sciences Krems, Krems, Austria
{larissa.neuburger,giancarlo.fedeli}@fh-krems.ac.at
[2] Northumbria University, Newcastle, UK
danielle.barbe@northumbria.ac.uk

Abstract. Social Media has become an important marketing tool for destinations due to its easy access, ability to reach broad audiences and capacity to act as a form of eWOM. Instagram in particular is one of the most popular channels for the visual marketing of a destination as well as for influencer marketing. Through Instagram, DMOs can create travel inspiration, and enhance interest in a destination. This study seeks to understand the tourists' perceptions of Instagram influencers as well as official DMO accounts and looks on their influence on tourists' participation and engagement on social media. A quantitative survey was conducted to analyze users' perceptions of DMO and influencer accounts on Instagram, as well as their participation behavior online. The study found that DMOs are perceived as being more trustworthy and credible than travel influencers. In addition, results indicate that active Instagram users are more likely to have positive perceptions of travel influencers, but online participation does not influence perceptions of DMOs.

Keywords: Influencer Marketing · Social Media · Destination Marketing · Instagram · Social Media Marketing

1 Introduction

In the early 2000s, the introduction of Web 2.0 and social media allowed Internet users to engage with one another more easily. The popularity of social media grew significantly over the next several years, also transforming the way tourism organizations operate, communicate with, and market to consumers. Tourism, as an 'information-intensive industry' [1] that relies on positive word-of-mouth (WOM), particularly experienced the tremendous impact of social media. Social media changed the way tourists search for, obtain, share, and produce information about tourism businesses, destinations and their experiences [2]. To adapt to these changes, Destination Management Organizations (DMOs) adopted social media into their marketing practices [3]. Today, the majority of DMOs are active on at least one social media platform for marketing and management purposes [4].

© The Author(s) 2024
K. Berezina et al. (Eds.): ENTER 2024, SPBE, pp. 410–420, 2024.
https://doi.org/10.1007/978-3-031-58839-6_42

Studies reviewing the literature on social media and tourism have found that the research focus lies mostly on social media platforms such as Facebook, Twitter (recently renamed as "X"), and review platforms such as TripAdvisor [5–7]. While Facebook continues to be the most popular platform with 2.9 billion monthly active users [8], Instagram quickly surpassed Twitter in the number of active users in 2014 and continues to be in the fourth most popular platform world-wide, whereas Twitter is no longer in the top ten most used platforms [8].

Despite Instagram's growth and popularity, tourism scholars are only recently focusing on its importance [4]. The emphasis has been heavily on destination image [9–11], likely due to the platform's visual focus. Tourists use Instagram to share photos or videos of their travel experiences with others and DMOs have similarly adopted Instagram accounts and use the visual emphasis of the platform to promote the destination through photos and videos. Hence through Instagram, DMOs can engage prospective travelers when they are likely looking for ideas, catch them while they are looking for inspiration, and thus increase their interest in the destination, as well as influence their visit intentions [12].

Due to its capabilities for sharing photos as well as shorter videos (stories) and longer videos (reels) in different formats, Instagram has become one of the most popular platforms for influencer marketing [13, 14]. Influencer marketing involves the marketing and promotion of products or services on social media through content and messages spread by influential users [15]. Unlike endorsements from well-known celebrities, such as artists, bands, singers or athletes, influencer marketing focuses on recommendations from 'ordinary people' who became popular through their visibility and the content they share on social media [14, 16]. Also known as 'micro-celebrities' or 'digital influencers' due to their connections and influence on their followers, these individuals are perceived as more trustworthy than 'real' celebrities and hence can be seen as a relevant instrument for electronic Word-of-Mouth (eWOM) [13]. Influencers on Instagram in particular vary from thousands to millions of followers [14] and have become increasingly popular for tourism marketing.

The impact of Instagram influencers on a destination as well as their influence on tourists' travel intention and destination image, has been a recent focus of tourism research [17–19]. However, there is little discussion surrounding the perceptions of travel influencers and the comparative impacts between influencer and DMO accounts.

The purpose of this research is to explore the perception of travel influencers in comparison to official Instagram accounts of DMOs. By understanding users' perceptions, DMOs can better cater their content to followers', as well as collaborate with influencers to address areas where users are not interested in following DMO accounts. In addition, this study seeks to examine how users current Instagram usage behavior influencer their perceptions of these accounts.

2 Literature Review

2.1 Social Media Marketing

Through the integration of social media channels on mobile devices and the possibility for users to receive and also to produce content, social media channels, such as Instagram, have become a powerful tool in tourism marketing – especially as a representation for real travel experiences [9]. Social media can be defined as platforms that enable user-generated-content (UGC) facilitating the communication between users, without the influence of marketers [20].

As the tourism and hospitality industry deals with intangible services that are associated with a high risk of purchase, WOM is an influential factor of travel decision-making [21, 22]. WOM in general appears to be more influential on customers than traditional advertising campaigns [21]. On social media, eWOM has emerged as a tool for direct communication. Managing and encouraging positive eWOM can generate more revenue, reinforce a positive destination image and enhance business activity [22].

Early on, the tourism industry integrated UGC in their marketing strategy such as travel blogs [23, 24] or the use of testimonials or reviews of customers [20]. Many studies have verified the impact of online reviews on consumer behavior of tourists [25]. [26] indicated that online reviews about hotels could enhance the awareness, attitudes of travelers or even increase the number of bookings [27].

In 2010, [20] predicted social media to change how tourism businesses and suppliers market to and communicate with their customers. More than ten years later, tourism marketing has in fact been shaped by the power of UGC and users who gain their popularity solely from the creation of content on various social media channels – influencers. Brands must compete with these influencers for the attention of potential consumers or tourists. Hereby, companies or DMOs often hire or collaborate with influencers to appear in their popular social media channels and promote their products or destinations [28]. Instagram can be seen as the main platform for influencer marketing [29].

2.2 Instagram Marketing in Tourism

The popular visual social media channels such as Instagram, YouTube or TikTok have been successfully used in tourism marketing. As tourism marketing focuses mostly on visual content [30], social media channels play an important role as sources of inspiration for travel decisions and information search [20]. Also from the demand side, images and videos are essential for tourists to remember and share their travel experiences [31, 32].

Research shows that photos cannot only change the perception of consumers towards a certain product or service [33] but also can be memorized easier than just text – especially when it comes to tourism destinations [34]. Therefore, the social media platform Instagram, which is mainly focusing on pictures and 'stories', can be seen as an important tool for visual destination marketing. A photo of a destination posted on Instagram can influence the image of a destination through a first visual impression [35]. Moreover, the type of picture and the uniqueness of the posted photo can create emotions towards the destination [35].

In tourism, Instagram is particularly popular by millennials to post selfies and pictures of their holiday destination, hotel or restaurant. Thereby, the 'Insta-worthiness' or 'Instagrammability' – describing the aesthetic and unique features, which make a place 'worth a picture' for Instagram – has become a central factor to choose a certain destination, hotel or restaurant.

2.3 Influencer Marketing in Tourism

Influencers can be defined as individuals who gained popularity online through their content and self-branding [16] and are often perceived as "expert friends giving opinions on the latest products [or services] on the market" [29]. Through their large network of followers [36] influencers use their influential power to promote their lifestyle, opinion as well as products or services [14]. Although most influencers are paid by brands and marketers to communicate their recent or past experiences with products and services, their content is still perceived as eWOM. This can explain the success of influencer campaigns and the impact on consumer behavior and even purchase intention [13].

Tourists reporting their experiences about new destinations and travel routes has been included in tourism theories since the 1970s and 80s [37–39]. Similarly, travel bloggers have been used for marketing purposes since the early 2000s [40, 41]. Travel influencers can be seen as the new opinion leaders in the world of social media and their success can be explained by their followers' perceived authenticity, their intense engagement with their followers as well as the perceived relevance of their content [28].

Along with destinations, also hotels and other tourism suppliers are already working together with influencers. In that way, hotels and destinations can work together to reach their goals of growing business and enhancing the image of a destination.

Despite those successful examples, DMOs need to cautiously weigh the positive and negative outcomes prior to working with influencers to market their destination. As influencer marketing on Instagram is still a growing phenomenon, little research has been done to explore the perceptions of followers of certain Instagram accounts and how this relates to those of DMO accounts.

2.4 Perceptions of Online Sources

With influencer marketing gaining prominence in tourism, understanding how tourists evaluate the credibility of influencers is increasingly important. As the easy access to social media facilitates ubiquitous information, the level of quality of content and information as well as the credibility and trustworthiness of information sources varies across platforms [41].

Several studies have explored the perceived credibility of different online sources such as websites [42], advertisement [43], online reviews [44], travel blogs [41] or travel related UGC [45] and found that users trust and believe official sources as well as traditional WOM more than eWOM. One of the factors for these low levels of credibility and trustworthiness of online content, reviews and other UGC is the anonymity of the contributor of the content. Even when the source of the comment or the photo is visible, the user may have no personal relationship or connection with the content creator [46]. In this case, influencer marketing can overcome this issue as influencers not only promote products or services but also show their personality, lifestyle and opinions. Therefore, the followers can establish a connection with the content creator. Due to the higher authenticity of influencer campaigns when compared with traditional advertising, the level of credibility can increase [47].

Other literature shows that trustworthiness is an additional factor that is important for the influencer-follower relationship [48]. Thereby, influencers seem to be more trustworthy and credible than celebrities based on a study among young females [49]. The perception of social media channels as credible or trustworthy can be seen as crucial antecedents for the engagement of users in any kind of following or participation behavior with brands on social media [50]. Therefore, it is suggested that the perception of Instagram accounts influences the reasons and motivations to follow certain accounts.

This study focuses on the perception of Instagram users towards travel-related accounts managed by Instagram influencers and official DMOs. Furthermore, this study looks at the differences in users' perception of those accounts and how their Instagram usage behavior (participation) influences these perceptions. To achieve the purpose of this study, this research answers the following research questions:

1. How do Instagram users perceive DMOs on Instagram compared to travel influencers?
2. How does Instagram usage behavior (participation) influence the perceptions of travel-related accounts on Instagram?

3   Method

For this study and in order to answer the respective research questions, a quantitative research design using an online survey was conducted. The study was pilot tested using a convenience sample (N = 63) and the questions were adapted to the feedback. The final survey was distributed using the platform Amazon Mechanical Turk. The survey questions were all adopted from pre-validated studies for validity and reliability purposes. At the beginning of the survey, participants were asked if they use Instagram on a regular basis (minimum once a week) in order to screen out non-users. In addition, participants were asked if they follow any travel-related accounts on Instagram.

Depending on their answer, participants were asked to rate only those accounts that they follow: DMO (n = 139, 68.8%) and/or influencers (n = 186, 92.1%). Therefore, the sample size of results varies throughout the study. Only 9 respondents (4.5%) follow only DMO accounts, whereas 56 respondents (27.7%) follow only influencers. The majority of respondents (n = 130, 64.4%) follow both influencers and DMO accounts.

3.1   Measures

As the purpose of this study is to understand the perceptions of travel-related accounts on Instagram, the main measurement items include: demographics, perceptions and Instagram behavior and participation.

Perceptions. The perception of influencers or DMOs through their accounts on Instagram were derived from prior literature about celebrity endorsement and consists of the four constructs 'expertise', 'trustworthiness', 'attractiveness' and 'self-congruity' [51–53]. Based on the results from the pre-test, due to DMOs being an organization and not an individual, attractiveness and self-congruity were not examined when looking at the perceptions of the DMO.

The variables were assessed using 14 items and adapted to the Instagram context of the study. Expertise, trustworthiness and attractiveness are assessed on a 7-point semantic differential scale (e.g. non-expert/expert, dishonest/honest, plain/elegant). A 7-point Likert scale was used to measure self-congruity of the user with the Instagram influencer or the DMO. Cronbach's Alpha indicated the reliability of the constructs as following: expertise ($\alpha = .93$), trustworthiness ($\alpha = .87$), attractiveness ($\alpha = .86$) and self-congruity ($\alpha = .87$).

Participation. Few studies have been published or have been conducted about participation in online environments. In order to explore the behavior of users on Instagram, the participation scale from [54] about participation behavior in online communities was used for this study and adjusted to the context of Instagram. Participants were asked to rate their level of agreement on a 7-point Likert scale (1 = strongly disagree, 7 = strongly agree) with four items as follows: I participate actively on Instagram, I use to contribute to the conversation on Instagram, I usually provide useful information to other Instagram users and I post messages and responses on Instagram with great excitement and frequency. Again, Cronbach's Alpha was used to indicate the reliability of the construct participation on Instagram ($\alpha = .90$).

To enhance the clarity of the data analysis, three groups (low/medium/high Instagram participation) were created. Respondents with mean participation scores of 1.00 to 2.99 were categorized as 'low participation', those with mean participation scores of 3.00 to 4.99 were categorized as 'medium participation', and those with mean participation scores of about 5.00 were categorized as 'high participation'.

4 Results

4.1 Sample Description

The sample of this study consisted of N = 202 final participants. The average study participant was at the age of 32 (M = 32.33, SD = 8.70), with most participants were younger than 30 (46.0%). Although the sample was specified on MTurk to those who are US residents, 25.9 per cent indicated they currently do not live in the US. Nearly half (48.5%) of participants have an undergraduate degree (48.5%), and 19.3 per cent have at least some college education. Most participants have an income of below $60,000 (55,4%). While only 18.9% of participants have their own passport, 17.8% of participants stated that they have never traveled outside of the US.

4.2 RQ1: How Do Instagram Users Perceive DMOs on Instagram Compared to Travel Influencers?

The respondents' perceptions of influencers were generally high, with expertise, trustworthiness, and attractiveness each above a mean of 5 out of 7 on the Likert-scale ratings, indicating that influencers were perceived as experts, being trustworthy, and attractive.

However, self-congruity with influencers was not as high (M = 4.68, SD = 1.30). The respondents' perceptions of DMO accounts were even greater than the influencers, with mean expertise and trustworthiness greater than 6.05.

A t-test was conducted to test whether the differences in perceptions between influencers and DMOs were statistically significant. Perceived expertise was significantly greater for DMOs (M = 6.05, SD = 1.12) than influencer accounts (M = 5.55, SD = 1.20): t(323) = −3.830, p < 0.000. Similarly, perceived trustworthiness was significantly greater for DMOs (M = 6.06, SD = 1.17) than influencer accounts (M = 5.71, SD = 1.17): t(323) = −2.703, p = 0.007.

4.3 RQ2: How Does Participation Influence the Perceptions of Travel-Related Accounts on Instagram?

ANOVA was used to examine whether the level of participation respondents have on Instagram influenced their perceptions of influencers and DMOs (Table 1). There was a statistically significant difference between groups of different participation levels (low/medium/high) for all perception variables for influencers. Homogeneity assumption was violated for influencer expertise, therefore Welch was used to evaluating significance (F(2,57.59) = 7.19, p = 0.002). The Tamhane post-hoc test revealed that those with high participation on Instagram perceived influencers as having significantly greater expertise than those with low (p = 0.031) or medium (p = 0.009) participation.

Table 1. Instagram Participation and Perceptions of Accounts

		Influencer			DMO		
		Low	Medium	High	Low	Medium	High
Expertise	MEAN	4.99	5.29	5.86	6.02	5.79	6.20
	SD	1.51	1.27	0.95	1.02	1.31	0.99
Trust	MEAN	5.46	5.40	5.97	3.48	4.38	5.19
	SD	1.33	1.08	1.13	1.20	1.13	1.16
Attractiveness	MEAN	5.59	5.41	5.89			
	SD	1.14	1.02	1.02			
Self-Congruity	MEAN	3.48	4.38	5.19			
	SD	1.20	1.13	1.16			

Tukey post-hoc tests were used to evaluate the results for trustworthiness (F(2,183) = 5.49, p = 0.005), attractiveness (F(2,183) = 4.63, p = 0.015), and self-congruity (F(2,183) = 25.08, p = 0.000), and found that those with high participation perceived influencers as being significantly more trustworthy (p = 0.006), attractive (p = 0.012), and self-congruent (p = 0.000) than those with medium participation. Self-congruity perceptions were also significantly different between those with low and high participation (p = 0.000) and low and medium participation (p = 0.004), whereby the greater the participation on Instagram the more the respondents feel that influencers are similar to them. Unlike influencer perceptions, participation on Instagram did not significantly affect the perceptions of DMO accounts.

5 Discussion and Conclusion

Despite the influx of influencer marketing and the research stating that influencers provide a greater ROI due to eWOM [13], the perceptions of DMO accounts on Instagram were significantly greater than perceptions of influencers in regard to expertise and trustworthiness. This indicates that respondents are aware that DMOs are experts on the destination, more so than a travel influencer. However, other factors could be more critical for influencers, such as their relatability.

As discussed previously, although DMOs are considered to be experts and more trustworthy, influencers may be more impactful because they are deemed more relatable. In the literature on celebrity endorsement, consumers were found to prefer brands with personalities congruent to their own [55]. Instagram influencers create their own self-brand through what they share on Instagram [56], and therefore Instagram users follow influencers who portray a lifestyle most similar to their own.

Finally, this study found that the level of participation predicts perceptions of influencers. This finding is somewhat intuitive as active Instagram users are likely to have greater perceptions of influencers they follow and engage more actively with. However, participation does not affect the perceptions of DMOs, perhaps as they are already perceived to be experts on their destination.

The theoretical implications of this study go beyond filling the gap in the literature on users' perceptions of travel-related accounts and provide a stepping stone to theory development on the unique phenomenon of influencer marketing in tourism. Understanding the differential perceptions of influencers and how these perceptions are stronger for active Instagram users, can inform researchers as to how consumer behavior influences opinions of online sources.

This study also increases knowledge of the industry, particularly for destination managers looking to understand influencer marketing. Influencer marketing can be an effective strategy for driving potential visitors to the DMOs Instagram pages, increasing awareness of the DMO. However, once the DMO has established an Instagram audience, influencer marketing may not prove as effective as influencers are not perceived as being as trustworthy and knowledgeable about the destination as the official DMO account.

A limitation of this study includes the use of Amazon's Mechanical Turk. Despite pretests, attention checks and open-ended questions to improve the quality of the data, it cannot be ensured that all participants filled out the questionnaire with due diligence. However, the data was filtered for double answers or IP addresses and invalid answers. Furthermore, research on Instagram and influencers is still emerging, especially as it relates to tourism, which presented itself as both a limitation and an opportunity. While this study provided insights into users' perception of travel influencers on Instagram, future research should consider whether these perceptions influence users' visit intentions, and if these findings are similar for different influencer platforms, such as TikTok.

References

1. Gretzel, U., Yuan, Y.L., Fesenmaier, D.R.: Preparing for the new economy: advertising strategies and change in destination marketing organizations. J. Travel Res. **39**(2), 146–156 (2000)
2. Sigala, M., Christou, E., Gretzel, U.: Social Media in Travel, Tourism and Hospitality: Theory, Practice and Cases. Ashgate Publishing Ltd, Surrey (2012)
3. Hays, S., Page, S.J., Buhalis, D.: Social media as a destination marketing tool: its use by national tourism organisations. Curr. Issue Tour. **16**(3), 211–239 (2013)
4. Uşaklı, A., Koç, B., Sönmez, S.: Social media usage among top European DMOs. In: Kozak, N., Kozak, M. (eds.) Tourist Destination Management: Instruments, Products, and Case Studies, pp. 1–14. Springer International Publishing, Cham (2019). https://doi.org/10.1007/978-3-030-16981-7_1
5. Chu, S.C., Deng, T., Cheng, H.: The role of social media advertising in hospitality, tourism and travel: a literature review and research agenda. Int. J. Contemp. Hosp. Manag. **32**(11), 3419–3438 (2020)
6. Lu, Y., Chen, Z., Law, R.: Mapping the progress of social media research in hospitality and tourism management from 2004 to 2014. J. Travel Tour. Mark. **35**(2), 102–118 (2018)
7. Nusair, K., Butt, I., Nikhashemi, S.R.: A bibliometric analysis of social media in hospitality and tourism research. Int. J. Contemp. Hosp. Manag. **31**(7), 2601–2719 (2019)
8. Statista: Ranking der größten Social Networks und Messenger nach der Anzahl der Nutzer im Januar (2023). https://de.statista.com/statistik/daten/studie/181086/umfrage/die-weltweit-groessten-social-networks-nach-anzahl-der-user/. Accessed 17 Aug 2023
9. Fatanti, M.N., Suyadnya, I.W.: Beyond user gaze: How Instagram creates tourism destination brand? Procedia Soc. Behav. Sci. **211**, 1089–1095 (2015)
10. Nixon, L., Popova, A., Önder, I.: How instagram influences visual destination image: a case study of Jordan and Costa Rica. In: Proceedings of ENTER2017 eTourism Conference, Rome, Italy (2017)
11. Shuqair, S., & Cragg, P.: The immediate impact of Instagram posts on changing the viewers' perceptions towards travel destinations. In: Proceedings of 1st International Conference on Advanced Research (ICAR-2017), Manama, Bahrain (2017)
12. Barbe, D., Neuburger, L., Pennington-Gray, L.: Follow us on Instagram! Understanding the driving force behind following travel accounts on Instagram. E-review Tourism Res. **17**(4), (2020)
13. Evans, N.J., Phua, J., Lim, J., Jun, H.: Disclosing Instagram influencer advertising: the effects of disclosure language on advertising recognition, attitudes, and behavioral intent. J Interact. Advert., 1–12 (2017)
14. Del Rowe, S.: Tapping into social's sphere of influence. CRM Mag. **22**(1), 26–30 (2018)
15. Carter, D.: Hustle and Brand: the sociotechnical shaping of influence. Soc. Media + Soc. **2**(3), 1–12 (2016)
16. Khamis, S., Ang, L., Welling, R.: Self-branding, 'micro-celebrity' and the rise of Social Media Influencers. Celebrity Stud. **8**(2), 191–208 (2017)
17. Chatzigeorgiou, C.: Modelling the impact of social media influencers on behavioural intentions of millennials: the case of tourism in rural areas in Greece. J. Tourism, Heritage Serv. Market. **3**(2), 25–29 (2017)
18. Ong, Y.X., Ito, N.: "I Want to Go There Too!" Evaluating social media influencer marketing effectiveness: a case study of Hokkaido's DMO. In: Pesonen, J., Neidhardt, J. (eds.) Information and Communication Technologies in Tourism 2019, pp. 132–144. Springer, Cham (2019). https://doi.org/10.1007/978-3-030-05940-8_11

19. Suciati, P., Maulidiyanti, M., Lusia, A.: Cultivation effect of tourism TV program and influencer's Instagram account on the intention of traveling. In: Proceedings of the 1st International Conference on Social Sciences (ICSS), Jakarta, Indoesia (2018)
20. Xiang, Z., Gretzel, U.: Role of social media in online travel information search. Tour. Manage. **31**(2), 179–188 (2010)
21. Bansal, H.S., Voyer, P.A.: Word-of-mouth processes within a services purchase decision context. J. Serv. Res. **3**(2), 166–177 (2000)
22. Litvin, S.W., Goldsmith, R.E., Pan, B.: Electronic word-of-mouth in hospitality and tourism management. Tour. Manage. **29**(3), 458–468 (2008)
23. Pan, B., MacLaurin, T., Crotts, J.C.: Travel blogs and the implications for destination marketing. J. Travel Res. **46**(1), 35–45 (2007)
24. Lin, Y.S., Huang, J.Y.: Internet blogs as a tourism marketing medium: a case study. J. Bus. Res. **59**, 1201–1205 (2006)
25. Gretzel, U., Yoo, K.H.: Use and impact of online travel reviews. In: O'Connor, P., Höpken, W., Gretzel, U. (Eds.) Information and Communication Technologies in Tourism vol. 2008, pp. 35–46 (2018)
26. Vermeulen, I.E., Seegers, D.: Tried and tested: the impact of online hotel reviews on consumer consideration. Tour. Manage. **30**(1), 123–127 (2009)
27. Ye, Q., Law, R., Gu, B.: The impact of online user reviews on hotel room sales. Int. J. Hosp. Manag. **28**(1), 180–182 (2009)
28. Gretzel, U.: Influencer marketing in travel and tourism. In: Sigala, M., Gretzel, U., (Eds.) Advances in Social Media for Travel, Tourism and Hospitality, pp. 147–156. Routledge (2017)
29. Activate. Double or Nothing: Betting Big on Influencer Marketing. State of Influencer Marketing Study. https://static1.squarespace.com/static/5a9ffc57fcf7fd301e0e9928/t/5c7 fd9c9f4e1fcc96b896b7e/1551882706715/ACTIVATE+2019+Influencer+Marketing+Study. pdf. Accessed 23 Oct 2023
30. Beeton, S.: Rural tourism in Australia – has the gaze altered? Tracking rural images through film and tourism promotion. Int. J. Tour. Res. **6**(3), 125–135 (2004)
31. Munar, A.M., Jacobsen, J.K.S.: Motivations for sharing tourism experiences through social media. Tour. Manage. **43**, 46–54 (2014)
32. Stepchenkova, S., Zhan, F.: Visual destination images of Peru: comparative content analysis of DMO and user-generated photography. Tour. Manage. **36**, 590–601 (2013)
33. Kim, M., Lennon, S.: The effects of visual and verbal information on attitudes and purchase intentions in internet shopping. Psychol. Mark. **25**(2), 146–178 (2008)
34. Babin, L.A., Burns, A.C., Biswas, A.: A framework providing direction for research on communications effects of mental imagery-evoking advertising strategies. Adv. Consum. Res. **19**(1), 621–628 (1992)
35. Hanan, H., Putit, N.: Express marketing of tourism destinations using Instagram in social media networking. In: Zainal, A. (ed.) Hospitality and Tourism: Synergizing Creativity and Innovation in Research, pp. 471–474. CRC Press (2013). https://doi.org/10.1201/b16064-93
36. De Veirman, M., Cauberghe, V., Hudders, L.: Marketing through Instagram influencers: the impact of number of followers and product divergence on brand attitude. Int. J. Advert. **36**(5), 798–828 (2017)
37. Cohen, E.: Toward a sociology of international tourism. Soc. Res. **39**, 164–182 (1972)
38. Plog, S.C.: Why destination areas rise and fall in popularity. Cornell Hotel Rest. Adm. Q. **14**(4), 55–58 (1974)
39. Butler, R.W.: The concept of a tourist area cycle of evolution: implications for management of resources. Can. Geographer/Le Géographe canadien **24**(1), 5–12 (1980)
40. Glover, P.: Celebrity endorsement in tourism advertising: effects on destination image. J. Hosp. Tour. Manag. **16**, 16–23 (2009)

41. Mack, R.W., Blose, J.E., Pan, B.: Believe it or not: credibility of blogs in tourism. J. Vacat. Mark. **14**(2), 133–144 (2008)
42. Freeman, K.S., Spyridakis, J.H.: An examination of factors that affect the credibility of online health information'. Tech. Commun. **51**(2), 239–263 (2004)
43. Greer, J.D.: Evaluating the credibility of online information: a test of source and advertising influence. Mass Commun. Soc. **6**(1), 11–28 (2003)
44. Hyung-Park, D., Lee, J., Han, I.: The effect of online consumer reviews on consumer purchase intention: the moderating role of involvement. Int. J. Electron. Commer. **11**(4), 125–148 (2007)
45. Cox, C., Burgess, S., Sellitto, C., Buultjens, J.: The role of user-generated content in tourists' travel planning behavior. J. Hosp. Market. Manag. **18**(8), 743–764 (2009)
46. Leung, D., Law, R., Van Hoof, H., Buhalis, D.: Social media in tourism and hospitality: a literature review. J. Travel Tour. Mark. **30**(1–2), 3–22 (2013)
47. De Vries, L., Gensler, S., Leeflang, P.S.H.: Popularity of brand posts on brand fan pages: an investigation of the effects of social media marketing. J. Interact. Mark. **26**(2), 83–91 (2012)
48. Lou, C., Yuan, S.: Influencer marketing: how message value and credibility affect consumer trust of branded content on social media. J. Interact. Advert. **19**(1), 58–73 (2019)
49. Djafarova, E., Rushworth, C.: Exploring the credibility of online celebrities' Instagram profiles in influencing the purchase decisions of young female users. Comput. Hum. Behav. **68**, 1–7 (2017)
50. Tsai, W.H.S., Men, L.R.: Motivations and antecedents of consumer engagement with brand pages on social networking sites. J. Interact. Advert. **13**(2), 76–87 (2013)
51. Ohanian, R.: Construction and validation of a scale to measure celebrity endorsers' perceived expertise, trustworthiness, and attractiveness. J. Advert. **19**(3), 39–52 (1990)
52. Van der Veen, R., Song, H.: Impact of the perceived image of celebrity endorsers on tourists' intentions to visit. J. Travel Res. **53**(2), 211–224 (2014)
53. Wang, S., Yu, E.: China's record-breaking glass bridge closes. https://www.cnn.com/travel/article/china-zhangjiajie-glass-bridge-closed/index.html. Accessed 23 Oct 2023
54. Casaló, L.V., Flavián, C., Guinalíu, M.: Antecedents and consequences of consumer participation in on-line communities: the case of the travel sector. Int. J. Electron. Commer. **15**(2), 137–167 (2010)
55. Aaker, J.L.: Brand Personality: Conceptualization, Measurement and Underlying Psychological Mechanisms. UMI, Ann Arbor (1995)
56. Eagar, T., Dann, S.: Classifying the narrated# selfie: genre typing human-branding activity. Eur. J. Mark. **50**(9/10), 1835–1857 (2016)

Influencers and Tourism: Story of a Recent and Revolutionary Phenomenon: What Does Bibliometric Analysis Reveal

Soufiane Benhaida[1]([✉]), Larbi Safaa[1], and Dalia Perkumiené[2]

[1] Higher School of Technology, Cadi Ayyad University, 40000 Essaouira, Morocco
s.benhaida.ced@uca.ac.ma
[2] Faculty of Bioeconomic Development, Vytautas Magnus University, 53361 Kaunas, Lithuania

Abstract. The field of tourism has recently undergone a revolutionary transformation, driven by the rapid expansion of digital platforms and the simultaneous rise of influencer culture. The convergence of these factors has led to a noticeable realignment in how tourists perceive travel destinations. Influencers now play a central role, leveraging genuine and superficial credibility and expertise in specific domains. This phenomenon has captured the attention of scholars, practitioners, and policymakers, catalyzing a wave of research aimed at delving into the multifaceted intersection of influencers and tourism. This article presents a comprehensive bibliometric analysis to examine the scholarly output related to influencers and tourism over the past decade. This methodology provides a comprehensive overview, unveiling an abundant and diverse work. The study identifies 196 articles published between 2005 and 2023, involving 504 authors across 123 journals. Cluster analyses highlight a dynamic and nuanced recomposition of subthemes, reflective of an evolving reality in the making.

Keywords: Influencers · Tourism · Tourist Destination · Social Networks · Bibliometric Analysis

1 Introduction

The integration of new technologies has brought about substantial changes in consumer preferences across various service industries, with the tourism sector being particularly impacted. The influence of digital technologies on tourist destinations is profound, challenging traditional economic and societal norms and reshaping the conventional perception of the tourism landscape [1]. This highlights the importance of destinations adapting to effectively manage their online presence, real-world reputation, and health and safety concerns [2]. The transformation potential of digital technologies in the tourism sector, including content distribution, the shift towards digital tourism offerings, and the restructuring of the value chain, is especially noteworthy [3]. Notably, these digital tools and platforms empower local service providers and destinations by enabling them to create and disseminate their digital content, granting them a level of autonomy [3].

© The Author(s) 2024
K. Berezina et al. (Eds.): ENTER 2024, SPBE, pp. 421–433, 2024.
https://doi.org/10.1007/978-3-031-58839-6_43

In summary, digital technologies have brought about significant transformations in the tourism industry, challenging traditional norms and opening up new opportunities for businesses and destinations [1]. However, these advancements have also given rise to challenges, including the need for businesses to adapt their models to align with 21st-century marketing strategies, particularly in the realm of digital marketing [4]. One such emerging strategy is influencer marketing, which involves collaborating with social media influencers to promote tourist destinations and experiences. It's noteworthy that the tourism literature does not always treat influencer studies as a distinct and separate domain [5].

The growing intersection of influencers and tourism has become a central focus in tourism studies. With the rapid expansion of digital platforms and social media, tourists now seek inspiration and advice through these channels, significantly impacting their behaviors [6–8]. Consequently, more tourist destinations are collaborating with influencers for promotional campaigns, selecting them based on their orientations, target demographics, and the desired image they wish to convey to travellers [9, 10].

To understand this complex research landscape, we employ bibliometric analysis as a valuable tool for mapping emerging research domains. This systematic analysis reveals trends, influential works, and evolving themes in influencer tourism research, emphasizing its interdisciplinary nature.

2 Literature Review

The concept of an influencer refers to an individual who possesses significant credibility, expertise, or social authority within a specific domain or industry. Influencers have the power to sway the opinions, behaviors, and purchasing decisions of those who follow them, primarily through their digital presence on platforms such as social media, blogs, vlogs, and more. This impact often stems from the perception of their sincerity, reliability, and the trust they have built with their audience over time [11]. The volume editors, usually the program chairs, will be your main points of contact for the preparation of the volume. The evolution of the influencer concept has resulted in the categorization of influencers into various types based on factors like follower count, specialization, and brand associations [12]. These influencer categories include macro-influencers, known for their wide reach and strong reputation; mega-influencers, typically celebrities with an even larger following; micro-influencers, who may have a smaller reach but boast high engagement rates; nano-influencers, known for their limited yet authentic reach; and advisers, specializing in particular domains. Micro-influencers often prioritize niche audiences with heightened engagement, while macro-influencers and celebrities aim for broader exposure. Furthermore, influencers specialize in diverse areas such as fashion, beauty, travel, fitness, and technology, depending on their personal passions and expertise [13]. This categorization highlights the diversity within the influencer landscape, each type serving different purposes in influencing consumer behavior and shaping various industries, including tourism.

The intricate relationship between tourism and influencers has garnered significant attention from researchers. In the contemporary digital landscape, the prominent role of influencers in the tourism industry has prompted scholars to delve deeply into this phenomenon. Influencers' ability to forge authentic connections with their audience through personalized narratives, genuine experiences, and visually appealing content has redefined conventional destination marketing and revolutionized consumer engagement strategies [14]. This shift underscores the transformative impact of influencers on the tourism sector, prompting extensive scholarly exploration to understand their role, influence, and implications.

Research has unveiled several key themes within the realm of tourism and influencers. These encompass diverse areas such as the impact of influencers on sustainable tourism, the integration of influencers into digital marketing strategies, the role of trust in consumer travel decisions, the growth of research into tourism forecasting using various prediction models and online data, and the analysis of pro-environmental behaviors in the tourism and hospitality sector. These subjects shed light on the multifaceted interplay between influencers and tourism, highlighting their influence and strategies on one side and consumer decision-making mechanisms and ethical and environmental considerations on the other.

3 Materials and Methods

3.1 Bibliometrie

In this study, a bibliometric analysis was conducted to quantify and measure the impact of research findings. Bibliometrics involves a quantitative analysis of scholarly publications, including articles, books, and conference proceedings, with the aim of evaluating research influence [15]. It utilizes statistical methods to dissect patterns and trends within the scientific literature, including citation analysis, co-citation analysis, and bibliographic coupling [16]. Additionally, bibliometrics serves as a tool to assess individual researchers, research groups, institutions, and countries in terms of productivity and impact [15], while also identifying emerging research domains and collaboration networks [16].

Bibliometric mapping, increasingly utilized across various disciplines, has gained prominence [17], potentially due to its synergy with scientific mapping [18]. The comprehensive bibliometric mapping analysis conducted in this study encompassed data collection, filtering, extraction, analysis, and processing.

3.2 Data Collection and Search Strategy

To retrieve relevant articles, we utilized the globally recognized Scopus database for assessing scientific production [19]. Data extraction took place on August 16, 2023. The search term "influencers and tourism" was queried across all indexers in the Scopus collection. Peer-reviewed articles, written in English, and published in indexed scientific journals were retained based on eligibility criteria. The initial query generated 208 document results. These results were filtered to eliminate non-relevant items according to the eligibility criteria.

TITLE-ABS-KEY ("influencers" AND "tourism") AND (EXCLUDE (LANGUAGE , "Spanish") OR EXCLUDE (LANGUAGE , "Portuguese") OR EXCLUDE (LANGUAGE , "German") OR EXCLUDE (LANGUAGE , "French")).

After meticulous application of inclusion and exclusion criteria, a total of 196 relevant data points were collected. The analysis focused on articles containing the keyword "influencers and tourism" in titles, abstracts, or keywords.

3.3 Data Analysis and Visualization

In our quantitative bibliometric research, we harnessed the open-source bibliometrix R-package developed by Aria and Cuccurullo [18]. This comprehensive package offers diverse tools for bibliometric analysis, including statistical and scientific mapping algorithms. It also includes Biblioshiny, a user-friendly web interface introduced in version 2.0, facilitating data input from sources like Scopus or Web of Science into formats like BibTex, CSV, or Plain Text. For our bibliometric analysis, we followed Donthu et al.'s (2021) framework [20]. Firstly, we conducted performance analysis to dissect the contributions of various research entities, including authors, institutions, countries, and journals, within this dynamic field [21]. Key parameters such as total publications (TP), academic publications (TP-A), industry publications (TP-I), publications from university-industry collaboration (TP-AI), and author count allowed us to assess productivity, impact, and collaboration dynamics, providing a nuanced understanding of research entity significance and performance[21, 22].

Moreover, we employed scientific mapping, a pivotal technique in bibliometric analysis, to portray the intricate web of relationships and connections among research components in the influencers and tourism domain [21]. This technique, providing a comprehensive view of the intellectual structure and knowledge domains, encompasses methodologies like citation analysis, co-citation analysis, bibliographic coupling, co-word analysis, and co-authorship analysis [23]. Often integrated with network analysis, these methods yielded visually intuitive representations like maps, graphs, or clusters, delivering invaluable insights into the structural dynamics and trends within the influencers and tourism research field. Table 1 provides an overview of the dataset, outlining the various document types included.

4 Results

4.1 Performance Analysis

This bibliometric study revealed a corpus of 196 publications, involving a total of 506 authors. Among these publications, there are journal articles (n = 129), conference papers (n = 27), reviews (n = 1), book chapters (n = 21), full-length books (n = 3), epistolary contributions in the form of letters (n = 3) and notes (n = 3), a singular case of retracted work, and a complete conference report.

In this study, we embark on a chronological journey, revealing the inception of research on mobile learning in 2005. However, the true focal point of our analysis lies in the significant upsurge in scholarly production after 2019. This increase notably intensified in 2022 (n = 46) and in 2023 (up to August 8, 2023) with a remarkable count of 43 publications. These findings shed light on the evolving landscape of research on the concept of influencers in the field of tourism over time.

Table 1. Main information about data.

Description	Results
MAIN INFORMATION ABOUT DATA	
Timespan	2005:2023
Sources (Journals, Books, etc.)	124
Documents	196
Annual Growth Rate %	23,24
Document Average Age	2,54
Average citations per doc	12,31
References	1
AUTHORS	
Authors	506
Authors of single-authored docs	23

In recent years, researchers' interest in influencers and their impact on the tourism sector has significantly escalated. This growing interest underscores the increasing importance of influencer marketing, which has become a highly effective strategy for enhancing the visibility of travel businesses and encouraging tourists to explore new destinations [24, 25]. This paradigm shift reflects a strong alignment with the evolving preferences and behaviors of modern tourists, who increasingly rely on influencer content for inspiration and travel decision-making [24]. In fact, our results illuminate the dynamic evolution of the "influencers" concept in tourism literature.

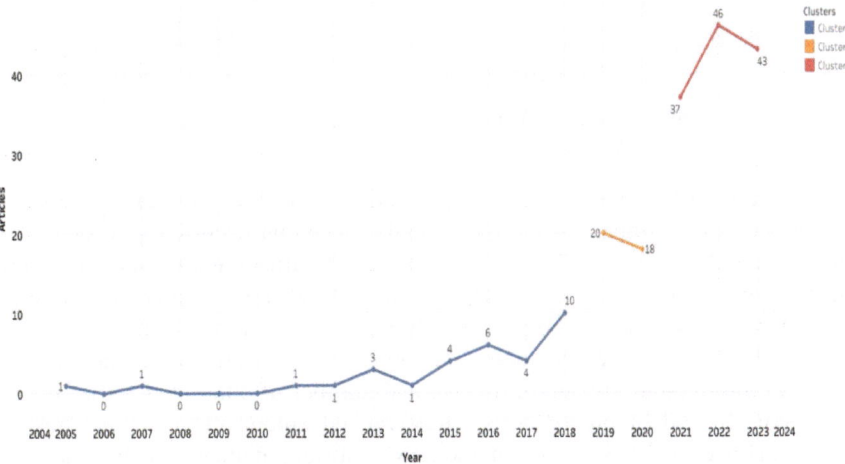

Fig. 1. Evolution of Research Interest Over Time.

Figure 1 provides a comprehensive overview of the research interest in the topic during three distinct periods. Initially, from 2005 to 2018, research activity experienced relatively slow growth, with the number of publications per year gradually increasing from a modest 1 to a modest 10. Next, the second period, spanning from 2019 to 2020, witnessed a moderate resurgence in interest, with the number of publications reaching 18 and 20, respectively. Finally, the most recent third period, from 2021 to 2023, saw an extraordinary peak in interest and engagement with the topic, as evidenced by the number of publications exceeding 40 per year. This three-phase evolution underscores the increasing significance and dynamism of the field over time.

Figure 2 illustrates the correlation between average citation rates and the number of publications for certain years within the study period (2005–2019). It highlights intriguing patterns where distinct peaks in average citations are associated with varying numbers of publications. Notably, in 2005 and 2011, a single publication garnered attention, resulting in average citations of 43 and 11, respectively. In contrast, in 2013, three publications achieved an average of 53.33 citations, indicating a set of high-impact research. Similarly, in 2018 and 2019, substantial averages of 33.80 and 32.45 citations, respectively, were aligned with 18 and 19 publications, indicating an increase in research production and its influence.

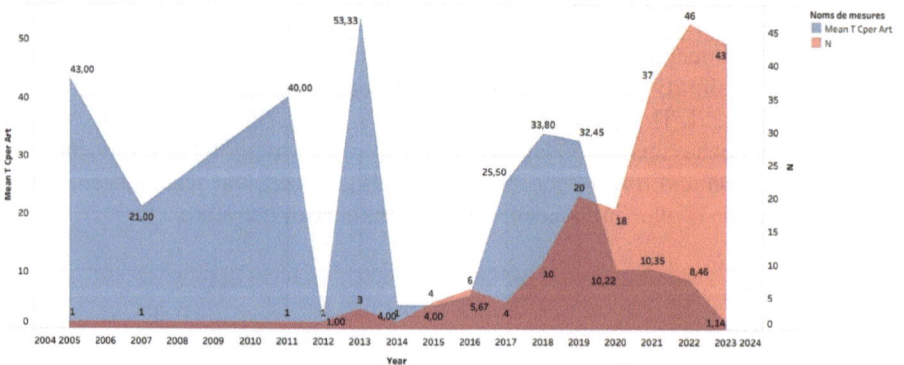

Fig. 2. Average Citations vs. Number of Publications.

Fluctuations in the average number of citations over the years are closely tied to the publication of significant articles, especially those that occupy top positions in the list of most-cited documents. This relationship can be illustrated by specific examples in our dataset. In 2005, for instance, Debbie Easterling's article emerged as one of the most-cited documents in our corpus. Similarly, in 2013, Tom Griffin's article stood out as the "third most-cited document." The publication of this influential work in the field had a considerable impact on the average number of citations for that year [26]. In 2018, Xu Xu and Stephen Pratt's article ranked among the top three most-cited documents. However, 2018 was also marked by a substantial increase in the total number of publications [26]. Therefore, while the presence of highly-cited articles continued to influence the average number of citations, the larger volume of publications exerted a counter-effect. A similar trend was observed in 2019, where the publication of significant articles contributed to a notable average number of citations. However, the increase in the number of publications that year again played a role in the overall average. This highlights the dynamic interaction between important articles that rank well in citation lists and the total number of publications, both of which collectively influence the average number of citations in a given year, thus underscoring the complex nature of scholarly impact and the multiple factors contributing to citation patterns in academic research.

Figure 3 provides an overview of key academic sources that have significantly contributed to the discourse on influencers and tourism. Notably, "Current Issues in Tourism" emerges as the predominant contributor with 15 related publications. Close behind is "Sustainability (Switzerland)" with 9 articles, followed by "Springer Proceedings in Business and Economics" with 8 publications. Several other journals have also played substantial roles in advancing research in this domain, including "Journal of Travel Research" and "Smart Innovation, Systems and Technologies," both with 5 publications. Furthermore, "Developments in Marketing Science: Proceedings of the Academy of Marketing Science," "Journal of Hospitality and Tourism Management," and "International Journal of Contemporary Hospitality Management" each published 4 articles. These diverse sources collectively reflect the interdisciplinary nature of influencers and tourism research, underscoring the growing academic and industry interest in this field.

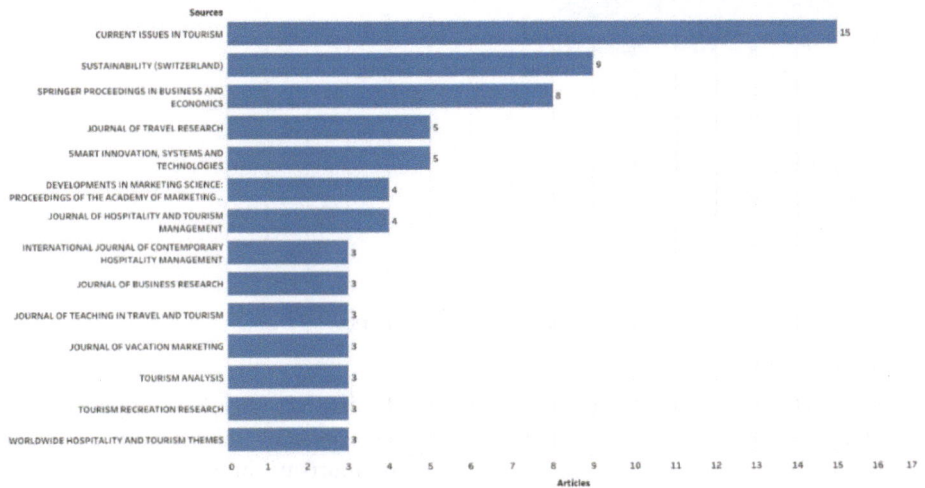

Fig. 3. Most relevant sources.

4.2 Science Mapping

Certainly, the mention of "NA NA" in Figure 4 as the most prolific author with 8 publications likely indicates that these publications are conference papers rather than journal articles or other types of scholarly works. This is a common practice in bibliometric analyses, where the author's names are anonymized or represented by placeholders like "NA NA" when the specific author information is not available or not disclosed, especially in the case of conference papers. So, in this context, "NA NA" is a representation of one or more authors who have contributed a significant number of conference papers to the field of influencers and tourism. Remarkably, all of these contributions take the form of conference papers, underscoring a significant presence in academic conferences dedicated to this topic. Following closely are authors such as C. Francalanci and A. Hussain, each with 4 publications, who have played pivotal roles in advancing the discourse on influencers and their impact on the tourism industry. Additionally, prominent researchers like U. Gretzel, P. Kumar, and AS Aloudat have each contributed to three publications, demonstrating their ongoing commitment to this rapidly evolving field of study. Collectively, these leading authors have significantly influenced the academic landscape of influencers and tourism, providing diverse perspectives and insights through a range of publication types, thus promoting an interdisciplinary and multidimensional approach to this dynamic field.

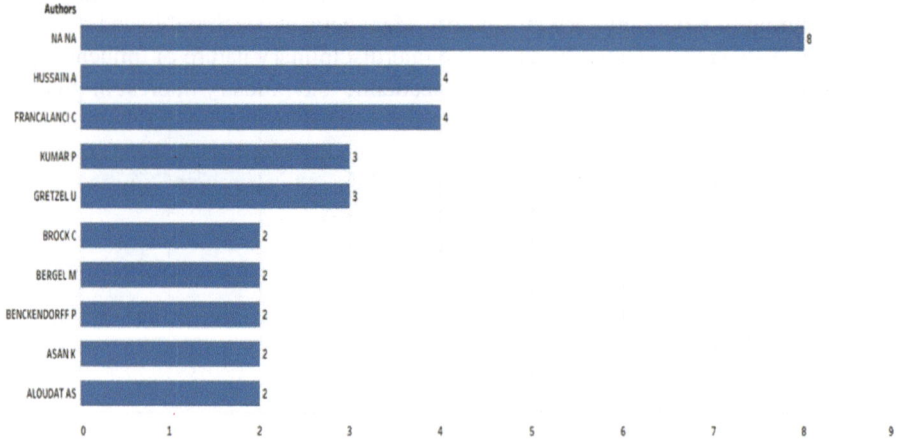

Fig. 4. Leading authors.

Figure 5 reveals the most frequent keywords in the field of research on influencers and tourism, providing valuable insights into the primary areas of interest in this domain. At the forefront are the words "social media" and "tourism," highlighting the central role of digital platforms in the context of the tourism industry. The term "marketing" closely follows, underscoring the crucial role played by influencer marketing in promoting tourist destinations. Additionally, keywords such as "perception," "tourist behavior," and "decision-making" emphasize the intricate exploration of tourist preferences and decision-making processes. In particular, the presence of terms like "China" and "Covid-19" underscores the significant impact of global events on this dynamic field. In summary, these keywords collectively encompass the diverse facets and multidisciplinary nature of research on influencers and tourism.

Our thematic analysis of documents published in the field of influencers and tourism reveals a diverse range of key themes. Figure 6 provides an overview of these foundational themes that form the basis of research, encompassing concepts such as "tourism," "influencer," "influencer marketing," "Instagram," "social media," "influencers," and the evolving impact of "Covid-19." These themes serve as cornerstones upon which much of the discourse rests. Within this thematic framework, certain driving themes have gained prominence, shaping the course of research. In particular, "destination image" and "digital influencers" emerge as dynamic drivers, reflecting their essential roles in contemporary tourism dynamics. Concurrently, several niche themes have carved out a place, adding depth and specificity to discussions. Themes such as "digital marketing," "netnography," "China," and "social media influencers" correspond to specialized areas of interest and research. In this evolving context, the analysis identifies themes that are either on the rise or declining. "Social media influencers" appear as a burgeoning area of interest, reflecting the increasing importance of this subset within the broader context of influencers and tourism. This thematic mapping illustrates the multiple facets of research on influencers and tourism, with different themes intersecting and evolving, thereby enriching our understanding of this dynamic field.

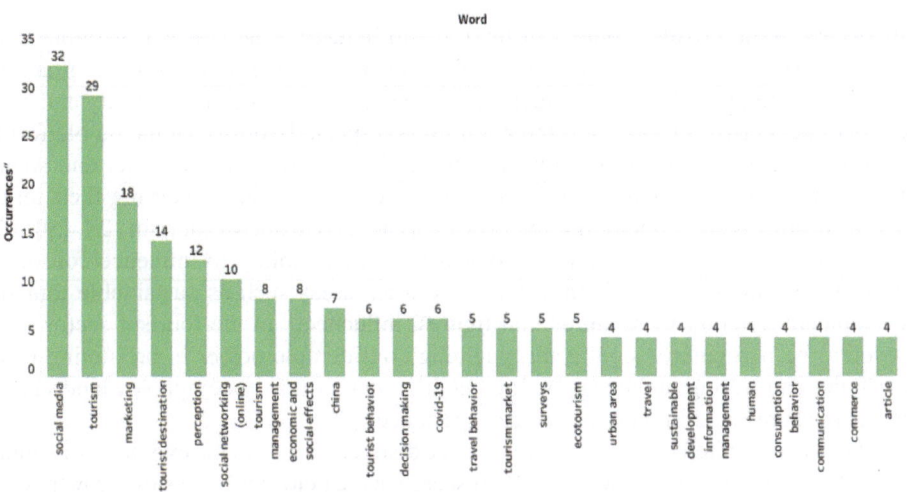

Fig. 5. The most frequent keywords.

5 Discussion

This article offers a comprehensive overview that meticulously traces the trajectory of research on the theme connecting influencers and tourism. It is a journey through time that reveals a fascinating narrative of the evolution of this field. What is clear is the remarkable growth and profound transformation that have characterized this subject over the years. This metamorphosis speaks volumes about the increasing importance of

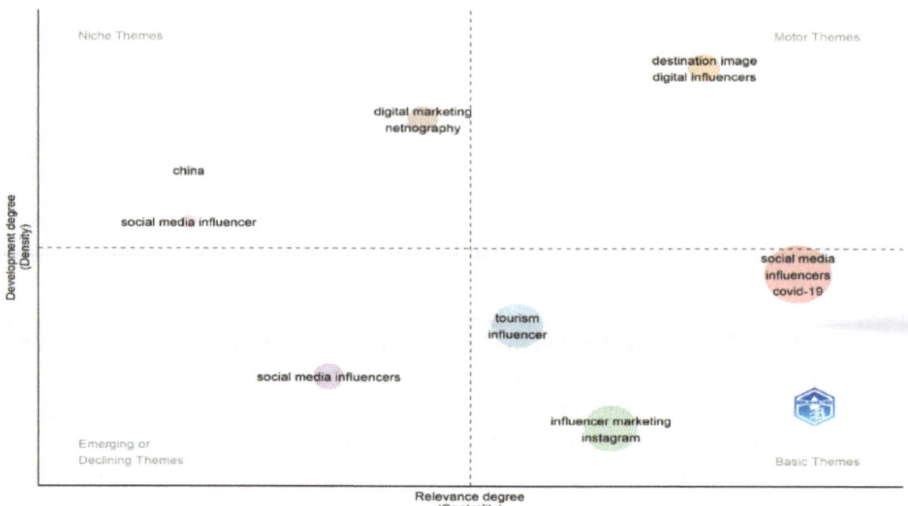

Fig. 6. Thematic map.

influencers in the broader context of the tourism industry. The concept of influencers in the tourism domain has undeniably evolved over time, tracing a fascinating path in the existing literature. Initially, influencers were seen as sources of credibility and conveyors of persuasive messages to their followers, especially on social media platforms like Instagram [27]. However, with the unprecedented rise of the Internet and social media, influencers gradually transformed into a formidable force, exerting their influence in various sectors, including the ever-evolving landscape of tourism [28, 29]. It's increasingly evident that influencers possess the unique ability to influence consumer attitudes, extending their influence even to critical areas such as sustainable tourism development. Among these influential figures, influencers in the tourism sector have proven to be particularly significant, wielding considerable power in promoting local travel and captivating audiences with engaging content that encompasses landscapes, artistic treasures, and immersive nature experiences [30].

The data presented in Figure 1 reveals three distinct periods in the evolution of annual research production. From 2005 to 2018, research in the field exhibited slow growth, with the number of publications per year gradually increasing from 1 to 10. This phase marked the initial exploration of the connection between influencers and tourism, often seen as a startup period. However, a significant turning point came in 2019, indicating the second period, characterized by a surge in interest. The number of publications skyrocketed, reaching 18 and 20 in 2019 and 2020, respectively, due to the growing recognition of influencer marketing's potential in the tourism sector. The most recent period, spanning from 2021 to 2023, saw a substantial increase in interest, with over 40 publications per year. This exponential growth underscores the field's dynamism and ongoing relevance.

Furthermore, thematic analysis reveals the dynamic and adaptive nature of research in the influencers and tourism field. Researchers have responded to global events like the Covid-19 pandemic, delved into fundamental questions regarding destination marketing and tourist behavior, explored innovative research methodologies like netnography, and shed light on specific subsets of influencers, especially those operating in the realm of social media. These collective efforts have enriched the body of knowledge and facilitated a more comprehensive understanding of influencers' role in the tourism landscape and the complex dynamics involved. While "core" and "driver" themes have persisted, emphasizing the role of influencers in shaping tourist choices and effective marketing, "emerging" and "niche" themes like "netnography" and "social media influencer" demonstrate the field's adaptability and exploration of new methodologies to comprehend online communities and the unique influence of social media influencers. Collectively, these findings underscore the dynamic and responsive nature of research in the influencers and tourism field, addressing contemporary challenges, fundamental questions, and emerging trends, enriching the field's knowledge. In conclusion, this comprehensive exploration of influencer marketing in tourism reveals a dynamic field that has evolved significantly over the years. It highlights the growing influence of influencers in shaping the tourism industry and emphasizes the need for adaptable marketing strategies. Furthermore, it underscores the interdisciplinary nature of research in this domain, encouraging collaboration among researchers from diverse backgrounds. While the study provides valuable insights, it also acknowledges its limitations, primarily its temporal scope and reliance on quantitative methods. Future research directions include investigating recent developments, cross-cultural analyses, and ethical considerations. Understanding the impact of influencer marketing and integrating emerging technologies in tourism campaigns will be essential in shaping the industry's future.

5.1 Future Research Lines and Limitations of the Study

Exploring post-2023 developments in influencer marketing is crucial for adapting to changing consumer behaviors and global events. Cross-cultural analyses assess how cultural factors influence influencer marketing effectiveness. Investigating tangible impacts through empirical studies provides insights, and ethical considerations, such as transparent and responsible influencer tourism promotion, gain significance. Examining how influencer content shapes consumer travel decisions offers research opportunities. This study has implications for stakeholders, emphasizing evolving trends and the need for adaptable strategies in the tourism sector. It informs strategies for destinations, travel companies, and influencers, fostering innovative approaches in this dynamic field.

References

1. Safaa, L., Oruezabala, G., Bidan, M.: Le tourisme à l'ère des technologies numériques. teoros 40 (2021). https://doi.org/10.7202/1084554ar
2. Safaa, L., Saoualih, A.: Des technologies et des destinations touristiques intelligentes: entre rhétorique et expérimentation. Études caribéennes (2022)
3. Tussyadiah, I.: A review of research into automation in tourism: launching the annals of tourism research curated collection on artificial intelligence and robotics in tourism. Ann. Tour. Res. **81**, 102883 (2020)

4. Saura, J.R., Palos-Sanchez, P., Blanco-González, A.: The importance of information service offerings of collaborative CRMs on decision-making in B2B marketing. J. Bus. Ind. Market. **35**, 470–482 (2019)

5. Calero, C., Turner, L.W.: Regional economic development and tourism: a literature review to highlight future directions for regional tourism research. Tour. Econ. **26**, 3–26 (2020). https://doi.org/10.1177/1354816619881244

6. Gursoy, D., Akova, O., Atsiz, O.: Understanding the heritage experience: a content analysis of online reviews of World Heritage Sites in Istanbul. J. Tourism Cult. Change **20**, 311–334 (2022)

7. Wang, W., Skovira, R.J.: Authenticity and Social Media. In: AMCIS 2017 PROCEEDINGS (2017)

8. Xiang, Z., Du, Q., Ma, Y., Fan, W.: A comparative analysis of major online review platforms: implications for social media analytics in hospitality and tourism. Tour. Manage. **58**, 51–65 (2017). https://doi.org/10.1016/j.tourman.2016.10.001

9. westling abby: The Truth Why Influencers And Entrepreneurs Are One And The Same. In: GREY Journal (2021). https://greyjournal.net/play/learn-culture/truth-why-influencers-and-entrepreneurs-are-same/. Accessed 14 May 2023

10. Cetin, G., Akova, O.: Creative Aspects of Package Tour Experiences in Destinations (2016)

11. Kaplan, A.M., Haenlein, M.: Users of the world, unite! the challenges and opportunities of social media. Bus. Horiz. **53**, 59–68 (2010)

12. Kim, J., Kim, M.: Rise of social media influencers as a new marketing channel: focusing on the roles of psychological well-being and perceived social responsibility among consumers. Int. J. Environ. Res. Public Health **19**, 2362 (2022). https://doi.org/10.3390/ijerph19042362

13. Djafarova, E., Rushworth, C.: Exploring the credibility of online celebrities' Instagram profiles in influencing the purchase decisions of young female users. Comput. Hum. Behav. **68**, 1–7 (2017)

14. Seddighi, H.R., Theocharous, A.L.: A model of tourism destination choice: a theoretical and empirical analysis. Tour. Manage. **23**, 475–487 (2002). https://doi.org/10.1016/S0261-5177(02)00012-2

15. Morandi, B.: La restauration des cours d'eau en France et à l'étranger : de la définition du concept à l'évaluation de l'action. Eléments de recherche applicables (2014)

16. Gimpl, K.: Evaluation von ausgewählten Altmetrics-Diensten für den Einsatz an wissenschaftlichen Bibliotheken (2017)

17. Aria, M., Cuccurullo, C.: Biblioshiny: Bibliometrix for no coders. Recuperado de: https://bibliometrix.org/biblioshiny/assets/player/KeynoteDHTMLPlayer.html(2020)

18. Aria, M., Cuccurullo, C.: Bibliometrix: an R-tool for comprehensive science mapping analysis. J. Informet. **11**, 959–975 (2017)

19. Baier-Fuentes, H., Hormiga, E., Miravitlles, P., Blanco-Mesa, F.: International entrepreneurship: a critical review of the research field. Eur. J. Int. Manag. **13**, 381–412 (2019)

20. Donthu, N., Kumar, S., Mukherjee, D., Pandey, N., Lim, W.M.: How to conduct a bibliometric analysis: an overview and guidelines. J. Bus. Res. **133**, 285–296 (2021)

21. Cobo, M.J., López-Herrera, A.G., Herrera-Viedma, E., Herrera, F.: Science mapping software tools: review, analysis, and cooperative study among tools. J. Am. Soc. Inf. Sci. **62**, 1382–1402 (2011). https://doi.org/10.1002/asi.21525

22. Fahimnia, B., Sarkis, J., Davarzani, H.: Green supply chain management: a review and bibliometric analysis. Int. J. Prod. Econ. **162**, 101–114 (2015)

23. Podsakoff, P.M., MacKenzie, S.B., Bachrach, D.G., Podsakoff, N.P.: The influence of management journals in the 1980s and 1990s. Strat. Mgmt. J. **26**, 473–488 (2005). https://doi.org/10.1002/smj.454

24. Femenia-Serra, F., Gretzel, U., Alzua-Sorzabal, A.: Instagram travel influencers in #quarantine: communicative practices and roles during COVID-19. Tour. Manag. **89**, 104454 (2022). https://doi.org/10.1016/j.tourman.2021.104454
25. Magno, F., Cassia, F.: The impact of social media influencers in tourism. Anatolia **29**, 288–290 (2018)
26. Xu (Rinka), X., Pratt, S.: Social media influencers as endorsers to promote travel destinations: an application of self-congruence theory to the Chinese generation Y. J. Travel Tour. Market. **35**, 958–972 (2018)
27. Yufada, E.M., Simanjuntak, T.N.: Evolving concept and popularity of influencers: a literature review. Jurnal Komunikasi Profesional **7**, 194–215 (2023)
28. Baltezarević, R., Baltezarević, B., Baltezarević, V.: The role of travel influencers in sustainable tourism development. Int. Rev. **3–4**, 125–129 (2022)
29. Razak, R.A., Mansor, N.A.: Instagram influencers in social media-induced tourism: Rethinking tourist trust towards tourism destination. In: Research Anthology on Social Media Advertising and Building Consumer Relationships. IGI Global, pp 1437–1446 (2022)
30. Berjozkina, G., Garanti, Z.: Emerging influencers promoting travel: the case of local tourism in Latvia. J. Region. Econ. Soc. Develop. **12**, 51–64 (2020)

The Complex World of Online Reviews: Criteria for Establishing a Global Index for Accommodation

Juan Pedro Mellinas[1] 🆔 and Eva Martin-Fuentes[2](✉) 🆔

[1] University of Murcia, Murcia, Spain
mellinas@um.es
[2] University of Lleida, Lleida, Spain
eva.martin@udl.cat

Abstract. Online reviews play a crucial role in shaping consumer decisions, particularly in the hospitality industry where the intangibility of services creates uncertainty. The lack of a standardized approach to measure the quality of hotels based on online reviews poses challenges for consumers and businesses alike. In the past, there have been various attempts to create a global index of average accommodation scores. However, all of them presented serious deficiencies in terms of transparency and level of dissemination, failing to achieve the expected success. To address these challenges, the study proposes the establishment of a rational reputation standard for accommodation services through online reviews. A Delphi method is proposed to seek consensus among academic experts and hotel managers, aiming to prioritize criteria for creating a transparent algorithm and a reliable global index for comparing accommodation establishments. The proposed rational reputation standard aims to empower consumers, allowing them to make informed decisions, while benefiting the hospitality industry by promoting transparency and credibility, as well as to allow public authorities with knowledge to establish a quality standard based on online reviews.

Keywords: Online reviews · transparency · hotel standards · criteria · index

1 Introduction

The intangibility of services creates uncertainty and insecurity for consumers, so they seek to obtain supplementary information to that provided by service suppliers, which helps to reduce that uncertainty. Tourism services have found in this ecosystem of online reviews an ideal environment for their development [1].

Travel-related platforms such as TripAdvisor or Online Travel Agencies such as Booking.com have become an indispensable source of information where most users consult them before booking a hotel. In fact, many tourists are unwilling to make a lodging reservation if there are no online reviews [2].

Online Travel Reviews (OTR), defined as "narratives, opinions, pictures, and ratings posted on travel related websites" [3], determine the level of quality perceived by potential customers. There are studies in the hotel sector that have been able to measure how

K. Berezina et al. (Eds.): ENTER 2024, SPBE, pp. 434–439, 2024.
https://doi.org/10.1007/978-3-031-58839-6_44

variations in the ratings of accommodations have effects on the levels of occupancy and prices of hotels [1].

Nevertheless, the use and analysis of this information is not without certain complexity for various reasons: each platform collects and displays information differently, they use different scoring scales, they use different adjectives to arbitrarily, they delete the oldest reviews or not, or even, what is the representativeness of visitors that write reviews, cultural differences are observed [1, 2, 4].

There is not a single standard to measure the quality of a hotel based on online reviews, and there is also a problem of lack of transparency in the algorithm used to calculate the average score on some platforms.

Well-known websites such as Kayak or Trivago provide a global accommodation score based on a kind of arithmetic mean of scores from various websites, while private companies offer similar global indices to their clients (Reviewpro, Olery, etc.). However, it is important to note that the calculation method for this overall score is not disclosed to the public (referred to as a secret algorithm). As a result, different platforms yield divergent global scores, all with the purported goal of providing an accurate and reliable global index [1]. Moreover, various national and international organizations have decided to address the challenges posed by the topic: Norway and Switzerland documented models of guest review integration into hotel classification, and regions of the United Arab Emirates, Germany and Australia tried to integrate online scores in their traditional stars system [5]. However, only the system implemented in Australia (with a global score calculated using a "secret algorithm" from a private company) is currently still in operation.

In 2014, reports from the United Nations World Tourism Organization [5] and the European Commission were published, offering a general vision and analysis of what was considered a matter of great importance to the sector [6]. Each of them focused on one of the aspects of debate around this phenomenon. Likewise, the European Commission has included specific references to online reviews in its Directive on Unfair Commercial Practices [7], while the ISO-20488 standard on online reviews was created in 2018 [8].

The aim of this study is to determine which reviews and which systems should be considered for the calculation of a future reliable global index that allows consumers, professionals and public bodies to compare accommodation establishments in a reliable way.

2 Methodology

For our research, a Delphi method is proposed as it allows to obtain reliable consensus from a group of experts, particularly in the context of problem-solving [9] with experts on accommodation online reviews from the academia, consultants, and hotel managers.

3 Results

It is expected to reach a consensus among academic experts, consultants and hotel managers consulted to determine which criteria to use when creating a transparent algorithm or global index to establish an overall accommodation score from online reviews. They will be asked about a series of specific issues, which will be decisive in the calculation of the algorithm.

3.1 Criteria for Scales Homogenization

Travel review sites use different rating scales. While TripAdvisor uses a rating of 1–5, others use a 10-point scale, or different scoring systems (e.g., HolidayCheck, 1–6, Agoda 2–10), that bring in ratings discrepancies among platforms as the design of the scale could influence the final score [4, 10]. Which scale should be used? And how the homogenization should be implemented?

3.2 Reviews Oldness

There are platforms such as Expedia and Booking.com that delete the reviews after three years since they were written, although they keep them longer if the hotel has few reviews. Google and TripAdvisor do not delete the old reviews, except on TripAdvisor that allows a business to remove all the past reviews only if they implemented structural changes such as new management, or total renovation of the lobby [11]. A decision should be made regarding the age of the reviews taken into consideration to calculate the global score.

3.3 Verified Reviews

There is a difference between platforms that only allow verified authors to write reviews through the reservation they have made and those in which anyone can write a review. Should we allow not verified reviews? What weight should each platform have to establish a global index?

3.4 Writing Reviews System

The way in which users fill out their experience is also significant, as are the changes in the platforms themselves over time. In this sense, TripAdvisor requests a general score first, followed by the title and contents of the review and, at the end, a rating for specific facets of the service (e.g., service, location, rooms, cleanliness, sleep quality). Instead, other platforms do not ask for a global rating, but request users to value several facets (e.g., cleanliness, comfort, facilities, staff, value for money, location) and then create a global score with the arithmetic average of these facets. Should we consider the global scores obtained by different systems in an equivalent way?

3.5 Reviews with Score, Text, or Image

There are platforms that allow users to publish a review indicating only the numerical score, while others force consumers to write a minimum of characters to publish it. In addition, some allow to publish images and videos together with the review. Should all reviews have the same weight? Or those that do not have a minimum of explanation, should they be given less weight? And to those who also provide images, should they be given more weight?

3.6 Minimum Reviews

Some platforms do not publish the average score of an accommodation establishment until it has achieved a minimum number of reviews, such as Booking.com, which only considers publishing the score if there are 5 reviews, but other platforms publish the average score from the first review. Should a minimum number of reviews be considered, equivalent to a minimum sample in a survey, to consider it appropriate to assign an overall score to a hotel?

3.7 Admitted Platforms to Calculate the Global Index

Not all platforms are used in the same way in different parts of the world, nor do they all have the same number of reviews or the same popularity. Some platforms should weight more than others? Do they have to have a minimum number of reviews to be able to enter in the global index? Should they be regional index worldwide? Should they be platforms used worldwide? Platforms must comply with legal systems, but what legislation (ISO-20488)? is it feasible? Should a series of objective parameters be established for websites to be accepted?

3.8 Reviewer Experience

There are users who have seniority and experience in writing reviews online. Should reviews from these reviewers carry more weight than reviews from new users? Should reviews from users who have only written one review on a website be accepted? Would it eliminate some of the potential fraud of writing fake reviews on platforms where the user is not verified?

3.9 Void Reviews and Reviewers

Sometimes there are organized attacks or inclusion of mass reviews that should be invalidated, in addition there are also reviewers suspected of attacking businesses or helping to increase reputation by buying reviews. Should all reviews from suspicious reviewers be invalidated? Do mass review entries have to be canceled?

4 Conclusions

In recent years, the traditional system of hotel stars has been surpassed by the scores of online reviews, despite the relative trust that many users have in online reviews [12]. Different organizations have suggested or promoted the implementation of a global score based on the reviews that would complement or replace the traditional star system. But this cannot be done using a "secret algorithm" that nobody knows which reviews include or the overall weight of each review or website.

The initial approach of our research involves making a series of decisions that lead to the creation of a global index that is perceived as fair, credible, transparent and useful for the accommodation sector. After this first step, an algorithm could be created, this time totally transparent, which could be applied to any accommodation in the world, even being established as a quality standard by public bodies, at the same level as the hotel star system.

Future research should focus on studying the level of acceptance that the algorithm, designed based on this study, could have within the sector. Similar investigations could also be implemented for other tourist services, such as restaurants, which also have a great dependence on online reviews, without there being a global index implemented either.

Acknowledgment. This research has been funded by the Spanish Ministry of Science and Innovation MCIN/AEI/https://doi.org/10.13039/501100011033/ FEDER, UE within the RevTour project Id PID2022-138564OA-I00, the Gastrotur Project Id TUR-RETOS2022-017, and by the INDEST-UdL within the ResTur project for the call 2023CRINDESTABC.

References

1. Mellinas J.P, Reino S.: Average scores integration in official star rating scheme. J. Hosp. Tour Technol. **10**(3), 339–350 (2019)
2. Schuckert, M., Liu, X., Law, R.: Hospitality and tourism online reviews: Recent trends and future directions. J. Travel Tour. Mark. **32**(5), 608–621 (2015)
3. Marine-Roig, E.: Content analysis of online travel reviews. In: Xiang, Z., Fuchs, M., Gretzel, U., Höpken, W. (eds.) Handbook of e-Tourism, pp. 1–26. Springer International Publishing, Cham (2020). https://doi.org/10.1007/978-3-030-05324-6_31-1
4. Martin-Fuentes, E., Mellinas, J.P., Parra, E.: Online travel review rating scales and effects on hotel scoring and competitiveness. Tour. Rev. **76**(3), 654–668 (2021)
5. World Tourism Organization: Online Guest Reviews and Hotel Classification Systems—An Integrated Approach. https://www.e-unwto.org/doi/pdf/10.1C8111/9789284416325. Accessed 28 July 2023
6. European Commission: Study on online consumer reviews in the hotel sector: Final report. https://data.europa.eu/doi/10.2772/32129. Accessed 28 July 2023
7. European Commission, Unfair commercial practices directive. https://ec.europa.eu/info/law/law-topic/consumer-protection-law/unfair-commercial-practices-law/unfair-commercial-practices-directive_en. Accessed 28 July 2023
8. ISO, ISO 20488:2018, Online consumer reviews—Principles and requirements for their collection, moderation and publication, https://www.iso.org/cms/render/live/en/sites/isoorg/contents/data/standard/06/81/68193.html. Accessed 28 July 2023
9. Okoli, C., Pawlowski, S.D.: The Delphi method as a research tool: an example, design considerations and applications. Inf. Manag. **42**(1), 15–29 (2004)
10. Leung R, Au N, Liu J, Law R. Do customers share the same perspective? J. Vacat. Mark, Apr, 24(2), 103–117 (2018)
11. TripAdvisor, Report a major renovation. https://www.tripadvisorsupport.com/en-US/hc/owner/articles/393. Accessed 25 July 2023
12. Gavilan, D., Avello, M., Martinez-Navarro, G.: The influence of online ratings and reviews on hotel booking consideration. Tour. Manag. **66**, 53–61 (2018)

The Cognitive Effect of YouTube Video and User-Generated Content: A Preliminary Study

Eunji Lee[1] , Seunghun Shin[2] , Hyeyeoun Joo[1] , and Chulmo Koo[1](✉)

[1] Kyung Hee University, Kyung Hee Dearo 26, Seoul, Republic of Korea
{edreamerj,hyes,helmetgu}@khu.ac.kr
[2] The Hong Kong Polytechnic University, 17 Science Museum Road, Tsim Sha Tsui East, Kowloon, Hong Kong
seung-hun.shin@khu.ac.kr

Abstract. Nowadays, video-sharing social media platforms have become essential sources of information for tourists. In line with this trend, many destination marketing organizations (DMOs) formulate marketing strategies utilizing video-sharing platforms. Nevertheless, despite the extensive research on the impacts of advertising video exposure, there is a notable absence of studies that delve into the influence of user-generated content on the cognitive effect of potential tourists on destinations. To address this gap, this study aims to identify the cognitive effects based on the presence of comments (vs. absent) and different positive comment types (absent vs. opinion vs. impression vs. compliment comments) through a field experiment design. We found that the cognitive effect of YouTube videos is higher when positive comments are available. Further, impression comments had a more significant cognitive effect than the other comment types. Building upon our research findings, we propose strategies for utilizing video social media platforms from the perspective of tourism destination marketers.

Keywords: YouTube Video · Tourism Destination Marketing · User Generated Content · Advertising Effectiveness

1 Introduction

Many destination marketing organizations (DMOs) are actively using a video-sharing social media platform, especially YouTube, as an advertising channel. The surveys regarding DMOs' usage of budgets showed that most DMOs kept increasing their budget for social media advertising from a few years ago [1]. With its increasing role in influencing tourists' choice of destination, developing an advertising strategy tailored to YouTube has become the spotlight for DMOs worldwide. One of the unique features of a video-sharing social media platform, which marketers have to consider for developing the platform-specific strategy, is the availability of others' opinions [2]. The users of a video-sharing platform can express their opinions about a certain video by leaving comments, and the comments are shown to others. YouTube users tend to consume a

K. Berezina et al. (Eds.): ENTER 2024, SPBE, pp. 440–445, 2024.
https://doi.org/10.1007/978-3-031-58839-6_45

video together with its comments by considering the comments as another part of the video.

It is important for DMOs to understand how the comments of a video-sharing social media platform affect viewers' perception of a video and the video's subject because it helps them develop platform-specific strategies [3]. Specifically, it can help DMOs realize the importance of managing comments on their content on a video-sharing social media platform and further specify how to do the management [4]. However, the effects of comments on a video-sharing social media platform on viewers' perception of a video and the video's subject have been scarcely discussed.

To respond this research call, this research aims to examine the effects of comments of a video-sharing social media platform on tourists' perception toward a video and a featured destination in the video. We examine the cognitive effect (i.e., increasing consumers' awareness or knowledge about a video and a featured product) of different types of comments. Targeting the most popular video-sharing social media platform (i.e., YouTube), we adopt a filed-experiment approach. This research contributes to the literature on destination advertising by explaining how tourists process video and comment on the platform, providing insights from a destination marketing perspective.

2 Literature Review and Hypothesis Development

2.1 The Cognitive Effect of DMO's YouTube Video: Presence of Comments

Previous studies found that the cognitive effect of an advertising post on a social media platform could be enhanced through its comments. Targeting a news-sharing social media platform, Witteman et al. [5] showed that while the post about home birth increased the readers' knowledge about the post and its topic, the level of increase became greater as the number of comments increased. Kim et al. [6] focused on the Facebook post promoting the flu vaccine and found that the post's positive impact on viewers' attention to the vaccine became stronger when positive comments were present. Schäfer et al. [7] investigated individuals' interest in a social issue (i.e., Diselgate) driven by Facebook posts and found that their interest further increased when comments were available. Based on these findings, we hypothesize the cognitive effect of comments to be present in a video-sharing social media platform. Thus, we propose the following hypothesis:

H1. The cognitive effect of DMOs' YouTube video is higher when positive comments are available than when not available.

H1a. The extent to which tourists become aware of the video is greater when the video is shown together with positive comments than when only the video is shown.

H1b. The extent to which tourists become aware of the featured destination is greater when the video is shown together with positive comments than when only the video is shown.

2.2 The Cognitive Effect of DMO's YouTube Video: Type of Comments

We also hypothesize the cognitive effect of comments to be contingent on their content type. According to Madden et al. [8], the positive comments available on YouTube can be classified by their content, such as those expressing positive sentiment, those expressing personal views on a video or topic, those complimenting a video creator, etc. We expect that DMOs' YouTube videos, including specific content types of positive comments, would have a higher cognitive effect than those including other types of positive comments. Thus, we hypothesized as follows:

H2. *The cognitive effect of positive comments varies by their content type.*

H2a. *A specific content type of positive comment is more effective in increasing tourists' awareness of the video than other types.*

H2b. *A specific content type of positive comment is more effective in increasing tourists' awareness of the featured destination than other types.*

3   Methodology

We utilized a YouTube video titled "Feel the Rhythm of Korea with BTS – DAEJEON ROCK N ROLL," created by the Korea Tourism Organization (KTO), as a stimulus. We collected comments written until April 30, 2023, for the relevant video and utilized them for the development of stimuli. We manually categorized the crawled comments in terms of positivity and content type based on the YouTube comment categorization scheme developed by Madden et al. [8] 200 Chinese undergraduate students from Kyung Hee University participated voluntarily, and after removing invalid cases, 161 cases were used for analysis. The participants were randomly assigned to one out of the four conditions (without comments vs. with opinion vs. with impression vs. with compliment). A brand recognition test is designed for measuring consumers' awareness toward an advertisement and a destination. As for a video, we asked participants 1) to choose the genre of background music among several options (In the video, a specific genre of music was played and emphasized in the title) and 2) to indicate a specific scene was in the video (Was the following scene in the video?). As for a destination, we asked participants 1) to choose the name of featured city among several options (Please choose the name of the city featured in the video among the following options) and 2) to indicate the correctness of spelling of the name (Is "Daegoen" the correct spelling for the name of the city featured in the video?). Since the second question was asked four times by showing different spelling, the correction rate was coded. All the measurements appeared to participants with delay through some distraction tasks (e.g., a list of short quizzes) because it could clear their short-term memory and, thus, measure their recognition more effectively.

4   Results

With the participants' responses to the first question about a video (In the video, a specific genre of music was played and emphasized in the title; Jazz/Blues/HipHop/Rock N Roll/Country), we conducted independent proportions test to compare the proportion of the participants with a correct answer across two conditions: 'video without positive comments' vs. 'video with positive comments.' The percentage of the 'video with positive comments' was more than twice higher than that of the 'video without positive comments' and the difference in proportions was significant across different test types ($Z = 3.03$, $p < 0.01$ in a Hauck-Anderson test; $Z = 3.00$, $p < 0.01$ in a Wald test).

Thus, H1a was supported. The same analysis was repeated with the first question about a destination (Is "Daegoen" the correct spelling for the name of the city featured in the video? Yes/No). Different from the awareness of a video, the difference in proportions was not significant: the percentage of the 'video with positive comments' = 76.1% and that of the 'video without positive comments' = 75.0% ($Z = 0.00, p = 0.50$ in a Hauck-Anderson test; $Z = 0.14, p = 0.88$ in a Wald test) (see Fig. 1). H1b was not supported. In conclusion, H1 was partially supported.

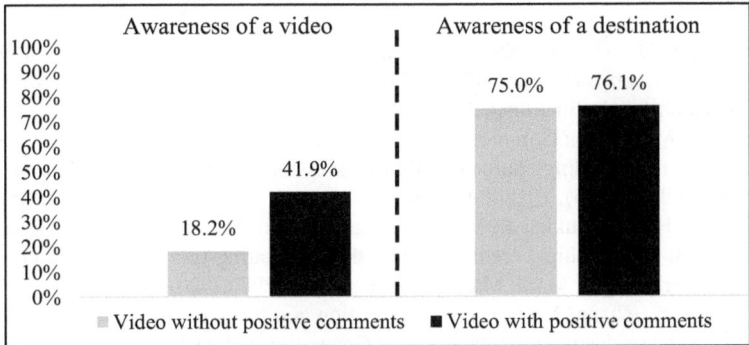

Fig. 1. Independent proportions test

With the participants' responses to the group of second questions about a video (Was the following scene in the video? Yes/No X 7 times with different scenes), we conducted one-way ANOVA to compare the correction rate across four conditions. The results showed a significant difference between the four conditions ($F (3, 157) = 4.174$, $p < 0.01$). Specifically, the correction rate of 'video with impression comments' was significantly higher than the other three conditions ($M_{impression} = 79.6, SD = 19.9$ vs. $M_{none} = 67.8, SD = 19.3; M_{opinion} = 64.5, SD = 16.4; M_{tribute} = 70.5, SD = 20.1$). Thus, H2a was supported. The same analysis was repeated with the group of second question about a destination (Is "Daegoen" the correct spelling for the name of the city featured in the video? Yes/No X 4 times with different spelling). According to the results, no significant difference was found across the conditions ($F (3, 157) = 0.137, p = 0.938$). H2b was not supported. Therefore, H2 was partially supported.

5 Conclusion

This preliminary study examined the cognitive effects of DMOs-provided YouTube videos and user-generated content on potential tourists. We offer both practical and academic implications. Firstly, while existing literature separates studies on YouTube videos or user-generated content, this study stands out by comparing the cognitive effectiveness of YouTube videos by considering the presence of comments and the types of comments. Indeed, these results are expected to provide DMOs with guidelines for managing comments to enhance destination advertising effectiveness. However, this study has limitations and future challenges. Initially, the participants in the preliminary study were limited to Chinese international students. In future research, it is necessary to compare effectiveness based on nationality or cultural dimensions and to investigate disparities in the impact of comments on video platforms other than YouTube. Furthermore, in future research, we anticipate that comparing elements that can impact users' emotional arousal, such as visual and audio components, apart from the effectiveness of comments, will provide valuable insights to tourism marketers and DMOs [9, 10].

References

1. Habtemariam, D.: TikTok's short-form video revolution gains traction in search for destinations. Skift, https://skift.com/2022/10/14/tiktoks-short-form-video-revolution-gains-traction-in-search-for-destinations/. Accessed 14 Oct 2022
2. Liao, M.-Q., Mak, A.K.: Comments are disabled for this video: a technological affordances approach to understanding source credibility assessment of CSR information on YouTube. Public. Relat. Rev. **45**(5), 101840 (2019)
3. Reinikainen, H., Munnukka, J., Maity, D., Luoma-Aho, V.: You really are a great big sister–parasocial relationships, credibility, and the moderating role of audience comments in influencer marketing. J. Mark. Manage. **36**(3–4), 279–298 (2020)
4. Hao, X., Xu, S., Zhang, X.: Barrage participation and feedback in travel reality shows: the effects of media on destination image among Generation Y. J. Dest. Mark. Manage. **12**, 27–36 (2019)
5. Witteman, H.O., Fagerlin, A., Exe, N., Trottier, M.-E., Zikmund-Fisher, B.J.: One-sided social media comments influenced opinions and intentions about home birth: an experimental study. Health Aff. **35**(4), 726–733 (2016)
6. Kim, H., Seo, Y., Yoon, H.J., Han, J.Y., Ko, Y.: The effects of user comment valence of Facebook health messages on intention to receive the flu vaccine: the role of pre-existing attitude towards the flu vaccine and psychological reactance. Int. J. Advert. **40**(7), 1187–1208 (2021)
7. Schäfer, S., Müller, P., Ziegele, M.: The double-edged sword of online deliberation: how evidence-based user comments both decrease and increase discussion participation intentions on social media. New Media Soc. **26**, 1403–1428 (2022). https://doi.org/10.1177/146144482 11073059
8. Madden, A., Ruthven, I., McMenemy, D.: A classification scheme for content analyses of YouTube video comments. J. Doc. **69**(5), 693–714 (2013). https://doi.org/10.1108/JD-06-2012-0078
9. Ma, J., Scott, N., Wu, Y.: Tourism destination advertising: effect of storytelling and sensory stimuli on arousal and memorability. Tour. Rev. **79**(3), 671–687 (2023)
10. Shen, H., Zhao, C., Fan, D.X., Buhalis, D.: The effect of hotel livestreaming on viewers purchase intention: exploring the role of parasocial interaction and emotional engagement. Int. J. Hosp. Manag. **107**, 103348 (2022)

Exploring the Impact of Music in Short-Form Travel Videos on Users' Emotional Resonance, Sharing Intention and Impulsive Travel Intention

Kaige Zhu[ID], Jiao Li[ID], Han Zhou[ID], and Juhyeok Jang[(✉)][ID]

Hokkaido University, Sapporo, Japan
jang.juhyeok@imc.hokudai.ac.jp

Abstract. The popularity of short-form video platforms and content creation tools has grown significantly in recent years, leading to increased consumption of travel-related visual content. A growing number of potential tourists are actively engaging with short-form travel videos (STVs). While previous studies have highlighted the importance of music in STVs, the research mechanisms and frameworks to investigate its impact remain unclear. Therefore, this study develops a research model based on resonance theory and the Stimulus-Organism-Response (SOR) model, aiming to investigate the influence of music congruity with various video elements (e.g., tempo, copywriting, style, destination attributes) within STVs presented on social media. Through a scenario-based experiment, this study attempts to confirm the role of music and video aesthetics as key factors in evoking emotional resonance and shaping users' behaviour. The findings could also suggest that emotional resonance could directly influence users' sharing intentions and impulsive travel intentions. These findings are expected to provide valuable insights for destination marketers and travel content creators.

Keywords: Short-Form Travel Videos (STVs) · Music Congruity · Video Aesthetics · Emotional Resonance

1 Introduction

In recent years, the importance of short-form travel videos (STVs) in destination marketing has been widely acknowledged [1]. These videos offer engaging and immersive travel experiences that can quickly evoke emotional responses in potential tourists, such as inspiration, memories and a desire to travel [2, 3]. STVs have become an integral part of the tourist experience and have a significant influence on tourists' decision-making processes [2, 4]. In China, one of the world's largest tourism source markets, 407 million users are interested in travelling on the Douyin, the Chinese version of TikTok [5]. More and more tourists are using short videos to share their travel experiences, seeking both social expression and emotional satisfaction [1, 2].

While many previous studies have focused on visual reference cues in STVs (e.g., [3]), the important role of music as an auditory reference cue has not been sufficiently

K. Berezina et al. (Eds.): ENTER 2024, SPBE, pp. 446–451, 2024.
https://doi.org/10.1007/978-3-031-58839-6_46

emphasised. As noted by Aufderheide [4], music can create an immersive environment, evoking experiences and emotions that drive purchase intentions and foster a sense of belonging. Recognised as a powerful sensory cue and environmental stimulus [6], music could act as a crucial bridge between the communication in short-form video content and the emotional engagement of the viewer. Specifically, the congruity between music and the elements in STVs, such as destination attributes and video types, may strongly influence video aesthetics and shape tourists' perceptions of destination-related emotions [2]. A classic example is the travel challenge hashtag '#fallingtrend' on the TikTok. User-generated 15-s STVs, precisely synchronised to the beat of Taylor Swift's song 'Love Story', motivated a significant number of potential tourists to spontaneously visit destinations and create travel-related content. However, the exact mechanism of music in STVs remains unclear at present. Considering the above, this study constructs a research model based on SOR theory and emotional resonance through a scenario-based experiment, aiming to address the following research questions:

RQ1: Does music congruity affect tourists' perception of the audiovisual environment (music cognition, video aesthetics) in virtual space?

RQ2: How do video aesthetics and music cognition evoke emotional resonance and influence the travel decision-making process of potential tourists?

2 Literature Review

2.1 The Audiovisual Environment in Short-Form Travel Videos

Mehrabian and Russell [7] introduced an influential theoretical framework known as the Stimulus-Organism-Response (SOR) model. This theory proposes that environmental stimuli can affect an individual's behaviour by influencing their emotional state. In the field of tourism, it has become an essential framework for researchers seeking to understand tourists' behaviour and emotions [6]. Although previous studies have recognised that stimuli in STVs include more than visual aesthetics, such as music-induced sensory experiences [3], and have confirmed the relationship between these stimuli and potential tourists' emotions, there is still a lack of quantitative studies investigating the relationship between the audiovisual environment in STVs and potential tourists' behavioural intentions. Furthermore, the interaction and impact of two key environmental factors, music [6, 8] and video aesthetics [3], in STVs remain unclear.

To address this research gap, this study conceptualises the audiovisual environment in short videos as 'Stimulus (S)', considers emotions as 'Organism (O)', and examines tourists' sharing intentions and impulsive travel intentions as 'Response (R)'.

2.2 Music Congruity

Music congruity is a complex and multidimensional concept. In the fields of psychology and marketing, many studies highlight the powerful emotional impact of music [e.g., 9, 10]. Specifically, the congruity between music and visual advertising could strongly influence positive emotional responses and attitudes towards the advertising [9]. Additionally, Baumgartner et al. [11] first used neuropsychological techniques to confirm that emotionally congruent musical excerpts significantly enhanced the emotional experience induced by visual stimuli. While the definition of music congruity may vary depending on the above research context, its practical value in tourism has been confirmed by its application in retail and offline tourism marketing [6, 8].

In recent years, tourists' travel content preferences have shifted towards virtual tourism on social media and digital audiovisual travel-related content [12]. This change in the habits of tourists has highlighted the importance of congruity between music and visual elements in videos [13]. In the context of tourism, Fang et al. [3] argues that it is essential to achieve a coordinated audiovisual experience. STVs can effectively evoke emotional responses in viewers, such as feelings of inspiration, only when there is optimal coordination. To achieve coordinated audiovisual experience in STVs, music may need to be coordinated with aesthetic design components such as copywriting, animation, and rhythm [3]. Therefore, in this study, music congruity is defined as the congruence between music and various video elements, including copywriting, video graphics, post-editing, and so on. Furthermore, while Raja et al. [8] introduced a conceptual framework for understanding the impact of music congruity on tourists' emotional resonance, further exploration of the mechanisms and quantitative models is needed.

2.3 Emotional Resonance and Behaviour Intentions

Previous studies have highlighted the critical role of emotional resonance in STVs for effective destination marketing [2]. Therefore, this study argues that emotions evoked by the audiovisual environment of STVs, as the key component of the 'environment-emotion-behaviour' pathway, are a necessary driver for the success of destination marketing campaigns. However, measuring emotional responses in STVs is challenging. This is due to the complex virtual audiovisual environment on social media platforms and the variety of video content available [14]. These factors may limit the effectiveness of traditional measures, such as the PAD scale, in accurately assessing the impact of emotions on STV users. To address this issue, Cheng et al. [2] investigated four main emotional resonance related factors (entertainment, inspiration, escapism, and self-congruence) in the context of STVs. Meanwhile, Cheng et al. [2] also confirmed the relationship between emotional resonance and engagement of STV users. However, Cheng et al. [2] did not consider the impact of music in STVs and did not use a scenario-based experiment. Furthermore, previous studies suggest that tourists' moods or emotional states influence their impulsive travel intentions [15] and sharing intentions [16].

Based on the above, Fig. 1 shows our research framework.

3 Proposed Methodology

The offline pilot and main surveys will be conducted in China, Japan and South Korea in October 2023. These countries were chosen because they are recognised by the UNWTO as major international tourist source countries. They also have rich cultural music resources and many short video users, making them ideal for our research design.

Due to the subjective nature of music congruity, and to minimise potential bias arising from participants' cultural backgrounds and inherent perceptions, firstly, we will employ convenience sampling and multigroup analysis (MGA). Our goal is to recruit 600 short video users (200 from each country) with travel experience, excluding those who have visited the destinations in sample videos. Secondly, we introduce music familiarity and demographic variables as control variables, according to Hadinejad et al. [10]. Thirdly, in terms of producing and selecting sample videos, we will collaborate with professional video production companies. Participants will be asked to watch 3 sample videos, each featuring a different themed tourist attraction. Each video will be paired with two types of background music: one congruent with the elements of the video, and another deliberately incongruent choice. This procedure serves as an experimental manipulation of music congruity.

To validate our music congruity manipulations, we will conduct manipulation checks focusing on two key aspects. First, we will measure participants' awareness of the music changes in the sample videos using music perception measures [6]. Second, participants will rate the appropriateness of the background music by considering elements such as video tempo, visual style, copywriting, and destination attributes.

Measurement items were developed from existing literature using a seven-point Likert scale (1 = strongly disagree; 7 = strongly agree). The measurement and structural models will be evaluated via Mplus or SmartPLS (version 4.0.8.7).

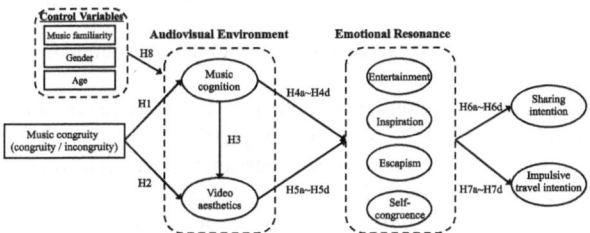

Fig. 1. Research Model.

4 Expected Results and Potential Implications

This study can examine the impact of multisensory congruity in online virtual environments, specifically how congruity between music and various video elements (e.g., tempo, copywriting, style, destination attributes) influences the emotional resonance and behavioural intentions of potential tourists. This research could provide valuable insights for marketers and content creators by focusing on the following key findings.

First, music congruity and incongruity may have opposite effects on the constitutive elements of the audiovisual environment (video aesthetics and music cognition) of STVs. Specifically, higher levels of congruity lead to increased stimulation perceived by users when interacting with the music and video content. These findings are consistent with previous studies [e.g., 9, 10] and could demonstrate the effectiveness of using scenario-based experiments, thereby extending the music congruity in the context of STVs. Marketers should consider the strategic use of music in STVs. For example, it is crucial to fine-tune the congruity between various video elements and music through test broadcasts prior to the formal release of STVs. Second, the emotional resonance evoked by the audiovisual stimuli in virtual environments could have a mediating effect. This is consistent with the SOR theory's proposition of an 'environment-emotion-behaviour' framework. Third, music and video are key factors in evoking emotional resonance and user behaviour, with emotional resonance directly influencing users' sharing intentions and impulsive travel intentions. Furthermore, marketers may need to consider factors such as nationality, cultural background and music familiarity when developing precise marketing strategies for different demographics.

References

1. Du, X., Liechty, T., Santos, C.A., Park, J.: I want to record and share my wonderful journey': Chinese millennials' production and sharing of short-form travel videos on TikTok or Douyin. Curr. Issues Tour. **25**(21), 3412–3424 (2022)
2. Cheng, Y., Wei, W., Zhang, L.: Seeing destinations through vlogs: implications for leveraging customer engagement behavior to increase travel intention. Int. J. Contemp. Hosp. Manage. **32**(10), 3227–3248 (2020)
3. Fang, X., Xie, C., Yu, J., Huang, S., Zhang, J.: How do short-form travel videos trigger travel inspiration? Identifying and validating the driving factors. Tour. Manage. Perspect. **47**, 101128 (2023)
4. Aufderheide, P.: Music videos: the look of the sound. J. Commun.Commun. **36**(1), 57–78 (1986)
5. Douyin: 2023 Douyin travel industry white paper (2023). https://trendinsight.oceanengine.com/arithmetic-report/detail/947. Accessed 9 Sep 2023
6. Min, Z., et al.: How destination music affects tourists' behaviors: travel with music in Lijiang. China. Asia Pac. J. Tourism Res. **25**(2), 131–144 (2020)
7. Mehrabian, A., Russell, J.A.: An Approach to Environmental Psychology. MIT Press (1974)
8. Raja, M.W., Anand, S., Allan, D.: Advertising music: an alternative atmospheric stimulus to retail music. Int. J. Retail Distrib. Manage. **47**(8), 872–892 (2019)
9. Morris, J.D., Boone, M.A.: The effects of music on emotional response, brand attitude, and purchase intent in an emotional advertising condition. ACR North Am. Adv. **25**(1), 518–526 (1998)
10. Hadinejad, A., Moyle, B.D., Kralj, A., Scott, N.: Physiological and self-report methods to the measurement of emotion in tourism. Tour. Recreat. Res.Recreat. Res. **44**(4), 466–478 (2019)
11. Baumgartner, T., Esslen, M., Jäncke, L.: From emotion perception to emotion experience: emotions evoked by pictures and classical music. Int. J. Psychophysiol.Psychophysiol. **60**(1), 34–43 (2006)
12. Munar, A.M., Jacobsen, J.K.S.: Motivations for sharing tourism experiences through social media. Tour. Manage. Manage. **43**, 46–54 (2014)
13. Maria, M., Adriana-Teodora, I.: Exploring the congruence level of music and product category. a content analysis on global musical ads. J. Media Res **16**(2 (46)), 46–61 (2023). https://doi.org/10.24193/jmr.46.3
14. Cheng, X., Su, X., Yang, B., Zarifis, A., Mou, J.: Understanding users' negative emotions and continuous usage intention in short video platforms. Electron. Commerce Res. Appl. **58**, 101244 (2023)
15. Yao, Y., Jia, G., Hou, Y.: Impulsive travel intention induced by sharing conspicuous travel experience on social media: a moderated mediation analysis. J. Hosp. Tourism Manage. **49**, 431–438 (2021)

16. Zhao, C., Shen, H., Zhang, Y.: The study on the impact of short video tourism vloggers at social media platform on online sharing intention. Front. Psychol. **13**, 905002 (2022)

Author Index

K. Berezina et al. (Eds.): ENTER 2024, SPBE, pp. 453–454, 2024.
https://doi.org/10.1007/978-3-031-58839-6